Leadership Roles and Management Functions in Nursing

Theory and Application

SECOND EDITION

$3\overset{\sim}{6}$.173

Bessie L. Marquis, RN, CNAA, MSN
Professor of Nursing
California State University
Chico, California

Carol J. Huston, RN, CNAA, MSN, DPA
Professor of Nursing
California State University
Chico, California

Lippincott
Philadelphia • New York

Acquisitions Editor: Jennifer Brogan
Editorial Assistant: Danielle DiPalma
Project Editor: Amy P. Jirsa
Production Manager: Helen Ewan
Production Coordinator: Kathryn Rule
Design Coordinator: Melissa G. Olson
Indexer: Patricia Perrier

Edition 2nd

Library of Congress Cataloging in Publication Data

Marquis, Bessie L.
    Leadership roles and management functions in nursing : theory and
  application / Bessie L. Marquis, Carol Jorgensen Huston. — 2nd ed.
        p.   cm.
    ISBN 0-397-55236-X (alk. paper)
    1. Nursing services—Administration.   2. Leadership.   I. Huston,
  Carol Jorgensen.   II. Title.
      [DNLM: 1. Nurse Administrators.   2. Nursing, Supervisory.
  3. Leadership.   WY 105 M357L   1996]
  RT89.M387   1996
  362.1'73'068—dc20
  DNLM/DLC
  for Library of Congress   95–36656
                                                                  CIP

The material contained in this volume was submitted as previously unpublished material, except in the instances in which credit has been given to the source from which some of the illustrative material was derived.

Any procedure or practice described in this book should be applied by the health-care practitioner under appropriate supervision in accordance with professional standards of care used with regard to the unique circumstances that apply in each practice situation. Care has been taken to confirm the accuracy of information presented and to describe generally accepted practices. However, the authors, editors, and publisher cannot accept any responsibility for errors or omissions or for any consequences from application of the information in this book and make no warranty, express or implied, with respect to the contents of the book.

The authors and publisher have exerted every effort to ensure that drug selection and dosage set forth in this text are in accordance with current recommendations and practice at the time of publication. However, in view of ongoing research, changes in government regulations, and the constant flow of information relating to drug therapy and drug reactions, the reader is urged to check the package insert for each drug for any change in indications and dosage and for added warnings and precautions. This is particularly important when the recommended agent is a new or infrequently employed drug.

Materials appearing in this book prepared by individuals as part of their official duties as U.S. Government employees are not covered by the above-mentioned copyright.

9   8   7   6   5   4

♾ This Paper Meets the Requirements of ANSI/NISO Z39.48–1992 (Permanence of Paper).

I dedicate this book to Carol Huston,
whose honesty, energy, determination, and creativity
have made our writing partnership successful.
Bessie L. Marquis

I dedicate this book to Bessie Marquis,
my mentor, colleague, and friend.
Carol Jorgensen Huston

Preface

This book's philosophy evolved during 16 years of teaching leadership and management. We entered academe from the community sector of the healthcare industry where we held nursing management positions. In our first effort as authors, *Management Decision-Making for Nurses: 101 Case Studies*, we used an experiential approach and emphasized management functions appropriate for first- and middle-level managers. The primary audience for that text was the nursing student.

Our second book, *Retention and Productivity Strategies for Nurse Managers*, focused on leadership skills necessary for managers to decrease attrition and increase productivity. This book was directed to the manager, rather than the student. The experience of completing research for the second book, coupled with our clinical observations, compelled us to incorporate more leadership content in our teaching and writing.

This book was also influenced by national events in business and finance—events that have led many to believe that a lack of leadership in management is widespread. It became apparent that if managers are to function effectively in the rapidly changing healthcare industry, enhanced managements skills are needed.

What we have attempted to do then, is combine these two very necessary elements: leadership and management. We do not see leadership as merely one role of management, nor management as only one role of leadership. We view the two as forever symbiotic. We have attempted to show this interdependent relationship by defining the leadership components and management functions inherent in all phases of the management process. Undoubtedly, a few readers will find fault with our divisions of management functions and leadership roles. Because the effective leader/manager must be skilled in both leadership and management, we felt it necessary to first artificially separate the two components for the reader, and then re-iterate the roles and functions. Adoption of this integrated role is critical for success in management.

The second concept that shaped this book was our belief in the teaching-to-think movement, especially our commitment to experiential learning and whole-brain thinking. Currently 80% of academic instruction is conducted in a teacher-lecturer/student-listener format, the least effective of all teaching strategies. Only about 20% of individuals learn best in this style. Most people learn best by methods that utilize concrete, experiential, self-initiated, and real world learning experiences.

In nursing, theoretical teaching is almost always accompanied by concurrent clinical practice, that allows concrete and real world learning experience. However, the exploration of leadership and management theory often omits this application through practicum, presenting theory in a lecture/listener format. The learner generally has limited opportunity to observe first- and middle-level managers in the leader/manager role in nursing practice. Because few individuals have a guided learning experience in this area, most novice managers have had little opportunity to practice their skills before assuming their first management position.

For us, there is little question that vicarious learning, or learning through mock experience, has tremendous value in the application of leadership and management theory. We propose that integrating leadership and management and using whole-brain thinking can be accomplished through the use of learning exercises. A type of experiential learning that has proven more effective than traditional lecture format, learning exercises strengthen problem solving and critical thinking skills.

Having gradually moved away from the lecture/listener format in our classes, we presently lecture only 20% to 30% of class time. Our students, once resistant to the experiential approach, are now our most enthusiastic supporters. We also find this enthusiasm for experiential learning apparent in the many workshops and seminars we provide for registered nurses. Experiential learning enables management and leadership theory to be fun and exciting, but most important, it facilitates retention of didactic material. Research we have completed on this approach to teaching supports these findings.

Although many leadership and management texts are available, this book meets an as-yet not fully addressed need; the need for emphasis on both leadership and management *and* the use of an experiential approach. More than 200 learning exercises taken from many different healthcare settings and a wide variety of learning modes give the reader many opportunities to apply theory, resulting in internalized learning.

Our faithful readers will find some of their favorite cases from our first edition and figures from our other books adapted for use in this text. Although we retained essential content, this second edition also includes contemporary research and theory to assure accuracy of the didactic material.

This book was written primarily for generic nursing students and registered nurses returning for a nursing baccalaureate degree; and for use by staff development instructors in management and leadership courses for new managers.

We have provided the instructor and learner with guidelines for using the experimental learning exercises in the text. The Instructor's and Reader's Guides can be omitted if individuals are well-versed in the experiential approach. We strongly urge the reader to use the learning exercises as they supplement the text.

The first unit of this book provides a broad background of management and leadership theory to assist with management/leadership problems presented in the text. The next five units are organized using the management process of planning, organizing, staffing, directing, and controlling. The final unit focuses on professional, ethical, and legal issues faced by nursing leaders and managers.

This book represents our philosophy about teaching leadership and management. We believe that leadership and management can and should be taught as an integrated whole; that this goal is best accomplished through a variety of experiential learning exercises; and that one of learning's goals is to strengthen the less dominant side of the brain to produce whole-brain thinking. We hope the text helps empower nurses and prepare them for the difficult task of leading and managing others.

Instructor's Guide

We have been involved with the teaching-to-think movement for some time. For many years we used a traditional lecturer/listener format to teach leadership and management. As we learned more about contemporary views of learning, we began to experiment with other teaching modes. Our first effort involved the use of case studies and resulted in the publication of a case study book. We felt, however, that other types of experiential learning were needed as well as exercises which developed writing skills and self-awareness in the reader. We also experimented with techniques to increase whole-brain thinking. This book is a result of our efforts. Although we realize that many educators are well grounded in contemporary learning theories, we have summarized these theories for those who have not used an experiential approach. We have also included suggestions for this book's use.

CONTEMPORARY LEARNING THEORIES

The idea that individuals need experiential learning was suggested by Kolb's research with different learning styles. Kolb (1976) identified four learning styles—three of which require nontraditional (non–lecture-listener format) methods for teaching to be effective.

Basically, the four different learning styles are 1) *Concrete Experience;* 2) *Reflective Observation;* 3) *Abstract Conceptualization;* and 4) *Active Experimentation.* Table A describes characteristics of each of the four learning styles. It is unlikely that anyone can be completely described by one of the learning styles because individuals combine learning styles.

TABLE A   Learning Styles

Learning Style		Characteristics
Active experimentation	=	Doing, practical, questioning, active, pragmatic, experimenting
Abstract conceptualizing	=	Involved, analytical, thinking, evaluative, logical, concrete
Reflective observation	=	Relevant, watching, risk taking, observing, reflecting, reserved
Concrete experience	=	Discriminating, intuitive, abstract, feeling, accepting, receptive

(Adapted from Kolb 1976.)

Following Kolb's work, researchers began to examine new teaching methods that would meet all learners' needs. McCarthy (1980) discovered that educators could actually increase competency in other, nonpreferred learning styles by using a variety of teaching modes. Later the concept of whole-brain learning and thinking (Edwards, 1980; Herrmann, 1981) was described.

Whole-brain research necessitated the discovery of teaching methods that incorporate a wide array of mental processes and encourage the use of both sides of the brain. These methods allow learners to strengthen the less-dominant hemisphere and become a whole-brain thinker. See Display A for appropriate learning activities for each quadrant of the brain.

TEACHING LEADERSHIP AND MANAGEMENT: AN EXPERIENTIAL APPROACH

Although studies as early as 1959 identified the need for students to focus on real managerial problems rather than focusing solely on management theory (Pierson, 1959; Gordon and Howell, 1959), the use of experiential learning in teaching leadership and management to nurses has been limited. Case study texts tended to focus on the executive nurse manager and not the novice.

For theoretical application to increase both whole-brain and critical thinking and facilitate the integration of leadership and management, two principles are needed. The first principle states that a sufficient number of learning exercises must exist so participants can begin to draw inferences. If a spectrum of vicarious experiences cannot be offered, Stevens (1982) believes that this approach is inappropriate.

Display A Learning Activities for Each Brain Quadrant

Left Cerebral

Written tests
Step-by-step procedures
Concrete problem solving
Reading the material in advance and
    coming prepared to class

Right Cerebral

Drawing maps, seeing pictures
Generating alternatives
Allowing for intuition and reflection
Seeing how the pieces fit
Future-oriented (abstract) problem
    solving

Left Limbic

Making checklists
Writing things down
Reading procedures
Taking time to organize
Seeking clear directions and
    expectations
Observing role models

Right Limbic

Debate
Case studies
Simulations
Role play
Thinking aloud
Negotiating
Seeking feedback
Active self-assessment

A variety of learning experiences reveals differences from norms and allows learners to draw generalizations and recognize patterns.

The second principle states that neither a totally right or wrong solution must exist. Although some solutions will be more successful when implemented, divergent ideas and solutions must be the goal.

Experiential learning in leadership and management is designed to look at four types of problems which can be used either individually or in groups (Willings, 1968). These types are individual problems, isolated incidents, organizational problems, and combinations of any or all three.

Individual problems. These exercises look at individuals who may have problems which affect not only their job, but the efficiency of the organization. Because managers spend so much time dealing with individual problems, identifying "universal problems" and alternative solutions is very beneficial.

Isolated incidents. These exercises identify incidents which are not covered by regulations or policy or procedure documents and which disrupt organizational functioning in some way. These exercises encourage managers to look for underlying causes and address problems, rather than symptoms of problems.

Organizational problems. The leader-manager is often personally involved in a problem and must include colleagues and subordinates in reaching an appropriate solution. The role of the organization versus the role of the worker frequently presents major conflicts.

Combinations of types of problems. These exercises present a realistic picture of problems common to managers. Individual needs and concerns, resulting isolated incidents, and organizational needs all present ramifications that must be considered.

A MODEL FOR TEACHING CRITICAL THINKING

We believe that the Marquis/Huston critical thinking teaching model (Figure A) can result in the desired learner outcomes of analysis, synthesis, and evaluation—all higher level cognitive skills. In using the model, it is important to know that each overlapping sphere is an *essential* component and all spheres must be incorporated in some way for maximum learner outcome.

The first sphere requires that the learner be introduced to formalized approaches to problem solving and critical thinking, such as the models presented in Chapter Two. If formalized problem solving is new to the learner, the instructor will need to role-model these approaches.

Secondly, there needs to be a theory component, such as the didactic material that precedes each learning exercise or set of exercises in this book. As new didactic material is presented, the learner should be given a chance to apply the theory through experiential learning exercises before moving on to new material.

The third component essential for successful implementation of the model is the use of the group process as depicted in the third sphere. Although frequently used in conjunction with group work, experiential learning is not synonymous with group work. However, we believe that the desired learner outcome for teaching critical thinking in leadership and management is an interaction between the learner

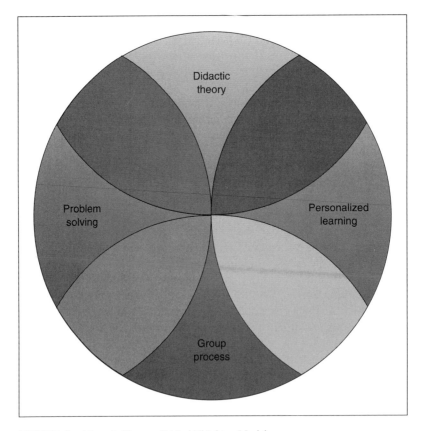

FIGURE A   Marquis-Huston Critical Thinking Model

and others that results in the ability to critically examine issues. Therefore, we believe that group process must be used with the learning exercises in this text.

Group process enhances both verbal and listening skills and encourages risk taking. Students learn to become better listeners and learn to give and receive constructive criticism. A student's ability to manipulate others toward personal and organizational goals improves and the group learns how to improve its collective performance. Groups may be used both in and out of the classroom. The use of groups increases the opportunities for individuals to learn. We have found the use of group learning to be a valuable tool in teaching learners to think.

The last sphere of the model requires that the learner be personally involved in the learning process. Personalizing the learning allows for learning to become internalized. Personalized learning occurs when the learner lives through the exercise as if it were happening to him or her, or when individuals are able to recall and use their own life experiences in problem solving. When the learner takes some sort of risk taking through sharing experiences, oral presentations or writing exercises, personalized learning also occurs. As students recall personal experiences through the use of written exercises, there is also increased writing proficiency and improved analytical thinking.

THE RESPONSIBILITIES OF THE FACILITATOR IN USING EXPERIENTIAL LEARNING

In using experiential learning exercises, certain responsibilities must be recognized by the group facilitator and/or instructor. There is little agreement, however, about how active or passive this role should be. The following suggestions are provided to assist educators or staff development instructors in facilitating the application of theory:

1. An essential prerequisite is planning. The instructor or facilitator switches places with the participant and asks: What would I learn from this exercise? How would I go about solving the problem? If I found myself faced with this situation, would I miss the real problem? What parts of this learning exercise would help me toward an understanding of the real problem? (Willings, 1968)

2. The group facilitator/instructor must be familiar with assigned exercises, and be able to identify learning objectives. When alternatives have not been formulated or issues have not been clarified, it may be difficult for group members to see what is involved. The facilitator must try to identify the universality or primary focus of the situation without squelching creativity in identifying solutions.

3. The facilitator must try to help groups beyond dependence on him or her as the leader and "solver" of the problem. The facilitator should become the "enabler" of the group.

4. With more experience in managerial and leadership problem-solving, it is easy for the facilitator to unconsciously direct group members toward a particular solution and to consider other solutions erroneous. Flexibility and objectivity, therefore, are essential. The facilitator must be willing to give up some control.

5. Time can be a constraint in any type of experiential learning. The facilitator should decide in advance how much time should be devoted to each learning exercise and how many exercises the time period allows. Factors to consider include the learning objectives and the maturity of group members.

Many generic nursing students know little about management theory and have limited exposure to management in a healthcare setting. Outside preparation and reading may be necessary before group members can solve the exercises. In addition, the facilitator should select exercises which provide an opportunity to apply all theory presented.

If exercises are used in a management seminar, the instructor must recognize that group members probably have varying levels of knowledge and expertise. Using knowledge of adult learner concepts, the facilitator should attempt to include the work experiences of group members, and focus on exercises which examine problems.

With RN students returning for their BSN, the facilitator's greatest challenge will be in determining how the learning exercises can best meet the needs of the majority of students. Generally, RN students possess life experiences and increased knowledge on which they can draw. Individual exercises may be alternated with those that encourage group members to add from their own knowledge and experience. In addition, group problem solving should encourage interpersonal relationships among the participants as well as allow more mature members to share their experiences and knowledge.

REFERENCES

Edwards, B. (1980). *Drawing on the Right Side of the Brain*. Los Angeles: JB Tarcher.

Gordon, R. A. and Howell, J. E. (1959). *Higher Education for Business.*, New York: Columbia University Press.

Herrmann, N. (1981). The Creative Brain. *Training and Development Journal*. Oct.

Kolb, D. A. (1976). *Learning Style Inventory*. Boston: McBer and Company.

Marquis, B. & Huston, C. J. (1994). *Management Decision-Making for Nurses, 2nd ed*. Philadelphia: J.B. Lippincott.

McCarthy, B. (1980). The 4MAT system: Teaching to learning styles with right/left mode techniques. Oak Brook, IL: Excel, Inc.

Pierson, F. C. (1959). *The Education of American Businessmen*. New York: McGraw Hill.

Stevens, B. J. (1982). *Educating the Nurse Manager*. Rockville, MD: Aspen Systems Corp.

Willings, D. R. (1968). *How To Use the Case Study in Training for Decision Making*. London: Business Publications Limited.

Reader's Guide

The authors of this text support the belief that theoretical teaching should almost always be accompanied by application in concurrent clinical practice. However, with leadership and management theory, this application is often limited. At best, the learner may have only observational experiences with leaders and managers. Therefore, most novice managers have had little opportunity to practice their management skills before assuming their first position.

These limitations can be overcome by allowing the learner to vicariously experience leadership and management problems through simulated learning. This book was developed with the perspective that vicarious learning, or experiential learning provides mock experiences and has tremendous value in applying leadership and management theory. We have included numerous learning exercises which allow the reader to experience the real world of leadership and management. However, in order for the book to have the desired outcomes, it is necessary that the reader actively participates in the book's various types of learning activities.

Schools of law and medicine have long used experiential learning. Case studies as a management learning tool originated at Harvard University in 1910, when the business school faculty invited corporate executives to their classes to describe the problems they faced in business. Students were asked to evaluate and develop proposals to deal with these problems. Case studies now represent a major portion of most business schools' experiential learning, with some students reading as many as 700 cases before graduating.

This book's learning exercises have been developed to increase whole-brain thinking. Some require left brain or analytical thinking; others, right brain thinking, or creative and intuitive thinking. Many require both. The learning exercises may supplement or be used in lieu of lecture. Designed to allow individuals to examine what is unique and what is common to all organizations, these exercises allow the novice manager to examine leadership problems in enough detail so that skills needed for effective leadership and management are attained.

The learning exercises in this text include case studies, writing exercises, specific management or leadership problems, staffing and budgeting calculations, group discussion or problem solving, and assessment of personal attitudes and values. Most exercises require some decision making. Some exercises include opinions, speculations, and value judgments, while others are more objective. The data in each learning exercise, however, are always incomplete to some degree, similar to a real life situation when a manager does not have all the facts.

An effective learning exercise is not just a device for instruction, it provides a means for new learning for both instructor and learner. Unlike abstract generalizations, learning exercises can demonstrate critical conditions in concrete terms. When a student can gather information and act on a problem, the discovery holds more meaning. The reader is able to vicariously make difficult decisions in a systematic and analytical manner. This allows the student to immediately apply and translate theory and principles into practice.

Additionally, learning exercises provide the opportunity for individuals to be recognized as mature, responsible human beings. By practicing leadership decision making, individuals gain confidence in their ability to solve problems and take risks. Because all successful leaders and managers are self-aware, understanding personal values, feelings, and perceptions and how they affect decision making is invaluable (Marquis and Huston, 1994).

GUIDELINES FOR USING THE LEARNING EXERCISES

Although the learning exercises presented in this book are designed for use by individuals or groups, experiential learning is frequently used in conjunction with group work. With group process, participants are able to not only solve the problem alone but to see how others would solve it. Feedback from other group members encourages the development of interpersonal skills and self-awareness. Sharing perceptions with others allows readers to more objectively evaluate their feedback as well as their own perceptions. Listening as well as verbal skills are therefore enhanced.

Group members in an experiential approach have certain responsibilities:

1. A willingness to listen to what other group members and the facilitator say. Group members need to listen to what is being said rather than focusing on their own rebuttal.

2. A responsibility to share ideas to allow mutual learning. Consistent participation in group discussions will strengthen verbal skills.

3. A responsibility to prepare assigned learning exercises. This includes carefully reading the exercises and completing the assigned didactic material before attempting problem solving.

4. A willingness to subject themselves to open debate and criticism. Little can be gained when nothing is risked. The ultimate goal of criticism is to assist other group members to make better future decisions. Criticism received must be viewed as the opportunity to learn when the risks are small and the potential for gain great.

LEARNING EXERCISE PREPARATION

Many of the learning exercises are uncomplicated and straightforward. Some involve simple mathematics. Others were developed to assist the individual in gaining personal insight and may require writing. Some of the exercises are complex and require reading for meaning which is different than skimming. Verifiable facts must be differentiated from unsupported opinions. Making brief written or mental notes will help categorize information and separate out critical information from superfluous data.

Ronstadt (1977) suggests asking a few fundamental questions when reading these types of exercises:

1. What do you think are the key issues?
2. Why was this problem assigned now?
3. Are there any hidden issues?
4. Are there any principle unassigned questions?
5. Must I make any creative assumptions?
6. What is unique about this problem? What is "universal"?
7. What is fact? What is opinion?

Data Gathering

To gain knowledge and insight into managerial problem solving, participants must reach outside their current sphere of knowledge in solving problems. Some data gathering sources include textbooks, periodicals, experts in the field, colleagues, and current research.

Questions that should be examined in data gathering are:

1. What was the setting?
2. What was the problem?
3. Where is it a problem?
4. When is it a problem?
5. Who is affected by the problem?
6. What was happening?
7. Why was it happening? What are the causes of the problem? Can the causes by prioritized?
8. What were the basic underlying issues? Areas of conflict?
9. What are the consequences of the problem? Which of these is most serious?

Solution Analysis

In analyzing possible solutions, group members may want to look at the following questions:

1. What factors can you influence? How can you make the positive factors more important? How can the negative factors be minimized?
2. What are the financial implications of each possible solution? Political implications? Departmental and interdepartmental consequences? Time involvement? Support available?
3. What are the criteria for action?
4. What are the alternative plans of action?
5. What are the weighting factors?
6. What should be done?
7. What is the "best" solution?
8. What is the means for evaluation?

Learning exercises may be prepared by groups outside of class, or may be used for individual projects. The exercises may also be presented during class, either by the facilitator, groups, or individuals. However, if the learning exercises are to promote critical thinking, encourage whole-brain thinking, and facilitate the integration of management functions and leadership roles, certain elements must be present:

1. The group process must be used in some way for problem solving.
2. Multiple alternatives for solving problems must be identified.
3. Individual accountability and decision making must be promoted as well as group problem solving.
4. Communication as well as problem solving should be a part of the critical thinking process.
5. The process of *analysis* must be stressed rather than finding the right answer.
6. *Many* learning exercises must be used, so there is ample opportunity to make decisions and develop analytical skills.

REFERENCES

Marquis, B. L. & Huston, C. J. (1994). *Management Decision-Making for Nurses: 118 Case Studies, 2nd ed.* Philadelphia: J.B. Lippincott.

Ronstadt, R. (1977). *The Art of Case Analysis.* Dover, MA: Lord Publishing.

Features of This Edition

The first edition of *Leadership Roles and Management Functions* created a stimulating learning experience by presenting the symbiotic elements of leadership and management with an emphasis on problem solving and critical thinking. The second edition maintains this precedent with a balanced presentation of a strong theory component with real world scenarios in the form of case studies, clinical situations, and experiential learning exercises.

LEARNING TOOLS

The second edition contains many pedagogical features designed to benefit both the student and instructor:

▶ **Tables, Displays, and Illustrations** are liberally applied throughout the text to reinforce learning as well as to help clarify complex information.
▶ **Numerous Learning Exercises** integrated in color throughout the text foster the reader's critical thinking skills and promote interactive discussions. **Additional Learning Exercises** are available at the end of each chapter for further study and discussion.
▶ **Key Concepts** summarize important information within every chapter.

NEW FEATURES

▶ More Case Studies have been included, further strengthening the problem-based element of this text. Many case studies have an increased emphasis on community-based situations.
▶ New information on transformational leadership and nursing care delivery systems for today's dynamic and ever-changing healthcare environment.
▶ New methods of organizing and prioritizing tasks are discussed in the extensively revised Chapter 5, "Time Management." New content on communication patterns is presented in Chapter 15, "Organizational and Interpersonal Communication."
▶ Combined Instructor's Manual and Test Bank.

Contents

UNIT I

A NEW APPROACH TO LEADERSHIP AND MANAGEMENT

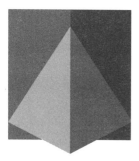

CHAPTER 1

Integrating Leadership Roles and Management Functions

Throughout history, nursing has been required to respond to changing technological and social forces. For example, managerial responsibilities have evolved in response to an increased emphasis on the business of healthcare, thus requiring managerial expertise in the financial and marketing aspects of their departments. Sullivan, Baumgardner, Henninger, and Jones (1994) stated that, given trends in healthcare delivery, the nurse manager role is becoming critical to effective, quality patient care; to confront these expanding responsibilities and demands, the manager must take on new dimensions to facilitate quality outcomes in patient care and meet other strategic institution goals and objectives.

The need to develop nursing leadership skills has never been greater. "Two of the foremost tasks of a new nursing leadership will be to raise the consciousness of nurses through an ongoing critique of the present system and to offer philosophical and practical rationales for fundamental change based on nursing values and the central role that nursing plays in the health care process" (Edwards, 1994, p. 20). Leadership skills also are necessary for team building at the organizational level. Ensuring

Bessie L. Marquis and Carol J. Huston:
LEADERSHIP ROLES AND MANAGEMENT FUNCTIONS IN NURSING, 2nd ed.
Lippincott-Raven Publishers © 1996

successful recruitment, retaining a cohesive nursing staff, and maintaining high quality practice depend on successful team building.

Stout-Shaffer and Larrabee (1992) have identified five paradigm shifts that will transform healthcare organizations within the next decade (Table 1.1). These changes will have a great impact on the nursing profession and represent a challenge to nursing leaders and managers.

DIFFERENCES IN LEADERSHIP AND MANAGEMENT

The relationship between leadership and management continues to prompt much debate for theorists. Tranbarger (1988) states that leadership is but one of management's many functions; yet Gardner (1986) asserts that leadership requires more complex skills than management and that management is only one role of leadership. Manthey (1990) delineates the two, stating that a manager guides, directs, and motivates, while a leader empowers others; therefore, every manager should be a leader.

McNeese-Smith (1992) states that management emphasizes *control*—control of hours, costs, salaries, overtime, use of sick leave, inventory, and supplies—and that leadership increases productivity by maximizing work force *effectiveness*. Farley (1990) implies that management preparation occurs before leadership when she states that young managers must be developed as leaders.

To define the manager, Holloman (1986) uses the term headship and distinguishes it from leadership. Holloman maintains that it is a mistake to refer to the dean of a school of nursing, a nursing supervisor, or a head nurse as a leader. These individuals are in a headship position, rather than a leadership position. A job title alone does not make a person a leader. Only a person's behavior determines if he or she occupies a leadership position.

Bennis and Nanus (1985) differentiate between leaders and managers in their argument that "managers are people who do things right and leaders are people who do the right thing." Bennis and Nanus also identify the manager as the individual who brings things about; the one who accomplishes, has the responsibility, and con-

TABLE 1.1   Paradigm Shifts in Health Care Organizations

Past	Future
Centralized hierarchies	Semiautonomous work units
Power vested in management	Empowerment of all
Distrust	Trust
Quantitative productivity	Intuition and creativity
Planning for patients	Planning with patients

Source: Stout-Shaffer, S., & Larrabee, J. (1992). Everyone can be a visionary leader. *Nursing Management, 23*(12), 54–58.

ducts. They define the leader as the individual who influences and guides direction, opinion, and course of action.

What then is the relationship between leadership and management? In an effort to understand better the relationship between leadership and management, it may be helpful to examine how they differ.

Managers

- Have an assigned position within the formal organization
- Have a legitimate source of power due to the delegated authority that accompanies their position
- Are expected to carry out specific functions, duties, and responsibilities
- Emphasize control, decision making, decision analysis, and results
- Manipulate individuals, the environment, money, time, and other resources to achieve organizational goals
- Have a greater formal responsibility and accountability for rationality and control than leaders
- Direct willing and unwilling subordinates

Leaders

- Often do not have delegated authority but obtain their power through other means, such as influence
- Have a wider variety of roles than do managers
- Are frequently not part of the formal organization
- Focus on group process, information gathering, feedback, and empowering others
- Emphasize interpersonal relationships
- Direct willing followers
- Have goals that may or may not reflect those of the organization

Historically, strong management skills have been valued more than strong leadership skills in the healthcare industry. Although greater emphasis has been placed on leadership skills in management in the last decade, research by Vincent, Brewer, Aslakson, and Swanson (1993) suggests that leadership may continue to be undervalued in nursing curricula and that internalization of the value of leadership should be increased. The National League for Nursing (1989) also supports the belief that leadership should be internalized by professional nurses and has recognized leadership as a criterion in their accreditation of baccalaureate programs in nursing.

In examining leadership and management, it becomes clear these two concepts have a symbiotic or synergistic relationship. For managers and leaders to function at their greatest potential, the two must be integrated. Every nurse is a leader and manager at some level, and the nursing role requires leadership and management skills. The need for visionary leaders and effective managers in nursing precludes the option of stressing one role over the other. Because rapid, dramatic change will continue in nursing and the healthcare industry, it has grown increasingly important for nurses to develop skill in leadership roles and management functions. Nurses must strive for the integration of leadership characteristics throughout every phase of the management process.

Gardner (1990) asserted that integrated leaders/managers distinguish themselves from the more traditional manager in six ways.

1. They think longer term. They are visionary and futuristic. They consider the effect their decisions will have years from now and their immediate consequence.
2. They look outward, toward the larger organization. They do not become narrowly focused. They are able to understand how their unit or department fits into the bigger picture.
3. They influence others beyond their own group. Effective leaders/managers rise above an organization's bureaucratic boundaries.
4. They emphasize vision, values, and motivation. They understand intuitively the unconscious and often nonrational aspects that are present in interactions with others. They are very sensitive to others and to differences in each situation.
5. They are politically astute. They are capable of coping with conflicting requirements and expectations from their many constituencies.
6. They think in terms of change and renewal. The traditional manager accepts the structure and processes of the organization, but the leader/manager examines the ever-changing reality of the world and seeks to revise the organization to keep pace.

This book is based on the premise that professional managerial judgment, critical thinking, and successful leadership decision making can be learned. How then can novice nurse managers learn important management functions and develop leadership skills? How do they become integrated leaders/managers?

This chapter explores the development of traditional management theory, examines leadership theory from historical and contemporary perspectives, and introduces whole-brain thinking as a method of integrating leadership and management.

HISTORICAL DEVELOPMENT OF MANAGEMENT THEORY

Management science, like nursing, develops a theory base from many disciplines, such as business, psychology, sociology, and anthropology. Because organizations are complex and varied, theorists' views of what successful management is and what it should be has changed repeatedly in the last 100 years.

Scientific Management (1900–1930)

Frederick W. Taylor, the "father of scientific management," was a mechanical engineer in the Midvale and Bethlehem Steel Plants in Pennsylvania in the late 1800s. Frustrated with what he called "systematic soldiering," where workers achieved minimum standards doing the least amount of work possible, Taylor postulated that if workers could be taught the "one best way to accomplish a task," productivity would increase. Borrowing a term coined by Louis Brandeis, a colleague of Taylor's,

Taylor called these principles "scientific management." The four overriding principles of scientific management as identified by Taylor (1911) follow:

1. Traditional "rule of thumb" means of organizing work must be replaced with scientific methods. In other words, by using time and motion studies and the expertise of experienced workers, work could be scientifically designed to promote greatest efficiency of time and energy.
2. A scientific personnel system must be established so that workers can be hired, trained, and promoted based on their technical competence and abilities. In other words, each employee's abilities and limitations would be identified so that the worker could be best matched to the most appropriate job.
3. Workers should be able to view how they "fit" into the organization and how they contribute to overall organizational productivity. This provides common goals and a sharing of the organizational mission. One way Taylor thought this could be accomplished was by the use of financial incentives as a reward for work accomplished. Because Taylor viewed humans as "economic animals," motivated solely by money, workers were reimbursed according to their level of production, rather than by an hourly wage.
4. The relationship between managers and workers should be cooperative and interdependent, and the work should be shared equally. Their roles, however, were not the same. The role of managers, or "functional foremen" as they were called, was to plan, prepare, and supervise. The worker was to do the work.

What was the result of scientific management? Productivity and profits rose dramatically. Organizations were provided with a rational means of harnessing the energy of the industrial revolution. Some experts have argued that Taylor was ahumanistic and that his scientific principles were not in the best interest of unions or workers. However, it is important to remember the era in which Taylor did his work. During the industrial revolution, laissez-faire economics prevailed, optimism was high, and a puritan work ethic was prevalent. To the end, Taylor maintained that he truly believed managers and workers would be satisfied if financial rewards were adequate as a result of increased productivity.

Max Weber, a well-known German sociologist developed similar ideas and expanded on Taylor's concepts. Weber saw the need for legalized, formal authority and consistent rules and regulations for personnel in different positions; he thus proposed bureaucracy as an organizational design. His essay, "Bureaucracy," was written in 1922 in response to what Weber perceived as a need to provide more rules, regulations, and structure within organizations to increase efficiency. Much of Weber's work and bureaucratic organizational design is still evident today in many healthcare institutions. His work is discussed further in Chapter 7.

Management Functions Identified (1925)

Henri Fayol (1925) first identified the management functions of planning, organization, command, coordination, and control. Luther Gulick (1937) expanded on Fayol's management functions in his introduction of the "seven activities of management"—planning, organizing, staffing, directing, coordinating, reporting, and budgeting—as denoted by the mnemonic POSDCORB.

Although often modified (either by including staffing as a management function or renaming elements), these functions or activities have changed little over time. Eventually, theorists began to refer to these functions as the management process.

The management process shown in Figure 1.1 is this book's organizing framework. Briefly, the five functions for each phase of the management process follow:

1. Planning encompasses determining philosophy, goals, objectives, policies, procedures, and rules; carrying out long- and short-range projections; determining a fiscal course of action; and managing planned change.
2. Organizing includes establishing the structure to carry out plans, determining the most appropriate type of patient care delivery, and grouping activities to meet unit goals. Other functions involve working within the structure of the organization and understanding and using power and authority appropriately.
3. Staffing functions consist of recruiting, interviewing, hiring, and orienting staff. Scheduling, staff development, and often employee socialization also are included as staffing functions.
4. Directing sometimes includes several staffing functions. However, this phase's functions usually entail human resource management responsibilities, such as motivating, managing conflict, delegating, communicating, and facilitating collaboration.

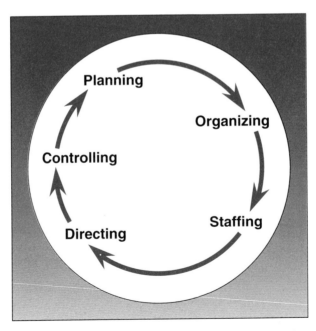

FIGURE 1.1   The management process.

5. Controlling functions include performance appraisals, fiscal accountability, quality control, legal and ethical control, and professional and collegial control.

Marquis and Huston (1994) assert that the management process is similar in many ways to the nursing process as shown in Figure 1.2. Both processes are cyclical, and many different functions may occur simultaneously. Suppose that a nurse-manager spent part of the day working on the budget (planning), met with the staff about changing the patient care management delivery system from primary care to team nursing (organizing), altered the staffing policy to include 12-hour shifts (staffing), held a meeting to resolve a conflict between nurses and physicians (directing), and gave an employee a job performance evaluation (controlling). Not only would the nurse-manager be performing all phases of the management process, but each function has a planning, implementing, and controlling phase. Just as nursing practice requires that all nursing care has a plan and an evaluation, so too does each function of management.

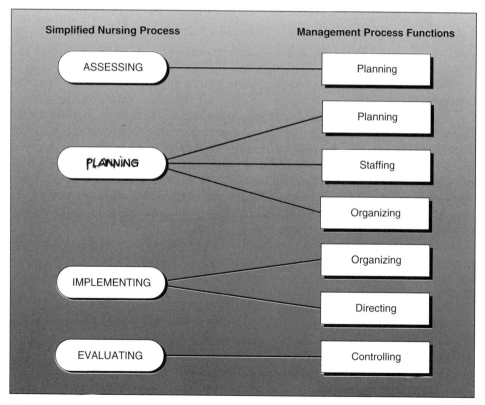

FIGURE 1.2   Integrating nursing and management processes.

Human Relations Management (1930–1970)

During the 1920s, worker unrest developed. The industrial revolution had resulted in great numbers of relatively unskilled laborers working in large factories on specialized tasks. Thus, management scientists and organizational theorists began to look at the role of worker satisfaction in production. This human relations era developed the concepts of participatory and humanistic management, emphasizing people rather than machines.

Mary Parker Follett was one of the first theorists to suggest basic principles of what today would be called "participative decision making" or "participative management." In her essay, "The Giving of Orders" (1926), Follett espoused her belief that managers should have authority with, rather than over, employees. Follett stated that to do so, a need existed for collective decision making.

The human relations era also attempted to correct what was perceived as the major shortcoming of the bureaucratic system—a failure to include the "human element."

Studies done at the Hawthorne Works of the Western Electric Company near Chicago between 1927–1932 played a major role in this shifting focus. The studies, conducted by Elton Mayo and his Harvard associates, began as an attempt to look at the relationship between light illumination in the factory and productivity.

Mayo and his colleagues discovered that when management paid special attention to workers, productivity was likely to increase, regardless of the environmental working conditions. This "Hawthorne effect" indicated that people respond to the fact that they are being studied, attempting to increase whatever behavior they feel will continue to warrant the attention. Mayo (1953) also found that informal work groups and a socially informal work environment were factors in determining productivity, and Mayo recommended more employee participation in decision making.

Douglas McGregor (1960) reinforced these ideas by theorizing that managerial attitudes about employees (and, hence, how managers treat those employees) can be directly correlated with employee satisfaction. He labeled this theory X and theory Y. Theory X managers believe that their employees are basically lazy, need constant supervision and direction, and are indifferent to organizational needs. Theory Y managers believe that their workers enjoy their work, are self-motivated, and are willing to work hard to meet personal and organizational goals. McGregor's contribution to motivation theory is discussed more fully in Chapter 14.

Chris Argyris (1964) supported McGregor and Mayo by saying that managerial domination causes workers to become discouraged and passive. He believed that if self-esteem and independence needs are not met, employees will become discouraged and troublesome or may leave the organization. Argyris stressed the need for flexibility within the organization and employee participation in decision making.

Abraham Maslow (1970) also did some of his work during the human relations era and contributed immensely to understanding human needs and motivation. Maslow developed a hierarchy of needs based on a lifetime study of normal human behavior. Needs embodied in each person include (1) physiological, (2) security or safety, (3) social or love, (4) ego or self-esteem, and (5) self-actualization. People generally first satisfy lower level needs before they move on to higher level needs.

Maslow's work reinforced the concept that human beings are complex creatures; managers, therefore, must recognize that employees are motivated by different things at different times in their lives.

Frederick Herzberg (1977), examining employee motivation, suggested that the factors that produce job satisfaction differ from those that produce job dissatisfaction. Growth or motivator factors intrinsic to the job are achievement, recognition for achievement, the work itself, responsibility, and growth or advancement. Dissatisfaction or hygiene factors extrinsic to the job include company policy and administration, supervision, interpersonal relationships, working conditions, salary, status, and security. Hygiene factors can cause dissatisfaction but do not lead to motivation. Herzberg stressed the need for organizations to include motivator factors for employee satisfaction. The work of the motivational theorists is discussed further in Chapter 14.

By the late 1960s, there was growing concern that the human relations approach to management was not without its problems (Marquis & Huston, 1994). Most people continued to work in a bureaucratic environment, making it difficult always to apply a participatory approach to management. The human relations approach was time consuming and often resulted in unmet organizational goals. In addition, not every employee liked working in a less-structured environment (Douglass, 1992).

Table 1.2 summarizes the development of management theory up to 1970. During the 1950s, leadership theory was developing separately from management science. It was not until the late 1960s that researchers began to understand how complex and intertwined management and leadership are.

HISTORICAL DEVELOPMENT OF LEADERSHIP THEORY

More than 10,000 books and articles, representing widely varying schools of thought, have been published on the topic of leadership (Yukl, 1989). To summarize what is known about this topic in one chapter is impossible. Instead, an effort is

TABLE 1.2   Management Theory Development

Theorist	Theory
Taylor	Scientific management
Weber	Bureaucratic organizations
Fayol	Management functions
Gulick	Activities of management
Follett	Participative management
Mayo	Hawthorne effect
McGregor	Theory X and Theory Y
Argyris	Employee participation

made to introduce the idea that leadership theory is dynamic; that is, what is "known" and believed about leadership has changed considerably during the last 100 years and will continue to change in the future. Conceptual definitions of leadership, the evolution of leadership theory, and contemporary theories of leadership are presented.

Defining Leadership

Although the term "leader" has been in use since the 1300s, the word "leadership" was not known in the English language until the first half of the nineteenth century (Marriner-Tomey, 1993). Despite its relatively new addition to the English language, leadership has many meanings. From Chapin's (1924) technical definition of leadership as "a point of polarization for group cooperation" to De Pree's (1987) abstract assertion that "leadership isn't a science or discipline; it is an art and as such, must be felt, experienced, created," it becomes clear that there is no single definition broad enough to encompass the total leadership process.

Selznick (1957, p. 25), in the classic *Leadership in Administration,* stated that leadership could be characterized by three guiding ideas: 1) it is work done to meet the needs of a social situation; 2) it is not equivalent to office holding, high prestige, authority or decision making; and 3) it is dispensable. "These premises emphasized the futility of attempting to understand leadership apart from the broader organizational experience of which it is a phase."

Kotter (1988), believing that leadership could occur outside of an organizational context, defined leadership as the process of moving a group or groups in some direction through mostly noncoercive means. Gardner (1990, p. 1) expanded this idea, defining leadership as "the process of persuasion and example by which an individual (or leadership team) induces a group to pursue objectives held by the leader or shared by the leader and his or her followers" (p. 1). Robbins (1991, p. 104) concurs, stating "leadership is the process of empowering beliefs and teaching others to tap their full capabilities by shifting the beliefs that have been limiting them" (p. 104). Bernhard and Walsh (1990, p. 16) define leadership simply as "a process used to move a group toward goal setting and goal achievement."

Because leadership researchers and theorists do not agree on exactly what leadership is, it is perhaps wiser to focus on what roles are inherent in leadership.

The following is a partial list of a leader's roles:

Decision maker	Teacher
Critical thinker	Communicator
Buffer	Evaluator
Advocate	Facilitator
Visionary	Risk taker
Forecaster	Mentor
Influencer	Energizer
Creative problem solver	Coach
Change agent	Counselor
Diplomat	Role model

LEARNING EXERCISE 1.1

In groups or individually, add roles to this list that you feel are examples of what a leader does. How many of the leadership roles listed previously, or others you have formulated, also are recognized as nursing roles?

THE EVOLUTION OF LEADERSHIP THEORY

The scientific study of leadership began in the 20th century. Early works focused on broad conceptualizations of leadership, such as the traits or behaviors of the leader. Contemporary research focuses more on leadership as a process of influencing others within an organizational culture and the interactive relationship of the leader and follower. To understand better today's beliefs about leadership, it is necessary to look at how leadership theory has evolved during the last century.

The Great Man Theory/Trait Theories

The great man theory and trait theories were the basis for most leadership research until the mid 1940s. The great man theory, from Aristotelian philosophy, asserts that some men are born to lead, while others are born to be led. Trait theories assume that some people have certain characteristics or personality traits that make them better leaders than others. To determine the traits that distinguish great leaders, researchers studied the lives of prominent men throughout history. The affect of followers and the impact of the situation itself were ignored. Contemporary opponents of these theories, such as Senge (1990) and Gardner (1990), argue that leadership skills can be developed, not just inherited.

Although trait theories have obvious shortcomings (ie, they neglect the impact of others or the situation on the leadership role), they are worth examining. Many of the characteristics identified in trait theories (see Display 1.1) are still used to describe successful leaders today.

Display 1.1 Characteristics of a Leader

Intelligence	Personality	Abilities
Knowledge	Adaptability	Able to enlist cooperation
Judgment	Creativity	Interpersonal skills
Decisiveness	Cooperativeness	Tact, diplomacy
Oral fluency	Alertness	Prestige
	Self-confidence	Social participation
	Personal integrity	
	Emotional balance and control	
	Nonconformity	
	Independence	

(Adapted from Huston, 1990; Swansburg, 1990; Bass, 1982.)

LEARNING EXERCISE 1.2

In groups or individually, list additional characteristics you feel an effective leader possesses. Which leadership characteristics from these lists do you have? Do you feel you were born with leadership skills, or have you consciously developed them during your lifetime?

Behavioral Theories

During the human relations era, many behavioral and social scientists studying management science also studied leadership. For example, McGregor's theories had as much influence on leadership research as they did on management science. As it developed in this era, leadership research moved away from studying what traits the leader had and placed greater focus on what he or she did—the leader's style of leadership.

A major breakthrough occurred when Lewin (1951) and White and Lippitt (1960) isolated common leadership styles. Later, these styles were called authoritarian, democratic, and laissez-faire.

The authoritarian leader is characterized by the following behaviors:

- Strong control is maintained over the work group.
- Others are motivated by coercion.
- Others are directed with commands.
- Communication flows downward.
- Decision making does not involve others.
- Emphasis is on difference in status ("I" and "you").
- Criticism is punitive.

Authoritarian leadership results in well-defined group actions that are usually predictable, reducing frustration in the work group and giving members a feeling of security. Productivity is usually high, but creativity, self-motivation, and autonomy are reduced. Authoritarian leadership, useful in crisis situations, is frequently found in very large bureaucracies, such as the armed forces.

The democratic leader exhibits the following behaviors:

- Less control is maintained.
- Economic and ego awards are used to motivate.
- Others are directed through suggestions and guidance.
- Communication flows up and down.
- Decision making involves others.
- Emphasis is on "we" rather than "I" and "you."
- Criticism is constructive.

Democratic leadership, appropriate for groups who work together for extended periods, promotes autonomy and growth in individual workers. This type of leadership is particularly effective when cooperation and coordination between groups are necessary.

Because many individuals must be consulted, democratic leadership takes more time and therefore may be frustrating for those who want decisions made rapidly. Studies have shown that democratic leadership is less efficient quantitatively than authoritative leadership.

The laissez-faire leader is characterized by the following behaviors:

- He or she is permissive with little or no control.
- Motivates by support when requested by the group or individuals.
- Little or no direction is provided.
- Communication is between members of group and upward and downward.
- Decision making is dispersed throughout the group.
- Emphasis is on the group.
- Criticism is not given.

Because it is nondirected leadership, the laissez-faire style can be frustrating; group apathy and disinterest can occur. However, when all group members are highly motivated and self-directed, this leadership style can result in much creativity and productivity. Laissez-faire leadership is appropriate when problems are poorly defined, and brainstorming is needed to generate alternative solutions.

An individual's leadership style has a great deal of influence on the climate and outcome of the work group. For some time, theorists believed that leaders had a predominant leadership style and used it consistently. During the late 1940s and early 1950s, however, theorists began to believe that most leaders did not fit a textbook picture of any one style, but rather fell somewhere on a continuum between authoritarian and laissez-faire. They also came to believe that leaders moved dynamically along the continuum in response to each new situation. This recognition was a forerunner to what is known as situational leadership theory.

Situational and Contingency Leadership Theories

The idea that leadership style should vary according to the situation or the employees involved was first suggested almost 100 years ago by Mary Parker Follett. Follett was one of the earliest management consultants and among the first to view an organization as a social system of contingencies. Her ideas, published in a series of books between 1896 and 1933, were so far ahead of their time, that they did not gain appropriate recognition in the literature until the 1970s. Follett (1926) stressed the need for "integration," which involved finding a solution that satisfied both sides without having one side dominate the other. Her "law of the situation," which said that the situation should determine the directives given after allowing everyone to know the problem, was contingency leadership in its humble origins.

Fiedler's (1967) contingency approach reinforced these findings, suggesting that no one leadership style is ideal for every situation. Fiedler felt that the interrelationships between the group's leader and its members were most influenced by the manager's ability to be a good leader. The task to be accomplished and the power associated with the leader's position also were cited as key variables.

In contrast to the continuum from autocratic to democratic, Blake and Mouton's (1964) grid shows the various combinations of concern or focus that managers had for or on productivity, tasks, people, and relationships. In each of these areas the manager/leader may rank high or low, resulting in numerous combinations of leadership behaviors. Various formations can be effective depending on the situation and the needs of the worker.

Hersey and Blanchard (1977) also developed a situational approach to leadership. Their tridimensional leadership effectiveness model predicts which leadership style is most appropriate in each situation based on the level of the followers' maturity. As individuals mature, leadership style becomes less task focused and more relationship oriented.

Tannenbaum and Schmidt (1983) built on the work of Lewin and White, suggesting that managers need varying mixtures of autocratic and democratic leadership behavior. They believed that the primary determinants of leadership style should include the nature of the situation itself, the skills of the manager, and the abilities of the group members.

CONTEMPORARY THEORIES OF LEADERSHIP

Although situational and contingency theories added necessary complexity to leadership theory and continue to be used effectively in management, by the late 1970s, theorists began arguing that effective leadership depended on an even greater number of variables, including organizational culture, the values of the leader and their followers, the work itself, the environment, the influence of the leader/manager, and the complexities of the situation (Tappen, 1995). Efforts to integrate these variables are apparent in contemporary interactional and transformational leadership theories.

Interactional Leadership Theories

The basic premise of interactional theory is that leadership behavior is generally determined by the relationship between the leader's personality and the specific situation. Ouchi (1981) was among the first researchers to introduce interactional leadership theory in his application of Japanese-style management to corporate America. Theory Z, the term Ouchi used for this type of management, is an expansion of McGregor's theory Y and supports democratic leadership. Characteristics of theory Z include consensus decision making, fitting employees to their jobs, job security, slower promotions, examining the long-term consequences of management decision making, quality circles, guarantee of lifetime employment, establishment of strong bonds of responsibility between superiors and subordinates, and a holistic concern for the workers (Ouchi, 1981; Viau, 1990). Ouchi was able to find components of Japanese-style management in many successful American companies.

Although theory Z was quite popular in the early 1980s, it has lost favor with some management theorists during the last decade. Glasser (1994) states that while American managers are well aware that they are losing market share to foreign competition, especially Japanese companies, they seem "unable to put these same ideas into practice in the United States. Instead, they continue to boss-manage workers in an attempt to make them do what they do not want to do." It is these types of differences between Japanese and American societies, values, and culture that have hindered the successful adoption of this management style in Western companies

(Strader, 1987). However, some American companies originally identified by Ouchi as having components of theory Z have continued to thrive.

Although theory Z is more comprehensive than many of the earlier theories, it too neglects some of the variables that influence leadership effectiveness. It has the same shortcomings as situational theories in inadequately recognizing the dynamics of the interaction between worker and leader.

Schein (1970) was the first to propose a model of humans as complex beings whose working environment was an open system to which they responded. A system may be defined as a set of objects with relationships between the objects and between their attributes. A system is considered open if it exchanges matter, energy, or information with its environment (Hall & Fagen, 1968). Schein's model, based on systems theory, had the following assumptions:

- People are very complex and highly variable. They have multiple motives for doing things. For example, a pay raise might mean status to one person, security to another, and both to a third.
- People's motives do not stay constant but change over time.
- Goals can differ in various situations. For example, an informal group's goals may be quite distinct from a formal group's goals.
- A person's performance and productivity are affected by the nature of the task and by his or her ability, experience, and motivation.
- No single leadership strategy is effective in every situation. To be successful, the leader must diagnose the situation and select appropriate strategies from a large repertoire of skills.

Hollander (1978) was among the first to recognize that both leaders and followers have roles outside the leadership situation and that both may be influenced by events occurring in their other roles. With leader and follower contributing to the working relationship and both receiving something from it, Hollander saw leadership as a dynamic two-way process. According to Hollander, a leadership exchange involves three basic elements:

- The leader, including his or her personality, perceptions, and abilities
- The followers, with their personalities, perceptions, and abilities
- The situation within which the leader and the followers function, including formal and informal group norms, size, and density

Leadership effectiveness, according to Hollander, requires the ability to use the problem-solving process; maintain group effectiveness; communicate well; demonstrate leader fairness, competence, dependability, and creativity; and develop group identification.

Nelson and Burns (1984) suggested that organizations and their leaders have four developmental levels and that these levels influence productivity and worker satisfaction. The first of these levels is reactive. The reactive leader focuses on the past, is crisis-driven, and is frequently abusive to subordinates. In the next level, responsive, the leader is able to mold subordinates to work together as a team, although the leader maintains most decision-making responsibility. At the proactive level, the leader and followers become more future oriented and hold common driving values.

Management and decision making are more participative. At the last level, high performance teams, maximum productivity, and worker satisfaction are apparent.

Brandt's (1994) interactive leadership model suggests that leaders develop a work environment that fosters autonomy and creativity through valuing and empowering followers. This leadership "affirms the uniqueness of each individual," motivating them to "contribute their unique talents to a common goal." The leader must accept the responsibility for quality of outcomes and quality of life for followers. Brandt states that this type of leadership affords the leader greater freedom while simultaneously adding to the burdens of leadership. The leader's responsibilities increase because priorities cannot be limited to the organization's goals, and authority confers not only power, but also responsibility and obligation. The leader's concern for each worker decreases the need for competition and fosters an atmosphere of collegiality, freeing the leader from the burden of having to resolve follower conflicts. Leaders in this model would understand what Drucker (1992) meant by his belief that leadership is a responsibility rather than a rank or privilege.

Wolf, Boland, and Aukerman (1994) also built an interactive leadership model in their creation of a "collaborative practice matrix." This matrix highlights the framework for the development and ongoing support of relationships between and among professionals working together. The "social architecture" of the work group is emphasized, as is how expectations, personal values, and interpersonal relationships affect the ability of leaders and followers to achieve the vision of the organization.

Kanter (1989) perhaps best summarized the work of the interactive theorists in the following quote:

> Position, title and authority are no longer adequate tools, not in a world where subordinates are encouraged to think for themselves and where managers have to work synergistically with other departments and even other companies.

Transformational Leadership

Burns (1978), a noted scholar in the area of leader–follower interactions, was among the first to suggest that both leaders and followers have the ability to raise each other to higher levels of motivation and morality. Identifying this concept as transformational leadership, Burns maintained that there are two types of leaders in management. The traditional manager, concerned with the day-to-day operations, was termed a *transactional leader*; the manager, on the other hand, who is committed, has a vision, and is able to empower others with this vision was termed a *transformational leader*. A composite of the two different types of leaders is shown in Display 1.2.

Bennis and Nanus (1985) built on this work when defining the transformational leader as a leader who commits people to action, who converts followers into leaders, and who converts leaders into agents of change.

Stout-Shaffer and Larrabee (1992) argue that the essence of transformational leadership is vision—the ability to see what is needed and to give the direction necessary to accomplish it. This vision implies the ability to picture some future state and describe it to others so they will begin "to share the dream." This new shared vision provides the energy required to move an organizational unit toward the future.

Wolf (1994, p. 38) defines transformational leadership as "an interactive relationship, based on trust, that positively impacts both the leader and the follower.

Display 1.2 Transactional and Transformational Leaders

Transactional Leader	Transformational Leader
Focuses on management tasks	Identifies common values
Is a caretaker	Is committed
Uses trade-offs to meet goals	Inspires others with vision
Shared values not identified	Has long-term vision
Examines causes	Looks at effects
Uses contingency reward	Empowers others

The purposes of the leader and follower become focused, creating unity, wholeness and collective purpose." Wolf says that the high-performing transformational leader demonstrates a strong commitment to the profession and the organization and is willing to tackle obstacles using group learning. This self-confidence comes from a strong sense of being in control. These transformational leaders also are able to create synergistic environments that enhance change. Change occurs because the transformational leader's futuristic focus values creativity and innovation. The transformational leader also values organizational culture and values strongly, perpetuating these same values and behaviors in their staff (Wolf, 1994).

Tyrrell (1994, p. 93) identifies "visioning" as a mark of the transformational leader, stating that "nurses at all levels are expected to demonstrate leadership in setting direction for nursing practice, and that visionary leadership allows nurses to create a picture of an ideal future. In sharing these visions, the transformational leader empowers staff to find common ground and a sense of connection."

Although the transformational leader is held as the current "ideal," many management theorists, including Bass, Avoliio, and Goodheim (1987) and Dunham and Klafehn (1990), sound a warning about transformational leadership. Although transformational qualities are highly desirable, they must be coupled with the more traditional transactional qualities of the day-to-day managerial role. Both sets of characteristics need to be present in the same individual in varying degrees. According to Bass, the transformational leader will fail without traditional management skills.

Bennis (1989) in *Why Leaders Can't Lead* sounds a different warning about the quest for transformational leadership in his assertion:

> There is an unconscious conspiracy in contemporary society that prevents leaders—no matter what their original vision—from taking charge and making changes. Within any organization, an entrenched bureaucracy with a commitment to the status quo undermines the wary leader. To make matters worse, certain social forces—the increasing tension between individual rights and the common good, for example—discourage the emergence of leaders (p. xii).

It is critical then to remember that the organization itself and the environment play a critical role in the development and support of the transformational and transactional leadership skills of its employees. The relationship must be symbiotic. Table 1.3 summarizes the development of leadership theory presented in this chapter.

TABLE 1.3 **Leadership Theory Development**

Theorist	Theory
Aristotle	Great man theory
Lewin and White	Leadership styles
Follett	Law of the situation
Fiedler	Contingency leadership
Blake and Mouton	Task versus relationship in determining leadership style
Hersey and Blanchard	Situational leadership theory
Tannebaum and Schmidt	Situational leadership theory
Selznick	Leadership as part of the organization
Kotter	Leadership as the movement of groups
Burns	Transactional and transformational leadership
Tyrrell	Visioning in transformational leadership
Gardner	The integrated leader/manager

LEADERSHIP FOR NURSING'S FUTURE

Seemingly insurmountable problems, a lack of resources to solve those problems, and individual apathy have been and will continue to be issues nurse leaders/managers face. Selznick (1957, p. vi) states the following:

> Our major institutions—political, legal, educational, industrial—are under pressure to perform in the short run and have little support, from within or without, for a longer view of what they are doing and where they are going . . . An understanding of leadership in both public and private organizations must have a high place on the agenda of social inquiry.

Gardner (1990, p. xii) repeats this theme 33 years later in *On Leadership*:

> We are faced with immensely threatening problems—terrorism, AIDS, drugs, depletion of the ozone layer, the threat of nuclear conflict, toxic waste, the real possibility of economic disaster. . . . Yet our response does not acknowledge the manifest urgency of these problems. We are anxious but immobilized. . . . Could it be that we have lost all conviction that we can do anything about these problems? . . . If so, the need for leadership has never been greater . . . and we can do better. Much, much better.

Becoming better leaders/managers begins with a basic understanding of what leadership is and how these skills can best be developed. The problem is that the skills needed to be an effective leader are dynamic and change constantly in response to the rapidly changing world in which we live. It is clear by looking at the evolution of leadership theory that what is considered "effective" or "desirable" leadership has changed virtually from decade to decade. Transformational leadership, interactional leadership theories, and "the learning organization" (Senge, 1990) are the 1990s' solutions to these problems. Will these strategies still be considered the answer to our problems in 2000? Can they solve the types of problems Selznick and Gardner described? Can they overcome the warnings sounded by Bass and Dunham?

The answer to these questions is probably not. We still have much to learn about the complexities of leadership. Many questions remain to be answered:

- If societal, group, organizational, and individual values conflict, what goals or objectives should guide the leader and his or her followers?
- What other variables that we have not even begun to consider yet may be a critical factor in understanding leadership?
- *Must* all followers be empowered? *Should* all followers be empowered?
- What safeguards should be used so that "shared vision" does not represent "group think," whereby all group members think alike?
- Can and should leader accountability be formalized? If so, how?

Gardner (1990) states "we have barely scratched the surface in our efforts toward leadership development. In the mid twenty-first century, people will look back on our present practices as primitive." It is imperative then, that nurse leaders/managers not only actively pursue leadership development, but that they make every effort possible to remain current in their understanding and application of contemporary leadership principles.

USE OF WHOLE-BRAIN THINKING TO INTEGRATE LEADERSHIP AND MANAGEMENT SKILLS

As discussed in the Instructor's and Reader's Guides, the left side of the brain is often considered the analytical side, while the right side is the artistic and speech center of the brain. Table 1.4 shows the functions of each hemisphere of the brain. It is obvious that the nursing profession and leadership and management practice depend on all four quadrants of the brain for maximum effectiveness.

Management traditionally has more highly valued left-brain functions, such as logic and measurement, and subordinated the more creative, intuitive, sensing, and artistic aspect of our nature (Covey, 1989; Veehoff, 1992). However, Murphy (1985) discovered that leadership responsibilities in management require right-brain thinking. Murphy found that the best managers tend to be multidominant, and by incorporating both hemispheres of the brain, they are able to use holistic thinking, relationships, and emotional considerations necessary for successful management. Herrmann (1982) maintains that with training and practice, people can move into an integrated mode of thinking, in which they are able to use both sides of the brain simultaneously.

No evidence exists that shows either right- or left-brain thinking is better than the other. Murphy (1985) asserts that each side is important, but each side also lacks something. Therefore, cultivating a whole-brain approach to management increases the individual's intelligence and ability. Venerable (1988, p. 19) sums up the need for whole-brain thinking in management in the following:

> We need managers who will catalyze our return to wholeness and balance—who recognize that productivity or profit goals in themselves are not enough. Unless the

TABLE 1.4   Right-and-Left-Brain Hemisphere Functions

Cerebral Left	Cerebral Right
Processes information and experiences logically	Recognizes spatial arrangements
Recognizes technical and mathematical details	Interprets pictures and other images
Looks for facts and details	Synthesizes pieces of the puzzle to see the whole
Seeks to solve concrete, immediate problems	Relies on intuition
	Seeks to solve abstract future-oriented problems

Limbic Left	Limbic Right
Responds favorably to rules and authority figures	Understands the meaning of interpersonal relationships
Concerned with what we *should* do as opposed to what we *want* to do	Accepts and understands emotions
Uses conservative and administrative guidelines for our behaviors	Appreciates the meaning of music
Functions in a controlling, planning, and organizing mode	Assigns meaning to spiritual beliefs

aim is set higher than the goals desired, the goals desired cannot be achieved. Therefore, when the aim of management is to nurture the human spirit, when the aim is to utilize both the analytical left brain and its artistic partner, the visual right brain, in complementation with one another, people automatically achieve the goals set before them. They become whole and productive without conscious effort.

With the current emphasis on creative right-brain leadership skills, the need to master traditional management functions may be neglected. It is critical to remember that being well-grounded in management techniques is as essential as being skilled in leadership roles.

The learning exercises in this book have been developed to foster whole-brain thinking. Some exercises require left-brain thinking, some require right-brain thinking, and many require both. An important part of the text, the learning exercises, should not be omitted. Their purpose is to supplement the text by providing an opportunity to apply theory and integrate leadership roles and management functions.

Management learning exercises provide a form of vicarious learning that allows the reader to examine what is unique and common to all organizations. Learning exercises and other forms of experiential learning can be used to teach any content but are especially useful in teaching leadership and management. If designed and used appropriately, learning exercises increase whole-brain thinking and provide an opportunity for the novice manager to examine leadership and management problems in detail so that the skills needed for effective leadership and management are cultivated.

Leadership and management skills can and should be integrated as they are learned. This union can best occur by 1) using experiential learning exercises designed to increase whole-brain thinking; 2) demonstrating the leadership component in all management functions; and 3) using a scientific approach to problem solving.

Chapter 2 in this unit provides a foundation for the further development of the integrated leader/manager. Chapter 2 focuses on the qualitative and quantitative decision-making technology needed to increase whole-brain thinking and facilitate the integration of leadership roles and management functions. The aim of the book is to produce an integrated leader/manager, an individual capable of managing the daily operation of a unit, displaying vision, and activating and empowering others. The integrated leader/manager is well-prepared to meet the future and deal appropriately with the challenges of a changing profession.

KEY CONCEPTS

▼ The management functions include planning, organizing, staffing, directing, and controlling. These are incorporated into what is known as the management process.

▼ Each management function has a planning and controlling phase.

▼ Classical, or traditional, management science focused on production in the workplace and on delineating organizational barriers to productivity. Workers were assumed to be motivated solely by economic rewards, and little attention was given to worker job satisfaction.

▼ The human relations era of management science grew out of the Hawthorne studies, which emphasized the needs of the worker and the needs of the organization. Concepts of participatory and humanistic management emerged during this era.

▼ Three primary forms of leadership styles have been identified: authoritarian, democratic, and laissez-faire.

▼ Research has shown that the leader/manager must assume a variety of leadership styles, depending on the needs of the worker, the task to be performed, and the situation or environment. This is known as situational or contingency leadership theory.

▼ Management and leadership have distinct differences and similarities and overlapping skills.

▼ Historically, strong management skills have been valued more than strong leadership skills in the healthcare industry. There is a critical need for leadership development in nursing.

▼ Leadership is defined as a process of persuading and influencing others toward a goal and is composed of a wide variety of roles.

▼ Early leadership theories focused on the traits and characteristics of leaders.

▼ Contemporary research focuses more on leadership as a process of influencing others within an organizational culture and the interactive relationship of the leader and follower.

▼ The basic premise of interactional theory is that leadership behavior is generally determined by the relationship between the leader's personality and the specific situation.

▼ The manager who is committed, has a vision, and is able to empower others with this vision is termed a transformational leader.

▼ The traditional manager, concerned with the day-to-day operations, is called a transactional leader.

▼ Transformational leaders and followers have the ability to raise each other to higher levels of motivation and morality.

▼ The organization itself and the environment play critical roles in the development and support of the transformational and transactional leadership skills of its employees.

▼ Integrating leadership skills with the ability to carry out management functions is necessary if an individual is to become an effective leader/manager.

▼ Management functions tend to require left-brain thinking.

▼ Leadership skills tend to require the use of right-brain functions.

▼ Whole-brain thinking is helpful for an integrated leader/manager.

▼ It is possible to promote whole-brain thinking by using exercises designed to increase the use of the less dominant side of the brain, thus becoming a whole-brain thinker.

ADDITIONAL LEARNING EXERCISES

These exercises may be explored individually or in groups and can be written or verbal assignments.

Learning Exercise 1.3

Recall times when you have been a manager. This does not only mean a nursing manager. Perhaps you were a head lifeguard or an evening shift manager at a fast-food restaurant. During those times, do you think you displayed more management skills or leadership skills?

Learning Exercise 1.4

Think of all the bosses that you have had. Which ones were the best? What made them better than others? Were their management skills or leadership skills better developed?

Learning Exercise 1.5

Make a list of your greatest leadership strengths, and then make a list of your management strengths.

Learning Exercise 1.6

One of the characteristics of transformational leadership is vision. How do you envision nursing changing in the next decade in response to healthcare reform? How will it affect you personally, and what steps have you taken to take to meet these changes proactively?

REFERENCES:

Argyris, C. (1964). *Integrating the individual and the organization*. New York: John Wiley and Sons.

Bass, B. M. (1982). *Stogdill's handbook of leadership*. New York: Free Press.

Bass, B. M., Avoliio, B. J., & Goodheim, L. (1987). Biography and the assessment of transformational leadership at the world-class level. Journal of Management, (Jan), 7-19.

Bennis, W. (1989). *Why leaders can't lead*. Jossey-Bass Publishers. San Francisco.

Bennis, W., & Nanus, B. (1985). *Leaders: The strategies for taking charge*. New York: Harper & Row.

Bernhard, L. A., & Walsh, M. (1990). *Leadership*. St. Louis: C.V. Mosby.

Blake, R. R., & Mouton, J. S. (1964). *The managerial grid*. Houston: Gulf Publishing.

Brandt, M. A. (1994). Caring leadership: Secret and path to success. *Nursing Management, 25*(8), 68–72.

Burns, J. M. (1978). *Leadership*. New York: Harper & Row.

Chapin, F. S. (1924). Socialized leadership. *Social Forces, 3,* 57–60.

De Pree, M. (1987). *Leadership is an art.* New York: Doubleday Books.

Douglass, L. M. (1992). *The effective nurse-leader and manager* (4th ed.). St. Louis: C.V. Mosby.

Drucker, P. F. (1992). *Managing for the future: The 1990's and beyond*. New York: Truman Talley/Dutton.

Dunham, J., & Klafehn, K. A. (1990). Transformational leadership and the nurse executive. *Journal of Nursing Administration, 20*(4).

Edwards, R. (1994). Image, practice, and empowerment: A call to new leadership for the invisible profession. *Revolution, 4*(1) 18–20.

Farley, S. (1990). Leadership. In R. C. Swansburg (Ed.), *Management and leadership for nurse managers*. Boston: Jones and Bartlett.

Fayol, H. (1925). *General and industrial management*. London: Pittman and Sons.

Fiedler, F. (1967). *A theory of leadership effectiveness*. New York: McGraw-Hill.

Follett, M. P. (1926). The giving of orders. In H. C. Metcalf (Ed.), *Scientific foundations of business administration*. Baltimore: William and Wilkins.

Gardner, J. W. (1986a). *The nature of leadership: Introductory considerations*. Washington DC: The Independent Sector.

Gardner, J. W. (1990). *On leadership*. New York: The Free Press.

Glasser, A. (1994). *The control theory manager*. New York: Harper Business

Gulick, L. (1937). Notes on the theory of the organization. In L. Gulick & L. Urwick (Eds.), *Papers on the science of administration* (pp. 3–13.) New York: Institute of Public Administration.

Hall, A. D., & Fagen, R. E. (1968). Definition of system. In W. Buckley (Ed.), *Modern systems research for the behavioral scientist*. Chicago: Aldine Publishing.

Herrmann, N. (1982). The creative brain II. *Training and Development Journal, 6,* 74–86.

Hersey, P., & Blanchard, K. (1977). *Management of organizational behavior: Utilizing human resources* (3rd ed.). Englewood Cliffs, NJ: Prentice Hall.

Herzberg, F. (1977). One more time: How do you motivate employees? In L. Carroll, R. Paine, & A. Miner (Eds.), *The management process* (2nd ed.). New York: Macmillan.

Hollander, E. P. (1978). *Leadership dynamics: A practical guide to effective relationships*. New York: The Free Press.

Holloman, C. R. (1969). Headship leadership. There is a difference. *Notes and Quotes, 365,* 4.

Huston, C. J. (1990). What makes the difference? Attributes of the exceptional nurse. *Nursing 90, 20*(5).

Kanter, R. M. (1989). The new managerial work. *Harvard Business Review, 67*(6), 85–92.

Kotter, J. P. (1988). *The leadership factor*. New York: The Free Press.

Lewin, K. (1951). *Field theory in social sciences.* New York: Harper & Row.

Manthey, M. (1990). The nurse manager as leader. *Nursing Management, 21*(6).

Marquis, B. L., & Huston, C. J. (1994). *Management decision-making for nurses: 101 Case studies* (2nd ed.). Philadelphia: J.B. Lippincott.

Marriner-Tomey, A. (1993). *Transformational leadership in nursing*. St. Louis: Mosby Year Book.

Maslow, A. (1970). *Motivation and personality* (2nd ed.). New York: Harper & Row.

Mayo, E. (1953). *The human problems of an industrialized civilization*. New York: Macmillan.

McGregor, D. (1960). *The human side of enterprise*. New York: McGraw-Hill.

McNeese-Smith, D. (1992). The impact of leadership upon productivity. *Nursing Economics, 10*(6) 393–401.

Murphy, E. C. (1985). Whole-brain management. Parts 1, 2. *Nursing Management, 16*(3, 4), Part 1:66; Part 2: 49.

National League for Nursing (1989). *Criteria for the appraisal of baccalaureate and higher degree programs in nursing.* New York.

Nelson, L., & Burns, F. (1984). High performance programming: A framework for transforming organizations. In J. Adams (Ed.), *Transforming work* (pp. 225–242). Alexandria, VA: Miles River Press.

Ouchi, W. G. (1981). *Theory Z: How American business can meet the Japanese challenge.* Reading, MA: Addison-Wesley.

Robbins, A. (1991). *Awaken the giant within.* New York: Fireside Books.

Schein, E. H. (1970). *Organizational psychology* (2nd ed.). Englewood Cliffs, NJ: Prentice-Hall.

Selznick, P. (1957). *Leadership in administration.* Berkeley, CA: University of California Press.

Senge, P. M. (1990). *The fifth discipline.* New York: Doubleday Books.

Strader, M. K. (1987). Adapting Theory Z to nursing management. *Nursing Management, 18*(4), 61–64.

Stout-Shaffer, S., & Larrabee, J. (1992). Everyone can be a visionary leader. *Nursing Management, 23*(12), 54–58.

Sullivan, P. D., Baumgardner, C. A., Henninger, D. E., & Jones, L. W. (1994). Management development: Preparing nurse managers for the future. *Journal of Nursing Administration, 24*(6), 32–38.

Swansburg, R. C. (1990). *Management and leadership for nurse managers.* Boston: Jones and Bartlett.

Tannenbaum, R., & Schmidt W. (1983). How to choose a leadership pattern. *Harvard Business Review, May/June.*

Tappen, R. M. (1995). *Nursing leadership and management.* Philadelphia. F.A. Davis.

Taylor, F. W. (1911). *The principles of scientific management.* New York: Harper & Row.

Tranbarger, R. (1988). The nurse executive in a community hospital. In M. Johnson (Ed.), *Series on nursing administration* (Vol. 1). Menlo Park, CA: Addison-Wesley.

Tyrrell, R. A. (1994). Visioning: An important management tool. *Nursing Economics, 12*(2), 93–95.

Veehoff, D. C. (1992). Whole brain thinking and the nurse manager. *Nursing Management, 23*(8), 33–34.

Venerable, G. (1988). Management: Right-brain vision for left-brain systems. *Topics in Health Records Management, March,* 9–19.

Viau, J. J. (1990). Theory Z: Magic potion for decentralized government? *Nursing Management, 21*(12), 34–36.

Vincent, P., Brewer, M. J., Aslakson, H., & Swanson, M. (1993). Are we teaching leadership as a value? *Nursing Management, 24*(7), 65–67.

White, R. K., & Lippitt R. (1960). *Autocracy and democracy: An experimental inquiry.* New York: Harper & Row.

Wolf, G. A., Boland, S., & Aukerman, M. (1994). A transformational model for the practice of professional nursing. Part II. *Journal of Nursing Administration, 24*(5) 38–46.

Yukl, G. A. (1989). *Leadership in organizations* (2nd ed.). Englewood Cliffs, NJ: Prentice Hall.

BIBLIOGRAPHY

Badaracco, J. L., & Ellsworth, R. R. (1993). *Leadership and the quest for integrity.* Boston: Harvard Business School Press.

Beck, J. D. W., & Yeager, N. M. (1994). *The leader's window: Mastering the four styles of leadership to build high performing teams.* New York: Wiley.

Blaney, D. R., Hobson, C. J., Meade, M. E., & Scodro, J. (1993). The assessment center: Evaluating managerial potential. *Nursing Management, 24*(2), 54–58.

Boston, C., & Forman, H. (1994). A time to listen: Staff and manager views on education, practice, and management. *Journal of Nursing Administration, 24*(2), 16–18.

Chemers, M. M. (1993). An integrative theory of leadership. In M. M. Chemers & R. Ayman (Eds.), *Leadership theory and research: Perspectives and direction.* San Diego: Academic Press.

Cottingham, C. (1990). Transformational leadership. In E. C. Hein & M. J. Nicholson (Eds.), *Contemporary leadership behavior* (3rd ed.). Glenview, IL: Scott, Foresman and Company.

Covey, S. R. (1989). *The 7 habits of highly effective people.* New York: Simon & Schuster.

Dunham, J., Fisher, E., & Kinion, E. (1993). Experiences, events people—Do they influence the leadership style of nurse executives? *Journal of Nursing Administration, 23*(7/8), 30–34.

Heifetz, R. A. (1994). *Leadership without easy an-*

swers. Cambridge, MA: Harvard University Press.

Hill, L. A. (1992). *Becoming a manager: Master of a new identity.* Cambridge, MA: Harvard Business School Press.

Hrebiniak, L. G. (1994). *The we-force in management: How to build and sustain cooperation.* New York: Lexington.

Huczynski, A. A. (1993). *Management gurus: What makes them and how to become one.* New York: Routledge, Chapman & Hall.

Kim, W. C., & Mauborgne, R. A. (1992). Parables of leadership. *Harvard Business Review, July/August,* 123–128.

Mark, B. A. (1994). The emerging role of the nurse manager. *Journal of Nursing Administration, 24*(1), 48–55.

McNeese-Smith, D. (1993). Leadership behavior and employee effectiveness. *Nursing Management, 24*(5), 38–39.

Merton, R. K. (1969). The social nature of leadership. *American Journal of Nursing, 69*(12), 2614–2618.

Pagonis, W. G. (1992). The work of the leader. *Harvard Business Review, 70*(6), 119–126.

Powell, G. N. (1993). Women and men in management (2nd ed.). Newbury Park, CA: Sage.

Rehfeld, J. E. (1994). Alchemy of a leader. New York: John Wiley and Sons.

Shamir, B., House, R. J., & Arthur, M. B. (1993). The motivational effects of charismatic leadership: A self-concept based theory. *Organization Science, 4,* 577–594.

Starratt, R. J. (1993). *The drama of leadership.* Bristol, PA: Falmer Press.

Stogdill, R. M. (1974). *Handbook of leadership: A survey of theory and research* (p. 8). New York: The Free Press.

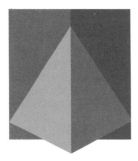

CHAPTER 2

Tools for Leadership and Management Problem Solving

The first chapter of this unit explores past and present theories of leadership and management and provides part of the foundation necessary for novices to become effective leaders/managers. Because decision making is often thought to be synonymous with management and is one of the criteria on which management expertise is judged (Corcoran, 1986), the second part of the management/leadership foundation, necessary for increasing effectiveness, is developing skills in decision making. Much of any manager's time is spent critically examining issues, solving problems, and making decisions. It is the authors' belief that problem solving, decision making, and critical thinking are learned skills that improve with practice. So that the processes can be consistently replicated, these learned skills rely heavily on established tools, techniques, and strategies.

This chapter introduces the reader to problem solving, decision making, and critical thinking; presents various management tools and techniques that assist managers in successful problem solving; and focuses on organizational and management decision making.

Bessie L. Marquis and Carol J. Huston:
LEADERSHIP ROLES AND MANAGEMENT FUNCTIONS IN NURSING, 2nd ed.
Lippincott-Raven Publishers © 1996

DECISION MAKING AND PROBLEM SOLVING

Decision making is a complex, cognitive process often defined as choosing a particular course of action. Webster's definition—to "judge or settle"—is another view of decision making (Websters, 1984). Both definitions imply that there was *doubt* about *several* courses of action and that a *choice* was made that eliminated the uncertainty.

Problem solving is part of decision making. A systematic process that focuses on analyzing a difficult situation, problem solving always includes a decision-making step.

Critical thinking is related to evaluation and has a broader scope than decision making and problem solving. Components of critical thinking include reasoning and creative analysis (Paul, 1992a; Ruggiero, 1995). Various theorists define critical thinking differently, but most agree that it is more complex than problem solving or decision making and involves higher order reasoning and evaluation. The authors believe that insight, intuition, empathy, and the willingness to take action are additional components of critical thinking. These same skills are necessary to some degree in decision making and problem solving.

Decision making, however, can occur without the full analysis required in problem solving. Although many educators use the terms problem solving and decision making synonymously, there is a small, yet important, difference between the two. Because problem solving attempts to identify the root problem in situations, much time and energy is spent on identifying the real problem. Decision making, on the other hand, is usually triggered by a problem but is often handled in a manner that does not eliminate the problem. For example, if an individual decided to handle a conflict crisis in some manner when it occurred but did not attempt to identify the real problem causing the conflict, only decision-making skills would be used. The decision maker might later choose to address the real cause of the conflict or might decide to do nothing at all about the problem. The decision has been made *not to problem solve*. This alternative may be selected because of a lack of energy, time, or resources to solve the real problem adequately. In some situations, this is an appropriate decision.

Here is an example of a decision *not* to solve a problem. A nursing supervisor has a staff nurse who has been absent a great deal during the last 3 months. However, the supervisor has reliable information that the nurse will be resigning soon to return to school in another state. Because the problem will soon no longer exist, the supervisor decides that the time and energy needed to correct the problem are not warranted.

THEORETICAL APPROACHES TO PROBLEM SOLVING AND DECISION MAKING

Although only one step in the problem-solving process, decision making is an important task that relies heavily on critical thinking skills. How do people become successful problem solvers and decision makers? Although successful decision making can be learned through life experience, not everyone learns to solve problems and judge wisely by this trial-and-error method because much is left to chance.

Some educators feel that people are not successful in these areas because students are not taught how to reason insightfully from multiple perspectives (Paul, 1992b). Carnevali and Thomas (1993) and Corcoran (1986) state that process and structure are beneficial to the process of decision making and force individuals to be specific about options and to separate probabilities from values. A structured approach to problem solving and decision making increases critical reasoning and is the best way to learn how to make quality decisions because it eliminates trial and error and focuses the learning on a proven process. A structured or professional approach involves applying a theoretical model in problem solving and decision making.

To improve decision-making ability, it is important to use an adequate process model as the theoretical base for understanding and applying critical thinking skills. Many acceptable problem-solving models exist, and most include a decision-making step; only three are reviewed here.

The Traditional Problem-Solving Process

The *traditional problem-solving model* is widely used and perhaps the most well known of the various models. The 7 steps follow. (Decision making occurs at step 5.)

1. Identify the problem.
2. Gather data to analyze the causes and consequences of the problem.
3. Explore alternative solutions.
4. Evaluate the alternatives.
5. Select the appropriate solution.
6. Implement the solution.
7. Evaluate the results.

Although the traditional problem-solving process is an effective model, its weakness lies in the amount of time needed for proper implementation. This process, therefore, is less effective when time constraints are a consideration. Another weakness is lack of an initial objective-setting step. Setting a decision goal helps to prevent the decision maker from becoming sidetracked.

The Managerial Decision-Making Process

The *managerial decision-making model,* a modified traditional model, eliminates the weakness of the traditional model by adding a goal-setting step. Harrison (1981) has delineated the following steps in the managerial decision-making process.

1. Set objectives.
2. Search for alternatives.
3. Evaluate alternatives.
4. Choose.
5. Implement.
6. Follow up and control.

The managerial decision-making process flows in much the same manner as the management process introduced in Chapter 1. A comparison of the management process, the nursing process, and an expanded model of management decision making is shown in Display 2.1.

The Nursing Process

The *nursing process* provides another theoretical system for solving problems and making decisions. It has a strength that the previous two models lack, namely its feedback mechanism. The arrows in Figure 2.1 show constant input into the process.

Educators have identified the nursing process as an effective decision-making model (Wales & Nardi, 1984). When the decision point has been identified, initial decision making occurs and continues throughout the process by using a feedback mechanism. Although the process was designed for nursing practice with regard to patient care and nursing accountability, it can easily be adapted as a theoretical model for solving leadership and management problems. Display 2.1 shows how closely the nursing process parallels the decision-making process.

The weakness of the nursing process, like the traditional problem-solving model, is in *not* requiring clearly stated objectives. Goals should be clearly stated in the planning phase of the process, but this step is frequently omitted or obscured.

However, because nurses are familiar with this process and its proven effectiveness, it continues to be recommended as an adapted theoretical process for leadership and managerial decision making.

Many other excellent problem-analysis and decision models exist. The model selected should be one with which the decision maker is familiar and one appropriate for the problem to be solved. Using models or processes consistently will increase the likelihood that critical analysis will occur. By cultivating a scientific approach, the

---

Display 2.1 Comparison of the Decision-Making Process with the Management and Nursing Processes

Decision-Making Process	Simplified Nursing Process	Management Process
Identify the decision. Collect data.	Assess	Planning
Identify criteria for decision. Identify alternatives.	Plan	Organizing
Compare alternatives with criteria. Choose alternative. Implement alternative.	Implement	Staffing Directing
Evaluate steps in decision.	Evaluate	Controlling

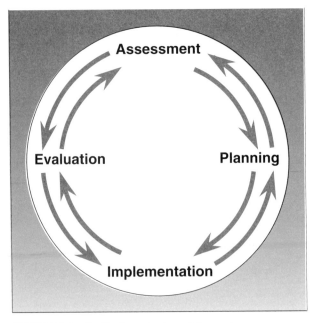

FIGURE 2.1   Feedback mechanism of the nursing process.

quality of one's management/leadership problem solving and decision making will improve tremendously.

INDIVIDUAL VARIATIONS IN DECISION MAKING

If each person receives the same information and uses the same scientific approach to solve problems, each one should make identical decisions. However, in practice this is not true. Because decision making involves perceiving and evaluating and individuals perceive by sensation and intuition and evaluate their perception by thinking and feeling, it is inevitable that individuality plays a part in decision making. Because everyone has different values and life experiences, and each person perceives and thinks differently, different decisions may be made given the same set of circumstances. No discussion of decision making would, therefore, be complete without a careful examination of the role of the individual in decision making.

Values and Decision Making

Individual decisions are based on each person's value system. No matter how objective the criteria, value judgments will always play a part in an individual's decision making, either consciously or subconsciously. The alternatives generated and the final choice selected are limited by each person's value system. For some, certain choices are not possible because of their beliefs. Because values also influence perceptions, they invariably influence information gathering and processing and outcome

(Marquis & Huston, 1994). Values also determine which problems in one's personal or professional life will be addressed or ignored.

Life Experiences and Decision Making

Each person brings to the decision-making task past experiences that include education and decision-making experience. The more mature the person and the broader his or her background, the more alternatives they can identify. Each time a new behavior or decision is observed, that possibility is added to the person's repertoire of choices. Recent research indicates that nurses' desire for autonomy varies widely (Dwyer, Swartz, & Fox, 1992). Therefore, it is likely that individuals seeking autonomy may have much more experience at making decisions than those who fear autonomy. Likewise, having made good or poor decisions in the past will influence an individual's decision making.

Individual Preference and Decision Making

With all the alternatives a person considers in decision making, one alternative may be preferred over another. The decision maker, for example, may see certain choices as involving greater personal risk than others and therefore may choose the safer alternative. Physical, economic, and emotional risks and time and energy expenditures are types of personal risk and costs involved in decision making. For example, an individual with limited finances or a reduced energy level may *decide* to select an alternative solution to a problem, which would not have been their first choice had they been able to overcome limited resources.

Individual Ways of Thinking and Decision Making

Evaluating information and alternatives to arrive at a decision is a thinking skill. Individuals think differently. It is believed that most individuals are either right- or left-brain dominant (Murphy, 1985). Although the authors encourage whole-brain thinking and studies have shown that individuals can strengthen the use of the less dominant side of the brain, most individuals continue to have a dominant side. Analytical, left-brain thinkers process information differently than intuitive, right-brain thinkers. The way one thinks has much to do with individual problem solving and decision making (Murphy, 1985).

OVERCOMING INDIVIDUAL VULNERABILITY IN DECISION MAKING

How do people overcome subjectivity in making decisions? This can never be completely overcome, nor should it. After all, life would be quite boring if everyone thought alike. However, managers and leaders must become aware of their own vulnerability and recognize how it influences and limits the quality of their decision

> ### LEARNING EXERCISE 2.1
>
> #### A Personal Decision Scenario
>
> You are an RN who graduated 3 years ago. During the last 3 years, your responsibilities in your first position have increased. Even though you enjoy your family (husband and one preschool-age child), you realize that you love your job, and your career is very important to you.
>
> Recently, you and your husband decided to have another baby. Last week, your supervisor told you that the charge nurse is leaving and that she wants to appoint you to the position. You were thrilled and excited about the new position. Yesterday you found out that you are pregnant.
>
> Last night you and your husband talked about your career future. He is an attorney whose practice has suddenly gained momentum. He feels you should work part time when the baby is born. This would mean that you could not take the new position.
>
> *Assignment:* Using a scientific approach, determine what you should do. After you have made your decision, get together in a group (4–6 people) and share your resolution.
>
> Were your decisions the same? How did you approach the problem solving differently from others in your group? Did some of the group members identify alternatives you had not considered? How did your personal views influence your decision?

making. Using the following suggestions will help decrease individual subjectivity and increase objectivity in decision making.

Values

Being confused and unclear about values may affect decision-making ability (Huston & Marquis, 1989). Overcoming a lack of self-awareness through value clarification decreases confusion. Deloughery (1991) maintains that individuals who understand their personal beliefs and feelings will have a conscious awareness of the values on which their decisions are based. This awareness is an essential component of decision making. Therefore, to be successful problem solvers, managers must periodically examine their values. Values clarification exercises are included in Chapter 3.

Life Experience

It is difficult to overcome inexperience when making decisions. Benner (1994) refers to this lack of experience as reason in transition. However, an individual can do some things to decrease this area of vulnerability. First, use available resources, including current research and literature, to gain a fuller understanding of the issues involved. Second, involve other people, such as experienced colleagues, trusted friends, or superiors, to act as sounding boards and advisors. Third, analyze decisions later to assess their success. By evaluating decisions, people learn from mistakes and are able to overcome inexperience.

Individual Preference

Overcoming this area of vulnerability involves self-awareness, honesty, and risk taking. The need for self-awareness was discussed previously, but it is not enough to be self-aware; people also must be honest with themselves about their choices and their preferences for those choices. Additionally, the successful decision maker must take some risks. Nearly every decision has some element of risk, and most involve consequences and accountability. Those who are able to do the right but unpopular thing and who dare to stand alone will thrive as leaders.

Individual Ways of Thinking

Individuals making decisions alone are frequently handicapped because they are not able to understand problems fully or make decisions from both an analytical and intuitive perspective. However, in most organizations, both types of thinkers may be found (Swansburg, 1990). Using the group process, talking management problems over with others, and developing whole-brain thinking also are methods for ensuring that both intuitive and analytical approaches will be used in solving problems and making decisions.

CRITICAL ELEMENTS IN PROBLEM SOLVING AND DECISION MAKING

Because decisions may have far-reaching consequences, problem solving and decision making must be of high quality. Even using a scientific approach to problem solving and overcoming personal areas of vulnerability in decision making do not ensure a quality decision. Special attention must be paid to other critical elements. The following elements, considered crucial in the problem-solving process, frequently result in poor quality decisions.

Clearly Defined Objective

Decision makers often forge ahead in their problem-solving process without first determining their goal. Even when decisions must be made quickly, there is time to pause and reflect on the purpose of the decision. If a decision lacks a clear objective or if an objective is not consistent with the individual's or organization's stated philosophy, a poor quality decision is likely.

Careful Data Gathering

Because decisions are based on knowledge and information available to the problem solver at the time the decision must be made, one must learn how to process and obtain accurate information. The acquisition of information begins with identifying the problem or the occasion for the decision and continues throughout the problem-solving process. Often the information is unsolicited, but most information is sought actively. Various tools have been designed to assist decision makers with the important task of information acquisition. Several of these tools are discussed later in this chapter.

Acquiring information always involves people, and no tool or mechanism is infallible to human behavior. Human values tremendously influence our perceptions. Therefore, as problem solvers gather information, they must be vigilant that their own preferences and those of others are not mistaken for facts. Remember that facts can be misleading if presented in a seductive manner, taken out of context, or are past-oriented. How many parents have been misled by the factual statement "Johnny hit me"? In this case, the information seeker needs to do more fact-finding. What was the accuser doing prior to Johnny hitting him? What was he hit with? Where was he hit? When was he hit? Like the parent, the manager who becomes expert at acquiring adequate, appropriate, and accurate information will have a head start in becoming an expert decision maker and problem solver.

LEARNING EXERCISE 2.2

Identify a poor decision you recently made because of faulty data gathering. Have you ever made a poor decision because someone withheld necessary information from you?

Generate Many Alternatives

The definition of decision making implies there are at least two choices in every decision. Unfortunately, many problem solvers limit their choices to two when many more options usually are available. The greater the number of alternatives that can be generated during this phase, the greater the chance that the final decision will be sound.

Several techniques can help generate more alternatives. Involving others in the process confirms the adage that two heads are better than one. Because everyone thinks uniquely, increasing the number of people working on a problem increases the number of alternatives that can be generated.

Brainstorming is another frequently used technique. The goal in brainstorming is to think of all possible alternatives, even those that may seem "off target." By not limiting the possible alternatives to only apparently appropriate ones, people are able to break through habitual or repressive thinking patterns and allow new ideas to surface. Although most often used by groups, brainstorming also may be used by individuals making decisions alone.

Think Logically

During the problem-solving process, one must draw inferences from information. An inference is part of deductive reasoning. Individuals must carefully think through the information and the alternatives. Faulty logic at this point may lead to poor quality decisions. People think illogically primarily in three ways.

LEARNING EXERCISE 2.3

In the personal choice scenario presented in Learning Exercise 2-1, some of the following alternatives could have been generated.

Do not take the new position.
Hire a full-time housekeeper, and take the position.
Have your husband reduce his job commitment.
Have an abortion.
Ask one of the parents to help.
Take the position, and do not hire child care.
Take the position and hire child care.
Have your husband quit his job and do child care.
Ask the supervisor if you can work 4 days a week and still have the position.
Take the position and wait and see what happens after the baby is born.

Assignment: How many of these alternatives did you or your group generate? What alternatives did you identify that are not included in this list?

1. Overgeneralizing. This type of "crooked" thinking occurs when one believes that because *A* has a particular characteristic, every other *A* also has the same characteristic. An example of this thinking is when stereotypical statements are used to justify arguments and decisions.
2. Affirming the consequences. In this type of illogical thinking, one decides that if *B* is good and he or she is doing *A*, then *A* must not be good. For example, if a new method is heralded as the best way to perform a nursing procedure and the nurses on your unit are not using that technique, it is illogical to assume that the technique used in your unit is wrong or bad.
3. Arguing from analogy. This thinking applies a component that is present in two separate concepts and then states that because *A* is present in *B*, then *A* and *B* are alike in all respects. An example of this would be to argue that because intuition plays a part in clinical and managerial nursing, then any characteristic present in a good clinical nurse also should be present in a good nurse–manager. However, this is not necessarily true; a good nurse–manager does not necessarily possess all the same skills as a good nurse–clinician.

Choose and Act Decisively

It is not enough to gather adequate information, think logically, select from among many alternatives, and be aware of the influence of one's values. In the final analysis, one must act. Many become vulnerable at this last point in the problem-solving process and choose to delay acting because they lack the courage to face the consequences of their choices. For example, if all managers granted *all* employee's requests for days off, they would have to accept the consequences of *their* decision by dealing with short staffing.

It may help the reluctant decision maker to remember that decisions, while often having long-term consequences and far-reaching effects, are not cast in stone. Judgments found to be ineffective or inappropriate often can be changed. By later evaluating decisions, managers can learn more about their abilities and where the problem solving was faulty. However, decisions must continue to be made, even though some are of poor quality because through continued decision making, individuals develop increased decision-making skills.

Although all experts do not agree, Huston (1990) suggests that the following are qualities of a successful decision maker:

- *Courage*. Courage is of particular importance and involves the willingness to take risks.
- *Sensitivity*. Good decision makers seem to have some sort of antenna that makes them particularly sensitive to situations and others.
- *Energy*. People must have the energy and desire to make things happen.
- *Creativity*. Successful decision makers tend to be creative thinkers. They develop new ways to solve problems.

MANAGEMENT DECISION MAKING

Thus far, the discussion has focused on the individual decision maker and on personal choices. What influence does the management or leadership position have on the decision-making process? What effect does the organization have on the decision maker?

Decision making is a manager's most important task and is present in every phase of the management process (Gillies, 1994). Johnson (1990, p. 35) maintains that "a manager's overall effectiveness is directly related to the effectiveness of their decision-making." If management and decision making are synonymous, it is important to understand how the organization influences the process.

The Effect of Organizational Power on Decision Making

Earlier in this chapter, the effect of the individual's values and preferences on decision making was discussed. Because organizations are made up of people with differing values and preferences, there is often conflict in organizational decision dynamics. Powerful individuals in organizations are more apt to have decisions made (by themselves or their subordinates) that are congruent with their own preferences and values. People holding little power in organizations must always consider the preference of the powerful when they make management decisions. Huston and Marquis (1989) maintain that power is frequently part of the decision factor. For instance, not only does the preference of the powerful influence decisions of the less powerful, but the powerful also are able to *inhibit* the preferences of the less powerful.

The ability of the powerful to influence individual decision making in an organization often requires adopting a *private personality* and an *organizational personality*. For example, some might feel that they would have made a different decision had they been acting on their own, but they went along with the organizational decision.

This "going along" in itself constitutes a decision; the individual chooses to accept an organizational decision that differs from their own preferences and values. The concept of power in organizations is discussed more fully in Chapter 8.

Rational and Administrative Decision Making

For many years, it was widely believed that most managerial decisions were based on a careful, scientific, and objective thought process and that managers made decisions in a rational manner. In the late 1940s, Herbert A. Simon's work revealed that most managers made many decisions that did not fit the objective rationality theory. Simon (1965) delineated two types of management decision makers: the *economic man* and the *administrative man*.

Managers who are successful decision makers attempt to make rational decisions, much like the economic man described in Display 2.2. Because they realize that restricted knowledge and limited alternatives directly affect a decision's quality, these managers gather as much information as possible and generate many alternatives. Simon (1965) believed that the economic model of man was an unrealistic description of organizational decision making. The complexity of information acquisition makes it impossible for the human brain to store and retain the amount of information that is available for each decision.

Because of time constraints and the difficulty of assimilating large amounts of information, most management decisions are made using the administrative man mode of decision making. The administrative man never has complete knowledge and generates fewer alternatives.

Simon (1965) argued that the administrative man carries out decisions that are

---

Display 2.2 Comparison of the Economic and Administrative Man

Economic Man	Administrative Man
1. Makes decisions in a very rational manner.	1. Makes decisions that are good enough.
2. Has complete knowledge of the problem or decision situation.	2. Because complete knowledge is not possible, knowledge is always fragmented.
3. Has a complete list of possible alternatives.	3. Because consequences of alternatives occur in the future, they are impossible to predict accurately.
4. Has a rational system of ordering preference of alternatives.	4. Usually chooses from among a few alternatives, not all possible ones.
5. Selects the decision that will maximize utility function.	5. The final choice is "satisficing" rather than maximizing.

(Adapted from Simon, 1976.)

only "satisficing," a term used to describe decisions that are not ideal but result in solutions that have adequate outcomes. These managers want decisions to be "good enough" so that they "work," but they are less concerned that the alternative selected is the optimal choice. The "best" choice for many decisions is often found to be too costly in terms of time or resources, so another less costly but workable solution is found.

MANAGEMENT DECISION-MAKING TECHNOLOGY

To assist the leader/manager in making decisions, management analysts have developed tools that provide order and direction in obtaining and using information or that are helpful in selecting who should be involved in making the decision. Because there are so many of these decision aids, this chapter presents selected technology that would be most helpful to a beginning manager. Some of these aids encourage analytical thinking, others are designed to increase intuitive reasoning, and a few encourage use of both hemispheres of the brain.

Quantitative Decision-Making Tools

Some management authors label management decision-making aids as *models;* others use the term *tools.* It is only important to remember that any decision-making aid always results in the need for the individual to make a final decision and that all aids are subject to human error.

DECISION GRIDS.   A decision grid allows one to visually examine the alternatives and compare each against the same criteria. Although any criteria may be selected, the same criteria are used to analyze each alternative. An example of a decision grid is depicted in Figure 2.2. When many alternatives have been generated or a group or committee is collaborating on the decision, these grids are particularly helpful to the process.

Alternative	Financial effect	Political effect	Departmental effect	Time	Decision
#1					
#2					
#3					
#4					

FIGURE 2.2   A decision grid.

This tool, for instance, would be useful when changing the method of managing care on a unit or when selecting a candidate to hire from a large interview pool. The unit manager or the committee of nursing staff would evaluate all the alternatives available using a decision grid. In this manner, every alternative is evaluated using the same criteria. It is possible to weight some of the criteria more heavily than others if some are more important. To do this, it is usually necessary to assign a number value to each criterion. The result would be a numeric value for each alternative considered.

PAY-OFF TABLES.   The decision aids that fall in this category have a cost–profit–volume relationship and are very helpful when some quantitative information is available, such as the item's cost or predicted use. To use pay-off tables, one must determine probabilities and use historical data, such as a hospital census or a report on the number of operating procedures performed.

To illustrate, a pay-off table might be appropriately used in determining how many participants it would take to make an in-service program break even. If the instructor for the class costs $400, the in-service director would need to charge each of the 20 participants $20 for the class, but for 40 participants, the class would only

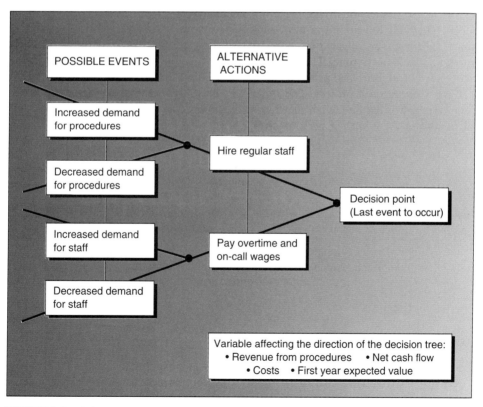

FIGURE 2.3   A decision tree.

cost $10 each. The in-service director would use attendance data from past classes and the number of nurses potentially available to attend to determine probable class size and thus how much to charge for the class. Pay-off tables do not guarantee that a correct decision will be made, but they assist in visualizing data.

DECISION TREES.   Because decisions are often tied to the outcome of other events, management analysts have developed decision trees. Used to plot a decision over time, decision trees allow visualization of various outcomes. The decision tree in Figure 2.3 compares the cost of hiring regular staff to the cost of hiring temporary employees. Here the decision is whether to hire extra nurses at regular salary to perform outpatient procedures on an oncology floor or to have nurses available to the unit on an on-call basis and pay them on-call and overtime wages. The possible consequences of a decreased volume of procedures and an increased volume must be considered. Initially costs would increase in hiring a regular staff, but over a longer period of time, this move would mean greater savings *if* the volume of procedures does not dramatically decrease.

PROGRAM EVALUATION AND REVIEW TECHNIQUE.   Program Evaluation and Review Technique (PERT) is a popular tool to determine timing of decisions. Developed by the Booz-Allen-Hamilton organization and the US Navy in connection with the Polaris Missile Program, PERT is essentially a flow chart that predicts when events and activities must take place if a final event is to occur. Figure 2.4 shows a PERT chart for developing a new outpatient treatment room for oncology procedures. The number of weeks to complete tasks is listed in optimistic time, most likely time, and pessimistic time. The critical path shows something that must occur in the sequence before one may proceed. PERT is especially helpful when a group of people are working on a project. The flow chart keeps everyone up-to-date, and problems are easily identified when they first occur. Flow charts are popular, and many individuals use them in their personal lives.

LEARNING EXERCISE 2.4

Think of some project you're working on; it could be a dance, a picnic, remodeling your bathroom, or a semester schedule of activities in a class.

Assignment: Draw a flow chart, inserting at the bottom the date activities for the event are to be completed. Working backward, insert critical tasks and their completion dates. Refer to your flow sheet throughout the project to see if you stay on target.

Selecting Decision-Making Styles

In addition to quantitative decision technology, management analysts have developed models that assist managers in choosing the correct decision-making style. A manager can be autocratic in making decisions and have little or no input from others or democratic and involve others in the process. Some managers develop patterns

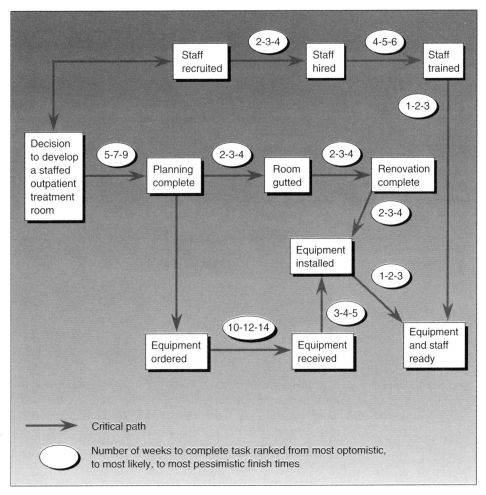

FIGURE 2.4   An example of a PERT flow diagram.

and use the same methods, rather than looking at the particular situation and then concluding which type of decision making is needed. Vroom and Yetton (1973) have developed a useful approach in selecting an appropriate decision-making style. They have identified five decision-making methods (Table 2.1).

There also are seven situation variables identified by Vroom (1973). These situation variables determine which of the five decision-making styles is appropriate in a situation (Table 2.2).

1. *The information rule.* If the quality of the decision is important and the leader does not possess enough information or expertise to solve the problem by himself or herself, AI is eliminated from the feasible set. (Its use risks a low-quality decision.)

TABLE 2.1   Types of Management Decision Styles

AI	You solve the problem or make the decision yourself, using information available to you at that time.
AII	You obtain the necessary information from your subordinate(s), then decide on the solution to the problem yourself. You may or may not tell your subordinates what the problem is when getting the information from them. The role played by your subordinates in making the decision is clearly one of providing the necessary information to you, rather than generating or evaluating alternative solutions.
CI	You share the problem with relevant subordinates individually, getting their ideas and suggestions without bringing them together as a group. Then *you* make the decision that may or may not reflect your subordinates' influence.
CII	You share the problem with your subordinates as a group, collectively obtaining their ideas and suggestions. Then *you* make the decision that may or may not reflect your subordinates' influence.
GII	You share a problem with your subordinates as a group. Together you generate and evaluate alternatives and attempt to reach agreement (consensus) on a solution. Your role is much like that of chairman. You do not try to influence the group to adopt "your" solution, and you are willing to accept and implement any solution that has the support of the entire group.

2. *The goal congruence rule.* If the quality of the decision is important and the subordinates do not share the organizational goals to be obtained in solving the problem, GII is eliminated from the feasible set. (Alternatives that eliminate the leader's final control over the decision reached may jeopardize the quality of the decision.)

3. *The unstructured problem rule.* When the quality of the decision is important, if the leader lacks the necessary information or expertise to solve the problem alone, and if the problem is unstructured (ie, he or she does not know exactly what information is needed and where it is located), the method used must provide a means not only to collect the information, but to do so in an efficient and effective manner. Methods that involve interaction among all subordinates with full knowledge of the problem are likely to be both more efficient and more likely to generate a high-quality solution to the problem. Under these conditions, AI, AII, and CI are eliminated from the feasible set. (AI does not provide for collection of the necessary information; AII and CI represent more cumbersome, less effective, and less efficient means of bringing the necessary information to bear on the solution of the problem than methods that do permit those with the necessary information to interact.)

4. *The acceptance rule.* If the acceptance of the decision by subordinates is critical to effective implementation and it is not certain that an autocratic decision made by the leader would receive that acceptance, AI and AII are eliminated from the feasible set. (Neither provides an opportunity for subordinates to participate in the decision, and both risk the necessary acceptance.)

TABLE 2.2 Problem Attributes Used in the Model

Problem Attributes	Diagnostic Questions
A. The importance of the quality of the decision	Is there a quality requirement such that one solution is likely to be more rational than another?
B. The extent to which the leader possesses sufficient information/expertise to make a high-quality decision by himself or herself	Do you have sufficient information to make a high-quality decision?
C. The extent to which the problem is structured	Is the problem structured?
D. The extent to which acceptance or commitment on the part of subordinates is critical to the effective implementation of the decision	Is acceptance of decision by subordinates critical to effective implementation?
E. The prior probability that the leader's autocratic decision will receive acceptance by subordinates	If you were to make the decision by yourself, is it reasonably certain that it would be accepted by your subordinates?
F. The extent to which subordinates are motivated to attain the organizational goals as represented in the objectives explicit in the statement of the problem	Do subordinates share the organizational goals to be obtained in solving this problem?
G. The extent to which subordinates are likely to be in conflict over preferred solution	Is conflict among subordinates likely in preferred solutions?

5. *The conflict rule.* If the acceptance of the decision is critical, an autocratic decision is not certain to be accepted, and subordinates are likely to be in conflict or disagreement over the appropriate solution, AI, AII, and CI are eliminated from the feasible set. (The method used in solving the problem should enable those who disagree to resolve their differences with full knowledge of the problem. AI, AII, and CI involve no interaction or only "one-on-one" relationships and therefore provide no opportunity for those in conflict to resolve their differences. Their use runs the risk of leaving some of the subordinates with less than the necessary commitment to the final decision.)

6. *The fairness rule.* If the quality of decision is unimportant and acceptance is critical and not certain to result from an autocratic decision, AI, AII, CI, and CII are eliminated from the feasible set. (The method used should maximize the probability of acceptance because this is the only relevant consideration in determining the effectiveness of the decision. In these circumstances, AI, AII, CI, and CII create less acceptance or commitment than GII. To use them is to run the risk of getting less than the needed acceptance of the decision.)

7. *The acceptance priority rule.* If acceptance is critical, not assured by an auto-

cratic decision, and subordinates can be trusted, AI, AII, CI, and CII are eliminated from the feasible set. (Methods that provide equal partnership in the decision-making process can provide greater acceptance without risking decision quality. Use of any method other than GII results in an unnecessary risk that the decision will not be fully accepted or receive the necessary commitment on the part of subordinates.)

(Reprinted, by permission of publisher, from Organizational Dynamics, Spring/1973. American Management Association, New York, p. 71. All rights reserved.)

KEY CONCEPTS

▼ The professional decision maker is self-aware, courageous, sensitive, energetic, and creative.
▼ The professional approach to problem solving begins with a fixed goal and ends with an evaluation process.
▼ The successful decision maker understands the significance that each individual's values, life experience, preferences, and way of thinking have on selected alternatives.
▼ The critical thinker is aware of areas of vulnerability that hinder successful decision making and makes efforts to avoid the pitfalls of faulty logic in their data gathering.
▼ The act of making and evaluating decisions increases the expertise of the decision maker.
▼ Several areas of organizational problem solving and decision making differ from personal or professional decision making.
▼ Two major considerations in organizational decision making are how power affects decision making and the assumption that management decision making needs only to be "satisficing."
▼ Management science has produced many tools and techniques for analyzing management problems and decision making. These tools can be very useful for the novice nurse-manager, but they are not foolproof and do not allow fully for the human element in management.

▲ ADDITIONAL LEARNING EXERCISES

Using the decision-making guidelines developed by Vroom and Yetton, decide what type of decision-making style should be selected for Additional Learning Exercises 2.5, 2.6, and 2.7.

Learning Exercise 2.5

You are the head nurse of a 30-bed medical unit. After consultation, you recently implemented a system for incorporating nursing diagnoses on the patient care plans. Although the system was expected to reduce report time between shifts and improve quality of patient care, to everyone's surprise, including your own, you find that the system is not working.

You do not think there is anything wrong with your idea. Many other hospitals in the area are using nursing diagnoses with success. You had a consultant come from another hospital and give an update to your nurses on use of the system. The consultant reported that your staff seemed very knowledgeable and appeared to understand their responsibilities in implementing the system.

You suspect that a few nurses might be sabotaging your efforts for planned change, but your charge nurses do not agree; they feel the failure may be lack of proper incentives or poor staff morale.

Your nursing director is anxious to implement the system in other patient care units but wants it to be working well in your unit first. You have just come from a head nurse meeting where your nursing director told you to solve the problem and report back to her within 1 week regarding the steps you had taken to solve your problem. You share your director's concern; how should you solve this problem? Select the most appropriate decision style.

Learning Exercise 2.6

(Adapted from La Monica & Finch, 1977.)

You are the evening shift charge nurse of the intensive care unit. Your supervisor is sending two nurses from each shift to an upcoming critical care conference in a nearby city. The supervisor wants each charge nurse to submit names of the selected nurses in 2 weeks.

All of the 12 full-time evening shift nurses would like to go; from a staffing standpoint, there is no reason why any of them could not go. All are active in the local critical care organization. Financial resources, however, limit your choice to two. How do you resolve this situation? Select the most appropriate decision style.

Learning Exercise 2.7

You are the day shift charge nurse on a surgical unit. Because of your related expertise, your supervisor has asked you to select a new type of blood warming unit. You want to be sure that you select the right one. Several companies have provided your staff with trial units. You have not received much feedback from the staff regarding their preferences.

Today your supervisor tells you that your selection and its price must be ready to accompany her budget, which is due in 2 days. What do you do? Select the most appropriate decision style.

Learning Exercise 2.8

Examine the process you used to decide to become a nurse. Would you describe it as fitting a profile of the *economic man* or the *administrative man*?

Learning Exercise 2.9

Describe the two best decisions you have made in your life and the two worst. What factors assisted you in making the wise decisions? What elements of critical thinking went awry in your poor decision making. How would you classify your decision-making ability?

Learning Exercise 2.10

Six nurses have just applied for a position in the open heart unit. Working with a group, develop an appropriate decision grid for selecting which nurse to hire. You may give each criterion weighted points so that the decision is a quantitative solution. For example, level of education could be weighted 5 to 10 points and experience, 10 to 30 points.

REFERENCES:

Benner, P. (1994, July 17). Engaged reasoning: Critical evaluation of critical thinking. Paper presented at *Improving the quality of thinking in a changing world, The Sixth International Conference on Thinking*. Massachusetts Institute of Technology, Cambridge.

Carnevali, D. L., & Thomas, M. D. (1993). *Diagnostic reasoning and treatment decision making in nursing*. Philadelphia: J.B. Lippincott.

Corcoran, S. (1986). Task complexity and nursing expertise as factors in decision-making. *Nursing Research, 35*, 107–112.

Deloughery, G. L. (1991). *Issues and trends in nursing*. St. Louis: Mosby Year Book.

Dwyer, D. W., Swartz, R. H., & Fox, M. L. (1992). Decision making autonomy in nursing. *Journal of Nursing Administration, 22*(2) 107–112.

Gillies, D. A. (1994). *Nursing management—A systems approach* (3rd ed.). Philadelphia: W.B. Saunders.

Harrison, E. F. (1981). *The managerial decision-making process* (2d ed.). Boston: Houghton Mifflin.

Huston, C. J. (1990). What makes the difference? Attributes of the exceptional nurse. *Nursing 90, 20*(5).

Huston, C. J., & Marquis B. L. (1989). *Retention and productivity strategies for nurse managers*. Philadelphia: J.B. Lippincott.

Johnson, L. J. (1990). The influence of assumptions on effective decision-making. *Journal of Nursing Administration, 20*(4), 35.

La Monica, E., & Finch, F. E. (1977). Managerial decision-making. *Journal of Nursing Administration, 7*.

Marquis, B. L., & Huston, C. J. (1994). Decisions, decisions. *Advanced Practice Nurse, 1*, March.

Murphy, E. C. (1985). Whole brain management part I. *Nursing Management, 16*(3), 66.

Paul, R. (1992a). *Critical thinking*. Santa Rosa, CA: Foundation for Critical Thinking.

Paul, R. (1992b). Overview—Reforming and restructuring education. *Critical Thinking: Shaping of the 21st Century, 1*(1), 1.

Ruggiero, V. (1995). *The art of thinking* (4th ed.). New York: Harper Collins College Publishers.

Simon, H. A. (1965). *The shape of automation for man and management*. New York: Harper Textbooks.

Swansburg, R. C. (1990). *Management and Leadership for nurse managers*. Boston: Jones and Bartlett.

Vroom, V. H. (1973). A new look at managerial decision-making: Organizational decision-making. *Organizational Dynamics, 1*(4), 66–80.

Vroom, V., & Yetton, P. W. (1973). *Leadership and decision-making*. Pittsburgh: University of Pittsburg Press.

Wales, C. E., & Nardi, A. (1984). *Successful decision-making*. West Virginia University: Center for Guided Design.

(1984). *Webster's II Riverside children's dictionary* (p. 165). Chicago, IL: Riverside Publishing.

BIBLIOGRAPHY

Baggs, J. G. (1993). Collaborative interdisciplinary bioethical decison making in intensive care units. *Nursing Outlook, 41*(3), 108–112.

Barhvte, D. Y., & Christman, L. P. (1987). Administrative decisions: Data are better than opinions. *Journal of Nursing Administration, 17*(5).

Etzioni, A. (1989). Humble decision making. *Harvard Business Review, 89*(4), 122–126.

Gambrill E. (1990). *Critical thinking in clinical practice: Improving the accuracy of judgements and decisions about clients*. San Francisco: Jossey-Bass Publishers.

Glendon, K., & Ulrich, D. (1992). Using cooperative decision making strategies in nursing practice. *Nursing Administrative Quarterly, 17*(1), 69–71.

Feldman, C., Olberding, L., Shortridge, L., Toole, K., & Zappin, P. (1993). Decision making in case management of home healthcare clients. *The Journal of Nursing Administration, 23*(1), 33–38.

Huston, C. J., & Marquis, B. L. (1995). Seven steps to successful decision-making. *American Journal of Nursing, 95*(5), 65–68.

Isenberg, D. J. (1986). Thinking and managing: A verbal protocol analysis of managerial problem solving. *Academic Management Journal, 29*(4).

Kaluzny, A. (1989). Revitalizing decision making at the middle management level. *Hospitals and Health Services Administration, 34*(1), 39–51.

Marquis, B. L., & Huston, C. J. (1994). *Management decison making for nurses.* Philadelphia: J.B. Lippincott.

Nagelkerk, J. M., & Henery B. M. (1990). Strategic decision making. *Journal of Nursing Administration, 20*(7/8).

Prescott, P., Dennis, K., & Jacob, A. (1987). Clinical decision making of staff nurses. *Image: Journal of Nursing Scholarship, 16,* 20–21.

Rew, L. (1988). Intuition in decision making. *Image, 20*(3), 150–154.

Umiker, W. (1989). Decision making and problem solving by the busy professional. *Health Care Supervisor, 7*(4), 33–40.

White, J. E., Nativio, D. G., Kobert, S. N., & Engberg, S. J. (1992). Content and process in clinical decision making. *Image, 24*(2), 153–158.

UNIT II

ROLES AND FUNCTIONS IN PLANNING

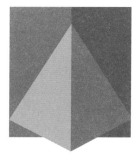

CHAPTER 3

Strategic Planning and the Planning Hierarchy

Bernhard and Walsh (1990, p. 83) define planning as "the determination of what is to be accomplished." Douglass (1992, p. 104) defines planning as "having a specific aim or purpose and mapping out a program or method beforehand for accomplishment of the goal." These definitions imply that planning is a proactive and deliberate process. It is a function required of all managers so that personal and organizational needs and objectives can be met. This cyclic process allows for unity of goals, continuity of energy expenditure (human and fiscal resources), and the opportunity to minimize uncertainty and chance. This process also directs attention to the objectives of the organization and provides the manager with a means of control.

Planning studies in the business sector have shown that although planning does not guarantee success, planners consistently out-perform nonplanners (Gehrman, 1989). Adequate planning provides the manager with a means of control and encourages the best use of resources. In effective planning, the manager must identify short- and long-term goals and changes that need to be undertaken to ensure that the unit will continue to meet its goals.

Identifying short- and long-term goals requires leadership skills, such as vision and creativity. It is impossible to plan what cannot be dreamed or envisioned. Likewise, planning requires flexibility and energy, two other leadership characteristics.

Bessie L. Marquis and Carol J. Huston:
LEADERSHIP ROLES AND MANAGEMENT FUNCTIONS IN NURSING, 2nd ed.
Lippincott-Raven Publishers © 1996

Planning is critically important to and precedes all other management functions. Without adequate planning, the management process will fail.

Unit 2 focuses on several aspects of planning, including strategic planning, the planning hierarchy, planned change, short-term planning, time management, and fiscal planning. This chapter deals with skills needed by the leader/manager for strategic planning and implementing the planning hierarchy. In addition, the leadership roles and management functions involved in developing, implementing, and evaluating that hierarchy are discussed (Display 3.1).

STRATEGIC PLANNING IN THE ORGANIZATION

Planning has several dimensions. Two of these dimensions are time span and complexity or comprehensiveness. Generally, complex organizational plans that involve a long period (usually 5 to 15 years) are referred to as long-range or *strategic* plans. At the unit level, any planning that is at least 6 months in the future may be considered long-range planning.

Berry (1994) defines strategic planning as a management process that combines four basic features:

1. A clear statement of the organization's mission
2. The identification of the agency's external constituencies or stakeholders and the determination of their assessment of the agency's purposes and operations
3. The delineation of the agency's strategic goals and objectives, typically in a 3- to 5-year plan
4. The development of strategies to achieve the goals

Thomas (1993) defines strategic planning as a long-range plan (including objectives) that identifies a department's environmental factors, while establishing its purpose, mission, philosophy, and goals. Fox and Fox (1983) and Paul and Taylor (1986) state that strategic planning should include an analysis of projected technological advances, internal and external environments, nursing and healthcare market and industry, economics of nursing and healthcare, availability of human and material resources, and judgments of top management.

Strategic planning requires managerial expertise in healthcare economics, human resource management, political and legislative issues affecting healthcare, and planning theory. Long-range planning also requires the leadership skills of being sensitive to the environment, being able to appraise accurately the social and political climate, and being willing to take risks.

Due to rapidly changing technology, increasing government involvement in healthcare, and scientific advances, healthcare organizations are finding it increasingly difficult to identify long-term needs appropriately and plan accordingly. Unlike the 20-year strategic plans of the 1960s and 1970s, most long-term planners today find it difficult to look even 5 or 10 years in the future. The healthcare system is in chaos, as is much of the business world. Traditional management solutions no longer apply; a lack of strong leadership in the healthcare system has limited the innovation needed to create solutions to new and complex problems. Because change is occurring so rapidly, managers can easily become focused on short-range plans and miss changes that can drastically alter specific long-term plans. Healthcare facilities are

Display 3.1 Leadership Roles and Management Functions in Strategic Planning and Implementing the Planning Hierarchy

Leadership Roles

1. Assesses the organization's internal and external environment in forecasting and identifying driving forces and barriers to planning
2. Demonstrates visionary, innovative, and creative thinking in organizational and unit planning, thus inspiring proactive, rather than reactive, planning
3. Influences and inspires group members to be actively involved in long-term planning
4. Periodically completes value clarification to increase self-awareness
5. Encourages subordinates toward value clarification by actively listening and providing feedback
6. Communicates and clarifies organizational goals and values to subordinates
7. Encourages subordinates to be involved in policy formation, including developing, implementing, and reviewing unit philosophy, goals, objectives, policies, procedures, and rules
8. Is receptive to new and varied ideas

Management Functions

1. Is knowledgable regarding legal, political, economic, and social factors affecting healthcare planning
2. Demonstrates knowledge of and uses appropriate techniques in both personal and organizational planning
3. Provides opportunities for subordinates, peers, competitors, regulatory agencies, and the general public to participate in planning
4. Coordinates unit-level planning to be congruent with organizational goals
5. Periodically assesses unit constraints and assets to determine available resources for planning
6. Develops and articulates a unit philosophy that is congruent with the organizational philosophy
7. Develops and articulates unit goals and objectives that reflect unit philosophy
8. Develops and articulates unit policies, procedures, and rules that operationalize unit objectives
9. Periodically reviews unit philosophy, goals, policies, procedures, and rules and revises them to meet the unit's changing needs

particularly vulnerable to external social, economic, and political forces; long-range planning, then, must address how these forces may change. It is imperative, therefore, that long-range plans be flexible, permitting change as external forces assert their impact on healthcare facilities.

If unit-level managers display one common fault, it is not developing adequate long-range plans. Many managers operate in a crisis mode. They do not use available historical patterns to assist them in planning, nor do they examine present clues and projected statistics, called *forecasting,* to determine future needs. Forecasting takes advantage of input from others, gives sequence in activity, and protects an organization against undesirable changes. With changes in technology, payment structures, and resource availability, the manager who is unwilling or unable to forecast accurately impedes the organization's efficiency and the unit's effectiveness. Increased competition, changes in government reimbursement, and decreased hospital revenues have reduced intuitive managerial decision making. Managers who are uninformed about the legal, political, economic, and social factors affecting healthcare make planning errors that may have disastrous implications for their professional development and the financial viability of the organization.

LEARNING EXERCISE 3.1

Identify six forces affecting today's healthcare system. You may include legal, political, economic, social, or ethical forces. Try to prioritize these forces in terms of how they will affect you as a manager or RN.

Long-range planning for the organization historically has been accomplished by top-level managers and the board of directors, with limited input from middle-level managers. There is increasing recognition, however, of the importance of subordinate input from all levels of the organization to give the strategic plan meaning and to increase the likelihood of its successful implementation. The first-level manager is generally more involved in long-range planning at the unit level. However, because the organization's strategic plans affect unit planning, managers at all levels must be informed of organizational long-range plans so that all planning is coordinated. Bombard (1993) suggests that all organizations establish annual strategic planning conferences, involving all departments and levels of the hierarchy; this action should promote increased effectiveness of nursing staff, better communication between all levels of personnel, a cooperative spirit relative to solving problems, and a pervasive feeling that the departments are unified, goal directed, and doing their part to help the organization accomplish its mission.

THE PLANNING HIERARCHY

There are many types of planning; in most organizations, these plans form a hierarchy, with the plans at the top influencing all the plans that follow (Fig. 3.1). The hierarchy as depicted in the pyramid in Figure 3.1 broadens at lower levels, representing an increase in the number of planning components. In addition, planning components at the top of the hierarchy are more general and lower components are more specific.

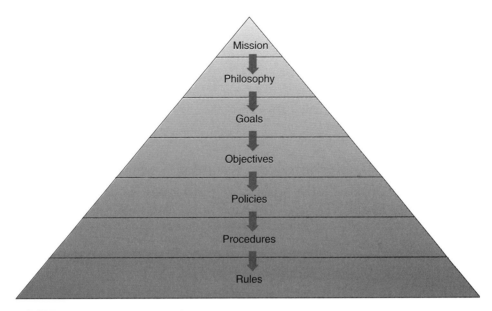

FIGURE 3.1 The planning hierarchy.

THE PURPOSE OR MISSION STATEMENT

The purpose or *mission* is a brief statement identifying the reason that an organization exists and its future aim or function. This statement identifies the organization's constituency and addresses its position regarding ethics, principles, and standards of practice. A sample mission statement for County Hospital, a teaching hospital, follows.

Mission Statement

County Hospital is a tertiary care facility and provides comprehensive, holistic care to all state residents who seek treatment. The purpose of County Hospital is to combine high quality, holistic healthcare with the provision of learning opportunities for students in medicine, nursing, and allied health sciences. Research is encouraged to identify new treatment regimens and to promote high quality healthcare for generations to come.

The mission statement is of highest priority in the planning hierarchy because it influences the development of an organization's philosophy, goals, objectives, policies, procedures, and rules. Managers employed by County Hospital would have two primary goals to guide their planning: 1) to provide high quality, holistic care, and 2) to provide learning opportunities for students in medicine, nursing, and other allied health sciences. To meet these goals, adequate fiscal and human resources would have to be allocated for preceptorships and clinical research. In addition, an employee's performance appraisal would examine the worker's performance in terms of organizational and unit goals.

THE ORGANIZATION'S PHILOSOPHY STATEMENT

The *philosophy* flows from the purpose or mission statement and delineates the set of values and beliefs that guide all actions of the organization. It is the basic foundation that directs all further planning toward that mission. A statement of philosophy can usually be found in policy manuals at the institution or is available on request. A philosophy that might be generated from County Hospital's mission statement follows.

Organizational Philosophy

The board of directors, medical and nursing staff, and administrators of County Hospital believe that human beings are unique, due to different genetic endowments, personal experiences in social and physical environments, and the ability to adapt to biophysical, psychosocial, and spiritual stressors. Thus, each patient is considered a unique individual, with unique needs. Identifying outcomes and goals, setting priorities, prescribing strategy options, and selecting an optimal strategy will be negotiated by the patient, physician, and healthcare team.

As unique individuals, patients provide medical, nursing, and allied health students invaluable diverse learning opportunities. Because the board of directors, medical and nursing staff, and administrators believe that the quality of healthcare provided directly reflects the quality of the education of its future healthcare providers, students are welcomed and encouraged to seek out as many learning opportunities as possible. Because high-quality healthcare is defined by and depends on technological advances and scientific discovery, County Hospital encourages research as a means of scientific inquiry.

The organizational philosophy provides the basis for developing nursing philosophies at the unit level and for nursing service as a whole. The *nursing service philosophy* may be described as an intentionally chosen set of values and purposes that is the basis for determining the means to accomplish nursing objectives (Douglass, 1992). Written in conjunction with the organizational philosophy, the nursing service philosophy should address fundamental beliefs about nursing and nursing care; the quality, quantity, and scope of nursing services; and how nursing specifically will meet organizational goals. Frequently, the nursing service philosophy draws on the concepts of holistic care, education, and research. County Hospital's nursing service philosophy might look something like this:

Nursing Service Philosophy

The philosophy of nursing at County Hospital is based on respect for the individual's dignity and worth. We believe all patients have the right to receive effective nursing care. This care is a personal service that is based on patients' needs and their clinical disease or condition. Recognizing the obligation of nursing to help restore patients to the best possible state of physical, mental, and emotional health and to maintain patients' sense of spiritual and social well-being, we pledge intelligent cooperation in coordinating nursing service with the medical and allied professional practitioners. Understanding the importance of research and teaching for improving patient care, the nursing department will support, promote, and participate in these activities. Using knowledge of human behavior, we shall strive for mutual trust and understanding between nursing service and nursing employees to provide an atmosphere for developing the fullest possible potential of each member of the nursing team. We believe that nursing personnel are individually accountable to patients and their families for the quality and compassion of the patient care rendered and for upholding the standards of care as delineated by the nursing staff (Marquis & Huston, 1994).

The *unit philosophy,* adapted from nursing service philosophy, specifies how nursing care provided on the unit will correspond with nursing service and organizational goals. This congruency in philosophy, goals, and objectives between the organization, nursing service, and unit is shown in Figure 3.2.

Although unit-level managers have limited opportunity to help develop organizational philosophy, they are active in determining, implementing, and evaluating the unit philosophy. *In formulating this philosophy,* the unit manager incorporates a knowledge of the unit's internal and external environments and an understanding of the unit's role in meeting organizational goals. The manager must understand the planning hierarchy and be able to articulate ideas in writing. Leaders/managers also must be visionary, innovative, and creative in identifying unit purposes or goals so that the philosophy not only reflects current practice, but incorporates a view of the future.

Statements of philosophy, in general, can be helpful only if they truly direct the work of the organization toward a specific purpose. Mallison (1989, p. 1021) emphasizes the difference between "lofty theoretical statements stored in nursing policy books and a *working* philosophy." She states that "a working philosophy is evident in a nursing department's decisions, in its priorities, and in its behavior within the organization." An individual should be able to identify exactly how the organization is implementing that philosophy by observing members of the nursing staff, reviewing the budgetary priorities, and talking to patients. "Whatever decisions are made in the nursing department make the philosophy of care visible to all—no matter what is espoused on paper" (Mallison, 1989, p. 1021). A philosophy that is not or cannot be implemented is useless.

LEARNING EXERCISE 3.2

Recover, Inc., a fictitious for-profit home health agency, provides complete nursing and supportive services for in-home care. Services include skilled nursing, bathing, shopping, physical therapy, occupational therapy, meal preparation, housekeeping, speech therapy, and social work. The agency provides round-the-clock care, 7 days a week to a primarily underserved rural area in northern California. The brochure the company publishes says that it is committed to satisfying the needs of the rural community and that it is dedicated to excellence.

Assignment: Based on this limited information, develop a brief philosophy statement that might be appropriate for Recover, Inc. Be creative and embellish information given in the learning exercise if appropriate.

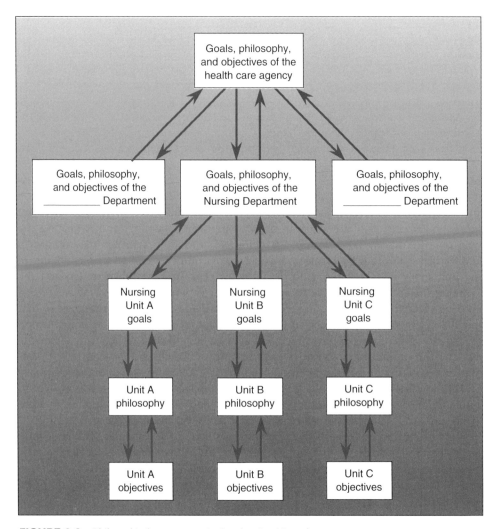

FIGURE 3.2   Philosophical congruence in the planning hierarchy.

SOCIETAL PHILOSOPHIES AND VALUES

Societies and organizations have philosophies or sets of beliefs that guide their behavior. These beliefs that guide behavior are called values. Mac Pherson (1987) defines a value as "a quality having intrinsic worth for a society or an individual" and identifies individualism, the pursuit of self-interests, and competition as some of the most strongly held American values. Bennis (1989, p. 46) states American society has always been at war with itself. "We have always dreamt of community and democracy, but always practiced democracy and capitalism. We have celebrated innocence, but sought power" Mac Pherson (1987) argues that these values have profoundly affected healthcare policy formation and implementation and that the result is a healthcare system that promotes structured inequalities. Despite more than 1 trillion dollars spent on healthcare in 1993, 38 million American citizens had *no* health insurance, and another 25 million Americans were underinsured.

While values seem to be of central importance for healthcare policy development and analysis, public discussion of this crucial variable is often neglected. Instead, healthcare policy makers tend to focus on technology, cost-benefit analysis, and cost-effectiveness. Mac Pherson argues that although this type of evaluation is important, it does not address the underlying values in this country that have led to unequal access to healthcare.

LEARNING EXERCISE 3.3

Both Canada and Germany have been held up as models in healthcare reform because they guarantee healthcare for all citizens. Drake, Fitzgerald, and Jaffe (1993), in their book *Hard Choices,* compare the healthcare systems in both these countries with that of the United States. At $2,867 per capita, 15% of the population in the United States is uninsured, and another 40% to 60% have inadequate coverage. At $1,915 per capita, Canadians receive hospitalization, doctor visits, and most dental work free of charge. At $1,659 per capita, Germany provides services at a level similar to Canada, but with an $8 per day copayment for hospitalization.

Unlike the emphasis on specialized care in the United States with limited choice of physicians, healthcare systems in Canada and Germany emphasize primary care, unlimited choice of physicians, free physician visits, and an emphasis on health promotion. With little financial incentive for physician specialization and a nationwide focus on health promotion, there are 500% more general practitioners per capita in Germany and Canada than in the United States.

At what cost is this healthcare offered? Canadians and Germans experience longer waits for some high-tech procedures, and the governments of those countries have limitations on the proliferation of technology. However, the United States continues to have a higher incidence of infant mortality and low birth weight than either country and the lowest life expectancy at birth. Despite the highest spending as a percent of gross domestic product, American consumers had the least number of physician visits and the shortest average hospital stay.

What is the bottom line? Canadian and German physicians and consumers are far more satisfied with their healthcare system than American citizens are with theirs; Americans feel "labeled and defined by the insurance" they hold (Drake, Fitzgerald, & Jaffe, 1993).

Assignment: In small groups, discuss the following:

Do you agree or disagree with Mac Pherson's assertion that the U.S. healthcare system represents societal values of individualism, the pursuit of self-interests, and competition? Do you believe the American people are willing to pay the costs required to pursue collectivism, cooperation, and equality in healthcare? Would you be willing to have less choices about your healthcare if access could be guaranteed to all? Do you feel the cost of universal coverage should be picked up by the consumer or by the employer? Recognize that both societal and individual values will affect your feelings.

INDIVIDUAL PHILOSOPHIES AND VALUES

As discussed in Chapter 2, values have a tremendous impact on decisions individuals make. For the individual, personal philosophies and values are shaped by the socialization processes experienced by that individual. All individuals should carefully examine their value system and recognize the role it plays in how they make decisions, resolve conflicts, and even how they perceive things. Therefore, the nurse-leader must be self-aware and provide subordinates with learning opportunities or experiences that foster increased self-awareness. At times, it is difficult to assess whether something is a true value.

McNally (1980) identified the following four characteristics that determine a true value.

1. It must be freely chosen from among alternatives only after due reflection.
2. It must be prized and cherished.
3. It is consciously and consistently repeated (part of a pattern).
4. It is positively affirmed and enacted.

If a value does not meet all four criteria, it is a *value indicator*. Most individuals have many value indicators but few true values. For example, many nurses assert that they value their national nursing organization, yet they do not pay dues or participate in the organization. True values require that the individual take action, while value indicators do not. Thus, the value ascribed to the national nursing organization is a value indicator for these nurses and not a true value.

In addition, because our values change with time, periodic clarification is necessary to determine how our values may have changed. Value clarification includes examining values, assigning priorities to those values, and determining how they influence behavior so that one's lifestyle is consistent with prioritized values. Hamilton and Kiefer (1986) identified seven steps to help determine and clarify values:

1. *Listen to your responses* (social, physical, intellectual, emotional, and spiritual). Before people can recognize their values, they must become aware of all their feelings.
2. *Differentiate internal sources from external sources.* Do your feelings come from within you (internally), or are they a result of what you've been told is right or wrong (externally)? True values encourage you to tune out external sources so that you can get a more honest response from within. You may, in fact, find that some values you have developed from external sources are right for you.
3. *Take time to experience full awareness of your internal responses.* Examine your responses, and pay attention to your reactions. Was your behavior consistent with your values? Are you satisfied with your behavior, or would you change it in some way?
4. *Act on your internal responses.* Now you must face up to your values and accept the need to change. You must be accountable for behaviors that conflict with your values.
5. *Evaluate your alternatives.* What alternative behaviors exist that allow you to be true to your value? Do compromise behaviors occur that do not conflict

with your values? Situations can be resolved in more than one way, even if your values are clearly defined and internalized.

6. *Establish behavior patterns consistent with your values.* Seek out behaviors that reflect your values and internal responses. This is a purposeful learning of new responses and behaviors.

7. *Trust your beliefs, preferences, likes, and dislikes.* Gain confidence in the decisions you make. Believe in yourself.

LEARNING EXERCISE 3.4

Using what you have learned about values, value indicators, and value clarification, answer the following questions. Take time to reflect on your values before answering. This may be used as a writing exercise.

1. List three or four of your basic beliefs about nursing.
2. Knowing what you know now, ask yourself, "Do I *value* nursing?" Was it freely chosen from among alternatives after appropriate reflection? Do you prize and cherish nursing? If you had a choice to do it over, would you still choose nursing as a career?
3. Are your personal and professional values congruent? Are there any values espoused by the nursing profession that are inconsistent with your personal values? How will you resolve resulting conflicts?

Sometimes values change as a result of life's experiences or newly acquired knowledge. Most of the values we have as children reflect our parents' values. Later, our values are modified by peers and role models. Although they are learned, values cannot be forced on an individual because they must be internalized. However, restricted exposure to other viewpoints also limits the number of value choices an individual is able to generate. Therefore, becoming more worldly increases our awareness of alternatives from which we select our values.

Occasionally, individual values are in conflict with those of the organization. Because the philosophy of an organization determines its priorities in goal selection and distribution of resources, nurses need to understand the organization's philosophy. For example, assume that a nurse is employed by County Hospital, which clearly states in its philosophy that teaching is a primary purpose for the hospital's existence. Consequently, medical students are allowed to practice endotracheal intubation on all people who die in the hospital, allowing the students to gain needed experience in emergency medicine. This practice disturbs the nurse a great deal; it is not consistent with his or her own set of values and thus creates great personal conflict.

Nurses who frequently make decisions that conflict with their personal values may experience confusion and anxiety. This intrapersonal struggle will lead ultimately to job stress and dissatisfaction, especially for the novice nurse who comes to the organization with inadequate value clarification.

As part of the leadership role, the manager should encourage all potential employees to read and think about the organization's mission statement or philosophy before accepting the job. The manager should give a copy of the philosophy to the prospective applicant prior to the hiring interview. The applicant also should be encouraged to speak to employees in various positions within the organization regarding how the philosophy is implemented at their job level. Finally, new employees should be encouraged to speak to community members about the institution's reputation for care. New employees who understand the organizational philosophy will not only have clearer expectations about the institution's purposes and goals, but will have a better understanding of how they fit into the organization.

Although all nurses should have a philosophy comparable with their employer's, it is especially important for the new manager to have a value system consistent with the organization. Institutional changes that closely align with the value system of the nurse-manager will receive more effort and higher priority than those that are not true values or that conflict with the nurse-manager's value system. It is unrealistic for managers to accept a position under the assumption that they can change the organization's philosophy to more closely match their personal philosophy. Such a change will require extraordinary energy and precipitate inevitable conflict because the organization's philosophy reflects the institution's historical development and the beliefs of those individuals who were vital in the institution's development.

Hodgetts (1986) states that not only do all managers have differing values, but these values change from generation to generation. Hodgetts argues that values regarding retention have changed tremendously in the last 5 years in response to organizational down-sizing. Other experts have argued that organizational and management values have changed as a result of the implementation of the Medicare Prospective Pricing System, the imposed reimbursement limits to hospitals for Medicare patients classified according to diagnosis-related groups, and the recent wave of healthcare consumerism (Curran & Boston, 1988). Perhaps organizational and managerial values have not really changed, but it is clear that contemporary changes in the healthcare system have required organizations and their managers to reexamine carefully their goals and purposes. Nursing managers must recognize that closely held values may be challenged by current social and economic constraints and that philosophy statements must be continually reviewed and revised to ensure ongoing accuracy of beliefs.

GOALS AND OBJECTIVES

Goals and objectives are the ends toward which the organization is working. All philosophies must be translated into specific goals and objectives if they are to result in action. Thus, goals and objectives "operationalize" the philosophy.

A *goal* may be defined as the desired result toward which effort is directed; it is the aim of the philosophy. Although institutional goals are usually determined by the organization's highest administrative levels, there is increasing emphasis on including workers in setting organizational goals. Goals, much like philosophies and values, change with time and require periodic reevaluation and prioritization.

Goals, although somewhat global in nature, should be measurable and ambitious, but realistic. Goals also should clearly delineate the desired end-product.

When goals are not clear, simple misunderstandings may compound, and communication may break down. Covey (1989) identified the cause of almost all relationship difficulties as conflicting or ambiguous expectations around roles and goals, which lead to misunderstanding, disappointment, and withdrawal of trust.

Organizations usually set long- and short-term goals for services rendered; economics; use of resources, including people, funds, and facilities; innovations; and social responsibilities. The more quantitative the goal, the more likely its achievement is to receive attention and the less likely it is to be distorted (Marriner-Tomey 1992). The following are sample goal statements:

> All nursing staff will recognize the patient's need for independence and right to privacy and will assess the patient's level of readiness to learn in relation to their illness.
>
> The nursing staff will provide effective patient care relative to patient needs insofar as the hospital and community facilities permit through the use of care plans, individual patient care, and discharge planning, including follow-up contact.
>
> An ongoing effort will be made to create an atmosphere conducive to favorable patient and employee morale and that fosters personal growth.
>
> The performance of all employees in the nursing department will be evaluated in a manner that produces growth in the employee and upgrades nursing standards.
>
> All nursing units within County Hospital will work cooperatively with other departments within the hospital to further the mission, philosophy, and goals of the institution.

Decker and Sullivan (1992) state that although goals may direct and maintain the behavior of an organization, there are several dangers in using goal evaluation as the primary means of assessing organizational effectiveness. The first danger is that goals may be in conflict with each other, creating confusion for employees and consumers. For example, the need for profit maximization in healthcare facilities today may conflict with some stated patient goals or quality goals. The second danger with the goal approach is that publicly stated goals may not truly reflect organizational goals. Organizational goals can be a facade for legitimizing unit goals and the career ambitions of employees (Decker & Sullivan, 1992). The final danger is that because goals are global, it is often difficult to determine whether they have been obtained.

Objectives are similar to goals in that they motivate individuals to a specific end and are explicit, measurable, observable or retrievable, and obtainable. Objectives, however, are more specific and measurable than goals because they identify *how* and *when* the goal is to be accomplished.

Goals usually have multiple objectives that are each accompanied by a targeted completion date. The more specific the objectives for a goal can be, the easier for all involved in goal attainment to understand and carry out specific role behaviors. This is especially important for the nurse-manager to remember when writing job descriptions; if there is little ambiguity in the job description, there will be little role confusion or distortion. Clearly written goals and objectives must be communicated to all those in the organization responsible for their attainment. This is a critical leadership role for the nurse-manager.

Objectives can focus either on the desired process or the desired result. *Process objectives* are written in terms of the method to be used, while *result-focused objectives* specify the desired outcome. An example of a process objective might be, "All patients will be oriented to the call light at the time of admission." An example of a result-focused objective might be, "All postoperative patients will perceive a decrease in their pain levels following the administration of parenteral pain medication." Writing good objectives requires time and practice.

Marrelli (1993) suggests that all objectives should have a specific time frame, be behaviorally stated, be objectively evaluated, and identify positive rather than negative outcomes.

As a sample objective, one of the goals at Mercy Hospital is "All registered nurses will be proficient in the administration of intravenous fluids." Objectives for Mercy Hospital might include the following:

1. All registered nurses will complete Mercy Hospital's course "IV Therapy Certification" within 1 month of beginning employment. The hospital will bear the cost of this program.
2. Registered nurses scoring less than 70% on a comprehensive examination in "IV Therapy Certification" must attend the remedial 4-hour course "Review of Basic IV Principles" not more than 2 weeks after the completion of "IV Therapy Certification."
3. Registered nurses unable to achieve a score of 70% or better on the comprehensive examination for "IV Therapy Certification" after completing "Review of Basic IV Principles" will not be allowed to perform IV therapy on patients. An individualized plan will be established by the unit manager and the employee who failed the examination.

The leader/manager clearly must be skilled in determining and documenting goals and objectives. Prudent managers assess the unit's constraints and assets and determine available resources before developing goals and objectives. The leader must then be creative and futuristic in identifying how goals might best be translated into objectives and thus implemented. The willingness to be receptive to new and varied ideas is a tremendous leadership skill. In addition, well-developed interpersonal skills allow the leader to involve and inspire subordinates in goal setting. The final step in the process involves clearly writing the identified goals and objectives, communicating changes to subordinates, and periodically evaluating and revising goals and objectives as needed.

▶ **LEARNING EXERCISE 3.5**

Practice writing goals and objectives for County Hospital based on the mission and philosophy statements in this chapter. Identify three goals and three objectives to operationalize each of these goals.

POLICIES AND PROCEDURES

Policies are plans reduced to statements or instructions that direct organizations in their decision making. These comprehensive statements, derived from the organization's philosophy, goals, and objectives, explain how goals will be met and guide the general course and scope of organizational activities. Megginson, Mosley, and Pietri (1988) define policies as broad general statements of expected actions that serve as guides to managerial decision making or to supervising the actions of subordinates. Thus, policies direct individual behavior toward the organization's mission and define broad limits and desired outcomes of commonly recurring situations, while leaving some discretion and initiative to those who must carry out that policy. While some policies are required by accrediting agencies, such as the Joint Commission on Accreditation of Healthcare Organizations, many policies are specific to the individual institution, thus providing management with a means of internal control.

Policies also can be implied or expressed. *Implied policies,* neither written or expressed verbally, have usually developed over time and follow a precedent. For example, a hospital may have an implied policy that employees should be encouraged and supported in their activity in community, regional, and national healthcare organizations. Another example might be that nurses who limit their maternity leave to 3 months can return to their former jobs and shifts with no status change.

Expressed policies are delineated verbally or in writing. Most organizations have many written policies that are readily available to all individuals and promote consistency of action. Expressed policies may include a formal dress code, policy for sick leave or vacation time, and disciplinary procedures.

Fiesta (1993) states that healthcare workers can be held liable in a court of law for failing to follow implied *or* expressed policies if patient injury occurs. Policies are necessary for consistency in care, and the court has *rejected* arguments that policies are only general goals, suggesting a desired course of action but not insisting on it. Fiesta (1993) also emphasizes that the only position worse than not having a policy is to have one but not follow it.

Policies are generally divided into four categories: 1) those that apply to patients; 2) those that apply to personnel; 3) those that apply to the environment in which patients receive care and in which personnel work; and 4) those that apply to relationships with other departments or disciplines (Swansburg, 1990). The manager is active in developing these policies. Although top-level nursing management is more involved in the setting of organizational policies (usually by policy committees), unit managers must determine how those policies will be implemented on their units. Input from subordinates in forming, implementing, and reviewing policy allows the leader/manager to develop guidelines that all employees will support and follow. Even if unit-level employees are not directly involved in policy setting, their feedback is crucial to its successful implementation.

After policy has been formulated, the leadership role of managers includes the responsibility for communicating that policy to all who may be affected by it. This information should be transmitted in writing and verbally. The relative value of the policy is often perceived in relation to how it is communicated.

Procedures are plans that have been reduced to a sequence of steps of required action. Procedures identify the process or steps needed to implement a policy and are generally found in manuals at the unit-level of the organization. Because procedural instructions involve elements of organizing, some textbooks place the development of procedures in the organizing phase of the management process. Regardless of where procedural development is formulated, there must be a close relationship with planning, the foundation for all procedures.

Procedures establish customary or acceptable ways of accomplishing a specific task by outlining a set of steps to follow and giving rationale for each set of activities. Grindol (1984) recommends following this sequence of events when developing procedure statements.

1. State the task or title.
2. Identify the need or stated purpose.
3. Make a draft of all the possible steps and substeps.
4. Consult with references and experts, including manufacturers.
5. Complete a second draft, including a standard format, related policies, equipment needed and its location, line drawings, and the ordering procedure. This draft should provide step-by-step instructions on performing the task, brief theory statements, and supporting documents.
6. Edit the final draft.
7. Assign an index code to the procedure.
8. Type the procedure, and distribute to reviewers (labeled with the word "draft" and with a deadline for feedback).
9. Revise the procedure after feedback is given.
10. Submit revised procedure for approval to authorities.
11. Have procedure printed and distributed.
12. Provide in-service training on the procedure to all appropriate personnel.

Again, involving the group in establishing procedures increases the quality of the end-product and the likelihood that the procedures will be implemented as desired. Established procedures save staff time, facilitate delegation, reduce cost, increase productivity, and provide a means of control.

The manager also has a responsibility to review and revise policies and procedure statements to ensure currency and applicability. Because most units are in constant flux, the needs of the unit and the most appropriate means of meeting those needs constantly change. For example, the unit manager is responsible for seeing that a clearly written policy regarding holiday and vacation time exists and that it is communicated to all those it affects. The unit manager also must provide a clearly written procedural statement regarding how to request vacation or holiday time on that specific unit. The unit manager would assess any long-term change in patient census or availability of human resources and revise the policy and procedural statements accordingly.

RULES

Rules and regulations are plans that define specific action or nonaction. Generally included as part of policy and procedure statements, rules describe situations that allow only one choice of action. Because rules are the least flexible type of planning in the planning hierarchy, there should be as few rules as possible in the organization. Existing rules, however, should be enforced to keep morale from breaking down and to allow organizational structure. Chapter 20 on discipline includes a more detailed discussion of rules and regulations.

BARRIERS TO IMPLEMENTING THE PLANNING HIERARCHY

Because planning is a complex and conscious process, it can be impeded by a number of factors. Lyles and Joiner (1986) have identified several barriers to good planning:

- Lack of knowledge and skill about how to plan
- Consistent use of reactive rather than proactive planning
- Lack of understanding about the external environment's impact on planning, thus excluding competitors, regulatory agencies, and the general public
- Inadequate intraorganizational support
- Inappropriate use of plans and overt resistance to change by individuals
- Too much or not enough detail in planning activities
- Plans used to control rather than inspire or lead

Because planning is essential, managers must be able to overcome these barriers. Benefits of effective planning include timely accomplishment of higher quality work and the best possible use of capital and human resources. For successful organizational planning, the manager must remember several points:

1. *The organization can be more effective if movement within it is directed at specified goals and objectives.* Because planning provides a basis for measuring organizational and individual performance, managers can evaluate the environment, resources, and employee effectiveness when the expected is known (Gehrman, 1989). Unfortunately, the novice manager frequently omits establishing a goal or objective. Setting a goal for a plan keeps managers focused on the bigger picture and saves them from getting lost in the minute details of planning. Just as the nursing care plan establishes patient care goals prior to delineating problems and interventions, managers must establish goals for their planning strategies that are congruent with goals established at higher levels.
2. *Because a plan is a guide to reach a goal, it must be flexible and allow for readjustment as unexpected events occur.* This flexibility is a necessary attribute for the manager in all planning phases and the management process.
3. *The manager should include in the planning process individuals and units that could be affected by the course of action.* Although time consuming, employee involvement in how things are done and by whom creates a feeling of ownership and therefore a strong commitment to goal achievement (Gehrman, 1989). Although not everyone will want to contribute to unit or organizational planning, all should be invited. The manager also needs to communicate clearly to all those responsible for carrying out the plans the goals and specific individual responsibilities so that work is coordinated.

4. *Plans should be specific, simple, and realistic.* A vague plan is impossible to implement. A plan that is too global or unrealistic discourages rather than motivates employees. If a plan is unclear, the nurse-leader must restate the plan in another manner or use group process to clarify common goals.

5. *Know when to plan and when not to plan.* It is possible to overplan and underplan. For example, one who overplans may devote excessive time to arranging details that might be better left to those who will carry out the plan. Underplanning occurs when the manager erroneously assumes that people and events will naturally fall into some desired and efficient method of production.

6. *Good plans have built-in evaluation checkpoints so that there can be a mid-course correction if unexpected events occur.* A final evaluation should always occur at the end of the plan. If goals were not met, the plan should be examined to determine why it failed. This evaluation process assists the manager in future planning.

INTEGRATING LEADERSHIP ROLES AND MANAGEMENT FUNCTIONS IN PLANNING

Clearly, the leader/manager must be skilled in determining, implementing, documenting, and evaluating all types of planning in the hierarchy. Managers draw on the philosophy and goals established at the organizational and nursing service levels in implementing planning at the unit level. Initially, managers must assess the unit's constraints and assets and determine its resources available for planning. The manager then draws on his or her leadership skills in creativity, innovation, and futuristic thinking to problem solve how philosophies can be translated into goals, goals into objectives, and so on down the planning hierarchy. The wise manager will develop the interpersonal leadership skills needed to inspire and involve subordinates in this planning hierarchy. The manager also must demonstrate the leadership skill of being receptive to new and varied ideas. The final step in the process involves articulating identified goals and objectives clearly; this learned management skill is critical to the success of the planning. If the unit manager lacks management or leadership skills, the planning hierarchy fails.

KEY CONCEPTS

▼ The planning phase of the management process is critical and precedes all other functions. Without adequate planning, the management process fails.

▼ Planning is a proactive function required of all nurses so that personal and organizational needs and objectives can be met.

▼ Plans should be specific, simple, and realistic.

▼ Because a plan is a guide for action in reaching a goal, it must be *flexible* and allow for readjustment as unexpected events occur.

▼ The manager should include in the actual planning process all individuals and organizational units that could be affected by the plan.

▼ Good plans have a time for evaluation built into them so that there can be a mid-course correction if unexpected events occur.

▼ Plans that involve a long time—usually 5 to 15 years—and are very complex are referred to as long-range or *strategic* plans.

▼ Most organizations use many types of plans that form a hierarchy from global to specific. The planning hierarchy in most healthcare institutions includes the elements of mission statement, philosophy, goals, objectives, policies, procedures, and rules.

▼ The *mission statement* identifies the reason an organization exists.

▼ The *philosophy* flows from the purpose or mission statement and delineates the set of values and beliefs that guides all organizational actions.

▼ A philosophy that is not, or cannot be, implemented is useless.

▼ Management functions include determining, implementing, and evaluating the unit philosophy, but leadership roles require an examination of values by managers and their subordinates.

▼ Although it is important for all nurses to have a philosophy comparable with the employing agency, it is especially important for the new manager to have a value system consistent with that agency. Nurses making frequent decisions that conflict with their personal values will experience job stress and anxiety.

▼ A *goal* may be defined as the desired result toward which effort is directed. A goal is the aim of the philosophy.

▼ *Objectives* are similar to goals because they motivate individuals to a specific end and are explicit, measurable, observable or retrievable, and obtainable. Objectives, however, are more specific and measurable than goals in that they identify *how* and *when* the goal is to be accomplished.

▼ *Policies* are plans reduced to statements or instructions that direct an organization in its decision making.

▼ *Procedures* are plans that have been reduced to a sequence of required actions.

▼ *Rules* and regulations are plans that define specific action or nonaction. Rules are generally included in policy and procedure statements and describe situations that allow only one choice of action.

▼ All planning must include an evaluation step. Philosophies, goals, objectives, policies, procedures, and the need for rules change with time and require periodic reevaluation and prioritization.

▼ All planning in the hierarchy must flow from, and be congruent with, planning done at higher levels in the hierarchy. That is, a nursing unit's goals cannot conflict with the overall philosophy of the central nursing administration or the mission of the organization.

▲ ADDITIONAL LEARNING EXERCISES

Learning Exercise 3.6

Susan is the supervisor of the 22-bed oncology unit at Memorial Hospital, a 150-bed hospital. Unit morale and job satisfaction are high, despite a unit occupancy rate of less than 50% in the last 6 months. Patient satisfaction on this unit is as high or higher than any other unit in the hospital. Susan's personal philosophy is that oncology patients have physical, social, and spiritual needs that are different from other patients. Both the unit and nursing service philosophy reflect this belief. Thus, nurses working in the oncology unit receive additional education, orientation, and socialization regarding their unique roles and responsibilities in working with oncology patients.

At this morning's regularly scheduled department head meeting, the chief executive nursing officer suggests that because of extreme budget shortfalls and continuing low census, the oncology unit should be closed and its patients merged with the general medical/surgical patient population. The oncology nursing staff would be reassigned to the medical/surgical unit with Susan as the unit's cosupervisor.

The idea received immediate support from the medical/surgical supervisor because of the current staffing shortage on her unit. Susan, startled by the proposal, immediately voiced her disapproval and asked for 2 weeks to prepare her argument. Her request was granted.

Assignment: What values or beliefs are guiding Susan, the chief executive nursing officer, and the medical/surgical unit supervisor? Determine an appropriate plan of action for Susan. What impact does a unit or nursing service philosophy have on the actions of management and employees?

Learning Exercise 3.7
(From Marquis & Huston, 1994.)

Conflict of Values

Following is a case study that deals with individual and organizational or professional values and how they may conflict. Read the case, and answer the questions that follow. Use some form of group process in your decision making.

Your next-door neighbor, Joe, is a 75-year-old with multiple chronic health problems. His history includes four prior myocardial infarctions, implantation of a pacemaker, open-heart surgery, an inoperable abdominal aneurysm, repeated episodes of congestive heart failure, and cardiac arrhythmias. Because of his poor health, he cannot operate the small business he owns or work for any length of time at his gardening or other hobbies. Both Joe and his wife talk about his "impending" death as a relief to his nearly constant discomfort and depression. Although his wife cares very much for him, the constant emotional and physical strain is very apparent. Joe is aware of this.

During the 3 years you have been Joe's neighbor, both he and his wife have called on you as a neighbor, friend, and nurse. Frequently, they request that you auscultate Joe's chest to confirm the recurrence of congestive heart failure. They rely on your judgment as to whether further medical care is needed. You have assisted and taught them about the multiple medications Joe takes daily. Your nursing assessments confirm the poor prognosis that Joe's doctor has given.

One weekend, as you are leisurely enjoying your lunch, Joe's granddaughter appears at your door, frantically begging you to come quickly because "something is wrong with Grandpa." When you arrive with your stethoscope, you find Joe lying on the floor in his hobby shop; he has no pulse or respirations. He is grossly cyanotic, cool, and has a small laceration on his chin that probably occurred when he fell. Joe had been noticeably absent for about 10 to 15 minutes before family members, visiting for the weekend, found him.

Joe's wife and family implore you to do something for him. "Do anything you can. Please help him. Hurry," Joe's wife states. As you begin cardiopulmonary resuscitation (CPR), you realize that many members of the family do not understand what is happening or what you are doing. Joe's wife, although shaken, is fairly calm and rational. She is reassuring her family that something is being done and that Joe's pain and suffering are almost over.

After 10 minutes of continuous CPR with no change in Joe's condition, you hear the distant approach of an ambulance. Joe's wife, also hearing the ambulance, places her hand on your back to signal your attention. She says she has had a chance to think now and wants you to stop CPR. "Let Joe be. His pain is over." You immediately wonder about the legal ramifications of stopping CPR without an order. At the same time, you reflect on the gentleness of this man and the quality of his life during the last few years. As the siren draws nearer, his wife becomes hysterical and begs for you to stop. After repeatedly asking her if she is sure, you stop CPR. A family member meets the ambulance at the driveway to inform the team that their services are not desired. His wife very tenderly takes Joe's head in her lap and says her goodbyes.

At that moment, the paramedics enter and tell Joe's wife that the law specifies that they must implement basic life support. They also inform her that once the emergency medical support system is activated, it cannot be canceled, leaving Joe's wife aghast and speechless. Although the paramedics have already restarted CPR, you repeat the patient's and spouse's wishes and the patient's medical history. You tell them that the arrest was unwitnessed and that 15 minutes had probably elapsed before CPR was started. You identify that CPR has just been stopped at the family's insistence. The paramedics make you feel as if you were somehow morally and legally negligent for stopping CPR.

You begin to feel helpless as IV lines are established, and drug therapy is initiated. Joe is intubated and defibrillated many times as his family watches this technical display with apparent horror. Joe's wife is quiet with resignation.

Joe is transported to the hospital by ambulance where he is pronounced dead, 2 hours after CPR was initiated. Three weeks later, the family receives a $1,200 bill for emergency services and hospital care.

Assignment: The "right" choice is one that accurately reflects your values and philosophy. What values are held by Joe, his wife, the neighbor? How would you have responded in this situation? What have you considered in your decision? Would your actions have been different if Joe was a stranger, and the same situation occurred? If you were the RN on the ambulance crew, how would you respond, and would this change your philosophy? Who should be responsible for the cost?

Learning Exercise 3.8

Assume that your career goal is to become a nurse-lawyer. You are currently an RN in an acute care facility in a large, metropolitan city. You have your BSN degree but will need to take at least 12 units of prerequisite classes for acceptance into law school. A law school within commuting distance of your home offers evening classes that would allow you to continue your current day job at least part time. Quitting your job entirely would be financially unfeasible.

Assignment: Identify at least four objectives you need to set to achieve your career goal. Be sure these objectives are explicit, measurable, observable or retrievable, and obtainable. Then, identify at least three actions for each objective that delineate how you will achieve them.

REFERENCES:

Bennis, W. (1989). *Why leaders can't lead.* San Francisco: Jossey-Bass.

Bernhard, L. A., & Walsh, M. (1990). *Leadership: The key to the professionalization of nursing* (2nd ed.). St. Louis, MO: C.V. Mosby.

Berry, F. S. (1994). Innovation in public management: The adoption of strategic planning. *Public Administration Review, 54*(4), 322–329.

Bombard, C. F. (1993). Strategic planning: A practical approach. *Journal of Nursing Administration, 23*(7/8), 41–45.

Covey, S. (1993). *The seven habits of highly effective people.* New York: Simon and Schuster

Curran, C., & Boston, C. M. (1988). New patterns of professional relationships external to the organization. In M. Johnson & J. McCloskey (Eds.), *Series on nursing administration, 1.* Menlo Park, CA: Addison-Wesley.

Decker, P. J., & Sullivan, E. J. (1992). *Nursing administration.* Norwalk, CT: Appleton and Lange.

Douglass, L. M. (1992). *The effective nurse: Leader and manager* (4th ed.). St. Louis: Mosby Year Book.

Fiesta, J. (1993). Legal aspects—Standards of care: Part I. *Nursing Management, 24*(7), 30–32.

Fox, D. H., & Fox, R. T. (1983). Strategic planning for nursing. *Journal of Nursing Administration, 13*(5), 11–16.

Gehrman, D. (1989). Why plan? In R. Kreitner (Ed.), *Management* (4th ed.). Boston: Houghton Mifflin.

Grindol, M. A. (1984). A manager's guide to procedure manuals. *Nursing Management, 15*(1), 12–14.

Hamilton, J., & Kiefer, M. (1986). *Survival skills for the new nurse* (p. 52). Philadelphia: J.B. Lippincott.

Hodgetts, R. M. (1986). *Management: Theory, process, and practice* (4th ed.). Orlando, FL: Academic Press.

Lyles, R., & Joiner, C. (1986). *Supervision in health care organizations.* New York: John Wiley and Sons.

Mallison, M. (1989). Putting your patient care philosophy to the test. *American Journal of Nursing, 89*(8), 1021

Marriner-Tomey, A. (1992). *Guide to nursing management* (4th ed.). St. Louis: Mosby Yearbook.

Marquis, B. L., & Huston, C. J. (1994). *Management decision making for nurses* (2nd ed.). Philadelphia: J.B. Lippincott.

Marrelli, T. M. (1993). *The nurse manager's survival guide.* St. Louis: Mosby Year Book.

McNally, M. (1980). Values. (Part 1). *Supervisor Nurse, 11,* 27–30.

Mac Pherson, K. I. (1987). Health care policy, values, and nursing. *Advances in Nursing Science, 9*(3).

Megginson, L. C., Mosley, D. C., & Pietri, P. H. Jr. (1986). *Management: Concepts and applications* (2nd ed.) (pp. 129–131). New York: Harper & Row.

Paul, R. N., & Taylor, J. W. (1986). The state of strategic planning. *Business, 36*(1), 37–43.

Swansburg, R. C. (1990). *Management and leadership for nurse managers.* Boston: Jones and Bartlett.

Thomas, A. M. (1993). Strategic planning: A practical approach. *Nursing Management, 24*(2), 34–38.

BIBLIOGRAPHY

Anderson, J. D. (1989). A hospital administration responds: Pursue long term solutions. *Journal of Christian Nursing, 6*(1), 8.

Brown, H. L. (1989). Strategic planning. *American Association of Occupational Health Nurses Journal, 37*(7), 284-285

Bluestein, R. (1988). Procedure manuals: The ultimate office organizer. *Professional Medical Assistant, 21*(5), 25–26.

Cox, A. R. (1989). Planning for the future of occupational health nursing: Strategic planning process (Part 1). *American Association of Occupational Health Nurses Journal, 37*(9), 352–355.

DeGeus, A. P. (1988). Planning as learning. *Harvard Business Review, 88*(2), 70–74.

Drake, D., Fitzgerald, S., & Jaffe, M. (1993). *Hard choices: Health care at what cost?* Kansas City: Andrews and Mc Meel

Fagin, C. M. (1987). Strategic planning-Outline of a plan. *Journal of Professional Nursing, 3*(2), 79, 124.

Graham, P., Constantini, S., Balik, B., et al., (1987). Operationalizing a nursing philosophy. *Journal of Nursing Administration, 17*(3), 14–18.

Haines, V. (1989). Strategic planning. *School Nurse, 5*(2), 5–6.

Johnson, J. E., Sparks, D. G., & Humphreys, C. (1988). Writing a winning business plan. *Journal of Nursing Administration, 18*(10), 15–19.

Jones, K. R. (1988). Strategic planning in hospitals: Applications to nursing administration. *Nursing Administration Quarterly, 13*(1), 1–10.

Kintgen-Andrews, J. (1988). Philosophy statements: Challenging beliefs and values. *Nursing and Health Care, 9*(8), 436–438.

Poteet, G. W., & Hills, A. S. (1988). Identifying the components of a nursing service philosophy. *Journal of Nursing Administration, 18*(10), 29–33.

Smith, M. J. (1987–1988). Valuing—A key to network quality nursing. *Nursing Forum, 23*(2), 56–59.

Teeple, K. L., Snyder, J. R., & Swanson, F. (1987). Using planning tools for reorganization. *Medical Laboratory Observer, 19*(4), 59–64.

Trexler, B. T. (1987). Nursing department purpose, philosophy, and objectives: Their use and effectiveness. *Journal of Nursing Administration, 17*(3), 8–12.

Vardi, Y., Wiener, Y., & Poppa, M. (1989). The value content of organizational mission as a factor in the commitment of members. *Psychological Reports, 65,* 27–34.

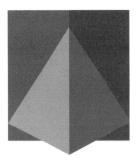

CHAPTER 4

Planned Change

Duck (1993) states that most organizations today find themselves undertaking a number of projects as part of a change effort. These projects are often directed at quality improvement, process and structure reengineering, and employee empowerment. The key to a successful change effort is not attending to each project in isolation but to connecting and balancing all the pieces. When one piece of the organization is changed, the rest of the organization changes as well. Duck (1993, pp. 110, 115) states the following:

> Managing change in an organization isn't like operating a machine or treating the human body one ailment at a time. Both of these activities involve working with a fixed set of relationships. The proper metaphor for managing change is balancing a mobile. . . . Managing these ripple effects is what makes managing change a dynamic proposition with unexpected challenges.

It becomes clear then that initiating and coordinating change requires well developed leadership and management skills. As stated in Chapter 3, leader/managers must be expert planners. This includes planning for changing needs. The failure to reassess goals proactively and initiate these changes results in misdirected and poorly used fiscal and human resources. Not only must leader/managers be visionary in identifying where change is needed in the organization, but they must be flexible in adapting to change they have directly initiated or by which they have been indirectly affected.

Planned change, in contrast to accidental change or change by drift, is change

Bessie L. Marquis and Carol J. Huston:
LEADERSHIP ROLES AND MANAGEMENT FUNCTIONS IN NURSING, 2nd ed.
Lippincott-Raven Publishers © 1996

that results from a well thought out and deliberate effort to make something happen. Tappen (1995) defines planned change as the deliberate application of knowledge and skills by a leader to bring about a change. This type of planning requires the leadership skills of problem solving and decision making and interpersonal and communication skills.

Planned change occurs because of an intended effort by a *change agent*—a person skilled in theory and implementation of planned change—to deliberately move the system. A change agent is the person responsible for moving others who are affected by the change through its stages. Changes are implemented slowly after consultation with others. In planned change, the manager is often the change agent. In some large organizations today, teams of individuals, called a transition management team (TMT), are committed full time to managing the change process (Duck, 1993). In such organizations, the TMT manages the conversation between the people leading the change effort and those who are expected to implement the new strategies. In addition, the TMT manages the organizational context in which change can occur and the emotional connections essential for any transformation.

Display 4.1 delineates selected leadership roles and management functions necessary for leader/managers acting in either the change agent role or as a coordinator of the TMT.

THE DEVELOPMENT OF CHANGE THEORY

Most of the current research on change builds on the classical change theories developed by Kurt Lewin in the mid-1900s. Lewin (1951) identified three phases through which the change agent must proceed before a planned change becomes part of the system. These stages include *unfreezing, movement,* and *refreezing.*

In the unfreezing stage, the change agent unfreezes forces that maintain the status quo. Thus, people become discontented and aware of a need to change. Unfreezing is necessary because before any change can occur, people must believe the change is needed. Unfreezing occurs when the change agent coerces members of the group to change or when guilt, anxiety, or concern can be elicited. For effective change to occur, the change agent needs to have made a thorough and accurate assessment of the extent of and interest in change, the nature and depth of motivation, and the environment in which the change will occur.

The second phase of planned change is movement. In movement, the change agent identifies, plans, and implements appropriate strategies, ensuring that driving forces exceed restraining forces. Whenever possible, change should be implemented gradually. Because change is such a complex process, it requires a great deal of planning and intricate timing. Recognizing, addressing, and overcoming resistance may be a lengthy process. Any change of human behavior, or the perceptions, attitudes, and values underlying that behavior, takes time. Therefore, any change must allow enough time for those involved to be fully assimilated in that change.

The last phase is refreezing. During the *refreezing* phase, the change agent assists in stabilizing the system change so that it becomes integrated into the status quo. If refreezing is incomplete, the change will be ineffective and the prechange behaviors will be resumed. For refreezing to occur, the change agent must be support-

Display 4.1 Leadership Roles and Management Functions in Planned Change

Leadership Roles

1. Is visionary in identifying areas of needed change in the organization and the healthcare system
2. Demonstrates risk taking in assuming the role of change agent
3. Demonstrates flexibility in goal setting in a rapidly changing health care system
4. Anticipates, recognizes, and creatively problem-solves resistance to change
5. Serves as a role model to subordinates during planned change by viewing change as a challenge and opportunity for growth
6. Role models high-level interpersonal communication skills in providing support for followers undergoing rapid or difficult change
7. Demonstrates creativity in identifying alternatives to problems
8. Demonstrates sensitivity to timing in proposing planned change

Management Functions

1. Forecasts unit needs with an understanding of the organization's and unit's legal, political, economic, social, and legislative climate
2. Recognizes the need for planned change and identifies the options and resources available to implement that change
3. Appropriately assesses the driving and restraining forces when planning for change
4. Identifies and implements appropriate strategies to minimize or overcome resistance to change
5. Seeks subordinates' input in planned change and provides them with adequate information during the change process to give them some feeling of control
6. Supports and reinforces the individual efforts of subordinates during the change process
7. Identifies and uses appropriate change strategies to modify the behavior of subordinates as needed

ive and reinforce the individual adaptive efforts of those affected by the change. Because change needs at least 3 to 6 months before it will be accepted as part of the system, change should never be attempted unless the change agent can make a commitment to be available until the change is complete.

It is important to realize that refreezing does not eliminate the possibility of further improvements to the change. Display 4.2 illustrates the change agent's responsibilities during the various stages.

Lippitt, Watson, and Westley (1958) built on Lewin's theories in identifying seven phases of planned change:

Display 4.2 Stages of Change and Responsibilities of the Change Agent

---

Stage 1—Unfreezing

a. Gather data.
b. Accurately diagnose the problem.
c. Decide if change is needed.
d. Make others aware of the need for change. (This often involves deliberate tactics to raise the group's discontent level.)

Do not proceed to Step 2 until the status quo has been disrupted, and the need for change is perceived by the others.

Stage 2—Movement

a. Develop a plan.
b. Set goals and objectives.
c. Identify areas of support and resistance.
d. Include everyone who will be affected by the change in its planning.
e. Set target dates.
f. Develop appropriate strategies.
g. Implement the change.
h. Be available to support others and offer encouragement through the change.
i. Use strategies for overcoming resistance to change.
j. Evaluate the change.
k. Modify the change, if necessary.

State 3—Refreezing

Support others so that the change remains.

---

1. The client must feel a need for change. Unfreezing occurs.
2. A helping relationship begins between the change agent and his or her clients.

Movement begins

3. The problem is identified and clarified. Data are collected.
4. Alternatives for change are examined. Resources are assessed.
5. Active modification or change occurs. Movement is complete.
6. Refreezing occurs as the change is stabilized.
7. The helping relationship ends, or a different type of continuing relationship is formed.

Perlman and Takacs (1990), building on Lewin's work, identified 10 emotional phases in the change process (Display 4.3). The phases of equilibrium, denial, anger, and bargaining reflect Lewin's unfreezing phase; chaos, depression, and resignation, the movement phase; and openness, readiness, and reemergence, the refreezing

---

Display 4.3   Ten Emotional Phases of the Change Process

---

1. Equilibrium	Characterized by high energy and emotional and intellectual balance. Personal and professional goals are synchronized.
2. Denial	Individual denies reality of the change. Negative changes occur in physical, cognitive, and emotional functioning.
3. Anger	Energy is manifested by rage, envy, and resentment.
4. Bargaining	In an attempt to eliminate the change, energy is expended by bargaining.
5. Chaos	Characterized by diffused energy, feelings of powerlessness, insecurity, and loss of identity.
6. Depression	Defense mechanisms are no longer operable. No energy left to produce results. Self-pity apparent.
7. Resignation	Change accepted passively but without enthusiasm.
8. Openness	Some renewal of energy in implementing new roles or assignments that have resulted from the change.
9. Readiness	Willful expenditure of energy to explore new event. Physical, cognitive, and emotional reunification occurs.
10. Reemergence	Individual again feels empowered and begins initiating projects and ideas.

---

phase. Regardless of the number of phases or their names, it is critical that the manager recognizes that organizations must consciously and constructively deal with the human emotions associated with all phases of planned change (Perlman & Takacs, 1990).

Driving and Restraining Forces

Lewin also theorized that individuals maintain a state of status quo or equilibrium by the simultaneous occurrence of both driving and restraining forces operating within any field. The forces that push the system toward the change are driving forces, whereas the forces that pull the system away from the change are called restraining forces (Tappen, 1995). Lewin's model maintained that for change to occur, the balance of driving and restraining forces must be altered. The driving forces must be increased or the restraining forces decreased.

Driving forces may include pressure from the manager, desire to please the manager, perception that the change will improve one's self-image, and the belief that the change will improve the situation (Marriner-Tomey, 1992). Restraining forces include conformity to norms, morals, and ethics; desire for security; perception of economic threat or threat to one's prestige and homeostasis; and regulatory mechanisms for keeping the situation fairly constant (Marriner-Tomey, 1992).

In Figure 4.1, the individual wishing to return to school must reduce the restraining forces or increase the driving forces to alter the present state of equilibrium.

FIGURE 4.1 Driving and restraining forces.

There will be no change or action until this occurs. Therefore, creating an imbalance within the system by increasing the driving forces or decreasing the restraining forces is one of the tasks required for a change agent.

LEARNING EXERCISE 4.1

Identify a change that you would like to make in your personal life (such as losing weight, exercising daily, or stopping smoking). List the restraining forces keeping you from making this change. List the driving forces that make you want to change. Determine how you might be able to change the status quo and make the change possible.

If the restraining forces are too great to overcome the driving forces, what should the change agent do? Elfrey (1982) outlined the following steps to take when change is blocked:

1. Discover the cause of the blockage or the magnitude of the restraining forces.
2. Get more data and build a better case.
3. Consult with others (peers and management).
4. Continue to do excellent work.
5. Develop and try an alternate plan.
6. Take care of your health.
7. Build small successes.
8. Hang in there, unless the situation proves to be unsalvageable. Then move on.
9. Accept the lesson learned.
10. Never panic.

Numerous factors affect successful implementation of planned change. Many good ideas are never realized because of poor timing or a lack of power on the part of the change agent. For example, both organizations and individuals tend to reject outsiders as change agents because they are perceived as having inadequate knowledge or expertise about the current status, and their motives are often not trusted. Therefore, there is less widespread resistance if the change agent is an insider. The outside change agent, however, tends to be more objective in his or her assessment, whereas the inside change agent's knowledge of how the organization functions is biased by personal experience (Decker & Sullivan, 1992).

Likewise, some greatly needed changes are never implemented because the change agent lacks sensitivity to timing. If the organization or the individuals within that organization have recently undergone a great deal of change or stress, any other change should wait until group resistance decreases.

CHANGE STRATEGIES

Three commonly used strategies for effecting change in others were described by Bennis, Benne, and Chinn (1969). The appropriate strategy for any situation depends on the power of the change agent and the amount of resistance expected from the subordinates. One of these strategies is to give current research as evidence to support the change. This group is often referred to as *rational–empirical* strategies. The change agent using this set of strategies assumes humans are rational beings who will change when given factual information documenting the need for change. This type of strategy is used when there is little anticipated resistance to the change or when the change is perceived as reasonable. Systems analysis, operations research, and implementation of research findings are consistent with empirical–rational strategies for change, as is long-range futuristic planning (Marriner-Tomey, 1992).

Because peer pressure is often used to effect change, another group of strategies that uses group process is called *normative–reeducative* strategies. These strategies use group norms to socialize and influence individuals so that change will occur. The change agent assumes humans are social animals, more easily influenced by others than by facts. This strategy does not require the change agent to have a legitimate power base. Instead, the change agent gains power by skill in interpersonal relationships. He or she focuses on noncognitive determinants of behavior, such as people's roles and relationships, perceptual orientations, attitudes, and feelings to increase their acceptance of change.

The third group of strategies, *power–coercive* strategies, is based on the application of power by legitimate authority, economic sanctions, or political clout of the change agent. These strategies include influencing the enactment of new laws and using group power for strikes or sit-ins. Using authority inherent in an individual position to effect change is another example of a power–coercive strategy. These strategies assume that individuals often are set in their ways and will change only when rewarded for the change or are forced by some other power–coercive method. Resistance is handled by authority measures; the individual must accept it or leave.

Often the change agent uses strategies from each of these three groups. An example would be the change agent who wants someone to stop smoking. The change agent might present the person with the latest research on cancer and smoking (the rational–empirical approach); at the same time, the change agent might have friends and family educate the person socially (normative–reeducative approach). The change agent also might refuse to ride in the car if the individual smokes while driving (power–coercive approach). By selecting from each set of strategies, the manager increases the chance of successful change. Hagerman and Tiffany (1994) suggest that the normative–reeducative strategy is the most appropriate for planned change in nursing.

REASONS FOR CHANGE

Change should be implemented only for good reasons. Because human beings have little control over many changes in their lives, the change agent must remember that individuals need a balance between stability and change in the workplace. Change for change's sake subjects employees to unnecessary stress and manipulation.

The following are three *good* reasons for change that are applicable to a wide variety of situations (Sullivan & Decker, 1988):

1. Change to solve some problem.
2. Change to make work procedures more efficient so that time will not be wasted on relatively unimportant tasks.
3. Change to reduce unnecessary workload.

LEARNING EXERCISE 4.2

Try to remember a situation in your own life that involved unnecessary change. Why do you feel the change was unnecessary? What types of turmoil did it cause?

RESISTANCE: THE EXPECTED RESPONSE TO CHANGE

Because change disrupts the homeostasis or balance of the group, resistance should always be expected. The level of resistance generally depends on the type of change proposed. Technological changes encounter less resistance than changes that are perceived as social or that are contrary to established customs or norms. This occurs because changes affecting social customs or values threaten individual self-esteem and the sense of security within the group (Ward & Moran 1984). For example, nursing staff are more willing to accept a change in the *type* of intravenous pump to be used than a change regarding *who* is able to administer certain types of IV therapy. Nursing leaders also must recognize that subordinates' values, educational levels, cultural and social backgrounds, and experiences with change (positive or negative) will have a tremendous impact on their degree of resistance.

It also is much easier to change an individual's behavior than it is to change an entire group's behavior (Hersey & Blanchard, 1988). It also is easier to change knowledge levels than attitudes.

In an effort to eliminate resistance to change in the workplace, managers historically used an autocratic leadership style with specific guidelines for work, an excessive number of rules, and a coercive approach to discipline. The resistance, which occurred anyway, was both covert (such as delaying tactics or passive–aggressive behavior) and overt (openly refusing to follow a direct command), and resulted in wasted managerial energy and time and a high level of frustration.

Today, resistance is recognized as a natural and expected response to change. Instead of wasting time and energy trying to eliminate opposition, contemporary managers immerse themselves in identifying and implementing strategies to minimize or manage this resistance to change. One such strategy is to encourage subordinates to speak openly so that options can be identified to overcome objections. Likewise, workers are encouraged to talk about their perceptions of the forces driving the planned change so that the manager can accurately assess change support and resources.

Silber (1993) suggests that the individual's ability to cope with change depends on four things:

1. Their flexibility to change
2. Their evaluation of the immediate situation
3. The anticipated consequences of the change
4. Their perceptions of what they have to lose or gain

Bushy and Kamphuis (1993), building on the work of Rodgers (1983), identified six behavioral patterns commonly seen in response to change: innovators, early adopters, early majority, late majority, laggards, and rejectors. *Innovators* are enthusiastic, energetic individuals who thrive on change and are almost obsessed with adventure. Described by some as disruptive radicals, they are able to effect change, often amidst controversy within the organization. *Early adopters* are open and receptive to new ideas, but are less obsessed with seeking out changes than innovators. *Early majority* adhere to the adage, "Be not the last to lay the old aside, nor the first by which the new is tried." Early majority people prefer the status quo but adopt new ideas shortly before the average person. *Late majority* are followers, skeptical of innovation, and frequently express their negative views. Only after a majority of the organization accepts an innovation will the late majority favor it. *Laggards,* the last to adopt an innovation, are dedicated to tradition. They interact primarily with other traditionalists and are highly suspicious of innovations and innovators. *Rejectors* openly oppose innovation and actively encourage others to do so. Although covert in nature, their activities may completely immobilize the change process, the change agent, or the system, even to the extent of sabotaging an innovation.

Perhaps the greatest factor contributing to the resistance encountered with change is a lack of trust between the employee and the manager or the employee and the organization. "One of the greatest paradoxes about change is that trust is hardest to establish at the times when you need it the most" (Duck, 1993, p. 114). Duck goes on to say that trust in a time of change is based on two things: *predictability*

LEARNING EXERCISE 4.3

Which behavioral pattern do you most commonly assume in response to change: Innovator, early adopter, early majority, late majority, laggard, or rejector? Is this behavioral pattern similar to your friends' and family's? Has your behavior always fit this pattern, or has the pattern changed throughout your life? If so, what life events have altered how you view and respond to change?

and *capability*. In any organization, workers want predictability; they want their work environment to be known and comfortable. They want security. That's why trust erodes when the ground rules change; as the assumed "contract" between the worker and the organization is altered. The leader/manager must remember that people tend to consider the effects of change on their personal lives, status, and future more than on the welfare of the organization (Marriner-Tomey, 1992).

The second factor in creating trust in the organization during change is capability. Both managers and workers must accurately understand and believe in the capability of the other to make the change successfully. Roles and responsibilities of each person involved in the change must be negotiated and accepted before each will trust the situation. Thus, the change must be personalized before the risks can be accepted.

PLANNED CHANGE AS A COLLABORATIVE PROCESS

Duck (1993) states that in most organizations, the change process is begun by a small group of individuals who closet themselves together to discuss a lot of "what-ifs." No effort is made to talk with anyone else in the organization. They agree among themselves that trying to keep everyone informed is a diversion from accomplishing their goal, "a luxury they cannot afford." They plan to let everyone know what they have figured out when their planning is complete.

This approach virtually guarantees that the change effort will fail. People abhor "information vacuums," and when there is no ongoing conversation about the change process, gossip usually fills the void. These rumors are generally much more negative than anything that is actually happening (Duck, 1993).

Whenever possible, all *those who may be affected* by a change *should be involved in planning for that change*. When change agents fail to communicate with the rest of the organization, they prevent people from understanding the principles that guided the change, what has been learned from prior experience, and why compromises have been made.

Likewise, those affected by the change should thoroughly understand the change and how it affects them as individuals. Good, open communication throughout the process can reduce resistance. Leaders must ensure that group members share perceptions about what change is to be undertaken, who is to be involved and in what role, and how the change will directly and indirectly affect each person in the organization.

The easiest way for the manager to ensure that subordinates share this perception is to involve them in the change process. When information and decision making are shared, subordinates feel that they have played a valuable role in the change. Brooten, Hayman, and Naylor (1988) believe that planned change can *never* be autocratic. The change agent and the elements of the system—the people or groups within it—openly work out the goals and strategies together. All have the opportunity to define their interest in the change, their expectation of its outcome, and their ideas on strategies for achieving change.

It is not always easy to attain grass roots involvement in planning efforts. Even when managers communicate that change is needed and that subordinate feedback is wanted, the message often goes unheeded. Some people in the organization may need to hear a message over and over before they hear, understand, and believe the message. "And if they don't like what they hear, then it takes even more time for them to come to terms with the concept of change. If there is a single rule of communication for leaders, it is that when you are so sick of talking about something that you can hardly stand it, then your message may be finally starting to get through" (Duck, 1993, p. 111).

THE LEADER/MANAGER AS A ROLE MODEL DURING PLANNED CHANGE

Leader/managers must act as role models to subordinates during the change process. The leader/manager must attempt to view change positively and to impart this view to subordinates. Marrelli (1993) argues that it is critical that managers not view change as a threat. Instead, it should be viewed as a *challenge* and the chance or opportunity to do something new and innovative.

Marrelli (1993) also encourages managers to believe that they can make a difference. This feeling of *control* is probably the most important trait for thriving in a changing environment. Friends, family, and colleagues should be used as a support network for managers during change. Likewise, managers should learn to recognize their own stress signals during change and intervene when the level gets too high.

Stern (1994) suggests 10 positive attitudes, which should be adopted by leader/managers regarding change:

1. Problems exist to be overcome.
2. Success involves the habit of changing habits.
3. Action cures fear.
4. The best way to escape a problem is to solve it.
5. Life changes occur only when beliefs change.
6. Look for opportunity, not guarantees.
7. Worry is negative and results from inaction.
8. Discovery consists of looking at the same thing as everyone else and thinking something different.
9. Effective people are not problem oriented, they are opportunity oriented.
10. You cannot operate on yesterday's standards and expect to be successful today.

ORGANIZATIONAL AGING— CHANGE AS A MEANS OF RENEWAL

Organizations progress through developmental stages, just as people do—birth, youth, maturity, and aging. As organizations age, structure increases to provide greater control and coordination. The young organization is characterized by high energy, movement, and virtually constant change and adaptation. Aged organizations have "established turf boundaries," function in an orderly and predictable fashion, and are rule and regulation focused. Change is limited. Other characteristics of aged organizations as identified by Willis (1968) and Schon (1971) include the following:

- Individual workers have difficulty perceiving how their work contributes to overall organizational goals.
- Loyalties are transferred from the total organization to subunits, and conflicts of interest develop.
- Overprogramming results in individuals performing their jobs in a perfunctory manner.
- Organizational subunits attempt to survive after having outlived their usefulness.
- There is a low rate of turnover.
- Predictable demands are made on the organization under time pressures, leading to stagnant technology and rigid procedures.

It is clear that organizations must find a critical balance between stagnation and chaos, between birth and death. In the process of maturing, workers within the organization can become prisoners of procedures, forget their original purposes and allow means to become the ends. Gardner (1990) argues that organizations must be "ever renewing." The ever-renewing organization is infantlike—curious and open to new experience and change. Gardner says that the only way to conserve an organization is to keep it changing. Without change, the organization may stagnate and die.

The other term Gardner (1990) uses to describe the aged organization is "organizational dry rot." Gardner states that organizational dry rot can be prevented by having effective programs for the recruitment and development of young talent; providing a hospitable organizational environment that fosters individuality; building in provisions for self-criticism by providing an atmosphere in which uncomfortable questions can be raised; and by being forward thinking. The organization needs to keep foremost what it is going to do, not what it has done.

LEARNING EXERCISE 4.4

Reflect on the organization in which you work or the nursing school you attend. Do you feel this organization has more characteristics of a young or aged organization? Diagram on a continuum from birth to death where you feel this organization would fall. What efforts have this organization taken to be ever-renewing? What further efforts could be made?

INTEGRATING LEADERSHIP ROLES AND MANAGEMENT FUNCTIONS IN PLANNED CHANGE

It should be clear that leadership and management skills are necessary for successful planned change to occur. The manager must understand the planning process and planning standards and be able to apply both to the work situation. The manager then is the mechanic who implements the planned change.

The leader, however, is the inventor or creator. Leaders today are forced to plan in a chaotic healthcare system that is changing at a frenetic pace. Out of this chaos, leaders must identify trends and changes that may affect their organizations and units and proactively prepare for these changes. Thus, the leader must retain a big picture focus while dealing with each part of the system. In the inventor or creator role, the leader displays such traits as flexibility, confidence, tenacity, and the ability to articulate vision through insights and versatile thinking (Sullivan & Decker, 1988).

Both leadership and management skills are necessary in planned change. The change agent fulfills a management function when identifying situations where change is necessary and appropriate and when assessing the driving and restraining forces affecting the plan for change. The leader is the role model in planned change; he or she is open and receptive to change and views change as a challenge and an opportunity for growth. Perhaps the most critical element in successful planned change are the change agent's leadership skills—interpersonal communication, group management, and problem-solving skills.

KEY CONCEPTS

- ▼ Change should not be viewed as a threat but as a challenge or the chance to do something new and innovative.
- ▼ Change should only be implemented for good reason.
- ▼ Because change disrupts the homeostasis or balance of the group, resistance should be expected as a natural part of the change process.
- ▼ The level of resistance to change generally depends on the type of change proposed. Technological changes encounter less resistance than changes that are perceived as social or that are contrary to established customs or norms.
- ▼ Perhaps the greatest factor contributing to the resistance encountered with change is a lack of trust between the employee and the manager or the employee and the organization.
- ▼ It is much easier to change an individual's behavior than it is to change an entire group's behavior. It also is easier to change knowledge levels than attitudes.
- ▼ Change should be planned and thus implemented gradually, not sporadically or suddenly.
- ▼ Those who may be affected by a change should be involved in planning for it. Likewise, workers should thoroughly understand the change and its affect on them.
- ▼ The feeling of *control* is critical to thriving in a changing environment.
- ▼ Friends, family, and colleagues should be used as a network of support during change.

▼ A *change agent* is a person skilled in theory and implementation of planned change. The change agent has the leadership skills of problem solving and decision making and has good interpersonal skills.

▼ In contrast to planned change, *change by drift* is unplanned or accidental.

▼ Historically, many of the changes that have occurred in nursing or have affected the profession are results of change by drift.

▼ Lewin identified three phases through which the change agent must proceed before the planned change becomes part of the system. These stages are *unfreezing*, *movement*, and *refreezing*.

▼ Individuals maintain status quo or equilibrium when both *driving* and *restraining forces* operating within any field simultaneously occur. For change to happen, this balance of driving and restraining forces must be altered.

▼ *Rational-empirical strategies* suggest change will result from giving information by using current data to support the change.

▼ *Normative-reeducative strategies* use the group to socialize and influence others for change.

▼ *Power-coercive strategies* use rewards or force to change behavior.

▼ Organizations are preserved by change and constant renewal. Without change, the organization may stagnate and die.

◣ ADDITIONAL LEARNING EXERCISES

Learning Exercise 4.5
(From Marquis & Huston, 1994.)

You are a Hispanic RN who has recently received a 2-year grant to establish a family planning clinic in a primarily Hispanic ghetto area of a large metropolitan city. The project will be evaluated at the end of the grant to determine whether continued funding is warranted. As project director, you have the funding to choose and hire three healthcare workers. You will essentially be able to manage the clinic as you see fit.

The average age of your clients will be 14 years, and many come from broken homes. In addition, the population with which you will be working has high unemployment, high crime and truancy levels, and great suspicion and mistrust of authority figures. You are aware that many restraining forces exist that will challenge you, but you feel strongly committed to the cause. You believe that the exorbitantly high teenage pregnancy rate and maternal and infant morbidity can be reduced.

Assignment:
1. Identify the restraining and driving forces in this situation.
2. Identify realistic short- and long-term goals for implementing such a change. What can realistically be accomplished in 2 years?
3. How might the project director use hiring authority to increase the driving forces in this situation?
4. Is refreezing of the planned change possible so that changes will continue if the grant is not funded again in 2 years?

Learning Exercise 4.6

Assume that morale and productivity are low on the unit where you are the new manager. In an effort to identify the root of the problem, you have informally been meeting with staff to discuss their perceptions of unit functioning and to identify sources of unrest on the unit. You feel that one of the greatest factors leading to unrest is limited advancement opportunity for your primary care nurses. You have a fixed charge nurse on each shift. This is how the unit has been managed for as long as everyone can remember. You would like to rotate the charge nurse position but are unsure of your staff's feelings about the change.

Assignment: Using the phases of change identified by Lewin, identify the actions you could take in unfreezing, movement, and refreezing. What are the greatest barriers to this change? What are the strongest driving forces?

Learning Exercise 4.7

You are the unit manager of a cardiovascular surgical unit. The work station on the unit is small, dated, and disorganized. The unit clerks have complained for some time that the chart racks on the counter above their desk are difficult to reach, that staff frequently impinge on their work space to discuss patients or to chart, that the call-light system is antiquated, and that supplies and forms need to be relocated. You ask all eight of your shift unit clerks to make a "wish list" of how they would like the work station to be redesigned for optimum efficiency and effectiveness.

Construction is completed several months later. You are pleased that the new work station incorporates what each unit clerk included in his or her "top three priorities" for change. There is a new revolving chart rack in the center of the work station, with enhanced accessibility to both staff and unit clerks. A new state-of-the-art call-light system has been installed. A small, quiet room has been created for nurses to chart and conference and new cubby holes and filing drawers now put forms within arm's reach of the charge nurse and unit clerk.

Almost immediately, you begin to be barraged with complaints about the changes. Several of the unit clerks find the new call-light system's computerized response system overwhelming and complain that patient lights are now going unanswered. Others complain that with the chart rack out of their immediate work area, charts can no longer be monitored and are being removed from the unit by physicians or left in the charting room by nurses. One unit clerk has filed a complaint that she was injured by a staff member who carelessly and rapidly turned the chart rack. She refuses to work again until the old chart racks are returned. The regular day shift unit clerk complains that all the forms are filed backwards for left-handed people and "that after 20 years, she should have the right to put them the way she likes it." Several of the nurses are complaining that the work station is "now the domain of the unit clerk" and that their access to the telephones and desk supplies is limited by the unit clerks. There have been some rumblings that several staff members feel that you favored the requests of some employees over others.

Today when you make rounds at change of shift, you find the day shift unit clerk and charge nurse involved in a heated conversation with the evening shift unit clerk and charge nurse. Each evening, the charge nurse and unit clerk reorganize the work station in the manner that they feel is most effective, and each morning, the charge nurse and unit clerk put back things the way they had been the prior day. Both feel that the other shift is undermining their efforts to "fix" the work station organization and that their method of organization is the best. Both groups of workers turn to you and demand that you "make the other shift stop sabotaging their efforts to change things for the better."

Assignment: Despite your intent to include subordinate input into this planned change, resistance is high, and worker morale is plummeting. Is the level of resistance a normal and anticipated response to planned change? If so, would you intervene in this conflict? How? Was it possible to have reduced the likelihood of such a high degree of resistance?

REFERENCES:

Bennis, W., Benne, K., & Chinn, R. (1969). *The planning of change* (2nd ed.). New York: Holt, Rinehart, and Winston.

Brooten, D. A., Hayman, L. L., & Naylor, M. D. (1988). *Leadership for change: An action guide for nurses* (2nd ed.). Philadelphia: J.B. Lippincott.

Bushy, A., & Kamphuis, J. (1993). Response to innovation: Behavioral patterns. *Nursing Management, 24*(3), 62–64.

Decker, P. J., & Sullivan, E. J. (1992). *Nursing administration.* East Norwalk, CT: Prentice Hall.

Duck, J. D. (1993). Managing change: The art of balancing. *Harvard Business Review,* November/December, 109–118.

Elfrey, P. (1982). *The hidden agenda—Recognizing what really matters at work.* New York: John Wiley and Sons.

Gardner, J. W. (1990). *On Leadership.* New York: The Free Press.

Hagerman, A. J., & Tiffany, C. R. (1994). Evaluation of two planned change theories. *Nursing Management, 25*(4), 57–62.

Hersey, P., & Blanchard, K. H. (1988). *Management of organizational behavior: Utilizing human resources* (5th ed.). Englewood cliffs, NJ: Prentice Hall.

Lewin, K. (1951). *Field theory in social sciences.* New York: Harper & Row.

Lippitt, R., Watson, J., & Westley, B. (1958). *The dynamics of planned change.* New York: Harcourt, Brace & World.

Marquis, B. L., & Huston, C. J. (1994). *Management decision making for nurses* (2nd ed.). Philadelphia: J.B. Lippincott.

Marrelli, T. M. (1993). *The nurse manager's survival guide.* St. Louis, MO: C.V. Mosby.

Marriner-Tomey, A. (1992). *Guide to nursing management* (4th ed.). St. Louis: Mosby Year Book.

Perlman, D., & Takacs, G. J. (1990). The ten stages of change. *Nursing Management, 21*(4), 33–38.

Rodgers, E. (1983), *Diffusion of innovations.* New York: The Free Press.

Schon, D. A. (1971). *Beyond the stable state.* New York: Random House.

Silber, M. B. (1993). The "Cs" in excellence: Choice and change. *Nursing Management, 24*(9), 60–62.

Stern, G. A. (1994). Meeting the challenges of care. *Revolution, 4*(2), 36–37.

Sullivan, E. J., & Decker, P. J. (1988). *Effective management in nursing* (2d ed.). Menlo Park, CA: Addison-Wesley.

Tappen, R. M. (1995). *Nursing leadership and management* (3rd ed.). Philadelphia: F.A. Davis.

Ward, M. J., & Moran, S. G. (1984). Resistance to change—Recognize, respond overcome. *Nursing Management, 15*(1), 30–33

Willis, R. H. (1968). On organizational aging. In E. Glatt & M. W. Shelly (Eds.), *The research society.* New York: Gordon and Breach.

BIBLIOGRAPHY

Amburgey, T. L., Kelly, D., & Barnett, W. P., (1993). Resetting the clock: The dynamics of organizational change and failure. *Administrative Science Quarterly, 38*(1), 51–73.

Blend, D. A. (1986). Change: Are you a resistor or creator? *Journal of Post Anesthesia Nursing, 1*(2), 92–96.

Brett, J. L. (1989). Organizational integrative mechanisms, and adoption of innovations by nurses. *Nursing Research, 38*(2), 105–110.

Cashman, J. (1989). Effecting change through the stream analysis process. *Journal of Nursing Administration, 19*(5), 37–44.

Chinn, P. L. (1992). Where and when does change begin? *Nursing Outlook, 40*(3), 102–103.

Curtin, L. (1993). Looking the snake in the eye. *Nursing Management, 24*(7), 7–8.

Davidhizar, R., & Kuipers, J. (1989). How to plan and implement change. *Advancing Clinical Care, 4*(3), 38–39.

Havenmen, H. A. (1992). Between a rock and a hard place: Organizational change and performance under conditions of fundamental environmental transformation. *Administrative Science Quarterly, 37*(1), 48–75.

Hendry, J., Johnson, G. & Newton, J. (Eds.) (1994). *Leadership and the management of change.* New York: John Wiley and Sons.

Kearns, K. P. (1988). Universal precautions: Employee resistance and strategies for planned organizational change. *Hospital Health Service Administration, 33*(4), 521–530.

Lutjens, L. R., & Tiffany, C. R. (1994). Evaluating planned change theories. *Nursing Management, 25*(3), 54–57.

Malkemes, L. C. (1989). Challenging yesterday's ideas . . . The nurse executive of the future. *Journal of Nursing Administration, 19*(10), 4–5.

Manion, J. (1993). Chaos or transformation? Managing innovation. *Journal of Nursing Administration, 23*(5), 41–48.

McClellan, M. A., Henson, R. H., & Schmele, J. (1994). Introducing new technology: Confusion or order? *Nursing Management, 25*(7), 38–41.

McSwain, C. J. & White, O. F. (1993). A transformational theory of organizations. *American Review of Public Administration, 23*(2), 81–98.

Muir, J. (1987). Room for change . . . Rights of managers and staff when change is in the air. *Nursing Times, 83*(21), 34–35.

Noone, J. (1987). Planned change: Putting theory into practice . . . Utilizing Lippitt's theory. *Clinical Nurse Specialist, 1*(1), 25–29.

Purdy, E., Wright, S., & Johnson, M. (1988). Change for the better . . . Nursing development unit. *Nursing Times, 84*(38), 34–35.

Schwartz, K., & Tiffany, C. R. (1994). Evaluating Bhola's configurations theory of planned change. *Nursing Management, 25*(6), 56–61.

Shortell, S. M., Morrison, E. M., & Friedman, B. (1992). *Strategic choices for America's hospitals: Managing change in turbulent times.* San Francisco, CA: Jossey-Bass.

Sovie, M. D. (1989). Clinical nursing practices and patient outcomes: Evaluation, evolution, and revolution (Legitimizing radical change to maximize nurses time for quality care). *Nursing Economics, 7*(2), 79–85.

Sturm, G. (1989). A nurse/patient responds: Be a change agent. *Journal of Christian Nursing, 6*(1), 6–7.

Thomas, P. (1988). Managing change. *Nursing Times, 84*(44), 58–59.

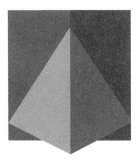

CHAPTER 5

Time Management

Another part of the planning process is *short-term planning*. This operational planning focuses on achieving specific tasks. Short-term plans involve a period of 1 hour to 3 years and are usually less complex than strategic or long-range plans. Short-term planning may be done annually, bimonthly, weekly, daily, or even hourly.

Previous chapters examined the need for prudent planning of resources, such as money, equipment, supplies, and labor. Time is an equally important resource. If managers are to direct employees effectively and maximize other resources, they must first be able to find the time to do so. *Time management* is making optimal use of available time. "Effective time management requires analysis of the characteristics of the work and the individual work habits of the team members, and intervention where a nonproductive use of time is found" (Tappen, 1995, p. 138).

Because time is a finite and valuable resource, learning how to use it wisely requires both leadership skills and management functions. The leader/manager must initiate an analysis of how time is managed on the unit level, involve team members and gain their cooperation in maximizing time use, and guide work to its conclusion and successful implementation (Tappen, 1995). The leader/manager also has a responsibility to decrease the costs associated with waste, rework, unnecessary complexity, and unreliability (Berwick, Godfrey, & Roessner, 1991). Leadership roles and management functions needed for effective time management are included in Display 5.1.

Bessie L. Marquis and Carol J. Huston:
LEADERSHIP ROLES AND MANAGEMENT FUNCTIONS IN NURSING, 2nd ed.
Lippincott-Raven Publishers © 1996

Display 5.1 Leadership Roles and Management Functions in Time Management

Leadership Roles

1. Is self-aware regarding personal blocks and barriers to efficient time management
2. Functions as a role model, supporter, and resource person in delegating tasks to subordinates
3. Encourages followers to use delegation as a time management strategy and team building tool
4. Assists followers in identifying situations appropriate for delegation
5. Assists followers in learning to manage time at work wisely
6. Eliminates environmental barriers to effective time management for unit staff

Management Functions

1. Appropriately prioritizes day-to-day planning to meet short-term and long-term unit needs
2. Accurately assesses subordinate capabilities and motivation when delegating
3. Delegates a level of authority necessary to complete delegated tasks
4. Develops and implements a periodic review process for all delegated tasks
5. Provides recognition or reward for the completion of delegated tasks
6. Builds time for planning into the work schedule

This chapter examines three aspects of time management: 1) managing time at work; 2) delegation; and 3) personal time management.

MANAGING TIME AT WORK

Being overwhelmed by work and time constraints leads to increased errors, the omission of important tasks, and general feelings of stress and ineffectiveness (Tappen, 1995). Although some people seem to be "naturals" with time management, the skill is learned and improves with practice. There are three basic steps to time management (Fig. 5.1) In the first step, time is allowed for planning and establishing priorities. The second step entails completing the highest priority task (as determined in step 1) whenever possible and finishing one task before beginning another. In the final step, the individual must reprioritize based on new information that may have been received. Because this is a cyclic process, all three steps must be accomplished sequentially.

Unfortunately, two mistakes common to novice managers are underestimating the importance of a daily plan and not allowing adequate time for planning. Daily planning is essential if the manager is to manage by efficiency rather than by crisis.

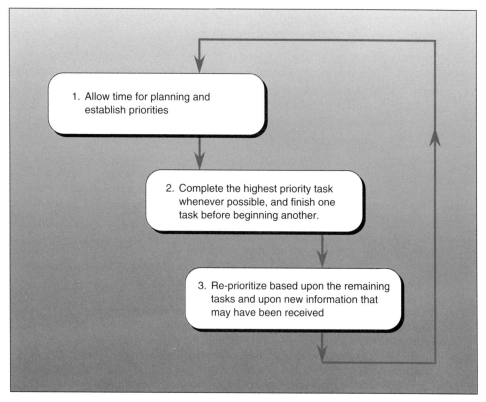

FIGURE 5.1 The three basic steps in time management.

Managers may feel they are unproductive if they sit at their desk designing the plan of care for the day, rather than accomplishing a specific task. Without adequate planning, however, the manager finds getting started difficult and begins to manage by crisis.

Planning takes time; it requires the ability to think, analyze data, envision alternatives, and make decisions. Setting aside time at the beginning of each day to plan the day allows the manager to spend time on high-priority tasks. During this planning time, the manager should review short-term, intermediate, and long-term goals and determine what progress will be made toward these goals.

Sometimes the manager does allow time for planning but has problems accurately predicting the length of time it will take to complete an activity. This management skill is acquired with experience (Bernhard & Walsh, 1990).

Swansburg (1990) suggests the following daily planning actions for the unit manager:

- In the morning, list all the actions to be accomplished that day.
- Plan ahead for meetings. Prepare and distribute advance agendas.
- Identify developing problems, and put them in the appropriate portion of the unit's short- or long-term plans.

• Review the short- and long-term plans of the unit regularly. Include colleagues and subordinates who the planning affects.

Examples of a charge nurse's day-to-day planning might include staffing schedules, patient care assignments, coordination of lunch and work break schedules, and interdisciplinary coordination of patient care.

▶ LEARNING EXERCISE 5.1

Assume that you are the RN leader of a team with one LVN and one nursing assistant on the 7 AM to 3 PM shift. The three of you are responsible for providing total care to 10 patients. Prioritize the following list of 10 things you need to accomplish this morning. Use a 1 for the first thing you will do and a 10 for the last. Be prepared to rationalize your priorities.

Check medication cards/sheets against the rand or kardex.
Listen to night shift report 0700–0720.
Take brief walking rounds to assess the night shift report and to introduce yourself to patients.
Hang four 0900 IV medications.
Set up the schedule for breaks and lunch among your team members.
Give 0845 pre-op on patient going to surgery at 0900.
Pass 0830 breakfast trays.
Meet with team members to plan schedule for the day and to clarify roles.
Read charts of patients who are new to you.
Check 0600 blood sugar lab results for 0730 insulin administration.

Because managers are inundated with many requests for their time and energy, the next step in time management is prioritizing. Covey (1989) argues that priority setting is the essence of time management and defines all activities as urgent or nonurgent and important or not important. Another means of prioritizing what is to be accomplished is to divide all such requests into three categories: "don't do," "do later," and "do now." The "don't do" items probably reflect problems that will take care of themselves, are already outdated, or are better accomplished by someone else. The manager either throws away the unnecessary information or passes it on to the appropriate person in a timely fashion. In either case, the manager removes unneeded clutter from his or her work area.

Some "do later" items reflect trivial problems or those that do not have immediate deadlines; thus, they may be procrastinated. Procrastination means to put off something until a future time, to postpone, or to delay needlessly. Chenevert (1993) identifies the three most common reasons for procrastination:

1. Not wanting to begin
2. Not knowing where to begin
3. Not knowing where to begin, even if you wanted to begin, which you don't

Although managers should selectively procrastinate, they should not avoid a task because it is overwhelming or unpleasant. Before setting "do later" items aside, the manager must be sure that large projects have been broken down into smaller projects and that a specific time line and plan for implementation are in place. The plan should include short-term, intermediate, and final deadlines. Likewise, a manager cannot ignore items without immediate time limits forever and must make a definite time commitment in the near future to address these requests.

The "do now" requests most commonly reflect a unit's day-to-day operational needs. These requests may include daily staffing needs, dealing with equipment shortages, meeting schedules, conducting hiring interviews, and giving performance appraisals. "Do now" requests also may represent items that had been put off earlier.

In prioritizing all the "do now" items, the manager may find preparing a written list helpful. Chenevert (1993) cautions, however, that sometimes making a list gives a false sense of accomplishment. A list is a plan, not a product. Although the manager may use monthly or weekly lists, a list also can assist in coordinating daily operations. This daily list, however, should not be longer than what can be realistically accomplished in one day; otherwise, it demotivates instead of assisting the manager. In addition, although the manager must be cognizant of and plan for routine tasks, it is not always necessary to place them on the list because they may only distract attention from other priority tasks. Lists should allow adequate time for each task and have blocks of time built in for the unexpected.

► LEARNING EXERCISE 5.2

Do you make a daily plan to organize what needs to be done? Develop a list of five items that must be accomplished today. Prioritize that list. Now make a list of five items that must be done this week. Prioritize that list also.

Periodically, the manager should review lists from prior days to see what was not accomplished or completed. If a task appears on a list for several successive days, the manager must reexamine it and assess why it was not accomplished. Some projects need to be removed from the list. A project may not be accomplished because it was not broken down into manageable tasks. For example, many well-meaning people begin thinking about completing their tax returns in early January but feel overwhelmed by a project that cannot be accomplished in one day. If preparing a tax return is not broken down into several smaller tasks with intermediate deadlines, it may be almost perpetually procrastinated.

► LEARNING EXERCISE 5.3

Think of the last major paper you wrote for a class. Did you set short-term and intermediate deadlines? Did you break the task down into smaller tasks to eliminate a last-minute crisis? What short-term and intermediate deadlines have you set to accomplish major projects that have been assigned to you this quarter or semester?

The manager must remember that a list is a planning tool, and there must be some flexibility in its implementation. In fact, the last step in time management is reprioritizing. Often the manager's priorities or list will change during a day, week, or longer because new information is received. If the manager does not take time to reprioritize after each major task is accomplished, other priorities set earlier may no longer be accurate.

In addition, no amount of planning can prevent an occasional crisis. If a crisis does occur, the manager should resort to crisis control, as described by Grohar-Murray and DiCroce (1992). In crisis control, the manager sets aside the original priorities for the day and reorganizes, communicates, and delegates a new plan reflecting the new priorities associated with the unexpected and untoward event causing the crisis.

Dealing With Interruptions

In a 1985 research study, Grantham, McKay, and Allison identified that lower level managers experience more interruptions than higher level managers. This occurs in part because first- and middle-level managers are more involved in daily planning than higher level managers and thus directly interact with a greater number of subordinates. In addition, many lower level managers do not have a quiet work space or clerical help to filter interruptions. Frequent work interruptions result in situational stress and lowered job satisfaction. Managers need to develop skill in preventing interruptions that prevent effective time management.

Lancaster (1984) has identified 10 external time wasters that keep managers from accomplishing their "do now" and "do later" lists. These external time wasters are listed in Display 5.2. Several of these items are discussed in previous chapters and others are discussed in later chapters. Three time wasters, however, warrant special attention here.

The first of these time wasters is *socializing*. Although socializing can help workers meet relationship needs or build power, it can tremendously deter productivity. Individuals can be discouraged from taking up managerial time with idle chatter in several ways.

Display 5.2   External Time Wasters

1. Telephone interruptions	7. Lack of adequately described policies and procedures
2. Socializing	
3. Meetings	8. Incompetent coworkers
4. Lack of information	9. Poor filing system
5. Poor communication	10. Paperwork and reading
6. Lack of feedback	

(Lancaster, 1984.)

1. *Don't make yourself overly accessible.* Make it easy for people to ignore you. Try not to "work" at the nursing station if this is possible. If charting is to be done, sit with your back to others. If you have an office, close the door. Have people make appointments to see you. All these behaviors will discourage casual socializers.

2. *Interrupt.* When someone is rambling on without getting to the point, break in and say gently, "Excuse me. Somehow I'm not getting your message. What exactly are you saying?"

3. *Avoid promoting socialization.* Having several comfortable chairs in your office, a full candy dish, and posters on your walls that invite comments encourage socializing in your office.

4. *Be brief.* Watch your own long-winded comments, and stand up when you are finished. This will signal an end to the conversation.

5. *Schedule long-winded pests.* If someone has a pattern of lengthy chatter and manages to corner you on rounds or at the nurse's station, say "I can't speak with you now, but I'm going to have some free time at 11 AM. Why don't you see me then?" Unless the meeting is important, the person who just wishes to chat will not bother to make a formal appointment.

6. If you would like to chat and have the time to do so, *use coffee breaks and lunch hours for socializing.*

Two other external time wasters that a manager must conquer are paperwork overload and a poor filing system. Managers are generally inundated with paper clutter, including organizational memos, staffing requests, quality assurance reports, incident reports, and patient evaluations. Because paperwork is often redundant or unnecessary, the manager needs to become an expert at handling it. Whenever possible, incoming correspondence should be handled the day it arrives; it should either be thrown away or filed according to the date to be completed. Try to address each piece of correspondence only once. Marriner-Tomey (1992) suggest using desk-organizing files, which are merely folders with such labels as urgent, return calls, dictate, read, file, and low priority to determine what to do each day.

An adequate filing system also is invaluable to handling paper overload. Keeping correspondence organized in easily retrievable files rather than disorganized stacks saves time when managers need to find specific information. If unsorted papers accumulate on the manager's desk, critical correspondence with short time lines may be missed (Tappen, 1995). The manager also may want to consider increased use of computerization and electronic mail.

DELEGATION

Delegation is a major element of the directing phase of the management process because much of the work accomplished by managers reflects not only their own efforts but those of their subordinates. *Delegation* can be defined as getting work done through others or as directing the performance of one or more people to accomplish organizational goals. For the manager, delegation is not an option but a necessity.

Frequently, there is too much work to be accomplished by one person. In these situations, delegation is indicated. Delegation should not limit the manager's control, prestige, and power but should extend his or her influence and capability by increasing what can be accomplished. In many cases, delegation is synonymous with productivity.

There are many good reasons for delegating. Sometimes managers must delegate routine tasks so they are free to handle problems that are more complex or require a higher level of expertise. Managers also should delegate work if someone else is better prepared or has greater expertise or knowledge about how to solve a problem. Delegation can be used to provide learning or "stretching" opportunities for subordinates. Subordinates who are not delegated enough responsibility will become bored, lazy, and ineffective (Bernhard & Walsh, 1990). Bennis (1989) states that "everyone needs to feel that he or she makes a difference to the success of the organization. The difference may be small, but when they are empowered, people feel that what they do has meaning and significance" (p. 23). Thus, in delegating, the leader/manager contributes to employees' personal and professional development.

Delegation is a major skill that must be learned. Frequent mistakes made by new managers in delegating include the following:

Underdelegating

This frequently stems from the manager's false assumption that delegation may be interpreted as a lack of ability on his or her part to do the job correctly or completely. Another frequent cause of underdelegating is the manager's desire to complete the whole job himself or herself—a lack of trust in the subordinates—because the manager believes he or she needs the experience or because he or she can do it better and faster than anyone else. It is important to remember that time spent in training another to do a job can be repaid tenfold in the future.

An additional cause of underdelegation is the fear that subordinates will resent having work delegated to them. Properly delegated work actually increases employee satisfaction and fosters a cooperative working relationship between managers and staff.

Managers also may underdelegate because they lack experience in the job or in delegation itself or because they have an excessive need to control or be perfect. A refusal to allow mistakes limits the opportunities available for subordinate growth and results in wasted time as the manager recompletes delegated tasks. If the manager requires a higher quality than "satisficing," this must be made clear at the time of the delegation. Not everything that is delegated needs to be handled in a maximizing mode.

Some novice managers emerging from the clinical nurse role underdelegate because they find it difficult to assume the manager role. This occurs in part because the nurses have been rewarded in the past for their own work and technical skills and not for their skill in leading other nurses (Swansburg, 1990). As managers come to understand and accept the need for the hierarchical responsibilities of delegation, they become more productive and develop more positive staff relationships.

Overdelegating

In contrast to underdelegating, which overburdens the manager, some managers overdelegate, burdening their subordinates. Some managers overdelegate because they are poor managers of time, spending most of it just trying to get organized. Others overdelegate because they feel insecure in their ability to perform a task. Managers also must be careful not to overdelegate to particularly competent employees, because they may become overburdened, frustrated, and resentful, all of which will adversely affect their performance (Decker & Sullivan, 1992).

Improperly Delegating

This includes such things as delegating at the wrong time, to the wrong person, or for the wrong reason. It also may include delegating tasks and responsibilities that are beyond the capability of the person to whom they are being delegated or which should be done by the manager.

Delegating decision making without providing adequate information also is an example of improper delegation. In many complex organizations, efforts have been made to delegate decision making to middle-level managers. When senior managers attempt to move a decision to a lower level in the organization, new channels for sharing information need to be established (Frohman & Johnson, 1993). Unfortunately, some top level managers balk at the idea of sharing more information.

Incomplete delegation also may occur when management divides a problem and assigns part of it to one department and part to another (Frohman & Johnson, 1993). When this occurs, the problem solvers at the middle-management level see only a part of the problem and must take action based on incomplete information.

LEARNING EXERCISE 5.4

Is it difficult for you to delegate to others? If so, do you know why? Are you more apt to underdelegate, overdelegate, or delegate improperly? Think back to the last thing you delegated. Was this delegation successful?

Managers should use the following steps to ensure effective delegation.

1. Plan ahead when identifying tasks to be accomplished.
2. Identify the skill or educational level necessary to complete the job.
3. Identify the person best able to complete the job in terms of capability and freedom of time to do so. It also is important that the person to whom the task is being delegated considers it important.
4. Clearly communicate exactly what is to be done, including the purpose for doing so. Include any limitations or qualifications that have been imposed. Although managers should specify the end-product desired, it is important to allow the subordinate feedback and an appropriate degree of autonomy in

deciding exactly how the work can be accomplished. Delegation is useless if the manager is unwilling to allow divergence in problem solving and thus redoes all work that has been delegated.

5. The manager must be sure to delegate the authority and the responsibility necessary to complete the task. Managers should encourage employees to attempt to solve problems themselves; however, the employee should be encouraged to ask questions about the task or to clarify the desired outcome.

6. Set time lines, and monitor how the task is being accomplished; this may be done through informal but regularly scheduled meetings. This shows an interest on the part of the manager, provides for a periodic review of progress, and encourages ongoing communication to clarify any questions or misconceptions. In addition, this monitoring keeps the delegated task before the subordinate and the manager, and both share accountability for its completion. Responsibility is shared when a task is delegated. Although the ultimate responsibility belongs to the manager, the subordinate accepting the task accepts responsibility for completing it appropriately and is accountable to the manager (Decker & Sullivan, 1992).

7. If the subordinate is having difficulty carrying out the delegated task, the leader should be available as a role model and resource in helping identify alternative solutions. Reassuming the delegated task should be a manager's last resort because this action fosters a sense of failure in the employee and demotivates rather than motivates. The manager also may need to delegate work previously assigned to an employee so that the employee has time to do the newly assigned task.

8. Evaluate the subordinate's performance after the task has been completed. Include positive and negative aspects of how the individual has completed the task. Be sure to reward appropriately a successfully completed task.

Delegation is a high-level skill essential to the manager that improves with practice. As managers gain the maturity and self-confidence needed to delegate wisely, they increase their impact and power both within and outside the organization. Subordinates gain self-esteem and increased job satisfaction from the responsibility and authority given to them, and the organization moves a step closer toward achieving its goals.

PERSONAL TIME MANAGEMENT

Personal time management refers in part to "the knowing of self." Self-awareness is a leadership skill. Managing time is difficult if a person is unsure of priorities for time management, including personal short-term, intermediate, and long-term goals. These goals give structure to what should be accomplished today, tomorrow, and in the future. However, goals alone are not enough; a concrete plan with time lines is needed. Plans outlined in manageable steps are clearer, more realistic, and attainable.

By being self-aware and setting goals accordingly, people determine how their time will be spent. If goals are not set, others often end up deciding how a person should spend his or her time and life. Think for a moment about last week. Did you accomplish all you wanted to accomplish? How much time was wasted by you or

You work in a public health agency. It is the agency's policy that several public health nurses are to be available in the office every day. Today is your turn to remain in the office. From 1 PM to 5 PM you will be the public health nurse at the scheduled immunization clinic; you hope to be able to spend some time finishing your end-of-month reports, which are due at 5 PM. The office stays open during lunch; you have a luncheon meeting with a cancer society group from noon to 1 PM today.

The RN in the office is to serve as a resource to the receptionist and handle client phone calls and drop-ins. In addition to the receptionist, you may delegate appropriately to a clerical worker. However, the clerical worker also serves the other clinic nurses and is usually fairly busy.

While you are in the office today trying to finish your reports, the following interruptions occur.

> 8:30 AM: Your supervisor comes in and requests a count of the diabetic and hypertensive clients seen in the last month.
>
> 9:00 AM: An upset client is waiting to see you about her daughter who just found out she's pregnant.
>
> 9:00 AM: Three drop-in clients are waiting to be interviewed for possible referral to the chest clinic.
>
> 9:30 AM: The public health physician calls you and needs someone to contact a family about a child's immunization.
>
> 9:30 AM: The dental department drops off 20 referrals and needs you to pull their charts.
>
> 10:00 AM: A confused client calls to find out what to do about the bills he has received.
>
> 10:45 AM: Six families have been waiting since 8:30 AM to sign up for food vouchers.
>
> 11:45 AM: A client calls about her drug use; she doesn't know what to do. She has heard about Narcotics Anonymous and wants more information now.

Assignment: How would you handle each interruption? Justify your decisions. Don't forget lunch for yourself and the two office workers. *Note: Attempt your own solution before reading the possible solution that follows.*

Analysis

TIME	TASK	RATIONALE
8:00 AM	Assign lunch breaks: 11:30–12:30—receptionist 12:30–1:30—clerical worker 12:00–1:00—you	Because you have a lunch engagement at noon, make sure other employees know when their lunch times must be.
	Finish reports	Because reports are due tonight, this would be the immediate task to be accomplished. Plan to finish these by 9 AM.
8:30 AM	Supervisor's request	Ask her when she needs the information. Tell her an estimate using primary diagnoses is now available but that an accurate figure that includes secondary diagnoses must

(continued)

LEARNING EXERCISE 5.5 (Continued)

		wait until you have time to go through your 150 family case files, which will be next week.
9:00 AM	Client with pregnant daughter/chest clinic drop-ins	The pregnancy takes priority over the chest clinic drop-ins. Ask the receptionist to start the paperwork on drop-ins while you spend 30 minutes with the mother.
9:30 AM	Phone call	Delegate this to the receptionist.
9:30 AM	Dental clinic referral	Delegate this duty to the clerical worker.
10:00 AM	Client call	Because this person is confused and you don't have available information, ask that he come in at 10 AM tomorrow with his bills.
10:45 AM	Families with food vouchers	Ask receptionist to finish paperwork and interviews on the families. Then quickly review information and sign vouchers. These families should not have had such a long wait. Make a note to find out what happened, and later counsel office staff about the delay.
11:45 AM	Drug call	Talk with client. Make a referral to a local drug clinic, and make an appointment for a part-time psychiatrist at the clinic. Do not get too involved on the phone with the client because it is better to make the appropriate referrals.

others? In your clinical practice, did you spend your time hunting for supplies and medicines instead of teaching your patient about his or her diabetes? Too often, irrelevant decisions and insignificant activities take priority over real purposes.

A study by Hendrickson, Doddato, and Kovner (1990) shows that within a typical 8-hour shift, nurses in six specialty units averaged only 31% of their time, or $2\frac{1}{2}$ hours, with patients—an average of 25 to 30 minutes per shift with each patient. This occurred despite an average of one nurse for every 4.8 patients during day shift and one nurse for every 6.9 patients on the evening shift. The results of this study raise several questions. If staffing levels were truly adequate to accomplish assigned work, did limited patient contact occur because the nursing staff managed their time poorly or because they did not value patient contact? Could work redesign or the use of another type of patient care delivery system increase the time spent in patient con-

LEARNING EXERCISE 5.6

You are an RN providing total patient care to four patients on an orthopedic unit during the 7 AM to 3 PM shift. Given the following patient information, prioritize your activities for the shift in eight 1-hour blocks of time. Be sure to include time for reports, planning your day's activities, breaks, and lunch. Be realistic about what you can accomplish. What activities will you delegate to the next shift? What overall goals have guided your time management? What personal values or priorities were factors in setting your goals?

101A—Ms. Jones, 84 years old. Fractured left hip secondary to fall at home. Disoriented since admission, especially at night. Soft restraints in use. Moans frequently. Being given IV pain medication every 2 hours prn. Vital signs and checks for circulation, feeling, and movement in toes ordered every 2 hours. Scheduled for surgery at 1030. Preoperative medications scheduled for 0930 and 1000. Consent yet to be signed. Family members will be here at 0800 and have expressed questions about the surgery and recovery period. Patient to return from surgery at approximately 1430. Will require postoperative vital signs every 15 minutes.

101B—Ms. Wilkins, 26 years old. Compound fracture of the femur with postoperative fat emboli, now resolved. 10 lb Buck's traction. Has been in the hospital 3 weeks. Very bored and frustrated with prolonged hospitalization. Upset about roommate who calls out all night and keeps her from sleeping. Wants to be moved to new room. Has also requested to have hair washed during bath today. Has IV running at 100 cc/h. IV antibiotic piggybacks at 0800 and 1200. Oral medications at 0800, 0900, and 1200.

102A—Mr. Jenkins, 47 years old. T-6 quadriplegic due to diving accident 14 years ago. Two days postoperative above-knee amputation due to osteomyelitis. Cultures have shown methicillin-resistant *staphylococcus aureus.* Strict wound isolation. Has been hospitalized for 2 weeks. Expressing great deal of anger and frustration to anyone who enters room. IV site red and puffy. IV needs to be restarted. Dressing change of operative site ordered daily. Heat lamp treatments ordered b.i.d. to small pressure sores on coccyx. IV antibiotic piggybacks at 0800, 1000, 1200, and 1400. Main IV bag to run out at 1000. 0600 lab work results to be called to physician this morning. Needs total assistance in performing activities of daily living, such as bathing and feeding self.

103A—Mr. Novak, 19 years old. Severe tear of rotator cuff in left shoulder while playing football. One day postoperative rotator cuff repair. Very quiet and withdrawn. Refusing pain medication, which has been ordered every 2 hours prn. Says he can handle pain and does not want to "mess up his body with drugs"; wants to be recruited into professional football after this semester. Nonverbal signs of grimacing, moaning, and inability to sleep suggest moderate pain is present. Physician states that likelihood of Mr. Novak ever playing football again is very low but has not yet told patient. Girlfriend frequently in room at patient's bedside. IV infusing at 150 cc/h. IV antibiotics at 0800 and 1400. Has not had a bath since admission 2 days ago.

Display 5.3 Time Inventory

5:00 A.M. _____
6:00 A.M. _____
6:30 A.M. _____
7:00 A.M. _____
7:30 A.M. _____
8:00 A.M. _____
8:30 A.M. _____
9:00 A.M. _____
9:30 A.M. _____
10:00 A.M. _____
10:30 A.M. _____
11:00 A.M. _____
11:30 A.M. _____
12:00 P.M. _____
12:30 P.M. _____
1:00 P.M. _____
1:30 P.M. _____
2:00 P.M. _____
2:30 P.M. _____
3:00 P.M. _____
3:30 P.M. _____
4:00 P.M. _____
4:30 P.M. _____
5:00 P.M. _____
5:30 P.M. _____
6:00 P.M. _____
6:30 P.M. _____
7:00 P.M. _____
7:30 P.M. _____
8:00 P.M. _____
8:30 P.M. _____
9:00 P.M. _____
9:30 P.M. _____
10:00 P.M. _____
11:00 P.M. _____
12:00 P.M. _____
1:00 A.M. _____
2:00 A.M. _____
3:00 A.M. _____
4:00 A.M. _____

Display 5.4   Internal Time Wasters

1. Procrastination
2. Poor planning
3. Failure to establish goals and objectives
4. Failure to set objectives
5. Inability to delegate

6. Inability to say no
7. Management by crisis
8. Haste
9. Indecisiveness
10. Open-door policy

(Lancaster, 1984.)

---

tact? Were the priorities for time management determined by individuals other than the nurses?

A study by Prescott, Ryan, and Thompson (1991) shows that hospital nurses inappropriately used their time doing the work of other departments, such as dietary, housekeeping, transportation, and pharmacy. They also were required to do the work of less-trained personnel, such as vocational nurses, aides, orderlies, unit clerks, and secretaries. Bassler and Goedde (1993) found that more than 30 hours each week of managerial time was spent on clerical work. Clearly, work redesign or a change in the type of care delivery system may alleviate some of these problems. However, the same general principle holds: Professional nurses who are self-aware and have clearly identified personal goals and priorities have greater control over how they expend their energy and what they accomplish.

In addition to goal setting, personal time management depends on self-awareness about how and when a person is most productive. Everyone avoids certain types of work or has methods of wasting time. Likewise, each person works better at certain times of the day or for certain lengths of time. The self-aware individual schedules complex or difficult tasks during the periods they are most productive and more simple or routine tasks during less productive times.

Because most people have an inaccurate perception of the time they spend on a particular task or the total amount of time they are productive during the day, a time inventory may be insightful. A time inventory is shown in Display 5.3. A time inventory provides an objective source of information about how an individual manages time (Tappen, 1995). Because the greatest benefit from a time inventory is being able to identify patterns of behavior, it may be necessary to maintain the time inventory for several days or even several weeks. It also may be helpful to repeat the time inventory every 6 months to 1 year and as work situations change to see if you have made any long-lasting changes in the use of your time (Tappen, 1995).

In addition to external time wasters, Lancaster (1984) has identified personal or internal time wasters. These are shown in Display 5.4.

Remember, there is no way to beg, borrow, or steal more hours in the day. The time we have is all the time available to us. Therefore, time often becomes our one real barrier because most other things are flexible. If time is habitually used ineffectively, being a manager will be very stressful.

LEARNING EXERCISE 5.7

Use the time inventory shown in Display 5-3 to identify your activities for a 24-hour period. Record your activities on the time inventory on a regular basis. Be specific. Do not trust your memory. Star the periods of time when you were most productive. Circle periods of time you were least productive. Do not include sleep time. Was this a typical day for you? Could you have modified your activity during your least productive time periods? If so, how?

INTEGRATING LEADERSHIP ROLES AND MANAGEMENT FUNCTIONS IN TIME MANAGEMENT

The leadership skills needed to manage time resources draw heavily on interpersonal communication skills. These communication skills are critical throughout the delegation process. The leader also is a resource and role model to subordinates in how to manage time. As has been stressed in other phases of the management process, the leadership skill of self-awareness also is necessary in time management. Leaders must understand their own value system, which influences how they use time and how they expect subordinates to use time.

The management functions inherent in using time resources wisely are more related to productivity. The manager must be able to prioritize activities of unit functioning to meet short- and long-term unit needs. This plan incorporates delegation as a means of increasing unit productivity and providing for subordinate accomplishment and enrichment. The right to delegate and the ability to provide formal rewards for successful completion of delegated tasks reflect the legitimate authority inherent in the management role.

Successful leaders/managers are able to integrate these leadership skills and management functions; they accomplish unit goals in a timely and efficient manner in a concerted effort with subordinates. They also recognize time as a valuable unit resource and share responsibility for the use of that resource with subordinates. Perhaps most importantly, the integrated leader/manager with well-developed time management skills is able to maintain greater control over time and energy constraints in his or her personal and professional life.

KEY CONCEPTS

▼ Because time is a finite and valuable resource, learning to use it wisely is essential to effective management.
▼ Time management can be reduced to three cyclic steps: 1) allow time for planning, and establish priorities; 2) complete the highest priority task, and whenever possible, finish one task before beginning the other; and 3) reprioritize based on remaining tasks and new information that may have been received.
▼ Setting aside time at the beginning of each day to plan the day allows the manager to spend appropriate time on high-priority tasks.

▼ Making lists is an appropriate tool to manage daily tasks. This list should not be any longer than what can realistically be accomplished in a day and must include adequate time to accomplish each item on the list and time for the unexpected.

▼ A common cause of procrastination is failure to break large tasks down into smaller ones so that the manager can set short-term, intermediate, and long-term goals.

▼ Lower level managers have more interruptions in their work than higher level managers. This results in situational stress and lowered job satisfaction.

▼ Although socializing can serve a purpose, such as meeting relationship needs of workers or power building, it can be a tremendous deterrent to productivity. Managers must learn strategies to cope with interruptions from socializing.

▼ Because so much paperwork is redundant or unnecessary, the manager needs to develop expertise at prioritizing it and eliminating unnecessary clutter at the work site.

▼ An efficient filing system is invaluable to handling paper overload.

▼ *Delegation* can be defined as getting work done through others or as directing the performance of one or more individuals to accomplish organizational goals.

▼ Delegation is not an option for the manager—it is a necessity.

▼ Delegation should be used for assigning routine tasks and tasks for which the manager does not have time. It also is appropriate as a tool for problem solving, changes in the manager's own job emphasis, and capability building in subordinates.

▼ Frequent mistakes made by new managers in delegating include underdelegation, overdelegation, and improper delegation.

▼ In delegation, managers must clearly communicate what they want done, including the purpose for doing so. Limitations or qualifications that have been imposed should be delineated. Although the manager should specify the end-product desired, it is important that the subordinate have an appropriate degree of autonomy in deciding how the work is to be accomplished.

▼ Managers must delegate the authority and the responsibility necessary to complete the task.

▼ *Personal time management* refers to "the knowing of self." Managing time is difficult if an individual is unsure of priorities, including personal short-term, intermediate, and long-term goals.

▼ Using a time inventory is one way to gain insight into how and when an individual is most productive. It also assists in identifying internal time wasters.

▲ ADDITIONAL LEARNING EXERCISES

Learning Exercise 5.8

You are the charge nurse on the 7 AM to 3 PM shift on an oncology unit. Immediately after report in the morning, you are overwhelmed by the following information:

- The nursing aide reports that Mrs. Jones has become comatose and is moribund. Although this is not unexpected, her family members are not present, and you know they would like to be notified immediately.

- There are three patients who need 0730 parenteral insulin administration. One of these patients had an 0600 blood sugar of 400.
- Mr. Johnson inadvertently pulled out his central line catheter when he was turning over in bed. His wife just notified the ward clerk by the call light system but states she is applying pressure to the site.
- The public toilet is overflowing, and urine and feces are pouring out rapidly.
- Breakfast trays arrived 15 minutes ago, and patients are using their call lights to ask why they do not yet have their breakfast.
- The medical director of the unit has just discovered that one of her patients has not been started on a chemotherapeutic drug she ordered 3 days ago. She is furious and demands to speak to you immediately.

Assignment: The other RNs are all very busy with their patients, but you do have the following people to whom you may delegate: yourself, a ward clerk, and an IV-certified LVN/LPN. Decide who should do what and in what priority. Justify your decision.

Learning Exercise 5.9
(From Marquis & Huston, 1994.)

It is October of your second year as coordinator of nursing management for the surgical department. A copy of your appointment calendar for Monday, October 27 follows.

You will review your unfinished business from the preceding Friday and look at the new items of business that have arrived on your desk this morning. The new items follow this assignment. The unit ward clerk is usually free in the afternoon to provide you with 1 hour of clerical assistance, and you have a charge nurse on each shift to whom you may delegate.

1. Assign a priority to each item with 1 being the most important and 5 being the least important.
2. Decide when you will deal with each item, being careful not to use more time than you have open on your calendar.
3. If the problem is to be handled immediately, explain how you will do this (eg, delegated, phone call).
4. Explain the rationale for your decisions.

Monday, October 27

8:00 AM	Arrive at work
8:15 AM	Daily rounds with each head nurse in your area
8:30 AM	Continuation of daily rounds with head nurses
9:00 AM	Open
9:30 AM	Open
10:00 AM	Department Head meeting
10:30 AM	United Givers committee
11:00 AM	United Givers committee continued
11:30 AM	Open
Noon	Lunch

12:30 PM	Lunch
1:00 PM	Weekly meeting with administrator—Budget and annual report due
1:30 PM	Open
2:00 PM	Infection Control meeting
2:30 PM	Infection Control meeting continued
3:00 PM	Fire drill and critique of drill
3:30 PM	Fire drill and critique of drill continued
4:00 PM	Open
4:30 PM	Open
5:00 PM	Off duty

Correspondence

ITEM 1

From the desk of M. Jones, personnel manager.

October 24

Dear Joan:

I am sending you the names of two new graduate nurses who are interested in working in your area. I have processed their applications; they seem well qualified. Could you manage to see them as early as possible in the week? I would hate to lose these prospective employees, and they are anxious to obtain definite confirmation of employment.

ITEM 2

From the desk of John Brown, purchasing agent.

October 23

Joan:

We really must get together this week and devise a method to control supplies. Your area has used three times the amount of thermometer covers as any other area. Are you taking that many more temperatures? This is just one of the supplies your area uses excessively. I'm open to suggestions.

ITEM 3

Roger Johnson, MD
chief of surgical department

October 24

Ms. Kerr:

I know you have your budget ready to submit, but I just remembered this week that I forgot to include an arterial pressure monitor. Is there another item that we can leave out? I'll drop by Monday morning, and we'll figure something out.

ITEM 4

October 23

Ms. Kerr:

The following personnel are due for merit raises, and I must have their completed and signed evaluations by Tuesday afternoon.

1. Mary Rocas
2. Jim Newman
3. Marge Newfield

M. Jones, personnel manager

ITEM 5

Roger Johnson, MD
Chief of surgical department

October 23

Ms. Kerr:

The physicians are complaining about the availability of nurses to accompany them on rounds. I feel you and I need to sit down with the doctors and head nurses to discuss this recurring problem. I have some free time Monday afternoon.

ITEM 6

5 AM

Joan:

Sally Knight (your regular night RN) requested a leave of absence due to her mother's illness. I told her it would be OK to take the next three nights off. She is flying out of town on the 9 AM commuter flight to San Francisco, so phone her right away if you don't want her to go. I felt I had no choice but to say yes.

Nancy Peters, Night Supervisor

P.S. You'll need to find a replacement for her for the next three nights.

ITEM 7

To: Ms. Kerr
From: Administrator
Re: Patient complaint

Date: October 23

Please investigate the following patient complaint. I would like a report on this matter this afternoon.

Dear Sir:

My mother Gertrude Boswich was a patient in your hospital, and I just want to tell you that no member of my family will ever go there again.

She had an operation on Monday, and no one gave her a bath for 3 days. Besides that, she didn't get anything to eat for 2 days, not even water. What kind of a hospital do you run anyway?

Elmo Boswich

ITEM 8

To: Joan Kerr
From: Nancy Newton, RN, Head Nurse
Re: Problems with x-ray department

Date: October 23

We have been having problems getting diagnostic x-ray procedures scheduled for patients. Many times, patients have had to stay an extra day to get x-ray tests done. I have talked to the radiology chief several times, but the situation hasn't improved. Can you do something about this?

ITEM 9

To: All department heads
From: Store room
Re: Supplies

Date: October 23

The store room is out of the following items:
Toilet tissue, paper clips, disposable diapers, and pencils.
We are expecting a shipment next week.

Telephone Messages

ITEM 10

Sam Surefoot, Superior Surgical Supplies, Inc., returned your call at 7:50 AM on October 27. He will be at the hospital this afternoon to talk about problems with defective equipment received.

ITEM 11

Donald Drinkley, Channel 32-TV, called at 8:10 AM on October 27 to say he will be here at 11:30 AM to do a feature story on the open-heart unit.

ITEM 12

Lila Green, director of nurses at St. Joan's Hospital, called at 8:05 AM on October 24 about a phone reference on Jane Jones, RN. Ms. Jones has applied for a job there. Isn't that the one we fired last year?

ITEM 13

Betty Brownie, Bluebird Troop 35, called at 8 AM on October 27 about the Bluebird troop visit to patients on Halloween with trick-or-treat candy. She will call again.

Learning Exercise 5.10

You are the supervisor of the oncology unit. One of your closest friends and colleagues is Paula, the supervisor of the medical unit. Frequently, you cover for each other in the event of absence or emergency. Today, Paula stops at your office to let you know that she will be gone for 7 days to a management workshop on the East Coast. She asks that you check on the unit during her absence. She also asks that you pay particularly close attention to Mary Jones, an employee on her unit. She states that Mary, an employee at the hospital for 4 years, has been counseled repeatedly about her unexcused absences from work and has recently received a written reprimand specifying that she will be terminated if there is another unexcused absence. Paula anticipates that Mary may attempt to break the rules during her absence. She asks that you follow through on this disciplinary plan in the event that Mary again takes an unexcused absence. Her instructions to you are to terminate Mary if she fails to show up for work this week for any reason.

When you arrive at work the next day, you find that Mary called in sick 20 minutes after the shift was to begin. The hospital's policy is that employees are to notify the staffing office of illness no less than 2 hours prior to the beginning of their shift. When you attempt to contact Mary by telephone at home, there is no answer.

Later in the day, you finally reach Mary and ask that she come in to your office early the next morning about her inadequate notice of sick time. Mary arrives 45 minutes late the next morning. You are already agitated and angry with her. You inform her that she is to be terminated for any rule broken during Paula's absence and that this action is being taken in accord with the disciplinary contract that had been established earlier.

Mary is furious. She states that you have no right to fire her because you are not her real boss and that Paula should face her herself. She goes on to say, "Paula told me that the disciplinary contract was just a way of formalizing that we had talked and that I shouldn't take it too seriously." Mary also says, "Besides, I didn't get sick until I was getting ready for work. The hospital rules state that I have 12 sick days each year." Although you feel certain that Paula was very clear about her position in reviewing the disciplinary contract with Mary, you begin to feel uncomfortable with being placed in the position of having to take such serious corrective action without having been involved in prior disciplinary review sessions. You are, however, also aware that this employee has been breaking rules for some time and that this is just one in a succession of absences. You also know that Paula is counting on you to provide consistency of leadership in her absence.

Assignment: Discuss how you will handle the situation. Was it appropriate for Paula to delegate this responsibility to you? Is it appropriate for one manager to carry out another manager's disciplinary plan? Would it matter if a written disciplinary contract had already been established?

REFERENCES:

Bassler, S., & Goedde, L. (1993). Clerical activities and the nurse manager. *Nursing Management, 24*(1), 63–64.

Bennis, W. (1989). *Why leaders can't lead.* San Francisco: Jossey-Bass.

Bernhard, L. A., & Walsh, M. (1990). *Leadership: The key to the professionalization of nursing* (2nd ed.). St. Louis: C.V. Mosby.

Berwick, D. M., Godfrey, A. B., & Roessner, J. (1991). Curing health care. San Francisco: Jossey-Bass Publishers.

Chenevert, M. (1993). *The pro-nurse handbook* (2nd ed.). St. Louis: Mosby Yearbook.

Covey, S. (1989). *The seven habits of highly effective people.* New York: Simon & Schuster.

Decker, P. J., & Sullivan, E. J. (1992). *Nursing administration.* East Norwalk, CT: Appleton and Lange.

Frohman, A. L., & Johnson, L. W. (1993). *The middle management challenge.* New York: McGraw Hill.

Grantham, M. A., McKay, R. C., & Allison, C. M. (1985). Job satisfaction and interruptions in planned time of nursing managers. *Journal of Nursing Administration, 15*(5), 7–10.

Grohar-Murray, M. E., & DiCroce, H. R. (1992). *Leadership and management in nursing.* Norwalk CT: Appleton and Lange.

Hendrickson, G., Doddato, T. M., & Kovner, C. T. (1990). How do nurses use their time? *Journal of Nursing Administration, 20*(3), 31–37.

Lancaster, J. (1984). Making the most of every minute: Reminders for nursing leaders. In M. S. Berger, D. Elhart, S. Firsich, S. Jordan, & S. Stone (Eds.), *Management for nurses.* St. Louis: C.V. Mosby.

Marquis, B. L., & Huston, C. J. (1994). *Management decision making for nurses* (2nd ed.). Philadelphia: J.B. Lippincott.

Marriner-Tomey, A. (1992). *Guide to nursing management* (4th ed.). St. Louis: Mosby Year Book.

Prescott, P. A., Ryan, J. W., & Thompson, K. O. (1991). Changing how nurses spend their time. *Image, 23*(1), 23–27.

Swansburg, R. C. (1990). *Management and leadership for nurse managers.* Boston: Jones and Bartlett.

Tappen, R. M. (1995). *Nursing leadership and management: Concepts and practice* (3rd ed.). Philadelphia: F.A. Davis.

BIBLIOGRAPHY

Bech, A. C. (1988). A manager's time shock. *Management World, 17*(2), 7–8.

Bice-Stephens, N. (1987). Overwhelmed?-You can cope. *Nursing Life, 7*(1), 30–32.

Comstock, L. G. & Moff, T. E. (1991). Cost-effective time efficient charting. *Nursing Management, 22*(7), 44–48.

DeBacca, V. (1987). So many patients, so little time. *RN, 50*(4), 32–33.

del Bueno, D. J. (1993). Delegation and the

dilemma of the democratic ideal. *Journal of Nursing Administration, 23*(3), 20–21, 25.

Del Bueno, D. J., & Freund, C. M. (1986). *Power and politics in nursing administration: A casebook.* Owing Mills, MD: National Health Publishing, Rynd Communications.

Falls, K. (1987). Time crunch: How one nurse avoids the squeeze. *Nursing Life, 7*(6), 34–36.

Feit, E. (1994). Upgrading systems: A new pager. *Nursing Management, 25*(12), 39.

Feri, R. S. (1987). In search of the excellent one-minute megatrend . . . or how to tolerate the five-minute burden. *American Journal of Nursing, 87*(1), 109–110.

Grainger, R. D. (1991). What does time mean to you? *American Journal of Nursing, 91*(7), 13.

Hayes, P. M. (1994). Non-nursing functions: Time for them to go. *Nursing Economics, 12*(3), 120–125.

Herrick, K. (1994). My license is not on the line: The art of delegation. *Nursing Management, 25*(2), 48–50.

Johnson, M., et al. (1989). Making every minute count: Effective time management. *Imprint, 36*(3), 75–77.

Kennison, M. M. (1989). Improving time management. *Critical Care Nurse, 9*(2), 70-73.

Lynch, M. (1991). P-A-C-E yourself: Tips on time management. *Nursing, 21*(3), 104, 106, 108.

Matejka, J. K., & Dunsing, R. J. (1987). Great expectations. *Management World, 17*(2), 16–17.

McAlvanah, M. F. (1988). Time management: A key to fulfilling job expectations. *Pediatric Nurse, 14*(6), 536.

Poteet, G. W. (1989). Nursing administrators and delegation. *Nursing Administration Quarterly, 13*(Spring), 12–32

Rhone, M. (1987). Try these time saving tips. *RN, 50*(8), 64.

Shubin, S. (1988). Making the most of your time. *Nursing Life, 8*(1), 39–41.

Webb, D. M. (1989). Time control: An introduction. *Hospital Topics, 67*(1), 38–39.

Webb, D. M. (1991). Interruptions and crises. *Hospital Topics, 69*(1), 43–44.

Wilkinson, R. (1991). Forget that meeting. *Nursing Management, 22*(12), 42.

Williamson, D. (1994). Automation at the point of care. *Nursing Management, 35*(7), 32–35.

CHAPTER 6

Fiscal Planning

Scarce resources and soaring healthcare costs have strained all healthcare delivery systems. There has never been a time when healthcare organizations needed to operate more efficiently or be more aware of cost containment. *Cost containment* refers to effective and efficient delivery of services while generating needed revenues for continued organizational productivity. Cost containment is the responsibility of every healthcare provider, and the survival of many healthcare organizations depends on their ability to do so (Campbell & Dowd, 1993).

It is critical that unit managers have expertise in managing costs. Of all the forms of planning, fiscal planning is often perceived as the most difficult and thus is frequently avoided by managers. Although familiar with the basics of fiscal planning, unit managers may encounter difficulty with forecasting costs based on current and projected needs. Sometimes this occurs because the manager has had little formal education or training on budget preparation. Fiscal planning, as is all planning, is a learned skill and improves with practice. It is essential that fiscal planning be included in nursing curricula and in management preparation programs. Campbell (1992) argues that healthcare economics education should be started in nursing school and that instructors and employers should empower nurses with the means to acquire fiscal accountability.

Historically, nursing management played a limited role in determining resource allocation in healthcare institutions. Nurse managers were given budgets without any rationale and were not allowed input. In addition, because nursing was classified as a

Bessie L. Marquis and Carol J. Huston:
LEADERSHIP ROLES AND MANAGEMENT FUNCTIONS IN NURSING, 2nd ed.
Lippincott-Raven Publishers © 1996

"non–income-producing" service, nursing input was shortchanged in the budget process.

During the last 20 years, healthcare organizations have grown to recognize the importance of nursing input in fiscal planning, and unit managers are now expected to be well versed in financial matters. Currently, nursing budgets account for up to 70% to 90% of the total expenses in healthcare institutions (Sullivan & Decker, 1988); therefore, participation in fiscal planning is viewed as a fundamental and powerful tool for nursing.

An essential feature of fiscal planning is *responsibility accounting,* which means that each of an organization's revenues, expenses, assets, and liabilities is someone's responsibility (Decker & Sullivan, 1992). As a corollary, the individual with the most direct control or influence on any of these financial elements should be held accountable for them. At the unit level, this accountability generally falls to the manager. The manager, then, should actively participate in the budget, have control over items charged against that budget, receive periodic and timely reports on actual results compared with the budget, and be held accountable for the financial results of the operating unit (Decker & Sullivan, 1992).

Unit managers play a critical role in forecasting trends in census and activity and supply and equipment needs at the unit level because they are involved in daily operations and see firsthand the unit's functioning. Forecasting involves making an educated budget estimate using data from the past to enhance judgment (Corley & Satterwhite, 1993). With forecasting, the unit-level manager can identify seasonal variations or trend behavior to schedule nursing and ancillary personnel, plan cleaning and renovation activities, establish space needs, and determine the need for other services (Kao & Pokladnik, 1978).

The unit manager also can best monitor and evaluate all aspects of a unit's budget control. "In an environment of tight budgets and the potential for ever diminishing resources, the success of unit managers will be measured by their ability to identify and balance cost/quality issues effectively while managing staffing under variable patient census and demanding patient acuity" (Dreisbach, 1994, p. 131).

The unit manager also has a responsibility to communicate budgetary planning goals to staff just as they do other types of planning. The more staff understand the budgetary goals and the plans to carry out those goals, the more likely goal attainment is. Sadly, 45% of staff nurses in a 1992 study had no knowledge of the nursing budget model applied by their hospital system (Wieseke & Bantz, 1992). In this study 88% of the respondents stated that healthcare costs could be reduced by involving them in decision making related to need identification and healthcare delivery; 92% felt healthcare costs could be reduced by better collaboration between the nurses and physicians.

This chapter discusses the unit manager's role in fiscal planning, identifies types of budgets, and delineates the budgetary process. Through experiential learning exercises, the reader will apply the basics of fiscal planning, forecasting, and budgetary monitoring.

Fiscal planning uses many of the same concepts and rules that are discussed in Chapters 3 and 4. For example, just as each individual's value system determines how personal resources are spent, fiscal planning reflects the philosophy, goals, and objectives of the organization. Fiscal planning must be proactive, flexible, and clearly stated in measurable terms; include short- and long-term planning; and involve as many individuals as feasible in the budgetary process. This type of planning also requires vision, creativity, and a thorough knowledge of the political, social, and economic forces that shape healthcare. The leadership roles and management functions inherent in fiscal planning are similar to those in other phases of the planning process. These roles and functions and are outlined in Display 6.1.

Display 6.1 Leadership Roles and Management Functions in Fiscal Planning

Leadership Roles

1. Is visionary in identifying or forecasting short- and long-term unit needs, thus inspiring proactive rather than reactive fiscal planning
2. Is knowledgable about political, social, and economic factors that shape fiscal planning in healthcare today
3. Demonstrates flexibility in fiscal goal setting in a rapidly changing system
4. Anticipates, recognizes, and creatively problem-solves budgetary constraints
5. Influences and inspires group members to become active in short- and long-range fiscal planning
6. Recognizes when fiscal constraints have resulted in an inability to meet organizational or unit goals and communicates this insight effectively, following the chain of command
7. Ensures that client safety is not jeopardized by cost containment

Management Functions

1. Identifies the importance of, and develops short- and long-range fiscal plans that reflect, unit needs
2. Articulates and documents unit needs effectively to higher administrative levels
3. Assesses the internal and external environment of the organization in forecasting to identify driving forces and barriers to fiscal planning
4. Demonstrates knowledge of budgeting and uses appropriate techniques
5. Provides opportunities for subordinates to participate in relevant fiscal planning
6. Coordinates unit-level fiscal planning to be congruent with organizational goals and objectives
7. Accurately assesses personnel needs using predetermined standards or an established patient classification system
8. Coordinates the monitoring aspects of budget control
9. Ensures that documentation of client's need for services and services rendered is clear and complete to facilitate organizational reimbursement

BASICS OF BUDGETS

A *budget* is a plan that uses numerical data to predict the activities of an organization over a period of time. The desired outcome of budgeting is maximal use of resources to meet organizational short- and long-term needs. The budget's value is directly related to its accuracy; the more accurate the budget blueprint, the better the institution can plan the most efficient use of its resources. Because a budget is at best a prediction, a plan, and not a rule, fiscal planning requires flexibility, ongoing evaluation, and revision.

In the budget, expenses are classified as *fixed* or *variable* and either *controllable* or *noncontrollable*. Fixed expenses do not vary with volume, while variable expenses do. Examples of fixed expenses might be a building's mortgage payment or a manager's salary; variable expenses might include the payroll of hourly wage employees and the cost of supplies. Controllable expenses can be controlled or varied by the manager, while noncontrollable expenses can not. For example, the unit manager can control the number of personnel working on a certain shift and the staffing mix; he or she cannot, however, control equipment depreciation, the number and type of supplies needed by patients, or overtime that occurs in response to an emergency.

 LEARNING EXERCISE 6.1

One of the oncologists on your unit (Dr. Jones) has offered to give you his old photocopier because his office is purchasing a new one.

As a condition of acceptance, he requires that all the oncologists and radiologists be allowed to use the copier free of charge.

Assignment:
1. Justify acceptance or rejection of the gift. What influenced your choice?
2. What are the fixed and variable costs?
3. What are the controllable and noncontrollable costs?
4. How much control will you as a unit manager have over the use of the copier?

Steps in the Budgetary Process

Douglass and Bevis (1983) have identified four steps in budget planning:

1. *Determine the requirements of the budget.* Historically, top-level managers frequently developed the budget for an institution without input from middle- or first-level managers. Because unit managers who participate in fiscal planning are more apt to be cost conscious and better understand the institution's long- and short-term goals, budgeting today generally reflects input from all levels of the organizational hierarchy. Unit managers develop goals, objectives, and budgetary estimates with input from colleagues and subordinates. Budgeting is most effective when all personnel using the resources are involved in the process. Managers, therefore, must be taught how to prepare a budget and must be supported by management throughout the budgeting

process. A composite of unit needs in terms of manpower, equipment, and operating expenses can then be compiled to determine the organizational budget. Display 6.2 lists some terms in fiscal planning that the manager should understand.

2. *Develop a plan.* The budget plan may be developed in many ways. A budgeting cycle that is set for 12 months is called a *fiscal-year budget.* This fiscal year, which may or may not coincide with the calendar year, is then usually broken down into quarters or subdivided into monthly, quarterly, or semiannual periods. Most budgets are developed for a 1-year period, but a *perpetual budget* may be done on a continual basis each month so that 12 months of future budget data are always available. Selecting the optimal time frame for budgeting also is important; a budget that is predicted too far in advance has greater probability for error. If the budget is short sighted, compensating for unexpected major expenses or purchasing capital equipment may be difficult.

3. *Analyze and control the operation.* Monitoring and analyzing the budget must be ongoing to avoid inadequate or excess funds at the end of the fiscal year. In most healthcare institutions, monthly computerized statements outline each department's projected budget and any deviations from that budget. Each unit manager is accountable for budget deviations in their unit. Most units can expect some change from the anticipated budget, but large deviations must be examined for possible causes, and remedial action must be taken if necessary. Some managers artificially inflate their department budgets as a cushion against budget cuts from a higher level of administration. If several departments partake in this unsound practice, the entire institutional budget may be ineffective. If a major change in the budget is indicated, the entire budgeting process must be repeated. Top-level managers must watch for and correct unrealistic budget projections before they are implemented.

4. *Review the plan.* The budget is reviewed periodically and modified as needed throughout the fiscal year. With each successive year of budgeting, managers can more accurately predict their unit's budgetary requirements. Managers develop a more historical approach to budgeting as they grow more adept at predicting seasonal variations in the population they serve or in their particular institution.

TYPES OF BUDGETS

There are three major types of expenditures that concern the unit manager: personnel, operating, and capital budgets.

The Personnel Budget

The largest of the budget expenditures is the *workforce* or *personnel* budget because healthcare is labor intensive. The prudent manager uses historical data about unit census fluctuations when forecasting short- and long-term personnel needs. Likewise, a manager must monitor the personnel budget closely to prevent understaffing

Display 6.2 Fiscal Terminology

Acuity index—A weighted statistical measurement that refers to severity of illness of patients for a given time. Patients are classified according to acuity of illness, usually in one of four categories. The acuity index is determined by taking a total of acuities and then dividing by the number of patients.

Assets—The financial resources that a healthcare organization receives, such as accounts receivable.

Baseline data—Historical information on dollars spent, acuity level, patient census, resources needed, hours of care, and so forth. This information is used as a basis on which future needs can be projected.

Break-even point—The point at which revenue covers costs. Most healthcare facilities have high fixed costs. Because per-unit fixed costs decrease with volume, hospitals need to maintain a high census to decrease unit fixed costs.

Case mix—This term refers to the type of patients served by an institution. A hospital's case mix is usually defined in such patient-related variables as diagnosis, personal characteristics, and patterns of treatment.

Cash flow—A rate at which dollars are received and dispersed.

Controllable costs—Costs that can be controlled or that vary. An example would be the number of personnel employed, the level of skill you require, wage levels, and quality of materials.

Cost-benefit ratio—The numerical relationship between the value of an activity or procedure in terms of benefits and the value of the activity's or procedure's cost. The cost-benefit ratio is expressed as a fraction.

Cost center—The smallest functional unit for which cost control and accountability can be assigned. A nursing unit is usually considered a cost center, but there may be other cost centers within a unit (orthopedics is a cost center, but often the cast room is considered a separate cost center within orthopedics).

Diagnostic related groups—Medical classification under which a medicare patient's diagnosis will be made. Each will have a set payment reimbursement rate. This rate may, in actuality, be higher or lower than the cost of treating the patient in a particular hospital.

Direct costs—Costs that can be attributed to a specific source, such as medications and treatments. Costs that are clearly identifiable with goods or service.

Fixed budget—A style of budgeting that is based on a fixed, annual level of volume, such as number of patient days or tests performed, to arrive at an annual budget total. These totals are then divided by 12 to arrive at the monthly average. The fixed budget does not make provisions for monthly or seasonal variations.

Fixed costs—Costs that do not vary according to volume. Examples of fixed costs are mortgage or loan payments.

For-profit organization—An organization in which the providers of funds have an ownership interest in the organization. These providers own stocks in the for-profit organization and earn dividends based on what is left when the cost of goods and of carrying on the business is subtracted from the amount of money taken in.

Full costs—The total of all the direct and indirect costs.

Full-time equivalent (FTE)—The number of hours of work for which a full-time employee is scheduled for a weekly period. For example, 1.0 FTE = five 8-hour days of staffing, which equals 40 hours of staffing per week. One FTE can be divided into different ways. For example, two part-time employees, each working 20 hours per week,

(*continued*)

would equal 1 FTE. If a position requires coverage for more than 5 days or 40 hours per week, the FTE will be greater than 1.0 for that position. Assume a position requires 7-day coverage, or 56 hours, then the position requires 1.4 FTE coverage (56 divided by 40 = 1.4) This means that more than one person is needed to fill the FTE positions for a 7-day period.

Health maintenance organization—An entity that is neither a private insurance nor healthcare contractor. It can be operated by some for-profit or not-for-profit organizations that provide healthcare in an organized system to subscribing members in a geographical area with a predetermined set of basic and preventive supplemental health maintenance and treatment services for a fixed, prepaid charge (Streff, 1994).

Hours per patient day (HPPD)—The hours of nursing care provided per patient per day by various levels of nursing personnel. HPPD are determined by dividing total production hours by the number of patients.

Indirect costs—Costs that cannot be directly attributed to a specific area. These are hidden costs and are usually spread among different departments. Housekeeping services are considered indirect costs.

Managed care—A term used to describe a variety of healthcare plans designed to contain the cost of healthcare services delivered to members while maintaining the quality of care. The case managers are clinicians who, as individuals or part of collaborative groups, oversee the management of care-type care (ie, DRGs) and are usually held accountable to some standard of cost effectiveness and quality (Zander, 1994).

Medicaid—A federally assisted and state-administered program to pay for medical services on behalf of certain groups of low-income individuals. Generally, these individuals are not covered by social security. Certain groups of people (ie, the elderly, blind, disabled, members of families with dependent children, and certain other children and pregnant women) also qualify for coverage if their incomes and resources are sufficiently low (Kelly, 1992).

Medicare—A nationwide health insurance program authorized under Title 18 of the Social Security Act that provides benefits to people 65 years of age or older. Part A is the hospital insurance program. Part B is the supplementary medical insurance program (Streff, 1994). Medicare coverage also is available to certain groups of individuals with catastrophic or chronic illness, such as patients with renal failure requiring hemodialysis, regardless of age.

Noncontrollable costs—Indirect expenses that you cannot usually control or vary. Examples might be rent, lighting, and depreciation of equipment.

Not-for-profit organization—This type of organization is financed by funds that come from several sources, but the providers of these funds do not have an ownership interest. Profits generated in the not-for-profit organization are frequently funneled back into the organization for expansion or capital acquisition.

Operating expenses—The daily costs required to maintain a hospital or healthcare institution.

Patient classification system—A method of classifying patients. Different criteria are used for different systems. In nursing, patients are usually classified according to severity of illness.

Preferred provider organization—A healthcare financing and delivery program with a group of providers, such as physicians and hospitals, who contract to give services on a fee-for-service basis. This provides financial incentives to consumers to use a select

(continued)

Display 6.2 Fiscal Terminology (Continued)

---

group of preferred providers and pay less for services. Insurance companies usually promise the preferred provider organization a certain volume of patients and prompt payment in exchange for fee discounts (Streff, 1994).

Production hours—The total amount of regular time, overtime, and temporary time. This also may be referred to as actual hours.

Revenue—A source of income or the reward for providing a service to a client.

RIM—One minute of nursing resource use. RIMs were developed in New Jersey to allocate nursing resources in a way that addresses the complaints that DRGs inadequately represent variability of nursing care requirements (Marriner-Tomey, 1992).

Staffing distribution—A determination of number of personnel allocated per shift, for example, 45% days, 35% evenings, and 20% nights. Hospitals vary on how staff are distributed.

Staffing mix—The ratio of RNs to other personnel. For example, a shift on one unit might have 40% RNs, 40% LPNs/LVNs, and 20% other. Hospitals vary on their staffing mix policies.

Turnover ratio—The rate at which employees leave their jobs for reasons other than death or retirement. The rate is calculated by dividing the number of employees leaving by the number of workers employed in the unit during the year and then multiplying by 100.

Variable costs—Costs that vary with the volume. Payroll costs are variable costs, for example.

Workload units—In nursing, workloads are usually the same as patient days. For some areas, however, workload units might refer to the number of procedures, tests, patient visits, injections, and so forth.

Zero-based budgeting—A type of budgeting that begins at zero each year. That means that every dollar that is to be spent needs to be justified. Established costs are not automatically continued from one year to the next. This style of budgeting ensures that the activities aren't continued simply because they were carried out in the past. In zero-based budgeting, objectives are very important, and they are listed according to priority. Zero-based budgeting also indicates what will happen if an objective is eliminated and which objectives could be accomplished for less money.

---

or overstaffing. As patient days or volume decreases, managers must decrease personnel costs in relation to the decrease in volume. For example, when the patient census drops below minimum staffing patterns and costs begin to exceed revenues, the unit manager must consider consolidating patients from partially filled units, or assigning patients in a manner that maintains a census on each unit that covers the fixed costs of minimum staffing patterns (Strasen, 1987).

In addition to numbers of staff, the manager must be cognizant of the staffing mix. The manager also must be aware of the institution's patient acuity so that the most economical level of nursing care that will meet patient needs can be provided. Although Unit 4 discusses staffing, it is necessary to briefly discuss here how staffing needs are expressed in the personnel budget.

Most staffing is based on a predetermined standard. This standard may be addressed in hours per patient day (medical units), visits per month (home health agencies), or minutes per case (the operating room). Because the patient census, number of visits, or cases per day never remain constant, the manager must be ready to alter staffing when volume increases or decreases. In addition, sometimes the population and type of cases change so that the established standard is no longer appropriate. For example, an operating room that begins to perform open-heart surgery would involve more nursing time per case; therefore, the standard (number of nursing minutes per case) would need to be adjusted. Normally the standard is adjusted upward or downward once a year, but staffing is adjusted daily depending on the volume.

The standard formula for calculating nursing care hours (NCH) per patient day (PPD) is shown in Figure 6.1. As the unit manager in an acute care facility, you might use this formula to calculate daily staffing needs. For example, assume that your budgeted nursing care hours are 6 NCH/PPD. You are calculating the NCH/PPD for today, January 31; at midnight it will be February 1. The patient census at midnight is 25 patients. In checking staffing, you find the following information:

Shift	*Staff on Duty*	*Hours Worked*
11 PM (1/30) to	2 RNs	8 hours each
7 AM (1/31)	1 LVN	8 hours
(last night)	1 CNA	8 hours each
7 AM to 3 PM	3 RNs	8 hours each
	2 LVNs	8 hours each
	1 CNA	8 hours
	1 ward clerk	8 hours
3 PM to 11 PM	2 RNs	8 hours each
	2 LVNs	8 hours each
	1 CNA	8 hours
	1 ward clerk	8 hours
11 PM (1/31)	2 RNs	8 hours each
to 7 AM (2/1)	2 LVNs	8 hours each
tonight	1 CNA	8 hours

Although you would ideally use 12 midnight to 12 midnight to compute the NCH/PPD for January 31, most staffing calculations based on traditional 8-hour

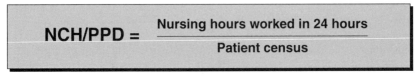

FIGURE 6.1 Standard formula for calculating nursing care hours (NCH) per patient day (PPD).

shifts are made beginning at 11 PM and ending at 11 PM the following night. Therefore, in this case, it would be acceptable to figure the NCH/PPD for January 31 using numerical data from the 11 PM to 7 AM shift last night and the 7 AM to 3 PM and 3 PM 11 PM shifts today.

The first step in this calculation requires a computation of total nursing care hours worked in 24 hours (including the ward clerk's hours). This can be calculated by multiplying the total number of staff on duty each shift by the hours each worked in their shift. Each shift total then is added together to get the total number of nursing hours worked in all three shifts or 24 hours:

$$
\begin{array}{rcl}
\text{Last night 11 PM to} \quad 7 \text{ AM} \quad 4 \text{ staff} \times 8 \text{ hours each} &=& 32 \text{ hours} \\
7 \text{ AM to} \quad 3 \text{ PM} \quad 7 \text{ staff} \times 8 \text{ hours each} &=& 56 \text{ hours} \\
3 \text{ PM to } 11 \text{ AM} \quad 6 \text{ staff} \times 8 \text{ hours each} &=& \underline{48 \text{ hours}} \\
&=& 136 \text{ hours}
\end{array}
$$

The nursing hours worked in 24 hours is 136 hours.

The second step in solving NCH/PPD requires that you divide the nursing hours worked in 24 hours by the patient census. The patient census in this case is 25. Therefore, 136 divided by 25 = 5.44.

The NCH/PPD for January 31 was 5.44, which is less than your budgeted NCH/PPD of 6.0. It would be possible to add up to 14 additional hours of nursing care in the next 24 hours and still maintain the budgeted nursing care hours standard. However, the unit manager must remember that the standard is flexible and that it would be necessary to assess the patient acuity and staffing mix to determine whether to add additional staff for February 1 and to determine what type of staff would be best and on what shift.

> ### ▶ LEARNING EXERCISE 6.2
>
> Calculate the NCH/PPD if the midnight census remained the same as above, but use the following as the number of hours worked:
>
> | | | |
> |---|---|---|
> | 12 midnight–12 noon | 2 RNs | 12 hours each |
> | | 2 LVNs | 12 hours each |
> | | 1 CNA | 12 hours |
> | | 1 ward clerk | 5 hours |
> | 12 noon–12 midnight | 3 RNs | 12 hours each |
> | | 2LVNs | 12 hours each |
> | | 1 CNA | 12 hours |
> | | 1 ward clerk | 11 hours |
>
> Now, calculate the NCH/PPD if the following staff were working.
>
> | | | |
> |---|---|---|
> | 12 midnight to 12 noon | 3 RNs | 12 hours each |
> | | 1 LVN | 12 hours |
> | 12 noon to 12 midnight | 2 RNs | 12 hours each |
> | | 1 LVN | 12 hours |
> | | 1 ward clerk | 4 hours |

The personnel budget includes actual worked time (also called *productive time* or *salary expense*) and time the organization pays the employee for not working (*nonproductive* or *benefit time*). Nonproductive time includes the cost of benefits, new employee orientation, employee turnover, sick and holiday time, and education time. It is critical that the unit manager monitor nonproductive and productive time.

The Operating Budget

The *operating* budget is the second area of expenditure that involves all managers. The operating budget reflects expenses that flex up or down in a predetermined manner to reflect variation in volume of service provided (Strasen, 1987). Included in this budget are such daily expenses as the cost of electricity, repairs and maintenance, and medical/surgical supplies.

Next to personnel costs, supplies are the second most significant component in the hospital budget. Barkholz (1985, p. 65) states "When labor costs are under control, supply buying and distribution becomes the focal point of a hospital's containment efforts." Effective unit managers should be alert to the types and quantities of supplies used in their unit. They also should understand the relationship of supplies used in the unit to patient mix, occupancy rate, technology requirements, and types of procedures performed on the unit; this way, they will be able to identify benchmarks for major supplies used on the unit (Dreisbach, 1994).

> ### LEARNING EXERCISE 6.3
>
> You are a unit manager in an acute care hospital. You are aware that staff occasionally leave at the end of the shift with forgotten hospital supplies in their pockets. You remember how often as a staff nurse you would unintentionally take home rolls of adhesive tape, syringes, pen lights, and bottles of lotion. Usually you remembered to return the items, but other times you did not.
>
> Recently, however, your budget has shown a dramatic and unprecedented increase in missing supplies, including gauze wraps, blood pressure cuffs, stethoscopes, surgical instruments, and personal hygiene kits. Although this increase represents only a fraction of your total operating budget, you feel it is necessary to identify the source of their use. An audit of patient charts and charges reveals that these items were not used in patient care.
>
> When you ask your charge nurses for an explanation, they reveal that a few employees have openly expressed that taking a few small supplies is, in effect, an expected and minor fringe benefit of employment. Your charge nurses do not feel that the problem is widespread, and they cannot *objectively* document which employees are involved in pilfering supplies. The charge nurses suggest that you ask all employees to document in writing when they see other employees taking supplies and then turn in the information to you anonymously for follow-up.
>
> Because supplies are such a major part of the operating budget, you feel that some action is indicated. You must determine what that action should be. Analyze your actions in terms of the desirable and undesirable effects on the employees involved in taking the supplies and those who are not. Is the *amount* of the fiscal debit in this situation a critical factor? Is it worth the time and energy that would be required to truly eliminate this problem?

Capital Budget

The third type of budget used by managers is the *capital* expenditure budget. Capital budgets plan for the purchase of buildings or major equipment, which include equipment that has a long life (usually greater than 5–7 years), is not used in daily operations, and is more expensive than operating supplies.

Capital budgets are composed of *long-term* planning, or a major acquisitions component, and a *short-term* budgeting component (Strasen, 1987). The long-term major acquisitions component outlines future replacement and organizational expansion that will exceed 1 year. Examples of these types of capital expenditures might include the acquisition of a computed tomography scanner or the renovation of a major wing in a hospital. The short-term component of the capital budget includes equipment purchases within the annual budget cycle, such as call-light systems, hospital beds, and medication carts.

Often the designation of capital equipment requires that the value of the equipment exceed a certain dollar amount. That dollar amount will vary from institution to institution, but $300 to $700 is common. Managers are usually required to complete specific capital equipment request forms either annually or semiannually and to justify their request.

COST EFFECTIVENESS AS A UNIT MANAGER'S GOAL

The desired result of careful fiscal planning is cost effectiveness. *Cost effective* does not mean cheap. It means getting the most for your money, or that the product is worth the price. Buying a very expensive piece of equipment may be cost effective if it can be shown that sufficient need exists for that equipment and that it was the best purchase to meet the need at that time. Cost effectiveness takes into account factors such as anticipated length of service, need for such a service, and availability of other alternatives.

BUDGETING METHODS

Budgeting is frequently classified according to how often it is done and the base on which budgeting takes place. Two of the most common budgeting methods are *incremental* budgeting, also called flat-percentile increase budgeting, and *zero-based* budgeting.

Incremental or the *flat-percentage increase* method is the simplest method for budgeting. By multiplying current year expenses by a certain figure, usually the inflation rate or consumer price index, this method arrives at the budget for the coming year. Although this method is simple, quick, and requires little budgeting expertise on the part of the manager, it is generally inefficient fiscally because there is no motivation to contain costs and no need to prioritize programs and services.

In comparison, managers who use zero-based budgeting must rejustify their program or needs every budgeting cycle. This method does not automatically assume that because a program has been funded in the past, it should continue to be funded. The use of a decision package to set funding priorities is a key feature of zero-based budgeting. Key components of decision packages are shown in Display 6.3.

Display 6.3   Key Components of Decision Packages in Zero-Based Budgeting

---

1. A listing of all current and proposed objectives or activities in the department
2. Alternative plans for carrying out these activities
3. The costs for each alternative
4. The advantages and disadvantages of continuing or discontinuing an activity

---

The following is an example of a decision package for implementing a mandatory hepatitis B vaccination program at a nursing school.

Objective: All nursing students will complete a hepatitis B vaccination series.

Driving forces: Hepatitis B is a severely disabling disease that carries a significant mortality. According to the National Centers for Disease Control and Prevention (NCDC), student nurses are at high risk for infection by hepatitis B. This vaccination will greatly reduce that risk.

The current vaccination series has been proven to have few serious side effects.

The nursing school risks liability if it does not follow NCDC recommendations to have all high-risk groups vaccinated.

Restraining Forces: The vaccination series costs $175 per student.

Some students do not want to have the vaccinations and feel requiring them to do so is a violation of free choice.

It is unclear whether the school is liable if a student experiences a damaging side effect as a result of the vaccinations.

The vaccine is not readily available in the rural area in which the school is located.

Alternative 1: Require the vaccinations, but because the school of nursing can not afford to pay for the cost of the series, require the students to pay for it.

Advantage: No cost to the school. All students receive the vaccinations.

Disadvantage: Many students cannot afford the cost of the vaccination and feel requiring it infringes on their right to control choices about their bodies.

Alternative 2: Do not require the vaccination series.

Advantage: No cost to anyone. Students have choice regarding whether or not to have the vaccinations and assume the responsibility of protecting their health themselves.

Disadvantage: Some nursing students will be unprotected against hepatitis B while working in a high-risk clinical setting.

Alternative 3: Require the vaccination series, but share the cost between the student and the school.

Advantage: Decreased cost to students. All students would be vaccinated.

Decision packages and zero-based budgeting are advantageous because they force managers to set priorities and use resources most efficiently. This rather lengthy and complex method also encourages participative management because information from peers and subordinates is needed to analyze adequately and prioritize the activities of each unit.

HEALTHCARE REIMBURSEMENT

Historically, healthcare institutions have placed little or no emphasis on budgeting. When budgeting was done, incremental budgeting was used. Because insurance carriers reimbursed fully on virtually a limitless basis, there was not a great deal of motivation to save costs and budget effectively. Organizations found it unnecessary to justify costs or prove that their services met client needs because they were not required to justify their charges. Reimbursement was based on costs incurred to provide the service with no ceiling placed on the amount that could be charged. High-quality care was the desired goal, and little thought was given to how raising costs would impact on total healthcare expenditures (Neumann, Suver, & Zelman, 1984).

With the advent of Medicare and Medicaid in the 1960s, healthcare costs sky-

 LEARNING EXERCISE 6.4

Given the following objective, develop a decision package to aid you in fiscal priority setting.

Objective

To have reliable, economic, and convenient transportation when you enter nursing school in 3 months.

Additional Information:

You currently have no car and rely on public transportation, which is inexpensive and reliable but not very convenient. Your current financial resources are limited, although you could probably qualify for a car loan if your parents were willing to cosign the loan. Your nursing school's policy states that you must have a car available to commute to clinical agencies outside the immediate area. You know that this policy is not enforced and that some students do carpool to clinical assignments.

Assignment: Identify at least 3 alternatives that will meet your objective. Choose the best alternative based on its advantages and disadvantages that you identify. You may embellish information presented in the case to help your problem-solving.

rocketed. As a result, the government began establishing regulations requiring organizations to justify the need for services and to monitor the quality of services. Healthcare providers were forced for the first time to submit budgets and justify costs. This new "big brother" surveillance and existence of external controls has had a tremendous effect on the industry.

The advent of diagnostic-related groups (DRGs) in the early 1980s added to the need for monitoring cost containment. DRGs were predetermined payment schedules that reflected historical costs for treatment of specific patient conditions. The first version of the DRG system included 383 categories, which were redefined because of the excessive number of outliers, or patients who did not fit into any category (Marriner-Tomey, 1992). By 1989, 468 DRGs or "product lines" had been established (Omachonu & Nanda, 1989). In October 1990, 13 new DRGs were proposed (Grimaldi, 1990). With DRGs, hospitals join the *prospective payment system* (PPS), whereby they receive a specified amount for each Medicare of Medicaid patient's admission, regardless of the actual cost of care.

As a result of the PPS and the need to contain costs, the length of stay for most hospital admissions has decreased greatly. Many argue that quality standards have been lowered and that patients are being discharged before they are ready. The nurse-leader is responsible for recognizing when cost containment begins to impinge on patient safety and taking appropriate action to guarantee at least the minimum standard of care. Chapter 17 further discusses the PPS and its impact on quality control.

Today, a significant number of patients treated in hospitals and other agencies are eligible for some type of federal or state healthcare reimbursement. Accompanying this funding has come an increase in regulations for facilities treating these patients and a system that rewards cost containment. Healthcare providers are encountering financial crises as they attempt to meet unlimited healthcare needs and services with limited fiscal reimbursement. Competition has intensified, driving prices down; technology has evolved, pushing prices up; outpatient services are now emphasized over inpatient care; and utilization controls have increased (Hollander, Smith, & Barron, 1992). Rapidly changing federal and state reimbursement policies make long-range budgeting and planning very difficult for such facilities.

The Health Maintenance Organization (HMO) Act of 1973, which authorized the spending of $375 million over 5 years to set up and evaluate HMOs in communities across the country, also has had a tremendous impact on healthcare reimbursement. HMOs provide healthcare in an organized system to subscribing members in a geographical area with an predetermined set of basic and preventive supplemental health maintenance and treatment services for a fixed, prepaid charge (Streff, 1994). Although HMOs were originally created in the 1970s as an alternative to traditional health insurance plans, some of the largest private insurers, including Blue Cross/Blue Shield, have created HMOs within their organization while maintaining their traditional indemnity plans. Other companies, such as Travelers, Aetna, and John Hancock, also have created such systems (Streff, 1994).

Another way that hospitals and physicians have coped with constantly changing reimbursement levels while ensuring an adequate population for services is to contract to become preferred providers. Preferred provider organizations (PPOs) render services on a fee-for-service basis. Financial incentives are offered to consumers (they pay less) when the preferred provider is used.

The establishment of the PPS, PPOs, and HMOs has led to the development of managed care. Broadly defined, managed care refers to any method of monitoring, tracking, and screening the use of health services (Kosterlitz, 1993). It also focuses on prevention, coordinates patient care, requires doctors to adhere to proven treatments, and keeps track of the results. The net effect, proponents maintain, is better care at a lower cost (Kosterlitz, 1993). This move to integrated health plans, in which doctors, hospitals, and insurers join forces to manage care, is a cornerstone of the "managed competition" approach to healthcare reform, suggested in President Clinton's Health Security Plan (1993) and other proposals now being considered.

Another aspect complicating healthcare reimbursement, through the PPS, an HMO, or a PPO, is that clear and comprehensive documentation of the need for services and actual services provided is mandatory. Provision of service no longer guarantees reimbursement. Thus, the fiscal accountability of nurses goes beyond planning and implementing; it includes responsible recording and communication of activities (Campbell & Dowd, 1993).

Maintaining quality care in an atmosphere of reduced resources strains the ingenuity, decision-making direction, and future planning of all managers (Vestal, 1988). It is critical in a cost-containment environment to ensure revenue collection for services rendered. To achieve nursing clinical objectives, precise financial management is not a goal, it is a requirement (Campbell & Dowd, 1993).

INTEGRATING LEADERSHIP ROLES AND MANAGEMENT FUNCTIONS IN FISCAL PLANNING

Managers must understand fiscal terminology, be aware of their budgetary responsibilities, and be accountable to the organization for maintaining a cost-effective unit. The ability to forecast unit fiscal needs with sensitivity to the organization's economic, social, and legislative climate is a high-level management function. In budgeting, managers also must be able to articulate unit needs to ensure sufficient funds for adequate nursing staff, supplies, and equipment. Finally, managers must be skillful in the monitoring aspects of budget control.

Leadership skills allow the manager to involve in fiscal planning all individuals who will be affected by the plan. Other leadership skills required in fiscal planning include flexibility, creativity, and vision regarding future needs. The skilled leader is able to anticipate budget constraints and act proactively.

In contrast, many managers allow budget constraints to dictate alternatives. In an age of inadequate fiscal resources, the leader is creative in identifying alternatives to meet client needs. The skilled leader, however, also ensures that cost containment does not jeopardize client safety.

Leaders also are assertive, articulate individuals who ensure that their department's budgeting receives a fair hearing. Because leaders can delineate unit budgetary needs in an assertive, professional, and proactive manner, they generally obtain a fair distribution of resources for their unit.

KEY CONCEPTS

▼ Fiscal planning, as in all types of planning, is a learned skill that improves with practice.

▼ Historically, nursing management played a limited role in determining resource allocation in healthcare institutions.

▼ Today, the nursing budget can account for up to 90% of the organization's total expenses; therefore, participation in fiscal planning is viewed as a fundamental and powerful tool for nursing.

▼ A *budget* is defined as a plan that uses numerical data and predicts an organization's activities for a set time.

▼ The desired outcome of budgeting is maximal use of resources to meet organizational short- and long-term needs.

▼ The budget's value to the institution is directly related to its accuracy.

▼ A budget is at best a forecast or prediction; it is a plan and not a rule. Therefore, a budget must be flexible and open to ongoing evaluation and revision.

▼ *Fixed* expenses do not vary with volume, while *variable* expenses do.

▼ *Controllable* expenses can be varied by the manager. *Noncontrollable* expenses cannot be varied.

▼ Three types of expenditures are of primary importance to the manager: the *personnel, operating,* and *capital* budgets.

▼ The largest expenditure is in workforce because healthcare is labor intensive.

▼ Most staffing is based on a predetermined standard that varies with each unit, department, organization, or service.

▼ Personnel budgets include actual worked time, *productive time* or *salary expense,* and time the organization pays the employee for not working, *nonproductive* or *benefit time.*

▼ The operating budget reflects expenses that flex up or down in a predetermined manner to reflect variation in volume of service provided.

▼ After to personnel costs, supplies are the second most significant component in the hospital budget.

▼ Capital budgets plan for the purchase of buildings or major equipment. This includes equipment that has a long life (usually greater than 5 years), is not used daily, and is more expensive than operating supplies.

▼ A budgeting cycle that is set for 12 months is a *fiscal-year budget.*

▼ A budget that is predicted too far in advance is open to greater error. If the budget is short sighted, compensating for unexpected major expenses or capital equipment purchases may be difficult.

▼ *Cost effective* does not mean cheap; it means getting the most for your money or that the product is worth the price.

▼ *Incremental budgeting* uses current year expenses and multiplies them by a certain figure, usually the inflation rate or consumer price index, to arrive at the budget for the coming year.

▼ Managers must rejustify their program or needs every budgeting cycle in *zero-based* budgeting. Using a "decision package" to set funding priorities is a key feature of zero-based budgeting.

▼ With the advent of state and federal reimbursement for healthcare in the 1960s, providers were forced to submit budgets and costs to payers that more accurately reflected their actual cost to provide these services.

▼ Cost containment refers to effective and efficient delivery of services while generating needed revenues for continued organizational productivity.

▼ DRGs, developed in the early 1980s, are predetermined payment schedules that reflect historical costs for treatment of specific patient conditions.

▼ With DRGs, hospitals join the PPS, whereby they receive a specified amount for each Medicare or Medicaid patient's admission, regardless of the actual cost of care.

▼ HMOs provide healthcare in an organized system to subscribing members in a geographical area with a predetermined set of basic and preventive supplemental health maintenance and treatment services for a fixed, prepaid charge.

▼ PPOs render services on a fee-for-service basis. Financial incentives are offered to consumers (they pay less) when the preferred provider is used.

▼ Managed care is broadly defined as any method of monitoring, tracking, and screening the use of health services that focuses on prevention, coordinates patient care, requires doctors to adhere to proven treatments, and keeps track of the results.

ADDITIONAL LEARNING EXERCISES

Learning Exercise 6.5

One of your goals as the Unit manager of a critical care unit is to prepare all your nurses to be certified in advanced cardiac life support. You currently have five staff nurses who need this certification.

You can hire someone to teach this class locally and rent a facility for $800.00; however, the cost will be taken out of the travel and educational budget for the unit, and this will leave you short for the rest of the fiscal year. It also will be a time-consuming effort because you must coordinate the preparation and reproduction of educational materials needed for the course and make arrangements for the rental facility.

A certification class also will be provided in the near future in a large metropolitan city approximately 150 miles from the hospital. The cost per participant will be $200.00. In addition, there would be travel and lodging expenses.

Assignment: You have several decisions to make. Should the class be held locally? If so, how will you organize it? Are you going to require your staff to have this certification or merely highly recommend that they do so? If it is required, will the unit pay the costs of the certification? Will you pay the staff nurses their regular hourly wage for attending the class on regularly scheduled work hours? Can this certification be cost effective? Use group process in some way to make your decision.

Learning Exercise 6.6
(From Marquis & Huston, 1994.)

You are the director of the local aging agency, which cares for ill and well elderly. You are funded by a private corporation grant, which requires matching of city and state funds. You have received a letter in the mail today from the state that says state funding will be cut by $15,000.00, effective in 2 weeks, when the state's budget year begins. This means that your private funding also will be cut $15,000.00 for a total revenue loss of $30,000.00. It is impossible at this time to seek alternative funding sources.

In reviewing your agency budget, you note that, as in many healthcare agencies, your budget is labor intensive. More than 80% of your budget is attributable to personnel costs, and you feel that the cuts must come from within the personnel budget. You may reduce the client population that you serve, although you do not really want to do so. You briefly discuss this communication with your staff, and no one is willing to reduce their hours voluntarily, and no one is planning to terminate their employment at any time in the near future.

Assignment: Given the following brief description of your position and each of your five employees, decide how you will meet the new budget restrictions. What is the rationale for your choice? What decision do you believe will result in the least disruption of the agency and of the employees in the agency? Should group decision making be involved in fiscal decisions such as this one? Can fiscal decisions such as this be made without value judgments?

> Your position is project director. As the project director, you coordinate all the day-to-day activities in the agency. You also are involved in long-term planning, and a major portion of your time is allotted to securing future funding for the agency to continue. As the project director, you have the authority to hire and fire employees. You are in your early 30s and have a master's degree in nursing and health administration. You enjoy your job and feel you have done well in this position since you started 4 years ago. Your yearly salary as a full-time employee is $48,000.
>
> Employee #1 is Mrs. Potter. Mrs. Potter has worked at the agency since it started 7 years ago. She is an RN with 30 years experience working with the geriatric population in public health nursing, care facilities, and private duty. She plans to retire in 7 years and travel with her independently wealthy husband. Mrs. Potter has a great deal of expertise she can share with your staff, although at times you feel that she overshadows your authority because of her experience and your young age. Her yearly salary as a full-time employee is $40,000.
>
> Employee #2 is Mr. Boone. Mr. Boone has B.S. degrees in both nursing and dietetics and food management. As an RN and RD, he brings a unique expertise to your staff, which is highly needed when dealing with a chronically ill and improperly nourished elderly population. In the 6 months since he joined your agency, he has proven to be a dependable, well-liked, and highly respected member of your staff. His yearly salary as a full-time employee is $36,000.
>
> Employee #3 is Miss Barns. Miss Barns is the receptionist/secretary in the agency. In addition to all the traditional secretarial duties, such as typing, filing, and transcription of dictation, she screens incoming telephone calls and directs individuals who come to the agency for information. Her efficiency is a tremendous attribute to the agency. Her full-time yearly salary is $16,000.
>
> Employee #4 is Mrs. Lake. Mrs. Lake is an LPN/LVN with 15 years of work

experience in a variety of healthcare agencies. She is especially empathetic to patient needs. Although her technical nursing skills are also good, her caseload frequently is more focused around elderly who need companionship and emotional support. She does well at patient teaching because of her outstanding listening and communication skills. Many of your clients request her by name. She is a single mother, supporting six children, and you are aware that she has great difficulty in meeting her personal financial obligations. Her full-time yearly salary is $24,000.

Employee #5 is Mrs. Long. Mrs. Long is an "elderly help aide." She has completed nurse aid training, although her primary role in the agency is to assist well elderly with bathing, meal preparation, driving, and shopping. The time Mrs. Long spends in performing basic care has decreased the average visit time for each member of your staff by 30%. She is widowed and feels that she needs this job to meet her social and esteem needs. Financially, her resources are adequate, and the money she earns is not a motivator for working. Mrs. Long works 3 days a week, and her yearly salary is $10,000.

Learning Exercise 6.7

Jane is the supervisor of a small cardiac rehabilitation program. The program includes inpatient cardiac teaching and an outpatient exercise rehabilitation program. Because of limited reimbursement by third-party insurance payers for patient education, there has been no direct charge for inpatient education. Outpatient program participants pay $120/month to attend three 1-hour sessions per week, although the revenue generated from the outpatient program still leaves an overall budget deficit for the program of approximately $1200/month.

Today, Jane is summoned to the Associate Administrator's office to discuss her budget for the upcoming year. At this meeting, the administrator states that the hospital is experiencing extreme financial difficulties due to DRGs and the prospective payment system. He states that the program must become self-supporting in the next fiscal year, or services must be cut.

On returning to her office, Jane decided to make a list of several alternatives for problem solving and to analyze each for driving and restraining factors. These alternatives include the following:

1. Implement a charge for inpatient education. This would eliminate the budget deficit, but the cost would probably have to be borne by the patient. (Implication: Only patients with adequate fiscal resources would select to receive vital education.)
2. Reduce department staffing. There are currently three staff in the department, and it would be impossible to maintain the same level or quality of services if staffing was cut.
3. Reduce or limit services. The inpatient education program or educational programs associated with the outpatient program could be eliminated. These are both considered valuable aspects of the program.
4. The fee for the outpatient program could be increased. This could easily result in a decrease in program participation, because many outpatient program participants do not have insurance coverage for their participation.

Assignment: Identify at least five program goals, and prioritize them as you would if you were Jane. Based on the priorities you have established, which alternative would you select? Explain your choice.

Learning Exercise 6.8

You are a single parent of two children younger than 5 years and are currently employed as a pediatric office nurse. You enjoy your job, but your long-term career goal is to become a pediatric nurse practitioner, and you have been taking courses part time preparing to enter graduate school in the fall. Your application for admission has been accepted, and the next cycle for admissions will not be for another 3 years. Your recent divorce and assignment of sole custody of the children has resulted in a need to reconsider your plan.

Restraining forces: You had originally planned to reduce your work hours to part time to allow time for classes and studying, but this will be fiscally impossible now. You also recognize that tuition and educational expenses will place a strain on your budget even if you continue to work full time. You have not looked into the availability of scholarships or loans and have missed the deadline for the upcoming fall. In addition, you have not yet overcome your anxiety and guilt about leaving your small children for even more time than you do now.

Driving forces: You also recognize, however, that gaining certification as a pediatric nurse practitioner should result in a large salary increase over what you are able to make as an office nurse and that it would allow you to provide resources for your children in the future that you otherwise may be unable to do. You also recognize that while you are not dissatisfied with your current job, you have a great deal of ability that has gone untapped and that your potential for long-term job satisfaction is low.

Assignment: Fiscal planning always requires priority setting, and often this priority setting is determined by personal values. Priority setting is made even more difficult when there are conflicting values. Identify the values involved in this case. Develop a plan that addresses these value conflicts and has the most desirable outcomes.

REFERENCES:

Barkholz, D. (1985). Cost consciousness gives managers a chance to standardize, centralize. *Modern Health Care, 15*(15), 65–66.

Campbell, B. (1992). Assessment of attitudes toward cost-containment needs. *Nursing Economics, 10*(6), 397–401.

Campbell, J. M., & Dowd, T. T. (1993). Success stories—Capturing scarce resources: Documentation and communication. *Nursing Economics, 11*(2), 103–106.

Clinton, W. (1993). *The president's health security plan.* New York: Times Books, Random House.

Corley, M. C., & Satterwhite, B. E. (1993). Forecasting ambulatory clinic workload to facilitate budgeting. *Nursing Economics, 11*(2), 77–81.

Decker, P. J., & Sullivan, E. J. (1992). *Nursing administration.* Norwalk, CT: Appleton and Lange.

Douglass, L. M. & Bevis, E. O. (1983). *Nursing management and leadership in action* (4th ed.). St. Louis: CV Mosby.

Dreisbach, A. M. (1994). A structured approach to expert financial management: A financial development plan for nurse managers. *Nursing Economics, 12*(3), 131–139.

Grimaldi, P. I. (1990). Thirteen new drugs and other proposed changes. *Nursing Management, 21*(7), 32–34.

Hollander, S. F., Smith, M., & Barron, J. (1992). Cost reductions part I: An operations improvement process. *Nursing Economics, 10*(5), 325–330.

Kao, E. P. C., & Pokladnik, F. M. (1978). Incorporating exogenous factors in adaptive forecasting of hospital census. *Management Science, 24,* 1677–1686.

Kelly, L. Y. (1992). *The nursing experience* (2nd ed.). New York: McGraw Hill.

Kosterlitz, J. (1993). All together now. *National Journal,* Nov. 13.

Marquis, B., & Huston, C. (1994). *Management decision making for nurses: 101 Case Studies* (2nd ed.). Philadelphia: J.B. Lippincott.

Marriner-Tomey, A. (1992). *Guide to nursing management* (4th ed.). St. Louis, MO: C.V. Mosby.

Neumann, B., Suver, J., & Zelman, W. (1984). *Financial management: Concepts and applications for health care providers.* Owings Mills: National Health Publishing.

Omachonu, V. K., & Nanda, R. (1989). Measuring productivity: outcome vs. output. *Nursing Management, 20*(4), 35–38, 40.

Strasen, L. (1987). *Key business skills for nurse managers.* Philadelphia: J.B. Lippincott.

Streff, M. B. (1994). Third-party reimbursement issues for advanced practice nurses in the '90s. In J. Mc Closkey & H. Grace (Eds.), *Current issues in nursing* (4th ed.). St. Louis: C.V. Mosby.

Sullivan, E. J., & Decker, P. J. (1988). *Effective management in nursing* (2nd ed.). Menlo Park, CA: Addison Wesley

Wieseke, A., & Bantz, D. (1992). Economic awareness of registered nurses employed by hospitals. *Nursing Economics, 10*(6), 406–412.

Zander, K. (1994). Nurses and case management. In J. Mc Closkey & H. Grace (Eds.), *Current issues in nursing* (4th ed.). St. Louis: C.V. Mosby.

BIBLIOGRAPHY

Applegeet, C. J. (1989). AORN's budget-planning and forecasting uncover future needs. *Association of Operating Room Nurses Journal, 50*(2), 212.

Bednar, B., Neff, M., & Randolph, G. (1988). Balancing financial principles and cost Containment for nurse managers. *American Nephrology Nurses Association Journal, 15*(6), 345–348

Cockerill, R., Pallas, L. O., Bolley, H., & Pink, G. (1993). Measuring nursing workload for case costing. *Nursing Economics, 11*(6), 342–349.

Coulter, S. J., Nadzam, D. M., & Caslow, A. Y. (1988). New leadership: A chance to analyze resource allocation. *Nursing Administration Quarterly, 13*(1), 19–25.

Francisco, P. D. (1989). Flexible budgeting and variance analysis. *Nursing Management, 20*(11), 40–43.

Huckabay, L. M. D. (1988). Allocation of resources and identification of issues in determining the cost of nursing services. *Nursing Administration Quarterly, 13*(1), 72–82.

Kersey, J. H. Jr. (1988). Increasing the nursing manager's fiscal responsibility. *Nursing Management, 19*(10), 30–32

Manthey, M. (1992). Budgeting: Controlling the ominous art. *Nursing Management, 23*(3), 14.

Masson, V. (1988). Slicing the salary pie. *Nursing Outlook, 36*(6), 264.

McAlvanah, M. (1989). Fiscal planning: The capital budget. *Pediatric Nursing, 15*(1), 70.

McGrail, G. R. (1988). Budgets: An underused resource. *Journal of Nursing Administration, 18*(11), 25–31.

Neff, M. L. (1988). General concepts of incremental and zero based budgeting. *American Nephrology Nurses Association Journal, 15*(6), 342–344.

Rosenstein, A. H., & Paluso, T. A. (1989). Effect of reimbursement changes on hospital based units: A case example. *Nursing Economics, 7*(1), 18–23.

Smeltzer, C. H., & Hyland, J. (1989). A working plan to understand and control financial pressures. *Nursing Economics, 7*(4), 208–214.

Solovy, A. (1989). Health care in the 1990's: Forecasts by top analysts. *Hospitals, 63*(14), 34–36

Swansburg, R. C., & Sowell, R. L. (1992). A Model for costing and pricing nursing service. *Nursing Management, 23*(2), 33–36.

Wilburn, D. (1992). Budget response to volume variability. *Nursing Management, 23*(2), 42–44.

UNIT III

ROLES AND FUNCTIONS IN ORGANIZING

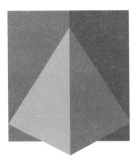

CHAPTER 7

Organizational Structure

The preceding unit provides a background in planning, the first phase of the management process. Organizing follows planning as the second phase and is explored in this unit. In the organizing phase, relationships are defined, procedures outlined, equipment readied, and tasks assigned (Marquis & Huston, 1994). Organizing also involves establishing a formal structure that provides the best possible coordination or use of resources to accomplish unit objectives.

This chapter looks at how the structure of an organization facilitates or impedes communication, flexibility, and job satisfaction. Chapter 8 examines the role of authority and power in organizations and how power may be used to meet individual, unit, and organizational goals; the last chapter in this unit looks at how human resources can be organized into groups to accomplish work.

Fayol (1949) suggested that an organization is formed when the number of workers is large enough to require a supervisor. Organizations are necessary because they accomplish more work than could be done by individual effort.

Because people spend most of their lives in social, personal, and professional organizations, they need to understand how they are structured. Organizational structure refers to the way in which a group is formed, its lines of communication, and its means for channeling authority and making decisions. Each organization has a formal and an informal organizational structure. The formal structure is generally highly planned and publicized, whereas the informal structure is unplanned and often concealed (Douglass, 1992). Formal structure, through departmentalization

Bessie L. Marquis and Carol J. Huston:
LEADERSHIP ROLES AND MANAGEMENT FUNCTIONS IN NURSING, 2nd ed.
Lippincott-Raven Publishers © 1996

and work division, provides a framework for defining managerial authority, responsibility, and accountability. In a well-defined formal structure, roles and functions are well defined and systematically arranged, different people have differing roles, and rank and hierarchy are evident (Ellis & Hartley, 1995).

Informal structure is generally social in nature with blurred or shifting lines of authority and accountability. Individuals need to be aware that informal authority and lines of communication exist in every group, even when they are never formally acknowledged (Marquis & Huston, 1994). The primary emphasis of this chapter, however, is on the leadership roles and management functions associated with formal organizational structure (Display 7.1).

Display 7.1 Leadership Roles and Management Functions Associated With Organizational Structure

Leadership Roles

1. Evaluates the organizational structure frequently to determine if management positions can be eliminated to reduce the chain of command
2. Encourages employees to follow the chain of command and gives counseling and guidance to enable them to do so
3. Supports personnel in advisory (staff) positions
4. Models responsibility and accountability for subordinates
5. Assists nursing staff to see how their roles are congruent with and complement the common organizational task
6. Facilitates informal group structure
7. Encourages upward communication
8. Explains organizational culture to subordinates
9. Counsels employees who do not follow chain of command

Management Functions

1. Is knowledgeable about the organization's structure, including personal and department authority and responsibilities within that structure
2. Provides the staff with an accurate unit organizational chart and assists with interpretation
3. When possible, maintains unity of command
4. Clarifies unity of command when there is confusion
5. Follows appropriate subordinate complaints upward through chain of command
6. Establishes an appropriate span of control
7. Is knowledgeable about the organization's culture
8. Uses the informal organization to meet organizational goals

ORGANIZATIONAL THEORY

Max Weber, a German social scientist mentioned in Chapter 1, is known as the father of organizational theory. Generally acknowledged to have developed the most comprehensive classic formulation on the characteristics of bureaucracy, Weber wrote from the vantage point of a manager, instead of from that of a scholar.

During the 1920s, Weber saw the growth of the large-scale organization and correctly predicted that this growth required a more formalized set of procedures for administrators. His statement on bureaucracy, published after his death, is still the most influential statement on the subject.

Weber postulated three "ideal types" of authority or reasons why individuals throughout history have obeyed their rulers. One of these, "legal-rational" authority, was based on a belief in the legitimacy of the pattern of normative rules and the rights of those elevated to authority under such rules to issue commands. Obedience then was owed to the legally established impersonal set of rules, rather than to a personal ruler. Therefore, power is vested in the office, rather than in the person who occupies it. It is this type of authority that is the basis for Weber's concept of bureaucracy.

Weber argued that the great virtue of bureaucracy—indeed, perhaps its defining characteristic—was that it was an institutional method for applying general rules to specific cases, thereby making the actions of management fair and predictable. Other characteristics of bureaucracies as identified by Weber include the following:

1. A clear division of labor; that is, all work must be divided into units that can be undertaken by individuals or groups of individuals competent to perform those tasks.
2. A well-defined hierarchy of authority in which superiors are separated from subordinates; on the basis of this hierarchy, remuneration for work is dispensed, authority recognized, privileges allotted, and promotions awarded.
3. Impersonal rules and impersonality of interpersonal relationships. In other words, bureaucrats are not free to act in any way they please. Bureaucratic rules provide systematic control of superiors over subordinates, thus limiting the opportunities for arbitrariness and personal favoritism.
4. A system of procedures for dealing with work situations (ie, regular activities to get a job done) must exist.
5. A system of rules covering the rights and duties of position incumbents must be in place.
6. Selection for employment and promotion is based on technical competence.

Bureaucracy was the ideal weapon to harness and routinize the energy and prolific production of the industrial revolution. Weber's work did not, however, consider the complexity of managing organizations in the 1990s. Weber wrote during an era when worker motivation was taken for granted and his simplification of manager and employee roles did not examine the bilateral relationships between employee and manager prevalent in most organizations today. Modern management theorists have learned much about human behavior, and most organizations have modified their structures to reduce rigidity and impersonality. However, almost 100 years after Weber's findings, components of bureaucratic structure continue to be found in the design of most large organizations.

COMPONENTS OF ORGANIZATIONAL STRUCTURE

Weber also is credited with the development of the *organization chart* to depict an organization's structure. Because the organization chart (Fig. 7.1) is a picture of an organization, the knowledgeable manager can derive much information by reading the chart. An organization chart can help identify roles and their expectations. By observing such elements as which departments report directly to the chief executive officer (CEO), the novice manager can make some inferences about the organization. For instance, an organization that has the top-level nursing manager reporting to an assistant executive officer rather than to the CEO might indicate the amount of value that organization places on nursing. Managers who understand an organization's structure and relationships will be able to expedite decision making and have a greater understanding of the organizational environment.

The organization chart defines formal relationships within the institution. Formal relationships, lines of communication, and authority are depicted on a chart by unbroken lines. These *line positions* can be shown by either horizontal or vertical unbroken lines. Horizontal unbroken lines represent communication between individuals with similar spheres of responsibility and power but different functions. Vertical unbroken lines between positions denote the official *chain of command*, the formal paths of communication and authority. Those having the greatest decision making and authority are located at the top; those with the least are at the bottom. The level of position on the chart also signifies status and power.

Dotted or broken lines on the organization chart represent *staff* positions. Because these positions are advisory, a staff member provides information and assistance to the manager but has limited organizational authority. Used to increase his or her sphere of influence, staff positions enable a manager to handle more activities and interactions than would otherwise be possible. These positions also provide for specialization that would be impossible for any one manager to achieve alone. Although staff positions can make line personnel more effective, organizations can function without them.

Advisory (staff) positions do not have inherent legitimate authority. Clinical specialists and in-service directors in staff positions lack the authority that accompanies a line relationship. Accomplishing the role expectations in a staff position is therefore more difficult because little authority accompanies it.

Unity of command is indicated by the vertical solid line between individuals. This concept is best described as one person/one boss: Each person has one manager to whom they report and to whom they are responsible. This greatly simplifies the manager/employee relationship because the employee needs only to maintain a minimum number of relationships and accept the influence of only one person as his or her immediate supervisor.

Unity of command is difficult to maintain in some large healthcare organiza-

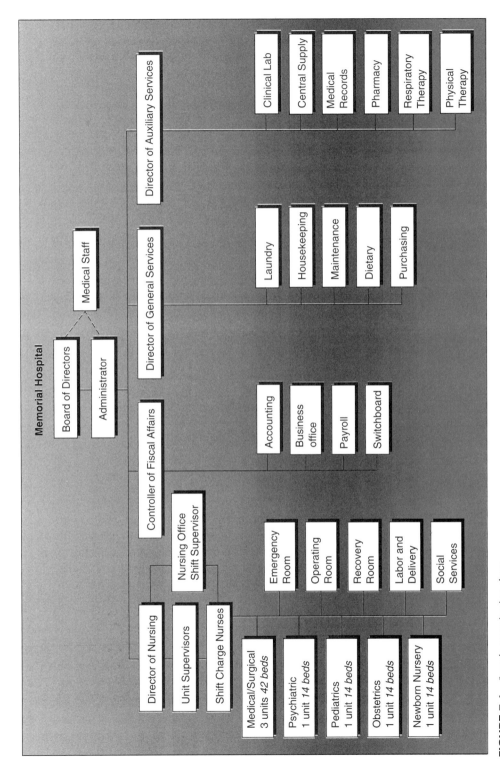

FIGURE 7.1 Sample organization chart.

tions because the nature of healthcare requires a multidisciplinary approach. Nurses frequently feel as though they have many bosses, including their immediate supervisor, their patient, the patient's family, central administration, and the doctor. All have some input in directing a nurse's work. Weber was correct when he determined that a lack of unity of command results in some conflict and lost productivity. This is demonstrated frequently when healthcare workers become confused about unity of command.

Span of control also can be determined from the organization chart. The number of people reporting to any manager represents that manager's span of control and determines the number of interactions expected of him or her. Theorists are divided on the question of the optimum span of control for any one manager. Quantitative formulas for determining the optimum span of control have been attempted; suggested ranges are from 3 to 50 employees. When determining an optimum span of control in an organization, the manager's abilities, employees' maturity, task complexity, geographic location, and level in the organization at which the work occurs must all be considered. The number of people reporting to any one supervisor must be the number that maximizes productivity and worker satisfaction. Too many people reporting to a single manager delays decision making, while too few results in an inefficient, top-heavy organization.

Until the last decade, the principle of narrow spans of control at top levels of management, with slightly wider spans at other levels was widely accepted. Now, with increased financial pressures on healthcare organizations to remain fiscally solvent, many have found it necessary to increase their spans of control (Pabst, 1993). As a result, many organizations have reduced the number of administrative levels in the organization.

In large organizations, several levels of managers often exist. *Top-level managers* look at the organization as a whole, coordinating internal and external influences, and generally make decisions with few guidelines or structures. Examples of top-level managers include the organization's CEO and the highest nursing administrator. Current nomenclature for top-level nurse-managers varies; this individual might be called vice president of nursing or patient care services, nurse administrator, director of nursing, chief nurse, assistant administrator of patient care services, or chief nurse administrator (CNO). Some top-level nurse-managers may be responsible for non-nursing departments. For example, a top-level nurse-manager might oversee the respiratory, physical, and occupational therapy departments in addition to all nursing departments. Likewise, the CEO might have various titles, such as president or director. It is necessary to remember only that the CEO is the organization's highest ranking individual and the top-level nurse-manager is its highest ranking nurse.

Responsibilities common to top-level managers include determining the organizational philosophy, setting policy, and creating goals and priorities for resource allocation. Top-level managers have a greater need for leadership skills and are not as involved in routine daily operations as are lower level managers.

Middle-level managers coordinate the efforts of lower levels of the hierarchy and are the channel between lower and top-level managers. Middle-level managers carry out day-to-day operations but are still involved in some long-term planning and in establishing unit policies. Examples of middle-level managers include nursing supervisors, nurse-managers, head nurses, and unit managers.

First-level managers are concerned with their specific unit's work flow. They deal with immediate problems in the unit's daily operations, with organizational needs, and with personal needs of the employee. The effectiveness of first-level managers tremendously affects the organization. First-level managers need good management skills. Because they are working so closely with patients and healthcare teams, first-level managers also have an excellent opportunity to practice leadership roles that will greatly influence productivity and subordinate satisfaction. Examples of first-level managers include primary care nurses, team leaders, case managers, and charge nurses. In many organizations, every registered nurse is considered a first-level manager. All nurses in every situation must manage themselves and those under their care.

One of the leadership responsibilities of organizing is to examine periodically the number of individuals in the chain of command. Organizations frequently add levels until there are too many managers. Therefore, the nursing manager should carefully weigh the advantages and disadvantages of adding a management level. For example, does having a charge nurse on each shift aid or hinder decision making? Does having this nurse solve or create problems?

Centrality refers to the location of a position on an organization chart where frequent and various types of communication occur. Centrality is determined by organizational distance. Employees with small relative organizational distance are able to receive more information than those who are more peripherally located. This is why the middle manager often has a broader view of the organization than other levels of management. A middle manager position has a large degree of centrality because it receives information upward, downward, and horizontally.

Because all communication involves a sender and a receiver, messages may not be received clearly because of the sender's hierarchical position. Similarly, status and power often influence the receiver's ability to hear information accurately.

An example of status' affect on communication is found in the "principal syndrome." Most people can recall panic at being summoned to the principal's office. Thoughts of "what did I do?" travel though one's mind. Even adults find discomfort in communicating with certain people who hold high status. This may be fear or awe, but both interfere with clear communication. The difficulties with upward and downward communication are more fully discussed in Chapter 15.

It is important then to be cognizant of how the formal structure affects overall relationships and communication. This is especially true because organizations change their structure frequently, resulting in new communication lines and reporting relationships. Unless one understands how to interpret a formal organization chart, confusion and anxiety will result when organizations are restructured.

Decision Making Within the Organizational Hierarchy

The decision-making hierarchy, or pyramid, is often referred to as a *scalar chain*. By reviewing the organization chart in Figure 7.1, it is possible to determine where decisions are made within the management hierarchy. Although every manager has

LEARNING EXERCISE 7.1

This learning exercise refers to the organization chart in Figure 7.1. Because Memorial Hospital is expanding, the board of directors has made several changes that require modification of the organization chart. The directors have just announced the following changes.

1. The name of the hospital has been changed to Memorial General Hospital and Medical Center.
2. State approval has been granted for open-heart surgery.
3. One of the existing medical-surgical units will be remodeled and will become two critical care units (one six-bed coronary and open-heart unit and one six-bed trauma and surgical unit).
4. A part-time medical director will be responsible for medical care on each critical care unit.
5. The hospital administrator's title has been changed to executive director.
6. An associate hospital administrator has been hired.
7. A new hospital-wide educational department has been created.
8. The old pediatric unit will be remodeled into a seven-bed pediatric wing and a seven-bed rehabilitation unit.
9. The nursing director's new title is vice president of patient care services.

Assignment: If the hospital is viewed as a large, open system, it is possible to visualize areas where problems might occur. In particular, it is necessary to identify changes anticipated in the nursing department and how these changes will affect the organization as a whole.

Depict all these changes on the old organization chart, delineating both staff and line positions. Give the rationale for your decisions. Why did you place the education department where you did? What was the reasoning in your division of authority? Where do you feel there might be potential conflict in the new organization chart? Why?

some decision-making authority, its type and level are determined by the manager's position on the chart.

In organizations with *centralized decision making,* decisions are made by a few managers at the top of the hierarchy. Thus, the more centralized the decision making, the longer the scalar chain.

Decentralized decision making diffuses decision making throughout the organization and allows problems to be solved by the lowest practical managerial level. Often this means that problems can be solved at the level at which they occur. In general, the larger the organization, the greater the need to decentralize decision making. This occurs because the complex questions that must be answered can best be addressed by a variety of people with distinct areas of expertise. In addition, leaving such decisions in a large organization to a few managers burdens those managers tremendously and could result in devastating delays in decision making. With decentralized organizations, the hierarchy of decision making is said to be flat, with a very short scalar chain.

Limitations of Organization Charts

Because it shows only formal relationships, what an organization chart can reveal about an institution is limited. The chart does not show the *informal structure* of the organization.

Every institution has in place a dynamic informal structure that can be powerful and motivating. Knowledgeable leaders never underestimate its importance because the informal structure includes employees' interpersonal relationships, the formation of primary and secondary groups, and the identification of group leaders without formal authority.

The informal structure also has its own leaders and its own communication channels, often referred to as "the grapevine." These groups are important in organizations because they provide a feeling of belonging. They also have a great deal of power in an organization; they can either facilitate or sabotage planned change. Their ability to determine a unit's norms and acceptable behavior has a great deal to do with the socialization of new employees.

Informal leaders are frequently found among long-term employees or individuals in select gate-keeping positions, such as the director of nurses' secretary. Frequently the informal organization evolves from social activities or from relationships that develop outside the work environment.

Organization charts also are limited in their ability to depict each line position's degree of authority. Additionally, equating *status* with authority frequently causes confusion. The degree of status is usually determined by the distance from the top of the organizational hierarchy; the closer to the top, the higher the status. Status also is influenced by skill, education, specialization, level of responsibility, autonomy, and salary accorded a position. Individuals frequently have status with little accompanying authority.

Because organizations are dynamic environments, an organization chart becomes obsolete very quickly. It also is possible that the organization chart may depict how things are supposed to be, when in reality, the organization is still functioning under an old structure because employees have not yet accepted new lines of authority.

Another limitation of the organization chart is that although it defines authority, it does not define responsibility and accountability. The manager should understand the interrelationships and differences among these three terms.

Authority is defined as the official power to act. It is power given by the organization to direct the work of others. A manager may have the authority to hire, fire, or discipline others. Because the use of authority, power building, and political awareness are so essential to functioning effectively in any structure, the next chapter discusses these organizational components in depth.

A *responsibility* is a duty or an assignment. It is the implementation of a job. For example, a responsibility common to many charge nurses is establishing the unit's daily patient care assignment. Managers should always be assigned responsibilities with concomitant authority. If authority is not commensurate to the responsibility, role confusion occurs for everyone involved. For example, supervisors may have the responsibility of maintaining high professional care standards among their staff. If

---

Display 7.2 Advantages and Limitations of the
Organizational Chart

Advantages
1. Maps lines of decision-making authority
2. Helps people understand their assignments and those of their coworkers
3. Reveals to managers and new personnel how they fit into the organization
4. Contributes to sound organizational structure
5. Shows formal lines of communication

Limitations
1. Shows only formal relationships
2. Does not indicate degree of authority
3. May show things as they are supposed to be or used to be rather than as they are
4. Possibility exists of confusing authority with status

---

the manager is not given the authority to discipline employees as needed, however, this responsibility is virtually impossible to implement.

Accountability is morally internalizing responsibility. It is an agreement to accept the consequences of actions. A nurse who reports a medication error is being accountable for the responsibilities inherent in the position. A manager cannot force employees to be accountable for their actions. Unfortunately, some individuals can and do accept responsibility without accepting accountability.

See Display 7.2 for the advantages and limitations of an organization chart.

ORGANIZATIONAL CULTURE

Organizational culture should not be confused with organizational climate—how employees perceive an organization. The organization's climate and its culture may differ. The organization chart helps shape the institution's culture. Thomas, Ward, Chorba, and Kumiega (1990) define organizational culture as a system of symbols and interactions unique to each organization. Cooke and Lafferty (1989) define it as the ways of thinking, behaving, and believing that members of a unit have in common. It is the total of an organization's values, language, history, formal and informal communication networks, rituals, and "sacred cows"—those few things present in an institution that are never to be discussed or changed. For example, the hospital logo that had been designed by the original board of trustees is an item that could never be considered for updating or change. Three types of organizational culture have been identified. Cooke and Lafferty (1989) call the first of these a positive culture. The positive culture is a constructive culture in which members are encouraged to interact with others and to approach tasks in proactive ways that will help them to meet their satisfaction needs. The constructive culture is based on achievement, self-actualization, encouragement of humanism, and afilliative norms.

In the other two cultures, passive-aggressive and aggressive-defensive, members interact in guarded and reactive ways and approach tasks in forceful ways to protect their status and security (Thomas, et al., 1990). These two cultures are based on approval, conventional, dependent, and avoidance norms and oppositional, power, competitive, and perfectionistic norms, respectively. In McDaniel and Stumpf's (1993) study of seven acute care hospitals in Western Pennsylvania, the constructive culture was slightly predominant. Organizational culture can become more performance enhancing with time; however, such a change is complex, takes time, and requires a great deal of leadership skill (Kotter & Heskett, 1992).

Sovie (1993) argues that because a constructive hospital culture is critical to accomplishing organizational goals, it is too important to be left to chance or to be a

---

Display 7.3 Characteristics of Consonant and Dissonant Cultures

Consonant Cultures	Dissonant Cultures
Collective spirit	Mismatch between professional and organizational goals
Golden rule norm	
One superordinate goal	Stronger union affiliations than organizational
Frequent staff–management interactions	
Clinical expertise valued	Little staff representation on committees
Professional and organizational goals similar	Low staff participation in decision making
Goals same across work units	Do not have primary care models
High cooperation between units	Competitive spirit
Primary care model promoting autonomy and independence	Them versus us norm
	Low staff–management interactions
Formal and informal systems to address conflicts	Staff feel undervalued
Match between values and outcomes	Mismatch between values and outcomes
All nurses seen as members of same occupational group	Management seen as outside occupation
All members seen as working toward same goal	Double standards for behaviors
Behavior norms same for everyone	Groups feel others not working toward common goal
	Myths, stories, symbols not caring or positive

Reprinted with permission from Fleeger (1993). Assessing organizational culture: A planning strategy. *Nursing Management, 24*(2), 39–41.

Display 7.4 Assessing the Organizational Culture

How does the organization view the physical environment?
1. Is the environment attractive?
2. Does it appear that there is adequate maintenance?
3. Are nursing stations crowded or noisy?
4. Is there an appropriate-size lobby? Are there quiet areas?
5. Is there sufficient seating for families in the dining room?
6. Are there enough conference rooms?

What is the organization's social environment?
1. Are many friendships maintained beyond the workplace?
2. Is there an annual picnic or holiday party that is well attended by the employees?
3. Do employees seem to generally like each other?
4. Do all shifts and all departments get along fairly well?
5. Are certain departments disliked or resented?
6. Are employees on a first-name basis with coworkers, doctors, charge nurses, and supervisors?

How supportive is the organization?
1. Is educational reimbursement available?
2. Are good low-cost meals available to employees?
3. Are there adequate employee lounges?
4. Are funds available to send employees to workshops?
5. Are employees recognized for extra effort?
6. Does the organization help pay for the holiday party or other social functions?

What is the organizational power structure?
1. Who holds the most power in the organization?
2. Which departments are viewed as powerful? Which are viewed as powerless?
3. Who gets free meals? Who gets special parking places?
4. Who carries beepers? Who wears lab coats? Who has overhead pages?
5. Who has the biggest office?
6. Who is never called by his or her first name?

How does the organization view safety?
1. Is there a well-lighted parking place for employees arriving or departing after dark?
2. Is there an active and involved safety committee?
3. Are security guards needed?

What is the communicative environment?
1. Is upward communication usually written or verbal?
2. Is there much informal communication?
3. Is there an active grapevine? Is it reliable?
4. Where is important information exchanged: the parking lot, the doctors' surgical dressing room, the nurses' station, the coffee shop, in surgery, or in the delivery room?

What are the organizational taboos and heroes?
1. Are there special rules and policies that can never be broken?
2. Are certain subjects or ideas forbidden?
3. Are there relationships that cannot be threatened?

by-product of institutional history. The leader must take an active role in creating the kind of organizational culture that will ensure success. Schein (1985) states that "one of the most decisive functions of leadership may well be the creation, the management, and—if and when that may become necessary—the destruction of culture" (p. 2). The more entrenched the culture and pattern of actions, the more challenging the change process is for the leader. In fact, Sovie (1993) argues that "if the culture is too entrenched, success in building a new culture may and often does require new leadership and a new leadership team, and, most frequently, leaders and team come from the outside" (p. 71). While assessing unit culture is a management function, building a constructive culture, particularly if a negative culture is in place, requires the interpersonal and communication skills of a leader.

Organizations, if large enough, also have subcultures that develop within specialized groups and departments. These subcultures also help shape perceptions, attitudes, and beliefs and influence how their members approach and execute their particular roles and responsibilities (Sovie, 1993). If the unit culture is in harmony with the organizational culture and the nursing culture is in harmony with the other professional cultures, *consonance* is said to exist (Fleeger, 1993). If the opposite is true, *dissonance* occurs. The characteristics of consonant and dissonant cultures are shown in Display 7.3. Managers must be able to assess their unit's culture and choose management strategies that encourage consonance and discourage dissonance.

Much of an organization's culture is not available to staff in a retrievable source and must be related by others. For example, feelings about collective bargaining, nursing education levels, nursing autonomy, and nurse–physician relationships differ from one organization to another. These beliefs and values, however, are not written down and never appear in a philosophy. Therefore, in addition to creating a constructive culture, a major leadership role is to assist subordinates in understanding the organization's culture. Display 7.4 identifies questions leaders and followers should ask when assessing organizational culture.

TYPES OF FORMAL ORGANIZATION STRUCTURES

Traditionally, nursing departments have used one of the following structural patterns: line organization, line-and-staff organization, functional organization, ad hoc organization, or matrix organization. The type of structure used in any healthcare facility affects communication patterns, relationships, and authority.

Line organization and *line-and-staff organization* are the most common structures in large healthcare facilities. Line organizations have no advisory positions; line-and-staff do use these positions. These two structures most resemble Weber's original design for effective organizations.

Because of most people's familiarity with these structures, there is little stress associated with orienting individuals to these organizations. In these structures, authority and responsibility are clearly defined, which leads to efficiency and simplicity of relationships. The organization chart in Figure 7.1 is a line-and-staff structure.

These formal designs have some disadvantages. They often produce monotony,

Having been with the county health department for 6 months, you are very impressed with the doctor who is the county health administrator. She seems to have a genuine concern for patient welfare. She has a tea for new employees each month to discuss the department's philosophy and her own management style. She says she has an open-door policy so employees are always welcome to visit her.

Since you have been assigned to the evening immunization clinic as charge nurse, you have become concerned with a persistent problem. The housekeeping staff often spend part of the evening sleeping on duty or socializing for long periods. You have reported your concerns to your health department supervisor twice.

Last evening, you found the housekeeping staff having another get-together. This mainly upsets you because the clinic is chronically in need of cleaning. Sometimes the public bathrooms get so untidy that they embarrass you and your staff. You frequently remind the housekeepers to empty overflowing waste baskets. You feel that this environment is demeaning to patients.

You also are upset by this because you and your staff work so hard all evening and rarely have a chance to sit down. You feel it is unfair to everyone that the housekeeping staff are not doing their share.

On your way to the parking lot this afternoon, the health administrator stops to chat and asks you how things are going. Should you tell her about the problem with the housekeeping staff? Is this an appropriate chain of command? Do you feel there is a dissonance between the housekeeping unit's culture and the nursing unit's culture? What should you do? List choices and alternatives. Decide what you should do and explain your rationale. *Note: Attempt to solve this problem before reading further because one approach has been provided for the reader.*

Analysis:

You should choose a goal before proceeding. If the goal is to relieve the immediate frustration of the situation, then going outside the chain of command might accomplish this. However, that goal appears to be selfish and meets only your immediate needs. A more appropriate goal would be to have the clinic clean and tidy. The first step then is to assess the data and identify possible risks. An assessment of this case's available information and rationale for decision making is outlined as follows.

Data Assessment

1. A copy of the organization chart was given to you when you were hired. The formal structure is a line and staff organization. The housekeeping department head is below the nursing director and the nursing section supervisor but at the same level as the immediate clinic supervisor. The housekeeping department head reports directly to the maintenance and engineering department head.
2. The county administrator has stated she has an open-door policy. You do not know if this means that bypassing department heads is acceptable or merely that the administrator is interested in the employees. An important reason for not skipping intermediate supervisors when communicating is that they must know what is going on in their departments. A manager's position, value, and status are strengthened if he or she serves as a vital and essential link in the vertical chain of command.
3. You have twice attempted to talk with your immediate supervisor; however, whether or not you followed up on the complaint is unclear.
4. You are a new employee and therefore probably do not know how the formal or informal structure works. This newness might render the complaints less credible.

(continued)

5. Possible risks include creating trouble for the housekeeping staff or their immediate supervisor, being labeled a troublemaker by others in the organization, and alienating your immediate supervisor.
6. Before proceeding, you need to assess your own values and determine what is motivating you to pursue this issue.

Alternatives for Action

There are many choices available to you.

1. You can do nothing. This is often a wise choice and should always be an alternative for any problem. Some problems solve themselves if left alone. Sometimes the time is not right to solve the problem.
2. You can talk with the county health administrator. Although this involves some risk, the possibility exists that the administrator will be able to take action. At the very least, you will have unburdened your problem on someone.
3. You can talk directly with the individual housekeepers by using "I" messages, such as "I get angry when the housekeeping staff take naps, and the bathrooms are dirty." Perhaps if feelings and frustrations were shared, you would learn more about the problem. Maybe there is a reason for their behavior; maybe they only socialize during their breaks. This alternative involves some risk. The housekeepers might look on you as a troublemaker.
4. Have all the evening staff sign a petition, and give it to the immediate supervisor. Forming a coalition often produces results. However, the supervisor could view this action as overreacting or meddlesome and might feel threatened.
5. Go to the housekeeping staff's department head and report them. In this way, you are saving some time and going right to the person who is in charge. However, this might be unfair to the housekeepers and certainly will create some enemies for you.
6. Follow up with the immediate supervisor. You could request permission to take action yourself and ask how best to proceed. This would involve your immediate supervisor and keep her informed. However, it also shows that you are willing to take risks and devote some personal time and energy to solving the problem.

Selecting an Alternative

This problem has no right answer. Under certain conditions, various solutions could be used. Under most circumstances, it is more fair to others and efficient for you to select alternative 3. However, because you are new and have little knowledge of the formal and informal organizational structure, your wisest choice would be alternative 6. New employees need to seek guidance from their immediate supervisors.

For this third session with the supervisor to be successful, you need to do the following.

1. Talk with the supervisor during a quiet time.
2. Admit to personally "owning" the problem without involving colleagues.
3. Acknowledge that legitimate reasons for the housekeepers' actions may exist.
4. Request permission to talk directly with the housekeepers. Role-play an appropriate approach with the supervisor.

You must accept the consequences of your actions. However, your attempt to correct the problem may motivate your supervisor to pursue the problem directly with the housekeeping staff's supervisor. If this is the action your supervisor takes, you should ask to speak with the housekeeping staff directly first. If after talking with the house-

(continued)

LEARNING EXERCISE 7.2 (Continued)

keeping staff, you decide a problem still exists and you elect to address that problem, then you should return to your immediate supervisor before proceeding.

Analysis of the Problem Solving

Would you have solved this problem differently? What are some other alternatives that could have been generated? Have you ever gone outside the chain of command and had a positive experience as a result?

Is it ever appropriate to go outside the chain of command? Of course, there are isolated circumstances when the chain of command must be breached. However, those rare conditions usually involve a question of ethics. In most instances, those being by-passed in a chain of command should be forewarned. Remember that unity of command provides the organization with a workable system for procedural directives and orders so that productivity is increased, and conflict is minimized.

alienate workers, and make adjusting rapidly to altered circumstances difficult. Another problem with line and line-and-staff structures, is their adherence to chain of command communication, which restricts upward communication. Good leaders encourage upward communication to compensate for this disadvantage. However, when line positions are clearly defined, going outside the chain of command for upward communication is usually inappropriate.

The *functional organization* structure allows advisory or staff positions to have some control over line employees. This is frequently done with advisory positions in areas such as nursing education, infection control, or hospital risk management. With some line authority, those in staff positions are able to apply their special expertise more effectively. In functional structure, however, the advising staff are never given total line authority. This design is sometimes depicted with a dotted and a solid line, denoting authority to implement job-related functions but no authority to hire, fire, or discipline.

The *ad hoc organization* structure was suggested by Alvin Toffler (1971) as a means of overcoming the inflexibility of line structure and as a way for professionals to handle the increasingly large amounts of available information. The ad hoc structure uses a project team or task approach. These teams operate within a more formal organization but allow for greater flexibility and cohesiveness among workers than does line structure. This structure's disadvantages are decreased strength in the formal chain of command and decreased employee loyalty to the parent organization.

A *matrix organization* structure uses the ad hoc approach but builds the team into a fully functional hierarchy. This structure has a formal vertical and horizontal chain of command. Although there are less formal rules and fewer levels of the hierarchy, a matrix structure is not without disadvantages. For example, in this structure, the nurse whose patient complained about vacuum cleaner noise would not be allowed to speak directly to the unit housekeeper but would need to talk with the housekeeping department's head.

Shared Governance:
The Organizational Design of the 1990s?

Shared governance, one of the most radical and idealistic of organization structures, was developed in the mid-1980s as an alternative to the traditional bureaucratic organizational structure. In shared governance (also called self-governance), the organization's governance is shared among board members, nurses, physicians, and management (Kovner, Hendrickson, Knickman, & Finkler, 1993). Thus, decision-making and communication channels are altered. Group structures, in the form of joint practice committees, are developed to assume the power and accountability for decision making, and professional communication takes on an equalitarian structure (Boeglin, 1993; Gessner, 1990).

The stated aim of shared governance is the empowerment of individuals within the decision-making system. In healthcare organizations, this empowerment is directed at increasing nurses' authority and control over nursing practice (Maas & Specht, 1994). Shared governance thus gives nurses more control over their nursing practice by being an accountability-based governance system for professional workers (Porter-O'Grady, 1987).

Although participatory management lays the foundation for shared governance, they are not the same. Participatory management implies that others are allowed to participate in decision making over which someone has control. Thus the act of "allowing" participation identifies for the participant the real and final authority (Porter-O'Grady, 1987).

There is no single model of shared governance, although all models share an underlying theme of the empowerment of staff nurses. In Porter-O'Grady's model, issues related to nursing practice are the responsibility of nurses, not managers, and nursing councils are used to organize governance. These nursing councils, elected at the organization and unit levels, use a congressional format organized like a representative form of government, with a president and cabinet.

The number of healthcare organizations using shared governance models is increasing, and research supports that shared governance improves staff nurses' perceptions of their job and practice environment (Jones, Stasiowski, Simons, Boyd, & Lucas, 1993; Ludemann & Brown, 1989). However, a major impediment to the implementation of shared governance has been the reluctance of managers to change their roles. The nurse manager's role becomes one of consulting, teaching, collaborating, and creating an environment with the structures and resources needed for the practice of nursing and shared decision making between nurses and the organization (Stichler, 1992). This new role is foreign to many managers and difficult to accept. In addition, consensus decision making takes more time than autocratic decision making, and not all nurses want to share decisions and accountability. De Baca, Jones, and Tornabeni (1993) also warn that although many positive outcomes have been attributed to implementation of shared governance, the expense of introducing and maintaining this model also must be considered. Thus, shared governance requires a substantial and long-term commitment on the part of the workers and the organization.

ORGANIZATIONAL EFFECTIVENESS

There is no one "best" way to structure an organization. One must always consider such variables as the size of the organization, the capability of its human resources, and the commitment level of its workers. Regardless of what type of organizational structure is used, certain minimal requirements can be identified:

1. The structure should be clearly defined so that employees know where they belong and where to go to for assistance.
2. The goal should be to build the fewest possible management levels and have the shortest possible chain of command. This eliminates friction, stress, and inertia.
3. The unit staff need to be able to see where their tasks fit common tasks of the organization.
4. The organizational structure should enhance, not impede, communication.
5. The organizational structure should facilitate decision making that results in the greatest work performance.
6. Staff should be organized in a manner that encourages informal groups to develop a sense of community and belonging.
7. Nursing services should be organized to facilitate the development of future leaders.

Despite the known difficulties of bureaucracies, including faceless decision making, impersonal management, lack of accountability, lack of flexibility, and organizational barriers in meeting work and personal goals (Kanter, 1989; Naisbitt & Aburdene 1987), it has been very difficult for organizations to move away from the bureaucratic model. Less rigid organizational designs continue to be developed but have not been extensively adopted by healthcare organizations. Although Guest predicted in 1986 that organizations in the future would be flexible and decentralized and that their authority would be derived from competence, progress toward this goal continues to be slow.

INTEGRATING LEADERSHIP ROLES AND MANAGEMENT FUNCTIONS ASSOCIATED WITH ORGANIZATIONAL STRUCTURE

The integrated leader/manager needs to look on organizational structure as the road map that tells them with whom to talk and who has authority in an organization; this way, the leader/manager can arrive at his or her destination efficiently and quickly. Without organizational structure, individuals would work in a chaotic environment. Structure becomes an important tool to facilitate order and enhance productivity.

The integrated leader/manager, however, goes beyond personal understanding of the larger organizational design. The leader/manager takes responsibility for ensuring that subordinates also understand the overall organizational structure and the structure at the unit level. This can be done by being a resource and a role model to subordinates. The role modeling includes demonstrating accountability and the appropriate use of authority.

The effective manager recognizes difficulties inherent in advisory positions and uses leadership skills to support staff in these positions. This is accomplished by granting sufficient authority to enable advisory staff to carry out the functions of their role.

Leadership requires that problems are pursued through appropriate channels, that upward communication is encouraged, and that unit structure is periodically evaluated to determine if it can be redesigned to enable more lower-level decision making. The integrated leader/manager also facilitates informal group structure. This may be done by encouraging staff to attend social planning meetings for the annual picnic or the holiday party or by allowing the posting of notices for unit parties, such as weddings or baby showers.

It is important for the manager to be knowledgeable about the organization's culture. It is just as important for the leader to promote the development of a constructive culture and to explain and communicate that culture to subordinates.

The integrated leader/manager understands the organization and recognizes what can be molded or shaped and what is constant. Thus, the interaction between the manager and the organization is dynamic.

KEY CONCEPTS

▼ A *bureaucracy,* as proposed by Max Weber, is characterized by a clear chain of command, rules and regulations, specialization of work, division of labor, and impersonality of relationships.

▼ An *organization chart* depicts formal relationships, channels of communication, and authority.

▼ *Line positions* are displayed by a solid line and *staff* or *advisory positions* by a broken line. Line positions have formal authority; staff positions do not.

▼ The *chain of command* follows a solid line and is called a *scalar chain.* The chain can be flat (in decentralized organizations) or tall (in centralized organizations). Going outside the chain of command is very risky in most organizations and should be done only in rare circumstances after other avenues have been exhausted.

▼ *Span of control* is characterized by the number of individuals reporting to one manager. The appropriate number depends on the organization, the maturity of the subordinates, and the type of work to be done. An inappropriate span of control can result in inefficiency.

▼ *Unity of command* means that each individual should have only one boss so that there is less confusion and greater productivity.

▼ *Centrality* refers to how centrally located a particular management position is along communication lines.

▼ In *centralized decision making,* decisions are made by a few managers at the top of the hierarchy. Thus, the more centralized the decision making, the longer the scalar chain.

▼ In *decentralized decision making,* decision making is diffused throughout the organization, and problems are solved by the lowest practical managerial level. Often this means that problems can be solved at the level at which they occur.

▼ *Authority* is the official power to act and direct the work of others.
▼ *Responsibility* is related to job assignment and must be accompanied by enough authority to accomplish the assigned task.
▼ *Accountability* is internal acceptance of the responsibilities that accompany a position.
▼ *Organizational culture* is the total of an organization's beliefs, history, taboos, formal and informal relationships, and communication patterns.
▼ Subunits of large organizations also have a culture. If the unit culture is in harmony with the organizational culture and the nursing culture is in harmony with the other professional cultures, *consonance* is said to exist. If the opposite is true, *dissonance* occurs.
▼ Informal groups are present in every organization. They are often powerful, although they have no formal authority. Informal groups determine norms and assist members in the socialization process.
▼ Many modern healthcare organizations continue to be organized around a *line* or *line-and-staff design* and have many attributes of a bureaucracy.
▼ Shared governance (also called *self-governance*) refers to an organizational design that empowers staff nurses by making them an integral part of patient care decision making and providing accountability and responsibility in nursing practice.
▼ Organizational structure affects how individuals perceive their roles and the status given to them by other individuals in the organization.
▼ Organizational structure is effective when 1) the design is clearly communicated; 2) there are as few managers as possible to accomplish goals; 3) communication is facilitated; 4) decisions are made at the lowest possible level; 5) informal groups are encouraged; and 6) future leaders are developed.

ADDITIONAL LEARNING EXERCISES

Learning Exercise 7.3

In groups or individually, analyze the following, and give an oral or written report.

1. Have you ever worked in an organization in which the lines of authority were unclear? Have you been a member of a social organization in which this happened? Did it interfere with the organization's functioning?
2. Do you feel that the "one boss per person" rule is a good idea? Don't hospital clerical workers frequently have many bosses? Have you ever worked in a situation in which you had more than one boss? What was the result?

Learning Exercise 7.4

You are the new head nurse of a hospital's acute care unit. You are very pleased to have this position and feel lucky to have been chosen from a field of four candidates. As head nurse, you have direct line authority over all unit staff. This authority includes responsibility for hiring, firing, performance appraisal, and discipline.

Your best friend, Mary, who works in the unit, also applied for the head nurse position. Mary seems sincerely happy for you, but you have some concerns about how your promotion will affect your friendship.

Shortly after you assume your new position, Mary begins making special requests for days off, taking extended dinner breaks, and asking you to give her top priority for low-census call-offs. In an effort to maintain the friendship, you have responded to these requests with a smile and by lightheartedly saying, "That wouldn't be fair to the other staff now, would it?" Mary has responded with a return smile and said, "It pays to have friends in high places."

Mary's behavior has become increasingly disruptive for you. You feel that she is taking advantage of your friendship. In addition, you wonder whether Mary has been speaking to other employees, implying your covert approval of her special privileges. When you have attempted to confront Mary with your concerns, she has dismissed them by saying, "I wouldn't do anything to hurt you in your new job; you are my best friend." You continue to feel that you are being sabotaged.

Assignment: Discuss how you will resolve this issue. Examine the appropriate place of friendship in a manager's life. This is a very difficult position, and there are no easy answers. In solving this problem, be sure and look at all the issues.

Learning Exercise 7.5
(Adapted from Marquis & Huston, 1994.)

You are the staff coordinator at a home health agency. There are 22 registered nurses in your span of control. In a meeting with the chief nursing officer (CNO) today, he tells you that he feels your span of control is too broad to be effective. Therefore, he has decided to decentralize the department. To accomplish this, he plans to designate three of your staff as shift coordinators. These shift coordinators will "schedule client visits for all the staff on their shift and be accountable for the staff they supervise." The CNO feels that this decentralization will give you more time for implementing a continuous quality improvement (CQI) program and promoting staff development.

Although you are glad to have the opportunity to begin these new projects, you are somewhat unclear about the role expectations of the new shift coordinators and how this will change your job description. Will these shift coordinators report to you? If so, will you have direct line authority or staff authority? Who should be responsible for evaluating the performance of the staff nurses now? Who will handle employee disciplinary problems? How involved should the shift coordinators be in strategic planning or determining next year's budget? What types of management training will be needed by the shift coordinators to prepare for their new role? Are you the most appropriate person to train them?

Assignment: There is great potential for conflict here. In small groups, make a list of 10 questions (not including the ones listed in the learning exercise) that you would want to ask the CNO at your next meeting to clarify role expectations. Discuss tools and skills you have learned in the preceding units that could make this role change less traumatic for all involved.

Learning Exercise 7.6

Review Display 7.3. Then select one of the following topics to discuss in small groups.

1. Identify key components of the professional nursing and medical cultures. Are the cultures of professional nursing and medicine consonant or dissonant? Give examples to support your position.
2. Identify key components of the registered nurse and licensed vocational nurse cultures. Are these two cultures consonant or dissonant? Do other members of the healthcare team (eg, respiratory therapists, dieticians, occupational therapists, physical therapists) have a consonant culture with nursing? Give examples to support your position.
3. (For RN to BSN students.) Have you found a difference between the culture of your baccalaureate nursing program and that of your ADN or diploma nursing program? If so, do you think this dissonance contributed to the failure of the 1985 American Nurses Association resolution to mandate the baccalaureate degree as the entry level to professional nursing practice?
4. Some clinicians have argued that nursing education is "carried out in an ivory tower, far removed from the real world of nursing practice." Do you feel there is dissonance between nursing education's culture and that of clinical practice? What are the key attributes of each of these cultures?

REFERENCES:

Boeglin, M. J. (1993). Shared governance. In A. Marriner-Tomey (Ed.), *Transformational leadership in nursing* (pp. 89–100). St. Louis: Mosby Year book.

Cooke, R., & Lafferty, J. (1989). Organizational culture inventory. Plymouth, MI: Human Synergistics.

De Baca, V., Jones, K., & Tornabeni, J. (1993). A cost-benefit analysis of shared governance. *Journal of Nursing Administration, 23*(7/8), 50–57.

Douglass, L. M. (1992). The effective nurse: Leader and manager (4th ed.). St. Louis: Mosby Year Book.

Ellis, J. R., & Hartley, C. L. (1995). Managing and coordinating nursing care (2nd ed.). Philadelphia: J.B. Lippincott.

Fayol, H. (1949). *General and industrial management* (C. Storrs, Trans.). London: Issac Pittman and Sons.

Fleeger, M. E. (1993). Assessing organizational culture: A planning strategy. *Nursing Management, 24*(2), 39–41.

Gessner, T. (1990). Organizations as work flow systems. In J. Dienemann (Ed.), *Nursing administration: Strategic perspectives and application.* Norwalk, CT: Appleton-Lange.

Guest, R. H. (1986). Management imperatives for the year 2000. *California Management Review, 26*(3).

Jones, C. B., Stasiowski, S., Simons, B. J., Boyd, N. J., & Lucas, M. D. (1993). Shared governance and the nursing practice environment. *Nursing Economics, 11*(4), 208–214.

Kanter, R. M. (1989). *When giants learn to dance: Mastering the challenges-Strategy, management and careers in the 1900s.* New York: Simon and Schuster.

Kotter, J. P., & Heskett, J. L. (1992). *Corporate culture and performance.* New York: The Free Press.

Kovner, C. T., Hendrickson, G., Knickman, J. R., & Finkler, S. A. (1993). Changing the delivery of nursing care. *Journal of Nursing Administration, 23*(11), 24–34.

Ludemann, R. S., & Brown, C. (1989). Staff perceptions of shared governance. *Journal of Nursing Administration, 13*(4).

Maas, M. L., & Specht, J. P. (1994). Shared governance in nursing: What is shared, who governs, and who benefits? In J. Mc Closkey & H. K. Grace (Eds.), *Current issues in nursing.* St. Louis: Mosby Year Book.

Marquis, B. L., & Huston, C. J. (1994). *Management decision making for nurses* (2nd ed.). Philadelphia: J.B. Lippincott.

McDaniel, C. & Stumpf, L. (1993). The organizational culture. *Journal of Nursing Administration, 23*(4):54–60.

Naisbitt, J., & Aburdene, P. (1987). *Reinventing the corporation.* New York: Random-Warner Books.

Pabst, M. K. (1993). Span of control on nursing inpatient units. *Nursing Economics, 11*(2), 87–90.

Porter-O'Grady, T. (1987). Shared governance and new organizational models. *Nursing Economics, 5*(6), 281–286.

Schein, E. H. (1985). *Organizational culture and leadership.* San Francisco: Jossey-Bass Publishers.

Sovie, M. D. (1993). Hospital culture-Why create one? *Nursing Economics, 11*(2), 69–75.

Stichler, J. F. (1992). A conceptual basis for shared governance. In T. Porter-O'Grady (Ed.), *Implementing shared governance: Creating a professional organization.* St. Louis: C.V. Mosby.

Swansburg, R. C. (1990). *Management and leadership for nurse managers* (p. 294). Boston: Jones and Bartlett.

Thomas, C., Ward, M., Chorba, C., & Kumiega, A. (1990). Measuring and interpreting organizational culture. *Journal of Nursing Administration, 20*(6).

Toffler, A. (1971). *Future shock.* New York: Bantam Books.

BIBLIOGRAPHY

Allen, R. F., & Kraft, C. (1987). *The organizational unconscious: How to create the culture you want and need.* Morristown, NJ: Human Resources Institute.

Banner, D. K., & Gagne, E. T. (1994). Designing effective organizations: Traditional and transformational views. Newbury Park, CA: Sage.

Brodbeck, K. (1992). Professional practice actualized through an integrated shared governance and quality assurance model. *Journal of Nursing Care Quality, 6*(2), 20–23.

Cooke, R., & Szumal, J. L. (1991). The reliability of the organizational culture inventory. Plymouth, MI: Human Synergistics.

Cooke, R., & Rousseau, D. (1987). Behavioral norms and expectations: A quantitative approach to the assessment of organizational culture. *Group Organizational Studies, 13*(3), 245–273.

Cox, C. L. (1980). Decentralization: Uniting authority and responsibility. *Supervisor Nurse, 11,* 28–35.

Dirschel, K. M. (1994). Decentralization or centralization: Striking a balance. *Nursing Management, 25*(9), 49–51.

Dutton, J. E., Dukerich, J. M., & Harquail, C. V. (1994). Organizational images and member identification. *Administrative Science Quarterly, 39*(June), 239–263.

Flarey, D. L. (1991). The social climate scale: A tool for organizational change and development. *Journal of Nursing Administration, 21*(4), 37–44.

Frohman, A. L., & Johnson, L. W. (1993). The middle management challenge: Moving from crisis to empowerment. New York: Mc-Graw Hill.

Hamada, T., & Sibley, W. E. (Eds) (1994). Anthropological perspectives on organizational culture. Lanham, MD: University Press of America.

Havens, D. S. (1992). Nursing involvement in hospital governance: 1990 and 1995. *Nursing Economics, 10*(5), 331–335.

Ingersoll, V. H., & Adams, G. B. (1992). *The tacit organization.* Greenwich, CT: JAI Press.

Jones, L., & Ortiz, M. (1989). Increasing nursing autonomy and recognition through shared governance. *Nursing Administration Quarterly, 13,* 11–16.

Kilduff, M. (1993). Deconstructing organizations. *Academy of Management Review, 18,* 13–31.

Korman, A. K., et al. (1994). *Human dilemmas in work organizations: Strategies for resolution.* New York: Guilford.

Kunda, G. (1992). *Engineering culture.* Philadelphia: Temple University Press.

Manfred, F. R., Kets de Vries, et al. (1991). *Organizations on the couch: Clinical perspectives on organizational behavior and change.* San Francisco, CA: Jossey-Bass.

Martin, J. (1992). *Cultures in organization: Three perspectives.* New York: Oxford University Press.

Mc Daniel, C. (1992). Ethics and culture in nursing service. Unpublished manuscript.

McGill, M. E., & Slocum, J. W. (1994). *The*

smarter organization: How to build a business that learns and adapts to the marketplace needs. New York: Wiley.

McMahon, J. (1992). Shared governance: The leadership challenge. *Nursing Administration Quarterly, 17*(1), 55–59.

Mentzer, M. S. (1994). Organization theory as ideological battleground in the year 2000. *International Journal of Public Administration, 17*(3&4), 589–605.

Minnen, T. G., Berger, E., Ames, A., Dubree, M., Baker, W., & Spinella, J. (1993). Sustaining work redesign innovations through shared governance. *Journal of Nursing Administration, 23*(7/8), 35–40.

Mularz, L. A., Maher, M., Johnson, A. P, Rolston-Blenman, B., & Anderson, M. A. (1995). Theory M: A restructuring process. *Nursing Management, 26*(1), 49–52.

O'Reilly, C., Chatman, J., & Caldwell, D. F. (1991). People and organizational culture: A profile comparison approach to assessing person-organization fit. *Academy of Management Journal, 34,* 487–516.

Ott, J. S., & Shafritz, J. M. (1994). Toward a definition of organizational incompetence: A neglected variable in organization theory. *Public Administration Review, 54*(4), 370–377.

Person, L. (1993). An educational blitz: Initiating shared governance. *Nursing Management, 24* (8), 61–62.

Peters, T. (1988). *Thriving on chaos.* New York: Alfred A. Knopf.

Rizzo, J. A., Gilman, M. P., & Mesermann, C. A. (1994). Facilitating care delivery redesign using measures of unit culture and work characteristics. *Journal of Nursing Administration, 24*(5), 32–37.

Sackmann, S. A. (1991). *Cultural knowledge in organizations: Exploring the collective mind.* Newbury Park, CA: Sage.

Sackmann, S. A. (1992). Culture and subcultures: An anlaysis of organizational knowledge. *Administrative Science Quarterly, 37*(1), 140–161.

Totten, N. W., & Scott, V. (1993). Who's on first? Shared governance in the role of the nurse executive. *Journal of Nursing Administration, 23*(5), 28–32.

Viau, J. J. (1990). Theory Z: "Magic potion" for decentralized management? *Nursing Management, 21*(12), 34–36.

Wilson, C. K. (1989). Shared governance: The challenge of change in the early phases of implementation. *Nursing Administration Quarterly, 13*(4), 29–33.

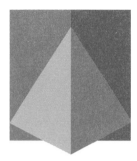

CHAPTER 8

Authority and Power in Organizations

Chapter 7 reviews organizational structure and introduces status, authority, and responsibility at different levels of the organizational hierarchy. In Chapter 8 the organization is examined further, with emphasis on the management functions and leadership roles inherent in effective use of authority, establishment of a personal power base, empowerment of staff, and the impact of organizational politics on power.

The word power is derived from the Latin verb "potere" (to be able); thus, power may be appropriately defined as that which enables one to accomplish goals. Covey (1989) defines power as the faculty or capacity to act, the strength and potency to accomplish something. Kippenbrock (1992) states that to possess power implies the ability to change the attitudes and behaviors of individual people and groups.

Authority, or the right to command, accompanies any management position and is a source of legitimate power, although components of management, authority, and power are also necessary, to a degree, for successful leadership. The manager knowledgeable about the wise use of authority, power, and political strategy is more effective at meeting personal, unit, and organizational goals. Likewise, powerful leaders are able to build high morale because they delegate more and build with a team effort. Thus, their followers become part of the growth and excitement of the

Bessie L. Marquis and Carol J. Huston:
LEADERSHIP ROLES AND MANAGEMENT FUNCTIONS IN NURSING, 2nd ed.
Lippincott-Raven Publishers © 1996

Display 8.1 Leadership Roles and Management Functions in Organizational Politics, Power Acquisition, and Authority

Leadership Roles

1. Creates a climate that promotes followership in response to authority
2. Recognizes the dual pyramid of power that exists between the organization and its employees
3. Uses a powerful persona to increase respect and decrease fear in subordinates
4. Recognizes when it is appropriate to have authority questioned *or* to question authority
5. Is personally comfortable with power in the political arena
6. Empowers other nurses
7. Assists staff in using appropriate political strategies

Management Functions

1. Uses authority to ensure that organizational goals are met
2. Uses political strategies that are complementary to the unit's and organization's functioning
3. Builds a power base adequate for the assigned management role
4. Maintains a small authority-power gap
5. Is knowledgeable about the essence and appropriate use of power
6. Maintains personal credibility with subordinates
7. Serves as a role model of the empowered nurse

organization as their own status is enhanced. The leadership roles and management functions inherent in the use of authority and power are shown in Display 8.1.

UNDERSTANDING POWER

Power may be feared, worshipped, or mistrusted. It is frequently misunderstood. McCurdy (1988) maintains that our first experience with power occurs in the family unit. Because children's roles are likened to later subordinate roles and the parental power position is similar to management, adult views of the management/subordinate relationship are influenced by how power was used in the family unit. A positive or negative familial power experience will greatly affect an individual's ability to deal with power systems in adulthood.

Successful leaders are aware of their views on the use and abuse of power. Women in particular often hold negative connotations of power and never learn to use power constructively. Edwards (1994) states that women have traditionally demonstrated at best ambivalence toward the concept of power and until quite recently, have openly eschewed the pursuit of power. McCurdy (1988) maintains that this has occurred because women have been socialized to view power differently than men. For women, power is viewed as dominance versus submission; is associated with personal qualities, not accomplishment; and is dependent on personal or physical attributes, not skill. McCurdy also maintains that women seldom feel they inherently possess power but instead, rely on others to acquire it. Rather than feeling capable of achieving and managing power, women often feel that power manages them (McCurdy, 1988).

Bunker and Seashore (1977, p. 358) concur, stating the following:

> The exercise of legitimate power requires behaviors that may not be well practiced by some women. It requires clear decision making, assertiveness, and accountability. It is sometimes a lonely task. Becoming more assertive, expressing her own views first rather than soliciting others, being proactive rather than reactive, indicating clearly the degree to which she is willing to share power, being decisive, all these behaviors are less a part of the socialization of women than of men.

Reimer, Morrissey, Mulcahy, and Bernat (1994), however, have found that nurse managers hold a positive view of power. The perception that power is good increases with the educational level of the manager, particularly for managers with master's degrees. Likewise, Porter (1991), in his participant observation study of power relations between nurses and doctors, found that nurses are becoming increasingly open in their contributions to decisions about care, although the physician continues to hold a power advantage.

In determining whether power is "good" or "bad," it may be helpful to look at its opposite: powerlessness. Most people agree that they dislike being powerless. Everyone needs some control in their lives. Powerlessness tends to breed bossiness. Thus, the leader/manager who feels powerless often creates an ineffective, petty, dictatorial, and rule-minded management style. Weins (1990, p.16) concurs, stating "Nurses who feel powerless become bossy and rules oriented with patients, visitors and staff. They become oppressive leaders; punitive and rigid in decision making, withhold information from others, and become difficult to work with." Although the adage that power corrupts might be true for some, it may be more correct to say that organizational powerlessness, not power, corrupts. Power is likely to bring more power in an ascending cycle, while powerlessness will only generate more powerlessness. Because the powerful have credibility to support their actions, they have greater capacity to get things accomplished and can enhance their base. As managers gain power, they are less coercive and rule-bound; thus, their peers and subordinates are more cooperative.

Apparently, then, power has a negative and a positive face. The negative face of power is the "I win; you lose" aspect of dominance versus submission. The positive face of power occurs when someone exerts influence *on behalf of* rather than *over* someone or something. Power, therefore, is not good or evil; how it is used and for what purpose makes it good or evil.

TYPES OF POWER

For leadership to be effective, some measure of power must often support it. This is true for the informal social group and the formal work group. French and Raven (1959) postulate that several bases, or sources, exist for the exercise of power: reward power, punishment or coercive power, legitimate power, expert power, and referent power.

Reward power is obtained by the ability to grant favors or reward others with whatever they value. The arsenal of rewards that a manager can dispense to get employees to work toward meeting organizational goals is very broad. Positive leadership through rewards tends to develop a great deal of loyalty and devotion toward leaders.

Punishment or *coercive power,* the opposite of reward power, is based on fear of punishment if the manager's expectations are not met. The manager may obtain compliance through threat (often implied) of transfer, layoff, demotion, or dismissal. The manager who shuns or ignores an employee is exercising power through punishment, as is the manager who berates or belittles an employee.

Legitimate power is position power. Authority also is called legitimate power. It is the power gained by a title or official position within an organization. As previously discussed, the socialization and culture of subordinate employees will influence to some degree how much power a manager has due to his or her position.

Expert power is gained through knowledge, expertise, or experience. Having critical knowledge allows a manager to gain power over others who need that knowledge. This type of power is limited to a specialized area. For example, someone with vast expertise in music would only be powerful in that area, not in another specialization.

Referent power is power an individual has because others identify with that leader or with what that leader symbolizes. Referent power is given to others through association with the powerful. People also may develop referent power because others perceive them as powerful. This perception could be based on personal charisma, the way the leader talks or acts, the organizations to which he or she belongs, or the people with whom he or she associates. Referent power is enjoyed by people others accept as role models or ideals. Physicians use referent power very effectively; society, as a whole, views them as powerful, and they carefully maintain this image.

Some theorists distinguish charismatic power from referent power. Willey (1990) states that charisma is a type of personal power, while referent power is gained only through association with powerful others.

Heineken and McCloskey (1985) add another type of power to the French and Raven power sources by identifying *informational power.* This source of power is obtained when individuals have information that others must have to accomplish their goals.

Morrison (1988) refers to all these types of power as patriarchal in that they imply power over others. Morrison prefers a power defined as *feminist power* or *self-power;* the power an individual gains over his or her own life. Barwick (1977) maintains that this power is a personal power that comes from maturity, ego integration, security in relationships, and confidence in one's impulse. The various sources of power are summarized in Table 8.1.

TABLE 8.1 Sources of Power

Type	Source
Referent	Association with others
Legitimate	Position
Coercive	Fear
Reward	Ability to grant favors
Expert	Knowledge and skill
Charismatic	Personal
Informational	The need for information
Self	Maturity, ego strength

THE AUTHORITY POWER GAP

If authority is the right to command, then a logical question is "Why do workers sometimes not follow orders?" The right to command does not ensure that employees will always follow orders. The gap that sometimes exists between a position of authority and subordinate response is called the authority-power gap. The term *manager power* may explain the subordinate response to the manager's authority. The more power subordinates *perceive* a manager to have, the smaller the gap between the right to expect certain things and the resulting fulfillment of those expectations by others.

The negative effect of a wide authority-power gap is that organizational chaos may develop. There would be little productivity if every order were questioned. The organization should rightfully expect that its goals will be accomplished. One of the core dynamics of civilization is that there will always be a few authority figures pushing the many for a certain standard of performance.

Individuals in this country are socialized very early to respond to authority figures. Children are conditioned to *accept* the directives of their parents, teachers, and community leaders. The traditional nurse educator has been portrayed as an authoritarian who demands unconditional obedience, and according to Meissner (1986), this view is true of many contemporary nurse educators as well. Educators who maintain a small authority-power gap reinforce dependency and obedience by emphasizing the ultimate calamity—the death of the patient (Carlson-Catalano, 1992). Thus, nursing students may be socialized to be overly cautious and to hesitate when making independent nursing judgments.

Because of these types of early socialization, the gap between the manager's authority and the worker's response to that authority tends to be relatively small. In other countries, it may be larger or smaller depending on how individuals are socialized to respond to authority.

This authority dependence that begins with our parents and is later transferred to our employers may be an important resource to managers. Although the authority-power gap continues to be small, it has grown in the last 20 years. Both the women's movement and the student unrest of the 1960s have contributed to the

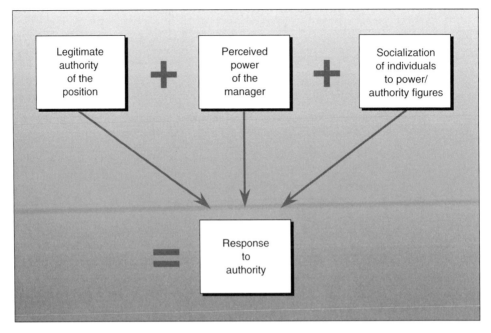

FIGURE 8.1 Interdependency of response to authority.

widening of the authority-power gap. This widening gap is evidenced when a 1970s college student asked her mother why she did not protest as a college student; the mother replied, "I didn't know we could."

At times, however, authority should be questioned by either the leader or the subordinates. This is demonstrated in healthcare by the increased questioning of the authority of physicians—many of whom feel they have the authority to command—by nurses. Figure 8.1 shows the dynamics of the relationships in organizational authority-power response.

LEARNING EXERCISE 8.1

Think back to your childhood. Who did you feel was most powerful in your family? Why did you think that person was powerful? If you are using group work, how many in your group named powerful male figures; how many named powerful female figures?

Did you grow up with a very small authority-power gap? Have your views regarding authority and power changed since you were a child? Do you feel that children today have authority-power gap similar to that you had as a child? Support your answer with examples.

BRIDGING THE AUTHORITY-POWER GAP

Sometimes subordinates feel badgered by very visible exercises of authority. Because overusing commands can stifle cooperation, naked commands should be used infrequently. Authority as a power tool, therefore, should be used as a last resort.

A method to bridge the gap is for the leader to make a genuine effort to know and care about each subordinate as a unique individual. This is especially important because each person has a limited tolerance of authority, and subordinates are better able to tolerate authority if they feel the leader cares about him or her as a person.

The manager needs to provide subordinates with enough information about organizational and unit goals that they understand how their efforts and those of their manager are contributing to goal attainment. If followers 1) perceive that the manager is doing a good job; 2) believe that the organization has their best interests in mind; and 3) do not feel controlled by authority, then the manager will have bridged the authority-power gap.

Finally, the manager must be seen as credible for the authority-power gap not to widen. Every manager begins their appointment with subordinates ready to believe them. This again is due to the socialization process that causes people to believe that those in power say what is true. However, the deference to authority will erode if the managers handle employees carelessly, are dishonest, or seem incapable of carrying out their duties. When a manager loses credibility, the power inherent in his or her authority decreases.

Another dimension of credibility that influences the authority-power relationship is "future promising." It is best to underpromise if promises must be made. Managers should *never* guarantee future rewards unless they have control of all possible variables. If managers revoke future rewards, they lose credibility in the eyes of the subordinates. However, managers *should* dispense present rewards to buy patronage, making the manager more believable and building greater power into his or her legitimate authority. A scenario that illustrates the difference in dispensing future and present awards follows.

> An RN requests a day off to attend a wedding, and you are able to replace her. You use the power of your position to reward her and give her the day off. The RN is grateful to you, and this increases your power.
>
> Another RN requests 3 months in advance to have every Thursday off in the summer to take a class. Although you promise this to her, on the first day of June, three nurses resign, rendering you unable to fulfill your promise. This nurse is very upset, and you have lost much credibility and therefore power. It would have been wiser for you to have said you could not grant her original request (underpromising) or to make it contingent on several factors. If the situation had remained the same and the nurses had not resigned, you could have granted the request. Less trust is lost between the manager and the subordinate when underpromising occurs than when a granted request is rescinded, as long as the subordinate believes the manager will make a genuine effort to meet his or her request.

EMPOWERING SUBORDINATES

The empowerment of staff is a hallmark of transformational leadership. Empowerment means to enable, develop, or allow. Hawks (1992) defines empowerment as an interactive process that develops, builds, and increases power through cooperation, sharing, and working together. Strader and Decker (1995) define empowerment as the process by which a manager or leader shares power with others. Empowerment occurs when leaders communicate their vision, employees are given the opportunity to make the most of their talents, and learning, creativity, and exploration are encouraged (Bass, Avolio, & Goodheim, 1987). Carlson-Catalano (1992) states that empowerment plants seeds of leadership, colleagueship, self-respect, and professionalism. In addition, it frees staff from mechanistic thinking and encourages critical thinking, problem solving, and the application of knowledge to practice.

Byrd (1987) states that leaders empower subordinates when they delegate assignments to provide learning opportunities and allow employees to share in the satisfaction derived from achievement. However, Tebbitt (1993) argues that empowerment is not the relinquishing of rightful power inherent in a position, nor is it a delegation of authority or its commensurate responsibility and accountability. Instead, the actions of empowered staff are freely chosen, owned, and committed to on behalf of the organization without any requests or requirements to do so. Thus, Tebbitt defines empowerment as creating and sustaining a work environment that speaks to values that facilitate the employee's choice to invest in and own personal actions and behaviors resulting in positive contributions to the organization's mission.

There are many barriers to creating an environment for empowerment in an organization. Seven barriers identified by Tebbitt (1993) include the following:

1. *Organizational beliefs about authority and status.* Empowerment is blocked if authority and power are viewed as the key motivational forces for achieving the organization's mission and strategic planning.
2. *Control perceptions, needs, and attitudes.* If managers emphasize rules, regulations, mandated policies, and procedures, little room is left for employee participation and empowerment. The individual who is unwilling to teach others and who does not want to see others succeed has been termed a *queen bee* and the activities and behaviors used to keep others from power, the *queen bee syndrome* (Spengler, 1976). The queen bee wants to be the main attraction and desires that subordinates remain powerless. Behaviors exhibited by nursing queen bees include identifying with others outside the profession (usually males who hold higher positions in the organization) and a disinterest in improving or changing the profession.
3. *Organizational inertia.* Empowerment does not happen "naturally." It occurs only as a result of an organizational commitment of time, energy, and resources.
4. *Personal and interdepartmental barriers.* Interdepartmental rivalries result in internal competition for resources. The more time managers must spend "defending their turf," the less organizational emphasis will be given to the empowerment process.
5. *Employee number, mix, and skill.* Larger organizations with greater staff diversity face a greater challenge in developing focused, yet flexible, strategies to empower their work force.
6. *A lack of ability and unwillingness of staff to assume responsibility and ac-*

countability for their attitudes and behaviors. Clarity of job roles or job expectations encourages empowerment as staff understand what is expected of them and can identify areas for improvement.

7. *Managerial incompetence.* The management skills required to empower staff are planning and goal setting, identifying and addressing problems, making decisions, defining priorities, implementing and managing change, forming interactive and self-directed teams, communicating, resolving conflict, fostering motivation, and building consensus.

Once organizational barriers have been eliminated, the leader/manager may use several strategies at the unit level to empower staff. The easiest strategy is to be a role model of an empowered nurse. Another strategy would be to assist staff in building their own personal power base. This can be accomplished by showing subordinates how their personal, knowledge, and referent power can be expanded. Empowerment also occurs when subordinates are involved in planning and implementing change; subordinates feel they have some input in what is about to happen to them and some control over the environment in which they will work in the future.

The key is for the leader/manager to be able to accomplish four separate tasks. A small authority power gap must be maintained, subordinates should be empowered whenever possible, authority should be used in such a manner that subordinates view what happens in the organization as necessary, and when needed, political strategies must be used to maintain power and authority.

BUILDING A PERSONAL POWER BASE

Managers must build a personal power base to further organizational goals, fulfill the leadership role, carry out management functions, and meet personal goals. A beginning manager or even a newly graduated nurse can begin to build a power base in many ways. Habitual behaviors resulting from early lessons, passivity, and focusing on wrong targets can be replaced with new power-gaining behaviors. Marquis and Huston (1994) suggest the following for enhancing power:

1. *Expand personal resources.* Power and energy go hand in hand. Effective leaders take sufficient time to unwind, reflect, rest, and have fun when they feel tired. Managers who do not take care of themselves begin to make mistakes in judgment that may result in terrible political consequences. Making time for significant relationships and developing outside interests are important so that other resources are available for sustenance when political forces in the organization drain energy.

2. *Present a powerful picture to others.* How individuals look, act, and talk influence whether others view them as powerful or powerless. The nurse who stands tall and is poised, assertive, articulate, and well-groomed presents a picture of personal control and power. The manager who looks like a victim will undoubtedly become one.

3. *Pay the entry fee.* Newcomers who stand out and appear powerful are those who do more, work harder, and contribute to the organization. They are not clock watchers or "nine-to-fivers." They attend meetings and in-

services, do committee work, and take their share of night shifts and weekend and holiday assignments without complaining. A power base is not achieved by slick, easy, or quick maneuvers but through hard work.

4. *Determine the powerful in the organization.* Understanding and working within the formal and informal power structures are necessary. Individuals must be cognizant of their limitations and seek counsel appropriately. One should know the names and faces of those with both formal and informal power. The powerful individuals in the informal structure are often more difficult to identify than those in the formal. When working with powerful people, look for similarities and shared values rather than focusing on differences.

5. *Learn the language and symbols of the organization.* Each organization has its own culture and value system. New members must understand this culture and be socialized into the organization if they are to build a power base. Being unaware of institutional taboos and sacred cows often results in embarrassment for the newcomer.

6. *Learn how to use the organization's priorities.* Every group has its own goals and priorities for achieving those goals. Those seeking to build a power base must be cognizant of organizational goals and use those priorities and goals to meet management needs. For example, a need for a new manager in a community health service might be to develop educational programs on chemotherapy because some of the new patient caseload includes this nursing function. If fiscal management is a high priority, the manager needs to show superiors how the cost of these educational programs will be offset by additional revenues. If public relations with physicians and clients is a priority, the manager would justify the same request in terms of additional services to clients and physicians.

7. *Increase professional skills and knowledge.* Because employees are expected to perform their jobs well, one's performance must be extraordinary to enhance power. One method of being extraordinary is to increase professional skills and knowledge until reaching an expertise level. Having knowledge and skill that others lack greatly augments a person's power base. Excellence that reflects knowledge and demonstrates skill enhances a nurse's credibility and determines how he or she is viewed by others.

8. *Maintain a broad vision.* Because individuals are assigned to a unit or department, they often develop a narrow view of the total organization. Power builders always look upward and outward. The successful manager not only recognizes how the individual unit fits within the larger organization, but also how the institution as a whole fits into the scheme of the total community. People without vision rarely become very powerful.

9. *Use experts and seek counsel.* Newcomers should seek out role models. By looking to others for advice and counsel, people demonstrate that they are willing to be team players, that they are cautious and want expert opinion before proceeding, and that they are not rash newcomers who think they have all the answers. Aligning oneself with appropriate veterans in the organization is excellent for building power.

10. *Be flexible.* Anyone wishing to acquire power should develop a reputation as someone who can compromise. The rigid, uncompromising newcomer is viewed as insensitive to the organization's needs.

11. *Develop visibility and a voice in the organization.* Newcomers must become active in committees or groups that are recognized by the organization as having clout. When working in groups, the newcomer must not monopolize committee time. Novice leaders and managers must develop observational, listening, and verbal skills. Their spoken contributions to the committee should be valuable and articulated well.

12. *Learn to toot your own horn.* Accepting compliments is an art. One should be gracious but certainly not passive when praised for extraordinary effort. Additionally, individuals should let others know when some special professional recognition has been achieved. This should be done in a manner that is not bragging but reflects the self-respect of one who is talented and unique.

13. *Maintain a sense of humor.* Appropriate humor is very effective. The ability to laugh at oneself and not take oneself too seriously is a most important power builder.

14. *Empower others.* Leaders need to empower others, and followers must empower their leaders. When nurses empower each other, they gain referent power. Huston and Marquis (1988) maintain that individual nurses and the profession as a whole do not gain their share of power because they allow others to divide them and weaken their base. Nurses can empower other nurses by sharing knowledge, maintaining cohesiveness, valuing the profession, and supporting each other.

LEARNING EXERCISE 8.2

The New Nurse Scenario
(From Marquis & Huston, 1994.)

You have been an RN for 3 years. Six months ago, you left your position as a day charge nurse at one of the local hospitals to accept a position at the public health agency. You really miss your friends at the hospital and find most of the public health nurses older and aloof.

However, you love working with your patients and have decided this is where you want to build a lifetime career. Although you feel you have some good ideas, you are aware that because you are new, you will probably not be able to act as change agent yet. You would like eventually to be promoted to agency supervisor and become a powerful force for stimulating growth within the agency. You decide that you can do a few things to build a power base. You spend a weekend plotting your political design.

Assignment: Make a power-building plan. Give 6 to 10 specific examples of things you would do to build a power base in the new organization. Give rationales for each selection. (Do *not* merely select from the general lists in the text. Outline *specific* actions you would take.) It might be helpful to consider your own community and personal strengths when solving this learning exercise.

THE POLITICS OF POWER

In *The Aquarian Conspiracy,* Ferguson (1987) defines politics as the use of power within the context of an organization. Diers (1985) defines politics as "the use of power for change" (p. 54). After the employee has built a power base through hard work, increased personal power, and knowledge of the organization, developing skills in the politics of power is necessary. Individuals often lose hard-earned power in an organization because they make political mistakes. Even seasoned leaders occasionally blunder in this arena. Although power is a universally available resource that does not have a finite quality, it can be lost as well as gained.

It is useless to argue the ethics or value of politics in an organization. Leininger (1978) maintains that politics exists in every organization, so nurses waste energy and remain powerless when they refuse to learn the art and skill of political maneuvers. Menke and Ogborn (1993, p. 35) state the following:

> Sometimes "the games being played" in our job settings cripple our ability to be powerful, effective participants in the world of work. Power, which is the ability to obtain, retain, and move resources, requires two sets of attributes: competence and political savoir-faire. Much attention is given to improving competence but little time is spent in learning the intricacies of political behavior. The most important strategy is to learn to "read the environment," through observation, listening, reading, detachment, and analysis.

Because power implies interdependency, nurses must not only understand the organizational structure in which they work, they also must be able to function effectively within that structure, including dealing effectively with the institution's inherent politics. Only when managers understand power and politics will they be capable of recognizing limitations and potential for change. Being in touch with one's own power can be frightening. Individuals may anticipate attacks from many fronts that will reduce their power. When these attacks occur, individuals who hold powerful positions may undermine themselves by regressing rather than progressing and by being reactive rather than proactive.

The following political strategies will help the novice manager negate the negative effects of organizational politics. These political strategies, along with power-building strategies, are summarized in Display 8.2.

1. *Become an expert handler of information and communication.* Beware that facts can be presented seductively and out of context. The manager must be cautious in accepting facts as presented because information is often changed to fit the others' needs. Managers must become adept at the art of acquiring information and questioning others.

    Decisions should be delayed until adequate and accurate information has been gathered and reviewed. Managers who fail to do the necessary homework may make decisions with damaging political consequences. Additionally, managers must not allow themselves to be trapped into discussing something about which they know very little. The politically astute manager says "I don't know" when inadequate information is available.

    This political astuteness in communication is often a difficult skill to mas-

---

Display 8.2 Power Building and Political Strategies

Power-Building Strategies	Political Strategies
Expand personal resources	Use information acquisition
Present a powerful persona	Communicate astutely
Pay the entry fee	Become proactive
Determine the powerful	Assume authority
Learn the organizational culture	Network
Use organizational priorities	Expand personal resources
Increase skills and knowledge	Maintain maneuverability
Have a broad vision	Develop conflict management
Use experts and seek counsel	and negotiation skills
Be flexible	Remain sensitive to people,
Be visible and have a voice	timing, and situations
Toot your own horn	Promote subordinates' identities
Maintain a sense of humor	Meet organizational needs
Empower others	Expand personal wellness

---

ter. Grave consequences can result from sharing the wrong information with the wrong people at the wrong time. Determining who should know, how much they should know, and when they should know requires great finesse.

One of the most politically serious errors one can make is lying to others within the organization. Although withholding or refusing to divulge information are both good political strategies, lying is not.

2. *Be a proactive decision maker.* Nurses have had such a long history of being reactive that they have had little time to learn how to be proactive. Although being reactive is better than being passive, being proactive means getting the job done better, faster, and more efficiently. The proactive leader prepares for the future instead of waiting for it to happen. He or she sees approaching change in the healthcare system, and instead of fighting those changes, *prepares* to meet them.

One way the nurse can become proactive is by assuming authority. Part of power is the *image* of power; a powerful political strategy also involves image. Instead of asking "May I?" leaders assume that they may. When people ask permission, they are really asking someone to take responsibility for them. If something is not expressly *prohibited* in the organization or in a job description, the powerful leader *assumes* that it may be done.

Politically astute nurses have been known to create new positions or new roles within a position simply by gradually assuming that they could do things that no one else was doing. In other words, they saw a need in the organization, and instead of asking if they could do something, they started doing it. The organization, through default, allowed expansion of the role. Individuals do need to be aware, however, that if they assume authority and something goes wrong, they will be held accountable, so this strategy is not without risk.

3. *Expand personal resources.* Because organizations are dynamic and the future is impossible to predict, the proactive nurse prepares for the future by expanding personal resources. Personal resources include economic stability, higher education, and a broadened skill base. This is often called the political strategy of having *maneuverability*. That is, the individual avoids having limited options. Individuals who have "money in the bank and gas in the tank" have a political freedom of maneuverability that others do not.

People lose power if others within the organization know that they cannot afford to make a job change or do not have the necessary skills to do so. Those who become economically dependent on a position lose political clout. Likewise, the nurse who has not bothered to develop additional skills or seek further education loses the political strength that comes from having the option of being able to find quality employment elsewhere.

4. *Develop political alliances and coalitions.* Nurses often can increase their power and influence by forming alliances with other groups. Individuals can form alliances with peers, sponsors, or subordinates. The alliances may be from within their own group or from without.

One of the most effective methods of forming alliances is through networking. Managers can sharpen their political skills by becoming involved with peers outside the organization. In this manner, the manager is able to keep abreast of current happenings and to use others for advice and counsel. Although networking works among many groups, for the nurse-manager, no group is as valuable as local and state nursing associations.

Networking—forming coalitions and alliances—also can be effective within the organization. This strategy is especially useful for some types of planned change. More power and political clout results from people working together rather than individuals acting alone. When an individual is under political attack by others in the organization, group power is very useful.

5. *Be sensitive to timing.* Successful leaders are sensitive to both the appropriateness and timing of their actions. The person who presents a request to attend an expensive nursing conference on the same afternoon that his or her supervisor just had extensive dental work is an example of someone with insensitivity to timing.

Besides being able to choose the right moment, the effective manager should develop skill in other areas of timing. One of these areas is knowing when is the appropriate time to do nothing. For example, in the case of a problem employee who is 3 months from retirement, time itself would resolve the situation.

The sensitive manager also learns when the time has come to stop requesting something, and that time should be before a superior has given a firm "no." Once this firm "no" has been reached, continuing to press the issue is politically unwise.

6. *Promote subordinate identification.* There are many ways a manager can promote the identification of subordinates. A simple "thank you" for a fine job

LEARNING EXERCISE 8.3

Case of Lemons
(From Marquis & Huston, 1994.)

This is based on a real event. The cast includes Sally Jones, the director of nursing; Jane Smith, the hospital administrator and CEO; and Bob Black, the assistant hospital administrator.

Sally has been in her position at Memorial Hospital for 2 years. She has made many improvements in the nursing department and is generally respected by the hospital administrator, the nursing staff, and the physicians.

The present situation involves the newly hired Bob Black. Previously too small to have an assistant administrator, the hospital has grown, and this position was created. One of the departments assigned to Bob is the personnel and payroll department. Until now, nursing, which comprises 45% of all personnel, has done its own recruiting, interviewing, and selecting. Since Bob has been hired, he has shown obvious signs that he would like to increase his power and authority.

Now Bob has proposed that he hire an additional clerk who will do much of the personnel work for the nursing department, although nursing administration will be able to make the final selections in hiring. Bob proposes that his department should do the initial screening of applicants, seeking references, and so on.

Sally has grown increasingly frustrated in dealing with the encroachment of Bob. Having just received Bob's latest proposal, she has requested to meet with Jane Smith and Bob to discuss the plan.

Assignment: What danger, if any, is there for Sally Jones in Bob Black's proposal? Explain two political strategies you feel Sally could use in the upcoming meeting. Is it possible to facilitate a win-win solution to this conflict? If so, how? If there is not a win-win solution, how much can Sally win? *Note: Attempt to solve this case before reading further.*

Analysis

In analyzing this case, one must forego feelings of resentment regarding Bob's obvious play for control and power. In reality, what real danger does his empire building pose for the director of nursing? Isn't Sally really just ridding herself and her staff of clerical duties and interruptions?

A certain amount of power is inherent in the ability to hire. Employees develop a loyalty for the person that actually hires them. Because Sally Jones or her designee will still actually make the final selection, Bob's proposal should result in little loss of loyalty or power.

Let's look at what the real Sally Jones did to solve this conflict. When she was able to see that Bob was not stripping her of any power, Sally was capable of using some very proactive strategies. Here was a chance for her to appear compromising, thereby increasing her esteem in the CEO's eyes and gain political clout in the organization.

When she met with Jane Smith and Bob, Sally began by complimenting Bob on his ideas. Then she suggested that because nurses were in the habit of coming to the nursing department to apply for positions and because personnel offices were rather cold and formal places, stationing the new personnel clerk in the nursing office would be more convenient and inviting. Sally knew that the personnel department lacked adequate space and that the nursing office had some extra room. She went on to say that

(continued)

LEARNING EXERCISE 8.3 (Continued)

because some of her unit clerks were very knowledgeable about the hospital organization, Bob might want to interview several of them for the new position. Although an experienced unit clerk would be difficult to replace, Sally said she was willing to make this sacrifice for the new plan to succeed.

The CEO, very impressed with Sally's generous offer, turned to Bob and said, "I think Sally has an excellent idea. Why don't you hire one of her clerks and station her in the nursing office?" Jane then said to Sally, "Now do we understand that the clerk will be Bob's employee and will work under him?" Sally agreed with this because she felt she had just pulled off a great power play. Let's examine what Sally won in this political maneuver.

1. She gained by not competing with Bob, therefore, not making him her enemy.
2. She gained by impressing the CEO with her flexibility and initiative.
3. She gained a new employee.

Although the new employee would be working for Bob with the salary charged to his cost center, the clerk would be Sally's former employee. Because the clerk would be working in the nursing office, she would have some allegiance to Sally. In addition, the clerk would be doing all the work that Sally and her assistants had been doing and at no cost to the nursing department.

When Sally first received Bob's memo, she was angry; her initial reaction was to talk to the CEO privately and complain about Bob. Fortunately, she did not do this. It is nearly always a political mistake for one manager to talk about another behind his or her back and without his or her knowledge. This generally reflects unfavorably on the employee with a loss of respect from the supervisor.

Another option Sally had was to compete with Bob and be uncooperative. Although this might have delayed centralizing the personnel department, in the end, Bob undoubtedly would have accomplished his goal, and Sally would not have been able to reap such a great political victory.

The later effects of this political maneuver were even more rewarding. The personnel clerk remained loyal to Sally and constantly leaked information to her regarding the personnel department and Bob. He became less adversarial and more cooperative with Sally on other issues. The CEO gave her a sly grin later in the week and said, "Great move with Bob Black." This case might be concluded by saying that this is an example of someone being given a lemon and then making lemonade.

works especially well when spoken in front of someone else. By calling attention to the extra effort of your subordinates, you are saying in effect, "Look what a good job we are capable of doing." Sending subordinates sincere notes of appreciation to their homes is another way of praising and promoting. Rewarding the excellent employee's work is an effective political strategy.

7. *View personal and unit goals in terms of the organization.* Even extraordinary and visible activities will not result in desired power unless those activities are used to meet organizational goals. Hard work for purely personal gain will become a political liability.

Frequently novice managers think only in terms of their needs and their problems rather than seeing the large picture. Additionally, people often look upward for solutions rather than attempting to find answers themselves. When problems are identified, it is more politically astute to take the problem *and* a proposed solution upward rather than just presenting the problem to the superior. Although the superior may not accept the solution, the effort to problem-solve will be appreciated.

8. *"Leave your ego at home in a jar."* Menke and Ogborn, (1993) warn managers not to take political muggings personally, because you may well be a bystander hit in a cross fire. Likewise, be careful about accepting credit for all political successes, because you may just have been in the right place at the right time. Be prepared as a manager to make political errors. The key to success is how quickly you rebound.

INTEGRATING LEADERSHIP ROLES AND MANAGEMENT FUNCTIONS WHEN USING AUTHORITY AND POWER IN ORGANIZATIONS

A manager's ability to gain and wisely use power is critical to his or her success. Nurses will never be assured of adequate resources until they gain the power to manipulate the needed resources legitimately. To do this, managers must be able to bridge the authority-power gap, build a personal power base, and successfully minimize the negative politics of the organization.

One of the most critical leadership roles in the use of power and authority is the empowerment of subordinates. The leader recognizes the dual pyramid of power and acknowledges the power of others, including that of subordinates, peers, and higher administrators.

Integrating the leadership role and the functions of management lessens the risk that power will be misused. Power and authority will be used to increase respect for the position and for nursing as a whole. The leader comfortable with power ensures that the goal of political maneuvers is cooperation, not personal gain. The successful manager who has integrated the role of leadership will not seek to have power over others but instead will empower others.

KEY CONCEPTS

▼ *Power* and *authority* are necessary components of leadership and management.
▼ An individual's response to authority is conditioned early through authority figures and experiences in the family unit.
▼ The gap that sometimes exists between a position of authority and subordinate response is called the authority-power gap. The smaller the *authority-power gap,* the greater the possibility that direct commands will *not* be required of a manager. Managers lose credibility and widen the authority-power gap when they lie or promise what they cannot deliver.
▼ The empowerment of staff is a hallmark of transformational leadership. Empow-

erment means to enable, develop, or allow. Empowerment also has been defined as an interactive process that develops, builds, and increases power through cooperation, sharing, and working together.

▼ Power has both a positive and a negative face. Traditionally, women have been socialized to view power differently than men.

▼ *Reward power* is obtained by the ability to grant rewards to others.

▼ *Coercive power* is based on fear and punishment.

▼ *Legitimate power* is the power inherent in one's position.

▼ *Expert power* is gained through knowledge or skill.

▼ *Referent power* is obtained through association with powerful others.

▼ *Charismatic power* results from a dynamic and powerful persona.

▼ *Information power* is gained when someone has information that another needs.

▼ *Feminist power* or *self-power* is gained through maturity, ego integration, confidence, and security in relationships.

▼ To acquire power in an organization, the novice manager should 1) present a powerful picture to others; 2) expand personal resources; 3) pay the entry fee; 4) determine who is powerful in the organization; 5) learn the organization's language and symbols; 6) learn how to use the organization's priorities; 7) increase professional skills and knowledge; 8) maintain a broad vision; 9) use experts and seek counsel; 10) be flexible; 11) develop visibility and a voice in the organization; 12) learn to toot his or her own horn; 13) maintain a sense of humor; and 14) empower others.

▼ Power gained may be lost because one is either politically naive or fails to use appropriate political strategies.

▼ Politics exist in every organization, so nurses waste energy and remain powerless when they refuse to learn the art and skill of political maneuvers.

▼ Political strategies helpful to the novice manager include 1) becoming an expert handler of information and communication; 2) becoming a proactive decision maker; 3) developing personal resources; 4) developing political alliances and coalitions; 5) being sensitive to timing; 6) promoting subordinate identification; and 7) viewing personal and unit goals in terms of the organization.

 ADDITIONAL LEARNING EXERCISES

Learning Exercise 8.4

After 5 years as a public health nurse, you have just been appointed supervisor of the western region of the county health department. There is one supervisor for each region, a nursing director, and an assistant director. You were selected over four other applicants. You have eight nurses who report directly to you.

You feel change is needed in the nurses' commitment to various area health committees. In the past, both the physician medical director and the nursing director have viewed this community responsibility as part of their own jobs and each supervisor's. Regular staff nurses have not been expected to serve on committees, such as the local hospice advisory board, the cardiac rehabilitation board, and the heart association education committee.

You would like your nurses to become more involved on such committees for several reasons. You want them to be more visible and have a greater voice in the organization. You also feel that nursing professionals should contribute to the community by volunteering.

Your first planned change, therefore, will be to increase the number of nurses on these committees. You thought that you would begin by asking one of the regular nurses to accompany you to the four committees you have been assigned to attend. At present, you are the only public health agency nurse who meets with each group, but other nurses do attend from the university and local hospitals. Not all the nurses who attend these meetings are classified as administrative.

Assignment: Devise a political strategy for successfully involving the public health nurses on your committees. Where is there danger of your plan being sabotaged? What change tactics can you use to ensure success? What are the political advantages and disadvantages of making a change fairly soon after being appointed a manager?

Learning Exercise 8.5

You are a middle-level manager in a public health department. One of your closest friends, Janie, is a registered nurse under your span of control. Today Janie calls and tells you that she injured her back yesterday during a home visit after she slipped on a wet front porch. She said that the home owners were unaware that she fell and that no one witnessed the accident. She has just returned from visiting her doctor who advises six weeks of bed rest. She requests that you initiate the paperwork for worker's compensation and disability, because she has no sick days left.

Shortly after your telephone conversation with Janie, you take a brief coffee break in the lounge. You overhear a conversation between Jon and Lacey, two additional staff members in your department. Jon says that he and Janie were water skiing last night, and she took a terrible fall and hurt her back. He planned to call her to see how she was feeling.

You initially feel hurt and betrayed by Janie because she has lied to you. You then want to call Janie and confront her. You plan to deny her request for worker's compensation and disability. You are angry that she has placed you in this position. You also are aware that proving Janie's injury is not work related may be difficult.

Assignment: How should you proceed? What are the political ramifications if this incident is not handled properly? How should you use your power and authority when dealing with this problem?

Learning Exercise 8.6

You are the day shift charge nurse for the intensive care unit. One of your nurses, Carol, has just requested a week off to attend a conference. She is willing to use her accrued vacation time for this and to pay the expenses herself. The conference is in 1 month, and you are a little irritated with her for not coming to you sooner. Carol's request conflicts with a vacation that you have given another nurse. This nurse requested her vacation 3 months ago.

You deny Carol's request, explaining that you will need her to work that week. Carol protests, stating that the educational conference will benefit the intensive care unit and repeating that she will bear the cost. You are firm but polite in your refusal.

Later, Carol goes to the supervisor of the unit to request the time. Although the supervisor upholds your decision, you feel that Carol has gone over your head in handling this matter.

Assignment: How are you going to deal with Carol? Decide on your approach, and support it with political rationale.

Learning Exercise 8.7

You are a 3 PM to 11 PM team leader on a medical unit of a small community hospital. When leaving the report room, John, the day shift team leader, tells you that Mrs. Jackson, a terminally ill patient with cancer, has decided to check herself out of the hospital "against medical advice." John states that he has already contacted Mrs. Jackson's doctor, who expressed his concern that the patient would have inadequate pain control at home and undependable family support. He feels that she will die within a few days if she leaves the hospital. He did, however, leave orders for home prescriptions and a follow-up appointment.

You immediately go in to Mrs. Jackson's room to asses the situation. She tells you that the doctor has told her that she will probably die within 6 weeks and that she wants to spend what time she has left at home with her little dog, who has been her constant companion for many years. In addition, she has many things "to put in order." She states that she is fully aware of her doctor's concerns and that she was already informed by the day shift nurse that leaving "against medical advice" may result in the insurance company refusing to pay for her current hospitalization. She states that she will be leaving in 15 minutes when her ride home arrives.

When you go to the nurse's desk to get a copy of the home prescriptions and follow-up doctor's appointment for the patient, the ward clerk states, "The hospital policy says that patients who leave against medical advice have to contact the physician directly for prescriptions and an appointment, because they are not legally discharged. The hospital has no obligation to provide this service. She made the choice—now let her live with it." She refuses to give a copy of the orders to you and places the patient's chart in her lap. Short of physically removing the chart from the ward clerk's lap, it is clear that you have no immediate access to the orders.

You confront the charge nurse, who states that the hospital policy does give that responsibility to the patient. She is unsure what to do and has paged the unit director, who appears to be out of the hospital temporarily.

You are outraged. You feel the patient has the "right" to her prescriptions because the doctor ordered them, assuming she would receive them before she left. You also know that if the medications are not dispensed by the hospital, there is little likelihood that Mrs. Jackson will have the resources to have the prescriptions filled.

Five minutes later, Mrs. Jackson appears at the nurse's station, accompanied by her friend. She states she is leaving and would like her discharge prescriptions.

Assignment: The power struggle in this scenario involves you, the ward clerk, the charge nurse, and organizational politics. Does the ward clerk in this scenario have informal or formal power? What alternatives for action do you have? What are the costs or consequences of each possible alternative? What action would you take?

REFERENCES:

Bass, B. M., Avolio, B. J., & Goodheim, L. (1987). Biography and the assessment of transformational leadership at the world class level. *Journal of Management, 13*(1).

Barwick, J. (1977). Some notes about power relationships in women. In A. Sargent (Ed.), *Beyond sex roles.* St. Paul: West Publishing.

Bunker, B., & Seashore, E. (1977). Power, collusion, intimacy-sexuality, support: Breaking the sex-role stereotypes in social and organizational settings (p. 358). In A. Sargent (Ed.), *Beyond sex roles.* St Paul: West Publishing.

Byrd, R. (1987). Corporate leadership skills: A new synthesis. *Organizational Dynamics, 16*(1): 34–43.

Carlson-Catalano, J. (1992). Empowering nurses for professional practice. *Nursing Outlook, 40*(3), 139–142.

Covey, S. R. (1989). *The seven habits of highly effective people.* New York: Simon and Schuster.

Diers, D. (1985). Policy and politics. In D. Mason & S. Talbott (Eds.), *Political action handbook for nurses.* Reading, MA: Addison-Wesley.

Edwards, R. (1994). Image, practice, and empowerment: A call to leadership for the invisible profession. *Revolution-Journal of Nurse Empowerment, 4*(1), 18–20, 87.

Ferguson, M. (1987). *The aquarian conspiracy.* Los Angeles: J.P. Tarcher.

French, J., & Raven, B. (1959). The bases of social power. In D. Cartwright (Ed.), *Studies in social power.* Ann Arbor, MI: University of Michigan.

Hawks, J. (1992). Empowerment in nursing education: Concept analysis and application to philosophy, learning, and instruction. *Journal of Advanced Nursing,* 17, 608–618.

Heineken, J., & McCloskey, J. (1985). Teaching power concepts. *Journal of Nursing Education, 24*(1).

Huston, C. J., & Marquis, B. L. (1988). Ten attitudes and behaviors necessary to overcome powerlessness. *Nursing Connections, 1*(2), 39–47.

Kippenbrock, T. A. (1992). Power at meetings: Strategies to move people. *Nursing Economics, 10*(4), 282–286.

Leininger, M. (1978). Political nursing: Essential for health service and educational systems of tomorrow. *Nursing Administration Quarterly,* Spring.

Marquis, B. L., & Huston, C. J. (1994). *Management decision making for nurses* (2nd ed.). Philadelphia: J.B. Lippincott.

McCurdy, J. F. (1988). Power is a nursing issue. In J. Muff (Ed.), *Socialization, sexism, and stereotyping.* Prospect Heights, IL: Waveland Press.

Meissner, J. (1986). Nurses: Are we eating our young? *Nursing, 16,* 51–53.

Menke, K., & Ogborn, S. E. (1993). Politics and the nurse manager. *Nursing Management, 24*(12), 35–37.

Morrison, E. G. (1988). Power and nonverbal behavior. In J. Muff (Ed.), *Socialization, sexism, and stereotyping.* Prospect Heights, IL: Waveland Press.

Porter, S. (1991). A participant observation study of power relations between nurses and doctors in a general hospital. *Journal of Advanced Nursing, 16,* 728–735.

Reimer, J. M., Morrissey, N., Mulcahy, K. A., & Bernat, A. L. (1994). Power orientation: A study of female nurse and non-nurse managers. *Nursing Management, 25*(5), 55–58.

Spengler, C. (1976). Other women. In M. Grissum & C. Spengler (Eds.), *Womanpower and health care.* Boston: Little, Brown.

Strader, M. K., & Decker, P. J. (1995). Role transition to patient care management. Norwalk, CT: Appleton and Lange.

Tebbitt, B. V. (1993). Demystifying organizational empowerment. *Journal of Nursing Administration, 23*(1), 18–23.

Weins, A. (1990). Expanded nurse autonomy: Models for small rural hospitals. *Journal of Nursing Administration, 20*(12), 15–22.

Willey, E. L. (1990). Acquiring and using power effectively. In E. C. Hein & M. J. Nicholson (Eds.), *Contemporary leadership behavior* (3rd ed.). Glenview, IL: Scott, Foresman/Little, Brown Higher Education.

BIBLIOGRAPHY

Alm, T. G. (1991). Power in nursing. *Journal of Advanced Nursing, 16*(5), 503.

Aroskar, M. A. (1987). The interface of ethics and politics in nursing. *Nursing Outlook, 35*(6).

Block, P. (1987). The empowered manager: Positive political skills at work. San Francisco: Jossey-Bass.

Bocchino, C. A., & Sharp, N. J. (1995). Health

care policy issues: Nursing politics and power. In K. W. Vestal (Ed.), *Nursing management: Concepts and issues* (2nd ed.). Philadelphia: J.B. Lippincott.

Booth, Z. (1987). Power: A negative or positive force in relationships? *Nursing Administration Quarterly, 7*(4).

Brown, C. L., & Schultz, P. R. (1991). Outcomes of power development in work relationships. *Journal of Nursing Administration, 21*(2), 45–48.

Chisholm, M. (1991). Use and abuse of power. *Clinical Nurse Specialist, 5*(1), 57.

Christy, K. A. (1987). Networks. *Nursing Management, 18*(4).

Cohen, W. J., & Milburn, L. T. (1988). *What every nurse should know about political action. Nursing and health care.* New York: National League for Nursing.

Dobos, C. L. (1990). Big fish in a big pool: Empowerment, assertiveness, and risk taking among nurses. *Today's OR Nurse, 12*(8), 12–16.

Ellis, J. R., & Hartley, C. L. (1995). *Nursing in today's world: Challenges, issues, and trends* (5th ed.). Philadelphia: J.B. Lippincott.

Eubanks, P. (1991). Employee empowerment key to culture change. *Hospitals, 65*(24), 40.

Gordon, S. (1991). Fear of caring: The feminist paradox. *American Journal of Nursing, 91*(2), 45–48.

Hawks, J. H. (1991). Power: A concept analysis. *Journal of Advanced Nursing, 16*, 754–762.

Hawks, J. H., & Hromek, C. (1992). Nursing practicum: Empowering strategies. *Nursing Outlook, 40*(5), 231–234.

Hoelzel, C. B. (1989). Using structural power sources to increase influence. *Journal of Nursing Administration, 19*(11).

Kanter, R. M. (1994). Collaborative advantage: The art of alliances. *Harvard Business Review, July/August*, 96–108.

Kerfoot, K. M. (1990). To manage by power or influence: The nurse manager's choice. *Nursing Economics, 8*(2), 117–118.

Kizlios, P. (1990). Crazy about empowerment? *Training, 27*(12), 47–56.

Maas, M. (1988). A model of organizational power: Analysis and significance to nursing. *Research in Nursing and Health, 11*, 153–163.

Manthey, M., & Miller, D. (1994). Empowerment through levels of authority. *Journal of Nursing Administration, 24*(7/8), 23.

Mason, D. J., Backer, B. A., & Georges, C. A. (1993). Toward a feminist model for the political empowerment of nurses. *Revolution, 3*(1):62.

Minett, S. (1992). *Power, politics, and participation in the firm.* Brookfield, VT: Ashgate.

Murphy, S. Z. (1994). Don't be a doormat: Personal empowerment in nursing. *Revolution, 4*(2), 66–68.

Pfeffer, J. (1992), *Managing with power: Politics and influence in organizations.* Boston: Harvard Business School Press.

Robbins, A. (1991). *Awaken the giant within.* New York: Simon and Schuster.

Thyen, M. N., Theis, R., & Tebbitt, B. V. (1993). Organizational empowerment through self governed teams. *Journal of Nursing Administration, 23*(1), 24–26.

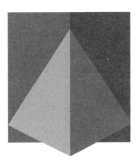

CHAPTER 9

Organizing Groups for Patient Care and Committee Work

First- and middle-level managers have their greatest influence on the organizing phase of the management process at the unit or department level. It is here that managers organize tasks to be done and appoint committee members. They frequently supervise committee work or serve as members of a committee in the larger organization. At the unit level, managers have a great influence on the organizational climate and in determining how patient care delivery is organized.

The unit leader/manager determines how best to plan work activities so that organizational goals are met effectively and efficiently. This involves using resources wisely, coordinating activities with other departments, and using committees appropriately. How activities are organized can impede or facilitate communication, flexibility, and job satisfaction.

For organizing functions to be productive and facilitate meeting organization needs, the leader must know the organization and its members well. Activities will be unsuccessful if there are inadequate resources or if their design does not meet group needs. The roles and functions of the leader/manager in organizing groups for patient care and committee work are shown in Display 9.1.

Bessie L. Marquis and Carol J. Huston:
LEADERSHIP ROLES AND MANAGEMENT FUNCTIONS IN NURSING, 2nd ed.
Lippincott-Raven Publishers © 1996

Display 9.1 Leadership Roles and Management Functions in Organizing Work and Using Committees

Leadership Roles
1. Periodically evaluates the effectiveness of the organizational structure for the delivery of patient care
2. Determines if adequate resources and support exist before making any changes in the organization of patient care
3. Examines the human element in work redesign and supports personnel during adjustment to changes
4. Uses committees to facilitate group goals, not to delay decisions
5. Teaches group members how to avoid "groupthink"
6. Inspires the work group toward a team effort

Management Functions
1. Organizes work activities to attain organizational goals
2. Groups activities in a manner that facilitates coordination within and between departments
3. Uses a patient care delivery system that maximizes resources, people, material, and time
4. Organizes work in a manner that facilitates communication
5. Uses committee structure to increase the quality and quantity of work accomplished
6. Uses knowledge of group dynamics for goal attainment

MODES OF ORGANIZING PATIENT CARE

The five primary means of organizing nursing care for patients are 1) case method nursing or total patient care; 2) functional nursing; 3) team nursing or modular nursing; 4) primary nursing; and 5) managed care or case management. Although some of these methods were developed to organize care in hospitals, most can be adapted to other settings. Choosing the most appropriate organizational mode to deliver patient care for each unit or organization depends on the skill and expertise of the staff, the availability of registered professional nurses, the economic resources of the organization, the acuity of the patients, and the complexity of the tasks to be completed.

Case Method Nursing

Case method nursing, or *total patient* care, is the oldest mode of organizing patient care. In this method, nurses assume total responsibility for meeting all the needs of assigned patients during their time on duty. At the turn of the 19th century, case nursing was practiced at home and in hospitals. Most medical and nursing care for the wealthy and middle class occurred in the home; hospitals at the time were used primarily by the poor and very acutely ill (Marquis & Huston, 1994).

During the depression of the 1930s, people could no longer afford home care and began using hospitals for care that had been performed by private duty nurses in the home. During that time, nurses and student nurses were the caregivers in hospitals and in public health agencies. As hospitals grew during the 1930s and 1940s, case method or total patient care continued as the primary means of organizing patient care. A diagram of case method structure is shown in Figure 9.1.

Case method is still widely used in hospitals and in home health agencies. Case nursing provides nurses with high autonomy and responsibility. Assigning patients is simple and direct and does not require the planning that other methods of patient care delivery do (Tappen, 1995). The lines of responsibility and accountability are clear. The patient theoretically receives holistic and unfragmented care during the nurse's time on duty. Each nurse caring for the patient can, however, modify the care regimen. Therefore, if there are three shifts, the patient could receive three different approaches to care, often resulting in confusion for the patient. To maintain quality care, this method requires more highly skilled and better paid personnel than some other forms of patient care. This method's opponents argue that some tasks performed by the primary caregiver could be accomplished by someone with less training and therefore at a lower cost.

The greatest disadvantage to case nursing occurs when the nurse is inadequately trained or prepared to provide *total* care to the patient. In the early history

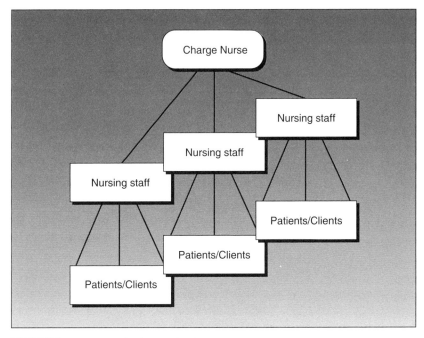

FIGURE 9.1 Case method or total patient care structure.

of nursing, there were only RNs, but now a variety of nursing care personnel work with patients, many of whom have no license and limited education. During nursing shortages, many hospitals assign healthcare workers who are not RNs to provide care using case nursing. Because the coassigned RN may have a heavy patient load, little opportunity for supervision exists. This potentially could result in unsafe care. Joel (1994) maintains that the large numbers of nonlicensed personnel used in hospitals as a recent effort to cut costs has resulted in a staff mix that is potentially unsafe.

Functional Nursing

The *functional method* of delivering nursing care evolved as a result of World War II. Because nurses were in great demand overseas and at home, many ancillary personnel were used to assist in patient care. These relatively unskilled workers were trained to do simple tasks and gained proficiency by repetition (Huston & Marquis, 1989). Personnel were assigned to complete certain tasks rather than care for specific patients. Examples of functional nursing tasks were checking blood pressures, administering medication, changing linens, and bathing patients. Functional nursing structure is shown in Figure 9.2.

This form of organizing patient care was thought to be temporary; when the war ended, hospitals would not need ancillary workers. However, the baby boom and resulting population growth immediately following World War II left the country short of nurses. Thus, employment of personnel with various levels of skill and

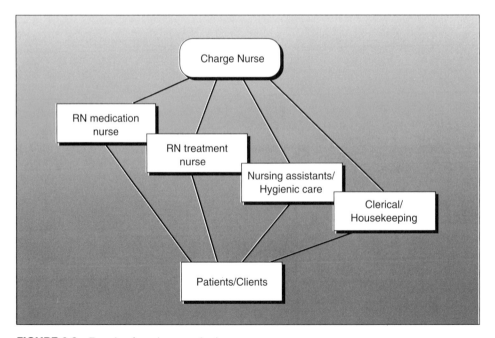

FIGURE 9.2 Functional nursing organization structure.

education proliferated as new categories of healthcare workers were created. Currently, most healthcare organizations have continued this practice.

Most administrators consider functional nursing an economical means of providing care. This is true if quality care and holistic care are not regarded as essential. A major advantage to functional nursing is its efficiency; tasks are completed quickly with little confusion regarding responsibilities. Functional nursing does allow care to be provided with a minimal number of registered nurses. In many areas, such as the operating room, the functional structure works well and is still very much in evidence.

Functional nursing may lead to fragmented care and the possibility of overlooking priority patient needs. Because some workers feel unchallenged and understimulated in their roles, functional nursing also may result in low job satisfaction. This type of organization may not be cost effective due to the need for many coordinators. Employees often focus only on their own efforts with less interest in overall results.

Team Nursing/Modular Nursing

Team nursing was developed in the 1950s in an effort to decrease the problems associated with the functional organization of patient care. Many felt that despite a continued shortage of professional nursing staff, a patient care system had to be developed that reduced the fragmented care that accompanied functional nursing. Team nursing structure is shown in Figure 9.3.

In team nursing, ancillary personnel collaborate in providing care to a group of patients under the direction of a professional nurse. As the team leader, the nurse is responsible for knowing the condition and needs of all the patients assigned to the team and for planning individual care. The team leader's duties vary depending on the patient's needs and the workload. These duties may include assisting team members, giving direct personal care to patients, teaching, and coordinating patient activities.

Through extensive team communication, comprehensive care can be provided for patients despite a relatively high proportion of ancillary staff. This communication occurs informally between the team leader and the individual team members and formally through regular team planning conferences. A team should consist of not more than five people or it will revert to more functional lines of organization.

Team nursing is usually associated with democratic leadership. Group members are given as much autonomy as possible when performing assigned tasks, although responsibility and accountability are shared by the team collectively. The need for excellent communication and coordination skills makes implementing team nursing organization difficult and requires great self-discipline on the part of team members.

Team nursing allows each member to contribute their own special expertise or skills. Team leaders, then, should use their knowledge about each member's abilities when making patient assignments. Recognizing the individual worth of all employees and giving team members autonomy result in high job satisfaction.

Disadvantages to team nursing are associated primarily with improper implementation rather than with the philosophy itself. Frequently, insufficient time is allowed for team care planning and communication. This can lead to blurred lines of responsibility, errors, and fragmented patient care. Joel (1994) states that while there

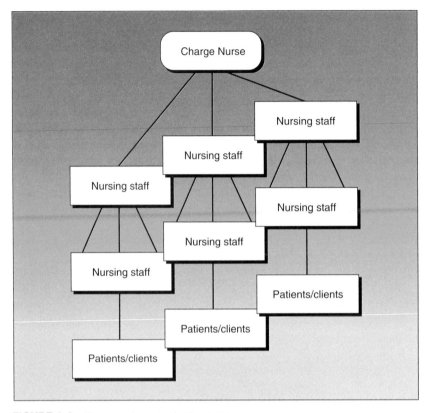

FIGURE 9.3 Team nursing organization structure.

is a demonstrated need for assistive personnel, such personnel should never be assigned to the patient but must always be assigned to the nurse. For team nursing to be effective, the leader must have good communication, organizational, and leadership skills and must be an excellent practitioner.

Team organization, as originally designed, has undergone much modification in the last 25 years. Most team nursing was never practiced in its purest form but was instead a combination of team and functional structure. Recent attempts to refine and improve team nursing have resulted in the concept of modular nursing, which is a miniteam (two to three members) approach. By keeping the team very small, greater involvement by the professional nurse in planning and coordinating care is hopefully possible. Additionally, a small team requires less communication, allowing members better use of their time for direct patient care activities.

Primary Nursing

Primary nursing, developed in the early 1970s, uses some of the concepts of case method. As originally designed, this method requires a nursing staff comprised totally of RNs. The RN *primary nurse* assumes 24-hour responsibility for planning the care of one or more patients from admittance or the start of treatment to discharge or the treatment's end. During work hours, the primary nurse provides total direct care for that patient. When the primary nurse is not on duty, care is provided by *associate nurses* who follow the care plan established by the primary nurse. Primary nursing structure is shown in Figure 9.4.

Although designed for use in hospitals, this structure lends itself well to home health nursing, hospice nursing, and other healthcare delivery enterprises. An integral responsibility of the primary nurse is to establish clear communication between the patient, the physician, the associate nurses, and other team members. Although the primary nurse establishes the care plan, feedback is sought from others in coordinating the patient's care. The combination of clear interdisciplinary group communication and consistent, direct patient care by relatively few nursing staff allows for holistic, high-quality patient care.

Although job satisfaction is high in primary nursing, this method is difficult to implement because of the degree of responsibility and autonomy required of the primary nurse. However, for these same reasons, once nurses develop skill in primary nursing care delivery, they feel challenged and rewarded.

Disadvantages to this method, as in team nursing, lie primarily in improper implementation. An inadequately prepared or educated primary nurse may be incapable of coordinating a multidisciplinary team or identifying complex patient needs and

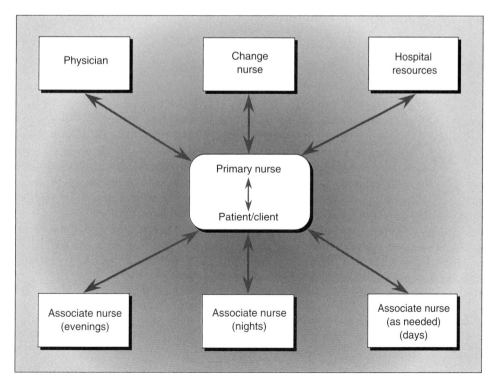

FIGURE 9.4 Primary nursing structure.

condition changes. Many nurses may be uncomfortable in this role (Marquis & Huston, 1994).

An all-RN nursing staff has not been proven to be more costly than other modes of nursing. There has, however, been some difficulty in recruiting and retaining all RNs, especially in times of nursing shortages. Currently, licensed vocational and practical nurses serve as associate nurses in some facilities, although the role of the primary nurse philosophically should be reserved for the RN.

Because this method's rationale is sound, some organizations are attempting to implement its underlying concepts by differentiating roles in their organization. This delivery system of patient care organization is termed *differentiated nursing practice*. RNs work within the role structure and assume responsibilities that correspond to the nurse's capabilities. Capabilities are assessed by skill, knowledge, and motivation rather than level of education. Differentiated nursing practice is still too new to determine if it has met its intended goals: improving nurse retention, quality of care, and fiscal outcomes (Malloch, Milton, & Jobes, 1990).

Managed Care and Case Management

Case management is the latest form of organizing activities to meet patient needs and is derived from the broader term *managed care*, although some writers use the terms interchangeably. Like the primary nursing method, one nurse is responsible for coordinating the activities and care of a patient. Zander (1988) lists four essential components of managed care: 1) clinical outcomes are achieved within a prescribed time frame; 2) the caregiver is the case manager; 3) episode-based nurse-physician group practice transcends units or departments; and 4) the patient and family are active in goal setting and evaluation.

Managed care differs from primary nursing in two very distinct ways. Although the case manager uses the nursing process, the primary focus is on planning, coordinating, and evaluating care. The case associates assigned to the care deal more with assessment and intervention. Secondly, unlike primary nursing, case management recognizes that not every patient needs managed care (Kramer, 1990).

Zander (1994) states that there will never be enough nurses with enough time to meet all the needs of a client. Therefore, the emphasis should be on managing a system that provides quality patient care. Although the nurse may be the manager of this system, the nursing role in managed care is one of collaboration rather than control of the patient. The emphasis in case management is on a multidisciplinary approach that saves time and money for the organization, while at the same time, facilitates improved quality of care for the consumer. The studies on this new method of managing patient care have been positive (Malloch, et al., 1990).

Selecting the Optimum Mode of Organizing Patient Care

Unfortunately, many nursing departments have a history of selecting methods of organizing patient care based on the most current popular mode rather than objectively determining the best method for a particular unit or department. Because

LEARNING EXERCISE 9.1

You are the head nurse of an oncology unit. At present, the patient care delivery mode on the unit is case method. You have a staff composed of 60% RNs, 35% practical nurses, and 5% clerical staff. Your bed capacity is 28, but your average daily census is 24. An example of day shift staffing follows:

One charge nurse who notes orders, talks with doctors, organizes care, makes assignments, and acts as a resource person and problem solver.

Three RNs who provide total patient care, including administering all treatments and medications to their assigned patients, giving IV medications to the practical nurses' assigned patients, and acting as a clinical resource person for the practical nurses.

Two practical nurses assigned to provide total patient care except for administering IV medications.

Your supervisor has just told all head nurses that because the hospital is having difficulty recruiting nurses, it has decided to hire nursing assistants. The nurses on your unit will have to assume more supervisory responsibilities and focus less on direct care. Your supervisor has asked you to reorganize the patient care management on your unit to best use the following day shift staffing: three RNs, which will include the present charge nurse position; two practical nurses; and two nursing assistants. You may delete the past charge nurse position and divide charge responsibility among all three nurses or divide up the work any way you choose.

Assignment: Draw a new patient care organization diagram. Who would be most affected by the reorganization? Evaluate your rationale, both for the selection of your choice and the rejection of others. Explain how you would go about implementing this planned change.

change is always stressful, evaluating the effectiveness of the mode of organizing patient care is important to determine if organizational change is absolutely necessary.

The leader should consider the following when evaluating the current system:

1. Is the method of patient care delivery providing the level of care stated in the organizational philosophy? Does the method facilitate or hinder other organizational goals?
2. Is the delivery of nursing care organized in a cost-effective manner?
3. Does the care delivery system satisfy patients and their families? (Satisfaction and quality care differ; either may be provided without the other being present.)
4. Does the organization of patient care delivery provide some degree of fulfillment and role satisfaction to nursing personnel?
5. Does the system allow implementation of the nursing process?
6. Does the method facilitate adequate communication between all members of the healthcare team?

If the present system reveals deficiencies, the manager needs to examine available resources and compare those with resources needed for the change. Nursing managers often elect to change to a system that requires a high percentage of RNs, only to discover resources are inadequate, resulting in a failed plan change. One of the leadership responsibilities in organizing patient care is to determine the availability of resources and support for proposed changes. There must be a commitment on the part of top-level administration and a majority of the nursing staff for a change to be successful. Because healthcare is multidisciplinary, the care delivery system used will impact heavily on many others outside the nursing unit; therefore, those affected by a system change must be involved in its planning. Change affects other departments, the medical staff, and the healthcare consumer.

Another mistake frequently made when changing modes of patient care delivery is not fully understanding how the new system should function or be implemented. Managers must carry out adequate research and be well versed in the system's proper implementation if the change is to be successful.

The leader also needs to examine the human elements that have great bearing on the success or failure of change in the work place. There are numerous pitfalls inherent in restructuring a job's design. Dwyer, Schwartz, and Fox (1992) state that every nurse does not desire a challenging job with the autonomy of personal decision making. Many forces interact simultaneously in an employee job design situation. Satisfaction does not occur only because of role fulfillment but also because of social and interpersonal relations. The change agent must consider the following:

1. How will the reorganization alter autonomy and individual and group decision making? Who will be affected? Will autonomy decrease or increase?
2. How will social interactions and interpersonal relationships change?
3. Will employees view their unit of work differently? Will there be a change from a partial unit of work to a whole unit? (For example, total patient care would be a whole unit of work, while team nursing would be a partial unit.)
4. Will the change require a wider or more restricted range of skills and abilities on the part of the caregiver?
5. Will the redesign change how employees receive feedback on their performance, either for self-evaluation or by others?
6. Will communication patterns change?

Change in the patient care delivery system will affect some or all of the above elements. That is not to say that change should not occur, but managers must evaluate all job variables before proceeding.

ORGANIZING OTHER UNIT ACTIVITIES

In addition to organizing patient care delivery, the unit manager needs to coordinate how other duties will be carried out and devise methods to make work simpler and more efficient. Often this includes simple tasks, such as organizing how supplies are stored or determining the most efficient lunch and break schedules for staff. The goal in organizing work and activities is to facilitate greater productivity and satisfaction.

> ### LEARNING EXERCISE 9.2
>
> *(From Marquis & Huston, 1994.)*
>
> To accommodate increasing numbers of personnel, Memorial Hospital has expanded its cafeteria hours. The cafeteria will now start serving lunch at 11 AM instead of 11:30 AM and will continue until 1:15 PM instead of 12:45 PM.
>
> As day charge nurse, you welcome this news. The new schedule will enable the unit to have fewer staff off the floor during any one time; more staff also will be available at lunchtime to assist with passing trays and feeding patients. However, you know that some employees probably will not like taking lunch at 11 AM, and some will dislike waiting until after 1 PM. The cafeteria is open from 8 AM to 10 AM for breakfast.
>
> Employees at Memorial Hospital are entitled to one 20-minute break in the morning, one 30-minute break for lunch, and one 10-minute break in the afternoon. During the short afternoon break, the unit is fairly quiet, and the staff use the conference room. During the morning and lunch breaks, the employees leave the unit.
>
> Each day, you have one ward clerk for clerical duties and one float aide to pass out water, answer call lights, and make beds. You do not take a patient assignment. Three RNs and three LVNs/LPNs are assigned to total patient care for an average of four patients each. Lunch trays arrive on your floor at 12:15 PM and breakfast trays at 7:45 AM.
>
> *Assignment:* Organize morning, afternoon, and lunch breaks for all personnel in a manner that is efficient and equitable. Support your decision with appropriate rationale.

The Relationship Between Planning and Organizing

Many nurses appear disorganized in their efforts to care for patients. Usually, however, this disorganization results from poor planning rather than poor organization. Planning occurs first in the management process because the ability to be organized develops from good planning. During planning, there should be time to think about the how the plans are going to be organized into action. The planner must pause and decide how people, activities, and materials are going to be put together to carry out the objectives. The following suggestions using industrial engineering principles assist in organizing work:

1. *Reduce travel to and from activities.* Gather all the supplies you will need before starting an activity.
2. *Group activities that are in the same location.* If you have walked a long distance down a hallway, attempt to do several things there before going back to the nurses' station.
3. *Use time estimates.* For example, if you know an intermittent intravenous medication (IV piggy back) will take 30 minutes to complete, then use that time estimate for planning some other activity in the patient's room at the end of 30 minutes.

COMMITTEE STRUCTURE IN AN ORGANIZATION

Managers also are responsible for designing and implementing appropriate committee structure. Poorly structured committees can be nonproductive for the organization and frustrating for committee members. However, there are many benefits to and justifications for well-structured committees (Gaynor, Reschak, & Verdin, 1994). To compensate for some of the difficulty in organizational communication created by line and line-and-staff structures, committees are used widely to facilitate upward communication. Additionally, the nature of formal organizations dictates a need for committees in assisting with management functions.

Committees may be advisory or may have a coordinating or informal function. Because committees communicate upward and downward and encourage participation of interested or affected employees, they assist the organization in receiving valuable feedback and important information. They generate ideas and creative thinking to solve operational problems or improve services and often improve the quality and quantity of work accomplished. Committees also can pool specific skills and expertise and help to reduce resistance to change.

However, all these positive benefits can be achieved only if committees are appropriately organized and led. If not properly used, the committee becomes a liability to the organizing process because it wastes energy, time, and money and can defer decision making and action taking. One of the leadership roles inherent in organizing work is to ensure that committees are not used to avoid or delay decisions but to facilitate organizational goals.

When organizing committees and making appointments, several factors should be considered:

1. The committee should be composed of individuals who want to contribute in terms of commitment, energy, and time.
2. The members should have a variety of work experience and educational backgrounds. Composition should, however, ensure expertise sufficient to complete the task.
3. Committees should have enough members to accomplish assigned tasks but not too many that discussion cannot occur. Six to eight members is usually ideal.
4. The tasks and responsibilities, including reporting mechanisms, should be clearly outlined.
5. Assignments should be given ahead of time with clear expectations that assigned work will be discussed at the next meeting.
6. All committees should have written agendas and effective committee chairs.

Stages of Groups

The chair of a committee should understand the issues of group dynamics, including the sequence through which each group must proceed before work can be accomplished. Tuckman (1965) has labeled these stages *forming, storming, norming, and performing.*

When individuals first gather, they must go through a process of meeting each other, the forming stage. Then they progress through a stage in which they chal-

TABLE 9.1   Stages of Group Process

Group Development Stage	Group Process	Task Process
Forming	Testing occurs to identify boundaries of interpersonal behaviors; establishing dependency relationships with leaders and other members; and determining what is acceptable behavior.	Testing to identify the tasks, appropriate rules, and methods suited to the task's performance
Storming	Resistance to group influence shown as members polarize into subgroups; conflict ensues and members rebel against demands imposed by the leader.	Resistance to task requirements and the differences regarding demands imposed by the task
Norming	Consensus evolves as group cohesion develops; norms develop; conflict and resistance are overcome.	Cooperation as differences are expressed and resolved
Performing	Interpersonal structure focuses on task and its completion; roles become flexible and functional; energies are directed to task performance.	Problems solved as the task performance improves; constructive efforts to complete task; more of group energies available for the task.

(Condensed from Luckman, 1965.)

lenge each other and establish individual identities, the storming stage. The group then begins to establish rules and design its work, the norming stage. Finally, during the performing stage, the work actually gets done. Table 9.1 summarizes each stage.

Northouse and Northouse (1986) add the termination phase as the last development in the working group. The leader guides members to summarize, express feelings, and come to closure. A celebration at the end of committee work is a good way to conclude group effort.

Because a group's work develops over time, the addition of new members to a committee can slow productivity. It takes some time for the group to accept new members. Some developmental stages will be performed again or delayed if several new members join a group. Therefore, it is important when assigning members to a committee to select those who can remain until the work is finished or until their appointment time is over.

 LEARNING EXERCISE 9.3

In discussion or as a writing exercise, identify the various groups or committees with which you are presently involved. Describe the stage of each one. Did it take longer for some of your groups to get to the performing stage than others? Describe what happened to the productivity level when membership on the committee changed.

GROUP DYNAMICS OF COMMITTEES

Benne and Sheats (1948) identify three sets of roles that group members also perform: *task roles, group building and maintenance roles,* and *individual roles.* Although no two are alike, groups do function in rather predictable ways. Managers should understand how groups carry out their specific tasks and roles.

Task Roles of Groups

Each group performs 11 tasks. A member may perform several tasks, but for the work of the group to be accomplished, all the necessary tasks will be carried out, either by members or the leader. These roles or tasks follow:

1. *Initiator-contributor.* Proposes or suggests group goals or redefines the problem. There may be more than one initiator during the group's lifetime.
2. *Information seeker.* Searches for a factual basis for the group's work.
3. *Opinion seeker.* Explores opinions that clarify or reflect the value of other members' suggestions.
4. *Information giver.* Offers an opinion of what the group's view of pertinent values should be.
5. *Elaborator.* Gives examples or extends meanings of suggestions given and how they could work.
6. *Coordinator.* Clarifies and coordinates ideas, suggestions, and activities of the group.
7. *Orienter.* Summarizes decisions and actions; identifies and questions departures from predetermined goals.
8. *Evaluator-critic.* Questions group accomplishments and compares them to a standard.
9. *Energizer.* Stimulates and prods the group to act and raises the level of its actions.
10. *Procedural technician.* Facilitates group action by arranging the environment.
11. *Recorder.* Records the group's activities and accomplishments.

Group Building and Maintenance Roles

The group task roles listed above all contribute to the work to be done; the group building roles that follow provide for the group's care and maintenance. Committees need to have a mix of members—enough individuals to carry out the work tasks but also individuals who are good at group building. One group member may perform task functions and group-building roles. The following are group-building roles:

1. *Encourager.* Accepts and praises all contributions, viewpoints, and ideas with warmth and solidarity.
2. *Harmonizer.* Mediates, harmonizes, and resolves conflict.
3. *Compromiser.* Yields his or her position in a conflict situation.
4. *Gatekeeper.* Promotes open communication and facilitates participation by all members.

5. *Standard setter.* Expresses or evaluates standards to evaluate group process.
6. *Group commentator.* Records group process and provides feedback to the group.
7. *Follower.* Accepts the group's ideas and listens to discussion and decisions.

Individual Roles of Group Members

Group members also carry out roles that serve their own needs. Group leaders must be able to manage member roles so that individuals do not disrupt meetings. The goal, however, should be management and not suppression. Not every group member has a need that results in the use of one of these roles. The eight individual roles follow:

1. *Aggressor.* Expresses disapproval of others' values or feelings through jokes, verbal attacks, or envy.
2. *Blocker.* Persists in expressing negative points of view and resurrects dead issues.
3. *Recognition seeker.* Works to focus positive attention on himself or herself.
4. *Self-confessor.* Uses the group setting as a forum for personal expression.
5. *Playboy.* Remains uninvolved and demonstrates cynicism, nonchalance, or horseplay.
6. *Dominator.* Attempts to control and manipulate the group.
7. *Help seeker.* Uses expressions of personal insecurity, confusion, or self-deprecation to manipulate sympathy from members.
8. *Special-interest pleader.* Cloaks personal prejudices or biases by ostensibly speaking for others.

RESPONSIBILITIES AND OPPORTUNITIES OF COMMITTEE WORK

Committees present the leader/manager with many opportunities and responsibilities. Managers need to be well grounded in group dynamics because meetings represent a major time commitment. Managers serve as members of committees and as leaders or chairpersons of committees.

Because major decisions are made by committees, managers should use the opportunities available at meetings to become more visible in the larger organization. The manager has a responsibility to select appropriate power strategies, such as coming to meetings well prepared, and to use skill in group process to generate influence and gain power at meetings (Kippenbrock, 1992).

Another responsibility is to create an environment at unit committee meetings that leads to shared decision making. Encouraging an interaction free of status and power is important. Likewise, an appropriate seating arrangement, such as a circle, will increase motivation for committee members to speak up.

The manager must not rely too heavily on committees or use them as a method to *delay* decision making. Numerous committee assignments exhaust staff, and committees then become poor tools for accomplishing work. An alternative that will decrease the time commitment for committee work is to make individual assignments and gather the entire committee only to report progress. Gaynor et al. (1994) recommend committee cost be built into the unit budget to allow more paid time off the unit for committee work and for support services, such as secretarial support.

In the leadership role, an opportunity exists for important influence on committee and group effectiveness. A dynamic leader inspires people to put spirit into working for a shared goal. Leaders demonstrate their commitment to participatory management by how they work with groups and committees. Leaders keep the group on course, draw out the shy, politely cut off the garrulous, and protect the weak. Committees may be chaired by an elected member of the group, appointed by the manager, or led by the department or unit manager. Informal leaders also may emerge from the group process.

It is important for the manager to be aware of the possibility for "groupthink" to occur in any group or committee structure. *Groupthink* is inappropriate conformity to group norms (Swansburg, 1990). It occurs when members fail to take adequate risks by disagreeing, being challenged, or assessing discussion carefully. If the manager is actively involved in the work group or on the committee, groupthink is less likely to occur. The leadership role includes teaching members to avoid groupthink by demonstrating critical thinking and being a role model who allows his or her own ideas to be challenged.

INTEGRATING LEADERSHIP ROLES AND MANAGEMENT FUNCTIONS IN THE ORGANIZATION OF WORK AND COMMITTEES

Organizing is an important management function. The work must be organized so that organizational goals are sustained. Activities must be grouped so that resources, people, materials, and time are used fully. The effective manager has an adequate knowledge of group dynamics and uses committees appropriately.

Integrating leadership roles and management functions ensures that the type of patient care delivery mode selected will provide quality care *and* staff satisfaction and that change in the mode of delivery will not be attempted without adequate resources and appropriate justification.

The integrated leader/manager groups activities to facilitate communication. Committees are used to increase productivity, not to delay decisions. All members of the work group should be assisted with role clarification. The leader's critical thinking and role-modeling behavior discourages groupthink among work groups or in committees.

Integrated leaders/managers also refrain from judging and encourage all members to participate and contribute, thus inspiring a group effort. This team effort in work activity increases productivity and worker satisfaction. The emphasis is on seeking solutions to poor organization of work, rather than finding fault.

When serving on committees, the opportunity should be used to gain influence to present the needs of clients and staff appropriately. The integrated leader/manager comes to meetings well prepared and contributes thoughtful comments and ideas.

KEY CONCEPTS

▼ *Case method,* or total patient care, is the oldest form of patient care organization and is still widely used today.

▼ *Functional nursing* organization requires the completion of specific tasks by different nursing personnel.

▼ *Team or modular nursing* organization uses a leader who coordinates team members in the care of a group of patients.

▼ *Primary care nursing* is organized so the patient is at the center of the structure. One nurse has 24-hour responsibility for the nursing care plan.

▼ *Differentiated* nursing practice delineates different roles for nurses based on their skill, knowledge, and motivation.

▼ *Case management* is similar to primary nursing and derived from *managed care.* The case manager in managed care focuses on coordinating, planning, and evaluating care; case management is used most frequently in complex patient care situations.

▼ The patient care structure should 1) facilitate meeting the goals of the organization; 2) be cost effective; 3) satisfy the patient; 4) provide role satisfaction to nurses; 5) allow implementation of the nursing process; and 6) provide for adequate communication among healthcare providers.

▼ When work is redesigned, it frequently has personal consequences for employees that must be considered. Social interactions, the degree of autonomy, the abilities and skills necessary, employee evaluation, and communication patterns are often affected by work redesign.

▼ Better organization of individual work can be accomplished by 1) grouping activities together; 2) reducing travel time; and 3) using time estimates to accomplish two tasks at once.

▼ Too many committees in an organization is a sign of a poorly designed organizational structure.

▼ Committees should have an appropriate number of members, prepared agendas, clearly outlined tasks, and effective leadership.

▼ Committees go through predictable developmental stages of *forming, storming, norming, and performing.* Committees also should include a termination phase when the work is completed.

▼ Appropriate committee assignment is crucial if the committee is to be productive. Members must have commitment and the necessary expertise.

▼ Adding new members to an established committee disrupts productivity and group development.

▼ Group members perform certain important tasks that facilitate work.

▼ Group members also perform roles that assist with group-building activities.

▼ Some group members will perform roles to meet their own individual needs.

▼ Managers must be well grounded in group dynamics because much of their work involves groups.

▼ Groupthink occurs when there is too much conformity to group norms, often resulting in opinions and ideas that may lack merit.

ADDITIONAL LEARNING EXERCISES

Learning Exercise 9.4

You are a 3 PM to 11 PM charge nurse on a surgical unit. Each week you have a short educational conference in which each staff member takes turns presenting a 15-minute summary of a topic of his or her choice. You also have two short staff meetings a week, one for general sharing and one for patient care conferences. Lately, you have found the meetings are not going well because one member of the group, Mary, tends to monopolize all the meeting time, except when someone is making a formal presentation. You have privately spoken to her about this, and although she apologizes, the behavior has continued. In all other respects, Mary is an excellent nurse and a good employee.

Assignment: Using your knowledge of group dynamics, outline the steps you would take to facilitate more group participation. Be specific; explain exactly what you would *do* the next time Mary takes over the meeting. Be able to support your selection of approach using theoretical rationale.

Learning Exercise 9.5

In groups or individually, investigate the types of patient care delivery in your area. Do not limit your investigation to hospitals. Assign one healthcare organization to a group. If possible, conduct interviews with nurses from a variety of delivery systems. Share the report of your findings with classmates. How many different modes of patient care delivery did you find? What is the most widely used method in healthcare facilities in your area? Does this vary from modes identified most frequently in current nursing literature?

Learning Exercise 9.6

In group discussion or as a writing exercise, choose one of following to examine in depth.

1. What has contributed to the productivity of committees on which you have served? What has made them nonproductive?
2. What roles do you normally carry out in group work?
3. Have you ever served on a committee that made recommendations on which the higher authority never acted? What was the effect on the group?

Learning Exercise 9.7

Many nurses learn organizing skills that help accomplish patient care activities. Some nurses fill their pockets with supplies they will need in the course of the day. Other nurses learn to group activities in an efficient manner. Some nurses use different colored pens to keep information organized on their clipboard. In groups, share the special organizing skills that have assisted you in carrying out the duties of your job.

REFERENCES:

Benne, K. D., & Sheats, P. (1948). Functional roles of group members. *Journal of Social Studies, 4.*

Dwyer, D. J., Schwartz, R. H., & Fox, M. L. (1992). Decision making autonomy in nursing. *Journal of Nursing Administration, 22*(2), 17–23.

Gaynor, S. E., Reschak, G. L. C., & Verdin, J. (1994). Evaluating a committee structure. *The Journal of Nursing Administration, 24*(7/8), 59–63.

Huston, C. J., & Marquis, B. L. (1989). *Retention and productivity strategies for nurse managers.* Philadelphia: J.B. Lippincott.

Joel, L. A. (1994). Changes in the hospital as a place to practice. In J. McCloskey & H. K. Grace (Eds.), *Current issues in nursing* (4th ed.). St. Louis: C.V. Mosby.

Kippenbrock, T. A. (1992). Power at meetings: Strategies to move people. *Nursing Economics, 10*(4), 282–286.

Kramer, M. (1990). The magnet hospitals: Excellence revisited. *Journal of Nursing Administration, 20*(9).

Tuckman, B. W. (1965). Developmental sequence in small groups. *Psychological Bulletin, 62*(6).

Malloch, K. M., Milton, A. D., & Jobes, M. O. (1990). A model for differentiated nursing practice. *Journal of Nursing Administration, 20*(2), 20–26.

Marquis, B. L., & Huston, C. J. (1994). *Management decision making for nurses: 118 Case studies* (2nd ed.). Philadelphia: J.B. Lippincott.

Northouse, L. L., & Northouse, P. G. (1986). *Health communication: A handbook for health professionals.* Englewood Cliffs, NJ: Prentice Hall.

Swansburg, R. C. (1990). *Management and leadership for nurse managers.* Boston: Jones and Bartlett.

Tappen, R. M. (1990). *Nursing leadership and management: Concepts and practice* (2nd ed.). Philadelphia: F.A. Davis.

Zander, K. (1988). Nursing care management: Strategic management of cost and quality outcomes. *Journal of Nursing Administration, 18*(5), 23–30.

Zander, K. (1994) To control or collaborate?. In J. McCloskey & H. K. Grace (Eds.), *Current issues in nursing* (4th ed.). St. Louis: C.V. Mosby.

BIBLIOGRAPHY

Bowers, K. (1991). *Case management by nurses.* Kansas City, Mo: American Nurses Association.

Brider, P. (1991). Who killed the nursing care plan? *American Journal of Nursing, 91*(5), 35–38.

Cronin, C. J., & Maklebust, J. (1989). Case-managed care: Capitalizing on the CNS. *Nursing Management, 20*(3).

Dahlen, A. L. (1978). With primary nursing we have it all together. *American Journal of Nursing, 78,* 426–428.

Ethridge, P., & Lamb, G. (1989). Professional nursing case management improves quality, access, and costs. *Nursing Management, 20*(3).

LeClair, C. L. (1991). Introducing and accounting for RN case management. *Nursing Management, 22*(3), 44–49.

Llewelyn, S., & Fielding, G. (1982). Forming, storming, norming and performing. *Nursing Mirror, 155.*

McKenize, C. B., Torkelson, N. G., & Holt, M. A. (1989). Care and cost: Nursing case management improves both. *Nursing Management, 20* (10).

Olivas, G. S., Del Togno-Armanasco, V., Erickson, J. R., & Jarter S. (1989). Case management: A bottom line care delivery model. Part 1: The concept. *Journal of Nursing Administration, 19*(11).

Olivas, G. S., Del Togno-Armanasco, V., Erickson, J. R., & Jarter S. (1989). Case management: A bottom line care delivery model. Part 2: Adaptation of the model. *Journal of Nursing Administration, 19*(12).

Rosenblum, E. H. (1982). Groupthink: The peril of group cohesiveness. *Journal of Nursing Administration, 12.*

Sheafor, M. (1991). Productive work groups in complex hospital units. *Journal of Nursing Administration, 21*(5), 25–30.

Sherman, R. O. (1990). Team nursing revisited. *Journal of Nursing Administration, 20*(11), 43–46.

Shukla, R. K. (1982). Primary or team nursing? Two conditions determine the choice. *Journal of Nursing Administration, 12,* 12–15.

Tucker, S. M. (1994). Death of the care plan. In J. McCloskey & H. K. Grace (Eds.), *Current issues in nursing.* St. Louis: C.V. Mosby.

UNIT IV

ROLES AND FUNCTIONS IN STAFFING

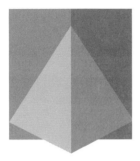

CHAPTER 10

Pre-employment Staffing Responsibilities

Staffing is the third phase of the management process. In staffing, the leader/manager recruits, selects, orients, and promotes personnel development to accomplish the goals of the organization (Marriner-Tomey, 1992). Staffing is an especially important phase of the management process in healthcare organizations because they are labor intensive; that is, they require many employees to accomplish their goals. Additionally, this large work force must be composed of highly skilled, competent professionals. Ensuring the adequacy of skilled staff to accomplish organizational goals is an important management function. Unit 4 reviews the manager's responsibilities in executing the staffing functions of the management process.

Staffing responsibilities begin with planning because the philosophy and fiscal resources of the organization influence the mix and numbers of staff. Staffing also is influenced by the system selected to deliver patient care because some types require a higher ratio of RNs to other nursing personnel.

The following are the sequential steps of staffing responsibilities, although each step has some interdependence with all staffing activities.

1. Determine the number and types of personnel needed to fulfill the philosophy, meet fiscal planning responsibilities, and carry out the chosen patient care management organization.

Bessie L. Marquis and Carol J. Huston:
LEADERSHIP ROLES AND MANAGEMENT FUNCTIONS IN NURSING, 2nd ed.
Lippincott-Raven Publishers © 1996

2. Recruit, interview, select, and assign personnel based on established job description performance standards.
3. Use organizational resources for induction and orientation.
4. Ascertain that each employee is adequately socialized to organization values and unit norms.
5. Use creative and flexible scheduling based on patient care needs to increase productivity and retention.
6. Develop a program of staff education that will assist employees with meeting the goals of the organization.

This chapter addresses the pre-employment functions of staffing, namely, determining present and future staffing needs and recruiting, interviewing, selecting, and placing personnel. The management functions and leadership roles inherent in these staffing responsibilities are shown in Display 10.1.

Display 10.1 Leadership Roles and Management Functions in Pre-employment Staffing

Leadership Roles

1. Plans for future staffing needs proactively
2. Predicts the future by being knowledgeable regarding current and historical staffing events
3. Identifies and recruits gifted individuals to the organization
4. Serves as a role model for recruitment
5. Is self-aware regarding personal biases during the pre-employment process
6. Uses the interview process as a means to promote the organization's image
7. Assigns new personnel to positions that facilitate success

Management Functions

1. Ensures that there is an adequate skilled work force to meet the goals of the organization
2. Shares responsibility for the recruitment of staff
3. Plans and structures appropriate interview activities
4. Uses techniques that increase the validity and reliability of the interview process
5. Applies knowledge of the legal requirements of interviewing and selection to ensure that the organization is not unfair in its hiring practices
6. Develops established criteria for selection
7. Uses knowledge of organizational needs and employee strengths to make placement decisions.

PLANNING FOR STAFFING

Planning is a major leadership role in staffing. Adequate planning to determine staffing needs is often a neglected part of the staffing process. Because the success of many staffing decisions greatly depends on previous decisions made in the planning and organizing phases, one must consider staffing when making other plans. Consideration must be given to the type of patient care management used, the education and knowledge level of staff to be recruited, budget constraints, and the historical background of staffing needs and availability.

Accurately predicting staffing needs is a valuable management skill because it enables the manager to avoid staffing crises. Managers should know the source of their nursing pool, how many students are currently enrolled in local nursing schools, the usual length of employment of new hires, peak staff resignation periods, and times when patient census is highest. Analyzing historical patterns, using computers to sort personnel statistics, and keeping accurate unit records are examples of proactive planning.

The manager also should be aware of the role economics plays in planning for staffing. Buerhaus (1993) states that a discussion of the RN labor market often focuses solely on noneconomic issues, such as autonomy, professional status, satisfaction, and gender conflicts; however, nurses do have economic self-interest, and the nurse market is strongly influenced by economic variables. For example, the national and local economy has a great impact on the nursing workforce. During the mid 1980s, when the national economy was on an upswing, a severe nationwide nursing shortage existed. However, as the economy worsened in the late 1980s and early 1990s, nursing jobs grew scarce. Many unemployed nurses returned to the workforce, and part-time nurses returned to full-time employment. In addition, dramatic increases in nursing wages served as a powerful retention tool during this time (Buerhaus, 1993).

During this same period, many healthcare organizations, hospitals in particular, began *downsizing,* or eliminating jobs in a cost-containment effort, and new graduate nurses experienced great difficulty in finding jobs. In a 1994 poll, 71% of nurses stated they did not feel secure in their jobs; 54% reported a hiring freeze in effect for nurses at their institution of employment; 32% reported RN lay-offs; and 40% stated that a hospital in their area had closed within the last 2 years (Meissner & Carey, 1994).

Some experts have suggested, however, that this country will again face a nursing shortage by the end of this decade and that it may be one of the most severe nursing shortages ever faced. Styles and Holzemer (1986) predicted that by 2000, there would be about one-half the number of nurses needed. This will occur as a result of the increased number of nurses (especially nurses with advanced degrees) needed to implement many of the healthcare reform proposals under consideration, the decrease in nursing school enrollments in the 1980s and early 1990s, and the short-sightedness of healthcare institutions (particularly hospitals) to recruit and hire RNs on a proactive basis.

Hurley (1994) suggests that nurses in the next decade will face increased needs for cross-training, an increased use of unlicensed assistive personnel, a shift from inpatient to outpatient services, an acceleration of acuity in the hospitalized patient, and the merger or alliance of healthcare organizations in a managed care environment. All of these changes have tremendous implications for strategic staffing planning.

RECRUITMENT

In complex organizations, work must be accomplished by groups of people; wise managers, therefore, try to surround themselves with people of ability, motivation, and promise. Unfortunately, some managers feel threatened by bright and talented individuals and surround themselves with mediocrity. The organization's ability to meet its goals and objectives is directly related to the quality of its employees. Excellent employees reflect well on the manager because they prevent stagnation and increase productivity within the organization. A leadership role in staffing includes identifying, recruiting, and hiring gifted individuals.

Recruiting is the process of actively seeking out or attracting applicants for existing positions. Although at any given time, an organization may have an adequate supply of RNs to meet demand, historical data support the idea that recruitment should be an ongoing process (Stratton, Dunkin, Juhl, Ludtke, & Geller, 1991).

The Nurse Recruiter

The manager may be greatly or minimally involved with recruiting, interviewing, and selecting personnel depending on 1) the size of the institution; 2) the existence of a separate personnel department; 3) the presence of a nurse recruiter within the organization; and 4) the use of centralized or decentralized nursing management.

Generally speaking, the more decentralized nursing management and the less complex the personnel department, the greater the involvement of the lower level manager in selecting personnel for individual units or departments.

When deciding whether to hire a nurse recruiter or decentralize the responsibility for recruitment, the organization needs to weigh benefits against costs. Costs include more than financial considerations. For example, an additional cost to an organization employing a nurse recruiter might be the eventual loss of interest by managers in the recruiting process. The organization loses if managers relegate their collective and individual responsibilities to the nurse recruiter. A collaborative relationship must exist between managers and the recruiter. Managers must be aware of recruitment constraints, and the recruiter must be aware of individual department needs and culture. Both parties must understand the organization's philosophy, benefit programs, salary scale, and other factors that influence employee retention.

Recruitment Strategies

Recruiting adequate numbers of nurses is relatively easy if the organization is located in a progressive community with a mild climate and several schools of nursing and if the organization has a good reputation for quality patient care and fair employment practices (Huston & Marquis, 1989). It is much more difficult to recruit nurses to rural areas that historically have experienced less appropriation of healthcare professionals per capita than urban areas (Stratton, et al., 1991). Factors contributing to this rural nursing shortage include substandard salaries, fewer opportunities for professional development and continuing education, and a shortage of ancillary healthcare professionals (American Nurses Association, 1989).

In their study of homecare nurses, deSavorgnani, Haring, and Galloway (1993) found that job satisfaction, flexible hours, salary, and working conditions are considered moderately to very important in recruiting. Items given less emphasis but still considered slightly to moderately important are availability of jobs, job location, weekend hours, orientation program, company polices, and job status. In addition, part-time RNs "value" pay more than full-time nurses and give less importance to professional status than their full-time counterparts (deSavorgnani, Haring, and Galloway, 1993). Other variables that affect recruitment include the availability of resources for advertising, the numbers of new and experienced nurses available, and the competitiveness of the organization's salaries and benefits, which is often influenced by budget constraints.

During nursing shortages, healthcare institutions frequently must recruit through advertisements in newspapers and national nursing journals. National searches can be expensive and time consuming. Generally, most healthcare institutions hiring nurses look first in their own geographic area. Often there is a potential pool of inactive local nurses. In addition, flyers should be sent to nursing schools for posting on recruitment bulletin boards.

Because some recruiting methods are expensive, healthcare organizations often seek less costly means of recruitment. One of the best ways to maintain an adequate employee pool is by word of mouth, the recommendation of the organization's own satisfied and happy staff. DeSavorgnani, Haring, and Galloway (1993), in their study of home care RNs, found that word-of-mouth referral was the most common recruitment method (52.3%), followed by newspaper advertisements (40.2%). Other inexpensive internal recruiting resources are hosting an open house for community nurses or using educational resources, especially at the local level.

Another less expensive recruitment strategy for healthcare organizations with local nursing schools is to participate in career day programs. If the organization does not have a recruiter, staff nurses may be asked to participate. Having an employee who is a recent graduate return to the school on a career day can be a good endorsement for a particular agency.

Having printed materials available to hand out or mail in response to inquiries is often a successful strategy for recruitment. These materials should list salaries, benefits, organizational philosophy, information about the community where the healthcare facility is located, and the name of the contact person in the agency.

The Relationship Between Recruitment and Retention

Some turnover is normal, and in fact, desirable. Turnover infuses the organization with fresh ideas. It also reduces the probability of "groupthink," in which all the individuals in the organization share similar thought processes, values, and goals (Mar-

LEARNING EXERCISE 10.1

Select one of the following.

1. Examine several nursing journals that carry job advertisements. Select three ads that particularly appeal to you. What do these advertisements say, or what makes them stand out? Are similar key words used in all three ads?
2. Select a healthcare agency in your area. Write an advertisement or recruitment poster that accurately depicts the agency and the community. Compare your completed advertisement or recruitment flyer with others in your group.
3. Write a recruitment poster or an advertisement for the healthcare agency where you are employed.

quis & Huston, 1994). However, excessive or unnecessary turnover is not only expensive, but reduces the ability of the organization to produce its end-product.

It is critical, then, that the manager recognize the link between retention and recruitment. Some healthcare organizations find it necessary to do external recruitment, partly because of their lack of attention to retention. Longo and Uranker (1987) state that hospitals should adopt the premise that "a nurse retained is a nurse recruited" and that the retention of a nurse exemplifies the hospital's protection of its investment. Wall (1988) states that recruited nurses should provide feedback regarding their career wants and needs so that the organization can make an effort to meet those criteria.

The closer the fit between what the nurse is seeking in employment and what the organization can offer, the greater the chance that the nurse will be retained. Often those recruiting during a nursing shortage inadvertently misrepresent the organization. At times, this behavior borders on unethical conduct but most often occurs because of the recruiter's overzealousness.

Interestingly, a 1993 study by Del Bueno shows that nurse executives change their employment status frequently and sometimes unexpectedly; although changes at the executive level may be disruptive personally and expensive organizationally, it appears inevitable in acute care hospitals regardless of their size or type.

INTERVIEWING

An *interview* may be defined as a verbal interaction between individuals for a particular purpose. Although other tools, such as testing and reference checks, may be used, the interview is frequently accepted as the foundation for selecting individuals for positions.

Beach (1980) maintains that the purposes, or goals, of the selection interview are threefold: 1) the interviewer seeks to obtain enough information to determine the applicant's suitability for the available position; 2) the applicant obtains adequate information to make an intelligent decision about accepting the job, should it be offered; and 3) the interviewer seeks to conduct the interview in such a manner that regardless of the interview's result, the applicant will continue to have respect for and good will toward the organization (Beach, 1980).

Interviews may be unstructured or structured. The unstructured interview requires little planning because the goals for hiring may be unclear, questions are not prepared in advance, and often the interviewer does more talking than the applicant (Tibbles, 1993). The structured interview requires greater planning time because questions must be developed in advance that address the specific job requirements, information must be offered about the skills and qualities being sought, examples of the applicant's experience must be received, and the willingness or motivation of the applicant to do the job must be determined (Tibbles, 1993).

Limitations of Interviews

The major defect of the interview is its subjectivity. Dorio (1994) suggests that one of the reasons for the popularity of the interview as a selection tool is that it allows us the freedom to exercise our personal judgment. Therefore we feel more confident in its results and view the interview as reliable. In reality, interviews generally require an interviewer to use judgments, biases, and values to make decisions based on a short interaction with an applicant in an unnatural situation. The applicant, trying to create a favorable impression, also may be unduly influenced by the interviewer's personality.

Research findings regarding the validity and reliability of interviews have been inconsistent. However, the following findings are generally accepted (Mayfield, 1964; Bouchard, 1976; Ghiselli, 1966; Jablin, 1975).

1. The same interviewer will consistently rate the interviewee the same. Therefore, the *intrarater reliability* is said to be high.
2. If two different interviewers conduct unstructured interviews of the same applicant, their ratings will not be consistent. Therefore, the inter-rater reliability is extremely low in unstructured interviews.
3. Inter-rater reliability is satisfactory if the interview is structured, and the same format is used by both interviewers.
4. Even if the interview has *reliability,* that is, it measures the same thing consistently, it still may not be valid. *Validity* occurs when the interview measures what it is supposed to measure, which, in this case, is the potential for productivity as an employee. Wright, Lichtenfels, and Pursell (1989) have found that structured interviews have a validity of 0.39, while the validity for unstructured interviews was only 0.14. Thus, the structured interview was found to be a much better predictor of job performance and overall effectiveness than the unstructured interview.
5. High *interview assessments* are not related to subsequent high-level job performance.
6. Validity increases when there is a team approach to the interview.
7. The attitudes and *biases* of interviewers greatly influence how candidates are rated. Although steps can be taken to reduce *subjectivity,* they cannot be eliminated entirely.
8. The interviewer is more influenced by unfavorable than by favorable information. *Negative information is weighed more heavily* than positive information about the applicant.

9. Interviewers tend to make up their minds about hiring applicants very early in the job interview. *Decisions are often formed in the first few minutes of the interview.*

10. *In unstructured interviews, the interviewer tends to do most of the talking,* while in structured interviews, the interviewer does only about 50% of the talking.

Regardless of the defects inherent in interviewing, the method remains a widely used and accepted way of selecting from among many applicants to fill a limited number of positions. By knowing the limitations of interviews and using findings from current research, interviews should be able to be conducted in a manner that will have an increased predictive value.

Overcoming Interview Limitations

Interview research has helped managers develop strategies for overcoming many of interviewing's inherent limitations. The following guidelines will assist the manager in developing an interview process that results in increased reliability and validity.

Use a Team Approach

Having more than one person interview the job applicant reduces the bias normally present in individual personalities. Staff involvement in hiring can be viewed on a continuum from no involvement to that described by Mills and Oie (1992) as an "autonomous staff selection team," whereby the team is empowered to make hiring decisions for all positions within the department without management influence or interference. When hiring a manager, using a staff nurse as part of the interview team is effective, especially if the staff nurse is mature enough to represent the interest and needs of the unit rather than his or her own self-interests.

Involving staff on hiring committees or panels to interview job applicants can involve a significant commitment of employee time and thus expense on the part of the organization. This expense may be justified if attrition rates are particularly high or if prior hiring outcomes have not been satisfactory to the organization. Any organization that has a high attrition rate should look very carefully at its selection process.

Develop a Structured Interview Format for Each Job Classification

Because each job has different position requirements, interviews must be structured to fit the position. The same structured interview should be used for all employees applying for the same job classification. A well-developed structured interview uses open-ended questions and provides ample opportunity for the interviewee to talk. The structured interview is advantageous because it allows the interviewer to be consistent and prevents the interview from becoming sidetracked. Display 10.2 is an example of a structured interview.

Display 10.2   The Structured Interview

Motivation
Why did you apply for employment with this company?

Physical
Do you have any physical limitations that would prohibit you from accomplishing the job?
How many days have you been absent from work during the last year of employment?

Education
What was your grade point average in nursing school?
What were your extracurricular activities and offices held?
For verification purposes, are your school records listed under the name on your application form?

Professional
In what states are you licensed to practice?
Do you have your license with you?
What certifications do you hold?
What professional organizations do you currently participate in that would be of value in the job for which you are applying?

Military experience
What are your current military obligations?
Which military assignments do you think have prepared you for this position?

Present employer
How did you secure your present position?
What is your current job title? What was your title when you began your present position?
What supervisory responsibilities do you currently have?
How would you describe your immediate supervisor?
What are some examples of success at your present job?
How do you get along with your present employer?
How do you get along with your present colleagues?
What do you like least about your present job?
What do you like most about your present job?
May we contact your present employer?
Why do you want to change jobs?
For verification purposes only, is your name the same as it was while employed with your current employer?

Previous position
Ask similar questions about recent past employment. Depending on the time span and type of other positions held, the interviewer does not usually review employment history that took place beyond the position just previous to the current one.

Specific questions for RNs
What do you like most about nursing?
What do you like least about nursing?
What is your philosophy of nursing?

(continued)

Display 10.2 The Structured Interview (Continued)

Personal characteristics

Which personal characteristics are your greatest assets?
Which personal characteristics cause you the most difficulty?

Professional goals

What are your career goals?
Where do you see yourself 10 years from now?

Contributions to organization

What can you offer this company?

Questions from interviewee

What questions do you have about the organization?
What questions do you have about the position?
What other questions do you have?

Evaluation

Evaluation should be objective and relate to the applicant's qualifications for the specific position.

Use Scenarios to Determine Decision-Making Ability

In addition to obtaining answers to a particular set of questions, the interview also should be used to determine the applicant's decision-making ability. This can be accomplished by designing scenarios that require problem-solving and decision-making skills. The same set of scenarios should be used with each category of employee. For example, a set could be developed for new graduates, critical care nurses, unit secretaries, and practical nurses. Patient care situations, as shown in Display 10.3, require clinical judgment and are very useful for this purpose.

Conduct Multiple Interviews

Many authorities suggest that most candidates should be interviewed more than once. For the process to be most effective, the applicant should be interviewed on separate days. This prevents applicants from being accepted or rejected merely because they were having a good or bad day. Dorio (1994) states the number of interviews needed depends to a large extent on two factors: the level of the job and the number of interviewers in the interview cycle. Regardless, the individual should be interviewed until all the interviewers' questions have been answered, and they feel confident they have enough information to make the right decision.

Display 10.3 Sample of Interview Questions Using Case Situations

Each recent graduate applying for a position at County Hospital will be asked to respond to the following.

Case 1

You are working on the evening shift of a surgical unit. Mr. Jones returned from the postanesthesia recovery room following a cholecystectomy 2 hours ago. While in the recovery room, he received 10 mg of morphine sulfate intravenously for incisional pain. Thirty minutes ago, he complained of mild incisional pain but then drifted off to sleep. He is now awake and complaining of moderate-to-severe incisional pain. His orders include the following pain relief order: M.S. 8–10 mg., IV push every 3 hours for pain. It has been two-and-a-half hours since Mr. Jones' last pain medication. What would you do?

Case 2

One of the practical nurses on your team seems especially tired today. She later tells you that her new baby kept her up all night. When you ask her about the noon finger stick blood glucose level on Mrs. White (82 years old), she looks at you blankly and then says quickly that it was 150. Later, when you are in Mrs. White's room, she tells you that she doesn't remember anyone checking her noon blood glucose. What do you do?

Provide Training in Effective Interviewing Techniques

Training should focus on communication skills and advice on planning, conducting, and controlling the interview. Mills and Oie (1992) suggest that training also should include instruction regarding the legalities of interviewing and selection, formulation of interview questions, and the mechanics of conducting an interview. Dorio (1994) suggests a combination of a 1- or 2-day course on interviewing, one-on-one coaching, and actual interview observations for interview training. It is unfair to expect a manager to make appropriate hiring decisions if he or she has never had adequate training in interview techniques. Unskilled interviewers often let subjective rather than objective data affect their hiring evaluation (Kinicki, Hom, Lockwood, & Griffeth, 1990). In addition, unskilled interviewers may place the organization at risk by asking discriminatory questions (Tibbles, 1993).

Planning, Conducting, and Controlling the Interview

Planning the interview in advance is vital to its subsequent success as a selection tool. If other interviewers are to be present, they should be available at the appointed time. The plan also should include adequate time for the interview. Before the interview, all interviewers should review the application, noting questions concerning information supplied by the applicant. Although it takes considerable practice, consistently using a planned sequence in the interview format will eventually yield a relaxed and spontaneous process. The following is a suggested interview format (Huston & Marquis, 1989):

1. Introduce yourself, and greet applicant.
2. Make a *brief* statement about the company and the available positions.
3. Ascertain the position for which the person is applying.
4. Discuss the information on the application, and seek clarification or amplification as necessary.
5. Discuss employee qualifications, and proceed with the structured interview format.
6. If applicant appears qualified, discuss the company and the position further.
7. Explain the subsequent procedures for hiring, such as employment physicals and hiring date. If the applicant is not hired at this time, discuss how and when he or she will be notified of the interview results.
8. Terminate the interview.

If the manager has opened well and the applicant is at ease, the interview will usually proceed smoothly. During the meeting, pause frequently to allow the applicant to ask questions. The format should always encourage and include ample time for questions from the applicant. Often interviewers are able to infer much about applicants by the types of questions they ask.

Moving the conversation along, covering questions on a structured interview guide, and keeping the interview pertinent but friendly becomes easier with experience. Methods that help reach the goals of the interview follow:

1. Ask only job-related questions.
2. Use open-ended questions that require more than a "yes" or "no" answer.
3. Pause a few seconds after the applicant has seemingly finished before asking the next question. This gives the applicant a chance to talk further.
4. Return to topics later in the interview on which the applicant offered little information initially.
5. Ask only one question at a time.
6. Restate part of the applicant's answer if you need elaboration.
7. Ask questions clearly, but do not verbally or nonverbally indicate the correct answer. By watching the interviewer's eyes and observing other body language, the astute applicant learns which answers are desired.
8. Always appear interested in what the applicant has to say. The interview should never be interrupted, nor should the interviewer's words ever imply criticism of or impatience with the applicant.
9. Language should be used that is appropriate for the applicant. Terminology or language that makes applicants feel the interviewer is either talking down to them or talking over their heads is inappropriate.

Display 10.4 lists questions that may be used in an interview and explains the importance of each question.

Display 10.4 How to Develop an Interview Guide

All questions on the application form and questions asked at the interview should have a specific purpose. Application forms and structured interviews should be reviewed periodically and revised as needed. Some examples of questions and explanations for their inclusion are given below. Managers should be able to provide similar explanations for all questions on their application forms and all questions asked at the interview.

How did you hear about us?
This question can help identify the effectiveness of various recruiting methods. If the organization is having difficulty with recruiting or wants to know which method is producing the best results, then this would be an important question to include on the application form or at the interview.

Is there any reason why you might not be able to work as regularly scheduled?
By asking this question, the interviewer is able to elicit information that would indicate any possible impediments to dependable attendance. The information also could be relevant in shift assignments.

In what community or professional activities are you involved?
This information may be helpful in identifying leadership abilities. Additionally, this question may establish a common ground of communication and induce a more relaxed atmosphere.

What kind of reference do you expect to get from your previous employers?
Ask this question to give the applicant the opportunity to discuss any possible problems that might be expected in obtaining references.

What was your attendance record at your previous job?
Because most healthcare organizations require dependability, the interviewer should be interested in past attendance. This question also affords the applicant an opportunity to discuss any previous attendance problems and state if these have been resolved.

A written record should be kept of all interviews. Note taking ensures accuracy and serves as a written record to recall the applicant. Keep note-taking or use of a checklist, however, to a minimum so that you do not create an uncomfortable climate.

As the interview draws to a close, the interviewer should make sure that all questions have been answered and that all pertinent information has been obtained. Usually applicants are not offered a job at the end of a first interview unless they are clearly qualified and the labor market is such that another applicant would be difficult to find. In most cases, interviewers need to analyze their impressions of the applicant, compare these perceptions with members of the selection team, and incorporate those impressions with other available data about the applicant. Frequently, the interviewer needs to consult with others in the organization before a job offer can be made. It is important, however, to let applicants know if they are being seriously considered for the position and how soon they can expect to hear a final outcome.

When the applicant is obviously not qualified, the interviewer needs to be extremely tactful. The interviewer should not give false hope but should advise the individual as soon as possible that he or she does not have the proper qualifications for the position. Such applicants should feel they have been treated fairly. The interviewer should, however, maintain records of the exact reasons for rejection in case of later discrimination charges.

Evaluation of the Interview

Interviewers should plan post-interview time to evaluate the applicant's interview performance. Interview notes are often taken in shorthand and may be difficult to read later. To avoid this problem, notes should be reviewed and necessary points clarified or amplified. Using a form to record the interview evaluation is a good idea. An example of such a form is shown in Display 10.5. The final question on the interview report form is a recommendation for or against hiring. In answering this question, two aspects must carry the most weight.

1. *The requirements for the job.* Regardless of how interesting or friendly people are, unless they have the basic skills for the job, they will not be successful at meeting the expectations of the position. Likewise, those overqualified for a position will usually be unhappy in the job.
2. *Personal bias.* Because completely eliminating the personal biases inherent in the interview is impossible, it is important for the interviewer to examine any

---

Display 10.5   Sample of Interview Evaluation Form

Interviewer's recommendation about Applicant

Interviewer #1 _____

_____

_____ Accept _____ Reject _____

Pending _____

Date _____   Interviewer's signature _____

Interviewer #2 _____

_____

_____ Accept _____ Reject _____

Pending _____

Date _____   Interviewer's signature _____

negative feelings that occurred during the interview. Often the interviewer discovers that the negative feelings have no relation to the criteria necessary for success in the position. Leadership requires that individual bias is minimized in personnel decisions.

Legal Aspects of Interviewing

The organization must ascertain that the application form does not contain questions that violate various employment acts. Likewise, managers must avoid unlawful inquiries during the interview. Inquiries cannot be made regarding age, marital status, children, race, sexual preference, financial or credit status, national origin, or religion (Swansburg, 1990). In addition to federal legislation, many states have specific laws pertaining to information that can be obtained during the process. For example, some states prohibit asking about a woman's ability to reproduce or her attitudes toward family planning. Table 10.1 lists subjects that are most frequently part of the interview process or applicant form, with examples of acceptable and unacceptable inquiries.

Managers who maintain interview records and receive applicants with an open and unbiased attitude have little to fear regarding charges of discrimination. Remember, the third goal of the interview process is that each applicant should feel good about the organization when the interview concludes. Regardless of the interview's outcome, each applicant and each interviewer should remember the experience as a positive one. It is a leadership responsibility to see that this goal is accomplished.

> ## ► LEARNING EXERCISE 10.2
>
> You are a new evening charge nurse on a medical floor in an acute care hospital. This is your first management position. You graduated 18 months ago from the local university with a nursing degree.
>
> Your immediate supervisor has asked you to interview two applicants who will be graduating from nursing school in 3 months. Your supervisor feels that they both are qualified. Because the available position is on your shift, she wants you to make the final hiring decision.
>
> Both applicants seem equally qualified in academic standing and work experience. Last evening, you interviewed Lisa and were very impressed. Tonight you interviewed John. During the meeting, you kept thinking that you knew John from somewhere but couldn't recall where. The interview went well, however, and you are equally impressed with John.
>
> Later, after John left, you suddenly remembered that one of your classmates used to date him, and he had attended some of your class parties. You recall that on several occasions, he appeared to abuse alcohol. This recollection bothers you, and you are not sure what to do. You know that tomorrow your supervisor wants to inform the applicants of your decision.
>
> *Assignment:* Decide what you are going to do. Support your decision with appropriate rationale. Explain how you would determine which applicant to hire. How great a role did your personal values play in your decision?

TABLE 10.1   Legal Interview Inquiries

Subject	Acceptable Inquiries	Unacceptable Inquiries
Name	If applicant has worked for the company under a different name. If school records are under another name. If applicant was convicted of a crime under another name.	Inquiries about name that would indicate lineage, national origin, or marital status.
Marital and family status	Whether applicant can meet specified work schedules or has commitments that may hinder attendance requirements. Inquiries as to anticipated stay in the position.	Any question about applicant's marital status or number or age of children. Information of child care arrangements. Any questions concerning pregnancy.
Address or residence	Place of residence and length resided in city or state.	Former addresses, names or relationships of people with whom applicant resides, or if owns or rents home.
Age	If over 18 or statement that hire is subject to age requirement. Can ask if applicant is between 18 and 70.	Inquiry of specific age or date or birth.
Birthplace	Can ask for proof of U.S. citizenship.	Birthplace of applicant or spouse or any relative.
Religion	No inquiries allowed.	
Race or color	Can be requested for affirmative action but not as employment criteria.	All questions about race are prohibited.
Character	Inquiry into actual conviction that relate to fitness to perform job.	Questions relating to arrests.
Relatives	Relatives employed in company. Names and addresses of parents if applicant is a minor.	Questions about with whom applicant lives. Number of dependents.
Notice in case of emergency	Name and address of a *person* to be notified.	Name and address of a *relative* to be notified.
Organizations	Professional organizations.	Requesting a list of all memberships.
References	Professional or character reference.	Religious references.
Physical condition	All applicants can be asked if they are able to carry out the physical demands of the job.	Employers must be prepared to justify any mental or physical requirements. Specific questions regarding handicaps are forbidden.
Photographs	Statement that a photograph may be required *after* employment.	Requirement that a photograph be taken prior to interview or hiring.
National origin	If necessary to perform job, languages applicant speaks, read, or writes.	Inquiries about birthplace, native language, ancestry, date of arrival in United States, or native language.
Education	Academic, vocational, or professional education. Schools attended. Ability to read, speak, and write foreign languages.	Inquiries into racial or religious affiliation of a school. Inquiry into dates of schooling.
Sex	Inquiry or restriction of employment is only for bona fide occupational qualification, which is interpreted very narrowly by the courts.	Cannot ask sex on application. Sex cannot be used as a factor for hiring decisions.

(continued)

TABLE 10.1 **Legal Interview Inquiries** (Continued)

Subject	Acceptable Inquiries	Unacceptable Inquiries
Credit rating	No inquiries.	Questions about car or home ownership also are prohibited.
Other	Notice may be given that misstatements or omissions of facts may be cause for dismissal.	

(Adapted from Huston & Marquis, 1989).

SELECTION

After applicants have been recruited, completed their applications, and been interviewed, the next step in the pre-employment staffing process is selection. Selection is the process of choosing from among applicants the best qualified individual(s) for a particular job or position. Jernigan (1988) maintains the following:

> The selection process is one of the most difficult of all personnel processes because not only must you find the best qualified individual who is willing to work for your salary and on the needed shift, but you must also predict successful work performance from an application form, some rather slanted references, and a few moments of conversation.

The selection process involves verifying the applicant's qualifications, checking his or her work history, and deciding if a good match exists between the applicant's qualifications and the organization's expectations. Can the applicant contribute to the organization in some unique way? Are the goals of the applicant and the institution compatible?

Educational and Credential Requirements

Consideration should be given to educational requirements and credentials for each job category as long as a relationship exists between these requirements and success of the job. If requirements for a position are too rigid, the job may remain unfilled for some time. Additionally, people who might be able to complete educational or credential requirements for a position are denied the opportunity to compete for the job. Therefore, many organizations have a list of preferred criteria for a position and a second list of minimal criteria. Frequently, organizations will accept substitution criteria in lieu of preferred criteria. For example, a position might require a bachelor's degree, but a master's degree is preferred. However, 5 years of nursing experience could be substituted for the master's degree.

Dorio (1994) warns that academic and professional credentials are the least checked items of a potential candidate's background. In a highly competitive job market, more and more candidates are succumbing to the pressure of telling "white lies" about their qualifications. It is imperative that the selector check with academic institutions and professional organizations prior to making a job offer.

Reference Checks

All applications should be examined to see if they are complete and to ascertain that the applicant is qualified for the position. At this point, references are requested, and employment history is verified. Usually the personnel department carries out some of these functions.

Excellent references do not necessarily guarantee excellent job performance. However, poor references can prevent a bad hiring decision (Dorio, 1994). Whenever possible, references should be checked and work experience and credentials should be verified before the interview. Some managers prefer to interview first so time is not wasted processing the application if the interview results in a decision not to hire. Although this is a personal choice, positions should *never* be offered until information on the application has been verified and references have been checked.

Occasionally, reference calls will reveal unsolicited information about the applicant. Information obtained by any method may not be used to reject an applicant *unless* a justifiable reason for disqualification exists. For example, if the applicant volunteers information about his or her driving record or if this information is discovered by other means, it cannot be used to reject a potential employee *unless* the position requires driving.

The Résumé

The résumé also is an important screening tool for selection. Often résumés are attached to the application but serve a somewhat different purpose. The application is designed by the employer and serves the needs of the organization, while the résumé is created by the applicant. When preparing a résumé, assessing one's own values, skills, and interests is an essential part of the process (Strader & Decker, 1995). Résumés should concentrate on what applicants like to do and what they do well.

When examining résumés, the selector must remember that applicants use the device to summarize their education and experience in the best possible light. Managers must look beyond the neat and well-prepared résumé and examine critical issues, such as length of time the applicant was employed in other positions and what positions were held. Developing as clear a picture of the recently graduated nurse or the nurse with little work experience is more difficult.

The application, résumé, and reference checks will usually give some clues as to the applicant's background. Résumé preparation is discussed more fully in Chapter 24.

Pre-employment Testing

Pre-employment testing is used only when such testing is directly related to the ability to perform a specific job. While testing is not a stand-alone selection tool, it can, when coupled with excellent interviewing and reference checking, provide additional information about a candidate to make the best selection possible (Dorio, 1994).

Because improper implementation and interpretation of pre-employment testing has been alleged, lawsuits have made employers shy away from pre-employment testing. Some major corporations but few healthcare organizations still use testing as a selection tool. Some healthcare organizations, however, do use postemployment testing to determine learning needs or skill deficiencies.

Physical Examination

A medical examination is generally a requirement for hiring. This examination determines if the applicant can meet the requirements for a specific job and provides a record of the physical condition of the applicant at the time of hire. The physical examination also may be used to identify applicants who will potentially have unfavorable attendance records or may file excessive future claims against the organization's health insurance.

Only those selected for hire can be required to have a physical examination, which is nearly always conducted at the employer's expense. If the physical examination reveals information that disqualifies the applicant, he or she is not hired. Most employers make job offers contingent on meeting certain health or physical requirements.

Making the Selection

When processing applications and determining the most appropriate person to fit the job, the manager must be sure that the same standards are used to evaluate all candidates. Final selection should be based on established criteria, not on value judgments and personal preferences.

Frequently, managers fill positions with internal applicants. These positions might be entry level or management. These applicants are interviewed in the same manner as newcomers to the organization; however, some organizations give special consideration and preference to their own employees. Every organization should have guidelines and policies regarding how transfers and promotions are to be handled. Transfers and promotions are discussed more fully in Chapter 24.

Finalizing the Selection

Once a final selection has been made, the manager is responsible for the following closure of the pre-employment process:

1. Follow up with applicants as soon as possible, thanking them for their applications and informing them when they can expect to be notified about a decision.
2. Candidates *not* offered a position should receive a timely written notice of their elimination. Whenever appropriate, applicants not being hired should be given reasons why they were not hired (eg, insufficient education or work experience), whether their application will be held for possible later employment, or if they should reapply in the future.

3. Applicants *offered* a position should be informed in writing of the benefits, salary, and placement. This avoids misunderstandings later regarding what employees think they were promised by the nurse recruiter or the interviewer.
4. Applicants who accept job offers should be informed as to pre-employment procedures, such as physical examinations, and supplied with the date to report to work.
5. Applicants who are offered positions should be requested to confirm in writing their intention to accept the position.

Because selection involves a process of reduction—that is, diminishing the number of candidates for a particular position—the person making the final selection has a great deal of responsibility. These decisions have far-reaching consequences, both for the organization and for the individuals involved. For these reasons, the selection process should be as objective as possible. The selection process is shown in Figure 10.1.

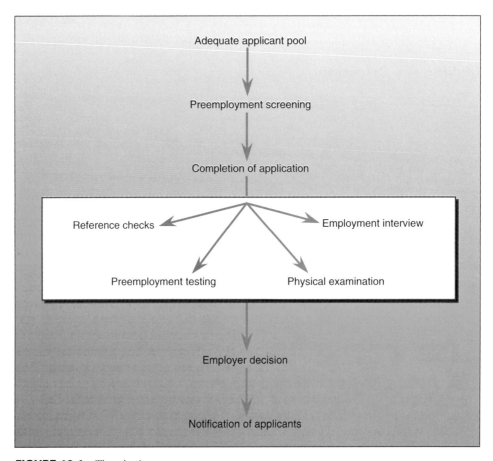

FIGURE 10.1 The selection process.

LEARNING EXERCISE 10.3

You are a home health nurse with a large caseload of low-income, inner-city families. Because of your spouse's job transfer, you have just resigned from your position of 3 years to take a similar position in another public health district.

Your agency supervisor has asked that you assist her with interviewing and selecting your replacement. Five applicants meet the minimum criteria. They each have at least 2 years acute care experience, a baccalaureate nursing degree, and a state public health credential.

Because you know the job requirements better than anyone, your supervisor has asked that you develop additional criteria and a set of questions to ask each applicant.

Assignment:
1. Use a decision grid (see Fig. 2-2) to develop additional criteria. Weight the criteria so the applicants will have a final score.
2. Develop an interview guide of six appropriate questions to ask the applicants.

SELECTING AN ASSISTANT

Because managers must delegate so many aspects of work, it is important that they trust subordinates and are able to work well with them. Often the manager who has a wide scope of responsibility, and thus does a great deal of delegation, needs to select an assistant. An example might be a head nurse appointing charge nurses for each shift or choosing an assistant head nurse; it also could be a supervisor selecting a head nurse or a director of nursing choosing an assistant. It could even mean hiring a ward clerk or secretary.

Regardless of the applicant's level of management, the manager should examine available candidates for any assistant position carefully. Del Bueno and Freund (1986) maintain that such selection has far-reaching implications, including a possible struggle for power at some future date. The following suggestions are helpful in selecting an assistant:

1. *Select someone with a similar philosophy.* Working closely with someone who views nursing and life extremely differently than you is difficult. The manager could end up wasting precious time arguing with the assistant about the value of decisions that should be made quickly. However, it is not necessary that the assistant be the manager's clone.
2. *Choose an assistant with different strengths and weaknesses than your own.* Selecting someone different than the existing manager makes it possible to compensate for each other's weaknesses and to complement each other's strengths. It is especially helpful for managers to have differences in leadership styles and abilities. Although this contrast may occasionally be a source of discomfort or conflict, if both parties act assertively, they can learn and grow from each other.
3. *Select an assistant who can be a good follower.* This does not mean a blind fol-

lower. A good follower will tell leaders when they are in error. A good follower is loyal but has the ego strength and wisdom to question inappropriate decisions of their leaders.

Once an assistant is chosen, the manager must give up some responsibility, authority, and power to the assistant for effective time management and delegation. In addition, the leader must spend time developing the assistant's leadership and management skills and acting as a role model.

Placement

The astute leader is able to assign a new employee to a position within his or her sphere of authority where the employee will have a reasonable chance for success. Nursing units and departments develop subcultures that have their own norms, values, and methods of accomplishing work. It is possible for one person to fit in well with an established group, while another equally qualified individual would never become part of it.

Additionally, many positions within a unit or department require different skills. For example, in a hospital, decision-making skills might be more necessary on a shift where leadership is less strong; communication skills might be the most highly desired skill on a shift where there is a great deal of interaction among a variety of nursing personnel.

Frequently, newcomers suffer feelings of failure because of inappropriate placement within the organization. This can be as true for the newly hired experienced employee as for the novice nurse. Appropriate placement is as vital to the organization's functioning as to the new employee's success. Faulty placement can result in sacrifices to organizational efficiency, increased attrition, threats to organizational integrity, and frustration of personal and professional ambitions.

Conversely, proper placement fosters personal growth, provides a motivating climate for the employee, maximizes productivity, and increases the probability of organizational goals being met. Managers who are able to match employee strengths to job requirements facilitate unit functioning, accomplish organizational goals, and meet employee needs.

INTEGRATING LEADERSHIP ROLES AND MANAGEMENT FUNCTIONS IN PRE-EMPLOYMENT STAFFING RESPONSIBILITIES

Productivity is directly related to the quality of an organization's personnel. Active recruitment allows institutions to bring in the most qualified personnel for a position. After those applicants have been recruited, managers using specified criteria have a critical responsibility to see that the best applicant is hired. To ensure that all applicants are evaluated using the same standards and that personal bias is minimized, the manager must be skilled in interviewing and other selection processes.

Pre-employment leadership roles include planning for future staffing needs and keeping abreast of changes in the healthcare field. Leadership also is necessary in the interview process to ensure that all applicants are treated fairly and that the interview terminates with applicants having positive attitudes about the organization. Because leaders are fully aware of nuances, strengths, and weaknesses within their sphere of authority, they are able to assign newcomers to areas that offer the greatest potential for success.

The integration of leadership roles and management functions in the organization ensures good public relations within the community because applicants know that they will be treated fairly. The pool of applicants will be sufficient because future needs are planned proactively. The leader/manager uses the selection and placement process as a means to increase productivity and retention, accomplish the goals of the organization, *and* meet the needs of new employees.

KEY CONCEPTS

▼ The first step in the staffing process is to determine the type and number of personnel needed.

▼ It is important to predict future staffing needs and proactively plan to meet those needs.

▼ Successfully recruiting an adequate work force depends on many variables, including financial resources, an adequate nursing pool, competitive salaries, the organization's reputation, the location's desirability, and the status of the national and local economy.

▼ Effective recruiting methods include advertisements, career days, and literature and the informal use of members of the organization as examples of satisfied employees.

▼ Managers share the responsibility for recruitment with nurse recruiters. The relationship between managers and recruiters must be collaborative.

▼ Despite their limitations, interviews are widely used as a method of selecting which employees to hire.

▼ Interview limitations include low reliability and validity. Validity, however, is higher with structured interviews than unstructured interviews.

▼ The interview should meet the goals of the applicant and the manager.

▼ Managers must be skilled in planning, conducting, and controlling interviews.

▼ Managers should evaluate applicants by completing a written form as soon as possible following the interview.

▼ Due to numerous federal acts that protect the rights of job seekers, managers must be cognizant of the legal constraints of interviews.

▼ In addition to the information obtained in the interview, résumés and references should be checked to determine the qualifications of the applicant.

▼ Selection should be based on the requirements necessary for the job; these criteria should be developed before beginning the selection process.

▼ Candidates should be thanked for applying and receive timely notification of the results of their application and interview.

▼ Applicants offered a position should confirm their acceptance in writing.

▼ Managers should assign new employees to the unit, department, and shift where they have the best chance of succeeding.

ADDITIONAL LEARNING EXERCISES

Learning Exercise 10.4

You are the head nurse of an intensive care unit and are interviewing Sam, a prospective charge nurse for your evening shift. Sam is currently the head nurse at Memorial Hospital, which is the other local hospital and your organization's primary competitor. He is leaving Memorial Hospital due to personal reasons.

Sam, well qualified for the position, has strong management and clinical skills. Your evening shift needs a strong manager with the excellent clinical skills that Sam also has. You feel fortunate that Sam is applying for the position.

Just before the close of the interview, however, Sam shuts the door, lowers his voice secretively, and tells you that he has vital information regarding Memorial's plans to expand and reorganize its critical care unit. He states that he will share this information with you if you hire him.

Assignment: How should you respond to Sam? Should you hire him? Identify the major issues in this situation. Support your hiring decision with rationale from the preceding chapter and other readings.

Learning Exercise 10.5

You are the head nurse of a surgical unit, a position you have held for 6 years. You are comfortable with your role and know your staff well. Recently, the day charge nurse resigned. Two of your staff, Nancy and Sally, have applied for the position.

Nancy, an older nurse, has been with the organization for 8 years but has been assigned to your department for only five 5 years. She has 12 years experience in acute care nursing. She performs her job competently and has good interpersonal relationships with the other staff and with patients and physicians. Although her motivation level is adequate for her current job, she has not demonstrated much creativity or initiative in helping the surgical unit establish a reputation for excellence, nor has she demonstrated specific skills in predicting or planning for the future.

Sally, a nurse in her mid-30s, has been with the organization and the unit for 3 years. She has been a positive driving force behind many of the changes that have occurred. She is an excellent clinician and highly respected by physicians and staff. The older staff, however, appear to resent her because they feel she attempted too much change before "paying her dues."

Both nurses have baccalaureate degrees and meet all the position qualifications for the job. Both nurses can be expected to work at least another 5 years in the new position. There is no precedent for your decision.

You must make a selection. If you do not use seniority as a primary selection criterion, many of the long-term employees may resent both Sally and you, and they may become demotivated. You are aware that Nancy is limited in her futuristic thinking and that the unit may not grow and develop under her leadership as it could under Sally's.

Assignment: Identify how your own values will affect your decision. Rank your selection criteria, and make a decision about what you will do. Determine the personal, interpersonal, and organizational impact of your decision.

Learning Exercise 10.6

The large teaching hospital in your area has a policy of limiting the hiring of new graduate nurses to 12 per graduating class (spring and fall). The hospital's rationale for this is to hire a variety of nurses from many schools to prevent inbreeding. Competition among your class of 62 is very keen because this hospital has an excellent reputation for high quality and innovative nursing. Your interview has been scheduled for next week.

Assignment: Using your knowledge of interviewing, outline an approach that makes the most of your interview. Support your plan with appropriate rationale. How can you convince the selection committee to hire you?

Learning Exercise 10.7
(From Marquis & Huston, 1994.)

You are the director of a small Native American health clinic. Other than yourself and a part-time physician, your only professional staff are two RNs. The remainder of your staff are from the Native American population and have been trained by you.

Because nurse Bennett, a 26-year-old female BSN graduate, has had several years experience working at a large southwestern community health agency, she is familiar with many of the clients' problems. She is hard working and extremely knowledgeable. Occasionally, her assertiveness is mistaken for bossiness among the Native American workers. However, everyone respects her judgment.

The other RN, nurse Mikiou, is a 34-year-old male Native American. He started as a medic in the Vietnam war and attended several career ladder external degree programs until he was able to take the RN examination. He does not have a baccalaureate degree. His nursing knowledge is occasionally limited, and he tends to be very casual about performing his duties. However, he is competent and has never shown unsafe judgment. His humor and good nature often reduce tension in the clinic. The Native American population is very proud of him, and he has a special relationship with them. However, he is not a particularly good role model because his health habits leave much to be desired, and he is frequently absent from work.

Nurse Bennett has come to find nurse Mikiou intolerable. She feels she has tried working with him, but this is difficult because she doesn't respect him. As the director of the clinic, you have tried many ways to solve this problem. You feel especially fortunate to have nurse Bennett on your staff. It is difficult to find many nurses of her quality willing to come and live on a desolate Native American reservation. On the other hand, if the Native American health concept is really going to work, the Native Americans themselves must be educated and placed in the agencies so that one day they can run their own clinics. It is very difficult to find educated Native Americans who want to return to this reservation.

Now you are faced with a management dilemma. Nurse Bennett has said either nurse Mikiou must go, or she will go. She has asked you to decide.

Assignment: List the factors bearing on this decision. Which choice will be the least damaging? Justify your decision.

REFERENCES:

American Nurses Association (1989). *Statement on rural nursing.* Kansas City, MO: Author.

Beach, D. S. (1980). *Personnel* (4th ed.). New York: Macmillan.

Bouchard, T. J. (1976). Field research methods: Interviewing questionnaires, participant observation, systematic observation, unobtrusive methods. In M. D. Dunnette (Ed.), *Handbook of industrial and organizational psychology.* Chicago: Rand McNally.

Buerhaus, P. (1993). Effects of RN wages and non-wage income on the performance of the hospital RN labor market. *Nursing Economics, 11*(3), 129–135.

Del Bueno, D. J. (1993). Nurse executive turnover. *Nursing Economics, 11*(1), 25–28.

Del Bueno, D. J. & Freund, C. M. (1986). *Power and politics in nursing administration: A casebook.* Owings Mills, MD: National Health Publishing, Rynd Communications.

deSavorgnani, A. A., Haring, R. D., & Galloway, S. (1993). Recruiting and retaining registered nurses in home healthcare. *Journal of Nursing Administration, 23*(6), 42–46.

Dorio, M. (1994). *Staffing: Problem solver for human resource professional and managers.* New York: John Willey and Sons.

Ghiselli, E. E. (1966). The validity of the personnel interview. *Personnel Psychology, 19*(4).

Hurley, M. L. (1994). Where will you work tomorrow? *RN, 57*(8), 31–35.

Huston, C. J., & Marquis, B. L. (1989). *Retention and productivity strategies for nurse managers.* Philadelphia: J.B. Lippincott.

Jablin, F. (1975). The selection interview: Contingency theory and beyond. *Human Resource Management, 4*(1).

Jernigan, D. K. (1988). *Human resource management in nursing.* Norwalk, CT: Appleton and Lange.

Kinicki, A. J., Hom, P. W., Lockwood, C. A., & Griffeth, R. W. (1990). Interviewer predictions of applicant qualifications and interviewer validity: Aggregate and individual analysis. *Journal of Applied Psychology, 75*(5), 477–486.

Longo, R. A., & Uranker, M. M. (1987). Why nurses stay: A positive approach to the nursing shortage. *Nursing Management, 18*(7), 78.

Marquis, B. L., & Huston, C. J. (1994). *Management decision making for nurses* (2nd ed.). Philadelphia: J.B. Lippincott.

Marriner-Tomey, A. (1992). Guide to Nursing Management (4th ed.). St. Louis: Mosby Year Book.

Mayfield, E. C. (1964). The selection interview: A re-evaluation of published research. *Personnel Psychology, 17.*

Mills, J., & Oie, M. (1992). Autonomous staff selection teams. *Journal of Nursing Administration, 22*(12), 57–63.

Meissner, J., & Carey, K. W. (1994). How's your job security? *Nursing 94, 24*(7), 33–38.

Strader, M. K., & Decker, P. J. (1995). Role transition to patient care management. Norwalk, CT: Appleton and Lange.

Stratton, T. D., Dunkin, J. W., Juhl, N., Ludtke, R. L., & Geller, J. M. (1991). Recruiting and retaining registered nurses in rural community hospitals. *Journal of Nursing Administration, 21*(11), 30–34.

Styles, M. M., & Holzemer, W. L. (1986). Educational remapping for a responsible future. *Journal of Professional Nursing, 2*(1), 64–68.

Swansburg, R. (1990). *Management and Leadership for Nurse Managers,* Boston: Jones and Bartlett.

Tibbles, L. R. (1993). The structured interview: An effective strategy for hiring. *Journal of Nursing Administration, 23*(10), 42–46.

Wall, L. L. (1988). Plan development for a nurse recruitment-retention program. *Journal of Nursing Administration, 18*(2).

Wright, P. M., Lichtenfels, P. A, & Pursell, E. D. (1989). The structured interview: Additional studies and meta-analysis. *Journal of Occupational Psychology, 62*(3), 191–199.

BIBLIOGRAPHY

Birkenstock, M. (1991). Recruitment and retention: Strategies for keeping good nurses. *Association of Operating Room Nurses Journal, 53*(1), 110–114, 116–118.

Bowin, R. B. (1987). *Human resource problem solving.* Englewood Cliffs, NJ: Prentice Hall.

Cassidy, J. (1991). Desperately seeking nurses: Recruitment and retention strategies. *Health Progress, 72*(4), 14–16.

Everson-Bates, S., & Fosbinder, D. (1994). Using an interview guide to identify effective nurse managers. *Journal of Nursing Administration, 24*(4S), 33–38.

Fenner, K. M., & Fenner, P. (1990). *Manual of*

nurse recruitment and retention. Rockville, MD: Aspen Publications.

Gulotta, K., & Matlock, K. (1990). Recruitment: Combining work and school. *Nursing Management, 21*(10), 72–78.

Jenks, J. M., & Zevnik, B. L. (1989). ABCs of interviewing. *Harvard Business Review, 67*(4), 38–42.

Jolma, D. J., & Weller, D. E. (1989). An evaluation of nurse recruitment methods. *Journal of Nursing Administration, 19*(4).

McLane, H. (1980). *Women executives.* New York: Van Nostrand Reinhold.

Nash, J. (1990). Turn it around: Make the interview work for you. *Today's OR Nurse, 12*(11), 12–16.

Ott, M. J., Esker, S., & Caserza, C. (1990). Peer interviews: Sharing the hiring process. *Nursing Management, 21*(11), 32–33.

Owen, J., & Leon, C. (1993). Career development: A vehicle for retention. *Nursing Management, 24*(8), 59–60.

Perry, L. (1989). Recruitment materials can impede hiring of nurses. *Modern Healthcare, 19*(3).

Schaffner, M. (1990). Interviewing, orientation and evaluation. *Gastroenterology Nursing, 12*(3), 172–178.

Sullivan, E. J., & Decker, P. J. (1990). *Effective management in nursing.* Menlo Park, CA: Addison-Wesley.

Voss, R. A. (1993). The challenge of filling vacancies. *Journal of Nursing Administration, 23*(4), 39.

Walters, J. (1987). An innovative method of job interviewing. *Journal of Nursing Administration, 17*(5), 25–29.

Warmke, D. L., & Weston, D. J. (1992). Employment interviews, techniques, panels, advantages, recommendations. *Personnel Journal, 71*, 120–126.

Whaley, B. A., Young, W. B., Adams, C. J., & Biordi, D. L. (1989). Targeting recruitment efforts for increased retention. *Journal of Nursing Administration, 19*(4).

Winland-Brown, J. E., & Pohl, C. (1990). Administrators attitudes about hiring disabled nurses. *Journal of Nursing Administration, 20*(4).

Yate, M. (1990). *Hiring the best.* Holbrook, MA: Bob Adams.

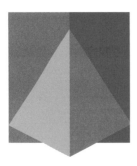

CHAPTER 11

Employee Indoctrination: Induction, Orientation, and Socialization

Indoctrination, as a management function, refers to the planned, guided adjustment of an employee to the organization and the work environment. Although the words induction and orientation are frequently used to describe this function, the indoctrination process includes three separate phases: induction, orientation, and socialization.

Indoctrination denotes a much broader approach to the process of employment adjustment than either induction or orientation. It seeks to 1) establish favorable employee attitudes toward the organization, unit, and department; 2) provide the necessary information and education for success in the position; and 3) instill a feeling of belonging and acceptance. Effective indoctrination programs result in higher productivity, fewer rule violations, less attrition, and greater employee satisfaction.

The employee indoctrination process begins as soon as an individual has been selected for a position and continues until the employee has been socialized to the norms and values of the work group. Effective indoctrination programs assist employees in having a successful employment tenure. The leadership roles and manage-

Bessie L. Marquis and Carol J. Huston:
LEADERSHIP ROLES AND MANAGEMENT FUNCTIONS IN NURSING, 2nd ed.
Lippincott-Raven Publishers © 1996

Display 11.1 Leadership Roles and Management Functions in Indoctrination

Leadership Roles

1. Periodically reviews induction and orientation programs to ascertain they are meeting unit needs
2. Generates enthusiasm in employees for organizational goals
3. Clarifies organizational and unit goals
4. Infuses a team spirit among employees
5. Serves as a role model to all employees and a mentor to select employees
6. Encourages mentorship between senior staff and junior employees
7. Observes carefully for signs of knowledge or skill deficit in new employees and intervenes appropriately
8. Supports employees having difficulty with resocialization
9. Assists employees in developing personal strategies to cope with role transition

Management Functions

1. Interprets information in employee handbook and provides input for handbook revisions
2. Participates actively in employee orientation
3. Ensures that each new employee understands appropriate organizational policies
4. Is aware of unit or department norms and values
5. Clarifies role expectations for all new employees
6. Uses positive and negative sanctions appropriately to socialize new employees
7. Intervenes proactively when employees experience difficulty in role transition
8. Carefully selects preceptors and encourages role modeling of the senior staff
9. Provides methods of meeting the special orientation needs of new graduates and experienced nurses changing roles

ment functions inherent in indoctrination are shown in Display 11.1. This Chapter addresses the specific activities and information that should be included in the indoctrination process, as shown in Display 11.2.

INDUCTION

Induction, the first phase of indoctrination, takes place after the employee has been selected but prior to performing the job role. The induction process includes all activities that educate the new employee about the organization and employment and personnel policies and procedures.

Display 11.2 Employee Indoctrination Content

1. Company history, mission, and philosophy
2. Company service and service area
3. Organizational structure, including department heads, with an explanation of the functions of the various departments
4. Employee responsibilities to the company
5. Organizational responsibilities to the employee
6. Payroll information, including how increases in pay are earned and when they are given (Progressive or unionized companzies publish pay scales for all employees.)
7. Rules of conduct
8. Tour of the company and of the assigned department
9. Work schedules, staffing and scheduling policies
10. When applicable, a discussion of the collective bargaining agreement
11. Benefit plans, including life insurance, health insurance, pension, and unemployment
12. Safety and fire programs
13. Staff development programs, including in-service, and continuing education for re-licensure
14. Promotion and transfer policies
15. Employee appraisal system
16. Work load assignments
17. Introduction to charting
18. Review of selection policies and procedures
19. Specific legal requirements, such as maintaining a current license, reporting of accidents, and so forth
20. Introduction to fellow employees
21. Establishment of a feeling of belonging and acceptance, showing genuine interest in the new employee

Note: Much of this content could be provided in an employee handbook, and the fire and safety regulations could be handled by a media presentation. *Appropriate* use of videotapes or film strips can be very useful in the design of a good orientation program. All indoctrination programs should be monitored to see if they are achieving their goals. Most programs need to be revised at least annually.

Induction activities are often performed during the placement and pre-employment functions of staffing or may be included with orientation activities. However, Holle and Blatchley (1987) see induction and orientation as separate entities and state that the employee suffers if content from either program is omitted. The most important factor is to provide the employee with adequate information.

Employee handbooks, an important part of induction, are usually developed by the personnel department. Managers, however, should know what information they contain and have input into their development. Most employee handbooks contain a form that must be signed by the employee, verifying that he or she has received and read it. The signed form is then placed in the employee's personnel file.

The handbook is important because employees cannot assimilate all the induction information, so they need a reference for later (Gillies, 1994). However, providing an employee with a personnel handbook is not sufficient for real understanding. The information must be followed with discussion by various individuals during the employment process, such as the personnel manager and staff development personnel during orientation. The most important link in promoting real understanding of personnel polices is the first-level manager.

ORIENTATION

Induction provides the employee with general information about the organization, while orientation activities are more specific for the position. Organizations may use a wide variety of orientation programs. For example, a first-day orientation could be conducted by the hospital's personnel department, which could include a tour of the hospital and all of the induction items listed in Display 11.2. The next phase of the orientation program could take place in the staff development department where aspects of concern to all employees, such as fire safety, accident prevention, and health promotion, would be presented. The third phase would be the individual orientation for each department. At this point, specific departments, such as dietary, pharmacy, and nursing, would each be responsible for developing their own programs. A sample distribution of responsibilities for indoctrination activities is shown in Display 11.3.

Because induction and orientation involve many different individuals from a variety of departments, they must be carefully coordinated and planned to achieve preset goals. The overall goals of induction and orientation include helping employees

---

Display 11.3 Responsibilities for Orientation

1. *Personnel Department:*
   Performs salary and payroll functions, insurance forms, physical exams, income withholding forms, tour of the organization, employee responsibilities to the organization and vice versa, additional labor–management relationships, and benefit plan.
2. *Staff Development Department:*
   Hands out and reviews employee handbook; discusses organizational philosophy and mission; reviews history of the organization; shows media presentation of various departments and how they function (if a media presentation is not available, introduce various department heads and share how departments function); discusses organizational structure, fire and safety programs, CPR certification and verifications; discusses available educational and training programs, reviews selected policies and procedures, and charts medication and treatment policies.
3. *The Individual Unit:*
   Tour of the department, introductions, review of specific unit policies that differ in any way from general policies, review of unit scheduling and staffing policies and procedures, work assignments, promotion and transfer policies, and establishment of a feeling of belonging, acceptance, and socialization.

by providing them with information that will smooth their transition into the new work setting (Bastien, Glennon, & Stein, 1987). Gillies (1994) maintains that the purpose of the orientation process is to make the employee feel a part of the team. A result of an effective orientation is the prevention of burnout, and new employees taking part in a formal orientation program reach independent and adequate functioning sooner and remain in the organization longer than employees who receive no orientation program (Huston & Marquis, 1989; Alspach, 1990). Therefore, other goals for orientation programs would be increasing retention and productivity.

It is important to look at productivity and retention as the orientation program is planned, structured, and evaluated. Organizations should periodically assess their induction and orientation program in light of organizational goals; programs that are not meeting organizational goals should be restructured. For example, if employees consistently have questions about the benefit program, this part of the induction process should be evaluated.

Too often various individuals having partial responsibility for induction and orientation "pass the buck" regarding failure of or weaknesses in the program. It is the joint responsibility of the personnel department, the staff development department, and each nursing service unit to work together to provide an indoctrination program that meets employee and organizational needs.

For some time, managers in healthcare organizations, especially hospitals, did not fulfill their proper role in the orientation of new employees. Managers assumed that between the personnel and staff development, or inservice, department, the new employee would become completely oriented. This often frustrated new employees because although they received an overview of the organization, they received little orientation to the specific unit. Because each unit has many idiosyncrasies, the new employee was left feeling inadequate and incompetent. The latest trend in orientation is for the nursing unit to take a greater responsibility for individualizing orientation (Tucker, 1987; Bastien, et al., 1986).

The unit manager must play a key role in the orientation of the new employee. An adequate orientation program minimizes the likelihood of rule violations, grievances, and misunderstandings; fosters feelings of belonging and acceptance; and promotes enthusiasm and morale. A sample 2-week orientation schedule is shown in Display 11.4.

SOCIALIZATION

Orientation is usually inadequate in itself to ensure that new employees are properly socialized into the organization. Socialization differs from orientation in that it involves little structured information. Rather, *socialization* is a sharing of the values and attitudes of the organization by the use of role models, myths, and legends. During the socialization phase of indoctrination, the leader introduces employees to unit values and culture.

Much has been written about the importance of socializing new members into their professional roles (Kramer, 1974; Schmalenberg & Kramer, 1979; Cherniss, 1980). The first socialization to the nursing role occurs through nursing education and continues after graduation. Because nurse administrators and nursing faculty

LEARNING EXERCISE 11.1

As a new head nurse, one of your goals is to reduce attrition. You plan to do this by increasing retention, thus reducing costs for orienting new employees. In addition, you feel the increased retention will provide you with a more stable staff.

In studying your notes from exit interviews, it appears that new employees seldom develop a loyalty to the unit but instead use the unit to gain experience for other positions. You feel one difficulty with socializing new employees might be your unit's orientation program.

Presently, the agency allows 2 weeks of orientation time (80 hours) when the new employee is not counted in the nursing care hours. These are referred to as nonproductive hours and are charged to the education department. Your unit has the following 2-week schedule for new employees.

Week One

Monday and Tuesday	9 AM–5 PM	Classroom
Wednesday, Thursday, and Friday	7 AM–11 AM	Assigned to work with someone on the unit

Week Two

Monday and Tuesday	7 AM–3:30 PM	Assigned to unit with an employee
Wednesday, Thursday, and Friday		Assigned to shift they will be working for orientation to that shift

Weekends are days off.

Following this 2-week orientation, the new employee is expected to function at 75% productivity for 2 or 3 weeks and then perform at full productivity.

The exception to this is the new graduate (RN) orientation. These employees spend 1 extra week on 7 AM–3 PM and 1 extra week assigned to their particular shift prior to being counted as staff.

Your nursing administrator has stated that you may alter the orientation program in any way you wish *as long as* you do not increase the nonproductive time and you ensure that the employee receives information necessary to meet legal requirements and that allows them to function safely.

Assignment: Is there any way for you to strengthen the new employee orientation to your unit? Outline your plans (if any), and give your rationale for your decision.

---

have been found to hold different values (Ulrich, 1987) and both of these groups assist in socializing the new nurse, there is potential for the new nurse to develop conflict and frustration (Johnson, 1994). However, less research exists in the special resocialization needs of nurses as they change roles throughout their professional careers.

Socialization into the organization is not only critical for the novice professional; adequate socialization of *all* employees has been shown to reduce attrition

---

Display 11.4 Sample Two-Week Orientation Schedule for Experienced Nurses

---

Week One

Day one, Monday:

8:00 AM–10:00 AM	Welcome by personnel department; employee handbooks distributed and discussed
10:00 AM–10:30 AM	Coffee and fruit served; welcome by staff development department
10:30 AM–12:00 PM	General orientation by staff development
12:00 PM–12:30 PM	Tour of the organization
12:30 PM–1:30 PM	Lunch
1:30 PM–3:00 PM	Fire and safety films; body mechanics demonstration
3:00 PM–4:00 PM	Afternoon tea and introduction to each unit supervisor

Day two, Tuesday:

8:00 AM–10:00 AM	Report to individual units Time with unit supervisor; introduction to assigned preceptor
10:00 AM–10:30 AM	Coffee with preceptor
10:30 AM–12:00 PM	General orientation of policies and procedures
12:00 PM–12:30 PM	Lunch
12:30 PM–4:30 PM	CPR recertification

Day three, Wednesday:	Assigned all day to unit with preceptor
Day four, Thursday:	Assigned all day to unit with preceptor
Day five, Friday:	Morning with preceptor, afternoon with supervisor and staff development for wrap-up

Week Two

Monday to Wednesday:	Work with preceptor on shift and unit assigned, gradually assuming greater responsibilities
Thursday:	Assign 80% of normal assignment with assistance and supervision from preceptor
Friday:	Carry normal workload. Have at least a 30-minute meeting with immediate supervisor to discuss progress

---

(Cherniss, 1980). During this phase of indoctrination, employees must be instilled with high morale and enthusiasm for the organization. A primary leadership role in indoctrination is this socialization process. Employees must be molded so they fit in the organization.

Kramer and Schmalenberg (1988) believe that one of the major roles of leaders in magnet hospitals is to generate enthusiasm down to the very last worker. The ability to instill and clarify the organization's value system to new employees creates the team approach that is found in excellent organizations.

The Socialization Process

There is no one theory of socialization. Among sociologists, the phenomenon of socialization has generally focused around role theory. That is, we learn the behaviors that accompany each role by using two simultaneous processes. One process is referred to as an *interactional process* and involves groups and significant others in a social context. The other is a *learning process* and includes such mechanisms as role playing, identification, modeling, operant learning, instruction, observation, imitation, trial and error, and role negotiation (Hardy & Conway, 1988).

This well-researched phenomenon is frequently neglected in formal indoctrination programs (Fitzpatrick & Abraham, 1987). Although, Kramer's (1974) research has been used as a foundation for new graduate intern programs, little attention has been paid to the resocialization needs of other employees (Hinshaw, 1982). Resocialization occurs when 1) new graduates leave the educational socialization process of nursing school and enter the work world; 2) the experienced nurse changes work settings, either within the same organization or in a new organization; and 3) the nurse undertakes new roles.

Brim (1966) states that resocialization would be more effective if efforts were made to determine why the individual was having difficulty in this area. He maintains that three areas of difficulty exist: 1) *ignorance of the particular role prescriptions and expectations;* 2) *inability to meet role demands;* and 3) *deficiencies in motivation.* Some employees adapt easily to the process of resocialization, but most experience some stress with role change (Hardy & Conway, 1988). Organizations can plan in advance to ease the stress of resocialization by the conscious use of appropriate interventions (Huston & Marquis, 1989).

CLARIFYING ROLE EXPECTATIONS IN RESOCIALIZATION

Role expectations can be clarified by using role models, preceptors, and mentors. While all three clarify roles through social interaction and educational processes, each has a different focus and uses different mechanisms. All have an appropriate place in employee socialization.

Role Models

Role models are examples of experienced, competent employees. The relationship between the new employee and the role model is a passive one; that is, employees see that role models are skilled and attempt to emulate them, but the role model does not actively seek this emulation. One of the exciting aspects of role models is their cumulative effect. The greater the number of excellent role models available for new employees to emulate, the greater the possibilities for new employees to perform well. This has been shown to contribute to quality performance (Kramer & Schmalenberg, 1988).

Preceptors

While the educational process in role modeling is passive, preceptoring is active and purposeful. The assumption that a one-on-one relationship increases learning is the basis for the use of preceptors (Schah & Polifroni, 1992). A preceptor is an experienced nurse who provides emotional support and is a strong clinical role model for the new nurse. An effective preceptor can role model and adjust the teaching to each learner's needs. There is an opportunity to answer questions and clarify role expectations (Clayton, Broome, & Ellis, 1989). To be effective, preceptors need to have an adequate knowledge of adult learning theory. Carefully selecting preceptors assists the organization in role clarification.

Mentors

Mentors take an even greater role in using education as a means for role clarification. Not every nurse will be fortunate enough to have a mentor to facilitate each new career role. Most nurses are lucky if they have one or two mentors throughout their careers. Madison Knight, and Watson (1993) describe mentoring as "a high level human relationship of some significance" and states that it is clearly different from the role model or preceptor role. Carden (1990) has documented the value of mentoring in the socialization process of adult career development. Mentors serve a particularly useful role in acclimating the nurse to the manager role. The roles of the mentor are shown in Display 11.5.

LEARNING EXERCISE 11.2

You have been selected to represent your unit on a committee to design a preceptor program for the nursing department. One of the committee's first goals is to develop a set of criteria for the selection of preceptors.

Assignment: Either individually or in groups, select a minimum of five and a maximum of eight criteria that would be appropriate for selecting preceptors on your unit.

ASSISTANCE IN MEETING ROLE DEMANDS IN RESOCIALIZATION

When meeting role demands, individuals generally need assistance in two areas. The first is the specific skills and knowledge requirements for the role, and the second is the values and attitudes that accompany any given role (Hardy & Conway, 1988). Organizations may use various means to assist the employee in meeting role demands.

Meeting Knowledge and Skill Requirements

To assist the employee in meeting the demands of the job, the manager needs to determine what those needs are. This requires more than just asking employees about

---

Display 11.5 Roles of the Mentor

---

1. *Model:* Someone you admire or want to emulate
2. *Envisioner:* Someone who can see and communicate a meaning of professional nursing and its potential
3. *Energizer:* Someone whose dynamism stimulates you to take action
4. *Investor:* Someone who invests their time and energy into your personal and professional growth
5. *Supporter:* Someone who offers you emotional support and builds self-confidence
6. *Standard prodder:* Someone who refuses to accept less than standards of excellence
7. *Teacher–Coach:* Someone who teaches you interpersonal, technical, or political skills essential for advancement
8. *Feedback giver:* Someone who gives honest positive and negative feedback for growth
9. *Eye-opener:* Someone who broadens your perspective and gives you new ways of viewing situations
10. *Door opener:* Someone who, by virtue of their position, can provide you with new opportunities or experiences
11. *Idea bouncer:* Someone who will listen and discuss your ideas
12. *Problem solver:* Someone who can help you examine problems and identify possible solutions
13. *Career counselor:* Someone who helps you to make short- and long-term career plans
14. *Challenger:* Someone who encourages you to investigate issues more critically or in greater detail

Adapted from Darling, 1984.

---

their knowledge deficits or giving employees a skills checklist or test; it requires careful observation by the manager and preceptor so deficiencies are identified and corrected before they handicap the employee's socialization. Careful observation is a leadership role. When such deficiencies are not corrected early, other employees often create a climate of nonacceptance that prevents assimilation of the new employee.

Meeting Value and Attitude Requirements

Johnson (1994) feels that nurses as a group do not possess strong discipline-specific values; therefore, values and attitudes may be a source of conflict as nurses learn new roles. However, organizations can assist new employees in meeting this requirement of socialization. Useful strategies are using role models; providing a safe climate for new employees to ventilate their frustration with value conflicts; clarifying differing role expectations that are held by physicians, patients, and other staff; and assisting new employees in developing strategies to cope with and resolve value and attitude conflicts.

LEARNING EXERCISE 11.3

Who or what has been the greatest influence on your socialization to the nursing role? Write a short essay (three or four paragraphs) describing this socialization. If appropriate, share this in a group.

OVERCOMING MOTIVATIONAL DEFICIENCIES IN RESOCIALIZATION

Brim (1966) suggests that if difficulties in resocialization occur because of motivational deficiencies, a planned reorientation program should occur through the use of rewards and punishment. Although *sanctions*—the bestowing of rewards and punishments—occur at many levels during the socialization process, they are rarely carried out on a systematic and planned basis, yet most employees learn what behavior is rewarded in an organization. For example, new employees determine quickly if getting off duty on time or excellent patient care receives reward sanctions. Effective leadership requires a conscious awareness of how unit values and behavior norms impact employee socialization.

Positive Sanctions

Positive sanctions can be used as an interactional or educational process of socialization. If deliberately planned, as Brim suggests, they become educational. However, sanctions given through the group process, or reference group, use the social interaction process. The reference group sets norms of behavior and then applies sanctions to ensure that new members adopt the group norms before acceptance into the group. These informal sanctions offer an extremely powerful tool for socialization and resocialization in the workplace. Managers should become aware of what role behavior they reward and what new employee behavior senior staff is rewarding.

Negative Sanctions

Punishment, like rewards, provides cues that enable people to evaluate their performance consciously and to modify behavior when needed. For positive or negative sanctions to be effective, they must result in the role learner internalizing the values of the organization. Negative sanctions are often applied in very subtle and covert ways. Making fun of a new graduate's awkwardness with certain skills or belittling a new employee's desire to use nursing care plans are very effective negative sanctions used to mold individual behavior to group norms. The manager should know what the group norms are and be observant of sanctions used by the group to make newcomers conform. This is not to say that negative sanctions should not be used. New employees should be told when their behavior is not an acceptable part of their role.

EMPLOYEES WITH SPECIAL SOCIALIZATION NEEDS

The previous discussion has focused on the problems that may occur in role adaptation for all new employees. However, some employees have special problems in socialization to new roles. These include the new nurse, employees with role status change, and the experienced nurse in transition. Managers providing appropriate socialization assistance for this group will increase the chance of a positive employment outcome.

The New Nurse

Kramer (1974) describes special fears and difficulties in adapting to the work setting that are common to new graduate nurses. Kramer believes that *reality shock* occurs because of conflict between a new graduate's expectations of the nursing role and the reality of the actual role in the work setting. Much of Kramer's work occurs in hospital settings where most new graduates are traditionally employed.

Kramer's work has been substantiated by other researchers who have studied professionals in their first year of employment (Wacker, 1979; Cherniss, 1980). No one is immune to a loss of idealism and commitment in response to stress in the work place, but in the first year of employment, the greatest change in attitude and behavior takes place (Cherniss, 1980).

Following the publication of Kramer's work, many hospitals began to look at methods that could be used in their orientation programs to alleviate some of the shock of entering the real world of nursing. Some hospitals developed prolonged orientation periods for new graduates that lasted from 6 weeks to 6 months. This extended orientation, or *internship,* contrasts sharply with the routine 1- to 2-week orientation that is normal for other employees. During this time, the graduate nurse is usually assigned to work with a preceptor and gradually takes on a patient assignment equal to that of the preceptor.

Some hospitals have discontinued internship programs due to their expense but have continued with the preceptor concept of teaming a new graduate with another nurse. In addition to providing orientation and socialization for the new graduate, a preceptorship provides recognition for experienced nurses who have demonstrated excellence.

Although internships appear to be one answer in reducing reality shock, such programs are not without hazards. Practices (1984) identified the following advantages and disadvantages of internships.

Advantages

1. The quality of patient care is increased as the intern has an opportunity to learn how to do more effective nursing assessments and interventions.
2. The intern is exposed to contrasting schools of thought about nursing.
3. Peer relationships with the staff are enhanced.
4. The intern is less likely to receive conflicting information when paired with a preceptor.

5. The duplication of information that occurs when more than one staff person is teaching is reduced.
6. The intern's self-confidence is increased.

Disadvantages

1. Internships may assist the new graduate nurse in coping with reality, but they do not attempt to fix the underlying problem of the gap between school and the work setting.
2. An internship may further delay a new graduate's adjustment to reality by allowing him or her to depend on a preceptor for a longer time.
3. Some internships attempt to rotate the nurse through too many specialty units in too short a time.
4. In programs in which the preceptor and intern have a prolonged formal relationship (more than 1 year), the intern may become overly dependent on the preceptor.

Many of the potential hazards of internship and preceptor programs can be overcome by 1) carefully selecting the preceptors; 2) selecting only preceptors who have a strong desire to be role models; 3) preparing preceptors for their role by giving formal classes in adult learning and other social/learning concepts; and 4) having either experienced staff development or supervisory personnel monitor the preceptor and new graduate closely to ensure that the relationship continues to be beneficial and growth producing for both.

The high costs of internship programs can be offset somewhat if the new graduate is paid a reduced salary during all or part of the internship. Organizations need to weigh carefully the cost effectiveness of such programs. If the program improves retention and quality of patient care, even expensive programs may be worth the cost.

Schmalenberg and Kramer (1979) suggest that there are four phases of role transition from student nurse to staff nurse: the honeymoon phase, followed by shock, recovery, and resolution phases. The researchers maintain that cultural conflict occurs because the values in the school and work subcultures differ.

As long as the novice nurse is sincerely welcomed into the workplace, the new nurse has little difficulty in the honeymoon phase. During the second phase of reality shock, however, there is often great personal conflict as the nurse discovers that many nursing school values are not prized in the work place. Usually the new graduate will be appropriately resocialized if the manager and the organization take sufficient action during the recovery and resolution phases.

Managers can use several mechanisms to ease the role transition of new graduates. Kramer suggests that anticipatory socialization carried out in educational settings prepares the new nurse for the inevitable reality shock (Kramer, 1974). However, managers should not assume that such anticipatory socialization has occurred. Instead, they should build into orientation programs opportunities for sharing and clarifying values and attitudes about the nursing role. Use of the group process is an excellent mechanism to promote the sharing that provides support for new graduates and assists them in recovering from reality shock.

Additionally, managers should be alert for signs and symptoms of the shock phase of role transition; they should intervene by listening to new graduates and helping them cope in the real world. Some of the new nurse's values should be supported and encouraged so that work and academic values can blend. New professionals need to understand the universal nature of role transition and know it is not limited to nurses. For example, Cherniss (1980) has found role transition difficult in all the helping professions. Providing a class on role transition also may assist new graduates in resocialization.

LEARNING EXERCISE 11.4

Talk with at least four nursing graduates that have been working as nurses for 3 months to 3 years. Make sure at least two of them are recent graduates and two of them have been working at least 18 months.

Ask them about their socialization to nursing after graduation. Did any of them experience reality shock? How long did it last? Did they recover from the shock? If so, how? Share your findings with other members of your group.

EMPLOYEES WITH ROLE STATUS CHANGE

Probably no other aspect of an employee's work life has as great an influence on productivity and retention as the quality of supervision exhibited by the immediate manager. Unfortunately, the orientation of new managers is often neglected by organizations. The lack of sufficient orientation to the new role may result in management errors.

There is a growing recognition that good managers do not emerge from the work force without a great deal of conscious planning on the part of the organization. A management development program should be ongoing. Every individual should receive some management development instruction prior to their appointment to a management position.

The new manager's orientation to the position by the outgoing manager should be relatively short. The previous manager usually spends no longer than 1 week working directly with the new manager, especially when the new manager is familiar with the organization. A short orientation by the outgoing manager allows the newly appointed manager to gain control of the unit quickly and establish his or her own management style. If the new manger has been recruited from outside the organization, the orientation period may need to be extended.

Frequently, a new manager will be appointed to a vacant or newly established position. In either case, no one will be readily available to orient the new manager. In such cases, the new manager's immediate superior appoints someone to assist the new manager in learning the role. This could be a manager from another unit, the manager's supervisor, or someone from the unit who is familiar with the manager's duties and roles.

A new manager's orientation does not cease following the short introduction to their various tasks. Every new manager needs guidance, direction, and continued orientation and development during the first year in this new role. This direction comes from several sources in the organization:

1. *The new manager's immediate superior.* This could be the unit supervisor if the new manager is a charge nurse, or it could be the chief nursing executive if the new manager is a unit supervisor. The immediate superior should have regularly scheduled sessions with the new manager to continue the ongoing orientation process.
2. *A group of the new manager's peers.* There should be a management group in the organization with which the new manager can consult. The new manager should be encouraged to use the group as a resource.
3. *A mentor.* New managers who are truly fortunate will be mentored by someone in the organization.

Clinical nurses who have recently assumed management roles often experience guilt when they decrease their involvement with direct patient care. When employees and physicians see a nurse-manager assuming the role of caregiver, they often make disparaging remarks, such as, "oh, you're working as a real nurse today." This tends to reinforce the nurse's value conflict in the new role.

Nurses moving into positions of increased responsibility also experience role stress created by role ambiguity and role overload. *Role ambiguity* describes the stress that occurs when job expectations are unclear. *Role overload* occurs when the demands of the role are excessive. Scalzi (1988) demonstrates that role overload is a major source of stress for nurse-managers. All of these factors make the role transition of nurses moving into higher status positions difficult.

Assistance With Role Status Change

In all resocialization, the use of role models, preceptors, and mentors is helpful, but in role status change, the use of mentors to facilitate resocialization is invaluable. Those lucky enough to find a mentor as they move into roles with increased responsibilities and status will find that resocialization will be much smoother. A mentor, as no other, is able to instill values and attitudes that accompany each role. In describing her mentor, one writer states, "I would have become a nurse without her, but never would I have sought the professionalism, the degree of compassion, the depth of humor, the height of empathy that are set as guidelines for me by the conduct of my mentor" (Schorr, 1979, p. 65).

The second most valuable mechanism that organizations use to assist in this type of resocialization is a clear understanding of role expectations. As nurses move into increased status positions, their job descriptions tend to become increasingly vague. Therefore, clarifying job roles becomes an important tool in the resocialization process.

THE EXPERIENCED NURSE IN A NEW POSITION

For many reasons, nurses make frequent career moves. Experienced nurses often make lateral transfers within the same organization. Others take new positions that are quite different from their previous role; these new positions may be in their present organization or with a new one. Specific orientation needs arise for these nurses:

> *Transition from expert to novice.* This is a very difficult role transition. Many nurses transfer or change jobs because they no longer find their present job challenging. However, this results in the necessity of assuming a learning role in their new environment. The employee assigned to orient them should be aware of the difficulties this nurse will experience. The transferred employee's lack of knowledge in the new area should never be belittled; whenever possible, the special expertise they bring from their former work area should be acknowledged and utilized.
>
> *Transition from familiar to the unfamiliar.* In their old surroundings, the employee knew everyone and where everything was located. In the new position, the employee will not only be learning new job skills, but will be in an unfamiliar environment.

The managers of departments that receive frequent transfers should prepare a special orientation for experienced nurses transferring to the department. In addition to providing necessary staff development content, these orientation programs should focus on efforts to promote the self-esteem of these nurses as they learn the skills necessary for their new role.

The special socialization needs of these new employees are often overlooked; these individuals need special attention that many organizations neglect. Hardy and Conway (1988) believe that organizations rarely address socialization problems that occur in job, position, or status change. They suggest that transition into new jobs would be associated with less role strain if programs were designed to facilitate role modification and role expansion (Hardy & Conway, 1988). For example, when a nurse moves from a medical floor to labor and delivery, the nurse does not know the group norms, is unsure of expected values and behaviors, and goes from being an expert to being a novice. All of these create a great deal of role strain. This same type of role stress occurs when experienced nurses move from one organization to another. Nurses often feel powerless during role transitions, which may culminate in anger and frustration as they seek to become socialized to a different role.

Assisting the Experienced Nurse in Role Transition

Hardy and Conway (1988) maintain that programs designed to assist the nurse with the role transition of position change should do more than just provide an orientation to the new position; they also should address specific values and behaviors necessary for the new roles. The values and attitudes expected in a hospice nursing role may be very different than those expected of a trauma nurse. Managers should not assume that the experienced nurse is aware of the new role's expected attitudes. Excellent companies, Peters and Waterman (1982) assert, have leaders who take responsibility for shaping the values of new employees. By instilling and clarifying organizational values, managers are able to create a homogeneous staff that functions as a team.

Employees adopting new values often experience role strain because they may need to give up a former value. Managers need to support employees during this value resocialization. Often negative sanctions are used by members of the reference group. For example, saying things like, "Well, we don't believe in doing that here" can make new, experienced employees feel as though the values held in other nursing roles were bad. Therefore, the manager should make efforts to see that formerly held values are not belittled.

INTEGRATING LEADERSHIP ROLES AND MANAGEMENT FUNCTIONS OF INDOCTRINATION

Socialization, a critical component of indoctrination, is a complex process directed at the acquisition of appropriate attitudes, cognitions, emotions, values, motivations, skills, knowledge, and social patterns necessary to cope with the social and professional environment (Hardy & Conway, 1988). Resocialization differs from orientation and induction and has a greater impact than either induction or orientation on subsequent productivity and retention.

Orientation, induction, and socialization all provide the organization with an opportunity to build loyalty and team spirit. This is the time to instill the employee with pride in the organization and the unit. This type of affective learning becomes the foundation for subsequent increased satisfaction and motivation.

The integrated leader/manager uses this opportunity to support employees with difficult role transitions. Mentoring and role modeling are encouraged, and role expectations are clarified.

The integrated leader/manager knows that a well-planned and implemented indoctrination program is a wise investment of organizational resources. It provides the opportunity to mold a team effort and infuse employees with enthusiasm for the organization. There is perhaps no other part of management that has as great an influence on reducing burnout as successful indoctrination. New employees' impressions of an organization during their adjustment period stay with them a long time. If the impressions are positive, they will be remembered in the difficult times that will ultimately occur during any long tenure of employment.

KEY CONCEPTS

▼ *Indoctrination* consists of induction, orientation, and socialization of employees.
▼ A well-prepared and executed *orientation program* educates the new employee about the desired behaviors and expected goals of the organization.
▼ The *induction* of a new employee should include all the activities that educate the employee about the company.
▼ A well-written *employee handbook* should be used as a tool in the induction process.
▼ There are many acceptable types of orientation structure.
▼ Various individuals assist with the orientation process, but the employee's immediate supervisor must take an active role.

▼ Research has shown that a successful orientation process reduces burnout.

▼ New graduates, new managers, and experienced nurses in new roles have unique orientation needs.

▼ The *socialization* of individuals into roles occurs with all roles and is a normal sociological process.

▼ Two methods used to socialize others are social interaction and education.

▼ *Socialization* and *resocialization* are often neglected areas of the indoctrination process.

▼ Although the terms *role model, preceptor,* and *mentor* are not synonymous, all play an important role in assisting with the socialization of employees.

▼ Most types of *role transition* create some stress during socialization and resocialization.

▼ Difficulties with resocialization usually center around unclear *role expectations,* inability to meet job demands, or deficiencies in motivation.

▼ Managers may use many effective interventions to assist employees during socialization and resocialization.

ADDITIONAL LEARNING EXERCISES

Learning Exercise 11.5

You are the supervisor of a critical care surgical unit. For the past several years, you have been experimenting with placing four newly graduated nurses directly into the unit, two from each spring and fall graduating class. These nurses are from the local BSN program. You consult closely with the nursing faculty and their former employers prior to making a selection.

Overall, this experiment has worked well. Only two new graduates were unable to develop into critical care nurses. Both of these nurses later transferred back into the unit after 2 years in a less-intensive medical-surgical area.

Because of the new graduates' motivation and enthusiasm, they have complemented your experienced critical care staff nicely. You feel your success with this program has been due to your well-planned and structured 4-month orientation and education program, careful selection, and appropriate shift placement.

This spring you have narrowed the selection down to four acceptable and well-qualified candidates. You plan to place one on the 3 PM to 11 PM shift and one on the 11 PM to 7 AM shift. You sit in your office and review the culture of each shift and your notes on the four candidates. You have the following information:

> 3 PM to 11 PM shift: A very assertive, all-female staff. Eighty-five percent RNs and 15% practical nurses. This is your most clinically competent group. They are highly respected by everyone, and although the physicians often have confrontations with them, the physicians also tell you frequently how good they are. The nurses are known as a group that lacks humor and does not welcome newcomers. However, once the new employee earns their trust, they are very supportive. They are very intolerant of anyone not living up to their exceptionally high standards. Your two unsuccessful new graduate placements were assigned to this shift.

11 PM to 7 AM shift: A very cohesive and supportive group. Although overall competent, this shift has some of your more clinically weak staff. However, it also is the shift that rates the highest with families and patients. They are caring and compassionate. Every new graduate you have placed on this shift has been successful. Thirty percent of the nurses on this shift are men. The group tends to be very close and has a number of outside social activities.

Your four applicants consist of the following:

John: A 30-year-old married man without children. He has had a great deal of emergency room experience as a medical emergency technician. He appears somewhat aloof. His definite career goals are 2 years in critical care, 3 years in emergency room, and then flight crew. Instructors praise his independent judgment but felt he was somewhat of a loner in school. Former employers have rated him as an independent thinker and very capable.

Sally: A 22-year-old unmarried woman. She is at the top of her class clinically and academically. She has not had much work experience until the last 2 years as a summer nursing intern at a medical center where her performance appraisal was very good. Instructors feel she lacks some maturity and interpersonal skills but praise her clinical judgment. She does not want to work in regular medical-surgical unit. She feels she can adapt to critical care.

Joan: A mature, divorced 38-year-old woman. She has no children. She has had a great deal of health-related work experience in counseling and has had limited clinical work experience (only nursing school). Former employers praise her attention to detail and her general competence. Instructors praise her interpersonal skills, maturity, and intelligence. She is quite willing to work elsewhere if not selected. She has a long-term commitment to nursing.

Mary: A dynamic 28-year-old married mother of two. She was previously a practical nurse and returned to school to get her degree. She did not do as well academically due to working and family commitments. Former employers and instructors speak of her energy, organization, and interpersonal skills. She appears to have less independent decision-making skills than the others. She previously worked in a critical care unit.

Assignment: Select the two new graduates, and place them on the appropriate shift. Support your decisions with rationales.

Learning Exercise 11.6

You are one of the care coordinators for a home health agency. One of your duties is to orient new employees to the agency. Recently the chief nursing executive hired Brian, an experienced acute care nurse, to be one of your team members. Brian seemed eager and enthusiastic. He confided in you that he was tired of acute care and wanted to be more involved with long-term patient and family case-loads.

During Brian's orientation, you became aware that his clinical skills were excellent, but his therapeutic communication skills were inferior to the rest of your staff.

You discussed this with Brian and explained how important communication is in gaining the trust of agency clients and that trust is necessary if needs of the clients and goals of the agency are to be met. You referred Brian to some literature that you felt might be helpful to him.

Following a 3-week orientation program, Brian began working unsupervised. It is now 4 weeks later. Recently, you received a complaint from one of the other nurses and one from a client regarding Brian's poor communication skills. Brian seems frustrated and has not gained acceptance from the other nurses in your work group. You suspect that some of the nurses resent Brian's superior clinical skills, while others feel he does not understand his new role and are becoming impatient with him. You are genuinely concerned that Brian does not seem to be fitting in.

Assignment: Could this problem have been prevented? Decide what you should do now. Outline a plan to resocialize Brian into his new role and make him feel a valued part of the staff.

Learning Exercise 11.7
(From Marquis & Huston, 1994.)

You have been working at Memorial Hospital for 3 months and have begun to feel fairly confident in your new role. However, one of the older nurses working on your shift constantly belittles your nursing education. Whenever you request assistance in problem solving or in learning a new skill, she says, "Didn't they teach you anything in nursing school?" Your charge nurse has given you a satisfactory 3-month evaluation, but you are becoming increasingly defensive regarding the comments of the other nurse.

Assignment: Explain how you plan to evaluate the accuracy of the older nurse's comments. How you will cope with this situation? What efforts can you make to improve your relationship? The article by Huston (1987) in the bibliography may be helpful to you.

REFERENCES:

Alspach, J. G. (1990). Critical care orientation: A discussion of survey results. *Critical Care Nurses, 10*(6), 12–4, 16.

Bastien, S., Glennon, P., & Stein, A. (1986). Orientation: Off toward a nurses "personal best." *Nursing Management, 17*(10), 64–66.

Brim, O. G. Jr. (1966). Socialization through the life cycle. In O. G. Brim, Jr. & S. Wheeler (Eds.), *Socialization after childhood: Two essays.* New York: John Wiley and Sons.

Carden, A. (1990). Mentering and adult career development: The evolution of a theory. *The Counseling Psycologist, 18*(2), 275–279.

Cherniss, C. (1980). *Professional burnout in human service organizations.* New York: Praeger Publishers.

Clayton, G., Broome, M., & Ellis, L. A. (1989). Relationship between a preceptorship experience and role socialization of graduate nurses. *Journal of Nursing Education, 28*(2).

Darling, L. A. (1984). What do nurses want in a mentor? *Journal of Nursing Administration, 14*(29).

Fitzpatrick, J. J., & Abraham, I. L. (1987). Toward the socialization of scholars and scientists. *Nurse Educator, 12*(3) 23–25.

Gillies, D. A. (1994). *Nursing management* (3rd ed.). Philadelphia: W.B. Saunders.

Hardy, M. E., & Conway, M. E. (1988). *Role theory: Perspectives for health professionals.* New York: Apple-Century-Crofts.

Hinshaw, A. S. (1982). Socialization and resocialization for professional nursing practice. In E. C. Hein & M. J. Nicholson (Eds.), *Contemporary leadership behavior: Selected readings.* Boston: Little, Brown.

Holle, M. L., & Blatchley, M. E. (1987). *Introduction to leadership and management in nursing* (2nd ed). Monterey, CA: Wadsworth Health Sciences Division.

Huston, C. J., & Marquis, B. L. (1989). *Retention and productivity strategies for nurse managers.* Philadelphia: J.B. Lippincott.

Johnson, M. (1994). Conflict and nursing professionalization. In J. McCloskey & H. K. Grace (Eds.), *Current issues in nursing* (4th ed.). St. Louis: C.V. Mosby.

Kramer, M. (1974). *Reality shock: Why nurses leave nursing.* St.Louis: C.V. Mosby.

Kramer, M., & Schmalenberg, C. (1988). Magnet hospitals: Part II. *Journal of Nursing Administration, 18*(2).

Madison, J., Knight, B. A., & Watson, K. (1993). Mentoring amongst academics in Australia: A case study. *Australian Educational Researcher, 20*(1), 18–32.

Marquis, B. L., & Huston, C. J. (1994). *Decision making in nursing management: 118 case studies* (2nd ed.). Philadelphia: J.B. Lippincott.

Peters, T. J., & Waterman, R. H. Jr (1982). *In search of excellence.* New York: Harper and Row.

(1984). *Practices.* Springhouse PA: NursesReference Library, Nursing 84 Books, Springhouse Corporation.

Scalzi, C. C. (1988). Role stress and coping strategies of nurse executives. *Journal of Nursing Administration, 18*(3).

Schah, H. S., & Polifroni, E. C. (1992). Preceptorship of CNS students: An exploratory study. *Clinical Nurse Specialist, 6*(1).

Schmalenberg, C., & Kramer, M. (1979). Coping with reality shock. Wakefield, MA: Nursing Resources.

Schorr, T. M. (1979).Mentor remembered. *American Journal of Nursing, 79*(1), 65.

Tucker, P. T. (1987). Recruiting nurses with an extern program. *Nursing Management, 18*(5), 90–94.

Ulrich, B. T. (1987). Value difference between practicing nurse executives and graduate educators. *Nursing Economics, 5*(6) 287–291.

Wacker, S. W. (1979). *Job stress and attitude change in teachers, lawyers, social workers, and nurses.* Unpublished doctoral dissertation, University of Michigan, Ann Arbor.

BIBLIOGRAPHY

Andrews, C. A. (1987). Orientation: Graduates' perceptions of initiation. *Nursing Management, 18*(11).

Asselin, M. E., & Barber, E. D. (1991). Unit orientation for experienced nurses. *Journal of Staff Development, 7*(3), 126–129.

Bethel, P. L. (1992). RN Orientation: Cost and achievement analysis. *Nursing Economics, 10*(5) 336–341.

Bayne, A. L. (1993). Reality Shock. *Graduating Nurse, Fall,* 12–15.

Holloran, S. D. (1993). Mentoring: The experience of nursing service executives. *Journal of Nursing Administration, 23*(2), 49–54.

Huston, C. J. (1987). A conflict born of insecurity. *Imprint, 34*(3).

Loudermilk, L. (1990). Role ambiguity and the clinical nurse specialist. *Nursing Connections, 3*(1).

May, K. M., Meleis, A. I., & Winstead-Fry, P.

(1982). Mentorship for scholarliness: Opportunities and dilemmas. *Nursing Outlook, 30*(1), 22–28.

Ponte, P. R., Higgins, J. M., James, R., Fay, M., & Madden, M. J. (1993). Development needs of adavance practice nurses in a managed care environment. *Journal of Nursing Administration, 23*(11), 13.

Rice, J. (1988). Transition from staff nurse to head nurse: A personal experience. *Nursing Management, 19*(4).

Sullins, M. L. (1989). The orientation process. *AORN Journal, 49*(2), 536–542.

Taylor, L. J. (1992). A survey of mentor relationships in academe. *Journal of Professional Nursing, 8*(1), 48–55.

Throwe, A. N., & Fought, S. G. (1987). Landmarks in the socialization process from RN to BSN. *Nurse Educator, 12*(6).

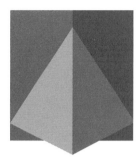

CHAPTER 12

Staffing Needs and Scheduling Policies

Once staff are appropriately selected and indoctrinated, the manager must ascertain that adequate numbers and an appropriate mix of personnel are available to meet daily unit needs and organizational goals. Because staffing patterns and scheduling policies directly affect the daily lives of all personnel, it is important that they be administered fairly and economically.

Scheduling policies and staffing patterns are directly related to the management phases of planning and organizing. For example, staffing ratios, availability of staff, and type of patient care organization greatly affect the successful implementation of staffing and scheduling options.

This chapter examines a variety of scheduling policies, staffing formulas, and staffing patterns. Included are the advantages and disadvantages of each. Unit fiscal responsibility is discussed with formulas and instructions for calculating daily staffing needs. Management responsibility for adequate and well-communicated staffing and scheduling policies is stressed. There is a focus on the leadership responsibility for developing trust through fair staffing and scheduling procedures. The leadership roles and management functions inherent in staffing and scheduling are shown in Display 12.1.

Bessie L. Marquis and Carol J. Huston:
LEADERSHIP ROLES AND MANAGEMENT FUNCTIONS IN NURSING, 2nd ed.
Lippincott-Raven Publishers © 1996

Display 12.1 Leadership Roles and Management Functions in Staffing and Scheduling

Leadership Roles

1. Identifies creative and flexible staffing methods to meet the needs of patients, staff, and the organization
2. Is knowledgeable regarding contemporary methods of scheduling and staffing
3. Assumes a responsibility toward staffing that builds trust and encourages a team approach
4. Periodically examines the unit standard of productivity to determine if changes are needed
5. Is alert to extraneous factors that impact on staffing
6. Is ethically accountable to patients and employees for adequate and safe staffing

Management Functions

1. Provides adequate staffing to meet patient care needs according to the philosophy of the organization
2. Uses organizational goals and patient classification tools to minimize understaffing and overstaffing as patient census and acuity fluctuate
3. Schedules staff in a fiscally responsible manner
4. Develops fair and uniform scheduling policies and communicates these clearly to all staff
5. Ascertains that scheduling policies are not in violation of local and national labor laws, organizational policies, or union contracts
6. Assumes accountability for quality and fiscal control of staffing
7. Evaluates scheduling and staffing procedures and policies on a regular basis

UNIT MANAGERS RESPONSIBILITIES IN MEETING STAFFING NEEDS

Although many organizations now use staffing clerks and computers to assist with staffing, the overall responsibility for scheduling continues to be an important function of first- and middle-level management. Each organization has different expectations regarding the unit manager's responsibility in long-range human resource planning and in short-range planning for daily staffing.

Some organizations decentralize staffing by having unit managers make scheduling decisions. Other organizations use centralized staffing with many decisions made by a central office or staffing center.

In organizations with *decentralized staffing,* the unit manager is often responsible for covering all scheduled staff absences, reducing staff during periods of decreased patient census or acuity, adding staff during high patient census or acuity, preparing monthly unit schedules, and preparing holiday and vacation schedules.

Advantages of decentralized staffing are that the unit manager understands the needs of the unit and staff intimately, which leads to the increased likelihood that sound staffing decisions will be made. Additionally, the staff feel more in control of their work environment because they are able to take personal scheduling requests directly to their immediate supervisor. Both Przestrzelski (1987) and Helmer and McKnight (1988) believe that decentralized scheduling and staffing lead to increased autonomy and flexibility, thus decreasing nurse attrition.

Decentralized staffing, however, carries the risk that employees will be treated unequally or inconsistently, which may result in negative staff reaction. Additionally, the unit manager may be viewed as granting rewards or punishments through the staffing schedule. Decentralized staffing also is time consuming for the manager and often promotes more "special pleading" than when staffing is centralized.

Organizations with *centralized staffing* use one individual or a computer to do the staffing and scheduling duties for all the units. The manager's role is limited to making minor adjustments and providing input. For example, the manager would communicate special staffing needs and assist with obtaining staff coverage for illness and sudden changes in patient census. Therefore, the manger in centralized staffing continues to have ultimate responsibility for seeing that adequate personnel are available to meet the needs of the organization.

In analyzing centralized staffing, Marquis and Huston (1994, p. 215) state, "This type of staffing is fairer to all employees because policies tend to be employed more consistently and impartially. In addition, the first-level manager is freed to complete other management functions and is more cost effective to the organization."

Centralized staffing, however, does not provide as much flexibility for the worker, nor can it account as well for a worker's desires or special needs. Additionally, managers may be less responsive to personnel budget control if they have little to do with staffing.

Centralized and decentralized staffing *are not* synonymous with centralized and decentralized management decision making. For example, a manager can work in an organization that has centralized staffing but decentralized organizational decision making. Regardless of whether the organization has centralized or decentralized staffing, all unit managers should understand scheduling procedures and the various options for scheduling and accept fiscal responsibility for personnel staffing.

Staffing and Scheduling Options

The requirement of night, evening, weekend, and holiday work that is frequently necessary in healthcare organizations is stressful and frustrating for some nurses. Inflexible scheduling is a major contributor to job dissatisfaction by nurses (Capuano, Fox, & Green, 1992). If nurses do not have input into work scheduling, they may feel demoralized as a result of lack of control. A feeling of powerlessness contributes to increased attrition rates and feelings of burnout among professional nurses (Marquis, 1989; Hinshaw, Smeltzer, & Atwood, 1987; Patterson & Goad, 1987). Scheduling, therefore, factors significantly in promoting job dissatisfaction or job satisfaction and subsequent nurse retention. Managers should periodically evaluate their staff's contentment with their present scheduling system. By helping employees feel that they do have some control over scheduling, shift options, and staffing policies, managers can improve job satisfaction.

It is beyond the scope of this book to discuss all of the creative staffing and scheduling options available. However, most options have positive and negative aspects. Therefore, in addition to obtaining input from employees, managers should examine options carefully before introducing change. Some of the more frequently used creative staffing and scheduling options are listed.

1. 10- or 12-hour shift
2. Premium pay for weekend work
3. A part-time staffing pool for weekend shifts
4. Cyclical staffing, which allows long-term knowledge of future work schedules (Fig. 12.1 shows a master staffing pattern that repeats every 4 weeks.)
5. Job sharing
6. Allowing nurses to exchange hours of work among themselves
7. Flextime
8. Use of supplemental nursing agencies for weekend coverage
9. Staff self-scheduling

There are advantages and disadvantages to each type of scheduling. Because some scheduling mandates overtime pay, the resultant nurse satisfaction must be weighed against the increased costs. Additionally, long shifts may result in clinical judgment errors when nurses become fatigued. For this reason, many organizations limit the number of consecutive days a nurse can work 12-hour shifts. Finally, the excessive use of part-time or supplemental nurses can result in poor continuity of nursing care.

However, many organizations are making an effort to shift the focus from worker adjustment to the organization to employer adjustment to meet the needs of a diverse work force (Jamieson & O'Mara, 1991). The two staffing options that appear to increase nurses' job satisfaction the most are flextime and self-scheduling (Wulff, 1994).

Flextime is a system that allows employees to select time schedules that best meet their personal needs, while still meeting work responsibilities. In the past, most flextime has been possible only for nurses in roles that did not require continuous coverage. However, staff nurses recently have been able to take part in a flextime system through prescheduled shift start times. Variable start times may be longer or shorter than the normal 8-hour work day. When a hospital uses flextime, units have employees coming and leaving the unit at many different times. Although flextime staffing creates greater employee choices, it may be difficult for the manager to coordinate and could easily result in overstaffing or understaffing.

Self-scheduling is the process that employees use to implement the work schedule collectively. With the help of the manager, staff set staffing guidelines that meet fiscal accountability and patient safety and use the guidelines to determine their own work schedules (Ringl & Dotson, 1989). Although this offers nurses greater control over their work environment, it is not an easy concept to implement. Success de-

Position	Name	Week I							Week II							Week III							Week IV						
		S	M	T	W	T	F	S	S	M	T	W	T	F	S	S	M	T	W	T	F	S	S	M	T	W	T	F	S
Full time	RN 1	X						X			X	X				X						X				X		X	
Full time	RN 2			X	X				X						X				X		X		X						X
Full time	RN 3	X						X			X		X			X						X			X	X			
Full time	RN 4			X		X			X						X			X	X				X						X
Full time	RN 5	X						X				X	X			X						X					X	X	
Full time	RN 6				X	X			X						X					X	X		X						X
Full time	RN 7	X						X		X				X		X						X		X			X		
Full time	RN 8		X				X		X						X		X			X			X						X
Part time	8 hrs/wk RN 9	On							On							On							On						
Part time	8 hrs/wk RN 10							On							On							On							On
Part time	8 hrs/wk RN 11	On							On							On							On						
Part time	8 hrs/wk RN 12							On							On							On							On
Total RNs on duty each day		6	7	6	6	6	6	6	6	7	6	6	6	6	6	6	7	7	6	6	6	6	6	7	7	6	6	6	6

Elements: Every other weekend off
Maximum days worked: 4
Minimum days worked: 2

Number of split days off each period: 2
Operates in multiples of 4, 8, 12...
Schedule repeats itself every 4 weeks

X: Scheduled day off

FIGURE 12.1   Four-week cycle master time sheet.

pends on the leadership skills of the manager to support the staff and demonstrate patience and perseverance throughout the implementation.

Wulff (1994) believes that while flextime and self-scheduling provide greater worker participation in decision making, they require greater worker involvement and management flexibility to be successful. Obviously all scheduling and staffing patterns, from traditional to creative, have shortcomings. Therefore, any changes in current policies should be evaluated carefully as they are implemented. It is wise to have a 6-month trial of new staffing and scheduling changes, with an evaluation at the end of that time to determine the impact on financial costs, retention, productivity, risk management, and employee and patient satisfaction.

LEARNING EXERCISE 12.1

You are the manager of an intensive care unit. Many of the nurses have approached you requesting 12-hour shifts. Other nurses have approached you stating that they will transfer out of the unit if 12-hour shifts are implemented.

You are exploring the feasibility and cost effectiveness of using both 8-hour shifts and 12-hour shifts so that staff could select which type of scheduling they wanted.

Assignment: Would this create a scheduling nightmare? Will you limit the number of 12-hour shifts staff could work in a week? Would you pay overtime for the last 4 hours of the 12 hour shift? Would you allow staff to choose freely between 8- and 12-hour shifts? What other problems may result from mixing 8- and 12-hour shifts?

Developing Staffing and Scheduling Policies

Nurses will be more satisfied in the work place if staffing and scheduling policies and procedures are clearly communicated to all employees (Huston & Marquis, 1989). Written policies provide a means for greater consistency and fairness. Personnel policies represent the standard of action that is communicated in advance so that employees are not caught unaware regarding personnel matters. In addition to being standardized, personnel policies should be written in a manner that allows some flexibility. A leadership challenge for the manager is to develop policies that focus on outcomes rather than constraints or rules that limit responsiveness to individual employee needs.

Scheduling and staffing policies should be reviewed and updated periodically. When formulating policies, management must examine its own philosophy and consider prevailing community practices. Unit-level managers will seldom have complete responsibility for formulating organizational personnel policies but should have some input as policies are reviewed. There are, however, nursing department and unit personnel policies that supervisors develop and implement.

The policies in Display 12.2 should be formalized by the manager and communicated to all personnel. To ensure that unit-level staffing policies do not conflict with higher level policies, they should have adequate input from the staff and be developed in collaboration with personnel and nursing departments (Gillies, 1994).

Display 12.2 Unit Checklist of Employee Staffing Policies

1. The person responsible for the staffing schedule and the authority of that individual if it is other than the employee's immediate supervisor
2. Type and length of staffing cycle used
3. Rotation policies, if shift rotation is used
4. Fixed shift transfer policies, if fixed shifts are used
5. Time and location of schedule posting
6. When shift begins and ends
7. Day of week schedule begins
8. Weekend off policy
9. Tardiness policy
10. Low census procedures
11. Policy for trading days off
12. Procedures for days-off requests
13. Absenteeism policies
14. Policy regarding rotating to other units
15. Procedures for vacation time requests
16. Procedures for holiday time requests
17. Procedures for resolving conflicts regarding requests for days off, holidays, or requested time off
18. Emergency request policies
19. Policies and procedures regarding requesting transfer to other units

---

For example, some states have labor laws that prohibit 12-hour shifts. Additionally, in organizations with union contracts, many staffing and scheduling policies are incorporated into the union contract. In such cases, staffing changes might need to be negotiated at the time of contract renewal.

The Impact of Standards of Productivity on Staffing

Requirements for staffing are based on the standard unit of measurement for productivity that the unit adopts. Standards of productivity, staffing formulas, and staffing terminology are discussed in Chapter 6. Refer to that chapter for help in solving some of the learning exercises presented here. The formula for calculating NCH/PPD is reviewed in Figure 12.2.

Patient classification is the grouping of patients according to specific characteristics because using the numbers of patients alone has proven to be an inaccurate method for determining nursing care assignments. Because other variables within the system impact on nursing care hours, it is usually not possible to transfer a patient classification system from one facility to another. Instead, each basic classification system must be modified to fit a specific institution.

Once an appropriate system is adopted, hours of nursing care must be assigned

$$\text{NCH/PPD} = \frac{\text{Nursing hours worked in 24 hours}}{\text{Patient census}}$$

FIGURE 12.2 Standard formula for calculating nursing care hours (NCH) per patient day (PPD).

for each patient classification. Although an appropriate number of hours of care for each classification is generally suggested by companies marketing patient classification systems, each institution should make the final decision regarding the number of care hours allotted (De Groot, 1989). There are many variables in any patient classification system, and none is without faults. Williams (1988) suggests that it is a mistake for managers to think that patient classification systems will solve all staffing problems. Although such systems provide a better definition of problems, it is up to people in the organization to use the information obtained by the system to solve staffing problems. A sample classification system can be illustrated in Table 12.1.

Standard units of measurement need to be reviewed periodically and adjusted if necessary. The middle-level manager must be alert to internal or external forces affecting unit needs that may not be reflected in the organization's patient care classification system. Examples of such forces could be a sudden increase in nursing or medical students using the unit, a lower skill level of new graduates, or cultural and language difficulties of recently hired foreign nurses.

The organization's classification system may prove to be inaccurate, or the hours allotted for each category or classification of patient may be inadequate. This does not imply that unit managers should not be held accountable for the standard unit of measurement, but rather they be cognizant of justifiable reasons for over-staffing or understaffing.

Fiscal and Ethical Accountability for Staffing

Regardless of the difficulties inherent in patient classification systems and the assignment of nursing care hours, it remains the best method for controlling the staffing function of management. As long as managers realize that all systems have weaknesses and as long as they periodically evaluate the system, managers will be able to initiate needed change. It is critical, however, that managers make every effort to base unit staffing on their organization's patient classification system. Nursing care remains labor intensive, and the manager is fiscally accountable to the organization for appropriate staffing. Accountability for a prenegotiated budget is a management function.

Growing federal and state budget deficits have resulted in increased pressure for all healthcare organizations to reduce costs. Because personnel budgets are large in healthcare organizations, a small percentage cut in personnel may result in large savings. It is important for managers to use staff to provide safe and effective care economically.

TABLE 12.1   Patient Care Classification Using Four Levels of Nursing Care Intensity

Area of Care	Category 1	Category 2	Category 3	Category 4
Eating	Feeds self or needs little food	Needs some help in preparing; may need encouragement	Cannot feed self but is able to chew and swallow	Cannot feed self and may have difficulty swallowing
Grooming	Almost entirely self-sufficient	Needs some help in bathing, oral hygiene, hair combing, and so forth	Unable to do much for self	Completely dependent
Excretion	Up and to bathroom alone or almost alone	Needs some help in getting up to bathroom or using urinal	In bed, needs bedpan or urinal placed; may be able to partially turn or lift self	Completely dependent
Comfort	Self-sufficient	Needs some help with adjusting position or bed (eg, tubes, IVs)	Cannot turn without help, get drink, adjust position of extremities, and so forth	Completely dependent
General health	Good—in for diagnostic procedure, simple treatment, or surgical procedure (D & C, biopsy, minor fracture)	Mild symptoms—more than one mild illness, mild debility, mild emotional reaction, mild incontinence, (not more than once/shift)	Acute symptoms—severe emotional reaction to illness or surgery, more than one acute illness, medical or surgical problem, severe or frequent incontinence	Critically ill—may have severe emotional reaction
Treatments	Simple—supervised ambulation, dangle, simple dressing, test procedure preparation not requiring medication, reinforcement of surgical dressing, x-pad, vital signs once/shift	Any Category 1 treatment more than once/shift, Foley catheter, care, I & O, bladder irrigations, sitz bath, compresses test procedures requiring medications or followups, simple enema for evacuation, vital signs every 4 hours	Any treatment more than twice/shift, medicated IVs, complicated dressings, sterile procedures, care of tracheotomy, Harris flush, suctioning, tube feeding, vital signs more than every 4 hours	Any elaborate or delicate procedure requiring two nurses, vital signs more often than every 2 hours

(continued)

TABLE 12.1 Patient Care Classification Using Four Levels of Nursing Care Intensity (Continued)

Area of Care	Category 1	Category 2	Category 3	Category 4
Medications	Simple, routine, not needing preevaluation or postevaluation; medications no more than once/shift	Diabetic, cardiac, hypotensive, hypertensive, diuretic, anticoagulant medications, prn medications, more than once/shift, medications needing preevaluation or postevaluation	Unusual amount of Category 2 medications; control of refractory diabetics (need to be monitored more than every 4 hours)	More intensive Category 3 medications; IVs with frequent, close observation and regulation
Teaching and emotional support	Routine follow-up teaching; patients with no unusual or adverse emotional reactions	Initial teaching of care of ostomies, new diabetics, tubes that will be in place for periods of time; conditions requiring major change in eating, living, or excretory practices; patients with mild adverse reactions to their illness (eg, depression, overly demanding)	More intensive Category 2 items; teaching of apprehensive or mildly resistive patients; care of moderately upset or apprehensive patients; confused or disoriented patients	Teaching of resistive paients, care and support of patients with severe emotional reaction.

Fiscal accountability to the organization is not incompatible with ethical accountability to patients and staff. It is possible to stay within a staffing budget and meet the needs of patients and staff. However, managers must increase staffing when patient acuity rises and decrease staffing when acuity is low; to do otherwise is demoralizing to the unit staff.

Some organizations require only that managers end the fiscal year within their budgeted nursing-care hours and pay less attention to daily or weekly nursing care hours. Shift staffing based on a patient acuity system does, however, allow for more consistent staffing and is better able to identify overstaffing and understaffing on a more timely basis. In addition, this is a fairer method of allocating staff.

The disadvantage of shift-based staffing is that it is time consuming and some-

LEARNING EXERCISE 12.2

Your flexible nursing care hours are budgeted at 8.2 hours per patient day (8.2 NCH/PPD). Each day you have a need for more or less staff depending on your patient census and patient acuity. The following is your acuity index based on the hospital's patient classification system and indicates the hours of nursing care needed for each acuity level:

	Days	Evenings	Nights
Category I acuity level	2.3	2.0	.5
Category II acuity level	2.9	2.3	1.0
Category III acuity level	3.4	2.8	2.0
Category IV acuity level	4.6	3.4	2.8

You must be overstaffed or understaffed by more than one-half of the hours a person is working to reduce or add staff. For example, for nurses working 8-hour shifts, the staffing must be over or under more than 4 hours to delete or add staff.

When you came on duty this morning, you had the following patients and classifications:

1 patient in category I acuity level
2 patients in category II acuity level
3 patients in category III acuity level
1 patient in category IV acuity level

Assignment: Calculate your staffing needs for the day shift. You have on duty one RN and one LVN/LPN working 8-hour shifts and a ward clerk for 4 hours. Are you understaffed or overstaffed? You have the same patients and acuity levels for the PM shift. Two RNs are scheduled for duty. Are you understaffed or overstaffed?

what subjective, because acuity or classification systems leave much to be determined by the individual assigning the acuity levels. The greater the degree of objectivity and accuracy in any system, the longer the time required to make staffing computations. Perhaps the greatest danger in staffing by acuity is that many organizations are unable to supply the extra staff when the system shows unit understaffing. However, the same organization may use the acuity-based staffing system to justify reducing staff on an overstaffed unit. Therefore, a staffing classification system can be demotivating if used inconsistently or incorrectly.

Employees have the right to expect a reasonable work load. Managers must ensure that adequate staffing exists to meet the needs of staff and patients. Managers who constantly expect employees to work extra shifts, stay overtime, and carry unreasonable patient assignments are not being ethically accountable.

Effective managers, however, do not focus totally on numbers of personnel, but look at all components of productivity; they examine nursing duties, job descriptions, and patient care organization. Such managers also use every opportunity to build a productive and cohesive team (Kirk, 1990).

Uncomplaining nursing staff have often put forth superhuman effort during periods of short staffing simply because they believed in their supervisor and in the organization. Just as often the opposite has occurred; units that were only moderately understaffed spent an inordinate amount of time and wasted energy complaining about their plight. The difference between the two examples has much to do with trust that such conditions are the exception, not the norm; that real solutions and not Band-aid approaches to problem solving will be used to plan for the future; that the management will work just as hard as the staff in meeting patient needs; and that the organization's overriding philosophy is based on patient interest and not financial gain.

INTEGRATING LEADERSHIP ROLES AND MANAGEMENT FUNCTIONS

The manager is responsible for providing adequate staffing to meet patient care needs. Attention must be paid to fluctuations in patient census and work load units to ensure that understaffing or overstaffing is minimized and to ensure fiscal accountability to the organization. The prudent manager involves employees when developing unit staffing and scheduling policies and ascertains that adopted policies are not in violation of organizational policies, union contracts, or labor laws.

When leadership roles are integrated with management functions, creative staffing and scheduling options can occur.

The leader keeps abreast of changes in community and national trends and uses contemporary methods of staffing and scheduling. The leader also assumes an ethical accountability to patients and employees for adequate and appropriate staffing. Unit policies are reviewed and revised on a timely basis. Additionally, the leader is alert for factors that affect the standard of productivity and negotiates changes in the standard when appropriate.

The effective leader/manager knows that establishing trust helps build the team spirit needed to deal with temporary staff shortages. The leader also looks for innovative methods to overcome staffing difficulties.

KEY CONCEPTS

▼ The manager must plan for adequate staffing to meet patient care needs.
▼ Efforts must be made to avoid *understaffing* and *overstaffing* as patient census and acuity fluctuate.
▼ Fair and uniform *staffing and scheduling policies* and procedures must be written and communicated to all staff.
▼ Staffing and scheduling policies must not violate labor laws or union contracts.
▼ Existing staffing policies must be examined periodically to determine if they meet the needs of the staff and the organization.
▼ The *patient classification system* should be reviewed to determine if it is a valid and reliable tool to measure staffing needs.
▼ Continued efforts should be made to use innovative and creative methods of staffing and scheduling.

▼ *Team building* and developing trust are effective methods of handling temporary staffing difficulties.
▼ *Flextime* is a concept modern organizations use to allow employees to have varying hours of starting and leaving times.
▼ *Self-scheduling* allows employees the opportunity and the responsibility to make their own work schedules.

 ## ADDITIONAL LEARNING EXERCISES

Learning Exercise 12.3

You are a member of a staffing committee in a small home health agency. The committee's function is to update staffing and scheduling policies and procedures.

There has been some dissatisfaction with how vacations are handled during the summer months. In particular, the staff who are married with school-age children feel that this should be a consideration in vacation requests. Others feel that seniority should count the most when requests are considered.

The unit supervisor has agreed to implement on a trial basis any policies regarding summer vacation requests that the committee formulates.

Assignment: Devise policies regarding summer vacation requests, and share them with others. If only one employee can leave at a time, how will you determine whose request will be filled? Be sure to discuss when and how requests are to be made and how conflicting requests will be handled.

Learning Exercise 12.4

A new rehabilitation unit has been added at Memorial Hospital. Although you have been given certain constraints in staffing the unit, you may choose any form of staffing that fits the constraints. Your constraints follow:

1. All staff must be licensed staff.
2. The ratio of LVNs/LPNs to RNs is one to one.
3. An RN must always be on duty.
4. Your budgeted NCH/PPD is 8.2.
5. You are not counted into the NCH/PPD, but ward clerks are counted.
6. Your unit capacity is seven, and you anticipate a yearly average census of six.
7. You may used any mode of patient care organization.

Your patients will be chronic, not acute, but will be admitted for an active 2- to 12-week rehabilitation program. The emphasis will be in returning the patient home with adequate ability to perform activities of daily living. Many other disciplines, including occupational and physical therapy, will be part of the rehabilitation team. A waiting list for the beds is anticipated because this service is needed in your community. You anticipate that the majority of your patients will have had cerebrovascular accidents, spinal cord-injuries, other problems with neurological deficits, and amputations.

You have hired four full-time RNs and two part-time RNs. The part-time RNs would like to have at least 2 days of work in a 2-week pay period, and in return for this work guarantee, they have agreed to cover for most sick days and vacations and some holidays for your regular RN full-time staff.

You also have hired three full-time LVNs/LPNs and two part-time LVNs/LPNs. However, the part-time LVNs/LPNs would like to work at least 3 days per week. You have decided not to hire a ward clerk but to use the pediatric ward clerk 4 hours each day to assist with various duties. Therefore, you need to calculate the ward clerk's 4 hours each day into the total hours worked.

You have researched various types of patient care management and various types of staffing patterns. Your newly hired staff is willing to experiment with any type of staffing and patient care management system you select.

Assignment: Determine what staffing pattern you will use. Explain why and how you made the choice you did. Next, show a 24-hour staffing pattern.

Learning Exercise 12.5

You are serving on an ad-hoc committee to examine the pros and cons of changing from permanently assigned fixed shifts to rotating shifts. The unit shifts are presently 7 AM to 3 PM, 3 PM to 11 PM, and 11 PM to 7 AM. The frequency that staff would be required to change from their present shift has not yet been discussed. At present, the committee is researching advantages and disadvantages of fixed versus rotating shift assignments.

Assignment: List five positive and five negative aspects of fixed shifts and rotating shifts. If shifts are fixed, what is a fair method for staff to obtain a change of shift? If shifts were changed to rotating, what length of time should be spent on each shift? Should evening shift be 3 PM to 11 PM? Should night shift be 11 PM to 7 AM? Could someone request to work only 11 PM to 7 AM as a permanent shift? Justify your decisions with rationale.

Learning Exercise 12.6

You graduated last year from your nursing program and were excited to obtain the job you wanted most. The unit where you work has a very progressive supervisor who believes in empowering the nursing staff.

Approximately 6 months ago, after considerable instruction, the unit began self-scheduling. You have enjoyed the freedom and control this has given you over your work hours. There have been some minor difficulties between staff, and occasionally the unit was slightly overstaffed or understaffed, but overall the self-scheduling has seemed to work well.

Today (September 15) you come to work on the 3 PM to 11 PM shift after 2 days off and see that the schedule for the upcoming Thanksgiving and Christmas holiday period has been posted, and many of the staff have already scheduled their days on and their days off. When you take a close look, it appears that no one has signed up to work Christmas Eve, Thanksgiving Day, or Christmas Day. You are very concerned because self-scheduling includes responsibility for adequate coverage.

There are still a few nurses, including yourself, who have not added their days to the schedule, but even if all the remaining nurses worked all three holidays, it would provide only scant coverage.

Assignment: What leadership role (if any) should you take in solving this dilemma? Should you ignore the problem and schedule yourself for only one holiday and let your supervisor deal with the issue? Remember, you are a new nurse both in experience and on this unit. List the options for decision making available to you, and using rationale to support your decision, plan a course of action.

REFERENCES:

Capuano, T. A., Fox, M. A., & Green, B. (1992). Staffing nurses according to episodic census variations. *Nursing Management, 23*(10), 34–37.

De Groot, H. (1989). Patient classification system evaluation: Part I: Essential system elements. *Journal of Nursing Administration, 19*(6), 30–35.

Gillies, D. A. (1994). *Nursing management—A systems approach.* Philadelphia: W.B. Saunders.

Helmer, F. T., & McKnight, P. (1988). One more time—Solutions to the nursing shortage. *Journal of Nursing Administration, 18*(11), 7–14.

Hinshaw, A. S., Smeltzer, C. H., & Atwood, J. R. (1987). Innovative retention strategies for nursing staff. *Journal of Nursing Administration, 17* (6), 8–16.

Huston, C. J., & Marquis, B. L. (1989). *Retention and productivity strategies for nurse managers.* Philadelphia: J.B. Lippincott.

Jamieson, M. L., & O'Mara, J. (1991) *Managing workforce 2000: Gaining the diversity advantage.* San Francisco: Josey Bass.

Kirk, R. (1990). Using workload analysis and acuity systems to facilitate quality and productivity.

Journal of Nursing Administration, 20(3), 21–30.

Marquis, B. (1989). Attrition: The effectiveness of retention activities. *Journal of Nursing Administration, 18*(3), 25–29.

Marquis, B. L., & Huston, C. J. (1994). *Management decision making for nurses* (2nd ed.). Philadelphia: J.B. Lippincott, 215.

Patterson, S. W., & Goad, S. (1987). Incentives for retention. *Nursing Management, 18*(2), 69–70.

Przestrzelski, D. (1987). Decentralization: Are nurses satisfied? *Nursing Administration, 18*(11):23–28.

Ringl, K. K., & Dotson, K. (1989). Self-scheduling for professional nurses. *Nursing Management, 20*(2), 42–44.

Williams, M. (1988). When you don't develop your own: Validation methods for patient classification systems. *Nursing Management, 19*(3), 90–96.

Wulff, K. S. (1994). flextime and self-scheduling. In J. McClosky & H. K. Grace (Eds.), *Current issues in nursing* (4th ed.). St. Louis: C.V. Mosby.

BIBLIOGRAPHY

Barnes, R. M. (1986). *Motion and time study design and measurement of work* (6th ed.). New York: John Wiley and Sons.

Becker, D., & Foster, R. (1988). Organizational determinants of nurse staffing patterns. *Nursing Economics, 21*(1), 27–29.

Heater, B. S., Olson, R. K., & Becker, A. M. (1990). Helping patients recover faster. *American Journal of Nursing, 90*(10).

Helberg, J. (1989). Reliability of the nursing clas-

sification index for home healthcare. *Nursing Management, 20*(3), 48–56.

Halloran, E., & Vermeersch, P. (1987). Variability in nurse staffing research. *Journal of Nursing Administration, 17*(2), 26–32.

Hausfeld, J., Gibbons, K., Holtmeier, A., Knight, M., Schulte, C., Stadtmiller, T., & Yeary, K. (1994). Self-staffing: Improving caaaare and staff satisfaction. *Nursing Management, 25*(10), 74–80.

Lafferty, K. (1987). Patient care systems vs. financial systems: The cost justification battle. *Nursing Management, 18*(7), 51–55.

Lawson, K. O., Formella, N. M., Smeltzer, C. H., & Walters, R. M. (1993). redefining the purpose of patient classification. *Nursing Economics, 11*(5), 298–302.

Ligon, R. (1990). A blueprint for involving staff in policy development. *Nursing Management, 21*(7).

Sullivan, E. J., & Decker, P. J. (1988). *Effective management in nursing.* Menlo Park, CA: Addison-Wesley.

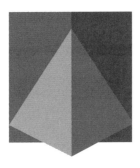

CHAPTER 13

Meeting Staff Development Needs

Once staff are selected and indoctrinated and the manager has adequately staffed the department or unit, staff must be appropriately trained. The leader/manager has a responsibility for maintaining a competent staff, but this responsibility is shared with other members of the organization. Because new equipment, procedures, and knowledge are constantly being introduced, the leader must develop skills in assessing staff learning needs.

Educational needs of staff are partially dependent on the staffing mix and position responsibilities that were developed during the organizing and planning phases of management. For example, the more experienced and educated the staff, the less educational and training needs they will have.

This chapter examines the responsibilities of the manager in educating and training employees. The delineation of the dual roles inherent in education and training staff are outlined. Various learning theories and needs of the adult learner are explored, and the concept of coaching as a staff development tool is introduced. Efforts of various organizations to define and certify competency and continuing education are briefly discussed. The leadership roles and management functions inherent in staff development are shown in Display 13.1.

Bessie L. Marquis and Carol J. Huston:
LEADERSHIP ROLES AND MANAGEMENT FUNCTIONS IN NURSING, 2nd ed.
Lippincott-Raven Publishers © 1996

Display 13.1 Leadership Roles and Management Functions in Staff Development

Leadership Roles

1. Applies adult learning principles when helping employees learn new skills or information
2. Coaches employees spontaneously regarding knowledge and skill deficits
3. Actively seeks out teaching opportunities
4. Uses teaching techniques that empower staff
5. Is sensitive to the learning deficits of the staff and creatively minimizes these deficits
6. Frequently assesses learning needs of the unit

Management Functions

1. Works with the education department to delineate shared individual responsibility for staff development
2. Ensures that there are adequate resources for staff development
3. Assumes responsibility for quality and fiscal control of staff development activities
4. Makes appropriate decisions regarding educational resource allocation in periods of fiscal constraints
5. Ensures that all staff are competent for roles assigned
6. Provides input in formulating staff development policies

STAFF DEVELOPMENT

The staff's knowledge level and capabilities are a major factor in determining the number of staff required to carry out unit goals. The better trained and more competent the staff, the less numbers of staff required. Staff development is a cost-effective method of increasing productivity.

Education and training are two components of staff development that occur after an employee's indoctrination and may occur either within or outside the organization. Only since World War II has a systematic program of education and training became a part of business and industrial management functions. Early staff development emphasized orientation and in-service training. In the last 20 years, however, other forms of education have become common in healthcare organizations. Management development, certification classes, and continuing education courses to meet relicensure requirements are now a part of many staff development programs. Because these forms of education also are the responsibility of the individual, they are discussed in the chapter on career development.

Training Versus Education

Managers have a greater responsibility for seeing that their staff are properly trained than they do for meeting educational needs. The terms may be defined in the following manner.

Training

Training may be defined as an organized method of ensuring that people have knowledge and skills for a specific purpose, that they have acquired the necessary knowledge to perform the duties of the job. The knowledge may require increased affective, motor, or cognitive skills. It is expected that acquiring new skills will increase productivity or create a better product. Managers at every level must assume some responsibility for training their employees.

Education

Education is more formal and broader in scope than training. While training has an immediate use, education is designed to develop the individual in a broader sense. Recognizing educational needs and encouraging educational pursuits are roles and responsibilities of the leader.

Managers may appropriately be requested to teach classes or courses; however, unless managers have specific expertise, they would not normally be responsible for an employee's formal education.

Responsibilities of the Education Department

Most education departments on the organization chart are depicted as having staff or advisory authority rather than line authority. Difficulties inherent in staff positions are discussed in Chapter 7. Because staff positions do not have line authority, education personnel generally have little or no authority over those for whom they are providing educational programs. Likewise, the unit manager has no authority over personnel in the education department.

Because of the ambiguity of overlapping roles and difficulties inherent in line and staff positions, educating and training employees may be neglected. If staff development activities are to be successful, it is necessary to delineate and communicate the authority and responsibility for all components of education and training.

Other difficulties arising from the shared responsibility among managers, personnel department staff, and educators for the indoctrination, education, and training of personnel are a frequent lack of cost effectiveness evaluation and little accountability for the quality and outcomes of the educational activities.

The following suggestions can help overcome difficulties inherent in a staff development system in which there is shared authority:

1. The nursing department must ensure that all parties involved in the indoctrination, education, and training of nursing staff understand and carry out their responsibilities in that process.
2. If the nursing department is not directly responsible for the staff develop-

ment department (in large institutions, a non-nursing administrator may have authority for this department), there must be input from the nursing department in formulating staff development policies and delineating duties.

3. An advisory committee with representatives from top-, middle-, and first-level management; staff development; and the personnel department should be formed. Representatives from all classifications of employees receiving training or education should be part of this committee (Ligon, 1990).
4. Accountability for various parts of the staff development program must be clearly communicated.
5. Some method of determining the cost and benefits of various programs should be used.

THEORIES OF LEARNING

Because all levels of management have a responsibility to improve employee performance through teaching, they must be familiar with learning theories. Understanding teaching/learning theories allows managers to structure training and use teaching techniques to change employee behavior and improve competence, which is the goal for all staff development (Huston & Marquis, 1989).

Adult Learning Theory

Many managers attempt to teach adults as they were taught in school, using *pedagogy* or child learning strategies. This type of teaching is usually ineffective for mature learners because adults have special needs. Malcom Knowles (1970) developed the concept of *androgogy,* or adult learning, to separate the adult learner from pedagogy. Display 13.2 summarizes the basic differences between the two learners. Adult learners are mature, self-directed individuals who have learned a great deal from life experiences and are focused toward solving problems that exist in their immediate environments.

Adult learning theory has contributed a great deal to the manner in which adults are taught. By understanding the assets adults bring to the classroom and the obstacles that might interfere with their learning, trainers and educators are able to

---

Display 13.2 Pedagogy and Androgogy Characteristics

Pedagogy	Androgogy
Learner is dependent.	Learner is self-directed.
Learner needs external rewards and punishment.	Learner is internally motivated.
Learner's experience is unimportant or limited.	Learner's experiences are valued and varied.
Subject-centered.	Task- or problem-centered.
Teacher-directed.	Self-directed.

Display 13.3 Obstacles to and Assets for Adult Learning

Obstacles to Learning	Assets to Learning
Institutional barriers	High self-motivation
Time	Self-directed
Self-confidence	A proven learner
Situational obstacles	Knowledge experience reservoir
Family reaction	Special individual assets
Special individual obstacles	

---

create an effective learning environment. Display 13.3 depicts the obstacles and assets to adult learning, and Display 13.4 shows how the child and adult learning environments should differ.

Sullivan and Decker (1988) suggest that Knowles' studies have the following implications for trainers and educators:

1. A climate of openness and respect will assist in the identification of what the adult learner wants and needs to learn.
2. Adults enjoy taking part in and planning their learning experiences.
3. Adults should be involved in the evaluation of their progress.
4. Experiential techniques work best with adults.
5. Mistakes are opportunities for adult learning.
6. If the value of the adult's experience is rejected, the adult will feel rejected.
7. Adult readiness to learn is greatest when they recognize that there is a need to know (such as in response to a problem).
8. Adults need the opportunity to apply what they have learned very quickly following the learning.
9. Assessment of need is imperative in adult learning.

Display 13.4 Learning Environment of Pedagogy and Androgogy

Pedagogy	Androgogy
The climate is authoritative.	The climate is relaxed and informal.
Competition is encouraged.	Collaboration is encouraged.
Teacher sets goals.	Teacher and class set goals.
Decisions are made by teacher.	Decisions are made by teacher and students.
Teacher lectures.	Students process activities and inquire about projects.
Teacher evaluates.	Teacher, self, and peers evaluate.

Readiness to Learn

Many people confuse readiness to learn with motivation to learn. Readiness refers to the maturational and experiential factors in the learner's background that influence learning. Maturation means that the learner has received the necessary prerequisites for the next stage of learning. The prerequisites could be behaviors or prior learning. Experiential factors are skills previously acquired that are necessary for the next stage of learning. For example, Hicks (1994) has determined that students who lack appropriate prerequisite math skills and those without necessary readiness to learn have a greater chance of failure when taking a posology course.

The implications gained from this theory are that it must be determined if learners have the necessary prerequisites prior to beginning the next stage of learning and learning should occur in sequential patterns that build on each other. Many training programs fail because prerequisite skills and knowledge were not considered.

Motivation to Learn

If learners are informed in advance about the benefits of learning specific content and adopting new behaviors, they are more likely to be motivated to attend the training sessions *and* learn. Telling employees *why* and *how* specific educational or training programs will benefit them personally is a vital management function in staff development.

Reinforcement also is important. Because a learner's first attempts are often unsuccessful, a preceptor is essential. Good preceptors are wonderful reinforcers. Once the behavior or skill is learned, it needs continual reinforcement until it becomes internalized. Managers and preceptors can influence the maintenance of new learning through rewards and benefits on the job.

Task Learning

Learning theory research (Wexley & Latham, 1981) has shown that when individuals are learning complex tasks, learning is facilitated when the task is broken down into parts, beginning with the simplest and continuing to the most difficult. It is necessary, however, to combine part learning with whole learning. When learning motor skills, spaced practice is more effective than massed practice. Overlearning also has been shown to be an effective method for teaching tasks.

Task learning research has been especially helpful in teaching healthcare workers, because much of the learning involves tasks and motor skills. Trainers teaching tasks should teach complex tasks in steps; teach in frequent, short sessions; and teach repeatedly until the task can be performed automatically.

Transfer of Learning

The goal of training is to transfer new learning to the work setting. For this to occur, there should first be as much similarity between the training context and the job as possible. Second, adequate practice is mandatory, and overlearning is recommended. Third, the training should include a variety of different situations so that the knowledge is generalized. Fourth, whenever possible, important features or steps in a process should be identified. Finally, the learner must understand the basic principles underlying the tasks and how a variety of situations will modify how the task is accomplished (Huston & Marquis, 1989).

Transfer of learning principles has many implications for healthcare managers. One of the reasons many in-service training sessions fail is because there is little transfer of classroom learning to the bedside due to inadequate reinforcement. Learning in the classroom will not be transferred without adequate practice in a simulated or real situation and without an adequate understanding of underlying principles.

Social Learning Theory

Social learning theory builds on reinforcement theory as part of the motivation to learn and has many of the same components as the theories of socialization discussed in previous chapters. Bandura (1977) suggests that individuals learn most behavior by direct experience and observation, and behaviors are retained or not retained based on positive and negative rewards.

Social learning theory involves four separate processes. First, people learn as a result of the direct experience of the effects of their actions. Second, knowledge is frequently obtained through vicarious experiences, such as by observing someone else's actions. Third, people learn by judgments voiced by others, especially when vicarious experience is limited. Fourth, people evaluate the soundness of the new information by reasoning through inductive and deductive logic. Social learning theory also acknowledges that anticipation of reinforcement influences what is observed and what goes unnoticed (Bandura, 1977). Figure 13.1 depicts the social learning theory process.

The soundness of social learning theory is demonstrated by the effectiveness of role models, preceptors, and mentors. Because the cognitive process is very much a part of social learning, observational learning will be more effective if the learner is informed in advance of the benefits of adopting a role model's behavior.

Span of Memory

The effectiveness of staff development activities depends to some extent on the ability of the participants to retain information. Many factors have been found to increase memory span.

Among effective strategies are the chance for repeated rehearsal, grouping items to be learned (three to four items for oral presentations and four to six visually), having the material presented in a well-organized manner, and chunking.

Chunking refers to presenting two independent items of information and grouping them together into one unit. The mind only has the ability to remember five to nine chunks of data, but Carnevali and Thomas (1994) believe that as clinical judgment increases, nurses are able to put much larger pieces of information into each chunk. Ashcroft (1989) refers to these larger chunks of data as enriched units. The manager must remember that inexperienced nurses will not be able to remember the amount of data that the expert clinician can remember; this is a skill that develops with time (Carnevali & Thomas, 1994).

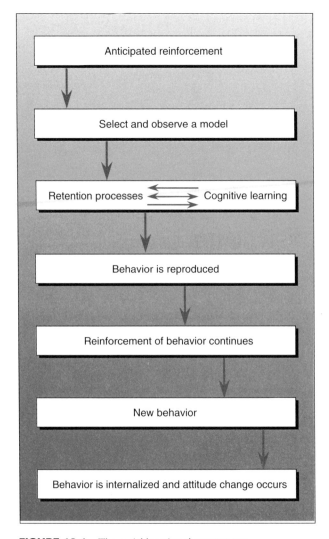

FIGURE 13.1 The social learning theory process.

Knowledge of Results

Research has demonstrated that people learn faster when they are informed regarding their accomplishments. Cromwell and Wutzdorff (1985) use knowledge of performance to enhance critical thinking skills. The knowledge of results must be automatic, immediate, and meaningful to the task at hand. People need to experience a feeling of progress, and they need to know how they are doing when measured against expected outcomes. Learning is facilitated when learners have some criterion by which to judge their progress.

LEARNING EXERCISE 13.1

You have been working in a home health agency for 3 years. During that time, the acuity of your case load has increased dramatically, and you find that teaching home health aides has become more difficult as the equipment they need to use has become more complex.

The home health aides seem motivated to learn, but you feel that part of the difficulty lies with how you are presenting the material. Many of them have a limited knowledge of nursing procedures.

One of your clients is Mr. Jones who has no family. A home health aide has been approved by his insurance company to visit every other day to bathe him and help him ambulate with a walker. Because of his chronic severe respiratory disease, he must be ambulated with oxygen but does not need it when resting. Today you have scheduled a session with Mr. Jones' home health aide for a demonstration and return demonstration on how to connect and disconnect the oxygen and how to use the walker for ambulation. The aide is very competent in basic hygiene skills but has not always used good body mechanics when providing patient care, and she seems intimidated by new equipment.

Assignment: Using your knowledge of learning theories presented in this chapter, design a teaching plan for this aide. Support your plan with appropriate rationale.

COACHING AS A TEACHING STRATEGY

Coaching as a means to develop and train employees is a teaching strategy rather than a learning theory. Coaching is one of the most important tools for empowering subordinates and changing behavior (Orth, Wilkinson, & Benfari, 1990). It is perhaps the most difficult role for a manager to master. Coaching is one person helping the other to reach an optimum level of performance. The emphasis is always on assisting the employee to recognize greater options, to clarify statements, and to grow. The following quote exemplifies coaching from an employee's viewpoint.

> Coaching isn't always noisy and obvious. The best coach I ever had used to come around and ask, "How's such and such going?" or "What do you think the customer wants?" Those question were perfectly aimed. I'd leave those little meetings believing I'd come up with the answers. Only later did I realize that he directed my attention with those questions of his, used them as rudders, to steer me in a certain direction. He never once came out and told me what to do; he led me there and made me feel like I'd figured it out on my own. He was never impatient or too busy to listen. But I think what I appreciated about him the most was that he never asked me to do something I didn't have the ability to do, even if I didn't realize it. He knew me well enough to judge my reach; that was his credibility. If he had put me in situations where I failed, I would have doubted his ability as a coach more than mine as a player. I knew he wanted me to succeed and that we could count on each other. After talking to him I felt empowered (Peters & Austin, 1985).

Coaching may be long term or short term. Short-term coaching is effective as a teaching tool, for assisting with socialization, and for dealing with short-term problems. Long-term coaching as a tool for career management and in dealing with disciplinary problems is different and is discussed in future chapters.

Short-term coaching frequently involves spontaneous teaching opportunities. Learning Exercise 13.2 is an example of how a manager can use short-term coaching to teach an employee in a new role.

ASSESSING STAFF DEVELOPMENT NEEDS

Although managers may not be involved in the implementation of all educational programs, they are responsible for the identification of learning needs. Staff development activities are normally carried out for one of three reasons: to establish competence, to meet new learning needs, and to satisfy interests the staff may have in learning in specific areas. If educational resources are scarce, staff desires for specific educational programs may need to be sacrificed to fulfill competency and new learning needs. Because managers and staff may identify learning needs differently, an educational needs assessment should be carried out prior to developing programs (Marquis & Huston, 1994).

Many staff development activities are generated to ensure that each level of worker is competent to perform the duties assigned to their position. Competence is defined as having the abilities to meet the requirements for a particular role. Healthcare organizations use many resources to determine competency. State board licensure, national certification, and performance review are some of the methods used to satisfy competency requirements. Other methods are self-administered checklists, record audits, and peer evaluation (Yocum, 1994). Many of these methods are explained in the unit on control. It is important for staff development purposes to remember that if competencies are found to be deficient, some staff development activity must take place to correct the deficiencies.

The other common learning need that occurs frequently in all healthcare organizations is the requirement of new learning to meet new technological and scientific challenges. Medical technology and science are developing rapidly, resulting in the need to learn new skills and procedures and acquire the knowledge necessary to operate complex equipment. Much of a manager's educational resources will be used to meet these new learning needs.

Some organizations implement training programs because they are faddish and have been advertised and marketed well. Educational programs are expensive and should not be undertaken unless a demonstrated need exists. Educational resources should be able to be justified. In addition to developing rationale for education programs, the use of an assessment plan will be helpful in meeting learner needs. The following plan outlines the sequence that should be used in developing an educational program:

1. Identify the desired knowledge or skills the staff should have.
2. Identify present level of knowledge or skill.
3. Determine deficit of desired knowledge and skills.
4. Identify resources available to meet needs.
5. Make maximum use of available resources.
6. Evaluate and test outcomes after use of resources.

LEARNING EXERCISE 13.2

Paul's Complaint

Paul is the 3 PM to 11 PM charge nurse on a surgical floor. One day he comes to work a few minutes early, as he occasionally does, so he can chat with his supervisor, Mary, prior to taking patient reports. Mary usually is in her office around this time. Paul enjoys talking over some of his work-related management problems with her because he is fairly new in the charge nurse role having been appointed 3 months ago. Today he asks Mary if she can spare a minute to discuss a personnel problem.

Paul: Sally is becoming a real problem to me. She is taking long break times and has not followed through on several medication order changes lately.

Mary: What do you mean by "long breaks" and not following through?

Paul: In the last 2 months, she has taken an extra 15 minutes for dinner three nights a week and has missed changes in medication orders eight times.

Mary: Have you spoken to Sally?

Paul: Yes, and she said she had been an RN on this floor for 4 years, and no one had ever criticized her before. I checked her personnel record, and there is no mention of those particular problems, but her performance appraisals have only been mediocre.

Mary: What do you recommend doing about Sally?

Paul: I could tell her that I won't tolerate her extended dinner breaks and her poor work performance.

Mary: What are you prepared to do if her performance does not improve?

Paul: I could give her a written warning notice and eventually fire her if her work remains below standard.

Mary: Well that is one option. What are some other options available to you? Do you think Sally really understands your expectations? Do you feel she might resent you?

Paul: I suppose I ought to sit down with Sally and explain exactly what my expectations are. Since my appointment to charge nurse, I've talked with all the new nurses as they have come on shift, but I just assumed the old-timers knew what was expected on this unit. I've been a little anxious about my new role; I never thought about her resenting my position.

Mary: I think that is a good first option. Maybe Sally interpreted your not talking with her, as you did all the new nurses, as a rejection. After you have another talk with her, let me know how things are going.

Analysis

The supervisor has coached Paul toward a more appropriate option as a first choice in solving this problem. Although Mary's choice of questions and guidance assisted Paul, she never "took over" or directed Paul, but instead let him find his own better solution. As a result of this conversation, Paul had a series of individual meetings with all his staff and shared with them his expectations. He also enlisted their assistance in his efforts to have the shift run smoothly.

Although he began to see an improvement in Sally's performance, he realized she was a marginal employee who would need a great deal of coaching. He reported back to Mary and outlined his plans for improving Sally's performance further. Mary reinforced his handling of the problem by complimenting Paul.

> ### ► LEARNING EXERCISE 13.3
>
> You are the evening charge nurse for a large surgical unit. Recently, your long-time and extremely capable unit clerk retired, and the manager of the unit has replaced her with 23-year-old Nancy, who does not have a healthcare background.
>
> Nancy received a 2-week unit clerk orientation that consisted of actual classroom time and working directly with the retiring clerk. She has been functioning on her own for 2 weeks, and you realize that her orientation has not been sufficient. Last evening after her 10th mistake, you became rather sharp with her, and she broke down in tears.
>
> You are very frustrated by this situation. Your unit is very busy in the evening with returning surgeries and surgeons making rounds and leaving a multitude of orders. On the other hand, you feel that Nancy has great potential. You realize that there is much to learn in this job, and without a healthcare background, learning the terminology, physicians' names, and unit routine is difficult. You spend the morning devising a training plan for Nancy.
>
> *Assignment:* Using your knowledge of learning theories, explain your teaching plan, and support your plan with appropriate rationale.

EVALUATION OF STAFF DEVELOPMENT ACTIVITIES

Because staff development includes participation and involvement from many departments, it is very difficult to control this important function effectively. Control, the evaluation phase of the management process, becomes extremely difficult when accountability is shared. It is very easy for the personnel department, middle-level managers, and the education department to "pass the buck" among each other for accountability regarding staff development activities.

The pendulum tends to swing regarding who has responsibility for a department's education and training. At one time, managers and in-service education shared this responsibility. In the 1970s, however, many education departments enlarged, and some managers willingly relinquished their responsibilities for the education and training of personnel.

Currently most organizations decentralize the responsibility for staff development to include the manager. This has occurred as a result of fiscal concerns, the awareness of the need to socialize new employees at the unit level, and recognition of the relationship between employee competency and productivity. It is now generally accepted that the ultimate responsibility for staff training and education rests with the manager, although the manager does not personally provide all aspects of staff development.

There are some difficulties associated with decentralized staff development (Gillies, 1994). One such difficulty is the conflict created by role ambiguity whenever two people share responsibility. Role ambiguity is sometimes lessened when staff development personnel and managers delineate the difference between training and education.

Evaluation of staff development consists of more than merely having class participants fill out an evaluation form at the end of the class session, signing an employee handbook form, or assigning a preceptor for each new employee. Evaluation of the three components of staff development (indoctrination, training, and education) should include the following four criteria:

1. *The learner's reaction.* How did the learner perceive the orientation, the class, the training, or the preceptor?
2. *The behavior change.* What behavior change occurred as a result of the learning? Was the learning transferred? Testing someone at the end of a training or educational program does not confirm that the learning changed behavior. There needs to be some method of follow-up to observe if behavior change occurred.
3. *Organizational impact.* Although it is often difficult to measure how staff development activities impact on the organization, efforts should be made to measure this criterion. Examples of measurements are assessing quality of care (Heater, Olson, & Becker, 1990), medication errors, accidents, quality of clinical judgment, turnover, and productivity.
4. *Cost effectiveness.* All staff development activities should be quantified in some manner. This is perhaps the most neglected aspect of accountability in staff development.

All staff development activities should be evaluated for quality control, impact on the institution, and cost effectiveness. This is true regardless of whether the education and training activities are carried out by the manager, the preceptor, the personnel department, or the education department.

INTEGRATING LEADERSHIP ROLES AND MANAGEMENT FUNCTIONS

The manager recognizes the ultimate responsibility for staff development and uses appropriate teaching theories to assist with teaching and training staff. There is a shared responsibility for assessing educational needs, educational quality, and fiscal accountability of all staff development activities.

The leader uses knowledge of androgogy in dealing with all employees, is able to coach spontaneously and effectively, and seeks opportunities to be personally involved with teaching, training, and staff development. By integrating the leadership role with the management functions of staff development, the manager is able to collaborate with in-service personnel and others so that the learning needs of unit employees are met.

The manager ensures that resources for staff development are used wisely. A focus of staff development should be keeping staff updated with new knowledge and ascertaining that all personnel remain competent to perform their roles. The integrated leader/manager is the role model of a good teacher, using teaching-learning theory to empower staff.

KEY CONCEPTS

▼ Training and education are important parts of staff development.

▼ Managers and education department staff have a shared responsibility for education and training.

▼ It is important that duties, responsibility, and accountability for all staff development activities be well delineated and communicated to all concerned.

▼ *Theories of learning* and principles of teaching must be considered if staff development activities are to be successful.

▼ *Adult learning theory* delineates the differences between child learning, called *pedagogy,* and adult learning, called *androgogy.*

▼ Complex tasks should be taught in steps, in short sessions, and repeated often.

▼ Overlearning is one of the best methods to ensure that there will be transfer of learning from the classroom to the practice setting.

▼ Learners who do not have the necessary prerequisites lack the readiness to learn.

▼ *Social learning theory* suggests that individuals learn most behavior by direct experience and observation.

▼ Educational programs for the adult learner should include a consideration of the learners' unique learning needs and the assets they bring to the learning process.

▼ Learners will learn best from testing if knowledge of results is shared very soon after the testing occurs.

▼ *Chunking* refers to grouping several small pieces of information into a larger chunk.

▼ A *needs assessment* to determine deficits in knowledge and skills is necessary prior to beginning any training or education activity.

▼ *Training* and *education* activities require justification.

▼ All staff development activities should be evaluated retrospectively for quality control and fiscal accountability.

◢◣ ADDITIONAL LEARNING EXERCISES

Learning Exercise 13.4

Assignment: Plan a continuing education program using the following events. Place the events in the proper order (from 0–10). Explain your rationale.

Event
Class begun
Date, time, place established
Program announced
Speaker selected
Audience defined
Evaluation form answered
Topic selected
Program conducted
Objectives formulated
Evaluation form written
Learning needs determined

Learning Exercise 13.5

Learning needs and the maturity of those in a class often influence course content and teaching methods. Look back at how your learning needs and maturity level have changed since you were a beginning nursing student. When viewed as a whole, were you and the other beginning nursing students child or adult learners? Compare Knowles' pedagogy and angrogogy characteristics to determine this.

Are pedagogical teaching strategies appropriate for beginning nursing students? If so, when does the nursing student make a transition from child to adult learner? If you were a nursing instructor during the first semester of a nursing program, what teaching modes do you feel would be most conducive to learning? Would this change as students progressed through the nursing program? Support your feelings with rationale.

Learning Exercise 13.6

You are on a committee representing the night shift for the purpose of developing minimal competencies necessary for intravenous venipuncture. The committee is to outline a minimum of four and a maximum of eight critical elements necessary for safely carrying out this procedure. The elements should be so important that their exclusion in the procedure would result in the employee being certified as incompetent in that procedure.

Assignment: List the criteria selected, and give rationale for inclusion. In discussion with classmates/colleagues, be prepared to justify the reasons other items were not deemed to be of critical importance.

REFERENCES:

Ashcroft, M. (1989). *Human memory and cognition.* Glenview, IL: Scott Foresman.

Bandura, A. (1977). *Social learning theory.* Englewood Cliffs, NJ: Prentice-Hall.

Carnevali, D. L., & Thomas, M. D. (1994). *Diagnostic reasoning and treatment decision making in nursing.* Philadelphia: J.B. Lippincott.

Cromwell, L., & Wutzdorff, A. (1985). Critical thinking in the classroom and in the curriculum. Presented at the Teaching Thinking Skills Conference at Rutgers University.

Gillies, D. A. (1994). *Nursing management—A systems approach.* Philadelphia: W.B. Saunders.

Heater, B. S., Olson, R. K., & Becker, A. M. (1990). Helping patients recover faster. *American Journal of Nursing, 90*(10), 19–20.

Hicks, C. (1994). *The relationship of basic mathematics assessment scores and posology post-test scores of selected vocational students.* Unpublished master's thesis, California State University. Chico, CA.

Huston, C. J., & Marquis, B. L. (1989). *Retention and productivity strategies for nurse managers.* Philadelphia: J.B. Lippincott.

Knowles, M. (1970). *The modern practice of adult education: Androgogy versus pedagogy.* New York: Association Press.

Ligon, R. (1990). A blueprint for involving staff in policy development. *Nursing Management, 21*(7).

Marquis, B. L., & Huston, C. J. (1994). *Management decision making for nurses* (2nd ed.). Philadelphia: J.B. Lippincott.

Orth, C. D., Wilkinson, H. E., & Benfari, R. C. (1990). The manager's role as coach and mentor. *Journal of Nursing Administration, 20*(9), 11–15.

Peters, T., & Austin, N. (1985). *A passion for excellence* (p. 362). New York: Random House.

Sullivan, E. J., & Decker, P. J. (1988). *Effective management in nursing.* Menlo Park, CA: Addison-Wesley.

Wexley, K. M., & Latham, G. P. (1981). *Developing and training human resources in organizations.* Glenview, Il: Scott Foresman.

Yocum, C. Y. (1994). Validating clinical competence. In J. McCloskey & H. K. Grace (Eds.), *Current issues in nursing* (4th ed.). St. Louis: C.V. Mosby.

BIBLIOGRAPHY

Bailey, K., Hoeppner, M., Jeska, S., Schneller, S., & Szalapski, J. (1989). A consortium approach to nursing staff development. *Nursing Economics, 7*(4), 195–199.

Beyrman, K., Phillips, K., & Lessner, J. (1987). Collaboration: Clinical education and hospital orientation. *Nursing Management, 18*(2), 64–66.

Callahan, L. (1988). Competency models: From theory to practice. *Journal of the American Association of Nurse Anesthetists, 56,* 387–389.

Huntsman, A. (1987). A model for employee development. *Nursing Management, 18*(2), 51–54.

Huston, C. J., & Marquis, B. L. (1987). Use of management and ethical case studies to improve decision-making skills in senior nursing student. *Journal of Nursing Education, 26*(5).

Janvrin, S. (1990). Introducing new graduates into pediatric intensive care. *Nursing Management, 21*(5).

Kane, M. (1992). The assessment of professional competence. *Evaluation & the Health Professions, 15,* 163–182

Mooney, V., Diver, B., & Schnackel, A. A. (1988). Developing a cost-effective clinical preceptor program. *Journal of Nursing Administration, 18*(1).

Ressler, K., Kruger, N., & Herb, T. (1991). Evaluating a critical care internship program. *Dimensions of Critical Care Nursing, 10*(3).

UNIT 5

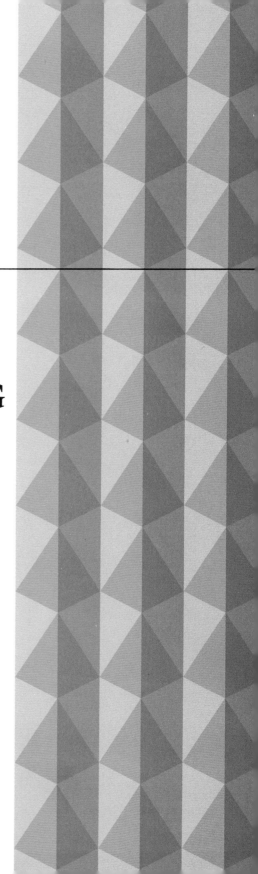

ROLES AND
FUNCTIONS
IN DIRECTING

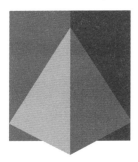

CHAPTER 14

Creating a Motivating Climate

This unit reviews the fourth phase of the management process: directing. This phase also may be referred to as *coordinating* or *activating*. Regardless of the nomenclature, this is the "doing phase" of management, requiring the leadership and management skills necessary to accomplish the goals of the organization. Managers direct the work of their subordinates during this phase. Components of the directing phase discussed in this textbook include creating a motivating climate, establishing organizational communication, managing conflict, facilitating collaboration, negotiating, and complying with union and legal constraints affecting management.

In planning and organizing, managers attempt to establish an environment that is conducive to getting work done. In directing, the manager sets those plans into action. This chapter focuses on creating a motivating climate as a critical element in meeting employee and organizational goals.

The amount and quality of work accomplished by managers directly reflect their motivation and that of their subordinates. Why are some managers or employees more motivated than others? How do demotivated managers affect their subordinates? What can the manager do to help the employee who is demotivated? Leah Curtin's (1990) editorial in the *American Journal of Nursing*, "How can I soar with the eagles when I work with turkeys?," addresses some of these questions. The motivational problems frequently encountered by the manager are complex. To respond

Bessie L. Marquis and Carol J. Huston:
LEADERSHIP ROLES AND MANAGEMENT FUNCTIONS IN NURSING, 2nd ed.
Lippincott-Raven Publishers © 1996

to staff complaints of "do something about the turkeys," managers need an understanding of the relationship between motivation and behavior.

Motivation comes from within the individual. Managers cannot directly motivate subordinates. The humanistic manager *can*, however, create an environment that maximizes the development of human potential. Management support, collegial influence, and the interaction of personalities in the work group can have a synergistic effect on motivation. The leader/manager must identify those components and strengthen them in maximizing motivation at the unit level.

All human beings have needs that motivate them. The *leader* focuses on the needs and wants of individual workers and uses motivational strategies appropriate for each person and situation. The leader also is the role model, listener, supporter, and encourager for demotivated employees.

Leaders should apply techniques, skills, and knowledge of motivational theory to help nurses achieve what they want out of work. At the same time, these individual goals should complement the goals of the organization (Swansburg, 1990). The *manager* bears primary responsibility for meeting organizational goals, such as reaching acceptable levels of productivity and quality.

The leader/manager then must create a work environment in which both organizational and individual needs can be met. Adequate tension must be created to maintain productivity while encouraging subordinates' job satisfaction. Thus, while the worker is achieving personal goals, organizational goals are being met. The leadership roles and management functions inherent in creating such an environment are included in Display 14.1.

This chapter examines motivational theories that have guided organizational efforts and resource distribution for the last 80 years. Special attention is given to the concepts of intrinsic versus extrinsic motivation and organizational versus self-motivation.

INTRINSIC VERSUS EXTRINSIC MOTIVATION

Motivation is the action individuals take to satisfy unmet needs. It is the willingness to put effort into achieving a goal or reward to decrease the tension caused by the need. *Intrinsic* motivation comes from within the individual, driving him or her to be productive. To be intrinsically motivated at work, the worker must value job performance and productivity.

The intrinsic motivation to achieve is directly related to a person's level of aspiration. Parents and peers play major roles in shaping a person's values about what he or she wants to do and be. Parents who set high but attainable expectations for their children and who constantly encourage them in a nonauthoritative environment tend to impart strong achievement drives in their children.

Even with a strong achievement drive, two other beliefs must be internalized before people are intrinsically motivated to behave in a certain way. Individuals must believe that improved performance will lead to outcomes congruent with their value system and that increased effort will lead to improved performance. Thus, the required energy expenditure will be worth the cost (Milkovich & Glueck, 1985).

Extrinsic motivation is motivation enhanced by the job environment or external

Display 14.1 Leadership Roles and Management Functions in Creating a Motivating Work Climate

Leadership Roles

1. Recognize each worker as a unique individual who is motivated by different things.
2. Identify the individual and collective value system of the unit, and implement a reward system that is consistent with those values.
3. Listen attentively to individual and collective work values and attitudes to identify unmet needs that can cause dissatisfaction.
4. Encourage workers to "stretch" themselves in an effort to promote self-growth and self-actualization.
5. Maintain a positive and enthusiastic image as a role model to subordinates in the clinical setting.
6. Encourage mentoring, sponsorship, and coaching with subordinates.
7. Devote time and energy to create an environment that is supportive and encouraging to the discouraged individual.
8. Develop a unit philosophy that recognizes the unique worth of each employee and promotes reward systems that make each employee feel like a winner.

Management Functions

1. Use legitimate authority to provide formal reward systems.
2. Use positive feedback to reward the individual employee.
3. Develop unit goals that integrate organizational and subordinate needs.
4. Maintain a unit environment that eliminates or reduces job dissatisfiers.
5. Promote a unit environment that focuses on employee motivators.
6. Create the tension necessary to maintain productivity while encouraging subordinate job satisfaction.
7. Clearly communicate expectations to subordinates.
8. Demonstrate and communicate sincere respect, concern, trust, and a sense of belonging to subordinates.
9. Assign work duties commensurate with employee abilities and past performance to foster a sense of accomplishment in subordinates.
10. Identify achievement, affiliation, or power needs of subordinates, and develop appropriate motivational strategies to meet those needs.

rewards. The reward occurs after the work has been completed. Although all individuals are intrinsically motivated to some degree, it is unrealistic for the organization to assume that all workers have adequate levels of intrinsic motivation to meet organizational goals. Thus, the organization must provide a climate that stimulates both extrinsic and intrinsic drives.

Because people constantly have needs and wants, individuals are always motivated

> **LEARNING EXERCISE 14.1**
>
> Think back to when you were a child. What rewards did your parents use to promote good behavior? Was your behavior more intrinsically or extrinsically motivated? Were strong achievement drives encouraged and supported by your family?
>
> If you have children, what rewards do you use? Are they the same rewards your parents used? Why or why not?

to some extent. In addition, because all human beings are unique and have different needs, they are motivated differently. The difference in motivation can be explained, in part, by our large and small group cultures. For example, because American culture values material goods and possessions more highly than many other cultures, rewards in this country are frequently tied to these values (Huston & Marquis, 1989).

Organizations also have cultures and values. Motivators vary between organizations and even between units in organizations. For example, competition has proven to be an effective motivator for company sales forces and for college graduates but appears to do little to motivate blue-collar workers (Beach, 1980). Competition may, however, be an effective motivator among blue-collar workers when it is used between groups and not individuals.

Because motivation is so complex, the leader faces tremendous challenges in accurately identifying individual and collective motivators. Even in similar or nearly identical work environments, large variation in individual and group motivation often exists. Much research has been undertaken by behavioral, psychological, and social scientists to develop theories and concepts of motivation. Economists and engineers have focused on extrinsic fiscal rewards to improve performance and productivity, while human relations scientists have stressed intrinsic needs for recognition, self-esteem, and self-actualization. To better understand the current view that both extrinsic and intrinsic rewards are necessary for high productivity and worker satisfaction, one needs to look at how motivational theory has evolved over time.

MOTIVATIONAL THEORY

Chapter 1 introduces traditional management philosophy that emphasizes paternalism, worker subordination, and bureaucracy as a means to predictable but moderate productivity. In this philosophy, high productivity means greater monetary incentives for the worker, and workers are viewed as being motivated primarily by economic factors. This traditional management philosophy is still in use today. Many factory and assembly line production jobs and jobs that use production incentive pay are based on these principles.

The shift from traditional management philosophy to a greater focus on the human element and worker satisfaction as factors in productivity began during the human relations era (1930–1970). The best known human motivation studies in this era were the Hawthorne studies conducted by Elton Mayo.

Continued focus on human motivation did not occur until Abraham Maslow's work in the 1950s. Most nurses are familiar with Maslow's hierarchy of needs and theory of human motivation. Maslow believed that people are motivated to satisfy certain needs ranging from basic survival to complex psychological needs and that people seek a higher need only when the lower needs have been predominantly met. Maslow's hierarchy of needs is depicted in Figure 14.1.

Although Maslow's work helps explain personal motivation, his early work unfortunately was not applied to motivation in the work place. His later work, however, offers much insight into motivation and worker dissatisfaction. Because of Maslow's work, managers began to realize that individuals are complex beings, not solely economic animals, and that they have many needs motivating them at any one time. It also became clear that motivation is internalized and that if productivity is to increase, management must help employees meet lower level needs. This shifting focus in what motivates employees has tremendously affected how organizations value workers today.

B. F. Skinner was another theorist in this era who contributed to our understanding of motivation, dissatisfaction, and productivity. Skinner's research on operant conditioning and behavior modification demonstrates that people can be conditioned to behave in a certain way based on a consistent reward or punishment system. Behavior that is rewarded will be repeated, and behavior that is punished or goes unrewarded is extinguished. Skinner's work continues to be reflected today in the way many managers view and use discipline in the work setting.

Frederick Herzberg believed that employees can be motivated by the work itself and that there is an internal or personal need to meet organizational goals. He felt that separating personal motivators from job dissatisfiers was possible. This distinction between hygiene or maintenance factors and motivator factors was called the *motivation-hygiene theory* or two-factor theory. Display 14.2 lists motivator and hygiene factors identified by Herzberg.

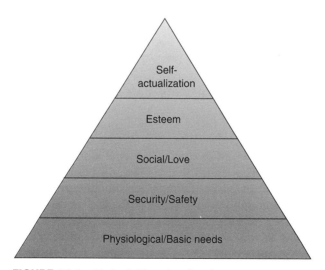

FIGURE 14.1 Maslow's hierarchy of needs.

Display 14.2 Herzberg's Motivator and Hygiene Factors	
Motivators	Hygiene Factors
Achievement	Salary
Recognition	Supervision
Work itself	Job security
Responsibility	Positive working conditions
Advancement	Personal life
Possibility for growth	Interpersonal relations/peers
Company policy	
Status	

Herzberg maintained that motivators or job satisfiers are present in work itself; they give people the desire to work and to do that work well. Hygiene or maintenance factors keep employees from being dissatisfied or demotivated but do not act as real motivators. It is important to remember that the opposite of dissatisfaction may not be satisfaction. When hygiene factors are met, there is a lack of dissatisfaction, not an existence of satisfaction. Likewise, the absence of motivators does not necessarily cause dissatisfaction.

For example, salary is a hygiene factor. Although it does not motivate in itself, when used in conjunction with other motivators, such as recognition or advancement, it can be a powerful motivator. If, however, salary is deficient, employee dissatisfaction can result. Some argue that money can truly be a motivator as evidenced by individuals who work insufferable hours at jobs they truly do not enjoy. Some theorists would argue that money in this case may be taking the place of some other unconscious need.

Some individuals in Herzberg's studies, however, did report job satisfaction solely from hygiene or maintenance factors. Herzberg asserts that these people are only temporarily satisfied when hygiene factors are improved, show little interest in the kind and quality of their work, experience little satisfaction from accomplishments, and tend to show chronic dissatisfaction with other hygiene factors, such as salary, status, and job security.

Herzberg's work suggests that although the organization must build on hygiene or maintenance factors, the motivating climate must actively include the employee. The worker must be given greater responsibilities, challenges, and recognition for work well done. The reward system must meet both motivation and hygiene needs, and the emphasis given by the manager should vary with the situation and employee involved. Although hygiene factors in themselves do not motivate, they are needed to create an environment that encourages the worker to move on to higher level needs. Hygiene factors also combat employee dissatisfaction and are useful in recruiting an adequate personnel pool.

Victor Vroom, another motivational theorist in the humanistic era, developed an *expectancy model*, which looks at motivation in terms of the individual's *valence* or preferences based on social values. In contrast to operant conditioning, which focuses on observable behaviors, the expectancy model says that a person's expectations about his or her environment or a certain event will influence behavior. In other words, individuals look at all actions as having a cause and effect; the effect may be immediate or delayed, but a reward inherent in the behavior exists to motivate risk taking. In Vroom's expectancy model (Fig. 14.2), people make conscious decisions in anticipation of reward; in operant conditioning, people react in a stimulus-response mode. Managers using the expectancy model must become personally involved with their employees to understand better the employees' values, reward systems, strengths, and willingness to take risks.

David McClelland has examined what motives guide a person to action. McClelland states that people are motivated by three basic needs: achievement, affiliation, and power. *Achievement-oriented* people actively focus on improving what is; they transform ideas into action, judiciously and wisely, taking risks when necessary.

In contrast, *affiliation-oriented* individuals focus their energies on families and friends; their overt productivity is less because they view their contribution to society in a different light than those who are achievement oriented. Research has shown that women generally have greater affiliation needs than men and that nurses generally have high affiliation needs. This may be a major reason many more women than men enter nursing (Simms, Price, & Ervin, 1985).

Power-oriented people are motivated by the power that can be gained as a result of a specific action. They want to command attention, get recognition, and control others. McClelland theorizes that managers can identify achievement, affiliation, or power needs of their employees and develop appropriate motivational strategies to meet those needs. Learning Exercise 14.2 is a self-evaluation tool that can be used to assess individual achievement, affiliation, and power needs.

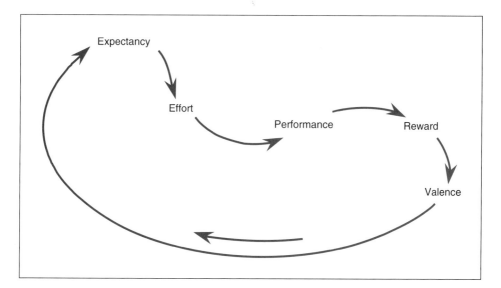

FIGURE 14.2 Vroom's expectancy model.

> ▶ **LEARNING EXERCISE 14.2**
>
> List six goals you hope to accomplish in the next 5 years. Identify which goals are most related to achievement needs, affiliation needs, and power needs. Remember that most people are motivated in part by all three needs, and no one motivational need is better than the others. However, each person must recognize and understand which basic needs motivate them most.

Saul Gellerman, another humanistic motivational theorist, has identified several methods to motivate people positively. One such method, *stretching*, involves assigning tasks that are more difficult than what the person is used to doing. Stretching must not be a routine or daily activity.

Another method, *participation*, entails actively drawing employees into decisions affecting their work. Gellerman strongly believed that motivation problems usually stem from the way the organization manages and not from the staff's unwillingness to work hard. According to Gellerman, most managers "overmanage"—they make the employee's job too narrow and fail to give the employee any decision-making power.

Douglas McGregor (1960) examined the importance of a manager's assumptions about workers on the intrinsic motivation of the workers. These assumptions, which McGregor labeled *theory X and theory Y* (depicted in Display 14.3, page 305), led to the realization in management science that how the manager views, and thus treats, the worker will have an impact on how well the organization functions.

McGregor did not consider theory X and theory Y as opposite points on the spectrum, but rather two points on a continuum extending through all perspectives of people. McGregor felt that people should not be artificially classified as always having theory X or theory Y assumptions about others; instead, most individuals fall within some point on the continuum. Likewise, McGregor did not promote either theory X or theory Y as being the one superior management style, although many managers have interpreted theory Y as being the ultimate management model. No one style is effective in all situations, at all times, and with all people. McGregor, without making value judgments, simply stated that in any situation, the manager's assumptions about people, whether grounded in fact or not, affect motivation and productivity.

The work of all these theorists has added greatly to the understanding of what motivates individuals in and out of the work setting. Research has revealed that motivation is extremely complex and that there is tremendous variation in what motivates different individuals. Research also has identified that some employee dissatisfaction and demotivation is job related (Gillies, 1994). Therefore, managers must understand what can be done at the unit level to create a climate that allows the worker to grow, increases motivation and productivity, and eliminates dissatisfiers that drain energy and cause frustration.

LEARNING EXERCISE 14.3

Crossword Puzzle: A Review of Motivational Theory

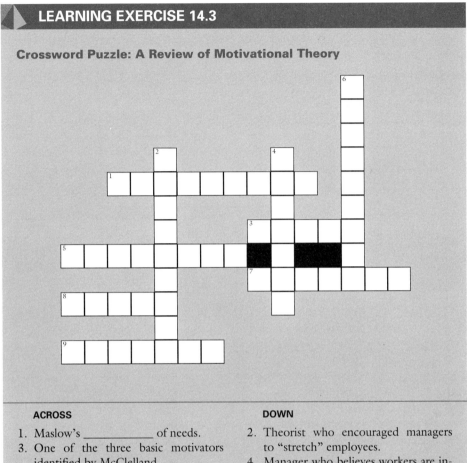

ACROSS

1. Maslow's _____ of needs.
3. One of the three basic motivators identified by McClelland.
5. Theorist who stated that one's assumptions about human nature influence his or her managerial behavior.
7. Factor that keeps the worker from being dissatisfied but is not a true motivator.
8. Developed the expectancy theory.
9. Described operant conditioning.

DOWN

2. Theorist who encouraged managers to "stretch" employees.
4. Manager who believes workers are inherently lazy, need total direction, and are externally motivated.
6. These studies were completed by Elton Mayo and suggested that individuals respond to the fact that they are being studied.

Puzzle solution is found on page 563.

CREATING A MOTIVATING CLIMATE

Because the organization has such an impact on extrinsic motivation, it is important to examine organizational climates or attitudes that directly influence worker morale and motivation. For example, organizations frequently overtly or covertly reinforce the image that each employee is expendable and that individual recognition is in some way detrimental to the employee and his or her productivity within the organization. Just the opposite is true. People who have a strong self-concept and perceive themselves as winners are willing to take risks and increase their productivity to achieve greater recognition. Peters and Waterman (1982) stress that organizations must be designed to make the individual employee feel like a winner; the focus must be on degrees of winning rather than on degrees of losing.

Some organizations, on the other hand, erroneously feel that if a small reward results in desired behavior, then a larger reward will result in even more of the desired behavior. Thus, an employee's motivation should increase proportionately with the amount of the incentive or reward. A study of navy recruits disproved this myth by finding little support for the concept that more incentives are a better motivator (Korman, Glickman, & Frey, 1981). More incentives were actually regarded as being less motivating, because they precipitated feelings of distrust or of being bought. Increasing incentives may be perceived as a violation of individual norms or as motivated by guilt (Bowin, 1987).

There appears to be a perceived threshold beyond which increasing the incentive results in no additional meaning or weight. Organizations must be cognizant of the need to offer incentives at a level where they are valued by employees. This requires that the organization and its managers understand employees' collective values and devise a reward system that is consistent with that value system. Managers also must be cognizant of an employee's individual values and attempt to reward each worker accordingly. The ability to recognize each worker as a unique individual who is motivated differently is a leadership skill.

In addition to the climate created by the organization's beliefs and attitudes, the supervisor or unit manager also has a tremendous impact on motivation at the unit level. Interpersonal relations between employees and their supervisors are critical factors affecting job satisfaction. Although managers cannot directly motivate employees, they can allow the free expression of innovation and creativity, which stimulates individual motivation (Moloney, 1992). Moraldo (1990) believes that nothing stifles motivation and productivity more quickly than not allowing employees to do what they are prepared to do. Managers, therefore, have an opportunity to motivate employees by providing a climate that encourages growth and productivity.

One of the most powerful motivators the manager can use to create a motivating climate, which is frequently overlooked or underused, is positive reinforcement. Peters and Waterman (1982) have identified the following simple approaches for an effective reward-feedback system that uses positive reinforcement.

1. *Positive reinforcement must be specific or relevant to a particular performance.*
   The manager should praise an employee for a specific task accomplished or

---

▶ **LEARNING EXERCISE 14.4**

Identify the greatest motivator in your life at this time. Has it always been the strongest motivator? Could you list the strongest motivator for the significant others in your life? If so, have you ever used this awareness to motivate those individuals to do something specific?

goal met. This praise should not be general. For example, saying "Your nursing care is good," has less meaning and reward than, "The communication skills you showed today as an advocate for Mr. Jones were excellent. I think you made a significant difference in his care."

2. *The positive reinforcement must occur as close to the event as possible.*
3. *The reward-feedback system must be achievable.* All performance goals must be attainable, and both large and small achievements should be recognized or rewarded in some way.
4. *Rewards should be unpredictable and intermittent.* If rewards are given routinely, they tend to lose their value.

Rewards being unpredictable and intermittent is an approach that is open to several interpretations. If Peters and Waterman are advocating inconsistency when granting rewards, we disagree because there must be consistency in how and when rewards are given. When rewards lack consistency, there is greater risk that the reward itself will become a source of competition and thereby lower morale. An attitude prevails that "there are a limited number of awards, and an award received by anyone else limits the chances of my getting one; thus, I cannot support recognition for my peer" (Huston & Marquis, 1989). Likewise, rewarding one individual's behavior and not another's who has accomplished a similar task at a similar level promotes jealousy and can demotivate.

If, however, Peters and Waterman mean that rewards and praise should be spontaneous and not relegated to predictable events, such as routine annual performance reviews or recognition dinners, then the authors agree. Reward and praise should be given whenever possible and whenever they are deserved.

If positive reinforcement and reward are to be used as motivational strategies, then rewards must represent a genuine accomplishment on the part of the individual and should be somewhat individual in nature (Huston & Marquis, 1989). For example, many managers erroneously consider annual merit pay increases as rewards that motivate employees. Most employees, however, recognize annual merit pay increases as a universal given; thus, this reward has little meaning and little power to motivate. Managers should promote excellence within achievable goals and reward performance in a way that is valued by their staff. These are the cardinal elements for a successful motivation-reward system for the organization.

Managers also can create a motivating climate by being a positive and enthusiastic role model in the clinical setting. Studies by Jenkins and Henderson (1984) demonstrate that the supervisor or manager's personal motivation is the most important factor affecting a staff's commitment to duties and morale. According to Jenkins and Henderson (p. 13), "Positive outlooks, enthusiasm, productivity, and accomplishment are contagious." Radzik (1985) stated that employees frequently gauge their job security and their employer's satisfaction with job performance by the expression they see on their manager's face. Managers who frequently project unhappiness to subordinates contribute greatly to low unit morale.

Besides being a role model for staff, managers must make an effort to mentor future managers and to encourage mentoring relationships between staff. Mentoring, which is discussed in Chapter 10, is one of the most successful motivational tools at the unit level. Kanter (1984) argues that all organizations seeking excellence need to encourage their managers to become mentors to employees. Likewise, Kotter (1985) states that managers must be mentors, sponsors, coaches, and especially role models if new employees are to succeed in their roles.

The Encouraging Manager

Sometimes fostering a subordinate's motivation is as simple as creating a supportive and encouraging environment. The cost of this strategy is only the manager's time and energy. Losoncy (1977) has identified the following characteristics of the *encouraging person* or *encouraging manager* that are essential for a motivating climate.

1. The encouraging person sees only individuals in the world. When faced with groups of people, each person is viewed as unique, with interests, problems, and goals that must be acknowledged.
2. The encouraging person is a safe, totally accepting person. He or she believes that the discouraged individual has not consistently experienced safe relationships and hence has developed a mask.
3. The encouraging person is skilled at looking for uniqueness or differences in an individual. This is almost a second-nature skill that the helper develops along the way. Once the individual's uniqueness is noticed, he or she begins to develop a sense of self-worth and finds the courage to take risks and change.
4. The encouraging person not only has faith in human nature but has faith in the discouraged individual.
5. The encouraging person is sincerely enthusiastic about the growth of the discouraged individual and communicates this enthusiasm to others.
6. The encouraging person is ultra-sensitive to the self-defeated person's goals, values, and purposes, believing that each behavior is significant and consequential. The encourager helps this person learn to see himself or herself in a more powerful light.
7. The encouraging person realizes that knowledge of the discouraged individual's past proud moments—his or her "claim to fame"—is important to building a new, more positive identity. Encouraged to feel worthwhile, the formerly defeated person will now take risks, formulate goals, and evaluate his or her own growth.
8. The encouraging person is sensitive to overdependency in the relationship and helps the discouraged person develop self-encouragement. As a result, this formerly discouraged person begins to develop new relationships in which he or she uses the same encouragement process with others. This person then becomes an encourager.

Strategies to Create a Motivating Climate

In addition to positive reinforcement, role modeling, and being an encouraging manager, the following strategies must be used consistently to create a motivating climate.

1. Have clear expectations for workers, and communicate these expectations effectively.
2. Be fair and consistent when dealing with all employees.
3. Be a firm decision maker using an appropriate decision-making style.
4. Develop the concept of teamwork. Develop group goals and projects that will build a team spirit.
5. Integrate the staff's needs and wants with the organization's interests and purpose.
6. Know the uniqueness of each employee. Let each know that you understand his or her uniqueness.
7. Remove traditional blocks between the employee and the work to be done.
8. Provide experiences that challenge or "stretch" the employee, and allow opportunity for growth.
9. When appropriate, request participation and input from all subordinates in decision making.
10. Whenever possible, give subordinates recognition and credit.
11. Be certain that employees understand the reason behind decisions and actions.
12. Reward desirable behavior; be consistent in how you handle undesirable behavior.
13. Let employees exercise individual judgment as much as possible.
14. Create a trustful and helping relationship with employees.
15. Let employees exercise as much control as possible over their work environment.
16. Be a role model for employees.

PROFESSIONAL SUPPORT SYSTEMS FOR THE MANAGER

The attitude and energy level of managers directly affect the attitude and productivity of employees. A burned-out, tired manager will develop a lethargic and demotivated staff. Therefore, managers must constantly monitor their own motivational level and do whatever is necessary to restore their motivation to be a role model to staff.

A 1987 to 1988 study of 1,870 white-collar employees of Westinghouse Electric Corporation showed that 36% of female managers and 23% of male managers qualified as clinically depressed at some point during their lives; 16.6% of the female and 8.6% of the male managers were clinically depressed at the time of the study (Bair, 1990, p. 6A). These figures exceed the 1986 depression rate of all Americans of 4.4%. The study concluded that middle-level managers are the group most often affected because they frequently find themselves "trapped between the gripes of their subordinates and the demands of their own bosses." In addition, the most commonly cited causes of depression were a lack of rewards, a cloudy job future, and specific events, such as pay cuts or bad evaluations.

For both managers and subordinates, motivation is closely tied to support from peers and significant others. If this support is lacking or inadequate, the manager may become overwhelmed with the responsibilities of the position and become less effective. It is very important then for the manager to identify a professional support system for reinforcement, information, and guidance in his or her professional development. The term *networking* is frequently used to describe the linking of professionals in a support system. As with mentoring, men have traditionally used the "old boy network" as a means for professional support and career growth, while women traditionally have worked as independent entities.

Hamilton and Kiefer (1986) have identified several prerequisites to successful networking:

1. Each individual in the network must have a basic self-interest: a desire to improve or get ahead.
2. Each individual must be willing to use other people and in return, be used by others. Each individual contributes or uses what is needed.
3. There must be a balance of power in the networking relationship. If one individual does all the giving, and one individual does all the taking, the relationship will die.
4. Individuals in networking must have a positive self-concept and feel that they can contribute to others.

In addition to networking, McFarland, Leonard, and Morris (1984) have identified the following strategies for the manager to reduce job-related stressors and keep motivation high:

1. Continue strengthening personal and professional skills and qualifications.
2. Distance yourself physically or emotionally from stress carriers whenever possible.
3. Avoid being a perfectionist; set realistic goals for yourself and your subordinates.
4. Enroll in stress management courses.
5. Use constructive outlets for emotions, such as physical exercise and talking.
6. Separate your personal life from your professional life.
7. Take appropriate breaks during the work day, and take regularly scheduled vacations.
8. Use strategies such as conflict management, time management, constructive use of power-oriented behavior, planned change, and communication skills.
9. Practice good health habits, such as a well-balanced diet, regular exercise, and adequate rest.
10. Reduce or replace self-defeating thoughts with positive ones.
11. Have a clear set of values and overall life goals that place stressors in their proper perspective.

Managers must be internally motivated before they can motivate others. In the Westinghouse study, 70% of the depressed managers did not seek treatment (Bair, 1990). It is imperative that discouraged or depressed managers acknowledge their own feelings and seek assistance accordingly. Managers are responsible to themselves and to subordinates to remain motivated to do the best job possible.

INTEGRATING LEADERSHIP ROLES AND MANAGEMENT FUNCTIONS

Most human behavior is motivated by a goal the individual wants to achieve. Identifying employee goals and fostering their attainment allow the leader to motivate employees to reach personal and organizational goals. The motivational strategy the leader uses should vary with the situation and the employee involved; it may be formal or informal. It also may be extrinsic, although because of a limited formal power base, the leader generally focuses on the intrinsic aspects of motivation.

The leader also must be a listener, supporter, or encourager to the discouraged employee. Perhaps the most important role the leader has in working with the demotivated employee, however, is that of role model. Leaders who maintain a positive attitude and high energy levels directly and profoundly affect the attitude and productivity of their followers.

When creating a motivating climate, the manager uses formal authority to reduce dissatisfiers at the unit level and to implement a reward system that reflects individual and collective value systems. This reward system may be formalized, or it may be as informal as praise. Managers, by virtue of their position, have the ability to motivate subordinates by "stretching" them intermittently with increasing responsibility and assignments they are capable of achieving. The manager's role then is to create the tension necessary to maintain productivity while encouraging subordinate job satisfaction. Therefore, the success of the motivational strategy is measured by the increased productivity and benefit to the organization and by the growth in the individual, which motivates him or her to accomplish again.

Display 14.3 McGregor's Theory X and Theory Y

Theory X	Theory Y
Employees	Employees
• avoid work if possible.	• like and enjoy work.
• dislike work.	• are self-directed.
• must be directed.	• seek responsibility.
• have little ambition.	• are imaginative and creative.
• avoid responsibility.	• have under-utilized intellectual capacity.
• need threats to be motivated.	• need only general supervision.
• need close supervision.	• are encouraged to participate in problem
• are motivated by rewards and punishment.	solving.

KEY CONCEPTS

▼ Because human beings have constant needs and wants, the individual is always motivated to some extent. All human beings are motivated differently, however, because they have different needs and desires.

▼ Managers cannot intrinsically motivate people because motivation comes from within the individual. The humanistic manager *can*, however, create an environment in which the development of human potential can be maximized.

▼ Maslow stated that people are motivated to satisfy certain needs ranging from basic survival to complex psychological needs and that people seek a higher need only when the lower needs have been predominantly met.

▼ Skinner's research on *operant conditioning* and *behavior modification* demonstrates that people can be conditioned to behave in a certain way based on a consistent reward or punishment system.

▼ Herzberg maintained that *motivators, or job satisfiers, are present in the work itself and encourage people to want to work and to do that work well. Hygiene or maintenance factors* keep the worker from being dissatisfied or demotivated but do not act as true motivators for the worker.

▼ Vroom's expectancy model says that people's expectations about their environment or a certain event will influence their behavior.

▼ McClelland's studies state that all people are motivated by three basic needs: achievement, affiliation, and power.

▼ Gellerman states that most managers in organizations "overmanage"—they make the responsibility of the employee too narrow and fail to give the employee any decision-making power.

▼ Douglas McGregor shows the importance of a manager's assumptions about workers on the intrinsic motivation of the worker. These assumptions, which McGregor labeled *theory X* and *theory Y,* influence worker motivation.

▼ *Intrinsic motivation* can be defined as the motivation that comes from within the individual and drives him or her to be productive. *Extrinsic motivation* is enhanced by the job environment or by external rewards.

▼ Peters and Waterman (1982) stress that organizations must be designed to make the individual employee feel like a winner. The focus must be on degrees of winning rather than on degrees of losing.

▼ There appears to be a perceived threshold beyond which increasing reward incentives results in no additional meaning or weight in terms of productivity.

▼ *Positive reinforcement* is one of the most powerful motivators the manager can use and is frequently overlooked or underused.

▼ The supervisor's or manager's personal motivation is an important factor affecting staff's commitment to duties and morale.

▼ Besides being a role model for staff, managers must try to mentor future managers and encourage mentoring relationships between subordinates.

▼ Managers should network with a professional support system for positive reinforcement, information, and guidance in their professional development.

▼ The success of a motivational strategy is measured by the increased productivity and benefit to the organization and by the growth in the individual, which motivates him or her to accomplish again.

ADDITIONAL LEARNING EXERCISES

Learning Exercise 14.5

You are the 3 PM to 11 PM charge nurse on the surgical unit. You have grown concerned about the behavior of one of the new RNs assigned to your unit. This new nurse, a recent graduate of a local BSN program, is named Sally Brown. Sally came to work at Memorial Hospital immediately after her graduation. She was assigned to work 7 AM to 3 PM for 2 months and appeared to be extremely hard-working, knowledgeable, well liked, and highly motivated. After a 2-month day orientation, she was assigned to permanent evening shifts or 3 PM to 11 PM shifts, which she has been working for the last 4 months.

Approximately 7 weeks ago, several small incidents happened to Sally. One of the physicians became very angry with her over a minor medication error she had made; Sally was already feeling badly about the error. Following this episode, a patient's husband began disliking Sally for no discernible reason; he then refused to allow Sally to care for his wife. Then 2 weeks ago, a patient died suddenly, and although no one was to blame, Sally apparently felt that if she had been more observant and skilled in assessment, she would have picked up the subtle changes in the patient's condition sooner.

Although you have been supportive of Sally, you recognize that she is in danger of becoming demotivated. Her once flawless appearance has been replaced by wrinkled uniforms; she is frequently absent from work; and her once pleasant personality has been exchanged for withdrawal from her coworkers.

Assignment: Using your knowledge of new role identification, assimilation, and motivational theory, develop a plan to assist this young nurse. What can you do to provide a climate that will remotivate her and decrease her job dissatisfaction? Explain what you think is happening to this nurse and the rationale behind your plan. Your plan should be realistic in terms of the time and energy you have to spend on one employee. Be sure to identify the responsibilities of the employee as well.

Learning Exercise 14.6

You are the chief nursing officer of County Hospital. Dr. Jones a cardiologist, has approached you about having an CU/CCU nurse make rounds with him each morning on all the patients in the hospital with a cardiac-related diagnosis. He feels this will probably represent a 90-minute commitment of nursing time daily. He is vague about the nurse's exact role or purpose, but you feel there is great potential for better and more consistent patient education and care planning.

Beth, one of your finest ICU/CCU nurses, agrees to assist Dr. Jones. Beth has always wanted to have an expanded role in teaching. However, because of personal constraints, she has been unable to relocate to a larger city where there are more opportunities for teaching. You warn Beth that it might be some time before this role develops into an autonomous position, but she is eager to assist Dr. Jones. The other ICU/CCU staff agree to cover Beth's patients while she is gone, although it is obviously an extension of an already full patient load.

After 3 weeks of making rounds with Dr. Jones, Beth comes to your office. She tearfully reports that rounds frequently take 2 to 3 hours and that making rounds with Dr. Jones amounts to little more than "carrying his charts, picking up his pages, and being a personal handmaiden." She has assertively stated her feelings to him and has attempted to demonstrate to Dr. Jones how their allegiance could result in improved patient care. She states that she has not been allowed any input into patient decisions and is frequently reminded of "her position" and his ability to have her removed from her job if she does not like being told what to do. She is demoralized and demotivated. In addition, she feels that her peers resent having to cover her workload because it is obvious that her role is superficial at best.

You ask Beth if she wants you to assign another nurse to work with Dr. Jones, and she says that she would really like to make it work but does not know what action to take that would improve the situation.

You call Dr. Jones, and he agrees to meet with you at your office when he completes rounds the following morning. At this visit, Dr. Jones confirms Beth's description of her role but justifies his desire for the role to continue by saying, "I bring $1,000,000 of business to this hospital every year in cardiology procedures. The least you can do is provide the nursing assistance I am asking for. If you are unable to meet this small request, I will be forced to consider taking my practice to a competitive hospital." However, after further discussion, he does agree that eventually he would consider a slightly more expanded role for the nurse after he learns to trust her.

Assignment: Do you meet Dr. Jones' request? Does it make any difference whether Beth is the nurse, or can it be someone else? Does the revenue Dr. Jones generates supersede the value of professional nursing practice? Should you try and talk Beth into continuing the position for a while longer? While trying to reach a goal, people must sometimes endure a difficult path, but at what point does the means not justify the end? Be realistic about what you would do in this situation. What do you perceive to be the greatest obstacles in implementing your decision?

Learning Exercise 14.7

You are a critical care nurse in a busy trauma unit. Your unit is understaffed, as are many critical care units across the nation due to the nursing shortage. Although hospital recruiters have been extremely active, there is little chance of resolving the staffing problem in the near future. The unit supervisor is extremely supportive of the staff's efforts but can do little to ease the actual shortage, other than to turn away patients or close the unit. Unfortunately, this unit is the only trauma facility in a 100-mile radius. As a result, all the nurses on the unit have been working at least 48 hours per week during the last 6 months; many have been working several double shifts and putting in many overtime hours each pay period.

Morale is deteriorating, and the staff have begun to complain. Most of the staff are feeling burned out and demotivated. Many of the staff have started refusing to work extra shifts or do overtime. You feel a responsibility to the patients, community, and organization and have continued to work the extra hours but are exhausted.

Today is your first evening off in 6 days. At 2 PM, the phone rings, and you suspect it is the hospital calling you to come in to work. You delay answering while you decide what to do. The answering machine turns on, and you hear your supervisor's voice. She says that they are desperate. There were two new patients admitted during the day from an auto accident, and the unit is full. She says she appreciates all the hours you've been working but needs you once again, although she is unable to give you tomorrow off in compensation.

You feel conflicting loyalties to the unit, patients, supervisor, and yourself.

Assignment: Decide what you will do. Will you agree to work? Will you return your supervisor's telephone call, or pretend you are not home? When do your loyalties to your patients and the organization end and your loyalties to yourself begin? Is the unit supervisor taking advantage of you? Are the other staff being irresponsible? What values have played a part in your decision making?

Learning Exercise 14.8

You are a school nurse and have worked in the same school for 2 years. Prior to that time, you had been a staff nurse at a local hospital working in pediatrics and later for a physician. You have been an RN for 6 years.

When you first began your job, it was so exciting. You felt you were really making a difference in children's lives. You started several good health promotion programs and worked hard upgrading your health aides' education and training.

Several months ago, funding for the school was drastically cut, and several of your favorite programs were eliminated. You have been very depressed about this and lately have been short tempered at work. Today one of your best health aides gave you her 2-week notice and said "this isn't a good place to work anymore." You realize many of the aides and several of the school teachers have picked up your negative attitude.

There is much you still love about your job, and you are not sure if the budget problems are temporary or long term. You go home early today and contemplate what to do.

Assignment: Should you stay in this job or leave? If you stay, how can you get remotivated? Can you remotivate yourself if the budget cuts are long term? Make a plan about what to do.

REFERENCES:

Bair, J. (1990). Study: Mid-managers get deep blues. *Chico Enterprise Record,* 6A.

Beach, D. (1980). *Personnel: The management of people at work* (4th ed.). New York: Macmillan.

Bowin, R. B. (1987). *Human resource problem solving.* Englewood Cliffs, NJ: Prentice Hall.

Curtin, L. (1990). The excellence within. *American Journal of Nursing, 90*(10), 7.

Gillies, D. A. (1994). *Nursing management* (3rd ed.). St Louis: C.V. Mosby.

Hamilton, J. M., & Kiefer, M. E. (1986). *Survival skills for the new nurse.* Philadelphia: J.B. Lippincott.

Huston, C. J., & Marquis, B. L. (1989). *Increasing retention and productivity through human resource management.* Philadelphia: J.B. Lippincott.

Jenkins, R. L., & Henderson, R. L. (1984). Motivating the staff: What nurses expect from their supervisors. *Nursing Management, 15*(2), 13–14.

Kanter, R. (1984). *The change masters.* New York: Simon and Schuster.

Korman, A. K., Glickman, A. S., & Frey, R. L. (1981). More is not better: Two failures of incentive theory. *Journal of Applied Psychology, 66,* 255–259.

Kotter, J. (1985). *Power and influence*. New York: The Free Press.

Losoncy, L. E. (1977). *Turning people on: How to be an encouraging person*. Englewood Cliffs, NJ: Prentice Hall.

McFarland, G., Leonard, H. S., & Morris, M. (1984). *Nursing leadership and management—Contemporary strategies*. New York: John Wiley & Sons.

McGregor, D. (1960). *The human side of enterprise*. New York: McGraw-Hill.

Milkovich, G. T., & Glueck, W. F. (1985). *Personnel, human resource management: A diagnostic approach*. Plano, TX: Business Publications.

Moloney, M. M. (1992) *Professionalization of Nursing*. Philadelphia: J.B. Lippincott.

Moraldo, P. (1990). The nineties: A decade in search of meaning. *Nursing and Health Care, 11*(1), 13.

Peters, T., & Waterman, R. H. (1982). *In search of excellence*. New York: Harper & Row.

Radzik, A. (1985). What managers want to know. *Nation's Business, 73*(8), 37.

Simms, L. M., Price, S. A., & Ervin, N. E. (1985). *The professional practice of nursing administration*. New York: John Wiley & Sons.

Swansburg, R. C. (1990). *Management and leadership for nurse managers*. Boston: Jones and Bartlett.

BIBLIOGRAPHY

Ash, A. M. (1988). Motivate before you delegate: An effective strategy. *Professional Medical Assistant, 21*(5), 16–18.

Beaulieu, L. P. (1988). Preceptorship and mentorship: Bridging the gap between nursing education and nursing practice. *Imprint, 35*(2), 111.

Burnard, P. (1988). Mentors: A supporting act. *Nursing Times, 84*(46), 24–27.

Chinn, P. L. (1987). Reflections on motivation and health care values. *Advances in Nursing Science, 9*(4), ix.

Darling, L. A. (1984). What do nurses want in a mentor? *Journal of Nursing Administration, 14*(10), 42–44.

Drucker, P. (1985). Getting things done—How to make people decisions. *Harvard Business Review, 63*, 22–25.

Herzberg, F., Mausner, B., & Snyderman, B. B. (1959). *The motivation to work*. New York: John Wiley & Sons.

Kirsch, J. (1988). *The middle manager and the nursing organization: Human resources, fiscal resources*. Norwalk, CT: Appleton and Lange.

Laurent, C. (1988). Mentors: On hand to help. *Nursing Times, 84*(46), 29–30.

Lewis, E. M., & Spicer, J. G. (1987). *Human resource management handbook: Contemporary strategies for nursing managers*. Rockville, MD: Aspen Publishers.

Longest, B. B. (1974). Job satisfaction for registered nurses in the hospital setting. *Journal of Nursing Administration, 4*(3), 46.

Madison, J. R. (1984). *A study to determine nurse administrator's perceptions of the mentoring relationship and its effect on their professional lives*. Unpublished master's thesis, University of Minnesota, School of Public Health.

Marquis, B. L., & and Huston, C. J. (1994). *Management decision making for nurses*. Philadelphia: J.B. Lippincott.

Maslow, A. H. (1943). A theory of human motivation. *Psychological Review, 50*, 370–396.

Maslow, A. H. (1971). *The farther reaches of human nature*. New York: Viking Press.

Orth, C. D., Wilkinson, H. E., & Benfari, R. C. (1990). The manager's role as coach and mentor. *Journal of Nursing Administration, 20*(9), 11–15.

Peters, T., & Austin, N. (1985). *A passion for excellence*. New York: Random House.

Quick, T. (1985). *The manager's motivation desk book*. New York: John Wiley & Sons.

Roberts, C. C. (1987). Managing motivation for quality care. *Journal of Post Anesthesia Nursing, 2*(1), 64–65.

Skinner, W. (1982). Big hat, no cattle: Managing human resources, Part 1. *Journal of Nursing Administration, 12*, 27–29.

Wysenki, N. J. (1986). Motivating your staff to do their best. *Nursing Life, 6*(1), 52–53.

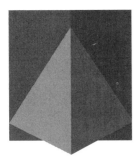

CHAPTER 15

Organizational and Interpersonal Communication

While some functions of management, such as planning, organizing, and controlling, can be reasonably isolated, communication forms the core of management activities and cuts across all phases of the management process. Organizational communication is a management function; it must be systematic, have continuity, and be fully integrated into the organizational structure, encouraging an exchange of views and ideas.

Depending on the manager's position in the organizational hierarchy, more than 80% of managerial time may be spent in some type of organizational communication. Sixteen percent of this time represents reading, 9% writing, 30% speaking, and 45% listening (Swansburg, 1990). Developing expertise in all aspects of communication is critical to managerial success.

Because 75% of managerial communication time is spent speaking and listening, it is clear that in a leadership role, one must have excellent interpersonal communication skills. These are perhaps the most critical leadership skills. The nursing leader communicates with clients, colleagues, superiors, and subordinates. In addition, because nursing practice tends to be group oriented, interpersonal communication be-

Bessie L. Marquis and Carol J. Huston:
LEADERSHIP ROLES AND MANAGEMENT FUNCTIONS IN NURSING, 2nd ed.
Lippincott-Raven Publishers © 1996

tween group members is necessary for continuity and productivity. The leader is responsible for developing a cohesive team to meet organizational goals. To do this, the leader must articulate issues and concerns so that workers will not become confused about priorities. Communicating effectively determines success as a leader/manager (Haimann, 1994).

Leadership skills and management functions inherent in organizational and interpersonal communication are listed in Display 15.1. This chapter examines both organizational and interpersonal communication. Barriers to communication in large-scale organizations and managerial strategies to overcome those difficulties are presented. Channels and modes of communication are compared and guidelines are

Display 15.1 Leadership Roles and Management Functions in Organizational and Interpersonal Communication

Leadership Roles

1. Understands and appropriately uses the informal communication network in the organization.
2. Communicates clearly and precisely in language others will understand.
3. Is sensitive to the internal and external climate of the sender or receiver and uses that awareness in interpreting messages.
4. Appropriately observes and interprets the verbal and nonverbal communication of followers.
5. Role models assertive communication and active listening.
6. Demonstrates congruency in verbal and nonverbal communication.
7. Recognizes status, power, and authority as barriers to manager/subordinate communication. Uses communication strategies to overcome those barriers.

Management Functions

1. Understands and appropriately uses the organization's formal communication network.
2. Determines the appropriate communication mode or combination of modes for optimal distribution of information in the organizational hierarchy.
3. Prepares written communications that are clear and uses language that is appropriate for the message and the receiver.
4. Consults with other departments or disciplines in coordinating overlapping roles and group efforts.
5. Differentiates between "information" and "communication" and appropriately assesses the need for subordinates to have both.
6. Is proficient in telephone communication skills.

given for managerial selection of the optimum channel or mode. In addition, assertiveness, nonverbal behavior, and active listening as interpersonal communication skills are discussed.

THE COMMUNICATION PROCESS

Lyles and Joiner (1986, p. 97) define communication as "the enabling process that allows information to be transferred and ideas to be translated into action." Vestal (1995, p. 34) defines communication as "the exchange of meanings between and among individuals through a shared system of symbols (verbal and nonverbal) that have the same meaning for both the sender and the receiver of the message." Both definitions impart a sense of the complexity involved in communication. For example, what if individuals do not share the same system of symbols? What if the verbal and nonverbal messages are not congruent? Does communication occur if an idea is transmitted but not translated into action?

Because communication is so complex, many models exist to explain how organizations and individuals communicate. Basic elements common to most models are shown in Figure 15.1. In all communication, there is at least one sender, one receiver, and one message. There also is a mode or medium through which the message is sent, such as verbal, written, or nonverbal.

An internal and an external climate also exist in communication. The internal climate includes the values, feelings, temperament, and stress levels of the sender and the receiver. Weather conditions, temperature, timing, and the organizational climate itself are a part of the external climate. The external climate also includes status, power, and authority as barriers to manager–subordinate communication.

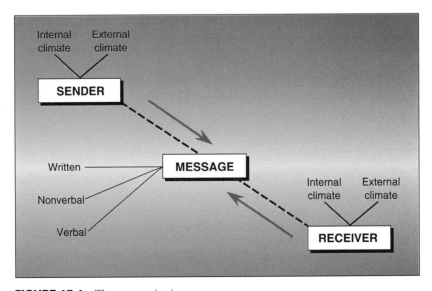

FIGURE 15.1 The communication process.

Both the sender and the receiver must be sensitive to the internal and external climate, because the perception of the message is altered greatly depending on the climate that existed at the time the message was sent or received. For example, an insecure manager who is called to meet with superiors during a period of stringent layoffs will probably view the message with more trepidation than a manager who is secure in his or her role. Fritz, Russel, and Shirk (1984) believe that external and internal climates either facilitate or inhibit communication.

Because each person is different and thus makes decisions and perceives differently, assessing external climate is usually easier than internal climate. In assessing internal climate, remember that the human mind perceives only what it expects to perceive. The unexpected is generally ignored or misunderstood. In other words, receivers cannot communicate if the message is incompatible with their expectations. Therefore, effective communication requires the sender to determine what receivers see and hear.

BARRIERS TO ORGANIZATIONAL COMMUNICATION

Gender is a significant factor in organizational communication. The healthcare industry has historically required communication between a predominantly male medical profession and a predominantly female nursing profession. The male role was generally recognized as active and vital, while the female role was passive and compliant. Manss (1994) characterizes traditional physician–nurse interactions as that of superior–subordinate. This occurs partly because women have different ways of speaking and a different relation to language (Sellers, 1991; Tannen, 1990). Feminist studies have argued that girls are socialized to use language and speech and the power they enable differently than men (Bartky, 1990). The combination of difference in use of language and difference in status has resulted in patterns of male dominance and female deference in communication. The majority of healthcare administrators continue to be male. Therefore, male physicians and male administrators may feel little incentive to seek a more enlightened, collaborative approach in communication that female nurses often desire. These differences in gender and in power and status continue to affect tremendously the types and quality of organizational and unit-level communication.

Formal organization structure also has an impact on communication. Joblin (1982), studying the effects of formal organization structure on superior–subordinate communication, found that subordinates at lower levels in the hierarchy perceive less openness in superior–subordinate communication than subordinates at higher levels. This may occur because higher level subordinates are more apt to be included in decision making. As the number of the employees increases (particularly more than 1,000 employees), the quantity of communication increases, but employees perceive it as increasingly closed.

In addition, in large-scale organizations, it is impossible for individual managers to communicate personally with each individual or group involved in organizational decision making. Jackson (1984) has identified the following characteristics of large-scale organizations that make communication particularly difficult.

1. *Spatial distance within an organization can be a barrier to communication.*
2. *Different subgroups or subcultures within the organization have their own value systems and identities.* Members within that subgroup form an allegiance to their own members. This results in different translations of messages from management, depending on the significance of the message to the things the subgroup values and is striving to accomplish.
3. *People are structured into different systems of relationships in organizations.* A work structure exists in which certain people are expected to complete tasks with other people. An *authority structure* exists when some workers are in charge of supervising others. A *status structure* determines which individuals have rights and privileges. A *prestige structure* allows some individuals to expect deferential treatment from others. The *friendship structure* encourages interpersonal trust. All of these systems influence who should communicate with whom and in what manner.
4. *Organizations are in a constant state of flux.* Relationships (subgroups or subcultures) and geographical locations constantly change. It is difficult to communicate decisions to all the people who are affected by them because of this constant state of change.

Managers must assess organizational communication. Who communicates with whom in the organization? Is the communication timely? Does communication within the formal organization concur with formal lines of authority? Are there conflicts or disagreements about communication? What modes of communication are used?

 LEARNING EXERCISE 15.1

Have you ever been employed in a large organization? Was the communication within that organization clear and timely? What or whom was your primary source of information? Were you a part of a subgroup or subculture? If so, how did that affect communication at the unit level?

ORGANIZATIONAL COMMUNICATION STRATEGIES

Although organizational communication is complex, the following strategies can increase the likelihood of clear and complete communication.

1. *Managers must understand the organization's structure and recognize who will be affected by decisions that are made.* Both formal and informal communication networks need to be considered. *Formal communication networks* follow the formal line of authority in the organization's hierarchy. *Informal communication networks* occur between individuals at the same or different levels of the organizational hierarchy but do not represent formal lines of authority or responsibility. For example, an informal communication network might occur between a hospital's CEO and her daughter who is a ward clerk on a medical wing. Although there may be a significant exchange of information about unit or organizational functioning, this communication network

would not be apparent on the organization chart. It is imperative then that managers be very careful of what they say and to whom until they have a good understanding of the formal and informal communication networks.

2. *Communication is not a one-way channel.* If other departments or disciplines will be affected by the communication, the manager must consult with those areas for feedback prior to the communication.

3. *The communication must be clear, simple, and precise.* The manager (sender) is responsible for ensuring the message is understood.

4. *Managers should seek feedback regarding whether their communication was accurately received.* One way to do this is to ask the receiver to repeat the communication or instructions. In addition, the sender should continue follow-up communication in an effort to determine if the communication is being carried out.

5. *Managers should not overwhelm subordinates with unnecessary information.* Although information and communication are different, they are interdependent. Swansburg (1990) defines *information* as logic that has no meaning; it is formal, impersonal, and unaffected by emotions, values, expectations, and perceptions. *Communication,* on the other hand, involves perception and feeling. It does not depend on information and may represent shared experiences. In contrast to information sharing, superiors must continually communicate with subordinates.

For example, most staff need little *information* about ordering procedures or organizational supply vendors as long as supplies are adequate and appropriate to meet unit needs. If, however, a vendor is unable temporarily to meet unit supply needs, the use of supplies by staff becomes an issue requiring close *communication* between managers and subordinates. The manager must communicate with the staff about which supplies will be inadequately stocked and for how long. In addition, the manager may choose to problem-solve this inadequacy of resources with the staff to identify alternative solutions.

CHANNELS OF COMMUNICATION

Because large organizations are so complex, communication channels used by the manager may be upward, downward, horizontal, diagonal, or through the "grapevine." In *upward* communication, the manager is a subordinate to higher management. Needs and wants are communicated upward to the next level in the hierarchy. Those at this higher level make decisions for a greater segment of the organization than the lower-level manager.

In *downward* communication, the manager relays information to subordinates. This is a traditional form of communication in organizations and helps coordinate activities in various levels of the hierarchy.

In *horizontal* communication, managers interact with others on the same hierarchical level as themselves who are managing different segments of the organization. The need for horizontal communication increases as departmental interdependence increases.

In *diagonal* communication, the manager interacts with personnel and managers of other departments and groups, such as physicians, who are not on the same level of the organizational hierarchy. Although these individuals have no formal authority over the manager, this communication is vital to the organization's functioning. Diagonal communication tends to be less formal than other types of communication.

The most informal communication network is often called the *grapevine*. Grapevine communication flows haphazardly between individuals at all hierarchical levels and usually involves three to four people at a time. Grapevine communication is subject to error and distortion because of the speed at which it passes and because the sender has little formal accountability for the message. Once managers understand how messages flow within their organization, they can begin promoting clear and efficient communication.

LEARNING EXERCISE 15.2

Assume that you are the project director of a small family planning clinic. You have just received word that your federal and state funding have been slashed and that the clinic will probably close in 3 months. Although an additional funding source may be found, it is improbable that it will occur within the next 3 months. The board of directors informed you that this knowledge is not to be made public at this time.

You have five full-time employees at the clinic. Because two of these employees are close friends, you feel some conflict about withholding this information from them. You are aware that another clinic in town currently has job openings and that the positions are generally filled quickly.

Assignment: It is important that you staff the clinic for the next 3 months. When will you notify the staff of the clinic's intent to close? Will you communicate the closing to all staff at the same time? Will you use downward communication? Should the grapevine be used to leak news to employees? When might the grapevine be appropriate to pass on information?

COMMUNICATION MODES

A message's clarity is greatly affected by the mode of communication used. In general, the more direct the communication, the greater the probability that it will be clear. The more people involved in filtering the communication, the greater the chance of distortion. The manager must evaluate each circumstance individually to determine which mode or combination of modes is optimum for each situation.

The following modes of communication are used most frequently by the manager.

1. *Written communication.* Written messages allow for documentation. They may, however, be open to various interpretations and generally consume more managerial time. Most managers are required to do a considerable amount of this type of communication and therefore need to be able to write clearly.

2. *Face-to-face communication.* Oral communication is rapid but may result in fewer people receiving the information than necessary. Managers communicate verbally upward and downward and formally and informally. They also communicate verbally in formal meetings, with individuals in peer work groups, and when making formal presentations.

3. *Nonverbal communication. Nonverbal communication includes facial expression, body movements, and gestures and is commonly referred to as body language.* Because nonverbal communication indicates the emotional component of the message, it is generally considered more reliable than verbal communication (Arnold & Boggs, 1989). There is significant danger, however, in misinterpreting nonverbal messages if they are not assessed in context with the verbal message. Nonverbal communication occurs any time managers are seen; for example, messages are transmitted to subordinates every time the manager communicates verbally or just walks down a hallway.

4. *Telephone communication.* A telephone call is rapid and allows the receiver to clarify the message at the time it is given. It does not, however, allow the receipt of nonverbal messages for either the sender or receiver of the message. Because managers today use the telephone so much, it has become an important communication tool, but it does have limits as an effective communication device.

► LEARNING EXERCISE 15.3

Which communication modes do you use most frequently? Which is your preferred mode and why? Which modes are most difficult for you to use and why?

WRITTEN COMMUNICATION WITHIN THE ORGANIZATION

Although communication may take many forms, written communication is used most often in large-scale organizations. By its nature, written communication suggests attention and deliberation on the part of the sender and gives receivers a record for reference and review (Palmer & Deck, 1987). Organizational policy, procedures, events, and change may be announced in writing. Job descriptions, performance appraisals, letters of reference, and memos also are forms of written communication.

The written communication issued by the manager reflects greatly on both the manager and the organization. Thus, the manager must be able to write clearly, professionally, and use understandable language. Writing is a learned skill that improves with practice. Because letters comprise much of a manager's writing, Health Care Education Associates (1988) composed the following suggestions for formal business letters:

1. *Know what you want to say before you start writing.* This requires that you think clearly before you can write clearly.

2. *Put people into your writing.* When you write about a subject, discuss it in terms of the people affected by it. Avoid words such as administration, authorization, and implementation because they are abstract and impersonal.

3. *Use action words.* Action verbs have a stronger impact.
4. *Write plainly.* Use familiar, specific, and concrete words. Plain writing is more easily understood and thus is more apt to be read.
5. *Use as few words as possible.* Find one good way to make a point, and trust that your reader will understand it.
6. *Use simple, direct sentences.* Keep sentences less than 20 words and only include one idea in each. Make positive statements that clearly delineate your position on an issue. Tell the pertinent facts first.
7. *Give the reader direction.* Be consistent in the tone of the message to establish a clear point of view.
8. *Arrange the material logically.* A logical presentation of facts increases the reliability that the reader attributes to the writer. The material may be organized deductively, inductively, by order of importance, from the familiar to the unfamiliar, in chronological order, by close relationship, or by physical location.
9. *Use paragraphs to lead readers.* A paragraph should not exceed 8 to 10 lines in a memo or five to six lines in a letter.
10. *Connect your thoughts.* To do this, you must add enough details, use repetition to tie thoughts together, and select transitional words to tell the reader when you are moving to a new thought.

▶ LEARNING EXERCISE 15.4

Read the following formal business letter. Assess the quality of the writing using the 12 criteria listed in the chapter. Rewrite the letter so that all criteria are met. Be prepared to read your letter to the class.

Mrs. Joan Watkins
October 19, 1991
Brownie Troop 407
Anywhere, USA 00000

Dear Mrs. Watkins:

I am the official Public Relations Coordinator for County Hospital and serve as correspondence officer for requests from public service groups. We have more than 100 requests such as yours every year, so I have a very busy job! You are welcome to come and visit our hospital anytime. My secretary told me you called yesterday and wondered whether we provide tours. There is no charge for our tours. My secretary also told me the average age of your Brownies is 8 years, so it might be most appropriate to have them visit our NICU, PICU, and ER. Please tell the kids about the units in advance so they'll be better prepared for what they will see. The philosophy at our hospital promotes community involvement, so this is one way we attempt to meet this goal. I'll be sure to arrange to have a nursing manager escort the group on your tour. Please call when you have a date and time in mind. I was a Brownie myself when I was 7 years old, so I think this is a terrific idea on your part.

Sincerely,

Ima Verbose, MSN
Personal Relations Coordinator
County Hospital

11. *Be clear.* Be certain your pronouns are clearly defined.
12. *Express similar thoughts in similar ways.* This will increase the continuity of the message.

Although a business letter's content is very important, its appearance or format also conveys a message. Adequate margins, clear typeface, and the use of appropriate greetings and salutations add to the message's professionalism. Display 15.2 shows the accepted basic format for any formal business letter.

Communication in a large organization requires tremendous intradepartmental and interdepartmental communication; much of this communication occurs in the form of memos. Memos, unlike letters, are distributed internally within the organization. The primary purpose of most memos is to either inform, instruct, recommend, or document. Health Care Education Associates (1988) suggests the following guidelines for writing effective memos:

Display 15.2 Business Letter Format

Skip four to eight lines, depending on the length of the letter
DATE
Skip four to eight lines
INSIDE ADDRESS—Check the spelling and address for accuracy.
Double space
RE: (pronounced ray or ree, means regarding)—This optional device alerts the reader to the subject of your letter.
Double space
SALUTATION—Write "Dear . . ." Abbreviate titles such as "Mr.," and "Dr."; spell out titles such as "Reverend" and "Senator."
Use a comma (,) for informal letters and a colon (:) for formal letters—if you are on a first-name basis, use a comma; otherwise, use a colon.
If you are uncertain as to the sex of the person to whom you are writing, address by title—"Dear Hospital Administrator" or "Dear Sir or Madam."
Double space
BODY OF LETTER—Single space within the paragraph, and double space between paragraphs. (If you use the indented form, you do not need to double space between paragraphs.)
Double space
COMPLIMENTARY CLOSING—Capitalize the first letter of the first word, and put a comma at the end—"Sincerely,"
Skip four lines if the letter is typed
SIGNATURE (typed)—Place your written signature above your typed name.
Double space
ENCLOSURES—If you are enclosing anything, indicate here, typically with "Enc." or "Encs."

(Reproduced with permission from HealthCare Education Associates [1988]. *Professional writing skills for health care managers,* p. 68.)

Display 15.3 Memo Format

Date:
> *Double space*

To: If the memo is to be distributed to more than one person, alphabetical order is the easiest method of listing. You may list by rank if you prefer.
> *Double space*

From:
> *Double space*

Subject: In a few words, state the reason you are writing the memo. This lets the reader know at a glance what you will be talking about.
> *Triple space*

Signature:
> *Triple space*

Copies: You may need to send copies of your memo to different people. You should indicate this here, using the abbreviation "cc:" followed by the names of those receiving copies of the memo.

(Reproduced with permission from HealthCare Education Associates [1988]. *Professional writing skills for health care managers*, p. 68.)

1. Memos should make the main point at the beginning.
2. Only essential information should be given in the memo.
3. The memo should be written simply, without inflated or authoritarian language.
4. Headings should be used in the memo to direct the reader to specific issues.

Most organizations have an established form for memos. This form is generally in a block format with no indentations from the left hand margin. Display 15.3 shows the standard format for an organizational memo.

The problem with letters and memos is there usually is no feedback mechanism available for the sender to clarify intent (Marquis & Huston, 1994). One way to minimize this danger is by having other supervisory personnel read and interpret written communication before distribution.

 LEARNING EXERCISE 15.5

You are a school nurse. In the last 2 weeks, nine cases of head lice have been reported in four different classrooms. The potential for spread is high, and both the teachers and parents are growing anxious. Compose a memo for distribution to the teachers. Your goals are to inform, reassure, and direct future inquiries. Be sure this memo uses the format shown in Display 15-3 and encompasses the guidelines for memo writing suggested in this chapter.

Unit managers are frequently asked to write letters of reference for employees who have been terminated. The information used in writing these letters comes from performance evaluations, personal interviews with staff and patients, evidence of continuing education, and personal observations. Assume that you are a unit manager and that you have collected the following information on Mary Doe, an RN who worked at your facility for 3 months before abruptly resigning with a 48-hour notice.

Performance Evaluation

Three-month evaluation scant. The following criteria were marked "competent": amount of work accomplished, relationships with patients and coworkers, work habits, and basic skills.

The following criteria were identified as "needing improvement": quality of work, communication skills, and leadership skills. No criteria were marked unsatisfactory or outstanding. Narrative comments were limited to the following: "has a bit of a chip on her shoulder," "works independently a lot," and "assessment skills improving."

Interviews With Staff

Coworker RN Judy: "She was OK. She was a little strange—she belonged to some kind of traveling religious cult. In fact, I think that's why she left her job."

Coworker LVN/LPN Lisa: "Mary was great. She got all her work done. I never had to help her with her meds or AM care. She took her turn at floating, which is more than I can say for some of the other RNs."

Coworker RN John: "When I was the charge nurse, I found I needed to seek Mary out to find out what was going on with her patients. It made me real uncomfortable."

Coworker LVN/LPN Joe: "Mary hated it here—she never felt like she belonged. The charge nurse was always hassling her about little things, and it really seemed unfair."

Patient Comments

"She helped me with my bath and got all my pills on time. She was a good nurse."

"I don't remember her."

"She was so busy—I appreciated how efficient she was at how she did her job."

"I remember Mary. She told me she really liked older people. I wish she had had more time to sit down and talk to me."

Notes from Personnel File

Twenty-four years old. Graduated from 3-year diploma school 2 years ago. Has worked in three jobs since that time. Divorced and mother of two small children.

Continuing Education

Current CPR card. No other continuing education completed at this facility.

Assignment: Mary Doe's prospective employer has requested a letter of reference to accompany Mary's application to become a hospice nurse/counselor. No form has been provided, so it is important that your response use an appropriate format, such as the one suggested in Display 15-2. Decide which information you should include in your letter and which should be omitted. Will you weigh some information more heavily than other information? Would you make any recommendations about Mary Doe's suitability for the hospice job? Be prepared to read your letter aloud to the class, and justify your rationale for the content you included.

INTERPERSONAL COMMUNICATION

Because it is impossible for the individual manager to communicate face-to-face with each member in the large organization, managers must develop other interpersonal communication skills. These skills include nonverbal communication, assertive communication, and listening skills.

Nonverbal Communication

Much of our communication occurs through nonverbal channels that must be examined in the context of the verbal content. Generally, if verbal and nonverbal messages are incongruent, the receiver will believe the nonverbal message.

Because nonverbal behavior can be and is frequently misinterpreted, receivers must validate perceptions with senders. The incongruence between verbal and nonverbal messages is the most significant difficulty in effective interpersonal communication (Sullivan & Decker, 1988).

The following is a partial list of nonverbal clues that can occur with or without verbal communication:

1. *Space.* The space between the sender and receiver influences what is communicated. Although distance implies a lack of trust or warmth, inadequate space, as defined by cultural norms, may make people feel threatened or intimidated. For example, North American, Indian, African-American, Pakistani, and Asian cultures generally require greater space between sender and receiver than Latin-American, Hispanic, Arab, and Southern European people (Richmond, McCroskey, & Payne, 1987). Likewise, the manager who sits beside employees during performance appraisals implies a different message than the manager who speaks to the employee from the opposite side of a large and formal desk. In this case, distance increases power and status on the part of the manager.
2. *Environment.* The area where the communication takes place is an important part of the communication process. Communication that takes place in a superior's office is generally taken more seriously than that which occurs in the cafeteria.
3. *Outward appearance.* Much is communicated by our clothing, hair styles, cosmetics, and attractiveness. The phrase "dressing for success" appropriately defines the impact of dress and appearance on role perception and power.
4. *Eye contact.* This nonverbal clue is often associated with sincerity. Richmond, McCroskey, and Payne (1987) state that eye contact constitutes an invitation or readiness to interact. Likewise, breaking eye contact indicates nonverbally that the interaction is about to cease. However, the manager must be aware that like space, the presence or absence of eye contact is strongly influenced by cultural standards.
5. *Body posture.* The weight of a message is increased if the sender faces the receiver, stands or sits appropriately close, and with head erect, leans toward the receiver.
6. *Gestures.* A message accented with appropriate gestures takes on added em-

phasis. Too much gesturing can, however, be distracting. For example, hand movement can emphasize or distract from the message.

7. *Facial expression.* Effective communication requires facial expression that agrees with your message. Managers who present a pleasant and open expression are perceived by staff as approachable. Likewise, a nurse's facial expression can greatly affect how and what clients are willing to relate.

8. *Timing.* Hesitation often diminishes the effect of your statement or implies untruthfulness.

9. *Vocal clues such as tone, volume, and inflection.* All of these clues add to the message being transmitted.

All nurses must be sensitive to nonverbal clues and their importance in communication. This is especially true for nursing leaders. Effective leaders are congruent in their verbal and nonverbal communication, so followers are clear about the messages they receive. Likewise, leaders are sensitive to nonverbal and verbal messages from followers and look for inconsistencies that may indicate unresolved problems or needs. Often organizational difficulties can be prevented because leaders recognize the nonverbal communication of subordinates and take appropriate and timely action.

Assertive Communication

Assertive behavior is a way of communicating that allows individuals to express themselves in direct, honest, and appropriate ways that do *not* infringe on another person's rights. A person's position is expressed clearly and firmly using "I" statements. In addition, assertive communication always requires that verbal and nonverbal messages be congruent. To be successful in the directing phase of management, the leader must have well-developed skills in assertive communication.

There are many misconceptions about assertive communication. The first is that all communication is either assertive or passive. Actually, at least four possibilities for communication exist: passive, aggressive, indirectly aggressive or passive-aggressive, or assertive. *Passive* communication occurs when a person suffers in silence, although he or she may feel strongly about the issue. *Aggressive* individuals express themselves in a direct and often hostile manner that infringes on another person's rights; this behavior is generally oriented toward "winning at all costs" or demonstrating self-excellence. *Passive-aggressive* communication is an aggressive message presented in a passive way. It generally involves limited verbal exchange (with incongruent nonverbal behavior) by an individual who feels strongly about a situation. This person feigns withdrawal in an effort to manipulate the situation.

The second misconception is that those who communicate or behave assertively get everything they want. This is untrue because being assertive involves rights and responsibilities. Display 15.4 lists the rights and responsibilities of the assertive person (Chenevert, 1988).

The third misconception about assertiveness is that it is unfeminine. Luke (1992) believes that women's lack of a voice in American society is a social consequence of history. Although the role of women in society in general has undergone tremendous change in the last 100 years, nursing continues to find great difficulty in accepting that the nurse plays an assertive, active, decision-making role.

Display 15.4 Rights and Responsibilities
of the Assertive Person

Rights	Responsibilities
To speak up	To listen
To take	To give
To have problems	To find solutions
To be comforted	To comfort others
To work	To do your best
To make mistakes	To correct your mistakes
To laugh	To make others happy
To have friends	To be a friend
To criticize	To praise
To have your efforts rewarded	To reward others' efforts
To be independent	To be dependable
To cry	To dry tears
To be loved	To love others

(Chenevert, 1988)

Assertive communication is not rude or insensitive behavior; rather, it is having an informed voice that insists on being heard. An assertive communication model helps individuals unlearn common self-deprecating speech patterns that signal insecurity and unassuredness (Holmes, 1990). Luciano and Darling (1985) believe nurses can begin to create change in the profession by providing a model of communication and behavior that sets standards of excellence for professional conduct. Eventually, a form of peer pressure can emerge that reshapes others and results in an assertive nursing voice.

A fourth misconception is that the term *assertive* and *aggressive* are synonymous. To be assertive is to not be aggressive. Even when faced with someone else's aggression, the assertive communicator does not become aggressive. When under attack by an aggressive person, an assertive person can do several things:

1. *Reflect.* Reflect the speaker's message back to him or her. Focus on the affective components of the aggressor's message. This helps the aggressor to clarify important feelings and experience them with an appropriate intensity in relation to a specific situation or event (Arnold & Boggs, 1989). For example, assume an employee enters a manager's office and begins complaining about a newly posted staff schedule. The employee is obviously angry and defensive. The manager might use reflection by stating: "I understand that you are very upset about your schedule. This is an important issue, and we need to talk about it."

2. *Repeat the assertive message.* Repeated assertions focus on the message's objective content. They are especially effective when the aggressor overgeneralizes or seems fixated on a repetitive line of thinking. For example, if a man-

ager requests that an angry employee step into his or her office to discuss a problem, and the employee continues his or her tirade in the hallway, the manager might say "I am willing to discuss this issue with you in my office. The hallway is not the appropriate place for this discussion."

3. *Point out the implicit assumptions.* This involves listening closely and letting the aggressor know that you have heard him or her. In these situations, managers might repeat major points or identify key assumptions to show that they are following the employee's line of reasoning.

4. *Restating the message by using assertive language.* Rephrasing the aggressor's language will defuse the emotion. Paraphrasing helps the aggressor focus more on the cognitive part of the message. The manager might use restating by changing a "you" message to an "I" message.

5. *Question.* When the aggressor uses nonverbal clues to be aggressive, the assertive person can put this behavior in the form of a question as an effective means of helping the other person become aware of an unwarranted reaction. For example, the desperate, angry employee may imply threats about quitting or transferring to another unit. The manager could appropriately confront the employee about his or her implied threat to see if it is real or simply a reflection of the employee's frustration.

Listening Skills

Research has shown that most people hear or actually retain only a small amount of the information given to them. Generally, although the average person spends 70% of his or her time listening, only one-third of the messages sent are retained. The active process of listening is as important, if not more important, than verbal skills to the leader.

To become a better listener, leaders must first become aware of how their own experiences, values, attitudes, and biases affect how they receive and perceive messages. Second, leaders must overcome the information and communication overload inherent in the middle management role. It is easy for overwhelmed managers to stop listening actively to the many subordinates who need and demand their time simultaneously.

Finally, the leader must continually work to improve listening skills. The leader who actively listens gives genuine time and attention to the sender, focusing on verbal and nonverbal communication. The leader's primary purpose then is to receive the message being sent rather than forming a response before the transmission of the message is complete.

INTEGRATING LEADERSHIP ROLES AND MANAGEMENT FUNCTIONS IN ORGANIZATIONAL AND INTERPERSONAL COMMUNICATION

Communication is critical to successful leadership and management. A manager has the formal authority and responsibility to communicate with many individuals in the organization. Because communication can be very complex, the manager must understand each unique situation well enough to be able to select the most appropriate internal communication network or channel.

After selecting a communication channel, the manager faces an even greater challenge communicating the message clearly, either verbally or in writing, in a language appropriate for the message and the receiver. To select the most appropriate communication mode for a specific message, the manager must determine what should be told, to whom, and when. Because communication is a learned skill, managers can improve their written and verbal communication with repetition.

The interpersonal communication skills are more reflective of the leadership role. Sensitivity to verbal and nonverbal communication; recognition of status, power, and authority as barriers to manager–subordinate communication; and consistent use of assertiveness techniques are all leadership skills. Nurse-leaders who are perceptive and sensitive to the environment and people around them have a keen understanding of how the unit is functioning at any time and are able to intervene appropriately when problems arise. Through consistent verbal and nonverbal communication, the nurse-leader is able to be a role model for subordinates.

Organizational communication requires both management functions and leadership skills. Management functions in communication ensure productivity and continuity through appropriate information sharing. Leadership skills ensure appraisal and intervention in meeting expressed and tacit human resource needs. Leadership skills in communication also allow the leader/manager to clarify organizational goals and direct subordinates in reaching those goals. Communication within the organization would fail if both leadership and management skills were not present.

KEY CONCEPTS

▼ Communication forms the core of management activities and cuts across all phases of the management process.

▼ Depending on the manager's position in the hierarchy, more than 80% of managerial time may be spent in some type of organizational communication; thus, organizational communication is a management function.

▼ Because 75% of managerial communication time is spent speaking and listening, managers must have excellent interpersonal communication skills. These skills are perhaps the most critical leadership role.

▼ Basic elements common to communication include the *sender, receiver, message, mode,* and *climate* of the interaction.

▼ Communication in large-scale organizations is particularly difficult due to their complexity and size.

▼ Managers must understand the structure of the organization and recognize whom their decisions will affect. Both formal and informal communication networks need to be considered.

▼ Communication channels used by the manager in the organization may be *upward, downward, horizontal, diagonal,* or through the "*grapevine.*"

▼ The clarity of the message is significantly affected by the mode of communication used. In general, the more direct the communication, the greater the probability of clear communication. The more people involved in filtering the communication, the greater the chance of distortion.

▼ Written communication is used most often in large-scale organizations.

▼ A manager's written communication reflects greatly on both the manager and the organization. Thus, managers must be able to write clearly and professionally and use understandable language.

▼ *Nonverbal communication* must be examined in the context of the verbal content. Generally, if verbal and nonverbal messages are incongruent, the receiver will believe the nonverbal message.

▼ The incongruence between verbal and nonverbal messages is the most significant barrier to effective interpersonal communication.

▼ Effective leaders are congruent in their verbal and nonverbal communication, so followers are clear about the messages they receive. Likewise, leaders are sensitive to nonverbal and verbal messages from followers and look for inconsistencies that may indicate unresolved problems or needs.

▼ Communication can be *passive, aggressive, indirectly aggressive* or *passive-aggressive,* or *assertive.*

▼ *Assertive behavior* is a way of communicating that allows people to express themselves in direct, honest, and appropriate ways that do *not* infringe on another's rights. To be successful in the directing phase of management, the leader must have well-developed skills in assertive communication.

▼ Most people hear or actually retain a small amount of the information given to them. *Active listening* is an interpersonal communication skill that improves with practice.

◢ ADDITIONAL LEARNING EXERCISES

Learning Exercise 15.7
(From Marquis & Huston, 1994.)

Decide if the following responses are an example of assertive, aggressive, passive-aggressive, or passive behavior. Change those that you identify as aggressive, passive, or passive-aggressive into assertive responses.

Situation	Response
1. A co-worker withdraws instead of saying what's on his mind. You say:	"I guess you are uncomfortable talking about what's bothering you. It would be better if you talked to me."
2. This is the third time in two weeks that your co-worker has asked for a ride home because her car is not working. You say:	"You're taking advantage of me and I won't stand for it. It's your responsibility to get your car fixed."
3. An attendant at a gas station neglected to replace your gas cap. You return to inquire about it. You say:	"One of the guys here forgot to put my gas cap back on! I want it found *now* or you'll buy me a new one."

4. You'd like to have a turn at being in charge on your shift. You say to your head nurse:

"Do you think that, ah, you could see your way clear to letting me be in charge once in a while?"

5. A committee meeting is being established. The proposed time is convenient for other people but not for you. The time makes it impossible for you to attend meetings regularly. When you asked about the time you said:

"Well, I guess it's OK. I'm not going to be able to attend very much but it fits into everyone else's schedule."

6. In a conversation, a doctor suddenly asks, "What do you women libbers want anyway?" You respond:

"Fairness and equality."

7. An employee makes a lot of mistakes in his work. You say:

"You're a lazy and sloppy worker!"

8. You are the one woman in a meeting with seven men. At the beginning of the meeting, the chair asks you to be the secretary. You respond:

"No. I'm sick and tired of being the secretary just because I'm the only woman in the group."

9. A physician asks to borrow your stethoscope. You say:

"Well, I guess so. One of you doctors walked off with mine last week and this new one cost me $35. Be sure you return it, OK?"

10. You are interpreting the I and O sheet for a physician and he interrupts you. You say:

"You could understand this if you'd stop interrupting me and listen."

Learning Exercise 15.8
(From Marquis & Huston, 1994.)

Mrs. White is the coordinator for the multidisciplinary mental health outpatient services of a 150-bed psychiatric hospital. She has been frustrated because the hospital is very centralized; she feels this keeps the hospital's therapists and nurse-managers from being as effective as they could if they had more authority. Therefore, she has worked out a plan to decentralize her department, giving the therapists and nurse-managers more control and new titles. She sent her new plan to the CEO, Mr. Short, and has just received this memo in return.

Dear Mrs. White:

The Board of Directors and I met to review your plan and think it is a good one. In fact, we have been thinking along the same lines for quite some time now. I'm sure you must have heard of our plans. Because we recently contracted with a physician's group to cover our crisis center, we feel this would be a good time to decentralize in other ways. We suggest that your new substance abuse coordinator report directly to the new chief of mental health. In addition, we feel your new director of the suicide prevention center should report directly to the chief of mental health. He then will report to me.

I am pleased that we are both moving in the same direction and have the same goals. We will be setting up meetings in the future to iron out the small details.

Sincerely,

Joe Short, CEO

Assignment: How and why did her plan go astray? Could it have been prevented? What communication mode would have been most appropriate for Mrs. White to use in sharing her plan with Joe Short? What should be her plan now? Explain your rationale.

Learning Exercise 15.9

You are a school nurse for kindergarten through sixth grades in a small community. The school board trustees who set policy are outspoken and conservative in their views. Recently, a policy was established regarding the admittance and education of children known to be human immunodeficiency virus (HIV) positive. This policy allows children who have tested positive for the virus to attend school, although physical segregation in the classroom is mandatory for children younger than 7 years. This policy is based on the belief that young children could inadvertently transmit body fluids in the course of spitting, drooling, urinating, and so on. The policy also requires that all school personnel involved with the child be aware of his or her healthcare status.

This policy has yet to be tested in the classroom. Although you are glad to see the district establish policy in this area, you feel that the current policy holds great potential for discriminating against and isolating HIV-positive children.

Recently, a new kindergarten student entered your district. He is a 5-year-old hemophiliac. His parents recently completed his health screening history and sent it to your office. At that time, they requested a copy of the district's HIV policy, which you sent them. One week later, you completed an initial screening visit on the child as part of the registration process. The child appeared pale and thin and was easily fatigued. On direct confrontation, the parents admitted that their son was positive for HIV, but implored you not to place this on his record. They have not yet discussed the HIV test results with their son, because they feel he is not old enough to understand the ramifications. They feel the current policy is discriminatory and that their son would be physically and socially ostracized from the other children. They also feel the community in general is conservative and would be unaccepting of their son and themselves.

Assignment: Who has a right to information in this case? To whom will you communicate this information and in what mode? How will you control the dissemination of that information? Can this communication be limited to the formal network? What safeguards can you build into your communication to protect all the individuals who might be affected?

REFERENCES:

Arnold, E., & Boggs, K. (1989). *Interpersonal relationships: Professional communication skills for nurses.* Philadelphia: W.B. Saunders.

Bartky, S. L. (1990). *Femininity and domination: Studies in the phenomenology of oppression.* New York: Routledge.

Chenevert, M. (1988). *Pro-nurse handbook* (3rd ed.). St. Louis: C.V. Mosby.

Fritz, P., Russel, C., & Shirk, F. (1984). *Interpersonal communication in nursing: An interactionist approach.* Norwalk, CT: Appleton-Century-Crofts.

Haimann, T. (1994). *Supervisory management for healthcare organizations.* Dubuque, IA: Wm. C. Brown.

HealthCare Education Associates (1988). *Professional writing skills for health care managers: A practical guide.* St. Louis: C.V. Mosby.

Holmes, J. (1990). Hedges and boosters in women's and men's speech. *Language and Communication, 10*(23), 185–205.

Jackson, J. M. (1984). The organization and its communication problems. In S. Stone, S. Firisch, S. Jordan, et al. (Eds.), *Management for nurses.* St. Louis: C.V. Mosby.

Joblin, F. M. (1982). Formal structural characteristics of organizations and superior-subordinate communication. *Human Communication Research, 9*(3), 338–347.

Luciano, K., & Darling, L. W. (1985). The physician as a nursing service customer. *Journal of Nursing Administration, 15*(6), 17–20.

Luke, C. (1992). Feminist politics in radical pedagogy. In C. Luke & J. Gore (Eds.), *Feminisms and critical pedagogy.* New York: Routledge.

Lyles, R. I., & Joiner, C. (1986). *Supervision in health care organizations* (p. 97). New York: John Wiley & Sons.

Manss, V. C. (1994). Effective communication: Gender issues. *Nursing Management, 25*(6) 79–80.

Marquis, B. L., & Huston, C. J. (1994). *Management decision making for nurses: 118 case studies* (2nd ed.). Philadelphia: J.B. Lippincott.

Palmer, M. E., & Deck, E. S. (1987). Assertiveness: Phone calls, memos, and "I" messages. *Nursing Management, 18*(1), 39–42.

Richmond, V., McCroskey, J., & Payne, S. (1987). *Nonverbal behavior in interpersonal relations.* Englewood Cliffs, NJ: Prentice Hall.

Sellers, S. (1991). *Language and sexual difference.* London: Macmillan.

Sullivan, E. J., & Decker, P. J. (1988). *Effective management in nursing* (3rd ed.). Menlo Park, CA: Addison-Wesley.

Tannen, D. (1990). *You just don't understand: Women and men in conversation.* New York: William Morrow.

Swansburg, R. C. (1990). *Management and leadership for nurse managers.* Boston: Jones and Bartlett.

Vestal, K. W. (1995). *Management concepts for the new nurse* (p. 34) (2nd ed.). Philadelphia: J.B. Lippincott.

BIBLIOGRAPHY

Alward, R. R., & Camutnas, C. (1990). Public relations: Part II—Strategies and tactics. *Journal of Nursing Administration, 20*(10), 31–42.

Anderson, M. A. (1987). Professionally speaking . . . Assertiveness is a hallmark of professional communication. *Pro Re Nata, Utah Nurses Association, 9*(1), 4.

Baugh, C. (1989). Practical ways to assert yourself. *Nursing 89, 19*(3), 57.

Bourhis, R. Y., Roth, S., & MacQueen, G. (1989). Communication in the hospital setting: A survey of medical and everyday language use amongst patients, nurses, and doctors. *Social Science and Medicine, 28*(4), 339–346.

Cerne, F. (1989). CEO shares information with his employees. *Hospitals, 63*(7), 54.

Chu, L.-K., & Chu, G. S. (1991). Feedback and efficiency: A staff development model. *Nursing Management, 22*(2), 28–31.

Cox, H. (1991). Verbal abuse nationwide, Part I: Oppressed group behavior. *Nursing Management, 22*(2), 32–35.

Czarniawska-Joerges, B., & Joerges, B. (1988). How to control things with words: Organizational talk and control. *Management Communication Quarterly, 2*(2), 170–194.

Farley, M. J. (1987). Power orientations and communication style of managers and non-managers. *Research in Nursing and Health, 10*(3), 197–202.

Frone, M. R., & Major, B. (1988). Communication quality and job satisfaction among managerial nurses. The moderating influence of job involvement. *Group and Organization Studies, 13*(3), 332–347.

Hodes, J. R., & Van Crombrugghe, P. (1990). Nurse-physician relationships. *Nursing Management, 21*(7), 73–74.

Jordana, A. M., (1989). Ineffective communication can thwart your practice. *Professional Medical Assistant, 22*(2), 12–13.

McConnell, C. R. (1989). Overcoming major barriers to true two way communication with employees. *Health Care Supervisor, 7*(4), 77–82.

McConnell, C. R. (1987). Making upward communication work for your employees: Processes and people. With emphasis on people, Part 3. *Health Care Supervisor, 5*(2), 71–80.

Nawrocki, H. (1988). How to tap into the employee grapevine. *Nursing 1988, 18*(12), 32C.

Pardue, S. F. (1980). Assertiveness for nursing. *Supervisor Nurse: The Journal for Nursing Leadership and Management, 11*, 47–48.

Shahoda, T., & Droste, T. (1987). Human resources: Employee communication softens merger's toll. *Hospitals, 61*(7), 80.

Wallace, H. (1989). How to improve your written communication. *Medical Laboratory Observer, 21*(3), 65–68.

Wilson-Barnett, J. (1988). Lend me your ear . . . Good communication and empathy. *Nursing Times, 84*(33), 51–53.

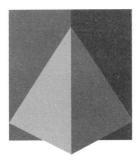

CHAPTER 16

Managing Conflict

Conflict is generally defined as the internal discord that results from differences in ideas, values, or feelings between two or more people. Because managers have interpersonal relationships with individuals having a variety of different values, beliefs, backgrounds, and goals, conflict is an expected outcome. Scarce resources and poorly defined role expectations also are frequent sources of conflict in an organization. Guy (1986) believes that conflict increases as complexity increases. Therefore, as organizations become larger and more complex, conflict and ambiguity increase.

Johnson (1994) maintains that cost containment, restructuring of healthcare organizations, and competition have given rise to increased conflict for nursing. Conflict is created when there are differences in economic and professional values and when there is competition among professionals.

Openly acknowledging that conflict is a naturally occurring and expected phenomenon in organizations reflects a tremendous shift from how sociologists viewed conflict 100 years ago. The current sociological view is that organizational conflict should be neither avoided nor encouraged, but managed. The manager's role is to create a work environment where conflict may be used as a conduit for growth, innovation, and productivity. When organizational conflict becomes dysfunctional, the manager must recognize it in its early stages and actively intervene so subordinate motivation and organizational productivity are not adversely affected. Appropriate conflict resolution requires leadership skills and management functions at all levels of

Bessie L. Marquis and Carol J. Huston:
LEADERSHIP ROLES AND MANAGEMENT FUNCTIONS IN NURSING, 2nd ed.
Lippincott-Raven Publishers © 1996

the organizational hierarchy. Leadership skills and management functions necessary for conflict resolution at the unit level are outlined in Display 16.1.

This chapter presents an overview of growth-producing versus dysfunctional conflict in the organization. The history of conflict management, categories of conflict, the conflict process itself, and strategies for successful conflict resolution are discussed. Negotiation as a conflict resolution strategy is emphasized.

Display 16.1 Leadership Roles and Management Functions in Conflict Resolution

Leadership Roles

1. Is self-aware and conscientiously works to resolve intrapersonal conflict.
2. Role models conflict resolution as soon as conflict is perceived and before it becomes felt or manifest.
3. Seeks a win-win solution to conflict whenever feasible.
4. Lessens the perceptual differences that exist between conflicting parties and broadens the parties' understanding about the problems.
5. Assists subordinates in identifying alternative conflict resolutions.
6. Recognizes and accepts the individual differences of staff.
7. Is sensitive to negotiation tactics and uses assertive communication skills to increase persuasiveness and foster open communication.

Management Functions

1. Creates a work environment that minimizes the antecedent conditions for conflict.
2. Appropriately uses legitimate authority in a competing approach when a quick or unpopular decision needs to be made.
3. When appropriate, formally facilitates conflict resolution involving subordinates.
4. Accepts mutual responsibility for reaching predetermined supraordinate goals.
5. Obtains needed unit resources through effective negotiation strategies.
6. Compromises unit needs only when the need is not critical to unit functioning and when higher management gives up something of equal value.
7. Is adequately prepared to negotiate for unit resources, including the advance determination of a bottom line and possible trade-offs.
8. Uses appropriate strategies during negotiation and addresses the need for closure and follow-up to the negotiation.

THE HISTORY OF CONFLICT MANAGEMENT

Early in the 20th century, conflict was considered to be an indication of poor organizational management, was deemed destructive, and was avoided at all costs. When conflict occurred, it was either ignored, denied, or dealt with immediately and harshly. The theorists of this era believed that conflict could be avoided if employees were taught the one right way to do things and if expressed employee dissatisfaction was met swiftly with disapproval.

In the mid-20th century, when organizations recognized that worker satisfaction and feedback were important, conflict was accepted passively and perceived as normal and expected. Attention centered on teaching managers how to resolve conflict rather than how to prevent it. Although conflict was considered to be primarily dysfunctional, it was believed that conflict and cooperation could happen simultaneously.

The interactionist theorists of the 1970s recognized conflict as an absolute necessity and actively encouraged organizations to promote conflict as a means of producing growth. This view has since been tempered by the realization that conflict in itself is neither good or bad and that it can produce growth or destruction depending on how it is managed. Greenhalgh (1986) states that because conflict is inevitable in the organization, it should be considered managed when it does not interfere with ongoing functional relationships.

Some level of conflict appears desirable, although the optimum level for a specific individual or unit at a given time is difficult to determine. Boulding (1962) first described the *quantitative* nature of conflict by asserting that there could be too little, too much, or just the right amount of conflict. Too little conflict results in organizational stasis, while too much conflict reduces the organization's effectiveness and eventually immobilizes its employees. Robbins (1984) says the following:

> Managers should stimulate conflict to achieve the full benefits from its functional properties, yet reduce its level when it becomes a disruptive force. But since we have yet to design a sophisticated measuring instrument for assessing whether a given conflict level is functional or dysfunctional, it remains for managers to make intelligent judgments regarding whether conflict levels in their units are optimal, too high, or too low.

Conflict can be *qualitative* and quantitative (Boulding, 1962). A person may be totally overwhelmed in one conflict situation yet be able to handle several simultaneous conflicts at a later time. The difference is in the quality or significance of that conflict to the person experiencing it.

Although quantitative and qualitative conflict produce distress at the time they occur, they can lead to growth, energy, and creativity by generating new ideas and solutions. If handled inappropriately, quantitative and qualitative conflict can lead to demoralization, decreased motivation, and lowered productivity.

Barton (1991) maintains that nursing managers can no longer afford to respond to conflict traditionally, that is to avoid or suppress conflict, because this is nonproductive. In an era of shrinking healthcare dollars, it has become increasingly important for managers to confront and manage conflict appropriately.

LEARNING EXERCISE 16.1

Do you generally view conflict positively or negatively? Does conflict affect you more cognitively, emotionally, or physically? Was open expression of conflict encouraged in your home when you were growing up? Do you presently feel that you have too much or too little conflict in your life? Do you have any control over the issues that are now causing conflict in your life?

CATEGORIES OF CONFLICT

Lewis (1976) has identified three categories of conflict: intrapersonal, interpersonal, and intergroup. *Intrapersonal conflict* occurs within the individual. It involves an internal struggle to clarify contradictory values or wants. For managers, intrapersonal conflict may result from the multiple areas of responsibility associated with the management role. Managers' responsibilities to the organization, subordinates, consumers, the profession, and themselves may sometimes conflict, and that conflict may be internalized. Being self-aware and conscientiously working to resolve intrapersonal conflict as soon as it is first felt is essential to the leader's physical and mental health.

Interpersonal conflict happens between two or more people with differing values, goals, and beliefs. The person experiencing this conflict may experience opposition in upward, downward, horizontal, or diagonal communication.

Intergroup conflict occurs between two or more groups of people, departments, or organizations. An example of intergroup conflict might be two political affiliations with widely differing or contradictory beliefs.

THE CONFLICT PROCESS

Before managers can or should attempt to intervene in conflict, they must be able to assess its five stages accurately. The first stage in the conflict process, *latent* conflict, implies the existence of *antecedent conditions,* such as short staffing and rapid change. In this stage, conditions are ripe for conflict, although none has actually occurred and may never occur. Much unnecessary conflict could be prevented or reduced if managers examined the organization more closely for antecedent conditions. For example, change and budget cuts almost invariably create conflict. Such events, therefore, should be well thought out so that interventions can be made before the conflicts created by these events escalate.

If the conflict progresses, it may develop into the second stage: *perceived* conflict. Perceived or substantive conflict is intellectualized and often involves issues and roles. It is recognized logically and impersonally by the individual as occurring. Sometimes conflict can be resolved at this stage before it is internalized or felt.

The third stage, *felt* conflict, occurs when the conflict is emotionalized. Felt emotions include hostility, fear, mistrust, and anger. It also is referred to as affective conflict. It is possible to perceive conflict and not feel it; that is, no emotion is attached to the conflict, and the individual views it only as a problem to be solved. A person also can feel the conflict but not perceive the problem; that is, he or she is unable to identify the cause of the felt conflict.

In the fourth stage, *manifest* conflict, also called overt conflict, action is taken. The action may be to withdraw, compete, debate, or seek conflict resolution. If conflict reaches this stage, it is difficult to bring about conflict resolution without the use of other resources (Booth, 1993).

People may learn patterns of dealing with manifest conflict early in their lives. Traditionally men are socialized to use competition, dominance, and aggression to resolve conflict as they are growing up, while women are more apt to be socialized either to avoid or use attempts to pacify conflict (Ronl, 1993). However, Chusmir and Mills (1989) have found no significant gender difference in *conflict resolution*. Conflict resolution, or problem solving, appears to be learned less frequently through developmental experiences and instead requires a conscious learning effort.

The final stage in the conflict process is *conflict aftermath*. This aftermath may be more significant than the original conflict if the conflict has not been handled constructively. There is always conflict aftermath, positive or negative. If the conflict is managed well, individuals involved in the conflict will feel that their position was given a fair hearing. If the conflict is managed poorly, the conflict issues frequently remain and may return later to cause more conflict. Figure 16.1 shows a schematic of this conflict process.

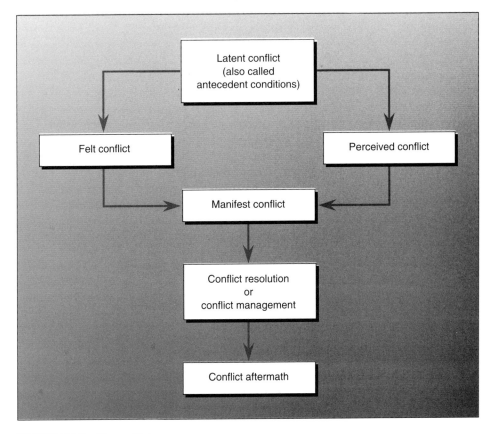

FIGURE 16.1 The conflict process.

CONFLICT MANAGEMENT

The optimal goal in resolving conflict is creating a win-win solution for all involved. This outcome is not possible in every situation, and often the manager's goal is to manage the conflict in a manner that lessens the perceptual differences that exist between the involved parties. A leader recognizes which conflict management or resolution strategy is most appropriate for each situation. The common conflict management strategies are identified in Display 16.2. The choice of the most appropriate strategy depends on many variables, such as the situation itself, the time urgency needed to make the decision, the power and status of the players, the importance of the issue, and the maturity of the individuals involved in the conflict.

In *compromising* a conflict resolution, each party gives up something it wants. Although many see compromise as an optimum conflict resolution strategy, antagonistic cooperation may result in a *lose-lose* situation because either or both parties perceive they have given up more than the other and may therefore feel defeated. For compromising not to result in a lose-lose situation, both parties must be willing to give up something of equal value.

The *competing* approach is used when one party pursues what it wants at the expense of the others. Because only one party wins, the competing party seeks the win regardless of the cost to others. Booth (1993) refers to this type of resolution as *forcing* because it imposes one's preference on another. *Win-lose* conflict resolution strategies leave the loser angry, frustrated, and wanting to get even in the future. Competing may be used by managers when a quick or unpopular decision needs to be made. It also may be used when one party has more information or knowledge about a situation than the other.

Cooperating is the opposite of competing. In the cooperating approach, one party sacrifices his or her beliefs and wants to allow the other party to win. The actual problem is usually not solved in this win-lose situation. *Accommodating* is another term that may be used for this strategy. The person cooperating or accommodating often collects I-owe-yous from the other party that can be used at a later date. Cooperating and accommodating are appropriate political strategies if the item in conflict is not of high value to the person doing the accommodating. *Smoothing* is used to manage a conflict situation. One individual smooths others involved in the conflict in an effort to reduce the emotional component of the conflict. Smoothing is often used by a manager to get someone to accommodate or cooperate with an-

Display 16.2 Common Conflict Resolution Strategies

Compromising
Competing
Cooperating-accommodating-smoothing
Avoiding
Collaborating

other party. Smoothing occurs when one party in a conflict attempts to compliment the other party or to focus on agreements rather than differences. Although it may be appropriate for minor disagreements, smoothing rarely results in resolution of the actual conflict.

In the *avoiding* approach, the parties involved are aware of a conflict but choose not to acknowledge it or attempt to resolve it. Avoidance may be indicated in trivial disagreements, when the cost of dealing with the conflict exceeds the benefits of solving it, when the problem should be solved by people other than yourself, and when the problem will solve itself.

Collaborating is an assertive and cooperative means of conflict resolution that results in a win-win solution. In collaboration, all parties set aside their original goals and work together to establish a *supraordinate* or *priority common goal*. In doing so, all parties accept mutual responsibility for reaching the supraordinate goal. Although it is very difficult for individuals truly to set aside original goals, collaboration cannot occur if this does not happen. For example, a couple experiencing serious conflict over whether or not to have a baby may first want to identify whether they share the supraordinate goal of keeping the marriage together. A nurse who is unhappy that she did not receive requested days off might meet with her supervisor and jointly establish the supraordinate goal that staffing will be adequate to meet patient safety criteria. If the new goal is truly a jointly set goal, each party will perceive that they have achieved an important goal and that the supraordinate goal is most important. In doing so, the focus remains on problem solving and not on defeating the other party.

Although Johnson (1994) believes that conflict is a pervasive force in healthcare organizations, only a small percentage of time is spent in true collaboration. Collaboration is rarely used when there is a wide difference in power between the groups or individuals involved (Johnson, 1994). Many think of collaboration as a form of cooperation, but this is not an accurate definition. In collaboration, problem solving is a joint effort with no superior/subordinate, order-giving/order-taking relationships.

Johnson (1994) maintains that collaboration is the best method to resolve conflict to achieve long-term benefits. However, because it involves others over which the manager has no control and because its process is lengthy, it may not be the best approach for all situations. Collaboration remains, however, the best alternative for complex problem solving involving others. Langford (1981) states that those who do choose this approach need to agree to the following:

LEARNING EXERCISE 16.2

It is important for managers to be self-aware regarding how they view and deal with conflict. In your personal life, how do you solve conflict? Is it important for you to win? When was the last time you were able to solve conflict by reaching supraordinate goals with another person? Are you able to see the other person's position in conflict situations? In conflicts with family and friends, are you least likely to compromise values, scarcities, or role expectations?

> ## ▶ LEARNING EXERCISE 16.3

(From Marquis & Huston, 1994.)

You have been working on the oncology unit since your graduation from the state college 1 year ago. Your performance has been complimented by your supervisor. Lately, she has allowed you to be relief charge nurse on the 3 PM to 11 PM shift when the regular charge nurse is not there. Occasionally, you have been asked to work other medical-surgical units when your department has a low census. Although you dislike leaving your own unit, you have cooperated because you felt you could handle the other clinical assignments and wanted to show your flexibility.

Tonight you have just come to work when the nursing office calls and requests that you help out in the busy delivery room. You protest that you don't know anything about obstetrics and that it is impossible for you to take the assignment. The supervisor from the nursing office insists that you are the most qualified person; she says, "Just go and do the best you can." Your own supervisor is not on duty, and the charge nurse says she does not feel comfortable advising you in this conflict. You feel torn between professional, personal, and organizational obligations. What should you do?

Select the most appropriate conflict resolution strategy. Give rationale for your selection and for your rejection of the others. After you have made your choice, read the analysis.

Analysis

You need to examine your goal, the supervisor's goal, and a goal on which you both can agree. Your goal might be that you want to protect your license and not to do anything that would bring harm to a patient. The supervisor's goal might be to provide assistance to an understaffed unit. A possible supraordinate goal would be for neither you nor the supervisor to do anything that would bring risk or harm to the organization.

The following conflict resolution strategies were among your choices.

ACCOMMODATING

Accommodating is the most obvious wrong choice. If you really feel that you are unqualified to work in the delivery room, this strategy could be harmful to patients and your career. Such a decision would not meet with your goal or the supraordinate goal.

SMOOTHING OR AVOIDING

Because you have little power and no one is available to intervene on your behalf, you are unable to choose either of these solutions. The problem cannot be avoided nor will you be able to smooth the conflict away.

COMPROMISING

In similar situations, you might be able to negotiate a compromise. For instance, you might say, "I cannot go to the delivery room but I will float to another medical-surgical area if there is someone on another medical-surgical unit who has OB experience." Alternatively, you could compromise by stating, "I feel comfortable working postpartum and will work in that area if you have a qualified nurse from postpartum that can be sent to the delivery room." It is possible that either solution could end the conflict depending on the availability of other personnel and how comfortable you would feel in the postpartum area. Often, someone attempting to problem solve, such as the supervisor in this case, becomes so overburdened and stressed that he or she is unable to see other alternatives.

(continued)

LEARNING EXERCISE 16.3 (Continued)

COLLABORATING

If time allows and the other party is willing to adopt a common goal, this is the preferred method of dealing with conflict. However, the power holder must view the other as having something important to contribute if this method of conflict management is to be successful. Perhaps you could convince the supervisor that the hospital and the supervisor could be at risk if an unqualified RN was assigned to an area requiring special skills. Once the supraordinate goal is adopted, you and the supervisor would be able to find alternative solutions to the problem. There are always many more ways to solve a problem than any one person can generate.

COMPETING

Normally, competing is not an attractive alternative for resolving conflict, but sometimes it is the only recourse. Before using competition as a method to manage this conflict, you need to examine your motives. Are you truly unqualified for work in the delivery room, or are you using your lack of experience as an excuse not to float to an unfamiliar area that would cause your anxiety? If you are truly convinced that you are unqualified, then you possess information that the supervisor does not have (a criterion necessary for the use of competing as a method of conflict resolution). Therefore, if other methods for solving the conflict are not effective, you must use competition to solve the conflict. You must win at the expense of the supervisor's losing. You risk much when using this type of resolution. The supervisor might fire you for insubordination, or at best, she may view you as uncooperative. The most appropriate method for using competition in this situation is an assertive approach. An example would be repeating firmly, but nonaggressively, "I cannot go to the delivery room to work because I would be putting patients at risk. I am unqualified to work in that area." This approach is usually effective. You must not work in an area where patient safety would be at risk. It would be morally, ethically, and legally wrong for you to do so. The legal implications of this case are discussed further in Chapter 23.

1. Define a supraordinate or common goal on which both groups can agree.
2. Mutually respect the knowledge and expertise of all parties.
3. Work together to review the goal once it is reached.
4. Communicate honestly and openly.
5. Have equitable, shared decision-making powers.
6. Share knowledge with each other.
7. Offer support to each other.
8. Have an understanding of the language and terms inherent in the problem to be solved.
9. Have mutually acceptable roles.

MANAGING UNIT CONFLICT

According to Ross and Pointer (1982), managing conflict effectively requires an understanding of its origin. Researchers identify the most common sources of organizational conflict as communication problems, organizational structure, and individual behavior within the organization. In addition to dealing with their own interpersonal conflicts, managers also are responsible for occasionally facilitating conflict resolution between others. Kotter (1990) states, "A central feature of modern organizations is interdependence, where no one has complete autonomy (p. 49)." Booth (1993) maintains that a consequence of this interdependence is increased tension and organizational conflict, which the manager must effectively manage. The following is a list of strategies a manager may use to deal effectively with organizational or unit conflict:

1. *Urging confrontation.* Many times subordinates inappropriately expect the manager to solve their interpersonal conflicts. Managers instead should urge the subordinates to attempt to handle their own problems.

2. *Third-party consultation.* Sometimes managers can be used as a neutral party to help others resolve conflicts constructively. This should be done only if both parties are motivated to solve the problem and if no differences exist in either party's status or power.

3. *Behavior change.* This is reserved for serious cases of dysfunctional conflict. Use of educational modes, training development, or sensitivity training can be used to solve conflict by developing self-awareness and behavior change in the involved parties.

4. *Responsibility charting.* When ambiguity results from unclear or new roles, it is often necessary to have the parties come together to delineate the function and responsibility of roles. If areas of joint responsibility exist, the manager must clearly define such areas as ultimate responsibility, approval mechanisms, support services, and responsibility for informing. This is a useful technique for elementary jurisdictional conflicts. An example of a potential jurisdictional conflict might arise between the house supervisor and unit manager in staffing or an inservice educator and unit manager in determining and planning unit educational needs or programs.

5. *Structure change.* Sometimes managers need to intervene in unit conflict by transferring or discharging individuals. Other structure changes may be moving a department under another manager, adding an ombudsman, or putting a grievance procedure in place. Often increasing the boundaries of authority for one member of the conflict will act as an effective structure change to resolve unit conflict. Changing titles and creating policies also are effective techniques.

6. *Soothing one party.* This is a temporary solution that should be used in a crisis when there is not time to handle the conflict effectively. The manager temporarily soothes one party so that cooperation will occur until the crisis is over. The manager must address the underlying problem later, or this technique will become dysfunctional.

NEGOTIATION

Negotiation in its most creative form is similar to collaboration and in its most poorly managed form, may resemble a competing approach. Negotiation frequently resembles compromise when it is used as a conflict resolution strategy. During negotiation, each party gives up something, and the emphasis is on accommodating differences between the parties. Because we live in a world with others, we have conflicting needs, wants, and desires that must be constantly compromised. Few individuals are able to meet all their needs or objectives. Most day-to-day conflict is resolved with negotiation. When one nurse says to another, "I'll answer that call light if you'll count narcotics," he or she is practicing the art of negotiation.

Although negotiation implies winning and losing for both parties, there is no rule that each party must lose and win the same amount. Most negotiators want to win more than they lose, but negotiation becomes destructively competitive when the emphasis is on winning at all costs. A major goal of effective negotiation is to make the other party feel satisfied with the outcome. The focus in negotiation should be to create a win-win situation.

Many small negotiations take place every day spontaneously and succeed without any advance preparation. However, Dirschel (1993) believes that few nurses are expert negotiators. If managers wish to succeed in important negotiations, for unit resources, they must 1) be adequately prepared, 2) be able to use appropriate negotiation strategies, and 3) apply appropriate closure and follow-up. To become more successful at negotiating, individuals need to do several things before, during, and after the negotiation.

Before the Negotiation

For managers to be successful, they must systematically prepare for the negotiation. As the negotiator, the manager begins by gathering as much information as possible regarding the issue to be negotiated. Because knowledge is power, the more informed the negotiator, the greater his or her bargaining power. Adequate preparation prevents others in the negotiation from catching the negotiator off guard or making him or her appear uninformed.

It also is important for managers to decide where to start in the negotiation. Because managers must be willing to make compromises, they should choose a strategy point that is high but not ridiculous. This selected starting point should be at the upper limits of their expectations, realizing that they may need to come down to a more realistic goal. Following is an example:

> You would really like four additional full-time RN positions and a full-time clerical position budgeted for your unit. You know that you could make do with three additional full-time RN positions and a part-time clerical assistant, but you begin by asking for what would be the most ideal.

It is almost impossible in any type of negotiation to escalate demands; therefore, the manager must start at an extreme but reasonable point. It also must be decided beforehand how much can be compromised. Can the manager accept one full-time RN position or two or three? The very least for which an individual will settle is often referred to as the *bottom line*.

The wise manager also has other options in mind when negotiating important resources. An *alternative option* is another set of negotiating preferences that can be used so that managers need not use their bottom lines but still meet their overall goal. The following scenario is an example of the use of an alternative option.

> You have requested four full-time RN positions and one full-time clerical position. You could get by with three full-time RNs and one part-time clerk. However, you feel strongly that you can't continue to provide safe patient care unless you are given two RNs and a part-time clerk—your bottom line. However, if the original negotiation is unsuccessful, reopen negotiations by saying that a second option that does not entail increasing the staff would be to float a ward clerk for 4 hours each day, implement a unit-dose system, require housekeeping to pass out linen, and have dietary pass all the patient meal trays. This way, the overall goal of providing more direct patient care by the nursing staff could still be met without adding additional nursing personnel.

The manager needs to consider other *trade-offs* that are possible in these situations. Trade-offs are secondary gains, often future oriented, that may be realized as a result of conflict. For example, while attending college, a parent may feel intrapersonal conflict because he or she is unable to spend as much time as desired with his or her children. The parent is able to compromise by considering the trade-off. Eventually everyone's life will be better because of the present sacrifices. The wise manager will consider possibly trading something today for something tomorrow as a means to reach satisfactory negotiations.

The manager also must look for and acknowledge *hidden agendas*—the covert intention of the negotiation. Usually, every negotiation has a covert and an overt agenda. For example, new managers may set up a meeting with their superior with the established agenda of discussing the lack of supplies on the unit. However, the hidden agenda may be that the manager feels insecure and is really seeking performance feedback during the discussion. Having a hidden agenda is not uncommon and is not wrong by any means. Everyone has them, and it is not necessary or even wise to share these hidden agendas. Managers, however, must be introspective enough to recognize their hidden agendas so that they are not paralyzed if the agenda is discovered and used against them during the negotiation.

If the manager's hidden agenda is discovered, he or she should admit that it is a consideration but not the heart of the negotiation. For example, although the hidden agenda for increasing unit staff might be to build the manager's esteem in the eyes of the staff, there may exist a legitimate need for additional staff. If, during the negotiations, the fiscal controller accuses the manager of wanting to increase staff just to gain power, the manager might respond by saying, "It is always important for a successful manager to be able to gain resources for the unit, but the real issue here is an inadequate staff." Managers who protest too strongly that they do not have a hidden agenda appear defensive and vulnerable.

During the Negotiation

Negotiation is psychological and verbal. The effective negotiator always looks calm and self-assured. At least part of this self-assurance comes from having adequately prepared for the negotiation. Part of the preparation should have included learning about the people with whom the manager is negotiating. There are many types of personalities, and it is necessary to negotiate with most of them. Some theorists suggest that some negotiators win by using specific tactics. These tactics might be conscious or unconscious but are used repeatedly because they have been successful for that person. Successful managers *do not use* negotiation tactics that are intimidating or manipulative, but because others with whom they negotiate may do so, they must be prepared to counter such tactics. Display 16.3 lists 14 negotiation tactics that Bakker and Bakker-Rabdan (1973) maintain are used by those wanting to win territory in negotiation. Individuals using these tactics take a competing approach to negotiation rather than a collaborative approach.

Ridicule

Ridicule is an especially effective weapon in negotiating because it undermines the psychological space of others. If you are negotiating with someone who uses ridicule, maintain a relaxed body posture, steady gaze, and patient smile. Body language changes must be prevented, or the other party gains power by capturing your psychological space.

Smoke Screen

The primary objective in smoke screen is to confuse the other party. This often takes the form of ambiguous or inappropriate questioning. For example, in one negotiating situation, the intensive care unit supervisor had requested additional staff to handle open-heart surgery patients. During her bargaining, the CEO suddenly said, "I never did understand the heart; can you tell me about the heart?" The supervisor did not fall into this trap and instead replied that the physiology of the heart was irrelevant to the issue. Because people tend to answer an authority figure, it is necessary to be on guard for this type of diversionary tactic.

Over the Barrel

This is a technique used when one party in the conflict knows the vulnerability of the other party and uses that vulnerability to force concessions. For example, if the man-

---

> **Display 16.3** Negotiation Tactics
>
> | | |
> |---|---|
> | 1. Ridicule | 8. Induction of guilt |
> | 2. Smoke screen | 9. Definition |
> | 3. Over the barrel | 10. Self-definition |
> | 4. Seduction | 11. Paternalism |
> | 5. Flattery | 12. Gifts |
> | 6. Sex | 13. Aggressive takeover |
> | 7. Illness-helplessness | 14. Pacifism |
>
> (Bakker and Bakker-Rabdan, 1973)

ager is especially vulnerable to crying or anger, then all the other party has to do is raise his or her voice or begin to cry and the manager will compromise. The first way to deal with this technique is to attempt to hide weak spots. In addition, managers must desensitize their areas of vulnerability if they are going to be effective negotiators.

Seduction

This is a highly successful negotiation tactic. It is exemplified by the individual who implies future promises. It is devious and therefore sometimes difficult to recognize. Two ingredients of seduction are providing a desirable gratification or creating the expectation of something good happening in the future. Flattery also is a part of seduction but often occurs without the other ingredients of seduction. An example of seduction would be a supervisor who promises future advancement or provides desired days off to keep charge nurses on the unit. This prevents the charge nurse from seeking a higher position elsewhere. Although these tactics may be used in good faith, the outcome is the same: a loss of negotiation power for the other party.

Flattery

Bakker and Bakker-Rabdan (1973) maintain that flattery is more potent than sexual desirability. The objective of flattery is to divert the attention of the other party. One method managers can use to discern flattery from other honest attempts to compliment is to be aware how they feel about the comment. If they feel unduly flattered by a gesture or comment, it is a good indication that they were being flattered. For example, asking for advice or instruction may be a subtle form of flattery, or it may be an honest request. If the request for advice is about an area in which the manager has little expertise, it is undoubtedly flattery. However, exchanging positive opening comments with each other when beginning negotiation is an acceptable and enjoyable practice performed by both parties.

Gender

Whenever negotiation involves two sexes, some degree of sexuality may be used as a weapon. This may be subtle or unsubtle, conscious or unconscious. For example, gender can be used as a weapon to stereotype in comments such as "women are all emotional." Some women may use their femininity to influence others into believing that they will be pushovers in negotiating. By behaving in a manner that makes them appear soft and fragile, women may attempt to gain an advantage in negotiating. Likewise, males may attempt to use their sexuality in a manner that gives them a negotiating edge.

Illness/Helplessness

Many managers are lured into losing because of others' illnesses or helplessness. Because of the nurturing nature of the profession, nurses can experience a great loss in any negotiation that involves a party who uses illness or helplessness as a tactic. Bakker and Bakker-Rabdan (1973) state that "a display of helplessness brings out an impulse to assist which is so strong that it takes a deliberate effort to refrain from doing so."

Induction of Guilt

Making one party feel guilty is another powerful negotiation tactic. "If you really loved me, you would do this" is a comment often used in interpersonal conflict situations. Likewise, nurses, in an effort to introduce guilt and therefore gain a powerful edge, may say, "If you really had the patient's or staff's best interests at heart. . . ." Sometimes guilt is more subtle. As a way to introduce guilt, a team member might say, "The assignment you gave me is so heavy, I'm not going to be able to go to lunch." Because the discomfort of guilt is usually recognized by self-aware managers, they then need to decide if the statement made to introduce guilt has legitimate merit.

Definition

This technique entails defining another by using a statement that has a pleasant quality. For example, if a negotiator says, "I know you are a reasonable person," he or she has now defined you as reasonable, so being unreasonable would be difficult. Using the process of definition is a method to limit the freedom of another. The manager must be alert whenever someone in a negotiating situation makes a definitive statement about them.

Self-Definition

Self-definition uses the same technique as definition but is directed toward self and is used to hide the truth. It is often used to justify one's behavior. "I am very temperamental" might be used to excuse an angry outburst during negotiations. Self-definition gives individuals the sense that they do not need to take responsibility for themselves. When dealing with these individuals, the other party must make it clear that they do not accept the self-definition as a legitimate excuse for behavior.

Paternalism

With this tactic, the aggressor in the conflict tries to convince the manager that his or her solution to the conflict would be in the manager's best interest. Individuals who insist, "I always know best," have convinced themselves that they have everyone's best interests at heart. Human beings have a great capacity for justifying their actions. If either party in a conflict situation feels they are doing something for the other person's own good, then the goals need to be reassessed.

Gifts

While flattery is one form of ingratiation, another is the use of gifts and favors to gain power in negotiation. Students who feel a conflict between the clinical instructor and themselves regarding a grade might give their instructor a gift prior to the grade conference. The student may perceive that this may give the student an advantage in negotiating the grade they desire.

Aggressive Takeover

Conflict is often resolved by someone assuming authority and rapidly resolving the conflict in a manner to suit him or her before other members realize what is happening. If managers feel this may be happening, they should call a halt to the negotiations before decisions are made. Saying simply "I need to have time to think this over" is a good method of stopping an aggressive takeover.

More often, there is a gradual takeover rather than a massive action. Gradual takeover can occur because others use their competence and willingness to do chores to gain power. This is particularly evident in role conflict because there are often overlapping responsibilities in roles in healthcare. The person who desires to negotiate a larger role for himself or herself can gradually develop expertise and assume authority until the role has greatly been expanded. By the time the situation reaches overt conflict, the person with the expanded role will be negotiating from a position of power.

Pacifism

Individuals who use pacifism win because they refuse to fight. Of all negotiation tactics, this is perhaps the most difficult to manage. When negotiating with the pacifist, the manager should ask for the resolution of the conflict in writing and do careful follow-up.

The manager needs to be aware of all of these negotiation tactics and develop strategies to overcome them. However, none of the previous tactics are recommended for personal use because most of them are destructively manipulative. Moreover, leaders need to become honest and self-aware regarding any manipulative negotiation strategies that they have used in the past and begin to develop strategies that are more conducive to a collaborative approach to negotiation. Leaders use an honest straightforward approach and develop assertive skills for use in conflict negotiation. Maintaining human dignity and promoting communication require that all conflict interaction be assertive, direct, and open. Conflict must be focused on the issues and resolved through joint compromise.

In addition to developing sensitivity to negotiation tactics and assertiveness skills, leaders can do several things during negotiation to increase their persuasiveness and foster open communication.

1. Use only factual statements that have been gathered in research.
2. Listen carefully, and watch nonverbal communication.
3. Keep an open mind because negotiation always provides the potential for learning. Don't prejudge. Establish a cooperative and not a competitive climate.
4. Try to understand from where the other party is coming. It is probable that one person's perception is different from another's. Concentrate on understanding and not just on agreeing.

5. Always discuss the conflict. Do not personalize the conflict by discussing the parties involved in the negotiation.
6. Try not to belabor how the conflict occurred or try to fix the blame for the conflict. Focus on preventing its recurrence.
7. Be honest.
8. Start tough so that concessions are possible. It is much harder to escalate demands in the negotiation than to make concessions.
9. When you are confronted with something totally unexpected in negotiation, do not attempt to deal with it at that time. Respond by saying, "I'm not prepared to discuss this right now" or "I'm sorry this was not on our agenda; we can set up another appointment later to discuss that." If asked a question that you do not know, simply say, "I don't have that information at this time."
10. Never tell the other party what you're willing to negotiate *totally*. You may be giving up the ship too early.
11. Know your bottom line, but try *never* to use it. If you use your bottom line, you must be ready to back it up, or you lose all credibility. If you reach your bottom line, tell the other party that you have reached an impasse and cannot negotiate further. Then encourage the other party to sleep on it and reconsider. Always leave the door open for further negotiation. Make another appointment. Be sure to allow the other party and yourself to save face.
12. If either party becomes angry or tired during the negotiation, take a break. Go to the bathroom or make a telephone call. Remember that neither party can effectively negotiate if they are enraged or fatigued.

Closure and Follow-up to Negotiation

Just as it is important to start the formal negotiation with some pleasantries, it is also good to close on a friendly note. Once a compromise has been reached, restate it so that everyone is clear about what has been agreed. If managers win more in negotiation than they anticipated, they should try to hide their astonishment. At the end of any negotiation, whether it is a short 2-minute conflict negotiation in the hallway with another RN or an hour-long formal salary negotiation, the result should be satisfaction by all parties that each has won something. It is a good idea to follow up formal negotiation in writing by sending a letter or a memo stating what was agreed.

INTEGRATING LEADERSHIP SKILLS AND MANAGEMENT FUNCTIONS IN MANAGING CONFLICT

The manager who creates a stable work environment that minimizes the antecedent conditions for conflict has more time and energy to focus on meeting organizational and human resource needs. When conflict does occur in the unit, managers must be able to discern constructive from destructive conflict. Conflict that is constructive will result in creativity, innovation, and growth for the unit. When conflict is deemed

LEARNING EXERCISE 16.4

You are one of a group of staff nurses who feel that part of your job dissatisfaction results from getting different patients every day. Your unit uses a system of total patient care, and assignments are made by the head nurse. Two staff nurses have gone to the head nurse and requested that she allow each nurse to pick his or her own patients based on the previous day's assignment and the ability of the nurse. The head nurse feels they are being uncooperative because she is responsible for seeing that all the patients get assigned and receive adequate care. She indicates that although she attempts to provide continuity of care, it is often inappropriate because many part-time nurses are used on the unit, and not all the nurses are able to care for every type of patient. At the end of the conference, the two nurses are angry, and the head nurse is irritated. However, the next day, the head nurse says she is willing to meet with the staff nurses. The other nurses feel this is a sign that the head nurse is willing to negotiate a compromise. They plan to get together tonight to plan the strategy for tomorrow's meeting.

Assignment: What are the goals for each party? What could be a possible hidden agenda for each party? What could happen if the conflict is escalated? Devise a workable plan that would accomplish the goals of both parties and develop strategies for implementation.

Analysis

The head nurse's goal is to be sure all patients receive safe and adequate care. She might have several hidden agendas. One might be that she does not want to relinquish any authority or she does not want to devote her energy to the planned change that has been proposed. The nurses have goals of job satisfaction and providing more continuity of care; however, their hidden agenda is probably the need for more autonomy and control of the work setting.

If the conflict is allowed to escalate, the staff nurses could begin to disrupt the unit because of their dissatisfaction, and the head nurse could transfer some of the "ring leaders" or punish them in some other way. The head nurse is wise in reconsidering these nurses' request. By demonstrating her willingness to talk and negotiate the conflict, she will be viewed by the staff nurses as cooperative and interested in their job satisfaction.

The staff nurses must realize that they are not going to obtain everything they want in this conflict resolution nor should they expect that result. To demonstrate their interest, they should develop some sort of workable policy and procedure for patient care assignments, recognizing that the head nurse will want to modify their procedure. Once the plan is developed, the nurses need to plan their strategy for the coming meeting. The following may be their outline.

1. Select a member of the group to be the spokesperson who has the best assertive skills but who is not abrasive or aggressive in his or her approach. This keeps the group from appearing overpowering to the head nurse. The other group members will be at the meeting lending their support but will speak only when called on by the group leader. Preferably the spokesperson also should be someone the head nurse knows well and whose opinion she respects.

2. The designated leader of the group should plan to begin her opening remarks by thanking the head nurse for agreeing to the meeting. In this way, the group acknowledges the authority of the head nurse.

(continued)

3. There should be a sincere effort by the group to listen to the head nurse and to follow modifications to their plan. They must be willing to give up something also, perhaps some modification in the staffing pattern.

4. As the meeting progresses, the leader of the group should continue to express the goal of the group—to provide greater continuity of patient care—rather than focusing on how unhappy the group is with the present system.

5. At some point, the nurses should show their willingness to compromise and offer to evaluate the new plan periodically.

6. Hopefully, the outcome of the meeting would be some sort of negotiated compromise in patient care assignment, which would result in more autonomy and job satisfaction for the nurses, enough authority for the head nurse to satisfy her responsibilities, and increased continuity of patient care assignment.

to be destructive, managers must deal appropriately with that conflict or risk aftermath, which may be even more destructive than the original conflict. Consistently using conflict resolution strategies with win-lose or lose-lose outcomes will create disharmony within the unit. Leaders who use optimal conflict resolution strategies with a win-win outcome promote increased employee satisfaction and organizational productivity.

Negotiation also requires both management functions and leadership skills. Well-prepared managers know with whom they will be negotiating and prepare their negotiation accordingly. They are prepared with trade-offs, multiple alternatives, and a clear bottom line to ensure that their unit acquires needed resources. Successful negotiation mandates the use of the leadership components of self-confidence and risk taking. If these attributes are not present, the leader/manager has little power in negotiation and thus compromises the unit's ability to secure desired resources. Other attributes that make leaders effective in negotiation are sensitivity to others and the environment and interpersonal communication skills. The leader's use of assertive communication skills, rather than tactics, results in an acceptable level of satisfaction for all parties at the close of the negotiation.

KEY CONCEPTS

▼ *Conflict* can be defined as the internal discord that results from differences in ideas, values, or feelings of two or more people.

▼ Because managers have a variety of interpersonal relationships with individuals with different values, beliefs, backgrounds, and goals, conflict is an expected outcome.

▼ Conflict theory has changed dramatically during the last 100 years. Currently, conflict is viewed as neither good nor bad because it can produce growth or destroy depending on how it is managed.

▼ Too little conflict results in organizational stasis, while too much conflict reduces the organization's effectiveness and eventually immobilizes its employees.

▼ The three categories of conflict are *intrapersonal, interpersonal,* and *intergroup.*

▼ The first stage in the conflict process is called *latent conflict.* Latent conflict implies the existence of antecedent conditions. Latent conflict may proceed to *perceived* or *felt* conflict. *Manifest* conflict also may occur. The last stage in the process is *conflict aftermath.*

▼ The optimal goal in conflict resolution is creating a win-win solution for everyone involved.

▼ When using *compromise* as an approach to conflict resolution, parties of equal power give up something that they want.

▼ The *competing* approach to conflict resolution is used when one party pursues what it wants at the expense of the other parties.

▼ In the conflict resolution strategy *accommodating,* one person sacrifices his or her beliefs and wants to allow the other party to win.

▼ *Smoothing* is a conflict resolution strategy used to reduce the emotional component of the conflict.

▼ In *avoiding,* the parties involved are aware of a conflict but choose not to acknowledge it or attempt to resolve it.

▼ *Collaborating* is an assertive and cooperative means of conflict resolution, which results in a win-win solution. Both parties set aside their original goals and work together to establish a *supraordinate* or *common goal.*

▼ The most common sources of organizational conflict are communication problems, organizational structure, and individual behavior within the organization.

▼ *Negotiation* may be competitive or collaborative, but collaborative negotiation generally has a more positive outcome.

▼ As a negotiator, it is important to win as much as possible, lose as little as possible, and make the other party feel satisfied with the outcome of the negotiation.

▼ Because knowledge is power, the more informed a negotiator, the greater his or her bargaining power.

▼ The manager must be able to recognize and counter negotiation tactics.

▼ The manager must know his or her *bottom line* but try *never* to use it.

▼ Closure and follow-up are important parts of the negotiation process.

◢ ADDITIONAL LEARNING EXERCISES

Learning Exercises 16.5
(From Marquis & Huston, 1994.)

In the following situations, choose the most appropriate approach to conflict resolution. Support your decision with rationale, and explain why other methods of conflict management were not used.

Situation 1

You are a circulating nurse in the operating room. Usually you are assigned to Room 3 for general surgery, but today you have been assigned to Room 4, the orthopedic room. You are unfamiliar with the orthopedic doctors' routines and attempt to brush up on them quickly before each case today by reading the doctors' preference cards prior to each case. So far, you have managed to complete two cases without incident. The next case comes in the room, and you realize everyone is especially tense; this patient is the wife of a local physician, and the doctors are performing a bone biopsy for possible malignancy. You prepare the area to be biopsied, and the surgeon, who has a reputation for a quick temper, enters the room. You suddenly realize that you have prepared the area with betadine, and this surgeon prefers another solution. He sees what you have done and yells, "You are a stupid, stupid nurse."

Situation 2

You are the intensive care unit charge nurse and have just finished an exhausting 8 hours on duty. Working with you today were two nurses who work 12-hour shifts. You have each been assigned two patients, all with high acuity levels. You are glad that you are going out of town tonight to attend an important seminar, because you are certainly tired. You also are pleased that you scheduled yourself an 8-hour shift today and that your relief is coming through the door. You will just have time to give report and catch your plane.

It is customary for 12-hour nurses to continue with their previous patients and for assignments not to be changed when 8-hour and 12-hour staff are working together. Therefore, you proceed to give report on your patients to the 8-hour nurse coming on duty. One of your patients is acutely ill with fever of unknown origin and is in the isolation room. It is suspected that he has meningitis. Your other patient is a multiple trauma victim. In the middle of your report, the oncoming nurse says that she has just learned that she is pregnant. She says, "I can't take care of a possible meningitis patient. I'll have to trade with one of the 12-hour nurses." You approach the 12-hour nurses, and they respond angrily. "We took care of all kinds of patients when we were pregnant, and we are not changing patients with just 4 hours left in our shift." When you repeat this message to the oncoming nurse, she says, "Either they trade or I go home!" Your phone call to the nursing office reveals that because of a flu epidemic, there is absolutely *no* personnel to call in, and all the other units are already short staffed.

Situation 3

You are the team leader for 10 patients. An LVN/LPN and nurse's aide also are assigned to the team. It is an extremely busy day, and there is a great deal of work to be done. Several times today you have found the LVN/LPN taking long breaks in the lounge or chatting at the desk despite the many patient needs that remain unmet. On these occasions, you have clearly delegated work tasks and timelines to her. Several hours later, you follow up on the delegated tasks and find that they are not completed. When you seek out the LVN, you find that she has gone to lunch without telling you or the aide. You are furious at her apparent disregard for your authority.

Learning Exercise 16.6

Often one group is more powerful or has greater status and refuses to relinquish this power position, thus making collaboration impossible. Therefore, negotiating a compromise to a win-win solution, rather than a lose-lose solution, becomes imperative. In the following situation, describe if you could and how you would go about negotiating a win-win solution to conflict.

You are a member of a senior baccalaureate nursing class. In your college, students may elect to accelerate through their course work by combining their last two semesters. Consequently, you find that you are one of 16 students electing to combine and have been placed in a class of 32 nonaccelerating seniors. The class has begun work on its end-of-program ceremony where the students receive nursing pins. Each group in this class (the 16-member group and the 32-member group) appears to have differing philosophies and values about nursing, and because this is the first time they have spent any time together, they do not know each other well. The committee meetings for the end-of-program ceremony have become a series of arguments and battles. The conflict has accelerated to the point where it has begun to be destructive as evidenced by some name calling.

The major conflict centers around traditionalists versus nontraditionalists. The 16 students who form the smaller group want a nontraditional ceremony, and the students who make up the larger group want a traditional ceremony.

The faculty member who is the liaison has become alarmed at the situation and has come to you as the leader of the smaller group and to the leader of the larger group and told both of you that she will *cancel* the ceremony if the conflict is not resolved. The faculty member agrees to give you 2 hours of class time to facilitate the resolution. The leader of the large group tells you she will give you the entire 2 hours to negotiate a compromise. She feels a need to compromise but feels your skill at facilitating a negotiated settlement is greater than hers. She wants the conflict resolved in a win-win situation so that no parties leave angry.

Assignment: How would you plan to approach the group? What strategies would you use? Explain your rationale. Remember you wish to negotiate a compromise, and although you desire a win-win solution, you are limited in time and may not be able to facilitate a total collaboration. What is your plan? What is your bottom line?

Learning Exercise 16.7

You are a woman who is a unit manager with a master's degree in health administration. You are about to present your proposed budget to the CEO. You have thoroughly researched your budget and have adequate rationale to support your requests for increased funding. Because the CEO is often moody, predicting his response is difficult.

You also are aware that the CEO has some very traditional views about women's role in the workplace, and generally this does not include a major management role. Because he is fairly paternalistic, he is charmed and flattered when asked to assist "his nurses with their jobs." Your predecessor was fired because she was perceived as brash, bossy, and disrespectful by the CEO. In fact, the former unit manager was one of a series of nursing managers who had been replaced in the last several years because of these characteristics. From what you have been told, these perceptions were not shared by the nursing staff.

You sit down and begin to plan your strategy for this meeting. You are aware that you are more likely to have your budgetary needs met if you dress conservatively, beseech his assistance and support throughout the presentation, and are fairly passive in your approach. In other words, you will be required to assume a traditionally feminine, helpless role. If you appear capable and articulate, you may not achieve your budgetary goals and may not even keep your job. It would probably not be necessary for you to continue to act this way, except in your interactions with the CEO.

Assignment: Are such behavioral tactics appropriate if the outcome is desirable? Are such tactics simply smart negotiation, or are they destructively manipulative? What would you do in this situation? Outline your strategy for your budget presentation, and present rationale for your choices.

Learning Exercise 16.8
(From Marquis & Huston, 1994.)

You are the head nurse of the new oncology unit. It is time for your first budget presentation to administration. You have already presented your budget to the director of nurses, and while she had a few questions, she was in general agreement. However, it is the policy at Memorial Hospital that each head nurse present her budget to the budget committee, consisting of the fiscal manager, the director of nurses, a member of the board of trustees, and the executive director. You know money is scarce this year because of the new building, but you really feel you need the increases you have requested in your budget. Basically, you have asked for the following:

1. Replace the 22% aides on your unit with 10% LVNs/LPNs and 12% RNs.
2. Increase educational time paid by 5% to allow for certification in chemotherapy.
3. Provide a new position of clinical nurse specialist in oncology.
4. Convert one room into a sitting room and minikitchen for patients' families.
5. Add shelves and a locked medication box in each room to facilitate primary nursing.
6. Provide no new equipment; replace existing equipment that is broken or outdated.

Assignment: Outline your plan. Include your approach, what is and what is not negotiable, and what arguments you would use. Give rationale for your plan.

REFERENCES:

Bakker, B. B., & Bakker-Rabdan, M. K. (1973). *No trespassing* (p. 186). San Francisco: Chandler and Sharp.

Barton, A. (1991). Conflict resolution by nurse managers. *Nursing Management, 22*(5), 83–86.

Booth, R. Z. (1993). The dynamics of conflict and conflict management. In D. J. Mason, S. W. Talbot, & J. K. Leavitt (Eds.), *Policy and politics for nurses* (2nd ed.). Philadelphia: W.B. Saunders.

Boulding, K. F. (1962). *Conflict and defense.* New York: Harper and Brothers.

Chusmir, L. H., & Mills, J. (1989). Gender differences in conflict resolution styles of managers: At work and at home. *Sex Roles, 20*(3–4), 149–163.

Dirschel, K. M. (1993). Principled negotiating. In D. J. Mason, S. W. Talbot, & J. K. Leavitt (Eds.), *Policy and politics for nurses* (2nd ed.). Philadelphia: W. B. Saunders.

Greenhalgh, L. (1986). Managing conflict. *Sloan Management Review, 27*(4), 45–51.

Guy, M. E. (1986). Interdisciplinary conflict and organizational complexity. *Hospitals and Health Services Administration, 31*(1), 111–121.

Johnson, M. (1994). Conflict and nursing professionalization In J. McCloskey & H. K. Grace (Eds.), *Current issues in nursing* (4th ed.). St Louis: C.V. Mosby.

Kotter, J. P. (1990). *A force for change.* New York: Free Press.

Langford, T. (1981). *Managing and being managed.* Englewood Cliffs, NJ: Prentice Hall.

Lewis, J. (1976). Conflict management. *Journal of Nursing Administration, 6*(10), 18–22.

Marquis, B. L., & Huston, C. J. (1994). *Management decision making for nurses* (2nd ed.). Philadelphia: J.B. Lippincott.

Robbins, S. P. (1984). *Management: Concepts and practices.* Englewood Cliffs, NJ: Prentice Hall.

Ronl, L. L. (1993). gender gaps within management. *Nursing Management, 24*(5), 65–66.

Ross, M., & Pointer, D. (1982). Health care manager's notebook—Conflict management. *Hospital Forum, 37.*

BIBLIOGRAPHY

Ambrose, J. (1989). Your nursing power to resolve conflict in the professional setting. *Today's OR Nurse, 11*(3), 13–21, 30–32.

Baker, C. M., Boyd, N. J., Stasiowski, S. A. et al. (1989). Interinstitutional collaboration for nursing excellence: Creating the partnership (Part 1). *Journal of Nursing Administration, 19*(2), 8–12.

Baker, C. M., Boyd, N. J., Stasiowski, S. A. et al. (1989). Interinstitutional collaboration for nursing excellence: Creating the partnership (Part 2). *Journal of Nursing Administration, 19*(3), 8–13.

Cavanagh, S. (1991). The conflict management style of staff nurses and nurse managers. *Journal of Advanced Nursing, 16*(8), 1254–1260.

Bishop, B. E. (1989). Collaboration: Needed more than ever. *Maternal Child Nursing, 14*(3), 153.

Bradford, R. (1989). Obstacles to collaborative practice. *Nursing Management, 20*(4), 72I, 72L–72M, 72P.

Burleson, E. J. (1987). Creative tension: Problem solving in conflict. *Nursing Management, 18*(5), 64J, 64L, 64N.

Davidhizar, R., (1989). How to disagree with your supervisor. *Advancing Clinical Care, 4*(5), 16–17.

Davidhizar, R., & Giger, J. (1990). When subordinates go over your head. *Journal of Nursing Administration, 20*(9), 29–34.

Davidhizar, R., & Bowen, M., (1988). Confrontation: An underused nursing management technique. *Health Care Supervisor, 7*(1), 29–34.

Hightower, T. (1986). Subordinate choice of conflict-handling modes. *Nursing Administration Quarterly, 11*(1), 29–34.

Loraine, K. (1989). Winning strategies when the game is confrontation. *RN, 52*(3), 18–20.

Marriner, A. (1987). How do you spell relief of conflict? Flexibility. *Nursing 87, 17*(3), 113–114.

Muller, P. A. (1989). A closer look at politics. *Journal of Post Anesthesia Nursing, 4*(5), 334–336.

Nazarey, P. (1988). Communication, cooperation, commitment: The challenges of collaboration. *Emphasis: Nursing, 3*(1), 7–10.

Rosen, L. F. (1987). Understanding and handling personal conflicts. *Today's OR Nurse, 9*(6), 31.

Schwab, T., & Simmons, R. (1989). Collaboration in action. *Nursing Connections, 2*(1), 35–42.

Silber, M. B. (1989). Managing confrontations: Once more into the breach. *Nursing Management, 15*(4), 54, 56–58.

Styles, M. (1988). Conflict and coalition strengthen nursing as a profession. *Orthopaedic Nursing, 7*(6), 9–11.

Todd, S. S. (1989). Coping with conflict. *Nursing 89, 19*(10), 100.

Toth, L. (1989). Collaboration is key. *SCI Nursing: American Association of Spinal Cord Injury Nurses, 6*(2), 24.

Woodtli, A. (1987). Conflict: Insights before intervention. *Nurse Educator, 12*(2), 22–26.

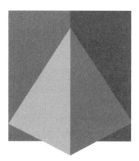

CHAPTER 17

Potential Constraints Affecting Directing: Unions and Employment Laws

Two constraints that may affect the directing aspects of management are collective bargaining and legislation concerning employment practices. It is possible to maximize these constraints, making them positive rather than negative influences. To accomplish this task, however, managers must first understand the impact of unionization on the healthcare industry and the proliferation of legislation regarding employment practices.

Managers must be able to see collective bargaining and employment legislation from four perspectives: 1) the organization, 2) the worker, 3) general historical and societal, and 4) personal. Managers able to gain this broad perspective will better understand how management and employees can work together within the areas of unionization and employment legislation. Many industrialized countries have adopted an attitude of acceptance and tolerance for the difficulties of managing under these constraints. However, in the United States, many organizations view these forces with resentment and hostility. This chapter examines the leadership roles

Bessie L. Marquis and Carol J. Huston:
LEADERSHIP ROLES AND MANAGEMENT FUNCTIONS IN NURSING, 2nd ed.
Lippincott-Raven Publishers © 1996

and management functions necessary to create a climate in which unionization and legislation are not a hindrance to the organization. These leadership roles and management functions are shown in Display 17.1.

UNIONS AND COLLECTIVE BARGAINING

Collective bargaining may be defined as activities occurring between organized labor and management that concern employee relations. Such activities include negotiation of formal labor agreements and day-to-day interactions between unions and management. Although first- and middle-level managers usually have little to do with negotiating the labor contract, they are greatly involved with the contract's daily implementation. The middle manager has the greatest impact on the quality of the relationship that develops between labor and management. Terminology associated with unions and collective bargaining is shown in Display 17.2.

Display 17.1 Leadership Roles and Management Functions in the Constraints of Directing

Leadership Roles

1. Is self-aware regarding personal attitudes and values regarding collective bargaining and employment legislation.
2. Recognizes and accepts reasons that individuals seek unionization.
3. Creates a work environment that eliminates the need for unionization to meet employees' needs.
4. Encourages upward communication.
5. Maintains an accommodating approach when dealing with unions and employment legislation.
6. Is a role model for fairness.
7. Is nondiscriminatory in all personal and professional actions.

Management Functions

1. Understands and appropriately implements union contracts.
2. Administers personnel policies fairly and consistently.
3. Works cooperatively with the personnel department and top-level administration when dealing with union activity.
4. Understands and follows labor and employment laws that relate to the manager's sphere of influence.
5. Ensures that the work environment is safe.
6. Is alert for discriminatory employment practices in the workplace.
7. Ensures that the unit or department meets state licensing regulations.

Display 17.2   Collective Bargaining Terminology

Agency shop: Also called an *open shop*. Employees are not required to join the union.

Arbitration: The terminal step in the grievance procedure. Always indicates the involvement of a third party. Arbitration may be voluntary on the part of management and labor or imposed by the government in a compulsory arbitration.

Collective bargaining: The relations between employers, acting through their management representatives, and organized labor.

Conciliation and mediation: Synonymous terms. They refer to the activity of a third party to help disputants reach an agreement. However, unlike an arbitrator, this individual has no final power of decision making.

Fact finding: Rarely used in the private sector but used frequently in labor–management disputes that involve government-owned companies. In the private sector, fact finding is usually performed by a board of inquiry.

Free speech: Public Law 101, Section 8 states that "the expressing of any views, argument, or dissemination thereof, whether in written, printed, graphic, or visual form, shall not constitute or be evidence of an unfair labor practice under any provisions of this Act, if such expression contains no threat of reprisal or force or promise of benefit."

Grievance: A perception on the part of a union member that management has failed in some way to meet the terms of the labor agreement.

Lockout: A lockout consists of closing a place of business by management in the course of a labor dispute for the purpose of forcing employees to accept management terms.

National Labor Relations Board: A labor board formed to implement the Wagner Act. Its two major functions are to 1) determine who should be the official bargaining unit when a new unit is formed and who should be in the unit and 2) adjudicate unfair labor charges.

Professionals: Professionals have the right to be represented by a union but cannot belong to a union that represents nonprofessionals unless a majority of them vote for inclusion in the nonprofessional unit.

Strike: A strike is a concerted withholding of labor supply to bring about economic pressure on employers and cause them to grant employee demands.

Supervisors: A supervisor is defined as someone who directs the work of others. Supervisors are excluded from protection under the Taft-Hartley Act and cannot be represented by a union.

Union shop: Also called a *closed shop*. All employees are required to join the union and pay dues.

HISTORICAL PERSPECTIVE OF UNIONIZATION IN AMERICA

Unions have been present in America since the 1790s. Skilled craftsmen formed early unions to protect themselves from wage cuts during the highly competitive era of industrialization. An examination of the history of the union movement reveals that union membership and activity increases sharply during high employment and prosperity, and decreases sharply during economic recessions and layoffs (Allen & Keavenly, 1983).

Periodically in this country, employment demand for nurses increases and decreases. High employment of nurses is tied directly to a healthy national economy (Marquis, 1988). When the demand for nurses is high, there is increased union activity. Therefore, using the history of unionization to forecast the future, it can be expected that during the next decade, there will be increased union activity in all nursing employment areas associated with a high demand for nurses and an improvement in the national economy.

However, a dramatic improvement in nurses' perceptions of the quality of their supervision could slow the unionization of nursing. A 1987 poll reveals that overwhelming numbers of nurses feel management does not listen to them or care about their needs (California Nursing Review, 1987). This discontentment provides a fertile ground for union organizers (Huston & Marquis, 1989). Unions thrive in a climate that perceives the organizational philosophy to be insensitive to the worker.

For many reasons, collective bargaining was slow in coming to the healthcare industry. Until labor laws were amended, unionization of healthcare workers was illegal. Nursing's long history as a service commodity further delayed labor organization in healthcare settings.

Initial collective bargaining in the profession took place in organizations that were deemed government or public. This was made possible by Executive Order 10988, authored in 1962. This order lifted restrictions preventing public employees from organizing. Therefore, collective bargaining by nurses at city, county, and district hospitals and healthcare agencies began in the 1960s.

In 1974, Congress amended the Wagner Act, extending national labor laws to private, nonprofit hospitals, nursing homes, health clinics, health maintenance organizations, and other healthcare institutions. These amendments opened the doors to much union activity for professions and the public employee sector. Indeed, a review of union membership figures readily shows that since 1960, most collective bargaining activity in the United States has occurred in the public and professional sectors of industry. There has been little growth of unionization in the private and blue-collar sectors since membership peaked in the 1950s. Table 17.1 outlines legislation that affected the union movement.

TABLE 17.1 Labor Legislation

Year	Legislation	Effect
1935	National Labor Act/ Wagner Act	Gave unions many rights in organizing; resulted in rapid union growth
1947	The Taft-Hartley Amendment	Returned some power to management; resulted in a more equal balance of power between unions and management
1962	Kennedy Executive Order 10988	Amended the 1935 Wagner Act to allow public employees to join unions
1974	Amendments to the Wagner Act	Allowed nonprofit organizations to join unions

From 1962 through 1989, there were slow but steady increases in the numbers of nurses represented by collective bargaining agents. In 1989, the National Labor Relations Board (NLRB) ruled that nurses could form their own separate bargaining units, and union activity increased (O'Connor, 1994). However, the American Hospital Association immediately sued the American Nurses Association (ANA), and the ruling was halted until the 1991 Supreme Court upheld the 1989 decision by the NLRB (*American Journal of Nursing*, 1991). Although union membership has increased since that time, only approximately 280,000 of the nation's nurses are represented by a collective bargaining agent; 150,000 by the ANA and 130,000 by other unions (Foley, 1993).

However, the increase in nursing union membership is significant when measured against the steady decline in blue-collar unionization (O'Connor, 1994). This consistent increase in union membership also is seen in other professions, most notably among faculty at institutions of higher education, teachers at primary and secondary levels, and physicians.

It is unclear at this time how the 1994 Supreme Court decision expanding the definition of "supervisor" will affect unionization in nursing. Prior to this decision, the NLRB definition of a supervisor required that they be in a capacity to hire, fire, determine pay raises, and the like. The new ruling defines a supervisor of nursing personnel as one who directs the work of others, such as nurses' aides. Because nurses classified as supervisors are excluded from joining a union and most nurses supervise the work of others, it could have a significant impact on union activity (Littler, Mendelson, Fastiff, Tichy, & Mathiason, 1994).

Various unions represent nurses and other healthcare workers. The following major organizations, listed in the order of those representing the largest number to the least number of nursing members, are collective bargaining agents for nurses: 1) ANA; 2) National Union of Hospital and Health Care Employees of Retail, Wholesale and Department Store Union, American Federation of Labor-Congress of Industrial Organizations (AFL-CIO); 3) Service Employees International Union, AFL-CIO; 4) American Federation of Government Employees, AFL-CIO; 5) American Federation of State, County, and Municipal Employees, AFL-CIO; and 6) American Federation of Teachers, AFL-CIO (Flanagan, 1984; Foley, 1993).

American Nurses Association and Collective Bargaining

One difficult issue faced by nurse-managers, not typically encountered in other disciplines, stems from the dual role of their professional organization, the ANA. This same organization at most state levels is recognized by the NLRB as a collective bargaining agent. The ANA represents more than 50% of union membership at healthcare organization bargaining tables.

The use of state associations as bargaining agents has been a divisive issue among American nurses. Some nurse-managers feel they have been disenfranchised by their professional organization. For many other members of the nursing profession, this issue presents no conflict. Regardless of individual values, there does appear to be some conflict in loyalty. Sullivan and Decker (1988) pose the question, "How can a manager, who is charged with the administration of the union contract, also belong to the same organization that serves as the bargaining agent for subordinates?" However, Rabban (1991) believes that unionization and professionalism are compatible when professional values are part of the bargaining agreement. There are no easy solutions to the dilemma created by the dual role held by the ANA. Clarifying these issues begins with the manager examining the motivation of nurses to participate in collective bargaining. The manager must at least try to hear and understand employees' points of view.

> ### ▶ LEARNING EXERCISE 17.1
>
> How do you feel about the American Nurses Association's (ANA's) certification as a collective bargaining agent? Do you belong to the state student nurses association? Do you plan to join your state ANA? Divide into two groups to debate the pros and cons of having the ANA, rather than other unions, represent nurses.

Motivation to Join or Reject Unions

Knowing that human behavior is goal directed, it is important to examine what personal goals union membership fulfills. Nurse-managers often tell each other that healthcare institutions differ from other types of industrial organizations. This is really a myth because most nurses work in large and impersonal organizations. The nurse frequently feels powerless and vulnerable as an individual alone in a complex institution. Therefore, five primary motivations for joining a union exist; the first is to *increase the power of the individual.* Employees know that singularly they are essentially dispensable. Because a large group of employees is much less dispensable, nurses greatly increase their bargaining power and reduce their vulnerability by joining a union. This is a particular strong motivating force for nurses when jobs are scarce and they feel vulnerable.

When there are nursing shortages, nurses feel less vulnerable, and other reasons to join unions become motivating factors. One motivator driving nurses in the 1990s toward unionization might be *to communicate their aims, feelings, complaints, and ideas to others.* Beach (1980) maintains that the need to make the organization listen is often a reason people join unions.

Because unions emphasize equality and fairness, nurses also join them because they need to *eliminate discrimination and favoritism.* This might be an especially strong motivator in groups that have experienced discrimination, such as women and minorities.

Many social factors also act as motivators to nurses regarding union activity. The fourth motivation for joining a union stems from the *social need to be accepted.* Sometimes this social need results from family or peer pressure. Because many working class families have a long history of strong union ties, children are frequently raised in a cultural milieu that promotes unionization.

Finally, nurses sometimes join unions because *the union contract dictates that all nurses belong to the union.* This has been a big driving force among blue-collar workers. However, the *closed shop,* or requirement that all employees belong to a union, has never prevailed in the healthcare industry. Most healthcare unions have *open shops,* allowing nurses to choose if they want to join the union.

Just as there are many reasons to join unions, there also are at least five reasons nurses reject unions. Perhaps the strongest are *societal and cultural factors.* Many people distrust unions; they feel they promote the welfare state and oppose the American system of free enterprise. Other reasons for rejecting unions might be one of five needs; the first is *a need to demonstrate that they can get ahead on their own merits.*

Professional employees have been slow in forming unions for several reasons that deal with class and education; they argue that unions were appropriate for the blue-collar worker but not for the university professor, physician, or engineer. Nurses rejecting unions on this basis usually are driven by *a need to demonstrate their individualism and social status.*

Beach (1980) states that many employees identify with management and thus frequently adopt its viewpoint toward unions. Such nurses, therefore, would reject unions because *their values more closely align with management than with workers.*

Although employees are protected under the National Labor Relations Act, many reject unions because of fears of employer reprisal. Nurses who reject unions on this basis could be said to be motivated most of all by *a need to keep their job.*

▶ LEARNING EXERCISE 17.2

List the reasons you would or would not join a union. Share this with others in your group, and examine the following questions. Would you feel differently about unions if you were a manager? What influences you the most in your desire to join or reject unions? Have you ever felt discriminated against or powerless in the workplace?

Once managers understand the drives and needs behind joining unions, they can begin to address those needs. It is certainly within managerial power to meet the first three needs for joining unions. Managers can encourage feelings of power by allowing subordinates' input into decisions that will affect their work. Managers also can listen to ideas, complaints, and feelings and take steps to ensure that favoritism and discrimination are not part of their management style. Additionally, the manager can strengthen the drives and needs that make nurses reject unions. By building a team effort, sharing ideas and future plans from upper management with the staff, and encouraging individualism in employees, the manager can facilitate identification of the worker with management.

Organizations with unfair management policies are more likely to become unionized. Leaders must be alert to employment practices that are unfair or insensitive to employee needs and must intervene appropriately before such issues lead to unionization. However, organizations offering liberal benefit packages and fair management practices may still experience union activity if certain social and cultural factors are present. If union activity does occur, managers must be aware of specific employee and management rights so the National Labor Relations Act is not violated by either managers or their employees.

Managers' Role During Union Organizing

Because of the healthcare industry's surge toward unionization, most nurses will probably be involved with unions in some manner during their careers. Managers who are not employed in a unionized healthcare organization should anticipate that one or more unions will attempt to organize nurses within the next few years. Display 17.3 shows a list of practices that the organization should have established *prior* to union activity. If the organization waits until the union arrives, it will be too late to perform these functions.

Employees have a right to participate in union organizing, and managers must not interfere with this right (Foley, 1993). However, if the astute manager picks up early clues of union activity, the organization may be able to take steps that will discourage unionization of its employees.

The first step in establishing a union is demonstrating an adequate level of desire for unionization by the employees. This usually involves at least 30% of employees signing cards requesting that an election for unionization be held. After a designated number of cards have been generated, the organization is forced to have an election. At that time, all employees of the same classification, such as registered nurses, would vote on whether they desired unionization. A choice in every such election is "no representation," which means that the voters do not want a union. The majority of employees must desire a union before unionization takes place.

Managers should never independently attempt to deal with union organizing activity. They should always seek assistance and guidance from higher level management and the personnel department.

The entire list of rights for management and labor during the organizing and

---

Display 17.3 Before the Union Comes

1. Know and care about your employees.
2. Establish fair and well-communicated personnel policies.
3. Use an effective upward and downward system of communication.
4. Ensure that all managers are well trained and effective.
5. Establish a well-developed formal procedure for handling employee grievances.
6. Have a competitive compensation program of wages and benefits.
7. Have an effective performance appraisal system in place.
8. Use a fair and well-communicated system for promotions and transfers.
9. Use organizational actions to indicate that job security is based on job performance, adherence to rules and regulations, and availability of work.
10. Have an administrative policy on unionization.

establishment phases of unionization is beyond the scope of this book. Throughout the years, Congress has amended various labor acts and laws so that power is balanced between management and labor. At times, the balance of power has shifted to management or labor, but Congress wisely eventually enacts laws that restore the balance. The manager must ensure that the rights of management and employees are protected. The two most sensitive areas of any union contract, once wages have been agreed on, are discipline and the grievance process, which are discussed in Unit 6.

Effective Labor-Management Relations

Before the 1950s, labor-management relations were turbulent. History books are filled with battles, strikes, mass-picketing scenes, and brutal treatment by management and employees. In the last 30 years, employers and unions have substantially improved their relationships. Although evidence is growing that contemporary management has come to accept the reality that unions are here to stay, businesses in the United States are still less comfortable with unions than their counterparts in many other countries. Likewise, unions have come to accept the fact that there are times when organizations are not healthy enough to survive aggressive union demands.

Once management is faced with dealing with a bargaining agent, it has a choice of either accepting or opposing the union. It may actively oppose the union by using various *union busting* techniques, or it may more subtly oppose the union by attempting to discredit it and win employee trust. Acceptance also may run along a continuum. The company may accept the union with reluctance and suspicion. Although they know the union has legitimate rights, managers often feel they must continually guard against the union encroaching further into traditional management territory.

There also is the type of union acceptance that Beach (1980) labels *accommodation*. Increasingly common, accommodation is characterized by management's complete acceptance of the union, with both union and management showing mutual respect. When these conditions exist, labor and management can establish mutual goals, especially in the areas of safety, cost reduction, efficiency, eliminating waste, and improving working conditions. Porter-O'Grady (1992) feels that this type of relationship has begun to be evidenced between unionized professional nurses and healthcare organizations and refers to this more cooperative interaction as a new model of collective relationship. Such cooperation represents the most mature and advanced type of labor-management relations.

The attitudes and the philosophies of the leaders in management and the union determine what type of relationship develops between the two parties in any given organization. When dealing with unions, managers must be flexible. It is critical that they do not ignore issues or try to overwhelm others with power. The rational approach to problem solving must be used.

Unionization of the healthcare industry will undoubtedly expand. It is important to learn how to deal with this potential constraint to effective management. Managers must learn to work with unions and develop the art of using unions to assist the organization in building a team effort to meet organizational goals.

LEARNING EXERCISE 17.3

You are a staff nurse in the intensive care unit in one of your city's two hospitals. You have worked at this hospital for 5 years, transferring to the intensive care unit 2 years ago. You love nursing but are sometimes frustrated in your job due to a short supply of nurses, excessive overtime demands, and the stress of working with such critically ill patients.

The hospital has a closed shop, so union dues are deducted from your pay even though you are not actively involved in the union. The present union contract is up for renegotiation, and union and management have not been able to agree on many issues. When management made its last offer, the new contract was rejected by the nurses. Now that the old contract has expired, nurses are free to strike if they vote to do so.

You had voted for accepting the management offer; you have two children to support, and it would be devastating to be without work for a long time. Last night, the nurses voted on whether to return to the bargaining table and try to renegotiate with management or to go out on strike

Again, you voted for no strike. You have just heard from your friend that the strike vote won. Now you must decide if you are going to support your striking colleagues or cross the picket line and return to work tomorrow. Your friends are pressuring you to support their cause. You know that the union will provide some financial compensation during the strike but feel it won't be adequate for you to support yourself and your children.

You agree with union assertions that the organization has overworked and underpaid you and that it has been generally unresponsive to nursing needs. On the other hand, you feel your first obligation is to your children.

Assignment: List all the reasons for and against striking. Decide what you will do. Use appropriate rationale from outside readings to support your final decision. Share your thoughts with the class. Take a vote in class to determine how many would strike and how many would cross the picket line.

EMPLOYMENT LEGISLATION

Like unionization, the many legal issues involved in hiring and employment impact the directing function. These potential constraints are present regardless of the presence of unions. The American industrial relations system is regarded as one of the most legalistic in the western world, and it continues to grow. Few aspects of the employment relationship are free from regulation by either state or federal law (Haimann, 1994). Many of these regulations relate to specific aspects of personnel management, such as the laws that deal with collective bargaining or the equal employment laws that regulate hiring. Some personnel regulations are discussed in previous chapters, and others are discussed later.

Some observers believe that employment and labor-management laws have become so prescriptive that they preclude experimentation and creativity on the part of management. Others believe that like collective bargaining, the proliferation of employment laws must be viewed from a historical standpoint to understand their need (Beach, 1980). Regardless of whether one feels such laws and regulations are necessary, they are a fact of each manager's life.

Being able to handle management's legal requirements effectively requires a comprehension of labor laws and their interpretation. The leader that embraces the intent of laws barring discrimination and providing equal opportunity becomes a role model for fairness. The feeling that the employer is fair to all will set the stage for the type of team building so important in effective management.

Employment laws, summarized in Table 17.2, fall into one of five categories:

1. *Labor standards.* These laws establish minimum standards for working conditions regardless of the presence or absence of a union contract. Included in this set are minimum wage, health and safety, and equal pay laws.
2. *Labor relations.* These laws relate to the rights and duties of unions and employers in their relationship with each other.
3. *Equal employment.* The laws that deal with employment discrimination are introduced in Chapter 10.
4. *Civil and criminal laws.* These are statutory and judicial laws that prescribe certain kinds of conduct and establish penalties.
5. *Other legislation.* Nursing managers have some legal responsibilities that do not generally apply to industrial managers. For instance, licensed personnel are required to have a current, valid license from the state in which they practice. Additionally, most states require that employers of nurses report certain types of substance abuse to the state licensing boards.

Labor Standards

Labor standards are regulations dealing with the conditions of the employee's work, including physical conditions, financial aspects, and the amount of hours worked. State and federal legislation often overlap; as a general rule, the employer must abide by the stricter of the two regulations. The following are the major labor standards.

Minimum Wages and Maximum Hours

More than 85% of all nonsupervisory employees are now covered by the Fair Labor Standards Act (FLSA). This law was first enacted by Congress in 1938 and estab-

TABLE 17.2   Employment and Labor Laws

Title of Legislation	Regulation
Fair Labor Standards Act (1938); has been amended many times since 1938	Sets minimum wage and maximum hours that can be worked before overtime is paid
Civil Rights Act of 1964	Sets equal employment practices
Executive Order 11246 (1965) and Executive Order 11375 (1967)	Sets affirmative action guidelines
Age Discrimination Act (1967) and 1978 amendment	Protects against forced retirement
Rehabilitation Act (1973)	Protects the handicapped
Vietnam Veterans Act (1973/1974)	Provides reemployment rights

lished an hourly minimum wage at that time of 25 cents. Since then, the law has been amended numerous times.

It is often said that in addition to putting a "floor under wages," the FLSA also puts a "ceiling over hours." The latter statement, however, is not quite accurate. The FLSA sets a maximum number of hours in any week beyond which a person may be employed *only if he or she is paid an overtime rate*. Some states have enacted a law that makes an exception to this weekly rule on overtime. The exception is an 80-hour 2-week pay period ceiling, after which the employee must receive overtime pay. Overtime pay can be significant, so it is imperative that managers know which standard their organization is using.

Hours worked includes all the time the employee is required to be on duty. Therefore, mandatory classes, orientation, conferences, and so on must be recorded as duty time and are subject to the overtime rules. The FLSA does not require time clocks but does require that some record be maintained of hours worked.

The FLSA also regulates the minimum amount of overtime pay, which is at least one and one-half times the basic rate. When state and federal laws differ on when overtime pay begins, the stricter rule usually applies. Some union contracts also have stricter overtime pay agreements than the FLSA.

Federal labor laws exempt certain employees from the minimum wage and overtime pay requirements. Executive employees, administrative employees, and professional employees are the three most notable white-collar exemptions. The functions of the position, rather than the title or the fact that employees are paid a monthly wage, differentiate an exempt employee. Certain students, apprentice learners, and other special circumstances also may qualify an employee for an exemption to FLSA regulations. The personnel department in any large organization is especially helpful to the manager in implementing these labor laws. Managers, however, should have a general understanding of how these laws restrict staffing and scheduling policies.

The Equal Pay Act of 1963 requires that men and women performing equal work receive equal compensation. Four equal pay tests exist: equal skill, equal effort, equal responsibility, and similar working conditions. This law had a great impact on nursing management when it was enacted. Before 1963, male "orderlies" were routinely paid a higher wage than female "aides" performing identical duties. Although this fact seems incredible today, at the time, many managers condoned this widespread practice of blatant wage discrimination. Most healthcare agencies now call

---

► **LEARNING EXERCISE 17.4**

Until the 1950s, most healthcare organizations did not require that employees use a time clock when arriving at or leaving work for meal breaks. Now time clocks are the norm for hospitals and some other, but not all, healthcare organizations.

Survey several community hospitals, clinics, and other organizations that employ nurses. How many of them require nurses to use time clocks? How do you feel about professionals being required to punch in and out for meal breaks? Discuss this issue in class and with nurses that you know.

these employees "nursing assistants," whether they are male or female, and all are paid the same wage.

However, Havens and Mills (1994) report that there continues to be pay inequity for nurses compared with other similar professions requiring similar skills and responsibilities.

Labor-Management Relations Laws

In addition to laws regarding collective bargaining, the manager needs to be aware of one section of the Wagner Act (1935) and the Taft-Hartley Amendment (1947), that deal with unfair labor practices by employers and unions.

The original Wagner Act listed and prohibited five unfair labor practices:

1. To interfere with, restrain, or coerce employees in a manner that interfered with their rights as outlined under the Act. Examples of these activities are spying on union gatherings, threatening employees with job loss, or threatening to close down a company if the union organizes.
2. To interfere with the formation of any labor organization or to give financial assistance to a labor organization. This provision was included to prohibit "employee representation plans" that were primarily controlled by management.
3. To discriminate with regard to hiring, tenure, and so on to discourage union membership
4. To discharge or discriminate against an employee who filed charges or testified before the NLRB
5. To refuse to bargain in good faith

The original Wagner Act gave so much power to the unions that it was necessary in 1947 to pass additional federal legislation to restore a balance of power to labor-management relations.

The Taft-Hartley Amendment retained the provisions under the Wagner Act that guaranteed employees the right to collective bargaining. However, the Taft-Hartley Amendment added the provision that employees have the right to *refrain* from taking part in unions. In addition to that provision, the Taft-Hartley Amendment added and prohibited the following six unfair labor practices of unions:

1. Requiring a self-employed individual or an employer to join a union
2. Forcing an employer to cease doing business with another person. This placed a ban on secondary boycotts, which were then prevalent in unions.
3. Forcing an employer to bargain with one union when another union has already been certified as the bargaining agent
4. Forcing the employer to assign certain work to members of one union rather than another
5. Charging excessive or discriminatory initiation fees
6. Causing or attempting to cause an employer to pay for unnecessary services. This prohibited *featherbedding,* a term used to describe union practices that prevented the displacement of workers due to advances in technology.

Equal Employment Opportunity Laws

Under the American free enterprise system, employers have historically been able to hire whomever they desired. Today the transplanted employer of the 1920s might be shocked to see that racial and ethnic minorities, women, the elderly, and the handicapped have acquired substantial rights in the workplace. The first legislation in the area of employment hiring practices resulted from years of discrimination toward minorities. More recent legislation has been aimed at eliminating discrimination that occurs because of sex, age, and physical impairment.

Equal employment opportunities have fostered many profound changes in the American workplace. Women, minorities, and the handicapped have been very successful in jobs previously denied to them. Beach (1980) states that if the government had not applied pressure through legislation to increase employment opportunities for these groups, it is highly unlikely that such change would have occurred. He suggests, however, that such legislative protection may result in a type of reverse discrimination and that this problem may never be solved to the satisfaction of all involved parties.

The manager should be familiar with the following five Equal Employment Opportunity (EEO) laws.

Civil Rights Act of 1964

This act laid the foundation for equal employment in the United States. The thrust of Title VII of the civil rights act is twofold: It prohibits discrimination based on factors unrelated to job qualifications, and it promotes employment based on ability and merit. The areas of discrimination specifically mentioned are race, color, religion, sex, and national origin. This act was strengthened by President Lyndon Johnson's Executive Order 11246 in 1965 and his Executive Order 11375 in 1967.

The executive orders sought to correct past injustices. Because the government felt that some groups had a long history of being discriminated against, it wanted to build in a mechanism that would assist those groups in "catching up" with the rest of the American work force. Therefore, they created an affirmative action component. Affirmative action plans are not specifically required by law but may be required by court order. In most states, affirmative action plans are voluntary unless government contracts are involved. Many organizations, however, have voluntarily put an affirmative action plan in place.

Affirmative action differs from equal opportunity. The EEO legislation is aimed at preventing discrimination. Affirmative action plans are aimed at *actively seeking* to fill job vacancies with groups who are underemployed, such as women, minorities, and the handicapped.

The Equal Employment Opportunity Commission (EEOC) is responsible for enforcing Title VII of the Civil Rights Act. The investigatory responsibility of the EEOC is broad. When it finds that a charge of discrimination is justified, the agency attempts to reach an agreement through persuasion and conciliation. When the EEOC is unable to reach an agreement, it has the power to bring civil action against the employer. When discrimination is found, the courts will order restoration of rightful economic status; this means that the employer may be ordered to restore back-pay for up to 2 years. In healthcare organizations, when discrimination was found (such as unequal pay for men and women in nursing assistant jobs), financial awards in class actions suits have been extraordinarily high. Managers must be alert for any such discriminatory practices. Some states have fair employment legislation that is more strict than the federal act. Again, the stricter regulations always apply.

Age Discrimination and Employment Act

Enacted by Congress in 1967, the Age Discrimination and Employment Act's (ADEA) purpose was to promote employment of older people based on their ability rather than age. In early 1978, the ADEA was amended to increase the protected age to 70. In 1987, Congress voted to remove even this age restriction except in certain job categories. Although many have been alarmed by the removal of mandatory age retirements, statistics show that the trend is toward earlier retirement (Ross, 1978). However, reversal of this trend may have serious consequences for some organizations. In particular, it could have a significant impact on organizations that are labor intensive, especially if those labor-intensive organizations also have demanding physical requirements, such as in nursing.

LEGISLATION AFFECTING AMERICANS WITH DISABILITIES

The Rehabilitation Act of 1973 required all employers with government contracts of more than $25,000 to take affirmative action to recruit, hire, and advance handicapped people who are qualified. Similar but less aggressive affirmative action steps

---

▶ LEARNING EXERCISE 17.5

You are the manager of a well-baby newborn nursery. Among your staff is a 69-year-old practical nurse, Mary Jones, who has worked for the hospitals for 30 years. No mandatory retirement age exists. This has not been a problem in the past, but Mary's general health is now making this a problem for your unit.

Mary has grown physically fragile. Cataracts have made her vision poor, and she suffers from hypertension. Last month, she began to prepare a little girl for circumcision because she did not read the arm band properly.

Your staff has become increasingly upset over Mary's inability to fulfill her job duties. The physicians, however, support Mary and found the circumcision incident humorous. Last week you requested that Mary have a physical examination, at hospital expense, to determine her physical ability to continue working.

You were not particularly surprised when she returned with medical approval. Her physician spoke very sharply with you, and although he admitted privately that Mary's health was rapidly failing, he told you that working was her only reason for living. He left you with these words: "Force Mary to retire, and she will die within the year."

Assignment: Using your knowledge of age discrimination, patient safety, employee rights, and management responsibilities, decide an appropriate course of action for this case. Be creative and think beyond the obvious. Be able to support your decisions.

were required for other companies doing business with the federal government, with specific requirements depending on the size of the company and the dollar amount of the contract. The Department of Labor was charged with enforcement of this act. Although initially there was very slow progress in getting companies to hire the handicapped, steady progress has been made. In 1990, Congress passed the Americans with Disabilities Act to eliminate discrimination against Americans with physical or mental disabilities in the workplace and in social life. Disability is defined as "any physical or mental impairment that limits any major life activity." This includes individuals with obvious physical disabilities, but also individuals with cancer, diabetes, human immunodeficiency virus, acquired immunodeficiency syndrome, and recovering alcoholics and drug users. The act not only prohibits discrimination, but also delineates clear, enforceable standards (Aiken & Catalano, 1994).

THE VIETNAM ERA VETERANS READJUSTMENT ASSISTANCE ACT

This act provides re-employment rights and privileges for veterans to positions they held prior to their entry in the armed forces. This act was used by some nurses during the nursing surplus following the Persian Gulf war to gain reemployment following military service.

OTHER LEGISLATION AFFECTING HUMAN RESOURCE MANAGEMENT

The manager needs to be especially cognizant of legislation imposed by the Occupational Health and Safety Act (OSHA) and state health licensing boards.

Occupational Safety and Health Act

This broadly written legislation speaks to the employer's requirements to provide a place of employment that is free from recognized hazards that may cause physical harm. The Department of Labor enforces this act. Because it is impossible for the Department of Labor to inspect physically all facilities, most inspections are brought about by employee complaint or employer request. The act allows fines to be levied if employers continue with unsafe conditions.

Since OSHA's inception, many companies have vehemently criticized the act, specifically its administration. Companies also have charged that the cost of meeting OSHA standards has excessively burdened American business.

On the other hand, unions have asserted that the federal government has never staffed or funded the Occupational and Health Administration adequately. They have charged that OSHA has been negligent in setting standards for toxic substances, carcinogens, and other disease-producing agents. This view is supported in the report of the Comptroller General of the United States (1977), which states that 390,000 new cases of occupational disease occur each year and that 100,000 people die because of these diseases.

Because the risk of discovery and the fine if found guilty are both low, employers often choose to ignore unsafe working conditions. Nurse-managers are in a unique position to call attention to hazardous conditions in the workplace and should communicate such concerns to higher authority. Evra (1992) believes that nurses are exposed to four types of hazards: biological, chemical, physical, and psychological. Public health scientists have estimated that 80% of all cancers stem from exposure to environmental factors (Ashford, 1976).

The current controversy regarding safety issues concerns the cost and effectiveness of universal precautions and hepatitis B vaccine immunizations. McPherson and Jackson (1994) report that although the cost of safety precautions is high (estimated by OSHA to be $322 million annually for U.S. hospitals), they ask, "What kind of price tag does an agency put on disease prevention when measured against the bottom line?"

Most states also have occupational and safety regulations. Again, the employer must comply with the more stringent regulations. Many of the state licensing boards have additional health regulations that differ from the federal regulations.

State Health Facilities Licensing Boards

In addition to health and safety requirements, many state boards have regulations regarding staffing requirements. It is the ultimate responsibility of top-level management to maintain the state license to operate. However, all managers are responsible for knowing and meeting the regulations that apply to their unit or department. For example, if the manager of an intensive care unit has a state staffing level that mandates 12 hours of nursing care per patient per day and requires that the ratio of registered nurses to other staff be 2:1, then the supervisor is obligated to staff at that level or greater. If, during times of short staffing, supervisors are unable to meet this level of staffing, they must apprise upper-level management so that there can be joint resolution.

The variation in state licensing requirements makes a lengthy discussion of them inappropriate for this book. However, managers must be knowledgeable about state licensing regulations that pertain to their level of supervision.

INTEGRATING LEADERSHIP SKILLS AND MANAGEMENT FUNCTIONS IN WORKING WITH UNIONS AND EMPLOYMENT LAWS

Unionization and legal constraints will seem less burdensome if managers remember that both primarily protect the rights of patients and employees. If managers perform their jobs well and work for organizations that desire to "do the right thing" by accepting their social responsibility, then managers need not fear unionization and legal constraints.

If the organization is nonunionized, the manager must use the leadership roles of communication, fairness, and shared decision making to ensure that employees do not feel unionization is necessary. The integrated leader/manager is a role model for fairness, knows unit employees well, and sincerely seeks to meet their needs.

When making decisions that deal with unions and employment legislation, the effective leader/manager always seeks to do what is just. Additionally, he or she seeks appropriate assistance before finalizing decisions that involve sensitive legal or contract issues. By incorporating the leadership role, the manager becomes fairer in personnel management. There is increased self-awareness and an understanding of an individual's need to seek unionization and of the necessity for employment legislation.

The effective manager maintains required staffing and ensures a safe working environment. Rights of the organization and the employee are protected as the manager uses personnel policies in a nondiscriminatory and consistent manner. The emphasis is on flexibility and accommodation of employment legislation and union contracts.

KEY CONCEPTS

▼ Historically, union activity is greater during labor shortages and economic upswings.
▼ The *ANA* acts as the *collective bargaining agent* for the largest number of nurses.
▼ Individuals are motivated to join or reject unions as a result of many needs and values.
▼ The middle-level manager has the greatest influence on preventing unionization in a nonunion organization.
▼ Managers have a very important role in establishing and maintaining effective management-labor relationships.
▼ It is possible to create a climate in which labor and management can work together to accomplish mutual goals.
▼ Many state and federal laws and regulations influence how employees are managed.
▼ Much of the human rights legislation concerning employment practices resulted because of documented *discrimination* in the workplace.
▼ Although some legislation makes the job of managing people more difficult for managers, it has resulted in increased job fairness and opportunities for women, minorities, the elderly, and the disabled.
▼ *Affirmative action* differs from *equal opportunity* in that the former seeks to correct past injustices, while the latter prevents current discrimination.
▼ The middle-level manager is in a good position to detect health hazards in the workplace.
▼ Nursing managers have additional areas of potential liability that are not found in all management roles because of the responsibilities that arise from their accountability for licensing and staffing requirements.

◤ ADDITIONAL LEARNING EXERCISES

Learning Exercise 17.6

Many employment laws generate emotion. Usually individuals feel strongly on at least one of these issues.

Select one of the following employment laws, and write a 250-word essay on why you support or disapprove of the law. Choose from the Equal Pay Act of 1963, equal opportunity laws, affirmative action, or age discrimination.

Learning Exercise 17.7
(Adapted from Marquis & Huston, 1994.)

At your hospital, it is a policy that licensed employees have a current valid license. This is in keeping with the state licensing code. It is always difficult to get people to bring their license in to verify its currency.

You have just come from a meeting with the director. He reminded you that you must not have people performing duties that require a license if the license has expired. You decide to issue a memo stating that you will hold payroll checks on all employees who have not verified their licenses with you.

Following this, all the LVNs/LPNs brought their licenses in for verification. However, one of the LVNs/LPNs has an expired date on her license. When she is questioned, she admits that she did not mail her payment for relicensure until after she had read your memo. She was hoping to delay showing her license. She was in a financial crisis and that is why she had delayed payment. You call the licensing board, and they state that it will be 6 weeks before the employee will receive her license. They *will not* verify her active license status over the telephone.

You consider the following facts. It is illegal to perform duties requiring a license without one. The LVN/LPN had prior knowledge of the licensing laws and hospital policy. The LVN/LPN has been a good employee with no record of prior disciplinary action.

Assignment: Decide what you should do. What alternatives do you have? Provide rationale for your decision.

Learning Exercise 17.8
(From Marquis & Huston, 1994.)

Betty Smith, a unit clerk, has come to see you, the nurse manager of the medical unit, to complain of flagrant discriminatory practices against female employees of University General Hospital. She alleges that women are denied promotional and training opportunities comparable to those made available to men.

She shows you a petition with 35 signatures supporting her allegations. Ms. Smith has threatened to forward this petition to the administrator of the hospital, the press, and the Department of Labor unless corrective action is taken at once. Being a woman yourself, you have some sympathy for Ms. Smith's complaint. However, you feel overall that employees at University General are treated fairly regardless of their sex.

Ms. Smith, a fairly good employee, has worked on your unit for 4 years. However, she has been creating problems lately. She has been reprimanded for taking too much time for coffee breaks. Personnel evaluations that recommend pay raises and promotions are due next week.

Assignment: How should you handle this problem? Is the personnel evaluation an appropriate time to address the petition? Outline your plan, and give your rationale.

REFERENCES:

Aiken, T. D., & Catalano, J. T. (1994). *Legal, ethical and political issues in nursing.* Philadelphia: F.A. Davis.

Allen, R. E., & Keavenly, T. J. (1983). *Contemporary labor relations.* Reading, MA: Addison-Wesley.

American Journal of Nursing (1989). *American Nurses Association News, 89*(9), 1223–1231.

(1991). Supreme Court hears debate on all RN units Association News. *American Journal of Nursing, 91*(5).

Ashford, N. A. (1976). *Crisis in the workplace: Occupational disease and injury.* Cambridge, MA. MIT Press.

Beach, D. (1980). *Personnel.* New York: Macmillan.

(1987). Job satisfaction: What nurses have to say. *California Nursing Review, 9*(4).

Comptroller General of the United States (1977). *Delays in setting workplace standards for cancer causing and other dangerous substances.* Washington D.C.: General Accounting Office.

Evra, G. (1992). Nurses in the OR. *Revolution, 2*(2), 64–66.

Flanagan, L. (1984). *Collective bargaining and the nursing profession.* Kansas City, MO: American Nurses Association.

Foley, M. E. (1993). The politics of collective bargaining. In D. J. Mason, S. W. Talbot, & J. K. Leavitt (Eds.), *Policy and politics for nursing* (2nd ed.), Philadelphia: W.B. Saunders.

Haimann, T. (1994). *Supervisory management* (5th ed.). St. Louis: W.C. Brown.

Havens, D. S., & Mills, M. E. (1994). Are nurses getting what they are worth? In J. McCloskey &

H. K. Grace (Eds). *Current issues in nursing* (4th ed.). St Louis: C.V. Mosby.

Huston, C. J., & Marquis, B. L. (1989). *Retention and productivity strategies for nurse managers.* Philadelphia: J.B. Lippincott.

Littler, Mendelson, Fastiff, Tichy & Mathiason (1994). *Health care labor report,* July.

Marquis, B. L. (1988). Attrition: The effectiveness of retention activities. *The Journal of Nursing Administration, 18*(8), 25–29.

Marquis, B. L., & Huston, C. J. (1994). *Management decision making for nurses: 118 Case studies* (2nd ed.). Philadelphia: J.B. Lippincott.

McPherson, D. C., & Jackson, M. M. (1994). The costs of safety precautions to reduce risk of exposure to bloodborne pathogens. In J. McCloskey & H. K. Grace (Eds.), *Current issues in nursing* (4th ed.). St Louis: C.V. Mosby.

O'Connor, K. S. (1994). Why are we seeing more unionization? In J. McCloskey & H. K. Grace (Eds.), *Current issues in nursing* (4th ed.). St Louis: C.V. Mosby.

Porter-O'Grady, T. (1992). Of rabbits and turtles: A time of change for unions. *Nursing Economics, 10*(3), 177–182.

Public Law 101 (also known as the Taft-Hartley Amendment). (1947, June 23), 80th Congress.

Rabban, D. (1991). Is unionization compatible with professionalism? *Industrial and Labor Relations Review, 45*(1), 97–110.

Ross, I. (1978). Retirement at seventy: A new trauma for management. *Fortune, 97*(9).

Sullivan, E., & Decker, P. (1988). *Effective management in nursing* (pp. 443–457). Menlo Park, CA: Addison-Wesley.

Wagner Act. 298 U.S.238, 1935.

BIBLIOGRAPHY

Baizer, R. D. (1989). Foreign nurses: Pending legislation may slow immigration procedures. *Nursing Management, 20*(11).

Cela, M. (1989). Management rights unionized hospitals. *Nursing Management, 20*(2), 82–83.

Cohen, A. (1989). The management rights clause in collective bargaining. *Nursing Management, 20*(11).

Cook, A. (1990). Comparable worth: An economic issue. *Nursing Management, 21*(2), 28–30.

Doebbeling, B. N., & Wenzel, R. P. (1990). The direct costs of universal precautions in a teaching hospital. *Journal of American Medical Association, 264,* 2083–2087.

Flarey, D., Yoder, S., & Barabas, M. (1992). Collaboration in labor relations. *Journal of Nursing Administration, 22*(9), 15–21.

Hunter, J. K., Bamberg, D., & Castaglia, P. T. (1986). Job satisfaction: Is collective bargaining the answer? *Nursing Management, 17*(3).

Hoerr, J. (1991). What should unions do? *Harvard Business Review,* May/June, 30–45.

Giovinco, G. (1993). When nurses strike: Ethical conflicts, *Nursing Management, 24*(5), 86–90.

Grelli, A. R. (1994). Nurses who direct aides are supervisors, High court decides. *The Philadelphia Inquirer, May*, 24.

McDonald, D. M. (1995). Labor relations issues. In K. W. Vestal (Ed.), *Nursing management* (2nd ed.). Philadelphia: J.B. Lippincott.

Hepner, J. O., & Zinner, S. E. (1991). Nurses and the new NLRB rules: Implications for health-care management. *Health Progress, 72,* 20–22.

Stickler, K. B. (1990). Union organization will be divisive and costly. *Hospitals, 64*(13), 68–70.

Wilson, N., Hamilton, C. L., & Murphy, E. (1990). Union dynamics in nursing. *Journal of Nursing Administration, 20*(2), 35–39.

UNIT 6

ROLES AND FUNCTIONS IN CONTROLLING

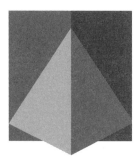

CHAPTER 18

Quality Control

Marriner-Tomey (1992) defines *controlling* as the function of management that involves setting standards, measuring performance against those standards, reporting the results, and taking action. Employees who feel they can influence their environment have some control over their destinies, thus increasing job satisfaction and motivation. Organizations also need some control over productivity, innovation, and quality outcomes. Controlling, then, should not be viewed as a means of determining success or failure but as a way to learn and grow, both personally and professionally.

This unit explores controlling as the fifth and final step in the management process. Because the management process, like the nursing process, is cyclic, controlling is not an end in itself; it is implemented throughout all phases of management. Examples of management controlling functions include the periodic evaluation of unit philosophy, mission, goals, and objectives; the measurement of individual and group performance against preestablished standards; the monitoring of expenses and use of supplies; and the auditing of client goals and outcomes.

Quality control, a specific type of controlling, refers to activities that evaluate, monitor, or regulate services rendered to consumers. In nursing, the goal of quality care would be to ensure quality while meeting intended goals. Quality control, when viewed simplistically, can be broken down into three basic steps:

1. The criterion or standard is determined.
2. Information is collected to determine if the standard has been met.
3. Educational or corrective action is taken if the criterion has not been met.

Bessie L. Marquis and Carol J. Huston:
LEADERSHIP ROLES AND MANAGEMENT FUNCTIONS IN NURSING, 2nd ed.
Lippincott-Raven Publishers © 1996

Although controlling is generally defined as a management function, effective quality control requires the manager to have skill in both leadership and management. Leadership roles and management functions inherent in quality control are delineated in Display 18.1.

To understand quality control, the manager must become familiar with the process and the terminology used in quality assurance. This chapter introduces quality control as a specific and systematic process. Audits are presented as tools to measure quality control. In addition, the historical impact of government reimbursement on the development and implementation of quality control programs in healthcare organizations is discussed. Quality control strategies, such as total quality management (TQM), outcome assessments, and minimum data set, are introduced.

Display 18.1 Leadership Roles and Management Functions in Quality Control

Leadership Roles
1. Encourages followers to be actively involved in the quality control process.
2. Clearly communicates standards of care to subordinates.
3. Encourages the setting of high standards to maximize quality, instead of setting minimum safety standards.
4. Implements quality control proactively instead of reactively.
5. Uses control as a method of determining why goals were not met.
6. Is politically active in communicating quality control findings and their implications to other health professionals and consumers.
7. Acts as a role model for followers in accepting responsibility and accountability for nursing actions.

Management Functions
1. In conjunction with other personnel in the organization, establishes clear-cut, measurable standards of care and determines the most appropriate method for measuring if those standards have been met.
2. Selects and uses process, outcome, and structure audits appropriately as quality control tools.
3. Accesses appropriate sources of information in data gathering for quality control.
4. Determines discrepancies between care provided and unit standards and seeks further information regarding why standards were not met.
5. Uses quality control findings as a measure of employee performance and rewards, coaches, counsels, or disciplines employees accordingly.
6. Keeps abreast of current government and licensing regulations that affect quality control.

QUALITY CONTROL AS A PROCESS

Measuring quantitative data is fairly simple. *Qualitative* data are, however, more elusive, and their measurement is more difficult. Accurate assessment of qualitative data requires managers to use consistently a specific and systematic process. Using a process such as that shown in Figure 18.1 reduces subjectivity and increases the validity and reliability of the measurements.

The first step in Figure 18.1 is the establishment of control criteria or standards. Measuring performance is impossible if standards have not been clearly established. Not only must standards exist, but the leader must see that all subordinates know and understand them. Because standards vary between institutions, employees must know the standard expected of them at their organization. Employees must be aware

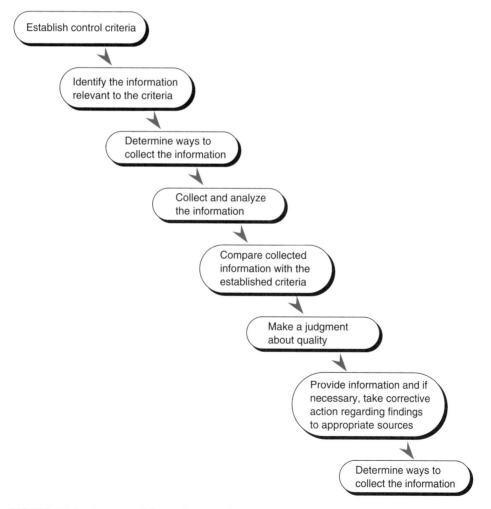

FIGURE 18.1 Steps in auditing quality control.

that their performance will be measured in terms of their ability to meet the established standard. For example, hospital nurses should provide postoperative patient care that meets standards specific to their institution. A nurse's performance can be measured only when it can be compared with a preexisting standard.

The second step in the quality control process includes identifying information relevant to the criteria. What information is needed to measure the criteria? In the example of postoperative patient care, this information might include the frequency of vital signs, dressing checks, and neurological or sensory checks.

The third step is determining ways to collect information. As in all data gathering, the manager must be sure to use all appropriate sources. When assessing quality control of the postoperative patient, the manager could find much of the information in the patient chart. Postoperative flow sheets, the physician orders, and the nursing notes would probably be most helpful. Talking to the patient or nurse also could yield information.

The fourth step in auditing quality control is collecting and analyzing information. For example, if the standards specify that postoperative vital signs are to be checked every 30 minutes for 2 hours and every hour thereafter for 8 hours, it is necessary to look at how often vital signs were taken the first 10 hours after surgery. The frequency of vital signs listed on the postoperative flow sheet are then compared with the standard set by the unit. The resulting discrepancy or congruency gives managers information with which they can make a judgment about the quality or appropriateness of the nursing care. If vital signs were not taken frequently enough to satisfy the standard, the manager would need to obtain further information regarding why the standard was not met and counsel employees as needed. Likewise, the manager should reward employees who provide nursing care that meets or exceeds organizational standards.

In addition to evaluating individual employee performance, quality control provides a tool for evaluating unit goals. If unit goals are consistently unmet, the leader must reexamine those goals and determine if they are inappropriate or unrealistic. There is great danger here that the leader, in a desperate effort to meet unit goals, may lower standards to the point where quality is meaningless. This reinforces the need to determine standards first and then evaluate goals accordingly.

The last step in Figure 18.1 is reevaluation. If quality control is measured on 20 postoperative charts and a high rate of compliance with established standards is found, the need for short-term reevaluation is low. If standards are consistently unmet or met only partially, frequent reevaluation is indicated. Remember that quality control should not be implemented solely as a reaction to a problem. Effective leaders ensure that quality control is proactive by identifying where care can be improved to maximal standards and by eliminating these problems in early stages before productivity or quality is compromised.

THE DEVELOPMENT OF STANDARDS

A *standard* is an predetermined baseline condition or level of excellence that comprises a model to be followed and practiced (Vestal, 1987). They have distinguishing characteristics; they are predetermined, established by an authority, and communicated to and accepted by the individuals affected by the standards. Because standards are used as measurement tools, they must be measurable and achievable (Larson & Lieske, 1992).

Because there is no one set of standards, each organization and profession must set standards and objectives to guide individual practitioners in performing safe and effective care. Standards for practice define the scope and dimensions of professional nursing. Since the 1930s, the American Nurses Association (ANA) has played a key role in developing standards for the profession. In 1973, the ANA Congress established *Standards for Nursing Practice*, which provides a means of determining the quality of nursing that a client receives regardless of whether such services are provided by a professional nurse alone or in conjunction with nonprofessional assistants. During the 1974 to 1975 biennium, ANA prioritized the implementation of the eight standards shown in Display 18.2.

The ANA publications *Standards for Organized Nursing Services, Standards of Nursing Practice,* and *Standards for Organized Nursing Services and Responsibilities of Nurse Administrators Across all Settings* exemplify optimal performance expectations for the nursing profession and have provided a basis for the development of organizational and unit standards nationwide.

Organizational standards outline levels of acceptable practice within the institution itself. For example, each organization develops a policy and procedure manual that outlines its specific standards. These standards may be minimizing or maximizing in terms of the quality of service expected. Standards of practice allow the organization to measure more objectively unit and individual performance. Koontz and Weihrich (1988) have identified the following eight types of standards that most organizations must establish:

1. *Physical standards,* which include patient acuity ratings to establish nursing care hours per patient day
2. *Cost standards,* which include the cost per patient day

Display 18.2 ANA Standards of Nursing Practice (1973)

1. The collection of data about the health status of clients is systematic and continuous. The data are accessible, communicated, and recorded.
2. Nursing diagnoses are derived from health status data.
3. The plan of nursing care includes goals derived from the nursing diagnoses.
4. The plan of nursing care includes priorities and the prescribed nursing approaches or measures to achieve the goals derived from the nursing diagnoses.
5. Nursing actions provide for client participation in health promotion, maintenance, and restoration.
6. Nursing actions help clients to maximize their health capabilities.
7. The client's progress or lack of progress toward goal achievement is determined by the client and the nurse.
8. The client's progress or lack of progress toward goal achievement directs reassessment, reordering of priorities, new goal setting, and a revision of the plan of nursing care.

3. *Capital standards,* which include the review of monetary investments or new programs
4. *Revenue standards,* which include the revenue per patient day for nursing care
5. *Program standards,* which guide the development and implementation of programs to meet client needs
6. *Intangible standards,* which include staff development or personnel orientation costs
7. *Goal standards,* which outline qualitative goals in short- and long-term planning
8. *Strategic plan standards,* which outline checkpoints in developing and implementing the organization's strategic plan

AUDITS AS A QUALITY CONTROL TOOL

Whereas standards provide the yardstick for measuring quality care, audits are measurement tools. An *audit* is a systematic and official examination of a record, process, or account to evaluate performance. Auditing in healthcare organizations provides managers with a means of applying the control process to determine the quality of services rendered. The audits most frequently used in quality control include outcome, process, and structure audits.

Outcome Audit

Naylor, Munro, and Brooten (1991) define outcomes as the "end results of care; the changes in the patient's health status that can be attributed to the delivery of health care services" (p. 210). Outcome audits determine what results, if any, occurred as a result of specific nursing interventions for clients. These audits assume the outcome accurately demonstrates the quality of care that was provided. Outcome *standards* are defined in terms of what the patient will know, do, express, or experience and reflect nursing goals for physiological, emotional, and mental well-being (Vestal, 1987). Many experts consider outcome measures to be the most valid indicators of quality care, but until recently evaluations of hospital care have focused on structure and process (Naylor, et al., 1991).

Examples of outcomes traditionally used to measure quality of hospital care include mortality, morbidity, and length of hospital stay. Naylor et al. (1991) suggest that outcome measures more clearly influenced by nursing could include functional status, mental status, stress levels, satisfaction with care, burden of care on families, and cost of care.

The Joint Commission for Accreditation of Healthcare Organizations (JCAHO) uses outcome criteria established for 24 hours prior to discharge when reviewing quality of care. Patient records are reviewed after discharge, but the review criteria are stated in terms of expected outcomes that should have occurred 24 hours prior to discharge.

Del Bueno (1993) warns, however, that outcome evaluations are always frustrating, because it is difficult to control the variables. She compares the outcome audit metaphorically to a black-box theory. It is clear what goes into the box (interventions, training, roles, geographic settings) and what comes out (length of stay, morbidity and mortality, employee satisfaction, productivity, and costs), but what goes on in the box (feelings, relationships, history, players' values and expectations) can be intuited but not directly or precisely measured.

Process Audit

Process audits are used to measure the process of care or how the care was carried out. Process audits are task oriented and focus on whether or not practice standards are being fulfilled. These audits assume that a relationship exists between the quality of the nurse and the quality of care provided. *Process standards* may be documented in patient care plans, procedure manuals, or nursing protocol statements. For example, a process audit might be used to establish whether fetal heart tones or blood pressures were checked according to an established policy. In a community health agency, a process audit could be used to determine if newborn teaching had been carried out during the first postpartum visit. Kaplan and Greenfield (1984) believe that process audits are especially appropriate for situations in which adverse outcomes occur infrequently, outcomes are ascribed to numerous factors beyond nursing control, patients have complex problems with multiple outcomes, long-term care is likely, terminal care is anticipated, and the population is small.

Structure Audit

This audit monitors the structure or setting in which patient care occurs, such as the finances, nursing service, medical records, and environment. Structure audits assume that a relationship exists between quality care and appropriate structure.

    Structural standards, which are often set by licensing and accrediting bodies, ensure a safe and effective environment but do not address the actual care provided. An example of a structural audit might include checking to see if patient call lights are in place or if patients can reach their water pitchers. It also might examine staffing patterns to ensure that adequate resources are available to meet changing patient needs.

    Outcome, process, and structure audits can occur retrospectively, concurrently, or prospectively. *Retrospective* audits are performed after the client receives the service. *Concurrent* audits are performed while the client is receiving the service. *Prospective* audits attempt to identify how future performance will be affected by current interventions.

WHO SHOULD BE INVOLVED IN QUALITY CONTROL?

Ideally, everyone in the organization should participate in quality control because each individual benefits from it. Quality control gives employees feedback about their current quality of care and how their care can be improved. As direct caregivers, staff nurses are in an excellent position to monitor nursing practice by identifying

LEARNING EXERCISE 18.1

You are a public health nurse in a small nonprofit visiting nurse clinic. The nursing director has requested that you chair the newly established quality assurance committee because of your experience with developing audit criteria.

Because a review of the patient population indicates that maternal/child visits make up the greatest percentage of visiting nurses' home visits, the committee chose to develop a retrospective process audit tool to monitor the quality of initial postpartum visits. The criteria specified that the clients to be included in the audit had been discharged with the infant after less than 12 hours in a birth center or obstetrical unit following uncomplicated vaginal delivery. The home visit would occur no longer than 72 hours after the delivery.

Assignment: Design an audit tool appropriate for this diagnosis that would be convenient to use. Specify percentages of compliance, sources of information, and number of clients to be audited. Limit your process criteria to 20 items. *Try solving this yourself before reading the possible solution that follows.*

POSSIBLE SOLUTION:

When writing audit criteria, define the client population as clearly as possible first so that information can be retrieved quickly. In this case, eliminate complicated births, abnormal newborns, cesarean section births, and home births because these clients will need more assessment and teaching. The performance expectations should be set at 100% compliance, but an allowance should be made for reasonable exceptions. One hundred percent is recommended because if any of these criteria are not recorded in the client's record, remedial actions should be taken. Select the client's record as the most objective source of information. It should be assumed that if criteria are not charted, they were not met. Audit 30 charts to give the agency enough data to make some assumptions, but not too many as to make it economically burdensome to review records. An audit form that could be developed follows.

NURSING AUDIT FORM FOR VISITING NURSES

Nursing Diagnosis: Initial home visit within 72 hours following uncomplicated vaginal delivery, with normal newborn, occurring in a birth center or obstetrical facility

Source of information: The client's record

Expected compliance: 100%, unless specific exceptions are noted

Number of records to be audited: 30

After the audit committee reviews the records, a summary should be made of the findings. A summary could look like this:

SUMMARY OF AUDIT FINDINGS

Nursing diagnosis: Initial home visit, within 72 hours following uncomplicated delivery, with normal newborn, occurring in a birth center or obstetrical facility.

Number of records audited: 30

Date of audit: 7/6/95

Summary of findings: 100% compliance in all areas except mother's temperature (50% compliance) and newborn assessment (70% compliance).

Suggestions for improving compliance: Remind nurses to record temperature of

(continued)

LEARNING EXERCISE 18.1 (Continued)

mother in record, even if normal. Time might be a factor in newborn assessment because temperature is frequently recorded on subsequent visit. Committee agrees that temperatures should be taken on first home visit and suggests an inservice and staff meeting regarding this area of noncompliance.

Signed, Chair of the Committee

The summaries should be forwarded to the individual responsible for the quality assurance, in this case, the director of the agency. At no time should individual public health nurses be identified as not having met the criteria. Quality assurance must always be separate from performance appraisal.

problems and implementing corrective actions that have the greatest impact on patient care (O'Brien, 1988). Naylor et al. (1991) state that nurses as major providers of healthcare must assume a leadership role when measuring the quality of their services and documenting their costs.

Although it is impractical to expect full staff involvement throughout the quality control process, staff should be involved in determining criteria or standards, reviewing standards, collecting data, or reporting. Heater, Olson, and Becker (1990) have shown that research-based nursing interventions can produce 28% better outcomes for 72% of patients.

Hughes (1987) states that patients or clients also must be actively involved in quality control. She maintains that only when patients are involved in the process can nurses truly understand the patient's point of view and see that patient rights are upheld.

Quality control also requires coordinating other professionals involved in client care. Professionals such as physicians, respiratory therapists, dietitians, and physical therapists contribute to client outcomes and therefore must be considered in the audit process. It is possible, however, to separate the contribution of nursing to the patient's outcome; recognition of this accountability in certain health outcomes is important in developing nursing as a profession. Cumulative evidence during the last decade has shown that nurse-delivered care can be substituted for physician services in many cases and that this care is generally more cost-effective (Fagin, 1990). If indeed nurses can accomplish outcomes that are as good as or better than those physicians achieve, and at a lower cost, the implications for third-party reimbursement for nursing care are enormous.

LEARNING EXERCISE 18.2

Develop three nursing criteria for outcome audit and three nursing criteria for process audit for the following nursing diagnosis: *Alterations in Comfort, acute pain.* In each criterion, show percentage of expected achievement or the exceptions to 100% achievement.

> ## LEARNING EXERCISE 18.3
>
> Some ill clients get better despite nursing care, not as a result of it. The quality of nursing care affects client outcomes tremendously. Do you feel that quality nursing care can make a difference in clients' lives? Identify five criteria you would use to define "quality nursing care." These criteria should reflect what you feel nurses do that makes the difference in client outcomes. Are the criteria you listed measurable? How?

THE IMPACT OF GOVERNMENT REIMBURSEMENT ON QUALITY CONTROL

Although few organizations would argue the significant benefits of well-developed and implemented quality control programs, quality control in healthcare organizations evolved primarily from government intervention and not as a voluntary monitoring effort. When Medicare and Medicaid (government reimbursement for the elderly, disabled, and financially indigent) were implemented in the early 1960s, healthcare organizations had little need to justify costs or prove that the services provided met patients' needs. Reimbursement was based on the costs incurred in providing the service, and no real ceilings were placed on the amount that could be charged for services. As the cost of these programs skyrocketed, the government established regulations requiring organizations to justify the need for services and to monitor the quality of services. Professional Standards Review Board legislation (PL 92-603), established in 1972, mandated a certification of need for the patient's admission and continued review of care; an evaluation of medical care; and an analysis of the patient profile, the hospital, and the practitioners.

This new "big brother" surveillance and the existence of external controls had a huge effect on the industry. Healthcare organizations began to question basic values and were forced to establish new methods for collecting data, keeping records, providing services, and accounting in general. Because government programs, such as Medicare and Medicaid, represent such a large group of today's patients, organizations that were unwilling or unable to meet these changing needs did not survive financially.

The advent of diagnostic-related groupings (DRGs) in the early 1980s added to the ever-increasing need for organizations to monitor cost containment yet guarantee a minimum level of quality (see Chap. 6). As a result of DRGs, hospitals became part of the *prospective payment* system, whereby they receive a specified amount for each patient's admission regardless of the actual cost of providing care. Because of the prospective payment system, patient acuity and nurse workload have increased, and the length of stay for most hospital admissions has decreased greatly (Kramer & Schmalenberg, 1987).

Fiesta (1992) argues that changing healthcare economics has resulted in a shift from clinical to financial control of medical decisions and that arguably, the standard of care should be divided into two elements: a clinical standard and a resource utilization standard. Kramer (1987) reports that DRGs have resulted in increased acuity levels of hospitalized patients, a decrease in the length of patient stay, and nurses' perception that patients are being discharged prematurely. All these factors have contributed to a greater dissatisfaction by nurses regarding the quality of care they provide. Van Hoesen's (1990) study of cardiovascular surgery patients, however, reports no significant change in patient acuity levels and quality of nursing care as a result of DRGs.

In the 1970s, JCAHO also became involved in quality assurance at the organizational level and mandated that each hospital have a quality assurance program in place by January 1, 1981. These quality assurance programs were to include a review of care provided by all clinical departments, disciplines, and practitioners; the coordination and integration of the findings of quality control activities; and the development of specific plans for known or suspected client problems. Again, in 1982, JCAHO established standards for nursing care as measured against written criteria; this comparison was to occur quarterly (Moloney, 1986). These standards emphasize quality and the need for continuous review and evaluation of care provided by professionals.

Current JCAHO guidelines state that a quality assurance program should be an integrated, systematic, institution-wide, quality review plan for all care-related services, support services, medical staff, and governing board (Bushy, 1991). According to JCAHO (1993), quality improvement in healthcare encompasses seven basic tenets:

1. There must be a commitment from the leadership to make quality a priority and to refocus on the consumer as the driving force behind the organization.
2. Leaders must define quality and incorporate it into the mission statement and planning documents (Sherman & Malkmus, 1994).
3. The needs and expectations of consumers must be explored and organizational changes made to meet those needs.
4. All employees must be involved in quality improvement, especially at the daily planning level.
5. The focus of improved quality must be directed toward work processes instead of individuals (Sherman & Malkmus, 1994).
6. Quality by design (prevention) must be emphasized over quality by inspection (correction).
7. Quality improvement is a scientific problem-solving process that requires data-driven decision making.

JCAHO now requires hospitals to use a quality assurance system resembling the industrial quality control models used in other industries (Burda, 1989). This *model* facilitates monitoring the entire organization and its processes, while emphasizing continuous measurement and improvements in clinical and service areas. JCAHO also has extended its benchmarking analyses to the clinical arena with automated collection of clinical indicators as part of its new *Agenda for Change* (Simpson, 1994).

Organizational accountability for the internal monitoring of cost containment and quality has increased during the last 30 years. Most healthcare organizations today have complete quality assurance programs and are actively involved in cost containment. Changing government regulations regarding quality control, however, continue to influence management decisions strongly. Managers must be cognizant of changing government and licensing regulations that affect their unit's quality control and standard setting. This awareness allows the manager to implement proactive rather than reactive quality control.

LEARNING EXERCISE 18.4

Is the quality of your patient care always as high as you would like it to be? What factors affect this quality? Which ones can you control? In your clinical experiences, have DRGs affected the quality of care provided? How?

TOTAL QUALITY MANAGEMENT/ CONTINUOUS QUALITY IMPROVEMENT

Total quality management (TQM), also referred to as continuous quality improvement (CQI), is a philosophy developed by Dr. W. Edward Deming. Considered the hallmark of highly successful Japanese management systems, TQM is being applied to American healthcare settings in an effort to provide a practical solution to the "best for less" dilemma (Arikian, 1991). TQM is based on the premise that the individual is the focal element on which production and service depend; that is, it must be a customer responsive environment. Quality is built into the service or product, rather than assuming that inspection of and removal of errors leads to quality (Kirk, 1992). Thus, identifying and doing the right things, the right way, the first time and problem prevention planning—not inspection and reactive problem solving—lead to quality outcomes. In TQM, this philosophy is incorporated into the organizational culture and is reflected in all attitudes regarding hierarchies, cost containment, and human relations (Arikian, 1991). Because ultimate responsibility for TQM belongs to top-level management, cooperation and support must be evident from top to bottom (LoPresti & Whetstone, 1993). For accreditation surveys as of January 1, 1992, all chief executives of hospitals were mandated by the JCAHO to be educated on CQI methods (Cesta, 1993).

Because TQM is a never-ending process, everything and everyone in the organization are subject to continuous improvement efforts. No matter how good the product or service is, the TQM philosophy says there is always room for improvement (Kirk, 1992). Customer needs and experiences with the end-product are constantly evaluated. This data collection is done by workers not by a central quality assurance department, thus providing a feedback loop between administration, workers, and consumers. Any problems encountered are approached in a preventive or proactive mode so that crisis management becomes unnecessary. It is critical in TQM that management assumes the responsibility for removing any barriers to quality, such as ineffective or inefficient policies, procedures, and systems (Kirk, 1992).

Another critical component of TQM is the empowerment of employees by providing positive feedback and reinforcing attitudes and behaviors that support quality and productivity (Arikian, 1991; Simpson, 1994). Based on the premise that employees have an in-depth understanding of their jobs, believe they are valued, and feel encouraged to improve product or service quality through risk taking and creativity, TQM trusts the employees to be knowledgeable, accountable, and responsible and provides education and training for employees at all levels (Arikian, 1991).

Although the philosophy of TQM emphasizes that quality is placed before profit, the resultant increase in quality of a well-implemented TQM program attracts more customers, resulting in increased profit margins and a financially healthier organization. Because the healthcare industry is so vulnerable to the forces of competition, changing technology, reimbursement, and dwindling resources, some experts propose that TQM may be one of the factors guaranteeing "survival of the fittest" in the future (Arikian, 1991). JCAHO in its publication *Agenda for Change* considers CQI the central conceptual framework for more meaningful quality of care evaluation (Roberts & Schyve, 1990).

The 14 quality management principles of TQM as outlined by Deming (1986) are summarized in Display 18.3.

 LEARNING EXERCISE 18.5

Think back to the organization for which you have worked the longest. How many of Deming's 14 principles for total quality management were used in that organization? Do you feel that some of the 14 principles are more critical than others, and why or why not? Could an organization have a successful quality management program if only some of the principles are used?

Merging Deming's 14 principles with his own control theory (whereby management gives up its traditional way of dealing with employees and substitutes it with a noncoercive approach), Glasser (1994) argues that five basic conditions must be met if workers are to do quality work:

1. The work environment must be warm and supportive. The workers must trust management.
2. Workers should be asked to do only useful or purposeful work. They should feel they are contributing to a worthwhile need.
3. Workers must be asked to do the best they can.
4. From the time workers are hired, lead-managers should guide the process of helping them learn to evaluate their work continually. Based on this ongoing evaluation, lead-managers will then encourage workers to improve the quality of what they do.
5. Quality work always feels good.

Glasser (1994) says that lead-managers must learn what quality actually is, teach it to all in the organization, and then listen carefully to any worker who has an idea of how it may be further improved. Likewise, everyone in the organization should be managed so that it is obvious to all workers that it is in their benefit to settle for nothing less than quality work.

Display 18.3 Total Quality Management Principles

1. Create a constancy of purpose for the improvement of products and service.
2. Adopt a philosophy of continual improvement.
3. Focus on improving processes, not on inspection of product.
4. End the practice of awarding business on price alone; instead, minimize total cost by working with a single supplier.
5. Improve constantly every process for planning, production, and service.
6. Institute job training and retraining.
7. Develop the leadership in the organization.
8. Drive out fear by encouraging employees to participate actively in the process.
9. Foster interdepartmental cooperation, and break down barriers between departments.
10. Eliminate slogans, exhortations, and targets for the work force.
11. Focus on quality and not just quantity; eliminate quota systems if they are in place.
12. Promote team work rather than individual accomplishments. Eliminate the annual rating or merit system.
13. Educate/train employees to maximize personal development.
14. Charge all employees with carrying out the total quality management package.

Source: Deming, 1986.

What are the costs of TQM? Simpson (1994) argues that the cost of quality is made up of the aggregate cost of *not* conforming plus the cost of conforming to customer requirements. Thus, the five elements that make up the cost of quality are the cost of preventing mistakes (employee training), the cost of appraisal (auditing and quality assurance), the cost of failure (errors and omissions), the cost of exceeding requirements (producing information nobody needs), and the cost of lost opportunities (lost market share and reduced revenues).

QUALITY CONTROL IN THE 1990s

For any quality control program to be effective, certain components need to be in place. First, the program needs to be supported by top-level administration; a quality control program cannot merely be an exercise to satisfy various federal and state standards. A sincere commitment by the institution, as evidenced by fiscal and human resource support, will be a deciding factor in determining and improving quality of services.

In addition, although the organization must be realistic about the economics of rendering services, if nursing is to strive for excellence, then developed criteria should be pushed to optimal levels rather than minimally acceptable levels. A study by Helt and Jelinek (1988) covering more than 8 million patient days suggests that the quality of nursing care has improved in the last decade, despite cost cutting and increased patient acuity. Nurses have responded to cost containment without sacrificing quality standards. As healthcare costs continue to spiral upward, organizations will increasingly be expected to provide high-quality yet cost-effective care.

Much is unknown about how the future will define quality care. Werley and Lang (1988) describe their efforts to establish uniform standards for evaluating outcomes. The nursing minimum data set (NMDS) represents their 10-year effort to establish such standards. Once in use, the NMDS will yield better data for quality control and for the costing of nursing services than ever before. Simpson (1991; p. 21) says that "the adoption of a Nursing Minimum Data Set is probably *the* most important step in the advancement of nursing through technology."

Other complex systems of quality measurement also are evolving. Naylor (1991) and Jones (1993) suggest the need for increased emphasis on outcome measurement in the future and the linking of outcomes to nursing practices. Waltz and Sylvia (1991) state that both the quantity and quality of the measurement efforts directed toward outcome assessment, especially as outcome relates to nursing effectiveness, have increased markedly during the last decade and will increase in the future as nurses attempt to document the worth of nursing programs and services.

Hurley (1994) argues that outcome management, along with the use of *critical pathways* (a strategic outline of a patient's expected progress from admission to discharge based on diagnosis) will be a major component of healthcare reform, fitting in with President Clinton's proposal for practice guidelines.

Omachonu and Nanda (1989) suggest a need for output measures in addition to outcome measures in the future. *Output measures,* in conjunction with DRGs, clarify healthcare costs and provide a consistent measure across all healthcare organizations. While *outcome measures* look at productivity in terms of efficacy or the ability to restore health through nursing or medical intervention, output measures focus on the dollar value of the services rendered and resources expended. Thus, output measures lend themselves to more objective quantification of results and eliminate the need for assuming there is a direct relationship between outcome and quality of care. Output measures also are more suitable to fiscal control than outcome measures.

Some theorists have questioned whether quality control in healthcare in the 1990s will be measured more by consumer satisfaction or actual quality of care (Carter & Mowad, 1988; Prehn, Mayo, & Weisman, 1989). Most industries create product lines based on consumer expectations and satisfaction, whereas nursing has been driven by quality standards set by the profession. At issue is whether consumer expectations and professional standards are compatible and whether quality care guarantees consumer satisfaction (Carter & Mowad, 1988).

Research by Eriksen (1987) demonstrates that the inverse is true. Consumer satisfaction increases as social courtesy and service are extended and not with an improvement in the quality of care. For example, consumer satisfaction with a hospital admission is often determined by the quality of food, provision of privacy, satisfaction with a roommate, or noisiness of the nursing station. In addition, consumer satisfaction may be adversely affected by long waits for call lights to be answered and for transport to ancillary services, such as x-ray. In reality, the quality of nursing care is probably reflected more accurately in terms of morbidity, incidence of nosocomial infection, length of hospital stay, client behavioral change as a result of new knowledge, and rehabilitation potential.

In another study of 139,830 former patients from 225 hospitals, not one of the top 15 factors determining patient satisfaction had anything to do with whether the patient's health improved during the stay (Modern Health Care, 1992). Patients were more concerned about staff provision of privacy, staff sensitivity to the inconvenience of hospitalization, overall cheerfulness of the hospital, and skill level and courtesy of technicians drawing blood.

INTEGRATION OF LEADERSHIP ROLES AND MANAGEMENT FUNCTIONS IN QUALITY CONTROL

Quality control findings pose many questions for leaders/managers. Should quality control plans be designed to measure consumer satisfaction or standards set by the profession? Should they integrate both criteria?

Accurately appraising quality control allows managers to change problem solving from an unsystematic, unscientific process to an accurate, analytical one (New, 1989). Managers must determine what standards will be used to measure quality care on their units and then develop and implement quality control programs that measure results against those standards. All managers are responsible for monitoring the quality of the product that their units produce; in healthcare organizations that product is client care. Managers also must assess and promote consumer satisfaction whenever possible.

The manager, however, cannot operate in a vacuum in determining what quality is and how it should be measured. Demands for hard data on quality have increased as regulatory bodies, consumers, payors, and hospital managers have required justification of services provided. Managers must be cognizant of rapidly changing quality control regulations and proactively adjust unit standards to meet these changing needs.

Inspiring subordinates to establish and achieve high standards of care is a leadership skill. Leaders role model high standards in their own nursing care and encourage subordinates to seek maximum rather than minimum standards. One way this can be accomplished is by involving subordinates in the quality control process itself. By studying direct cause-effect relationships, subordinates learn to modify individual and group performance to better the quality of care provided.

Vision is another leadership skill inherent in quality control. The visionary leader looks at what is and determines what should be. This future focus allows leaders to shape unit goals proactively and improve the quality of care.

KEY CONCEPTS

▼ Controlling is implemented throughout all phases of management.
▼ *Quality control* refers to activities that evaluate, monitor, or regulate services rendered to consumers.
▼ To assess qualitative data accurately, managers must consistently use a specific and systematic process for quality control.
▼ A *standard* is a predetermined baseline condition or level of excellence that comprises a model to be followed and practiced.
▼ Because there is no one set of standards, each organization and profession must

set standards and objectives to guide individual practitioners in performing safe and effective care.

▼ The ANA has played a key role in developing standards for the nursing profession since the 1930s.

▼ Standards may be minimizing or maximizing in terms of the quality of service expected.

▼ An *audit* is a systematic and official examination of a record, process, or account to evaluate performance.

▼ *Outcome audits* determine what results, if any, resulted from specific nursing interventions for clients.

▼ *Process audits* are used to measure the process of care or how the care was carried out.

▼ *Structure audits* monitor the structure or setting in which patient care occurs (such as the finances, nursing service structure, medical records, and environmental structure).

▼ Outcome, process, and structure audits can occur retrospectively, concurrently, or prospectively.

▼ Quality control in healthcare organizations has evolved primarily from government intervention and not as a voluntary effort to monitor the quality of services provided.

▼ TQM, also called CQI, is based on the premise that the consumer is the focal element on which production and service depend. Quality is built into the service or product, rather than assuming that inspection of and removal of errors lead to quality.

▼ Some experts advocate that outcome management, along with the use of *critical pathways* (a strategic outline of a patient's expected progress from admission to discharge based on diagnosis) will be a major component of quality control in the 1990s.

▼ The NMDS represents an effort to establish uniform standards for evaluating outcomes. Proponents of the NMDS argue that it will yield better data for quality control and for estimating the cost of nursing services than ever before.

▼ Ideally, everyone in the organization should participate in quality control because each person benefits from it.

▼ As direct caregivers, staff nurses are in an excellent position to monitor nursing practice by identifying problems and implementing corrective actions that have the greatest impact on patient care.

◢◣ ADDITIONAL LEARNING EXERCISES

Learning Exercise 18.6

You are a staff nurse at Mercy Hospital. The hospital's patient census and acuity have been very high for the last 6 months. Many of the nursing staff have resigned; a coordinated recruitment effort to refill these positions has been largely unsuccessful. The nursing staff is demoralized, and staff frequently call in sick or fail to show up for work. Today you arrive at work and find that you are again being asked to work short-handed. You will be the only RN on a unit with 30 patients. Although you have two LVNs and two CNAs assigned to work with you, you are concerned that patient care safety could be compromised. A check with the central nursing office ascertains that no additional help can be obtained.

You feel that you have reached the end of your rope. The administration at Mercy Hospital has been receptive to employee feedback about the acute staffing shortage, and you feel that they have made some efforts to try to alleviate the problem. You also feel, however, that the efforts have not been at the level they should have been, and that the hospital will continue to expect nurses to work short-handed until some major force changes things. Although you have thought about quitting, you really enjoy the work you do and feel morally obligated to your coworkers, the patients, and even your superiors. Today, it occurs to you that you could anonymously phone the State Licensing Bureau and turn in Mercy Hospital for consistent understaffing of nursing personnel, leading to unsafe patient care. You feel this could be the impetus needed to improve the quality of care. You also are aware of the action's political risks.

Assignment: Discuss whether or not you would take this action. What is your responsibility to the organization, to yourself, and to patients? How do you make decisions such as this one, which have conflicting moral obligations?

Learning Exercise 18.7

You have been the nursing coordinator of cardiac services at a medium-size urban hospital for the last 6 months. Among the hospital's cardiac services are open-heart surgery, invasive and noninvasive diagnostic testing, and a comprehensive rehabilitation program. The open-heart surgery program was implemented just more than 1 year ago. During the last 3 months, you have begun to feel uneasy about the mortality rate of postoperative cardiac patients at your facility. An audit of medical records shows a unit mortality rate that is approximately 30% above national norms.

You approach the unit medical director with your findings. He becomes very defensive and states that there have been a few freakish situations to skew the results but that the open-heart program is one of the best in the state. When you question him about examining the statistics further, he becomes very angry and turns to leave the room. At the door, he stops and says, "Remember that these patients are leaving the operating room alive. They are dying on your unit. If you stir up trouble, you are going to be sorry."

Assignment: Outline your plan. Identify areas in your data gathering that may have been misleading or that may have skewed your findings. If you feel action is still warranted, what are the personal and professional risks involved? How well developed is your power base to undertake these risks? To whom do you have the greatest responsibility?

Learning Exercise 18.8

You are the director of a baccalaureate nursing program. In the early 1980s, your school averaged approximately 200 applicants for the 50 student openings each semester. This resulted in the school being very selective about which students would enter the program. Because entering students traditionally had high grade point averages and had completed almost all non-nursing requirements, the attrition and dropout rate was fairly low, and academic failure was rare.

Currently, because of a severe national nursing shortage coupled with a marked decrease in the number of students seeking nursing as a career, barely enough students apply to fill each entering class. As a result, students meeting only minimal grade point average requirements and many that haven't met general studies course requirements are accepted into the program. You have seen the attrition and dropout rate quadruple in the last 3 years with much of this attrition attributable to academic failure.

Recently, the faculty members have begun discussing changing the academic failure policy in an effort to increase student retention. The current policy results in automatic dismissal from the program if students fail two courses in the major.

Faculty members are concerned that teaching positions will be cut as a result of the decreased enrollment and high attrition. You are aware that university administration feels that nursing is an expensive major, that this situation is not going to improve in the near future, and that budget cuts may indeed soon be mandated.

You, however, have grave concerns about eliminating or altering the academic failure policy because you feel you are in effect lowering program standards and thus the quality of its end-product. You do not feel that students failing two courses in the major would be safe practitioners. You also feel that students in academic difficulty are taking a disproportionate amount of faculty time and energy at the expense of better students.

Assignment: What options are available to you? What obligations do you have to your faculty, to the students, to the public as consumers of healthcare, and to university administration? How do you determine an appropriate course of action when these duties conflict?

REFERENCES:

American Nurses Association (1973). *Standards of nursing practice*. Kansas City, MO: Author.

Arikian, V. L. (1991). Total quality management: Applications to nursing service. *Journal of Nursing Administration, 21*(6), 46–50.

Burda, D. (1989). JCAHO plans quality requirements. *Modern Healthcare, 19*(12), 4.

Bushy, A. (1991). Quality assurance in rural hospitals. *Journal of Nursing Administration, 21*(10), 34–39.

Carter, S., & Mowad, L. (1988). Is nursing ready for consumerism? *Nursing Administration Quarterly, 12*(3), 74–78.

Cesta, T. G. (1993). The link between continuous quality improvement and case management. *Journal of Nursing Administration, 23*(6), 55–61.

Del Bueno, D. J. (1993). Outcome evaluation: Frustration or fertile field? *Journal of Nursing Administration, 23*(7/8), 12–13, 19.

Deming, W. E. (1986). *Out of the crisis.* Cambridge, MA: MIT Press.

Eriksen, L. (1987). Patient satisfaction: An indicator of nursing care quality? *Nursing Management, 18*(7), 31–35.

Fagin, C. M. (1990). Nursing's value proves itself. *American Journal of Nursing, 90*(10), 17–18.

Fiesta, J. (1992). Cost standards, quality and technology. *Nursing Management, 23*(2), 16–17.

Glasser, W. (1994). *The control theory manager.* New York: Harper Business.

Heater, B. S., Olson, R. K., & Becker, A. M. (1990). Helping patients recover faster. *American Journal of Nursing, 90*(10), 19–20.

Helt, E. H., & Jelinek, R. C. (1988). In the wake of cost cutting, nursing productivity and quality improve. *Nursing Management, 19*(6), 36–48.

Hughes, F. S. Y. (1987). Quality assurance in home care services. *Nursing Management, 18*(12), 33–36.

Hurley, M. L. (Ed.) (1994). Focusing on outcomes. *RN, 57*(5), 57–60.

Joint Commission on Accreditation of Health Care Organizations (1993). *What is quality improvement? (Q1-102).* Oakbrook Terrace, IL: Author.

Jones, K. R. (1993). Outcomes analysis: Methods and issues. *Nursing Economics, 11*(3), 145–152.

Kaplan, S. H., & Greenfield, S. (1984). Criteria mapping: Using logic in evaluation of processes of care. *Quality Review Bulletin, 10,* 462–466.

Kirk, R. (1992). The big picture—Total quality management and continuous quality improvement. *Journal of Nursing Administration, 22*(4), 24–31.

Koontz, H., & Weihrich, H. (1988). *Management.* New York: McGraw Hill.

Kramer, M. (1987). Magnet hospitals talk about the impact of DRGs on nursing care: Part I. *Nursing Management, 18*(9), 38–42.

Kramer, M., & Schmalenberg, C. (1987). Magnet hospitals talk about the impact of DRGs on nursing care: Part 2. *Nursing Management, 18*(10), 33–40.

Larson, S., & Lieske, A. (1992). *Standards: The basis of a quality assurance program. Improving quality: A guide to effective programs.* Gaithersburg, MD: Aspen Publication.

LoPresti, J., & Whetstone, W. R. (1993). Total quality management: Doing things right. *Nursing Management, 24*(1), 34–36.

Marriner-Tomey, A. (1992). Guide to nursing management (4th ed.). St. Louis: Mosby Year Book.

Modern HealthCare (1992). "Outliers—What the patients think. June 1, 44.

Moloney, M. M. (1986). *Professionalization of nursing: Current issues and trends.* Philadelphia: J.B. Lippincott.

Naylor, M. D., Munro, B. H., & Brooten, D. A. (1991). Measuring the effectiveness of nursing practice. *Clinical Nurse Specialist, 5*(4), 210–215.

New, N. A. (1989). Quality measurement: Quick, easy and unit based. *Nursing Management, 20*(10), 50–51.

O'Brien, B. (1988). QA: A commitment to excellence. *Nursing Management, 19*(11), 33–40.

Omachonu, V. K., & Nanda, R. (1989). Measuring productivity: Outcome vs. output. *Nursing Management, 20*(4), 35–38, 40.

Prehn, R. A., Mayo, H., & Weisman, E. (1989). Determining the validity of patient perceptions of quality care. *Quality Review Bulletin, 15*(3), 74–76.

Roberts, J., & Schyve, M. (1990). From QA to QI: The views and role of the joint commission. *The Quality Letter for Health Care Leaders, 2*(4), 9–12.

Sherman, J. J., & Malkmus, M. A. (1994). Integrating quality assurance and total quality management/quality improvement. *Journal of Nursing Administration, 24*(3), 37–41.

Simpson, R. L. (1991). Adopting a nursing minimum data set. *Nursing Management, 22*(2), 20–21.

Simpson, R. L. (1994). How technology enhances total quality management. *Nursing Management, 25*(6), 4041.

VanHoesen, N. S., & Eriksen, L. R. (1990). The impact of diagnosis-related groups of patient acuity, quality of care, and length of stay. *Journal of Nursing Administration, 20*(9), 20–23.

Vestal, K. W. (1987). *Management concepts for the new nurse.* Philadelphia: J.B. Lippincott.

Waltz, C. F., & Sylvia, B. M. (1991). Accountability and outcome measurement: Where do we go from here? *Clinical Nurse Specialist, 5*(4), 202–203.

Werley, H. H., & Lang, N. M. (1988). *The nursing minimum data set: Benefits and implications. Perspectives in nursing 1987-1989.* New York: Springer Publishing.

BIBLIOGRAPHY

Anderson, C. (1994). Advanced practice: Quality control. *Nursing Outlook, 42*(2), 54–55.

Bobnet, N. L., Ilcyn, J., Milanovich, P. S., Ream, M. A., & Wright, K. (1993). Continuous quality improvement: Improving quality in your home care organization. *Journal of Nursing Administration, 23*(2), 42–28.

Broome, L. (1993). The goal is quality improvement. *Nursing Management, 24*(1), 51–52.

Carefoote, R. (1994). Total quality management implementation in home care agencies: Common questions and answers. *Journal of Nursing Administration, 24*(10), 31–37.

Chassie, M. B. (1987). Risk management and

quality assurance. In K. W. Vestal (Ed.), *Management concepts for the new nurse* (pp. 153–183). Philadelphia: J.B. Lippincott.

Cumberland, A. (1993). Making the transition to a TQM system. *Nursing Management, 24*(8), 62–63.

Davis, S. L., & Adams-Greenly, M. (1994). Integrating patient satisfaction with a quality improvement program. *Journal of Nursing Administration, 24*(12), 28–31.

Eubanks, P. (1992). TQM/CQI: The CEO experience. *Hospitals, 66*(11), 24–36.

Fanucci, D., Hammill, M., Johannson, P., Leggett, J., & Smith, M. J. (1993). Quantum leap Into continuous quality improvement. *Nursing Management, 24*(6), 28–30.

Fitzpatrick, J. J. (1994). Performance improvement through quality improvement teams. *Journal of Nursing Administration, 24*(12), 20–27.

Flarey, D. L. (1993). Quality improvement through data analysis. *Journal of Nursing Administration, 23*(12), 2121–2130.

Gaucher, E. J., & Coffey, R. J. (1993). *Total quality in health care: From theory to practice.* San Francisco: Jossey-Bass.

Green, E., & Katz, J. (1989). A quality assurance tool that works overtime. *RN, 52*(9), 30–31.

Greene, J. (1989). Maintaining, improving quality are at top of board's agendas. *Modern Healthcare, 19*(4), 26–27.

Grudnicki, S. M. (1988). Quality assurance and effective nursing leadership. *Dimensions in Oncology Nursing, 2*(1), 13–15.

Harris, S. H., Kreger, S. M., & Davis, M. Z. (1989). A problem-focused quality assurance program. *Nursing Management, 20*(2), 54–56.

Hoebeke, L. (1994). *Making work systems better: A practitioner's reflections.* New York: Wiley.

Kennedy, M. (1992). Combining the best of QA and TQM. *Quality Management Update, 2*(1), 1, 10–14

Krenz, M. (1989). Linking nursing diagnosis, quality assurance and nursing standards. *Journal of Advanced Medical-Surgical Nursing, 1*(3), 53–61.

Law, M., Ryan, B., Townsend, E., et al. (1989). Criteria mapping: A method of quality assurance. *American Journal of Occupational Therapy, 43*(2), 104–109.

MacStravic, R. S. (1988). Outcome marketing in health care. *Health Care Management Review, 13*(2), 53–59.

Marquis, B. L., & Huston, C. J. (1994). *Management decision making for nurses* (2nd ed.). Philadelphia: J.B. Lippincott.

Masters, M. L., & Masters, R. J. (1993). Building TQM into nursing management. *Nursing Economics, 11*(5), 274–278.

McCabe, W. J. (1992). Total quality management in a hospital. *QRB, 18*(4), 134–140.

Mitchell, M. K. (1989). The power of standards: The glory days of nursing yet to come? *Nursing and Health Care, 10*(6), 306–309.

Puta, D. F. (1989). Nurse-physician collaboration towards quality. *Journal of Nursing Quality Assurance, 3*(2), 11–18.

Robinson, M. L. (1989). JCAHO emphasizes patient outcomes. *Hospitals, 63*(14), 21.

Salvage, J. (1989). A measure of care: Audit. *Nursing Times, 85*(18), 25.

Statland, B. E. (1989). Quality management: Watchword for the 90s . . . Managing for quality rather than for productivity. *Medical Laboratory Observer, 21*(7), 33–35, 38–40.

Taban, H. A., & Cesta, T. G. (1994). Developing case management plans using a quality improvement model. *Journal of Nursing Administration, 24*(12), 49–58.

Taunton, R. L., Kleinbeck, S. V., Stafford, R., Woods, C. Q., & Bolt, M. (1994). Patient outcomes: Are they linked to registered nurse absenteeism, separation or work load? *Journal of Nursing Administration, 24*(4S), 48–55,

Thurston, N. E., Watson, L. A., & Reimer, M. A. (1993). Research or quality improvement? *Journal of Nursing Administration, 23*(7/8), 4649.

Ventura, M. R., Rizzo, J., & Lenz, S. (1993). Quality indicators: Control maintains-propriety improves. *Nursing Management, 24*(1), 46–50.

Western, P. (1994). QA/AI and nursing competence: A combined model. *Nursing Management, 25*(3), 44–46.

Yaws, J. Y., & Deruvo, S. S. (1989). Utilization management: Improving patient care while maintaining cost control. *Journal of Nursing Quality Assurance, 3*(2), 53.

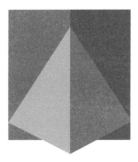

CHAPTER 19

Performance Appraisal

An additional managerial controlling responsibility is determining how well employees carry out the duties of their assigned jobs. This is done through performance appraisals. In performance appraisal, actual performance should be evaluated, not just good intentions (Tappen, 1995). McMurray (1993) states that performance appraisals not only evaluate performance, but they also let employees know where they stand and what is expected of them. They also generate information for salary adjustments, promotions, transfers, disciplinary actions, and terminations.

Marquis and Huston (1994) state that none of the manager's actions are as personal as appraising the work performance of others. Because work is an important part of one's identity, people are very sensitive to opinions about how they perform. For this reason, performance appraisal becomes one of the greatest tools an organization has to develop and motivate staff. When used correctly, performance appraisal can motivate staff and increase retention and productivity; in the hands of an inept or inexperienced manager, however, the appraisal process may discourage and demotivate staff.

Because a manager's opinions and judgments are used for far-reaching decisions regarding the employee's work life, they must be determined in an objective, systematic, and formalized manner. Beach (1980) maintains that the difference between an informal and a formal appraisal system is that in a formal system, managers are encouraged to observe their staff constantly to provide adequately for their training and

Bessie L. Marquis and Carol J. Huston:
LEADERSHIP ROLES AND MANAGEMENT FUNCTIONS IN NURSING, 2nd ed.
Lippincott-Raven Publishers © 1996

development and to gather information for appraisal. Using a formal system of performance review also reduces the appraisal's subjectivity.

The more professional a group of employees is, such as nurses, the more complex and sensitive the evaluation process becomes. The skilled leader/manager who uses a formalized system appropriately builds a team approach to patient care.

This chapter focuses on the relationship between performance appraisal and motivation, and discusses how performance appraisals can be used to determine developmental needs of staff. Emphasis is given to appropriate data gathering, proper implementation of management by objectives (MBO), and peer review. The performance appraisal interview also is explored. The leadership roles and management functions inherent in performance appraisal are shown in Display 19.1.

Display 19.1 Leadership Roles and Management Functions in Performance Appraisal

Leadership Roles

1. Uses the appraisal process to motivate employees and promote growth.
2. Uses techniques to reduce the anxiety inherent in the appraisal process.
3. Involves employees in all aspects of performance appraisal.
4. Is self-aware of own biases and prejudices.
5. Develops employee trust by being honest and fair when evaluating performance.
6. Encourages the peer review process among professional staff.
7. Uses appraisal interviews to facilitate two-way communication.
8. Provides ongoing support to employees attempting to correct performance deficiencies.
9. Uses coaching techniques that promote employee growth in work performance.

Management Functions

1. Uses a formalized system of performance appraisal.
2. Gathers data for performance appraisals that are fair and objective.
3. Uses the appraisal process to determine staff education and training needs.
4. Bases performance appraisal on documented standards.
5. Is as objective as possible in performance appraisal.
6. Maintains appropriate documentation of the appraisal process.
7. Follows up on identified performance deficiencies.
8. Conducts the appraisal interview in manner that promotes a positive outcome.
9. Provides frequent informal feedback on work performance.

USING THE PERFORMANCE APPRAISAL TO MOTIVATE EMPLOYEES

Although systematic employee appraisals have been used in management since the 1920s, using the appraisal as a tool to promote employee growth did not begin until the 1950s. Most formal appraisals focus on the professional worker and the manager rather than on the hourly paid worker. Because hourly workers are frequently locked into merit increases through union contracts, performance appraisal may be less effective as a motivational tool for them (Beach, 1980). There is evidence, however, that even when pay raises are automatic, performance appraisal can increase productivity if used appropriately (Huntsman, 1987). A performance appraisal wastes time only if it is merely an exercise to satisfy regulations, and the goal is not employee growth.

The evolution of performance appraisals is reflected in its changing terminology. At one time, the appraisal was called a *merit rating* and was tied fairly closely to salary increases. More recently, it was termed *performance evaluation,* but because the term "evaluation" implies that personal values are being placed on the performance review, that term is used infrequently. Some organizations continue to use both of these terms or others, such as *effectiveness report* or *service rating.* Most healthcare organizations, however, use the term performance appraisal because this term implies an appraisal of how well employees perform the duties of their job as delineated by the job description.

An important point to consider if the appraisal is to have a positive outcome is how the employee views the appraisal. If employees feel the appraisal is based on their job description, rather than on whether the manager approves of them, they are more likely to view the appraisal as relevant. Management research has shown that the following factors influence whether the appraisal ultimately results in increased motivation and productivity (Huston & Marquis, 1989).

1. The employee must feel that the appraisal is based on a standard to which other employees in the same classification are held accountable. This standard, which must be communicated clearly to employees at the time they are hired, may be a job description or individual goals set by staff on a regular basis, as in MBO. The concept of MBO is discussed later in this chapter.
2. The employee should have some input into developing the standards or goals on which his or her performance is judged. This is *imperative* for the professional employee.
3. The employee must know in advance what happens if the expected performance standards are not met.
4. The employee needs to know how information will be obtained to determine performance. The appraisal tends to be more accurate if various sources and types of information are solicited (Marquis & Huston, 1994). Sources could include peers, coworkers, nursing care plans, patients, and personal observation. Employees should be told which sources will be used and how such information will be weighted.
5. The appraiser should be one of the employee's direct supervisors. For example, the charge nurse who works directly with the staff nurse should be in-

volved in the appraisal process and interview. It is appropriate and advisable in most instances for the head nurse and supervisor also to be involved. However, employees must feel that the person doing the major portion of the review has actually observed their work.

6. The outcome of the performance appraisal is more likely to have a positive outcome if the appraiser is viewed with trust and professional respect. This increases the chance that the employee will view the appraisal as a fair and accurate assessment of work performance.

LEARNING EXERCISE 19.1

During your lifetime, you probably have had many performance appraisals. These may have been evaluations of your clinical performance during nursing school or as a paid employee. Reflect on these appraisals. How many of them encompassed the six recommendations listed in the chapter? How did the inclusion or exclusion of these recommendations influence your acceptance of the results?

Assignment: Select one of the six recommendations about which you feel strongly. Write a three paragraph essay on your personal experience involving this recommendation.

STRATEGIES TO ENSURE ACCURACY AND FAIRNESS IN THE PERFORMANCE APPRAISAL

If the employee views the appraisal as valuable and valid, it can have many positive effects. Information obtained during the performance appraisal can be used to develop the employee's potential, to assist the employee in overcoming difficulties he or she has in fulfilling the job's role, to point out strengths of which the employee may not be aware, and to aid the employee in setting goals. Because inaccurate and unfair appraisals are negative and demotivating, it is critical that the manager use strategies that increase the likelihood of a fair and accurate appraisal. Although some subjectivity is inescapable, the following will assist the manager in arriving at a fairer and more accurate assessment.

The appraiser should develop an awareness of his or her own biases and prejudices. This helps guard against subjective attitudes and values influencing the appraisal. Appraiser gender also may influence the accuracy of the performance appraisal. McMurray (1993) states that because women generally have higher affiliation needs than men, female managers are more apt to give a favorable evaluation during performance appraisal than male managers in an effort to please others, avoid confrontation, and increase social acceptance. On the other hand, male managers tend to have lower affiliation needs and higher achievement needs; thus, they may be more willing to give constructive criticism even if they expect the employee to be defensive.

Consultation should be sought frequently. Another manager should be consulted when a question about personal bias exists and in many other situations. For example, it is very important that new managers solicit assistance and consultation when they complete their first performance appraisals. Even experienced managers may need to consult when an employee is having great difficulty fulfilling the duties of the job. Consultation also must be used when employees work several shifts so that information can be obtained from all the shift supervisors.

Data should be gathered appropriately. Not only should many different sources be used in gathering data about employee performance, but the data gathered needs to reflect the entire time period of the appraisal. Frequently, managers gather data and observe an employee just before completing the appraisal, which gives an inaccurate picture of performance. Because all employees have periods when they are less productive and motivated, data should be gathered systematically and regularly.

Information should be written down and not trusted to memory. The manager should make a habit of keeping notes about observations, others' comments, and their periodic review of charts and nursing care plans. When *ongoing* anecdotal notes are not maintained throughout the evaluation period, the appraiser is more apt to experience the "recency effect," in which the importance of recent issues outweighs past performance (McMurray, 1993).

Collected assessments should contain positive examples of growth and achievement and areas of needed development. Nothing delights an employee more than discovering their immediate supervisor is aware of their growth and accomplishments and can cite specific instances in which good clinical judgment was used. Too frequently, collected data concentrate on negative aspects of performance.

The appraiser needs to guard against the three common pitfalls of assessment: "halo effect," "horns effect," and "central tendency." The *halo effect* occurs when the appraiser lets one or two positive aspects of the assessment or behavior of the employee unduly influence all other aspects of the employee's performance. The *horns effect* occurs when the appraiser allows some negative aspects of the employee's performance influence the assessment to such an extent that other levels of job performance are not accurately recorded. The manager who falls into the *central tendency* trap is hesitant to risk true assessment and therefore rates all employees as average. These appraiser behaviors lead employees to discount the entire assessment of their work.

Some effort must be made to include the employee's own appraisal of his or her work. Self-appraisal may be performed in several appropriate ways. Employees can be instructed to come to the appraisal interview with some informal thoughts about their performance, or they can work with their managers in completing a joint assessment. One advantage of MBO—the use of personalized goals to measure individual performance—is the manner in which it involves the employee in assessing his or her work performance and in goal setting.

PERFORMANCE APPRAISAL TOOLS

Since the 1920s, many appraisal tools have been developed. Certain types of tools or review techniques have been popular at different times. Presently, the JCAHO advocates that performance review be developed using the employee's job description as the standard. The following is an overview of some of the appraisal tools used in healthcare institutions.

> ### LEARNING EXERCISE 19.2
>
> Mrs. Jones is a new LVN/LPN and has been working 3 PM to 11 PM on the long-term care unit where you are the PM charge nurse. It is time for her 3-month performance appraisal. In your facility, each employee's job description is used as the standard of measure for performance appraisal.
>
> Essentially, you feel Mrs. Jones is performing her job well but are somewhat concerned because she still relies on the RNs for even minor patient care decisions. While you are glad that she does not act completely on her own, you would like to see her become more independent. The patients have commented favorably to you on Mrs. Jones' compassion and on her follow-through on all their requests and needs.
>
> Mrs. Jones gets along well with the other LVNs/LPNs, and you sometimes feel they take advantage of her hardworking and pleasant nature. On a few occasions, you felt they inappropriately delegated some of their work to her.
>
> When preparing for Mrs. Jones' upcoming evaluation, what can you do to make the appraisal as objective as possible? You want Mrs. Jones' first evaluation to be growth producing.
>
> *Assignment:* Plan how you will proceed. What positive forces are already present in this scenario? What negative forces will you have to overcome? Support your plan with readings from the bibliography at the end of this chapter.

Trait Rating Scales

A *rating scale* is a method of rating an individual against a set standard, which may be the job description, desired behaviors, or personal traits. The rating scale is probably the most widely used of the many available appraisal methods.

Rating personal traits and behaviors is the oldest type of rating scale. Many experts, however, argue that the quality or quantity of the work performed is a more accurate performance appraisal method than the employee's personal traits and that trait evaluation relies far too much on the opinions and preferences of the individual conducting the appraisal (McMurray, 1993). Rating scales also are subject to central tendency and halo and horns effect errors and thus are not used as often today as they were in the past. Instead, many organizations use two newer rating methods, namely the job dimension scale and the behaviorally anchored rating scale (BARS). Display 19.2 shows a portion of a trait rating scale with examples of traits that might be expected in a registered nurse.

Job Dimension Scales

This technique requires that a rating scale be constructed for each job classification. The rating factors are taken from the context of the written job description. Although job dimension scales share some of the same weaknesses as trait scales, they do focus on job requirements rather than on ambiguous terms, such as quantity of work. Display 19.3 shows an example of a job dimension scale for an industrial nurse.

Display 19.2 Sample of a Trait Rating Scale

Job Knowledge

Serious gaps in essential knowledge	Satisfactory knowledge of routine	Adequately informed on most phases	Good knowledge of all phases of job	Excellent understanding of the job
1	2	3	4	5

Judgment

Decisions are often wrong on issues	Makes some decision errors	Good decisions made often	Sound and logical thinker	Makes good, complex decisions
1	2	3	4	5

Attitude

Resents suggestions, no enthusiasm	Apathetic but cooperative	Generally cooperative and accepting of new ideas	Openly cooperates and accepts new ideas	Consistently helpful and enthusiastic
1	2	3	4	5

Behaviorally Anchored Rating Scales

BARS, sometimes called behavioral expectation scales, overcome some of the weaknesses inherent in other rating systems. As in the job dimension method, the BARS technique requires that a separate rating form be developed for each job classification. Then, as in the job dimension rating scales, employees in specific positions work with management to delineate key areas of responsibility. However, in BARS,

---

Display 19.3 Sample Job Dimension Rating Scale for an Industrial Nurse

Job Dimension	5	4	3	2	1
Renders first aid and treats job-related injuries and illnesses					
Holds fitness classes for workers					
Teaches health and nutrition classes					
Performs yearly physicals on workers					
Keeps equipment in good working order and maintains inventory					
Keeps appropriate records					
Dispenses medication and treatment for minor injuries					

(5 = Excellent; 4 = Good; 3 = Satisfactory; 2 = Fair; and 1 = Poor.)

many specific examples are defined for each area of responsibility; these examples are given various degrees of importance by ranking them from 1 to 9. If the highest ranked example of a job dimension is being met, it is less important that a lower ranked example is not.

Because separate BARS are needed for each job, the greatest disadvantage to the BARS method is the time and expense required to involve large numbers of employees in determining the dimensions of effective performance and behavioral examples of various levels of performance for each variable (Marriner-Tomey, 1992). It also is primarily applicable to physically observable skills rather than to conceptual skills. However, it is an excellent tool because it focuses on specific behaviors, allows employees to know exactly what is expected of them, and reduces rating errors. In addition, employees are more committed to this appraisal system because of their own involvement in designing it (Marriner-Tomey, 1992).

Although all rating scales are prone to weaknesses and interpersonal bias, they do have some advantages. Many may be purchased, and although they must be individualized to the organization, there is little need for expensive worker hours to develop them. Rating scales also force the rater to look at more than one dimension of work performance, which eliminates some bias.

Checklists

There are several types of checklist appraisal tools. The *weighted scale,* the most frequently used checklist, is composed of many behavioral statements that represent desirable job behaviors. Each of these behavior statements has a weighted score attached to it. Employees receive an overall performance appraisal score based on behaviors or attributes. Often merit raises are tied to the total point score; that is, the employee needs to reach a certain score to receive an increase in pay.

Another type of checklist, *the forced checklist,* requires that the supervisor select an undesirable and a desirable behavior for each employee. Both desirable and undesirable behaviors have quantitative values, and the employee again ends up with a total score on which certain employment decisions are made.

Another type of checklist is the *simple checklist.* The simple checklist is composed of numerous words or phrases describing various employee behaviors or traits. These descriptors are often clustered to represent different aspects of one dimension of behavior, such as assertiveness or interpersonal skills. The rater is asked to check all those that describe the employee on each checklist (Dienemann, 1990).

A major weakness of all checklists is that there are no set performance standards. In addition, specific components of behavior are not addressed. Checklists do, however, focus on a variety of job-related behaviors and avoid some of the bias inherent in the trait rating scales.

Essays

This appraisal method is often referred to as the *free form review.* The appraiser describes in narrative form employee strengths and areas where improvement or growth is needed. Although this method can be unstructured, it usually calls for certain items to be addressed.

This technique has some strengths because it forces the appraiser to focus on positive aspects of the employee's performance. However, a greater opportunity for supervisor bias undoubtedly exists.

Many organizations combine various types of appraisals to improve the quality of their review processes. Because the essay method does not require exhaustive development, it can quickly be adapted as an adjunct to any type of structured format. This then gives the organization the ability to decrease bias *and* focus on employee strengths.

Self-Appraisals

There are advantages and disadvantages to using self-appraisal as a method of performance review. Marquis and Huston (1994) maintain that although introspection and self-appraisal result in growth when the individual is self-aware, even mature individuals require external feedback and performance validation.

Some employees may look on their annual performance review as an opportunity to receive positive feedback from their supervisor, especially if the employee receives infrequent praise on a day-to-day basis. Asking these employees to perform their own performance appraisal would probably be viewed negatively rather than positively.

In addition, some employees undervalue their accomplishments or may feel uncomfortable giving themselves high marks in many areas. Using such a self-analysis as the only appraisal tool could provide an inaccurate picture of the worker's performance and negatively influence the manager's appraisal. Blakely's (1993) study of undergraduate business majors shows that when subordinates give themselves low self-evaluations (even when undeserved), supervisors tended to modify their original ratings, which were more positive. In an effort to avoid this potential influence on their rating, managers may wish to complete the performance appraisal tool prior to reading the employee's self-analysis, or they should view the self-appraisal as only one of a number of sources of data that should be collected when evaluating worker performance. When self-appraisal is not congruent with other data available, the manager may wish to pursue the reasons for this discrepancy during the appraisal conference. Such an exchange may provide valuable insight regarding the worker's self-awareness and ability to view himself or herself objectively.

Management by Objectives

MBO is an excellent tool for determining individual employee progress because it incorporates the assessments of the employee and the organization. Drucker's MBO concepts are discussed in Chapter 5; therefore, the focus here is on how these concepts are used as an effective performance appraisal method, rather than on their use as a planning technique.

MBO was developed for appraising the performance of managers and autonomous professionals (Beach, 1980). Although it is not used frequently in healthcare, MBO is an excellent method to appraise the performance of the registered nurse in a manner that promotes individual growth and excellence in nursing. The following steps delineate how MBO can be used effectively in performance appraisal:

1. The employee and supervisor meet and agree on the principle duties and responsibilities of the employee's job. (The job description serves as a guide only.) This is done as quickly as possible after beginning employment.
2. The employee sets short-term goals and target dates in cooperation with the supervisor or manager. The manager guides the process so that it relates to the position's duties. In addition, the goals identified must be meaningful and congruent with the goals of the organization (Tappen, 1995).
3. Both parties agree on the criteria that will be used for measuring and evaluating the accomplishment of goals. In addition, a time frame is set for completing the objectives, which depends on the nature of the work being planned. Common time frames used in healthcare organizations include 1 month, 3 months, 6 months, and 1 year (Tappen, 1995).
4. Regularly, but more than once a year, the employee and supervisor meet to discuss progress. At these meetings, some modifications can be made to the original goals if both parties agree. Tappen (1995) states that concern about external factors that slow progress of work toward a stated objective has led to the development of a somewhat more complex MBO system. In this system, any major obstacles that stand in the way of completing the objectives within the time frame are listed separately to recognize the possibility of their occurrence. In addition, the resources and support needed from others are identified. Separating these factors allows the appraiser to use the employee's objectives more fairly as evaluation criteria, even if the goal has not been met (Tappen, 1995).
5. The manager's role is supportive, assisting the employee to reach goals by coaching and counseling.
6. During the appraisal process, the manager determines whether the employee has met the goals.
7. The entire process focuses on outcomes and results and not on personal traits.

Beach (1980) states that one of the many advantages of MBO is that the method creates a vested interest in the employee to accomplish goals. This occurs because employees are able to set their own goals. Additionally, defensive feelings are minimized, and a spirit of teamwork prevails. In MBO, the focus is on the controllable present and future rather than the uncontrollable past.

There are disadvantages to MBO as a performance appraisal method. Highly directive and authoritarian managers find it difficult to lead employees in this manner. Also, the marginal employee frequently attempts to set easily attainable goals. However, research has shown that MBO, when used correctly, is a very effective method of performance appraisal.

Peer Review

When monitoring and assessing work performance is carried out by peers rather than by supervisors, it is referred to as *peer review*. The concept of collegial evaluation of nursing practice is closely related to maintaining professional standards. Curtin

(1994) states that one of the most effective ways to promote excellence in nursing practice is for nurses to offer information, support, guidance, criticism, and direction to one another. Although the prevailing practice in most organizations is to have managers evaluate employee performance, there is much to be said for collegial review.

Most likely, the manager's review of the employee is not complete unless some type of peer review data are gathered. Peer review, when implemented properly, provides the employee with valuable feedback that can promote growth. It also can provide learning opportunities for the peer reviewers. Martin (1994) found that peer reviewers who critiqued patient records completed by their peers increased the accuracy and precision of their own patient records by decreasing unnecessary, confusing, and illegible entries.

Peer review is widely used by colleges and universities and by physicians but is not as widely used by business and industry (Andrusyszyn, 1990). Healthcare organizations also have been slow to adopt peer review for the following five reasons (Marquis & Huston, 1994).

1. *Staff are poorly oriented to the peer review method.* Peer review is viewed as very threatening when inadequate time is spent orienting employees to the process and when necessary support is not provided throughout the process.
2. *Peers feel uncomfortable sharing feedback with people with whom they work closely, so they omit needed suggestions for improving the employee's performance.* Thus, the review becomes more advocacy than evaluation.
3. *Peer review is viewed by many as more time consuming* than traditional superior/subordinate performance appraisals.
4. Because much socialization takes place in the workplace, *friendships often result in inflated evaluations,* or interpersonal conflict may result in unfair appraisals.
5. Because peer review shifts the authority away from management, *the insecure manager may feel threatened.*

Peer review has its shortcomings, as is evidenced by some university teachers receiving unjustified tenure or the failure of physicians to maintain adequate quality control among some individuals in their profession. Additionally, peer review involves much risk taking, is time consuming, and requires a great deal of energy.

However, Waldo, Hofschulte, Magno, and Colleran (1993) argue strongly for placing the responsibility for quality control in the hands of professional members. Because performance appraisal may be viewed as a type of quality control, it seems reasonable to expect that nurses should have some input into the performance evaluation process of their profession's members.

Peer review can be carried out in several ways. The process may require the reviewers to share the results only with the individual being reviewed or the results may be shared with the employee's supervisor *and* the employee. The review would never be shared only with the employee's supervisor.

The results may or may not be used for personnel decisions. The number of observations, number of reviewers, qualification and classification of the peer reviewer, and procedure need to be developed for each organization. If peer review is to succeed, the organization must overcome its inherent difficulties by doing the following before implementing a peer review program:

- Peer review appraisal tools must reflect standards to be measured, such as the job description.
- Staff must receive a thorough orientation to the process prior to its implementation. The role of the manager should be clearly defined.
- Ongoing support, resources, and information must be made available to the staff during the process.
- Data for peer review need to be obtained from predetermined sources, such as observations, charts, and patient care plans.
- A decision must be made about whether anonymous feedback will be allowed. This is controversial and needs to be addressed in the procedure.
- Decisions must be reached on whether the peer review will affect personnel decisions and if so, in what manner.

Peer review has the potential to increase the accuracy of performance appraisal. It also can provide many opportunities for increased professionalism and learning and ensure appropriate rewards for high performance levels and professionalism on the job (Tappen, 1995). The use of peer review in nursing should continue to expand as nursing increases its autonomy and professional status.

LEARNING EXERCISE 19.3

Even in organizations that have no formal peer review process, professionals must take some responsibility for colleagues' work performance, even if informally. The following scenario illustrates the need for peer involvement.

Since your graduation from nursing school, you have worked at Memorial Hospital. Your school roommate, Mary, also has worked at Memorial since her graduation. For the first year, you and Mary were assigned to different units, but you both were transferred to the oncology unit 6 months ago.

You both work 3 PM to 11 PM, and it is the policy for the charge nurse duties to alternate among three RNs assigned to the unit on a full-time basis. Both you and Mary are among the nurses assigned to rotate to the charge position. You have noticed lately that when Mary is in charge, her personality seems to change; she barks orders and seems tense and anxious.

She is an excellent clinical nurse, and many of the staff seek her out in consultation about patient care problems. You have, however, heard several of the staff grumbling about Mary's behavior when she is in charge. As Mary's good friend, you do not want to hurt her feelings, but as her colleague you feel a need to be honest and open with her.

Assignment: This is a very difficult situation when personal and working relationships are combined. Describe what, if anything, you would do. Use the readings from the bibliography to assist you in making a plan.

EFFECTIVE USE OF APPRAISAL DATA

The most accurate and thorough appraisal will fail to produce growth in employees if the information gathered is *not* used appropriately. Many appraisal interviews have negative outcomes because the manager views them as a time to instruct the employee only on what they are doing wrong, rather than looking at strengths as well.

Difficulties with Appraisal Interviews

Managers often dislike the appraisal interview more than the actual data gathering. One of the reasons managers dislike the appraisal interview is because of their own negative experiences when they have been judged unfairly or criticized personally. Both parties in the appraisal process tend to be anxious before the interview, and thus the appraisal interview remains an emotionally charged event. For many employees, past appraisals have been traumatizing. Although little can be done to eliminate completely the often negative emotions created by past experiences, the leader/manager can manage the interview in such a manner that individuals will not be traumatized further.

Overcoming Appraisal Interview Difficulties

Feedback, perhaps the greatest tool a manager has for changing behavior, must be given in an appropriate manner (Huston & Marquis, 1989). There is a greater chance that the performance appraisal will have a positive outcome if certain conditions are present before, during, and following the interview (Marquis & Huston, 1994).

Before the Interview

1. Make sure that the conditions mentioned previously have been met; for example, the employee knows the standard by which his or her work will be evaluated, and he or she has a copy of the appraisal form.
2. Select an appropriate time for the appraisal conference. Do not choose a time when the employee has just had a traumatic personal event or is too busy at work to take the time needed for a meaningful conference.
3. Give the employee a 2- to 3-day advance notice of the scheduled appraisal conference so that he or she can be prepared mentally and emotionally for the interview.
4. Be personally prepared mentally and emotionally for the conference. If something should happen to interfere with your readiness for the interview, it should be canceled and rescheduled.
5. Schedule uninterrupted interview time. Hold the interview in a private, quiet, and comfortable place.
6. Plan a seating arrangement that reflects collegiality rather than power. Having the individual seated across a large desk from the appraiser denotes a power/status position; placing the chairs side by side denotes collegiality.

During the Interview

1. Greet the employee warmly, showing that the manager and the organization have a sincere interest in his or her growth.
2. Begin the conference on a pleasant, informal note.
3. Ask the employee to comment on his or her progress since the last performance appraisal.
4. Avoid surprises in the appraisal conference. The effective leader coaches and communicates informally with staff on a continual basis, so there should be little new information at an appraisal conference.
5. Use coaching techniques throughout the conference.
6. When dealing with an employee who has several problems—either new or long-standing—don't overwhelm him or her at the conference. If there are too many problems to be addressed, select the major ones.
7. Conduct the conference in a nondirective and participatory manner. Input from the employee should be solicited throughout the interview. McMurray (1993) suggests that relinquishing some control and involving the employee at every stage of the performance appraisal process will encourage employee participation.
8. Focus on the employee's performance and not his or her personal characteristics.
9. Avoid vague generalities, either positive or negative, such as "you're doing fine" or "your assessment skills could improve" (McMurray, 1993). Be prepared with explicit performance examples. Be liberal in the positive examples of employee performance; use examples of poor performance sparingly. Use several examples only if the employee has difficulty with self-awareness and requests specific instances of a problem area.
10. When delivering performance feedback, be straightforward, and state concerns directly (McMurray, 1993). Indirectness and ambiguity are more likely to inhibit communication rather than enhance it, and the employee is left unsure about the significance of your message.
11. Never threaten, intimidate, or use status in any manner. The appraiser must make sure that the individual's self-esteem is not threatened because this will prevent the nurturing of a meaningful and constructive relationship between the manager and employee.
12. Let the employee know that the organization and the manager are aware of his or her uniqueness, special interests, and valuable contributions to the unit. Remember that all employees make some special contribution to the workplace.
13. Make every effort to ensure that there are no interruptions during the conference.
14. Use terms and language that are clearly understood and carry the same meaning for both parties. Avoid words that have a negative connotation. Do not talk down to employees or use language that is inappropriate for their level of education.
15. Mutually set goals for further growth or improvement in the employee's

performance. Decide how goals will be accomplished and evaluated and what support is needed.

16. Plan on being available for employees to return retrospectively to discuss the appraisal review further. There is frequently a need for the employee to return for elaboration if the conference did not go well or if the employee was given unexpected new information. This is especially true for the new employee.

Following the Interview

1. Both the manager and employee need to sign the appraisal form to document that the conference was held and that the employee received the appraisal information. This does not mean that the employee is agreeing to the information in the appraisal; it merely means the employee has read the appraisal. An example of such a form is shown in Display 19.4. There should be a place for comments by both the manager and the employee.
2. End the interview on a pleasant note.
3. Document the goals for further development that have been agreed on by both parties. The documentation should include target dates for accomplishment, support needed, and when goals are to be reviewed. This documentation is often part of the appraisal form.
4. If the interview reveals specific long-term coaching needs, the manager should develop a method of follow-up to ensure such coaching takes place.

COACHING: A MECHANISM FOR INFORMAL PERFORMANCE APPRAISAL

As noted previously, the employee's formal evaluation should not contain surprises because the effective manager and astute leader is aware that day-to-day feedback regarding performance is one of the best methods for improving work performance and building a team approach. The word *coaching* (described in Chap. 13) has become a contemporary term to convey the spirit of the manager's role in informal day-to-day performance appraisals. Coaching techniques also should be used in the formal appraisal interview but are especially effective for encouraging and correcting daily work performance. Haas and Gold (1993) suggest that managers use the often "neglected art of administrative rounds" to provide regular opportunities for coaching staff.

When coaching is combined with informal performance appraisal, the outcome is usually a positive modification of behavior. For this to occur, however, the leader must establish a climate in which there is a free exchange of ideas. For this coaching feedback to be effective and improve work performance, it should be delivered in the following manner (Orth, Wilkinson, & Benfari, 1990):

1. Be specific, not general in describing behavior that needs improvement.
2. Be descriptive, not evaluative, when describing what was wrong with the work performance.

Display 19.4 Performance Appraisal Documentation Form

Performance appraisal for:

Name: _____

Unit: _____

Prepared by: _____

Reason: _____
                          (Merit, terminal, end of probation, general reviews)

Date of evaluation conference: _____

Comments by employee.

                                    Employee's signature: _____
(Signature of employee denotes that the evaluation has been read. It *does not* signify acceptance or agreement. Space is provided for any comments employee wishes to make.)

Comments by evaluator:
(These comments are to be written at the time of the evaluation conference and in the
presence of the employee.)

_____   _____   _____
Employee's signature   Date   Evaluator's signature

(From Huston & Marquis, 1989.)

---

3. Be certain that the feedback is not self-serving but meets the needs of the
   employee.
4. Direct the feedback toward behavior that can be changed.
5. Use sensitivity in timing the feedback.
6. Make sure the employee has clearly understood the feedback and that the
   employee's communication also has been clearly heard.

   When employees believe that their manager is interested in their performance
and personal growth, they will have less fear of the work performance appraisal.
When that anxiety is reduced, the formal performance interview process can be used
to set mutual performance goals.

INTEGRATING LEADERSHIP ROLES AND MANAGEMENT FUNCTIONS IN CONDUCTING PERFORMANCE APPRAISALS

Performance appraisal is a major responsibility in the controlling function of management. The ability to conduct meaningful, effective performance appraisals requires an investment of time, effort, and practice on the part of the manager (McMurray, 1993). Although performance appraisal is never easy, if used appropriately, it produces growth in the employee and increases productivity in the organization.

To increase the likelihood of successful performance appraisal, managers should use a formalized system of appraisal and gather data about employee performance in a systematic manner, using many sources. The manager also should attempt to be as objective as possible, using established standards for the appraisal. The result of the appraisal process should provide the manager with information for meeting training and educational needs of employees. By following up conscientiously on identified performance deficiencies, employee work problems can be corrected before they become habitual.

Integrating leadership into this part of the controlling phase of the management process provides an opportunity for sharing, communicating, and growing. The integrated leader/manager is self-aware regarding his or her own biases and prejudices. This self-awareness leads to fairness and honesty in evaluating performance. This, in turn, increases trust in the manager and promotes a team spirit among employees.

The leader also uses day-to-day coaching techniques to improve work performance and reduce the anxiety of performance appraisal. When anxiety is reduced during the appraisal interview, the leader/manager is able to establish a relationship of mutual goal setting, which has a greater potential to result in increased motivation and corrected deficiencies. The result of the integration of leadership and management is a performance appraisal that facilitates employee growth and increases organizational productivity.

KEY CONCEPTS

▼ The employee *performance appraisal* is a sensitive and important part of the management process, requiring much skill.

▼ When accurate and appropriate appraisal assessments are performed, the outcomes can be very positive.

▼ Performance appraisals are used to determine how well employees are performing their job, using the job description as a standard of measurement.

▼ There are many different types of appraisal tools. While some appraisal tools are better designed than others, all have advantages and disadvantages.

▼ The employee must be involved in the appraisal process and must view the appraisal as accurate and fair.

▼ MBO has proven to increase productivity and commitment in employees.

▼ *Peer review*, although infrequently used in the appraisal process, has great potential for developing professional accountability.

▼ Unless the appraisal interview is carried out in an appropriate and effective manner, the performance appraisal data will be useless.

▼ Due to past experiences, performance appraisal interviews are highly charged, emotional events for most employees.

▼ Showing a genuine interest in the employee's growth and seeking his or her input at the interview will increase the likelihood of a positive outcome from the appraisal process.

▼ Performance appraisals should be signed to show that feedback was given to the employee.

▼ Informal work performance appraisals are an important management function.

▼ Leaders should routinely use appropriate *coaching* techniques to improve work performance on an informal basis.

 ADDITIONAL LEARNING EXERCISES

Learning Exercise 19.4

You are the director of a home health agency. You have just returned from a management course and have been inspired by the idea of requesting input from your subordinates about your performance as a manager.

You realize that there are some risks involved but feel the potential benefits from the feedback outweigh the risks. However, you want to provide some structure for the evaluation, so you spend some time designing your appraisal tool and developing your plan.

Assignment: What type of tool will you use? What is your overall goal? Will you share the results of the appraisal with anyone else? How will you use the information obtained? Would you have the appraisal forms signed or anonymous? Who would you include in the group evaluating you? Be able to support your ideas with appropriate rationale.

Learning Exercise 19.5
(From Marquis & Huston, 1994.)

You are the new night shift charge nurse in a large intensive care unit composed of an all-RN staff. When you were appointed to the position, your supervisor told you that there had been some complaints regarding the manner in which evaluation sessions had been handled by the previous charge nurse.

Not wanting to repeat the mistakes, you draw up a list of things you could do to make the evaluation interviews less traumatic. Because the evaluation tool appears adequate, you feel the problems must lie with the interview itself. You put at the top of your list that you will make sure each employee has advance notice of the evaluation.

Assignment: How much advance notice should you give? What additional criteria would you add to the list to help eliminate much of the trauma that frequently accompanies performance appraisal (even when the appraisal is very good)?

Add six to nine items to the list. Explain why you think each of these would assist in alleviating some of the anxiety associated with performance appraisals. Do not just repeat the guidelines listed in this chapter. You may make the guidelines more specific or use the bibliography for assistance in developing your own list.

Learning Exercise 19.6

Patty Brown is an LVN/LPN who has been employed on your unit for 10 years. She is an older woman and is very sensitive to criticism. Her work is generally of high quality, but in reviewing her past performance appraisals, you notice that during the last 10 years, at least seven times she has been rated unsatisfactory for being on duty promptly and eight times for not attending staff development programs. Because you are the new charge nurse, you would like to help Patty grow in these two areas.

You have given Patty a copy of the evaluation tool and her job description and have scheduled her appraisal conference for a time when the unit will be quiet. You can conduct the appraisal in the conference room.

Assignment: How would you conduct this performance appraisal? Outline your plan. Include how you would begin. What innovative or creative way would you attempt to provide direction or improvement in areas mentioned? How would you terminate the session? Be able to give rationale for your decisions.

Learning Exercise 19.7
(From Marquis & Huston, 1994.)

Mr. Jones, a 49-year-old automobile salesman, was admitted with severe back pain. As his primary care nurse, you have established a rapport with Mr. Jones. He has a type A personality and has been very critical of much of his hospitalization. He also was very upset by the quality and quantity of his pain following his laminectomy.

You agreed to ambulate him on your shift three times (at 4 PM, 7 PM, and 10:30 PM) so that he would need to be ambulated only once during the day shift. He does not care for many of the day staff and feels that you help ambulate him better than anyone else. You noted the ambulating routine on his nursing orders.

Yesterday, Joan Martin, a day nurse, felt his bowel sounds were somewhat diminished. She urged him to ambulate more on the day shift, but he refused to do so. (The doctor had ordered ambulation q.i.d.) When Mr. Jones' physician visited, nurse Martin told him that Mr. Jones ambulated only once on the shift. She did not elaborate further to the doctor. The physician proceeded to talk very sternly with Mr. Jones, telling him to get out of bed three times today. Joan did not mention this incident to you in report.

By the time that you arrived on duty and received report, Mr. Jones was very angry. He threatened to sign himself out against medical advice. You talked with his doctor, got the order changed, and finally managed to calm Mr. Jones down. You then wrote a nursing order that read "nurse Martin is not to be assigned to Mr. Jones again."

When Joan Martin came on duty this morning, the night shift pointed out your notation. She was very angry and went to see the head nurse.

Assignment: Should you have done anything differently? If so, what? Could the evaluation of clinical performance by you and Joan Martin have been done in a manner that would not have resulted in conflict? If you were nurse Martin, what could you have done to prevent the conflict? Be able to discuss this case in relation to professional trust, peer review, and assertive communication.

Learning Exercise 19.8
(From Marquis & Huston, 1994.)

You are a senior baccalaureate nursing student. This is your sixth week of a medical-surgical advanced practicum. Your instructor assigns two students to work together caring for four to six patients. The students alternate fulfilling leader and follower roles and providing total patient care. This is the second full day you have worked as a team with Sally Brown.

Last week, when you were assigned with Sally, she was the leader and made numerous errors in judgment. She got a patient up who was on strict bed rest. She made an intravenous medication error by giving a medication to the wrong patient. She gave morphine too soon because she forgot to record the time in the medication record and she frequently did not seem to know what was wrong with her patients.

Today you have been the leader and have observed her contaminate a dressing and forget to check arm bands twice when she was giving medications. When you asked her about checking placement of the nasogastric tube, she did not know how to perform this skill. You have heard some of the other students complain about Sally.

Assignment: What is your obligation to your patients, your fellow students, the clinical agency, and your instructor? Outline what you would do. Give rationale for your decisions.

REFERENCES:

Andrusyszyn, M. A. (1990). Faculty evaluation: A closer look at peer review. *Nurse Educator Today, 10*(6), 410-—414.

Beach, D. (1980). *Personnel.* New York: Macmillan.

Blakely, G. L. (1993). The effects of performance rating discrepancies on supervisors and subordinates. *Organizational Behavior and Human Decision Process, 54*(5), 57–80.

Curtin, L. (1994). Collegial ethics of a caring profession. *Nursing Management, 25*(8), 28–30.

Dienemann, J. (1990). *Nursing administration.* Norwalk, CT: Appleton and Lange.

Haas, S., & Gold, C. (1993). Administrative rounds—A neglected art. *Journal of Nursing Administration, 23*(9), 65–69.

Huntsman, A. J. (1987). A model for employee development. *Nursing Management, 18*(2).

Huston, C. J., & Marquis, B. L. (1989). *Retention and productivity strategies for nurse managers.* Philadelphia: J.B. Lippincott.

Marquis, B. L., & Huston C. J. (1994). *Decision making for nurses: 101 Case studies* (2nd ed.). Philadelphia: J.B. Lippincott.

Marriner-Tomey, A. (1992). *Guide to nursing management* (4th ed.). St. Louis: Mosby Year Book.

Martin, K. (1994). How can the quality of nursing practice be measured? In J. M. McCloskey & H. K. Grace (Eds.), *Current issues in nursing* (4th ed.). St. Louis: C.V. Mosby.

McMurray, C. (1993). Performance appraisal: A measure of effectiveness. *Nursing Management, 24*(11), 94–95.

Orth, C. D., Wilkinson, H. E., & Benfari, R. C. (1990). The manager's role as coach and mentor. *Journal of Nursing Administration, 20*(9), 11–15.

Tappen, R. M. (1995). *Nursing leadership and management* (3rd ed.). Philadelphia: F.A. Davis.

Waldo, J. M., Hofschulte, L. E., Magno, L. T., & Colleran, M. A. (1993). Peer review for nurse managers. *Nursing Management, 24*(9), 58–59.

BIBLIOGRAPHY

American Nurses Association (1988). *Peer review guidelines.* Kansas City, MO: Author.

Anderson, P. A., & Davis, S. E. (1987). Nursing peer review: A developmental process. *Nursing Management, 18*(1).

Beck, R. A. (Ed.) (1986). *Performance assessment.* Baltimore: Johns Hopkins University Press.

Billings, C. V. (1987). Employment setting barriers to professional actualization in nursing. *Nursing Management, 18*(11).

Buechlein-Telutki, M. S., Bilak, Y., Merrick, M., Reich, M., & Stein, D. (1993). Nurse manager performance appraisal: A collaborative approach. *Nursing Management, 24*(10), 48–50.

Cocheu, T. (1986). Performance appraisal: A case in points. *Personnel Journal, Sept. 1,* 48–55.

Davidhizar, D. (1990). The manager as coach. *Advancing Clinical Care, 5*(3), 42–44.

Flarey, D. L. (1991). Management compensation: A reward systems approach. *Journal of Nursing Administration, 21*(7/8), 39–46.

Gellerman, S. W., & Hodgson, W. G. (1988). Cyanamid's new table on performance appraisal. *Harvard Business Review, 88*(3), 36–41.

Haas, S. H. (1992). Coaching: Developing key players. *Journal of Nursing Administration, 22*(6), 54–55.

Harmon, S. (1991). Giving constructive criticism with aplomb. *Medical Laboratory Observer, 23*(3), 24–27.

Hoeppner, M., & Schneller, S. (1995). Coaching: The staff nurse committee member. *Nursing Management, 26*(1), 53.

Maratea, J. M. (1991). If performance palls, look below the surface. *Medical Laboratory Observer, 23*(5), 19.

McGee, K. G. (1992). Making performance appraisals a positive experience. *Nursing Management, 23*(8), 36–37.

Nauright, L. (1987). Toward a comprehensive personnel system: Performance appraisal. *Nursing Management, 18*(8), 67–77.

Pelle, D., & Greenhalgh, L. (1987). Developing the performance appraisal system. *Nursing Management, 18*(12).

Schultz, A. W. (1993). Evaluation for clinical advancement system. *Journal of Nursing Administration, 23*(2), 13–19.

Smith, M. L. (1993). Defendable performance approvals. *Journal of Management Engineering, 9*(2), 128–135.

Sullivan, E. J., & Decker, P. J. (1990). *Effective management in nursing.* Menlo Park, CA: Addison-Wesley.

Yochem, B. (1991). Counseling: A "how to" for new nurse managers. *Pediatric Nursing, 17*(2), 201–202.

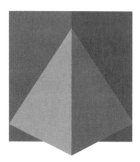

CHAPTER 20

Creating a Growth-Producing Work Environment Through Discipline

As unique individuals, employees' perceptions of what they owe the organization and what they owe themselves vary. At times, organizational and individual needs, wants, and responsibilities are in conflict. The coordination and cooperation needed to meet organizational goals requires leaders/managers to control the individual urges of subordinates that are counterproductive to these goals. Subordinates do this by self-control. Managers do this by enforcing established rules, policies, and procedures. Leaders do this by creating a supportive and motivating climate.

When employees are unsuccessful in meeting organizational goals, managers must attempt to identify reasons for this failure and counsel employees accordingly. If employees fail because they are unwilling to follow rules or established policies and procedures or they are unable to perform their duties adequately despite assistance and encouragement, the manager has an obligation to discipline the employee. *Discipline* can be defined as a training or molding of the mind or character to bring about desired behaviors. Thus, discipline allows one individual to have some control

Bessie L. Marquis and Carol J. Huston:
LEADERSHIP ROLES AND MANAGEMENT FUNCTIONS IN NURSING, 2nd ed.
Lippincott-Raven Publishers © 1996

over another. Display 20.1 identifies several of the leadership roles and management functions necessary to achieve discipline in the workplace.

This chapter focuses on discipline as a necessary and positive tool in promoting subordinate growth and meeting organizational goals. The normal progression of steps taken in disciplinary action is delineated. The chapter also reviews suggested components of disciplinary and termination conferences and strategies for administering discipline fairly and effectively. The need for an informal and formal system of handling employee grievances that result from the disciplinary process also is discussed.

CONSTRUCTIVE VERSUS DESTRUCTIVE DISCIPLINE

Scientific management theory viewed discipline as a necessary means for controlling an unmotivated and self-centered work force. Because of this traditional philosophy, managers primarily used threats and fear to control behavior. Written warnings and threats of termination were rampant, making the employee always alert to impending penalty or termination. This "big stick" approach to management focused on eliminating all behavior that could be considered to conflict with organizational goals, without regard for employee growth (Huston & Marquis, 1989).

Although this approach may be successful on a short-term basis, it is demotivating and reduces long-term productivity. This occurs because individuals will achieve only at the level they feel is necessary to avoid punishment. This approach also is destructive and demoralizing because discipline is often arbitrarily administered and is unfair either in the application of rules or in the resulting punishment. "In examining the history of crime, punishment has never been shown to be an effective deterrent. The individual who breaks rules does not plan that far ahead. They are not thinking of the consequences of their actions, only their immediate needs" (Beach, 1980).

Constructive discipline uses discipline as a means of helping the employee grow, not as a punitive measure. Punishment is frequently included when defining discipline, but it also can be defined as training, educating, or molding. In fact, the word *discipline* comes from the Latin term *disciplina*, which means teaching, learning, and growing. In constructive discipline, punishment may be applied for improper behavior, but it is carried out in a supportive, corrective manner. Employees are reassured that the punishment given is because of their actions and not because of who they are.

The primary emphasis in constructive discipline is assisting employees to behave in a manner that allows them to be self-directive in meeting organizational goals. Before employees can focus energy on meeting organizational goals, they must feel secure in the workplace. This security develops only when employees know and understand organizational rules and penalties and when rules are applied in a fair and consistent manner. In an environment that promotes constructive discipline, employees generally are self-disciplined to conform with established rules and regulations, and the primary role of the manager becomes that of coordinator and helper, rather than enforcer.

Display 20.1 Leadership Roles and Management Functions in Discipline and Limit Setting

Leadership Roles

1. Encourages employees to be self-disciplined in conforming with established rules and regulations.
2. Assists employees to identify with organizational goals, thus increasing the likelihood that the standards of conduct deemed acceptable by the organization will be accepted by its employees.
3. Humanistically uses discipline as a means of promoting employee growth.
4. Periodically assesses the need for existing rules and regulations and suggests modifications as necessary.
5. Is self-aware regarding the power and responsibility inherent in having formal authority to set rules and discipline employees.
6. Demonstrates sensitivity to the environment in which discipline is given.
7. Serves in the role of coach in performance deficiency coaching.

Management Functions

1. Ensures that rules and regulations are clearly written and communicated to subordinates.
2. Discusses rules and policies with subordinates, explaining the rationale for their existence and encouraging questions.
3. Enforces established rules in a fair and consistent manner.
4. Judiciously uses formal authority to take progressively stronger forms of discipline when employees continue to fail to meet expected standards of achievement.
5. Carefully documents employee behavior(s) that prompts disciplinary action and any attempts to counsel the employee.
6. Uses well-developed communication skills to do the following:
   a. Clearly explain the nature or seriousness of disciplinary problems
   b. Allow employees feedback in the disciplinary process
   c. Explain disciplinary actions to be taken and why
   d. Describe expected behavioral changes and what the consequences of failure to change will be
   e. Reach agreement and acceptance of the disciplinary plan with the employee
7. Disciplines union employees in accordance with the steps, penalties, and time frames established in the union contract.
8. Advises employees in seeking disciplinary action redress through informal and formal grievance procedures.

LEARNING EXERCISE 20.1

Think back to when someone in authority, such as a parent, teacher, or boss, set limits or enforced rules in such a way that you became a better child, student, or employee. What made this disciplinary action growth producing instead of destructive? What was the most destructive disciplinary action you ever experienced? Did it modify your behavior in any way?

SELF-DISCIPLINE AND GROUP NORMS

The highest level and most effective form of discipline is self-discipline. When employees feel secure, safe, validated, and affirmed in their essential worth, identity, and integrity, the natural growth process of self-discipline is encouraged (Covey, 1989). Ideally, all employees have adequate self-control and are self-directed in their pursuit of organizational goals. Unfortunately, this is not always the case.

Group norms are group-established standards of expected behavior that are enforced by social pressure. Group norms have a tremendous effect on the organizational climate and thus on individual behavior. The leader who understands group norms is able to work within those norms to mold group behavior. This modification of group norms, in turn, affects individual behavior and thus self-discipline.

Although self-discipline is internalized, the leader plays an active role in developing an environment that promotes self-discipline in employees. Health Care Education Associates (1987) have identified four factors that must be present to foster a climate of self-discipline. The first of these factors is *employee awareness and an understanding of rules and regulations that govern behavior.* Managers must discuss clearly written rules and policies with subordinates, explain the rationale for the rules' existence, and encourage questions. It is impossible for employees to have self-control if they do not understand the acceptable boundaries for their behavior, nor can they be self-directed if they do not understand what is expected of them.

The second factor that must exist is an *atmosphere of mutual trust.* Managers must believe that employees are capable of and actively seek self-discipline. Likewise, employees must respect their managers and perceive them as honest and trustworthy. Employees lack the security to self-discipline if they do not trust their manager's motives.

The third factor is that *formal authority must be used judiciously.* If formal discipline is quickly and widely used, subordinates do not have the opportunity to self-discipline.

 LEARNING EXERCISE 20.2

Think back to "rule breakers" you have known. Were they a majority or minority in the group? How great was their impact on group behavior? What characteristics did they have in common? Did the group modify the rule breaker's behavior, or did the rule breaker modify group behavior?

The fourth factor important in self-discipline is that *employees should identify with organizational goals.* When employees accept the goals and objectives of an organization, they are more likely to adopt the standards of conduct deemed acceptable by that organization.

FAIR AND EFFECTIVE RULES

Several rules must be followed if discipline is to be perceived by subordinates as growth producing and not punitive. This does not imply that subordinates enjoy being disciplined or that discipline should be a regular means of promoting employee growth. However, discipline, if implemented correctly, should not permanently alienate or demoralize subordinates.

McGregor (1967) has developed four rules to make discipline as fair and growth producing as possible. These rules are called *hot stove rules* because they can be applied to someone touching a hot stove:

1. All individuals must be *forewarned* that if they touch the hot stove (break a rule), they will be burned (punished or disciplined). They must know the rule beforehand and be aware of the punishment.
2. If the person touches the stove (breaks a rule), there will be *immediate* consequences (getting burned). All discipline should be administered immediately after rules are broken.
3. If the person touches the stove again, he or she will again be burned. Therefore, there is *consistency;* each time the rule is broken, there are immediate and consistent consequences.
4. If any other person touches the hot stove, he or she also will get burned. Discipline must be *impartial,* and everyone must be treated in the same manner when the rule is broken.

Unfortunately, most rule breaking is not enforced using McGregor's rules. For example, many people exceed the speed limit when driving. Generally, individuals are aware of speed limit regulations, and signs are posted along the roadway as reminders of the rules; thus, there is forewarning. There is not, however, immediacy, consistency, or impartiality. Many individuals exceed the speed limit for long periods before they are stopped and disciplined, or they may never be disciplined at all. Likewise, an individual may be stopped and disciplined one day and not the next even though the same rule is broken. Finally, the punishment is inconsistent because some individuals are punished for their rule breaking, and others are not. Even the penalty varies between individuals (Huston & Marquis, 1989).

Imagine that automobiles have been developed that require drivers to place a built-in electronic sensor on the end of their fingers before the automobile will operate. The purpose of this sensor would be to deliver a low-charge but painful electrical shock every time the car exceeds the posted speed limit. The driver would be forewarned of the consequences of breaking the speed limit rule. If each time the rule was broken, the driver immediately received an electrical shock and if all automobiles included this feature, speeding would probably be eliminated.

If a rule or regulation is worth having, it should be enforced (Marquis & Huston, 1994). When rule breaking is allowed to go unpunished, other individuals tend to replicate the behavior of the rule breaker. Likewise, the average worker's natural inclination to obey rules can be dissipated by lax or inept enforcement policies, because employees develop contempt for managers who allow rules to be disregarded. The enforcement of rules using McGregor's guide for rule fairness keeps morale from breaking down and allows structure within the organization.

An organization should, however, have as few rules and regulations as possible. A leadership role involves regularly reviewing all rules, regulations, and policies to see if they should be deleted or modified in some way. If managers find themselves spending all their time enforcing one particular rule, it would be wise to reexamine the rule and consider whether there is something wrong with the rule or how it is communicated.

> ### LEARNING EXERCISE 20.3
>
> Rules quickly become outdated and need to be deleted or changed in some way. Think of a policy or rule that needs to be updated. Why is the rule no longer appropriate? What could you do to update this rule? Does the rule need to be replaced with a new one?

DISCIPLINE AS A PROGRESSIVE PROCESS

Further action must be taken when employees continue undesirable conduct, either in breaking rules or in not performing their job duties adequately. Managers have the formal authority and responsibility to take progressively stronger forms of discipline when employees fail to meet expected standards of achievement. Most progressive discipline systems incorporate four steps.

Generally, the first step of the disciplinary process is *informal reprimand* or *verbal admonishment*. This reprimand includes an informal meeting between the employee and manager to discuss the broken rule or performance deficiency. The manager suggests ways in which the employee's behavior might be altered to keep the rule from being broken again. Often, informal reprimand is all that is needed for behavior modification.

The second step is *formal reprimand* or *written admonishment*. If rule breaking recurs after verbal admonishment, the manager again meets with the employee and issues a written warning about the behaviors that must be corrected. This written warning is very specific about what rules or policies have been violated and the potential consequences if behavior is not altered to meet organizational expectations. The written admonishment also should include any reference to previous informal reprimands, the employee's explanation of the incidents in question, a plan of action to achieve expected change or improvement, and the employee's opinion of that plan (Health Care Education Associates, 1987). Both the employee and the manager should sign the warning to signify that the problem or incident was discussed. The employee's signature does not imply that the employee agrees with everything on the report, only that it has been discussed. The employee must be allowed to respond in writing to the reprimand, either on the form itself or to attach comments to the disciplinary report; this allows the employee to air any differences in perception between the manager and the employee. One copy of the written admonishment is then given to the employee, and another copy is retained in the employee's personnel file. Display 20.2 presents a sample reprimand form.

The third step in progressive discipline is usually a *suspension from work without pay*. If the employee continues the undesired behavior despite verbal and written warnings, the manager should remove the employee from his or her job for a brief time, generally a few days to several weeks. Sometimes, a suspension gives an employee needed time to reflect and make some self-corrections or behavior modifications (Ellis & Hartley, 1995).

The last step in progressive discipline is *involuntary termination* or *dismissal*. In reality, many people will terminate their employment voluntarily before reaching this step, but the manager cannot be certain that this will occur (Ellis & Hartley, 1995). Termination should always be the last resort when dealing with poor performance. However, if the manager has given repeated warnings and rule breaking or policy violation continues, the employee should be terminated. Although this is difficult and traumatic for the employee, the manager, and the unit, the cost in terms of managerial and employee time and unit morale for keeping such an employee is enormous.

When using progressive discipline, the steps are followed progressively only for repeated infractions of the same rule. For example, even though an employee has previously received a formal reprimand for unexcused absences, discipline for a first-time offense of tardiness should begin at the first step of the process. Also remember that although discipline is generally administered progressively, some rule breaking is so serious that the employee may be suspended or dismissed with the first infraction. Table 20.1 presents a progressive discipline guide for managers.

When using progressive discipline in all but the most serious infractions, the slate should be wiped clean at the conclusion of a predesignated period, generally 1 to 2 years (Beach, 1980). Little justification exists for holding infractions against employees in perpetuity if the employee has modified his or her behavior.

DISCIPLINARY STRATEGIES FOR THE NURSE-MANAGER

It is vital that managers recognize their power in evaluating and correcting employees' behavior. Because a person's job is very important to him or her—often as a part of self-esteem and as a means of livelihood—disciplining or taking away an individual's job is a very serious action and should not be undertaken lightly (Marquis & Huston, 1994). The manager can implement several strategies to ensure that discipline is fair and growth producing.

The first strategy the manager must use is to investigate thoroughly the situation that has prompted the employee discipline. Has this employee been involved in a situation like this before? Was he or she disciplined for this behavior? What was his or her reaction to the corrective action? How serious or potentially serious is the current problem or infraction? Who else was involved in the situation? Does this em-

Display 20.2 Sample Written Reprimand Form

Employee name _____

Position _____ Date of hire _____

Person completing report _____

Position _____ Date report completed _____

Date of incident(s) _____ Time _____

Description of incident:

Prior attempts to counsel employee regarding this behavior (cite date and results of disciplinary conferences):

Disciplinary contract (plan for correction) and timelines:

Consequences of future repetition:

Employee comments: (Additional documentation or rebuttal may be attached)

_____   _____
Signature of individual   Employee signature
making the report

_____   _____
Date   Date

Date and time of follow-up appointment to review disciplinary contract:

TABLE 20.1   Guide to Progressive Discipline

Offense	First Infraction	Second Infraction	Third Infraction	Fourth Infraction
Gross mistreatment of a patient	Dismissal			
Discourtesy to a patient	Verbal admonishment	Written admonishment	Suspension	Dismissal
Insubordination	Written admonishment	Suspension	Dismissal	
Intoxication while on duty (this offense is difficult to prove)	Verbal admonishment	Written admonishment	Dismissal	
Use of intoxicants while on duty	Dismissal			
Neglect of duty	Verbal admonishment	Written admonishment	Suspension	Dismissal
Theft or willful damage of property	Written admonishment	Dismissal		
Falsehood	Verbal admonishment	Written admonishment	Dismissal	
Unauthorized absence	Verbal admonishment	Written admonishment	Dismissal	
Abuse of leave	Verbal admonishment	Written admonishment	Suspension	Dismissal
Deliberate violation of instruction	Verbal admonishment	Written admonishment	Suspension	Dismissal
Violation of safety rules	Verbal admonishment	Written admonishment	Dismissal	
Fighting	Verbal admonishment	Written admonishment	Suspension	Dismissal
Inability to maintain work standards	Verbal admonishment	Written admonishment	Suspension	Dismissal
Excessive unexcused tardiness*	Verbal admonishment	Written admonishment	Dismissal	

*The first, second, and third infractions do not mean the first, second, and third time an employee is late, but the first, second, and third time that unexcused tardiness becomes excessive as determined by the manager. (From Marquis, B., & Huston, C.J. [1994]. Management decision making for nurses: 101 case studies. Philadelphia: J.B. Lippincott.)

ployee have a history of other types of disciplinary problems? What is the quality of this employee's performance in the work setting? Have other employees in the organization also experienced the problem? How were they disciplined? Could there be a problem with the rule or policy? Were there any special circumstances that could have contributed to the problem in this situation? What disciplinary action is suggested by organizational policies for this type of offense? Will this type of disciplinary action keep the infraction from recurring? The wise manager will ask all these questions so that a fair decision can be reached about an appropriate course of action.

> ### LEARNING EXERCISE 20.4
>
> You are the supervisor of a neurological care unit. One morning you receive report from the night shift RNs. Neither of the nurses reports anything out of the ordinary except that the young head-injury patient has been particularly belligerent and offensive in his language. This young man was especially annoying because he appeared rational and then would suddenly become abusive. His language was particularly vulgar. You recognize that this is fairly normal behavior in a head-injury patient, but yesterday morning his behavior was so offensive to his neurosurgeons that one of them threatened to wash his mouth out with soap.
>
> After both night nurses leave the unit, you receive a phone call from the house night supervisor. She relates the following information: When the supervisor made her usual rounds to the neuro unit, nurse Caldwell was on a coffee break and Nurse Jones was in the unit with two LVNs/LPNs. Nurse Jones reported that nurse Caldwell became very upset with the head-injury patient because of his abusive and vulgar language and had taped his mouth shut with a 4-inch piece of adhesive tape. Nurse Jones had observed the behavior and had gone to the patient's bedside and removed the piece of tape and suggested that nurse Caldwell go get a cup of coffee. The supervisor observed the unit several times following this, and nothing else appeared to be remiss. She stated that nurse Jones said no harm had come to the patient and that she was reluctant to report the incident but felt perhaps one of the supervisors should counsel Nurse Caldwell. You thank the night supervisor and consider the facts in this case, which follow:
>
> Nurse Caldwell has been an excellent nurse but is occasionally judgmental.
> Nurse Caldwell is a very religious young woman and has led a rather sheltered life.
> Taping a patient's mouth with a 4-in piece of adhesive tape is very dangerous, especially for someone with questionable chest and abdominal injuries and neurologic injuries.
> Nurse Caldwell has never been reprimanded before.
>
> You call the physician and explain what happened. He says that he feels there was no harm done. He agrees with you that it is up to you whether to discipline the employee and to what degree. However, he feels most of the medical staff would want the nurse fired.
>
> You phone the nurse and arrange for a conference with her. She tearfully admits what she did. She states that she lost control. She asks you not to fire her, although she agrees this is a dischargeable offense. You consult with the administration, and everyone agrees that you should be the one to decide the disciplinary action in this case.
>
> *Assignment:* Decide what you would do. You have a duty to your patients, the hospital, and your staff. List at least four possible courses of action. Select from among these choices, and justify your decision.

Another strategy the manager should use is always to consult with either a superior or the personnel department prior to dismissing an employee. Most organizations have very clear policies about which actions constitute grounds for dismissal and how that dismissal should be handled. To protect themselves from charges of willful or discriminatory termination, managers should carefully document the behavior that occurred and any attempts to counsel the employee. Managers also must be careful not to discuss the reasons for terminating an employee with another employee or to make negative comments about past employees, which may discourage other employees or reduce their trust in the manager (Health Care Education Associates, 1987).

Performance Deficiency Coaching

Performance deficiency coaching is another strategy that the manager can use to create a disciplined work environment. As discussed in Chapter 13, coaching may be ongoing or problem centered. Problem-centered coaching is less spontaneous and requires more managerial planning than ongoing coaching. In performance deficiency coaching, the manager actively brings areas of unacceptable behavior or performance to the attention of the employee and works with him or her to establish a plan to correct deficiencies. Because the role of coach is less threatening than that of enforcer, the manager becomes a supporter, enabler, and helper. Orth, Wilkinson, and Benfari (1990) state that performance deficiency coaching should not be viewed as a one-time way of solving problems but as a way of helping employees, over time, improve (change) their performance (behavior and results) to the highest level of which they are capable. As such, the development, use, and mastery of performance deficiency coaching should result in improved performance for all. The scenario depicted in Display 20.3 is an example of performance deficiency coaching.

LEARNING EXERCISE 20.5

You are the professional staff coordinator of a small emergency care clinic. Historically, the clinic is busiest on weekend evenings, when the majority of drunk driving injuries, stabbings, and gunshot wounds occur. In addition, many use the clinic on weekends to take care of nonemergency medical needs that were not addressed during regular physician office hours during the week. Jane has been an RN at the clinic since it opened 2 years ago. She is well liked by all the employees and provides a sense of humor and lightheartedness in what is usually a highly stressful environment.

Jane has a reputation for being a "party animal." She is known to begin partying after work on Friday night and close down the bars Saturday morning. During the last 3 months, Jane has called in sick five of the seven Saturday evenings she was scheduled to work. The other employees have worked understaffed on what is generally the busiest night of the week, and they are becoming angry. They have asked you to talk to Jane or to staff an additional employee on the Saturday evenings Jane is assigned to work.

Assignment: You have decided to begin performance deficiency coaching with Jane. Write a possible coaching scenario that includes the following:

1. The problem stated in behavioral terms.
2. An explanation to the employee of how the problem is related to organizational functioning
3. A clear statement of possible consequences of the unwanted behavior
4. A request for input from the employee
5. Employee participation in the problem solving
6. A plan for follow-up on the problem

Display 20.3 Performance Deficiency Coaching Scenario

Coach: I am concerned that you have been regularly coming into report late. This interrupts the other employees who are trying to hear report and creates overtime as the night shifts must stay and repeat report on the patients you missed. It also makes it difficult for your modular team members to prioritize their plan of care for the day if the entire team is not there and ready to begin at 0700. Why is this problem occurring?

Employee: I've been having problems lately with an unreliable babysitter and my car not starting. It seems like it's always one thing or another and I'm upset about not getting to work on time, too. I hate starting my day off behind the eight ball.

Coach: This hospital has a longstanding policy on attendance, and it is one of the criteria used to judge work performance on your performance appraisal.

Employee: Yes, I know. I'm just not sure what I can do about it right now.

Coach: What approaches have you tried in solving these problems?

Employee: Well, I'm buying a new car, so that should take care of my transportation problems. I'm not sure about my babysitter though. She's young and not very responsible, so she'll call me at the last minute and tell me she's not coming. I keep her though because she's willing to work the flexible hours and days that this job requires, and she doesn't charge as much as a formal day care center would.

Coach: Do you have family in the area or close friends you can count on to help with child care on short notice?

Employee: Yes, my mother lives a few blocks away and is always glad to help, but I couldn't count on her on a regular basis.

Coach: There are employment registry lists at the local college for students interested in providing child care. Have you thought about trying this option? Often, students can work flexible hours and charge less than formal day care centers.

Employee: That's a good idea. In fact, I just heard about a child care referral service that also could give me a few ideas. I'll stop there after work. I realize that my behavior has affected unit functioning, and I promise to try to work this out as soon as possible.

Coach: I'm sure these problems can be corrected. Let's have a follow-up visit in 2 weeks to see how things are going.

The Disciplinary Conference

When coaching is unsuccessful in modifying behavior, the manager must take more aggressive steps and use more formal measures, such as a disciplinary conference. After thoroughly investigating employee offenses, managers must confront employees with their findings. This occurs in the form of a disciplinary conference. Health Care Education Associates (1987) have identified the following steps in the disciplinary conference:

1. *State the problem clearly and specifically, and refer to previous discussions of the rule violation.* The manager must not be hesitant or apologetic. Novice man-

agers often feel uncomfortable with the disciplinary process and may provide unclear or mixed messages to the employee regarding the nature or seriousness of a disciplinary problem. Managers must assume the authority given to them by their role. A major responsibility in this role is evaluating employee performance and suggesting appropriate action for improved or acceptable performance. Disciplinary problems, if unrecognized or ignored, generally do not go away; they get worse.

2. *Ask the employee why there has been no improvement.* Give the employee the opportunity to explain any limiting or extraneous factors of which you may not be aware. Allowing employees feedback in the disciplinary process ensures them recognition as a human being and reassures them that your ultimate goal is to be fair and promote their growth.

3. *Explain the disciplinary action you are going to take and why you are going to take it.* Although the manager must keep an open mind to new information that may be gathered in the second step, preliminary assessments regarding the appropriate disciplinary action should already have been made. This discipline should be communicated to the employee. The employee who has been counseled at previous disciplinary conferences should not be surprised at the punishment, because it should have been discussed at the last conference.

4. *Describe the expected behavioral change, and list the steps needed to achieve this change. Explain the consequences of failure to change.* Again, the manager must not be apologetic or hesitant, or the employee will be confused about the seriousness of the threat. Because they lack self-control, employees who have repeatedly broken rules need firm direction. It must be very clear to the employee that timely follow-up will occur.

5. *Get agreement and acceptance of the plan. Give support, and let the employee know that you are interested in him or her as a person.* Because discipline is administered to promote employee growth rather than to punish, the leader/manager is a humanist. Although the expected standards must be very clear, the leader imparts a sense of genuine concern for and desire to help the employee grow. This approach helps the employee recognize that the discipline is directed at the offensive behavior and not at the individual. The leader must be cautious, however, not to relinquish the management role in an effort to nurture and counsel. The leadership role is to provide a supportive environment and structure so that the employee can make the necessary changes.

In addition to understanding what should be covered in the disciplinary conference, the leader must be sensitive to the environment in which discipline is given. All discipline, even informal admonishments, should be conducted in private. Although the employee must receive feedback about his or her rule breaking or inappropriate behavior as soon as possible after it has occurred, the manager should never discipline in front of patients or peers. If more than an informal admonishment is required, the manager should inform the employee of the unacceptable action and then schedule a formal disciplinary conference later.

All formal disciplinary conferences should be scheduled in advance at a time agreeable to both the employee and manager. Both will want time to reflect on the situation that has occurred. Allowing lag time should reduce the situation's emotionalism and promote employee self-discipline, because employees often identify their own plan for keeping the behavior from recurring.

In addition to privacy and advance scheduling, the length of the disciplinary conference is important; it should not be so long that it degenerates into a debate, nor so short that both the employee and manager cannot state their positions. The facts of the situation should be stated, and each party should provide input. If the employee seems overly emotional or if great discrepancies exist between the manager's and employee's perceptions, an additional conference should be scheduled. Employees often need time to absorb what they have been told and to develop a plan that is not defensive.

The Termination Conference

At times, the disciplinary conference must be a termination conference. Although many of the principles are the same, the termination conference differs from a disciplinary conference in that planning for future improvement is eliminated. The following steps should be followed in the termination conference (Health Care Education Associates, 1987):

1. *Calmly state the facts of the situation, and explain the reasons for termination.* The manager must not appear angry or defensive. Although managers may express regret that the outcome is termination, they must not dwell on this or give the employee reason to think the decision is not final. The manager should be prepared to give examples of the behavior in question.

2. *Explain the termination process.* State the date of termination and the employee's and organization's role in the process.

3. *Ask for employee input, and respond calmly and openly.* Listen to the employee, but do not allow yourself to be drawn emotionally into his or her anger or sorrow. Always stay focused on the facts of the case.

4. *End the meeting on a positive note.* The manager should wish the employee success in the future. The manager also should inform the employee what, if any, references will be supplied to prospective employers. Finally, it is usually best to allow the employee who has been terminated to leave the organization immediately. If the employee continues to work on the unit after termination has been discussed, it can be demoralizing for all the employees who work on that unit.

"GRIEVING" DISCIPLINARY ACTION

Growth can occur only when employees perceive that the feedback and discipline given to them is fair and just. When employees' perceptions of "fair" and "just" differ from those of their managers, the discrepancy can usually be resolved by a more formal means called a *grievance procedure*. The grievance procedure is essentially a statement of wrongdoing or a procedure to follow when one feels that a wrong has been committed. This procedure is not limited to resolving discipline discrepancies; it can be used by employees any time they feel they have not been treated fairly by management. This chapter, however, focuses specifically on grievances that result from the disciplinary process.

Most grievances or conflicts between employees and management can be resolved informally through communication, negotiation, compromise, and collaboration. Generally, though, even informal resolution has well-defined steps that should be followed.

If the employee and management are unable to resolve their differences informally, a formal grievance process begins. The steps of the formal grievance process are generally outlined in all union contracts or administrative policy and procedure manuals. Generally these steps include the progressive lodging of formal complaints up the chain of command. If resolution does not occur at any of these levels, a formal hearing is usually held. Several individuals or a small group are impaneled, much in the same way as a jury, to make a determination of what should be done. Ellis and Hartley (1995) warn managers that in disciplinary hearings, there is a tendency to favor the small "powerless" individual over the "powerful" institution. This tendency reinforces the need for the manager to have clear, objective, and comprehensive written records regarding the problem employee's behavior and attempts to counsel.

If the differences cannot be settled through a formal grievance process, the matter may finally be resolved in a process known as *arbitration*. In arbitration, both sides agree on the selection of a professional mediator who will review the grievance, complete fact finding, and interview witnesses prior to coming to a decision. About half of the grievance cases appealed to an arbitrator by labor unions involve disciplinary actions. In about half of these cases, management either reversed or modified its decision when the individual's appeal was upheld (Marriner-Tomey, 1992).

Although grievance procedures extract a great deal of time and energy from both the employee and the manager, these procedures serve several valuable and needed purposes. Grievances can settle some problems before they escalate into even larger ones. They also are a source of data to focus attention on ambiguous contract language for labor/management negotiation at a later date. Perhaps the most important outcome of a grievance is the legitimate opportunity it provides for employees to resolve conflicts with their superiors. Employees who are not given an outlet for resolving work conflicts become demoralized, angry, and dissatisfied. These emotions affect unit functioning and productivity. Even if the outcome is not in the favor of the individual filing the grievance, the grieving person will know that the opportunity was given to present the case to an objective third party, and the chances of constructive conflict resolution are greatly increased. In addition, managers tend to be fairer and more consistent when they know that employees have a method of redress for arbitrary managerial action.

Rights and Responsibilities in Grievance Resolution

Employees and managers have some separate and distinct rights and responsibilities in grievance resolution, but many overlap. Although it is easy to be drawn into the emotionalism of a grievance that focuses on one's perceived rights, the manager and employee must remember that they both have rights and that these rights have concomitant responsibilities. For example, although both parties have the right to be heard, both parties are equally responsible to listen without interrupting. The employee has the right to a positive work environment but has the responsibility to communicate needs and discontent to the manager. The manager has the right to expect a certain level of productivity from the employee but has the responsibility to provide a work environment that makes this possible. The manager has the right to expect employees to follow rules but has the responsibility to see that these rules are clearly communicated and fairly enforced.

Both the manager and the employee must show good will in resolving grievances. This means that both parties must be open to discussing, negotiating, and compromising and attempt to resolve grievances as soon as possible. The ultimate goal of the grievance should not be to win, but to seek a resolution that satisfies both the individual and the organization. In many cases, the manager can eliminate or reduce his or her risk of being involved in a grievance by fostering a work environment that emphasizes clear communication and fair, constructive discipline. Employees also can eliminate or reduce their risk of being involved in a grievance by being well informed about the labor contract, policies and procedures, and organizational rules. If both employee and employer recognize their rights and responsibilities, the incidence of grievances in the workplace should decrease. When mutual problem solving, negotiation, and compromise are ineffective at resolving conflicts, the grievance process can provide a positive and growth-producing resolution to disciplinary conflict.

DISCIPLINING THE UNIONIZED EMPLOYEE

It is essential that all managers be fair and consistent in disciplining employees regardless of whether a union is present. The presence of a union does, however, usually entail more procedural, legalistic safeguards in administering discipline and a well-defined grievance process for employees who feel they have been disciplined unfairly. For example, the manager of nonunionized employees has greater latitude in selecting which disciplinary measure is appropriate for a specific infraction. Although this gives the manager greater flexibility and latitude, discipline between employees may be inconsistent. On the other hand, unionized employees generally must be disciplined according to specific, preestablished steps and penalties within an established time frame. For example, the union contract may be very clear that excessive unexcused absences from work must be disciplined first by a written reprimand, then a 3-day work suspension, and then termination. This type of discipline structure is generally fairer to the employee but allows the manager little flexibility in evaluating each case's extenuating circumstances.

Another aspect of discipline that may differ between unionized and nonunionized employees is following due process in disciplining union employees. *Due process* means that management must provide union employees with a written statement outlining disciplinary charges, the resulting penalty, and reasons for the penalty. Employees then have the right to defend themselves against such charges and to settle any disagreement through formal grievance hearings (Beach, 1980).

Another difference between unionized and nonunionized employee discipline lies in the burden of proof. In disciplinary situations with nonunionized employees, the burden of proof typically falls on the employee. With union employees, the burden of proof for the wrongdoing and need for subsequent discipline fall on management. This means that managers disciplining union employees must keep detailed records regarding misconduct and counseling attempts.

The contract language used by unions regarding discipline may be very specific or very general. Most contracts recognize the right of management to discipline, suspend, or dismiss employees for just cause. *Just cause* is defined as "having substantial reasons to justify the actions taken" (Vestal, 1995, p. 347). For just cause to exist, the manager must be able to prove three things: 1) this employee did commit this offense or breach of rule; 2) the offense does, in fact, need some corrective action or penalty; and 3) the proposed penalty is appropriate to the offense (Metzger & Pointer, 1972). These contracts also generally recognize the right of the employee to submit grievances when they feel these actions have been taken unfairly or are discriminatory in some way.

Each manager is responsible for knowing all union contract provisions that affect how discipline is administered on their units. Managers also should work closely with others employed in human resource or personnel positions in the organization. These professionals generally prove to be invaluable resources for dealing with union employees.

INTEGRATING LEADERSHIP ROLES AND MANAGEMENT FUNCTIONS TO CREATE A GROWTH-PRODUCING WORK ENVIRONMENT THROUGH DISCIPLINE

When discipline is constructive, fair, and consistent, it provides the structure needed for high unit morale and productivity. When discipline is destructive, vindictive, and inconsistent, unit morale and productivity plummet. The skills of the leader/manager play a key role in determining the climate for discipline and how discipline is administered at the unit level.

The leader has the greatest impact on the disciplinary climate because he or she is responsible for actively shaping group norms and promoting self-discipline. The leader is a supporter, motivator, enabler, and coach. The humanistic attributes of the leadership role make employees want to follow the rules of the leader and thus the organization.

Management functions are more controlling because they involve the enforcement of established rules, policies, and procedures. Although good managerial practice greatly reduces the need for discipline, some employees still need external direction and discipline to accomplish organizational goals. Discipline allows the violating employee and all the employees on the unit to understand clearly the expectations of the organization and the penalty for failing to meet those expectations.

The integrated leader/manager is able to balance the need for employee growth and organizational structure. When discipline is deemed necessary, the integrated leader/manager administers that discipline in a constructive manner and ensures an outcome that is growth producing for all involved.

KEY CONCEPTS

▼ Discipline is a necessary and positive tool in promoting subordinate growth.

▼ In examining the history of crime, punishment alone has never emerged as an effective deterrent.

▼ The optimal goal in *constructive discipline* is assisting employees to behave in a manner that allows them to be self-directive in meeting organizational goals.

▼ To ensure fairness, rules should include the components of *forewarning, immediate application, consistency,* and *impartiality.*

▼ If a rule or regulation is worth having, it should be enforced. When rule breaking is allowed to go unpunished, groups generally adjust to and replicate the low-level performance of the rule breaker, and the average worker's natural inclination to obey rules is dissipated.

▼ As few rules and regulations as possible should exist in the organization. All rules, regulations, and policies should be regularly reviewed to see if they should be deleted or modified in some way.

▼ Except for the most serious infractions, discipline should be administered in progressive steps, which include *verbal admonishment, written admonishment, suspension,* and *termination.*

▼ In *performance deficiency coaching,* the manager actively brings areas of unacceptable behavior or performance to the attention of the employee and works with him or her to establish a short-term plan to correct deficiencies.

▼ The role of coach is less threatening than that of enforcer; thus, the manager becomes a supporter, enabler, and helper.

▼ The *disciplinary conference* provides the opportunity for the manager to delineate clearly to the employee what behavior is unacceptable to the organization and to work together in making a plan to alter that behavior.

▼ Although many of the principles are the same, the *termination conference* differs from a disciplinary conference in that planning for future improvement is eliminated.

▼ Growth can occur only when employees perceive that the feedback and discipline given to them are fair and just.

▼ The *grievance procedure* is essentially a statement of wrongdoing or a procedure to follow when one feels that a wrong has been committed. All employees should have the right to grieve disciplinary action that they feel has been arbitrary or unfair in some way.

▼ The presence of a union generally entails more procedural, legalistic safeguards for administering discipline and a well-defined grievance process for employees who feel they have been disciplined unfairly.

▲ ADDITIONAL LEARNING EXERCISES

Learning Exercise 20.6

You are the supervisor of a pediatric acute care unit. One of your patients, Joey, is a 5-year-old boy who sustained 30% third-degree burns, which have been grafted and are now healing. He has been a patient in the unit for approximately 2 months. His mother stays with him nearly all the waking hours and generally is supportive of both him and the staff.

In the last few weeks, Joey has begun expressing increasing frustration with basic nursing tasks, has frequently been uncooperative, and has in your staff's opinion become very manipulative. His mother is frustrated with Joey's behavior but feels that it is understandable given the trauma he has experienced. She has begun working with the staff on a mutually acceptable behavior modification program.

Although you have attempted to assign the same nurses to care for Joey as often as possible, it is not possible today. This lack of continuity is especially frustrating today because the night shift has reported frequent tantrums and uncooperative behavior. The nurse you have assigned to Joey is Monica. Monica is a good nurse but has lacked patience in the past with uncooperative patients. During the morning, you are aware that Joey is continuing to act out. Although Monica begins to look more and more harried, she states that she is handling the situation appropriately.

When you return from lunch, Joey's mother is waiting at your office. She furiously reports that Joey told her that Monica hit him and told him he was "a very bad boy" after his mother had gone to lunch. His mother feels physical punishment was totally inappropriate and that she wants this nurse to be fired. She also states that she has contacted Joey's physician and that he is on his way over.

You call Monica in to your office, where she emphatically denies all the allegations. Monica states that during the lunch hour, Joey refused to allow her to check his dressings and that she followed the behavior modification plan and discontinued his television privileges. She feels his accusations further reflect his manipulative behavior. You then approach Joey who tearfully and emphatically repeats the story he told to his mother. He is consistent about the details and swears to his mother that he is telling the truth. None of your staff were within hearing proximity of Joey's room at the time of the alleged incident. When Joey's doctor arrives, he demands that Monica be fired.

Assignment: Determine your action. You do not have proof to substantiate either Monica's or Joey's story. You feel that Monica is capable of the charges but are reluctant to implement any type of discipline without proof. What factors contribute the most to your decision?

Learning Exercise 20.7

Susie has been an RN on your medical surgical unit for 18 months. During that time, she has been a competent nurse in terms of her assessment and organizational skills and her skills mastery. Her work habits, however, need improvement. She frequently arrives 5 to 10 minutes late for work and disrupts report when she arrives. She also frequently extends her lunch break 10 minutes beyond the allotted 30 minutes. Her absence rate is twice that of most of your other employees.

You have informally counseled Susie about her work habits on numerous past occasions. Last month, you issued a written reprimand about these work deficiencies and placed it in Susie's personnel file. Susie acknowledged at that time that she needed to work on these areas but that her responsibilities as a single parent were overwhelming at times and that she felt demotivated at work. Every day this week, Susie has arrived 15 minutes late. The staff are complaining about Susie's poor attitude and have asked that you take action.

You contemplate what additional action you might take. The next step in progressive discipline would be a suspension without pay. You feel that this action could be supported given the previous attempts to counsel the employee without improvement. You also realize that many of your staff are closely watching your actions to see how you will handle this situation. You also recognize that suspending Susie would leave her with no other means of financial support and that this penalty is somewhat uncommon for the offenses described. In addition, you are unsure if this penalty will make any difference in modifying Susie's behavior.

Assignment: Decide what type of discipline, if any, is appropriate for Susie. Support your decision with appropriate rationale. Discuss your actions in terms of the effects on you, Susie, and the department.

Learning Exercise 20.8
(From Marquis & Huston, 1994.)

You are the coordinator of a small, specialized respiratory rehabilitation unit. Two other nurses work with you. Because all of the staff are professionals, you have used a very democratic approach to management and leadership. This approach has worked well, and productivity has always been high. The nurses work out schedules so that there are always two nurses on duty during the week, and they take turns covering the weekends, at which time there is only one RN on duty. With this arrangement, it is possible for three nurses to be on duty one day during the week, if there is no holiday or other time off scheduled by either of the other two RNs.

Several months ago, you told the other RNs that the State Licensing Board was arriving on Wednesday, October 16, to review the unit. It would, therefore, be necessary for both of them to be on duty because you would be staying with the inspectors all day. You have reminded them several times since that time. Today is Monday, October 14, and you are staying late preparing files for the impending inspection. Suddenly, you notice that only one of the RNs is scheduled to work on Wednesday. Alarmed, you phone Mike, the RN who is scheduled to be off. You remind him about the inspection and state that it will be necessary for him to come to work. He says that he is sorry that he forgot about the inspection but that he has scheduled a 3-day cruise and has paid a large, nonrefundable deposit. After a long talk, it becomes obvious to you that Mike is unwilling to change his plans. You say to him, "Mike, I feel this borders on insubordination. I really need you on the 16th, and I am requesting that you come in. If you do not come to work, I will need to take appropriate action." Mike replies, "I'm sorry to let you down. Do what you have to do. I need to take this trip, and I will not cancel my plans."

Assignment: What action could you take? What action should you take? Outline some alternatives. Assume it is not possible to float in additional staff because of the specialty expertise required to work in this department. Decide what you should do. Give rationale for your decision.

REFERENCES:

Beach, D. S. (1980) *Personnel: The management of people at work* (4th ed.). New York: Macmillan.

Covey, S. R. (1989). The 7 habits of highly effective people. New York: Simon and Schuster.

Ellis, J. R., & Hartley, C. L. (1995). Managing and coordinating care (2nd ed.). Philadelphia: J.B. Lippincott.

Health Care Education Associates (1987). *Models of excellence for nurse managers.* St. Louis: C.V. Mosby.

Huston, C. J., & Marquis, B. L. (1989). *Retention and productivity strategies for nurse managers.* Philadelphia: J.B. Lippincott.

Marquis, B. L., & Huston, C. J. (1994). *Management decision making for nurses: 101 Case studies.* Philadelphia: J.B. Lippincott.

Marriner-Tomey, A. (1992). Guide to nursing management (4th ed.). St. Louis: Mosby Year Book.

McGregor, D. (1967). *The professional manager.* New York: McGraw Hill.

Metzger, N., & Pointer, D. (1972). *Labor management relations in the health service industry.* New York: The Science and Health Publications.

Orth, C. D., Wilkinson, H. E., & Benfari, R. C. (1990). The manager's role as coach and mentor. *Journal of Nursing Administration, 20*(9), 11–15.

Vestal, K. W. (1995). Nursing management: Concepts and issues (2nd ed.). Philadelphia: J.B. Lippincott.

BIBLIOGRAPHY

Anthony, C. E., & del Bueno, D. (1993). A performance-based development system. *Nursing Management, 24*(6), 32–34.

Beletz, E. E. (1986). Discipline: Establishing just cause for correction. *Nursing Management, 17*(8), 63–67.

Bellocq, J. A. (1988). Student dismissal: How much documentation is enough? *Journal of Professional Nursing, 4*(3), 147, 230.

Brooke, P. S. (1990). Firing for cause. *Journal of Nursing Administration, 20*(9), 45–50.

Davidhizar, R., & Giger, J. (1990). When subordinates go over your head: The manipulative employee. *Journal of Nursing Administration, 20*(9), 29–34.

Glende, N. H. (1987). Constructive criticism: Building blocks to improved performance. *Nursing Life, 7*(2), 46–48.

Holle, M. L. (1986). What to do when your staff won't follow your lead. *Nursing Life, 6*(6), 48–50.

Jernigan, D. (1986). Keeping the gears meshing: Five steps for managing the problem employee. *Nursing Life, 6*(2), 50–54.

Klann, S. (1990). Procedures for disciplining employees. *OR Manager, 6*(4), 14, 16.

Manthey, M. (1989). Discipline without punishment; Part I. *Nursing Management, 20*(10), 19.

Manthey, M. (1989). Discipline without punishment; Part 2. *Nursing Management, 20*(11), 23.

Martin, B. J. (1990). A successful approach to absenteeism. *Nursing Management, 21*(8), 45–49.

Pozgar, G. D. (1989). Wrongful discharge and discipline. *Health Care Supervisor, 8*(1), 57–67.

Rogers, J. E., Hutchins, S. G., & Johnson, B. J. (1990). Non-punitive discipline: A method of reducing absenteeism. *Journal of Nursing Administration, 20*(7/8), 41–43.

Vestal, K. (1990). Fired! Managing the process. *Journal of Nursing Administration, 20*(June), 14–16.

Wieczorek, B. (1990). An alternative approach to discipline. *Pediatric Nursing, 16*(6), 587–588.

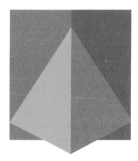

CHAPTER 21

Employees With Special Needs

Chapter 20 discusses the need for progressive discipline when dealing with employees who fail to follow established rules or procedures or to meet organizational goals. However, progressive discipline is inappropriate for employees who are impaired as a result of disease, degree of ability, or energy. These employees have special needs and require active coaching, support, and sometimes professional counseling to maintain productivity. Managers must be able to distinguish between employees needing progressive discipline and those who are impaired so that the employee can be managed most appropriately.

This chapter focuses on three types of employees with special needs: the chemically impaired employee, the marginal employee, and the disruptive superachiever. *Chemical impairment* refers to impairment due to drug or alcohol addiction. The scope of chemical addiction among nurses is discussed in this chapter, and behaviors common to chemically impaired nurses are presented to aid the manager in identifying these employees. In addition, the manager's role in confronting and assisting the chemically impaired employee is included. Steps in the recovery process and the reentry of the recovering chemically impaired nurse into the work force also are discussed.

Marginal employees are those whose quantity or quality of work standards con-

Bessie L. Marquis and Carol J. Huston:
LEADERSHIP ROLES AND MANAGEMENT FUNCTIONS IN NURSING, 2nd ed.
Lippincott-Raven Publishers © 1996

sistently meets only minimal standards considered acceptable by the unit or organization. These employees disrupt unit functioning because they are unable to carry their share of the workload. This chapter presents common coping methods used by managers working with marginal employees. Strategies for determining the best possible coping method for different situations are presented.

Disruptive superachievers, although at times productive and creative employees, cause unit turmoil with a controlling style, unwillingness to work with others, lack of flexibility, overdomination, and refusal to be a team player. The disruptive superachiever has a need to produce at a high level regardless of the cost. In their zeal to achieve, they alienate coworkers and create a tense and rigid work environment. Because these employees can be so productive, however, the manager is reluctant to take action. This chapter presents managerial strategies appropriate for coping with disruptive superachievers.

Assisting employees with special needs to become effective and productive members of the work force should not be viewed as an altruistic or benevolent action on the part of the manager. The cost of absenteeism, work-related accidents, lowered productivity, and turnover of these employees is immense. J.T. Wrich (1989) reports that the sick time, absenteeism, and general decreased productivity from impaired nursing practice is estimated to cost $5,000 per year, per employee. These employees place the organization at greater liability for patient care errors in judgment and reduce group morale and unit efficiency. LaGodna and Hendrix (1989) state the following:

> Nursing administrators may face no management problem more costly or emotionally draining than that of nurses whose practice is impaired by substance abuse or psychological dysfunction. The impact of impaired practice is felt in turnover and retention rates, benefits, staff morale and high level management time, as well as in quality of care.

Effective management demands that the organization take an active role in helping employees with special needs. Planning strategies that counsel and assist these employees in an effort to return them as productive members of the work force are not only humanistic, but cost effective and necessary. Leadership roles and management functions required to meet the special needs of these employees are shown in Display 21.1.

CHEMICAL IMPAIRMENT: SCOPE OF THE PROBLEM

Chemical dependency in the health professions was first documented in studies by Modlin and Montes (1964) in the late 1940s, although there is little doubt that chemical dependency has been around as long as alcohol and drugs have been. Substance abuse accounts for almost 70% of nurses who have their licenses withdrawn or revoked (Curtin, 1987). The American Nurses Association (1987) and Stammer (1988) estimate that 6% to 8% of nurses use alcohol or other drugs to an extent sufficient to impair their professional performance. Landry (1987) estimates that 8% to 10% of all registered nurses and licensed practical nurses in the United States have ei-

Display 21.1 Leadership Roles and Management Functions in Working with Employees with Special Needs

Leadership Roles

1. Recognizes and reinforces the intrinsic self-worth of each employee and the role of successful work performance in maintaining a positive self-image.
2. Is proactive in recognizing and appropriately intervening with impaired employees.
3. Takes an active interest in the well-being of each employee.
4. Is self-aware regarding values, biases, and beliefs about chemical abuse.
5. Uses active listening as a support tool in working with impaired subordinates.
6. Has the self-confidence and ego strength needed to modify the behavior of disruptive superachievers.
7. Recognizes own limitations in counseling and refers impaired employees to outside experts for appropriate counseling.

Management Functions

1. Uses legitimate authority appropriately to see that all employees contribute to unit functioning.
2. Clearly identifies performance expectations for all employees and confronts employees when those expectations are not met.
3. Assigns employees to work roles and situations that successfully challenge or intermittently "stretch" the employee. Does not allow employees to fail repeatedly.
4. Seeks out and completes extensive education about chemical abuse in the work setting. Provides these same opportunities to staff.
5. Acts as a resource to impaired employees regarding professional services or agencies that provide counseling and support services.
6. Collects and records adequate objective data when suspicious of employee chemical impairment.
7. Maintains control when employees are confronted with evidence of impaired behavior.
8. Focuses employee confrontations on performance deficits and not the cause of the underlying problem or addiction.
9. Works with the chemically impaired, marginal, and disruptive superachiever employee to develop a remedial plan for action. Ensures that the employee understands the performance expectations of the organization and the consequences of not meeting these expectations.

ther a drug or alcohol dependency; this equates to approximately 135,000 to 170,000 impaired nurses. These statistics suggest that at least 1 in 20 hospital nurses is working under the influence of some sort of mood-altering drug (Robinson & Spicer, 1987). The rate of narcotic addiction among nurses is estimated to approximate that of physicians—30 to 100 times that of the general population (Curtin, 1987; Murray, 1974).

The nursing profession as a whole has a 50% higher risk of becoming chemically addicted than other professions (Robinson & Spicer, 1987). This risk is greater in part because nursing is primarily a female occupation and current literature documents women's greater susceptibility to drug abuse than men. This may occur because women use more prescription mood-altering drugs, such as tranquilizers, than men do (Naegle, 1988; Robinson & Spicer, 1987). Women also are more apt to see their physician for medical and emotional problems and as a result, have more than twice as many prescriptions filled as men (Robinson & Spicer, 1987). Studies also have shown that most chemically addicted nurses first began abusing with legally prescribed drugs that were legitimately obtained for physical, emotional, personal, or job-related problems (Poplar, 1969).

Demerol and alcohol are the most commonly abused chemicals. Hughes and Smith (1994) report that of drugs other than alcohol, meperidine was by far the most commonly abused drug. Ninety-four percent of the members of the San Francisco Support Group for Chemically Dependent Nurses reported Demerol as their primary drug as well (Buxton & Jessup, 1983). Other abused chemicals frequently include the benzodiazepines, such as Valium, and other narcotic drugs, such as morphine and pentazocine (Talwin; Landry, 1987). Barbiturates may replace alcohol in the workplace so that the employee may feel a similar effect without having alcohol detectable on their breath. Likewise, addicted nurses may combine amphetamines and central nervous system depressants to facilitate their performance and mediate the depressed effect (Landry, 1987).

Clearly, the incidence of chemical impairment in health professionals is substantial. On a personal level, a person suffers from an illness that may go undetected and untreated for many years. On a professional level, the entire healthcare system is affected by the chemically impaired employee. Patient care is jeopardized by nurses with impaired skills and judgment. The chemically impaired nurse also compromises teamwork and continuity as colleagues attempt to pick up the slack of their impaired team member. The personal and professional cost of chemical impairment demands that nursing leaders and managers recognize the chemically impaired employee as early as possible and provide intervention.

Recognizing the Chemically Impaired Employee

Although most nurses have finely tuned assessment skills for identifying patient problems, they generally lack sensitivity in identifying behaviors and actions that could signify chemical impairment of an employee or colleague. Sensitivity to others and to the environment is a leadership skill. As drug dependency behaviors manifest in the employee, complex emotional barriers develop between the manager, the impaired employee, and other staff members (Robinson & Spicer, 1987). It is essential

---

Display 21.2 Common Personality/Behavior Changes of the Chemically Impaired Employee

- Increased irritability with patients and colleagues, often followed by extreme calm
- Social isolation; eats alone, avoids unit social functions
- Extreme and rapid mood swings
- Euphoric recall of events or elaborate excuses for behaviors
- Unusually strong interest in narcotics or the narcotic cabinet
- Sudden dramatic change in personal grooming or any other area
- Forgetfulness ranging from simple short-term memory loss to blackouts
- Change in physical appearance, which may include weight loss, flushed face, red or bleary eyes, unsteady gait, slurred speech, tremors, restlessness, diaphoresis, bruises and cigarette burns, jaundice, and ascites
- Extreme defensiveness regarding medication errors

---

that the nursing leader identify and intervene as soon as chemical impairment is reasonably suspected.

The profile of the impaired nurse may vary greatly, although several behavior patterns and changes have been frequently noted. These behavior changes can be grouped into three primary areas: personality/behavior changes, job performance changes, and time and attendance changes (Landry, 1987). Displays 21.2, 21.3, and 21.4 show characteristics of each of these categories.

As the employee progresses into a deeper stage of chemical dependency, managers can more easily recognize these behaviors. Typically, in the earliest stages of chemical dependency, the employee uses the addictive substance primarily for plea-

---

Display 21.3 Common Job Performance Changes of the Chemically Impaired Employee

- Difficulty meeting schedules and deadlines
- Illogical or sloppy charting
- High frequency medication errors or errors in judgment affecting patient care
- Frequently volunteers to be medication nurse
- Has a high number of assigned patients who complain that their pain medication is ineffective in relieving their pain
- Consistently meeting work performance requirements at minimal levels or doing the minimum amount of work necessary
- Judgment errors
- Sleeping or dozing on duty
- Complaints from other staff members about the quality and quantity of the employee's work

Display 21.4 Common Time and Attendance Changes of the Chemically Impaired Employee

- Increasingly absent from work without adequate explanation or notification; most frequent absence on a Monday or Friday
- Long lunch hours
- Excessive use of sick leave or requests for sick leave after days off
- Frequent calling in to request compensatory time
- Arriving at work early or staying late for no apparent reason
- Consistent lateness
- Frequent disappearances from the unit without explanation

sure, and although the alcohol or drug use is excessive, it is primarily recreational and social. Thus, generally substance use does not occur during work hours, although some effects of its use, such as absenteeism, judgment errors, and changes in interpersonal relationships, may be apparent (Robinson & Spicer 1987).

As chemical dependency deepens, the employee develops tolerance to the chemical and must use the substance in greater quantities and more frequently to achieve the same effect. At this point, the individual has made a conscious lifestyle decision to use chemicals. There is a high use of defense mechanisms, such as justifying, denying, and bargaining about their drug use (Hutchinson, 1987). Often the employee in this stage begins to use the chemical substance at and away from work. Drugs are often supplied by stealing patient medications and substituting other drugs (Ashton & Bay, 1994). In a study of 80 nurses who abused drugs, 61 (76%) took them from work either by taking a patient's prescription or by forging prescriptions (Sullivan, 1987). By this stage of chemical dependency, work performance generally declines in the areas of attendance, judgment, quality, and interpersonal relationships, and an appreciable decline in unit morale, as the result of an unreliable and unproductive worker, begins to be apparent (Robinson and & Spicer, 1987).

In the final stages of chemical dependency, the employee must continually use the chemical substance, even though they no longer gain any pleasure or gratification. The employee, physically and psychologically addicted, harbors a total disregard for self and others. In fact, two-thirds of chemically dependent nurses studied have seriously considered taking their own lives, compared with fewer than one in five nondependent nurses (Hughes & Smith, 1994).

Because the need for the substance is so great in this stage, the employee's personal and professional lives are focused around their need for drugs, and the employee becomes totally unpredictable and undependable in the work area. Assignments are incomplete or not done at all; charting may be sloppy or illegible; frequent judgment errors occur. Because the employee in this stage must use drugs frequently, there are often signs of drug use during work hours. Narcotic vials are missing. The employee may be absent from the unit for brief periods of time with no plausible excuse. Mood swings are excessive, and the employee often looks physically ill. As managers gain greater expertise in identifying the chemically impaired employee, it is easier to recognize and remove such employees from the work setting prior to this final stage.

The manager also must examine in which clinical area the suspected impaired nurse has been working. Buxton and Jessup (1983) found that 55% of addicted female nurses and 75% of addicted male nurses first self-administered a psychoactive drug while working in critical care areas, such as the intensive care unit, critical care unit, and emergency room. Whether these nurses took these drugs because of their inability to cope with the higher stress levels associated with these clinical areas or sought work in these areas because psychoactive drugs are more readily available is unclear.

Another factor that makes identifying impaired employees more difficult is that most managers have preconceived ideas about what the chemically impaired nurse looks like or acts like. Frequently these preconceptions include unkempt, marginally bright employees with a history of poor work performance and little self-motivation.

In reality, Bissell (1979) found that in a study of 100 alcoholic nurses, that most of them had the following characteristics:

- Were in the top third of their class
- Held advanced degrees
- Held demanding and responsible jobs
- Were highly respected for excellent work that continued long after they began to drink heavily
- Were ambitious and achievement oriented

These characteristics generally do not fit the stereotype managers have of a chemically impaired individual, especially a chemically impaired nurse. Surveys indicate that most nurses view substance abuse as a treatable disease unless the abuser is a colleague. With colleagues, nurses tend to believe that such behavior results from a moral defect (Curtin, 1987). Leaders/managers must be self-aware regarding their values, biases, and beliefs about chemical abuse before they can recognize and implement an appropriate strategy to help the impaired nurse overcome this disease.

In addition, both managers and subordinates clearly need extensive education about chemical abuse. Sixty-one percent of employers in a recent study said that they do not or have not provided staff education programs on substance abuse (Naegle, 1988). Nursing schools' courses generally focus on the physiological effects of alcohol and other drugs and deal little with the psychological process of addiction and even less with chemical dependency in nurses (Hughes & Smith, 1994) Because of

---

▶ LEARNING EXERCISE 21.1

Has your personal or professional life been affected by a chemically impaired person? In what ways have you been affected? Has it colored the way you view chemical abuse and chemical impairment? Do you feel you will be able to separate your personal feelings about chemical abuse from the actions you must take as a manager in working with chemically impaired employees?

this limited knowledge about chemical impairment, nurses today feel ill prepared to deal with drug impairment (Ashton & Bay, 1994).

Humanistic leaders recognize the intrinsic self-worth of each individual employee and strive to understand the unique needs these workers have. If the leader genuinely cares about and shows interest in each employee, employees learn to trust, and the helping relationship has a chance to begin.

Confronting the Chemically Impaired Employee

Unlike most alcoholics or intravenous narcotic users, healthcare professionals do not achieve clandestine peer approval for their addictive behavior. In contrast to other non-nurse addicts, studies have shown that nurses usually use their drugs in private, rather than with friends, to protect their professional identity (Poplar, 1969). Thus, physicians and nurses are much less likely to admit, even to colleagues, that they are using, much less that they are addicted to, a controlled substance (Landry, 1987). Frequently, they deny their chemical impairment even to themselves.

This self-denial is perpetuated because nurses and managers traditionally have been slow to recognize and reluctant to help these colleagues. Leffler (1986) carries this thought one step further when she contends that addicted nurses have not been discovered or confronted because of a "conspiracy of silence." "The impaired nurse is a personal as well as a professional embarrassment and if they can be kept out of sight, they will be out of mind" (Leffler, 1986, p. 41).

This attitude is slowly changing. Addicted nurses are finally being recognized as having a treatable disease, which is what drug or alcohol addiction is (Leffler, 1986). Baywood (1990) poses a strong argument for intervening with chemically impaired colleagues based on the ethical responsibility nurses have to "do no harm." She states, "We have a professional responsibility to our patients to assure them quality care, as well as a personal responsibility to our colleagues to help them overcome their impairment" (Baywood, 1990, p. 40). As managers gain more information about chemical impairment, how to recognize it, and how to intervene, more employees are being confronted with their impairment.

> ### LEARNING EXERCISE 21.2
>
> Have you ever suspected a work colleague of chemical abuse? What, if anything, did you do about it? If you did suspect a colleague, would you approach him or her with your suspicions before talking to the unit manager? Describe the risks involved in this situation.

The first step of confronting the impaired employee actually occurs before the confrontation process. In the data- or evidence-gathering phase, the manager collects as much hard evidence as possible to document his or her suspicions of chemical impairment in the employee. All behavior, work performance, and time and attendance changes presented in the displays in this chapter should be noted objectively and recorded in writing. If possible, a second person should be asked to validate the manager's observations. In suspected drug addiction, the manager also may examine unit narcotic records for inconsistencies and check to see that the amount of narcotic the nurse signed out for each patient is congruent with the amount ordered for that patient (Leffler and Doyle, 1986).

Proving alcohol impairment is more difficult because an employee can generally hide alcoholism more easily than drug addiction (Doyle, 1986). Because few nurses drink while on duty, the manager will have to observe for more subtle clues, such as the smell of alcohol on the employee's breath. If the organization's policy allows for it, the manager may wish to require an employee suspected of alcohol impairment while on duty to have a serum alcohol analysis. If the employee refuses to cooperate, the organization's policy for documenting and reporting this incident should be followed (Leffler and Doyle, 1986).

If at any time the manager suspects that an employee is chemically influenced and thus presents a potential hazard to patient safety, the employee must be immediately pulled off the unit and privately confronted with the manager's perceptions. The manager should decisively and unemotionally tell the employee that he or she will not be allowed to return to the work area because of the manager's perception that the employee is chemically impaired. The manager should arrange for the employee to be taken home so that he or she is not allowed to drive while impaired. A formal meeting to discuss this incident should be scheduled within the next 24 hours.

This type of direct confrontation between the manager and the employee is the second phase in dealing with the employee suspected of chemical impairment. Although some employees admit their problem when directly confronted, many use defense mechanisms (including denial) because they may not have admitted the problem to themselves. Denial and anger should be expected in the confrontation, and the manager must assume responsibility for controlling the situation (Robinson & Spicer, 1987). If the employee denies having a problem, documented evidence demonstrating a decline in work performance should be shared. The manager must be careful to keep the confrontation focused on the employee's performance deficits and not allow the discussion to be directed to the cause of the underlying problem or addiction. These are issues and concerns that the manager is unable to address. The manager also must be careful not to preach, moralize, scold, or blame.

Confrontation should always occur before the problem escalates too far. However, in some situations, the manager may have only limited direct evidence but still feel that the employee should be confronted because of rapidly declining employee performance or unit morale. There is, however, a greater risk that confrontation at this point may be unsuccessful in terms of helping the employee. If direct confrontation is unsuccessful, it may have been too early; the employee may not have been desperate enough or may still be in denial. In these situations, job performance will probably continue to be marginal or unsatisfactory, and progressive discipline may be necessary. If the employee continues to deny chemical impairment, and work performance continues to be unsatisfactory despite repeated constructive confrontation, it may be necessary to terminate the employee (Robinson & Spicer, 1987).

The last phase of the confrontation process is outlining the organization's plan or expectations for the employee in overcoming the chemical impairment. This plan is similar to the disciplinary contract discussed in Chapter 20, in that it is usually written and outlines clearly the rehabilitative measures that should be undertaken by the employee and consequences if remedial action is not sought. Although the employee is generally referred informally by the manager to outside sources to help deal with the impairment, the employee is responsible for correcting his or her work deficiencies. Time lines are included in the plan, and the manager and employee must agree on and sign a copy of the contract.

LEARNING EXERCISE 21.3

There have been rumors for some time that Mrs. Clark, one of the night nurses on the unit you supervise, has been coming to work under the influence of alcohol. Fellow staff have reported the odor of alcohol on her breath, and one staff member stated that her speech is often slurred. The night supervisor states that she feels "this is not her problem," and your night charge has never been on duty when Mrs. Clark has shown this behavior.

This morning, one of the patients whispered to you that he thought Mrs. Clark had been drinking when she came to work last night. When you question the patient further, he states, "Mrs. Clark seemed to perform her nursing duties OK, but she made me nervous." You have decided you must talk with Mrs. Clark. You call her at her home and ask her to come to your office at 3 PM.

Assignment: Determine how you are going to approach Mrs. Clark. Outline your plan, and give rationale for your choices. What flexibility have you built into your plan? How much of your documentation will be shared with Mrs. Clark?

The Manager's Role in Assisting the Impaired Employee

Because of the general nature of nursing, many managers find themselves wanting to nurture the impaired employee, much as they would any other person who is sick. However, this nurturing can quickly become enabling (Navarra, 1995). In addition, the employee who already has a greatly diminished sense of self-esteem and a perceived loss of self-control may ask the manager to participate actively in his or her recovery. This is one of the most difficult aspects of working with the impaired employee. The manager must be very careful *not* to assume the role of counselor or treatment provider. Others who have greater expertise and objectivity should assume this role.

The manager also must be careful not to feel the need to diagnose the cause of the chemical addiction or to justify its existence. Protecting patients must be the top priority, taking precedence over any tendency to protect or excuse subordinates. The manager's role is to identify clearly performance expectations for the employee and to confront the employee when those expectations are not met. This is not to say that the manager should not be humanistic in recognizing the problem as a disease and not a disciplinary problem or that he or she should be unwilling to refer the employee for needed help. Although the manager may suggest appropriate help or refer the impaired employee to someone, a manager's primary responsibility is to see that the employee becomes functional again and can meet organizational expectations before returning to the unit.

In addition, the manager can play a vital role in creating an environment that decreases the chances of chemical impairment in the work setting. This may be done by controlling or reducing work-related stressors whenever possible and by providing mechanisms for employee stress management. The manager also should control drug accessibility by implementing, enforcing, and monitoring policies and procedures related to medication distribution. Finally, the manager should provide opportunities for the staff to learn about substance abuse, its detection, and available resources (Robinson & Spicer, 1987).

The Recovery Process

Although most authors disagree on the name or number of steps in the recovery process, they do agree that certain phases or progressive observable behaviors suggest that the individual is recovering from the chemical impairment (Veatch, 1987). The first of these four phases is called the *premotivation phase*. In this phase, the impaired employee continues to deny the significance or severity of the chemical impairment but does reduce or suspend chemical use to appease family, peers, or managers. These employees hope to reestablish their substance abuse in the future.

The second phase of recovery is the *breakthrough phase*. As denial subsides, the impaired employee begins to see that the chemical addiction is having a negative impact on his or her life and begins to want to change. Frequently, individuals in this phase are buoyant with hope and commitment but lack maturity about the struggles they will face. This phase generally lasts about 3 months.

The third phase of recovery is *early recovery*. During this phase, the individual examines his or her values and coping skills and works to develop more effective coping skills. Frequently, this is done by aligning himself or herself with support groups that reinforce a chemical-free lifestyle. In this stage, the person realizes how sick he or she was in the active stage of the disease and is often fraught with feelings of humiliation and shame.

The last phase of recovery is called *extended recovery*. In this phase, individuals gain self-awareness regarding why they became chemically addicted, and they develop coping skills that will help them deal more effectively with stressors. As a result of this self-awareness, self-esteem and self-respect increase. When this happens, the individual is able to decide consciously whether he or she wishes to and should return to the work place.

Reentry of the Chemically Impaired Employee Into the Workplace

Because chemically impaired nurses recover at varying rates, predicting how long this process will take is difficult. Many experts feel that impaired employees must devote at least 1 year to their recovery.

With active treatment programs, employees return to the workplace as productive members in 85% to 90% of the cases (Robbins, 1987). Their success in reentering the work force depends on factors such as the extent of their recovery process and individual circumstances. Again, although managers must show a genuine personal interest in their employee's rehabilitation, their primary role is to be sure that the employee understands that the organization has the right to insist on unimpaired performance in the workplace. Buxton, Jessup, and Landy (1985) and Curtin (1987) suggest the following reentry guidelines for the recovering nurse:

- The employee must be told that no psychoactive drug use will be tolerated.
- The employee should be assigned to day shift for the first year.
- The employee should be paired or "buddied" with a successful recovering nurse whenever possible.
- The employee should be willing to consent to random urine screening twice weekly, with toxicology or alcohol screens.
- The employee should agree to participate in weekly nurse's group meetings with the option of open communication with facilitators.
- The employee must give evidence of continuing involvement with support groups, such as Alcoholics Anonymous or Narcotics Anonymous. Employees should be encouraged to attend meetings four times each week.
- The employee should be encouraged to participate in a structured aftercare program.
- The employee should be encouraged to seek optional individual psychotherapy.
- The employee should be encouraged to take Antabuse or Naltrene on the recommendation of his or her physician (optional).

These guidelines should be a part of the employee's return to work contract. Mandatory drug testing, however, invokes questions about privacy rights and generally should not be implemented without advice from human resources personnel or legal counsel (Robinson & Spicer, 1987).

Managers have the responsibility to be proactive in identifying and confronting chemically impaired employees. Prompt and appropriate intervention by managers is essential for positive outcomes. With 10% of the nursing work force chemically impaired, organizations must actively assist these employees to return as productive members of the work force.

THE MARGINAL EMPLOYEE

Retaining and coping with marginal or ineffective employees is unfortunately a common management task. All organizations have at least a few such employees. Employees become marginal for various reasons. Jernigan (1988) suggests that performance deficiencies result most frequently from burnout, boredom, job dissatisfaction, resentment of the need to work for economic reasons, personal problems, knowledge deficits, inability to learn, emotional disturbances, and failing health.

A study by Schniederjans and Stoeberl (1985) shows that 85% of managers use one of the five following coping methods when dealing with marginal employees.

1. *Terminate.* The manager either terminates the employee or talks him or her into an early retirement or resignation.
2. *Transfer.* The manager transfers the employee to another department, section, or unit.
3. *Counsel.* The manager attempts to improve the employee's performance through active coaching and counseling.
4. *Lack of resolution.* The manager explores possible solutions while problems remain unresolved.
5. *Work around.* The manager basically ignores the marginal employee and works around him or her.

The measure most often chosen varies with the level of the manager dealing directly with the marginal employee. "Lack of resolution" and "work around" are passive measures and are considered more successful by lower level managers. Higher level managers feel the more active measures of counsel, transfer, and terminate are more successful.

In addition to management level, the nature of the organization is key in determining the most frequent measure. Government-controlled organizations are more apt to use passive measures, while managers in organizations with other sponsors are more apt to use active measures.

The trend since 1980 has been toward passive managerial coping strategies with marginal employees (Schniederjans & Stoeberl, 1985). However, the manager must remember that each individual and situation is different and that the most appropriate strategy depends on many variables. Learning Exercise 21.4, which has been solved for the reader, depicts alternatives managers may consider in dealing with the marginal employee.

THE DISRUPTIVE SUPERACHIEVER

A problem employee is one who exhibits chronic disruptive behavior (Douglass, 1992). Certainly, the disruptive superachiever must be viewed as a problem employee. Paradoxically, these employees can account for a large percentage of unit output and frequently provide the technical know-how that leads to advances in nursing practice; however, they also can cause management problems that equal or exceed their productivity (Russell, 1989). With marginal employees, the manager is more apt to consider transfer or termination. With superachievers, the manager is more apt to tolerate unwanted behaviors or attempt to modify them, because the superachiever's contribution to unit productivity and functioning is unquestionable.

Russell (1989) has identified three categories of disruptive superachievers: bulls or A-bombs, killer angels, and know-it-alls. *Bulls or A-bombs,* the most common type of superachiever, believe that their thoughts, beliefs, ideas, and ways of doing things are the only feasible possibility. Because they believe they are truly superior, they treat colleagues in a demeaning or patronizing manner. Their interactions are abusive, abrupt, intimidating, and always overwhelming and are almost always directed at individuals who lack self-confidence and assertiveness. This unrelenting behavior leads others to acquiesce despite their better judgment. A-bombs use tantrums rather than the direct attack used by bulls, but the outcome is the same.

The first thing managers must do when dealing with A-bombs is realize that the

The Marginal Employee

You are the oncology supervisor in a 400-bed hospital. There are 35 beds on your unit, which is generally full. It is an extremely busy unit, and your staff need high-level assessment and communication skills in providing patient care. Because the nursing care needs on this floor are unique and because you use primary nursing, it has been very difficult in the past to float staff from other units when additional staffing was required. Although you have been able to keep the unit adequately staffed on a day-to-day basis, there are two open positions for registered nurses on your unit that have been unfilled for almost 3 months.

Historically, your staff have been excellent employees. They enjoy their work and are highly productive. Unit morale has been exceptionally good. However, in the last 3 months, the staff have begun complaining about Judy, a full-time employee who has been on the unit for about 4 months. Judy has been a registered nurse for about 15 years and has worked in oncology units at other facilities. References from former employers identified Judy's work as competent, although little other information was given. At Judy's 6-week and 3-months performance appraisals, you coached her regarding her barely adequate work habits, assessment and communication skills, and decision making. Judy responded that she would attempt to work on improving her performance in these areas, because working on this unit was one of her highest career goals. Although Judy has been receptive to your coaching and has verbalized to you her efforts to improve her performance, there has been little observable difference in her behavior. You have slowly concluded that Judy is probably currently working at as high a level as she is capable and that she is a marginal employee at best. The other staff feel that Judy is not carrying her share of the workload and have asked that you remove her from the unit.

Try to solve this exercise on your own before reading the following solution. The traditional problem-solving process is used as a decision-making tool in this solution.

Analysis

1. *Identify the problem.* The marginal performance of one employee is affecting unit morale.
2. *Gather data to analyze the causes and consequences of the problem.* The following information should be gathered and considered by the nursing manager.

Judy has been a registered nurse for 15 years and probably has always been a marginal employee.

Judy states she is highly motivated to be an oncology nurse.

Judy has been coached on several occasions regarding how she might improve her performance, and no improvement has been seen.

It is difficult to recruit and retain staff nurses for this unit.

The unit is already short two full-time RN positions.

Judy's performance is not unsatisfactory; it is only marginal.

The other nurses on the floor considered Judy's performance to be disruptive enough to ask you to remove her from the floor.

Identify alternative solutions

Alternative 1—Terminate Judy's employment.
Alternative 2—Transfer Judy to another floor.

(continued)

Alternative 3—Continue coaching Judy, and help her identify specific and realistic goals about her performance.

Alternative 4—Do nothing and hope that the problem resolves itself

Alternative 5—Work with the other staff nurses to create a work environment that will make Judy want to be transferred from the unit.

Evaluate the Alternatives

Alternative 1—Although this would provide a rapid solution to the problem, there are many negative aspects to this alternative. Judy, although performing at a marginal level, has not done anything that warrants discipline or termination. Even though some staff have requested her removal from the unit, this action could be viewed as arbitrary and grossly unfair by a silent minority. Thus, employees' sense of security and unit morale could decrease even more. In addition, it would be difficult to fill Judy's position.

Alternative 2—This alternative would immediately remove the problem from the supervisor and would probably please the staff. This alternative merely transfers the problem to a different unit, which is counterproductive to organizational goals. This might be an appropriate alternative if the supervisor could show that Judy could be expected to perform at a higher level on another unit. It is difficult to predict how Judy would feel about this alternative. Judy is probably aware of the other staff's frustration with her, and a transfer would provide at least temporary shelter from her colleagues' hostility. In addition, although Judy would be pleased that she was not terminated, she would appropriately view the transfer as her failure. This recognition is demoralizing, and the opportunity for her to fulfill a long-term career goal would be denied.

Alternative 3—This alternative requires a long-term and time-consuming commitment on the part of the manager. There is inadequate information in the case to determine whether the supervisor can make this type of commitment. In addition, there is no guarantee that setting short-term, specific, and realistic goals will improve Judy's work performance. It should, however, increase Judy's self-esteem and reinforce her supervisor's interest in her as a person. It also retains a registered nurse who is difficult to replace. This alternative does not address the staff's dissatisfaction.

Alternative 4—There are few positive aspects to this alternative other than that the supervisor would not have to expend energy at this point. The problem, however, will probably snowball, and unit morale will get worse.

Alternative 5—Although most would agree that this alternative is morally corrupt, there are some advantages. Judy would voluntarily leave the unit, and the supervisor and staff would not have to deal with the problem. The disadvantages are similar to those cited in Alternative 1.

Select the Appropriate Solution

As in most decisions with an ethical component, there is no one right answer, and all the alternatives have desirable facets. Alternative 3 probably presents the least number of undesirable attributes. The cost to the supervisor is in time and effort. There is really little to lose in attempting this plan to increase employee productivity, because there are no replacements to fill the position anyway. Losing Judy by termination or transfer merely increases the workload on the other employees due to short staffing. It also cannot help the employee.

(continued)

LEARNING EXERCISE 21.4 (Continued)

Implement the Solution

In implementing Alternative 3, the supervisor should be very clear with Judy about her motives. She also must be sure that the goals they set are specific and realistic. Although the staff may continue to verbalize their unhappiness with Judy's performance, the supervisor should be careful not to discuss confidential information about Judy's coaching plan with them. The manager should, however, reassure the staff that she is aware of their concerns and that she will follow the situation closely.

Evaluate the Results

The supervisor elected to review her problem solving 6 months after the plan was implemented. She found that although Judy was satisfied with her performance and appreciative of her supervisor's efforts, her performance had not improved appreciably. Judy continued to be a marginal employee but was meeting minimal competency levels. The supervisor did find, however, that the staff seemed more accepting of Judy's level of ability and rarely verbalized their dissatisfaction with her anymore. In general, unit morale increased again.

behaviors of the individual disrupting the unit will not just go away. Managers must calmly and assertively stand up to these disruptive superachievers. They must not argue but assertively and repeatedly state whatever messages they feel must be imparted. The manager must keep his or her voice low when dealing with an A-bomb. The louder the difficult person talks, the softer the manager must answer (Lewis-Ford, 1993). Using this strategy will require the A-bomb to calm down to hear what the manager is saying.

Lewis-Ford (1993) also warns that managers must be careful to guard their perspective. The A-bomb's outburst should not be taken personally. Likewise, if emotionally shaken by the confrontation, the manager should find some excuse to leave briefly to compose himself or herself. It is imperative that the manager not be reduced to tears. "Crying is like bleeding: when attackers smell blood, they keep on coming" (Lewis-Ford, 1993, p. 36).

The manager also must have enough self-confidence and ego not to wage a battle over who has the most official control. Managers have official power and authority by virtue of their position, but it is not necessary to laud this over the bull. In fact, the wise manager will assign tasks to disruptive superachievers that keep them challenged, thus eliminating the constant need for bulls to prove themselves.

Killer angels have the same goal as bulls and A-bombs but accomplish their goals in a manner that requires less personal risk taking (Russell, 1989). Killer angels are generally passive-aggressive in their interactions and use well-chosen digs or snide comments to put down others. In an effort to attain superiority, killer angels go out of their way to make others look bad in front of management. It is important for the manager to confront killer angels openly with their behavior because they usually back down when confronted with their passive-aggressive behavior because of their distaste for social embarrassment. Managers must provide a forum for killer angels to openly air their feelings and ideas. In addition, the manager should seek the advice and help of killer angels whenever possible, meeting their needs to feel important and valuable.

Know-it-alls are the least dangerous of all the disruptive superachievers (Russell, 1989). These employees truly believe they are authorities in their field and willingly offer advice about anything and everything to anyone who will listen. The manager who is able to filter selectively the expertise continually received from the know-it-all allows this type of disruptive superachiever to save face and gains access to some valuable information.

INTEGRATING LEADERSHIP ROLES AND MANAGEMENT FUNCTIONS IN WORKING WITH EMPLOYEES WITH SPECIAL NEEDS

The leader recognizes each employee's intrinsic worth and assists them in reaching their maximal potential. Because individual abilities, achievement drives, and situations vary, the leader recognizes each employee as an individual with unique needs and intervenes according to those specific needs. The leader is a coach, a resource person, an enabler. The leader is not a counselor, disciplinarian, or authority figure.

The management role is more controlling. Because chemically impaired, marginal employees, and disruptive superachievers affect unit functioning and thus productivity, the manager's primary obligation is to see that productivity is adequate to meet unit goals. The manager uses the authority inherent in his or her position to provide positive and negative sanctions for employee behavior in an effort to meet these goals.

The integrated leader/manager blends human resource needs and unit productivity needs. The leader/manager creates an environment that recognizes and supports individual employee needs and maintains productivity. Chemically impaired, marginal, and disruptive superachievers pose tremendous challenges. All these employees can draw an inordinate amount of time and energy from the manager that may not always yield the desired outcome. Likewise, selecting and implementing appropriate strategies to maintain and promote employee productivity are complex. The leader/manager, however, believes that each employee has the potential to be a successful and valuable member of the unit and intervenes accordingly to meet each one's special needs.

KEY CONCEPTS

▼ It is essential that managers be able to distinguish between employees needing progressive discipline and those who have special needs so that the employee can be managed in the most appropriate manner.
▼ Because chemical impairment is a disease, traditional progressive discipline is inappropriate because it cannot result in employee growth.
▼ Planning strategies that counsel and assist chemically impaired employees in an effort to return them as productive members of the work force are not only humanistic, but cost-effective.

▼ Current estimates are that there are 40,000 to 75,000 chemically impaired nurses in the work force. Eight to ten percent of all registered nurses and licensed practical nurses in the United States have either a drug or alcohol dependency.

▼ As a profession, the rate of narcotic addiction among nurses is estimated to be 30 to 100 times that of the general population.

▼ The profile of the impaired nurse may vary greatly, although typically behavior changes are seen in three areas: personality/behavior changes, job performance changes, and time and attendance changes.

▼ Nurses and managers traditionally have been slow to recognize and reluctant to help chemically impaired colleagues.

▼ Proving alcohol impairment in an employee is more difficult because generally it is easier for an employee to hide alcoholism than drug addiction.

▼ Confronting an employee suspected of chemical impairment should always occur before the problem escalates and before patient safety is jeopardized.

▼ The manager should *not* assume the role of counselor or treatment provider or feel the need to diagnose the cause of the chemical addiction. The manager's role is to identify clearly performance expectations for the employee and to confront the employee when those expectations are not met.

▼ The manager should be able to detect phases or progressive observable behaviors when evaluating whether the recovering impaired employee is ready to return to work. Many experts feel that impaired employees must devote at least 1 year to their recovery without the stresses of drug availability, overtime, and shift rotation.

▼ Marginal employee performance results most frequently from burnout, boredom, job dissatisfaction, resentment of the need to work for economic reasons, personal problems, knowledge deficits, inability to learn, emotional disturbances, and failing health.

▼ Managers typically use one of the five following coping methods when dealing with marginal employees: terminate, transfer, counsel, lack of resolution, or work around. The method deemed most successful varies with management level, the nature of the healthcare organization, and the current prevailing attitude toward passive or active intervention.

▼ Disruptive superachievers can account for a large percentage of unit output and frequently provide the technical know-how that leads to advances in nursing practice. They also can cause management problems that equal or exceed their productivity.

▼ Russell (1989) has identified three categories of superachievers: bull or A-bombs, killer angels, and know-it-alls.

◢ ADDITIONAL LEARNING EXERCISES

Learning Exercise 21.5

You are a staff nurse at a public health department. Marva, one of your closest friends since childhood, also is a staff nurse at the health department. During the last 6 months, you have noticed a dramatic change in Marva's behavior and work performance. Her appearance, which was once exemplary, is now frequently disheveled, and she appears gaunt and pale. Because you have noticed Marva's car in her driveway on your way to make early morning client visits, you suspect that she is either missing or arriving late for her own morning client visits. One day, you visit a client who reports that Marva has not shown up for their last three weekly appointments. The client's health status has declined appreciably, and her foot ulcer is seriously infected. After returning to the health department, you check the patient files and find that Marva has charted that visits were made on those days and that there was no change in the patient's condition. You immediately confront Marva with your observations. She tearfully admits that she "has been using cocaine recreationally and that it had gotten a little out of hand lately." She says she will never again allow it to interfere with her work. She begs you as her best friend not to report her.

Assignment: What do you do? What personal and professional values are at stake here? Identify at least three alternatives for handling this situation. What are the possible ramifications of each alternative?

Learning Exercise 21.6

You are the supervisor of a medical-surgical unit. Annabelle, a former employee who was terminated after 3 years of progressively deteriorating work habits due to a drinking problem has requested a letter of reference from you for her new employer. In the 5 years prior to Annabelle's drinking problem, she had been one of your best employees. She states that she is no longer drinking, although you personally doubt this and are aware that she did not complete the rehabilitation program to which you referred her; this is why you have not hired her back.

Annabelle tells you that her husband has left her with four small children to support and that she needs this new job to survive. She asks that you provide a letter of reference regarding her work performance which reflects her work habits before she began drinking. She also asks that you not mention her drinking, or she will not be able to get the job. Because her work for you was her only previous employment, getting a work reference from any other source is impossible. You like this person very much as an individual but would not be willing to hire her back as an employee yourself.

Assignment: What moral obligation do you have to yourself, Annabelle, and her potential employers? What are the power issues involved? Should managers have the power to influence the economic and social livelihood of past employees?

Learning Exercise 21.7

You are the PM charge nurse on a medical unit. Ruby is one of the RNs assigned to your shift. Despite intensive personal coaching on your part, Ruby continues to have difficulty carrying her share of the workload. Most of the staff complain that when they are assigned to "buddy" with Ruby, they feel they have to pick up a fair amount of her work. You also recognize that Ruby is not capable of being assigned to provide patient care autonomously. Ruby's prior performance evaluations indicate that this is the fifth unit on which she has worked in the 2 years she has been at the hospital. All unit evaluations indicate that Ruby has been a marginal employee at best, although she is motivated to learn and become the "best nurse possible." It is now time to complete your evaluation of Ruby's performance and make recommendations regarding her probationary status. You recognize the significant investment of time and energy that will be required of you and your staff to coach Ruby to make her a functional employee. You also recognize that the hospital is experiencing a severe nursing shortage and that it would be somewhat difficult to replace Ruby in the near future.

Assignment: What recommendations do you make regarding Ruby's retention? What factors weighed most heavily in your decision? Is there a limit to the number of marginal employees a manager can commit to coaching?

Learning Exercise 21.8

You are the day-shift coordinator of a home health agency. John is an RN on the day shift and has been so for 3 years. He carries one of the heaviest caseloads of any of your nurses and has always received high evaluations from clients. Because this is a small agency, there are generally only three RNs assigned to any one day shift. It is now August, and it will soon be time for the student nurses to return to school. They have been using your agency as a clinical practice site for the last year. Six students are assigned at a time to work in the agency, and you generally assign two students per nurse. Assigning more than two students per nurse would diminish the opportunities for individual learning experiences.

You are aware that several students have reported bad experiences working with John. They say he openly ignores them in front of clients, and they feel he destroys any rapport or credibility they might otherwise have with the clients. They say he belittles the charting they do, and when their instructor is not present he tells them to "go back to the simulation lab where you belong." The nursing instructor has asked what you can do to intervene with John.

Assignment: You feel John has many of the characteristics of a disruptive super-achiever. You must decide whether or not to assign nursing students to work with John. If you do, will you say anything to John? What would you say or do? Will you say anything to the nursing students? How will you respond to the nursing instructor? Be realistic about your plan. What are the risks in taking any action?

REFERENCES:

American Nurses Association (1987). Impaired nursing practice. *ANA News Release, March.*

Ashton, J. T., & Bay, J. (1994). Investigating narcotic diversion. *Nursing Management, 25*(3), 35–37.

Baywood, R. (1990). Substance abuse and obligations to colleagues. *Nursing Management, 21*(8), 40–41.

Bissell, L. (1979). Alcoholism and the health professional. Paper presented at the Summer School on Alcohol Studies. Rutgers University.

Buxton, M., & Jessup, M. (1983). Unpublished survey in the San Francisco Support Group for Chemically Dependent Nurses. San Francisco.

Buxton, M., Jessup, M., & Landry, M. (1985). Treatment of the chemically dependent health professional. In H. Milkman & H. Shaffer (Eds.), *The addictions: Multi-disciplinary perspectives and treatments.* Lexington, MA: Lexington Books, D.C. Heath.

Curtin, L. (1987). Throw away nurses: Editorial opinion. *Nursing Management, 18*(7), 7–8.

Douglass, L. M. (1992). *The effective nurse: Leader and manager* (4th ed.). St. Louis: Mosby year Book.

Hughes, T. L., & Smith, L. L. (1994). Is your colleague chemically dependent? *American Journal of Nursing, 94*(9), 31–35.

Hutchinson, S. A. (1987). Chemically dependent nurses: Implications for nurse executives. *Journal of Nursing Administration, 17*(9), 23–29.

Jernigan, D. K. (1988). *Human resource management in nursing.* East Norwalk, CT: Appleton and Lange.

LaGodna, G. E., & Hendrix, M. J. (1989). Impaired nurses: A cost analysis. *Journal of Nursing Administration, 19*(9), 13–18.

Landry, M. (1987). The impaired nurse. *California Nursing Review, 9*(6), 14–18.

Leffler, D. (1986). Addicted nurses: How you can lend them a helping hand. *Nursing Life, 6*(3), 41–43.

Lewis-Ford, B. (1993). Management techniques: Coping with difficult people. *Nursing Management, 24*(3), 35–38.

Modlin, H. C., & Montes, A. (1964). Narcotics addiction in physicians. *The American Journal of Psychiatry, 121*, 358–363.

Murray, R. M. (1974). Psychiatric illnesses in doctors. *Lancet, 1*, 1211–1213.

Navarra, T. (1995). Enabling behavior: The tender trap. *American Journal of Nursing, 95*(1), 50–52.

Naegle, M. A. (1988). Drug and alcohol abuse in nursing: An occupational hazard? *Nursing Life, 8*(1), 42–54.

Neill, M. M. (1987). Impaired employee—Administrative strategy. In E. M. Lewis & J. G. Spicer (Eds.), *Human resource management handbook.* Rockville, MD: Aspen Publications.

Poplar, J. F. (1969). Characteristics of nurse addicts. *American Journal of Nursing, 69*(1), 117–119.

Robbins, C. E. (1987). A monitored treatment program for impaired health care professionals. *Journal of Nursing Administration 17*(2), 17–21.

Robinson, M., & Spicer, J. G. (1987). Impaired employee-Confrontation process. In E. M. Lewis & J. G. Spicer (Eds.), *Human resource management handbook.* Rockville, MD: Aspen Publications.

Russell, L. N. (1989). Managing the super achiever nurse. *Nursing Management, 20*(2), 38–39.

Schniederjans, M. J., & Stoeberl, P. A. (1985). Coping with ineffective subordinates. *Nursing Management, 16*(11), 51–52.

Stammer, M. E. (1988). Understanding alcoholism and drug dependency in nurses. *Quality Review Bulletin, 14*(3), 75–80.

Sullivan, E. J. (1987). A descriptive study of nurses recovering from chemical dependency. *Archives of Psychiatric Nursing, 1*(3), 194—200.

Veatch, D. (1987). When is the recovering impaired nurse ready to work? A job interview guide. *Journal of Nursing Administration, 17*(2), 14–16.

Wrich, J. T. (1989). *The employee assistance program.* Minneapolis, MN: Hazelden Research Services.

BIBLIOGRAPHY

Billings Farley, P., & Hendrix, M. J. (1993). Impaired and nonimpaired nurses during childhood and adolescence. *Nursing Outlook, 41*(1), 25–31.

Black, C. (1992). Double duty: Chemically dependent. New York: Ballantine Books.

Brennar, S. J. (1991). Recognizing and assisting the impaired nurse: Recommendations for nurse managers. *Nursing Forum, 26*(2), 12–16.

Buxton, M., & Jessup, M. (1982). The development of peer support group in California: Recovery is possible. Unpublished paper.

Charter Medical Corporation. *How a chemically dependent employee behaves.* Roswell, GA: Addictive Disease Division.

Creighton, H. (1988). Legal implications of the impaired nurse—Part 2. *Nursing Management, 19*(2), 20–21.

Crosby, L. R. (1990). Demystifying the intervention process. *Addictions Nursing Network, 2*(4), 13–16.

Cutler, A. (1984). The Illinois study profiling the impaired professional nurse: An examination of cases of reported substance abuse. Unpublished master's thesis.

Ensor, J., & Giovinco, G. (1991). Ethical issues related to chemical dependency. *Imprint, 38*(4), 85–87.

Fiesta, J. (1993). Liability for drug testing. *Nursing Management, 24*(5), 2224.

Gelfand, G., Long, P., McGill, D., & Sheerin, C. (1990). Prevention of chemically impaired nursing practice. *Nursing Management, 21*(7), 76–78.

Green, P. (1989). The chemically dependent nurse. *Nursing Clinics of North America, 24*(1), 81–94.

Hughes, T. L., & Solari-Twadell, A. (1989). A response to chemical impairment: Policy and program initiatives. In M. R. Haack and T. L. Hughes (Eds.), *Addiction in the nursing profession: Approaches to intervention and recovery.* New York: Springer Publishing Co.

Huston, C. J., & Marquis, B. L. (1989). *Retention and productivity strategies for nurse managers.* Philadelphia: J.B. Lippincott.

Klick, G. A. R. (1991). Collegial support for the addicted nurse. *Imprint, 38*(4), 76–81.

Lash, C. L. (1990). Tapping information sources when dealing with an impaired nurse. *Nurse Manager's Bookshelf, 2*(2), 141–146.

Lewis, E. M., & Spicer, J. G. (1987). *Human resource management handbook: Contemporary strategies for nursing managers.* Rockville, MD: Aspen Publications.

Little, M. (1991). When Judy fell, she didn't know she was in a trap. *Tennessee Nurse, 54*(3), 31–33.

Lopez, D. (1993). Surviving verbal abuse: A win-win game plan. *Nursing Management, 24*(5), 80–82.

Naegle, M. A. (1989). Patterns and implications of drug use by students of nursing. *Imprint, 36*(2), 85, 87–88.

Naegle, M. A. (1991). Impaired nursing practice: Evolution of a professional issue. *Imprint, 38*(4), 69–70.

Polk, D., Glendon, K., & Devore, C. (1994). The chemically dependent student nurse: Guidelines for policy development. *Nursing Outlook, 41*(4), 166–170.

Shaffer, S. (1988). Attitudes and perceptions held by impaired nurses. *Nursing Management, 19*(4), 46–50.

Sisney, K. F., & Taylor, P. A. (1991). Conquering the challenges of student chemical dependence. *Imprint, 38*(4), 71–75.

Skinner, K. (1990). Drug abuse: A step-by-step guide. *Nursing Management, 21,* 14–15.

Sullivan, E. J. (1992) Impaired nursing performance: Ethical issues. *The Kansas Nurse, 67*(6), 1–3.

UNIT 7

PROFESSIONAL AND SOCIAL ISSUES IN LEADERSHIP AND MANAGEMENT

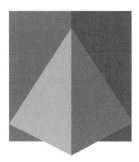

CHAPTER 22

Ethical Issues

Unit 7 examines ethical, professional, social, legal, and legislative issues affecting leadership and management. This chapter focuses on applied ethical decision making and advocacy as a professional and ethical issue. Chapter 23 focuses primarily on the impact of legislation and the law on leadership and management, and Chapter 24 examines career development of leaders/managers and their subordinates.

Ethics is the systematic study of what a person's conduct and actions ought to be with regard to himself or herself, other human beings, and the environment; it is the justification of what is right or good and the study of what a person's lives and relationships ought to be, not necessarily what they are (Aroskar, 1987).

Applied ethics requires application of normative ethical theory to everyday problems. The normative ethical theory for each profession arises from the purpose of the profession (Veatch & Fry, 1987). The values and norms of the nursing profession, therefore, provide the foundation and the filter from which ethical decisions are made (Powers & Vogel, 1980). The nurse-manager, however, has a different ethical responsibility than the clinical nurse and does not have as clearly a defined foundation to use as a base for ethical reasoning.

Because management is a discipline and not a profession, it does not have a defined purpose, such as medicine or the law; therefore, it lacks a specific set of norms to guide ethical decision making. Instead, the organization reflects norms and values to the manager, and the personal values of managers are reflected through the organization. The manager's ethical obligation is tied to the organization's purpose, and

Bessie L. Marquis and Carol J. Huston:
LEADERSHIP ROLES AND MANAGEMENT FUNCTIONS IN NURSING, 2nd ed.
Lippincott-Raven Publishers © 1996

the purpose of the organization is linked to the function it fills in society and the constraints society places on it. Therefore, the responsibilities of the nurse-manager emerge from a complex set of interactions. Society helps define the purposes of various institutions, and the purposes in turn help ensure that the institution fulfills specific functions. However, the specific values and norms in any particular institution determine the focus of its resources and shape its organizational life. The values of people within institutions influence actual management practice. In reviewing this set of complex interactions, it becomes evident that arriving at appropriate ethical management decisions is a difficult task.

Not only is nursing management ethics distinct from the ethics of clinical nursing, but it also is distinct from other areas of management. Although there are many similar areas of responsibility between nurse-managers and non-nurse-managers, many leadership roles and management functions are specific to nursing. These differences require the nurse-manager to deal with unique obligations and ethical dilemmas that are not encountered in non-nursing management.

In an era of markedly limited physical, human, and fiscal resources, nearly all decision making by nurse-managers involves some ethical component. However, the following forces ensure that ethics will become an even greater dimension in management decision making in the 1990s: increasing technology, regulatory pressures, and competitiveness among healthcare providers; national nursing shortages; reduced fiscal resources; spiraling costs of supplies and salaries; and the public's increasing distrust of the healthcare delivery system and its institutions (McCloskey & Grace, 1994).

In addition, because personal, organizational, subordinate, and consumer responsibilities differ, there is great potential for managers to experience intrapersonal conflict. Multiple advocacy roles and accountability to the profession further increase the likelihood that managers will be faced with ethical dilemmas in their practice.

To make appropriate ethical decisions, the manager must use a professional approach that eliminates trial and error and focuses on proven decision-making models or problem-solving processes. Using a systematic approach allows managers to make better decisions and increases the probability that they will feel good about decisions they have made.

Systematic approaches presented in this chapter include ethical frameworks and principles and theoretical problem-solving and decision-making models. In addition, Chapter 22 examines the need for managerial advocacy for clients, subordinates, and the profession. Leadership roles and management functions involved in these ethical issues are shown in Display 22.1.

ETHICAL DILEMMAS

Individual values, beliefs, and personal philosophy play a major role in the moral or ethical decision making that is part of the daily routine of all managers. How do managers decide what is right and what is wrong? What does the manager do if no right or wrong answer exists? What if both answers are right or wrong?

Ethical dilemmas can be defined as having to choose between two equally desirable or undesirable alternatives. Curtin (1982) maintains that for a problem to be an ethical dilemma, it must have three characteristics. First, the problem cannot be

Display 22.1 Leadership Roles and Management Functions in Ethics and Advocacy

Leadership Roles

1. Is self-aware regarding own values and basic beliefs about the rights, duties, and goals of human beings.
2. Accepts that some ambiguity and uncertainty must be a part of all ethical decision making.
3. Accepts that negative outcomes occur in ethical decision making despite high quality problem solving and decision making.
4. Demonstrates risk taking in ethical decision making.
5. Role models ethical decision making, which is congruent with the American Nurses Association Code of Ethics and Interpretive Statements.
6. Actively advocates for clients, subordinates, and the profession.
7. Clearly communicates expected ethical standards of behavior.

Management Functions

1. Uses a systematic approach to problem solving or decision making when faced with management problems with ethical ramifications.
2. Identifies outcomes in ethical decision making that should always be sought or avoided.
3. Uses established ethical frameworks to clarify values and beliefs.
4. Applies principles of ethical reasoning to define what beliefs or values form the basis for decision making.
5. Is aware of legal precedents that may guide ethical decision making and is accountable for possible liabilities should they go against the legal precedent.
6. Continually reevaluates quality of own ethical decision making, based on the *process* of decision making or problem solving used.
7. Recognizes and rewards ethical conduct of subordinates.
8. Takes appropriate action when subordinates use unethical conduct.

solved using only empirical data. Second, the problem must be so perplexing that deciding what facts and data need to be used in making the decision is difficult. Third, the results of the problem must affect more than the immediate situation; there should be far-reaching effects.

Remember that the way managers approach and solve ethical dilemmas is influenced by their values and basic beliefs about the rights, duties, and goals of all human beings. Self-awareness, then, is a vital leadership role in ethical decision making, just as it is in so many other aspects of management.

No rules, guidelines, or theories exist that cover all aspects of the ethical dilemmas that managers face. Curtin (1982) maintains that values and morals are individual, and only the person can ascertain if he or she has acted within his or her beliefs. Quinn and Smith (1987, p. 53) state, "In the end, ethical individuals must be prepared to live with a certain amount of ambiguity and uncertainty. The professional who accepts uncertainty in practice situations avoids the paralysis that comes from postponing action until all information is available." However, Quinn and Smith also assert, "Although there is value in learning to tolerate uncertainty, there is a point at which excessive tolerance amounts to neglect of professional and ethical commitments." To tolerate uncertainty at all times and under all circumstances is to ignore the value of knowledge and dismiss the ability to think critically.

Thinking critically occurs when the manager is able to engage in an orderly process of ethical problem solving to determine the rightness or wrongness of courses of action. Learning systematic approaches to ethical decision making and problem solving reduces personal bias, facilitates better decision making, and lets managers feel more comfortable about decisions they have made.

ETHICAL PROBLEM SOLVING AND DECISION MAKING

Because problem solving and decision making are discussed in Chapter 2, only a brief review is included here. Much of the difficulty individuals have in making ethical decisions can be attributed to a lack of formal education about problem solving. Trial and error decision making helps some managers learn to make good decisions, but much is left to chance. The cost of poor ethical decisions is measured in terms of human and fiscal resources.

Another error made by managers in ethical problem solving is using the outcome of the decision as the sole basis for determining the quality of the decision making. Although decision makers should be able to identify desirable or undesirable outcomes, outcomes alone cannot be used to assess the quality of the problem solving. Many variables affect outcome, and some of these are beyond the control or foresight of the problem solver. Even the most ethical courses of action can have undesirable and unavoidable consequences. The quality of ethical problem solving should be evaluated in terms of the *process* used to make the decision. If a structured approach to problem solving is used, data gathering is adequate, and multiple alternatives are analyzed, then regardless of the outcome, the manager should feel comfortable that the best possible decision was made at that time with the information and resources available.

The Traditional Problem-Solving Process

Although not recognized specifically as an ethical problem-solving model, one of the oldest and most frequently used tools for problem solving is the traditional problem-solving process. This process, which is discussed in Chapter 2, consists of seven steps with the actual decision being made at step five (Display 22.2). Although many use at least some of these steps in their decision making, they frequently fail to generate an adequate number of alternatives or to evaluate the results—two essential steps in the process.

Display 22.2   Traditional Problem-Solving Process

---

1. Identify the problem.
2. Gather data to analyze the causes and consequences of the problem.
3. Explore alternative solutions.
4. Evaluate the alternatives.
5. Select the appropriate solution.
6. Implement the solution.
7. Evaluate the results.

The Nursing Process

Another problem-solving model not specifically designed for ethical analysis but appropriate for it is the nursing process. Most nurses are aware of the nursing process and the cyclic nature of its components of assessment, planning, implementation, and evaluation (Fig. 22.1). However, most nurses do not recognize its use as a decision-making tool. The cyclic nature of the process allows for feedback to occur at any step. It also allows the cycle to repeat until adequate information is gathered to make a decision. It does not, however, require clear problem identification. Learning Exercise 22.2 shows how the nursing process might be used as an ethical decision-making tool.

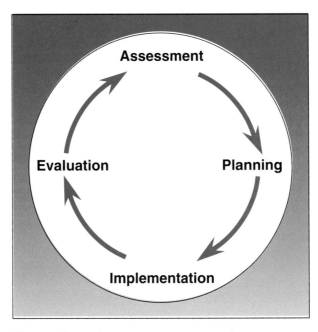

FIGURE 22.1   The nursing process.

LEARNING EXERCISE 22.1

(From Marquis & Huston, 1994.)

You are a nurse on a pediatric unit. One of your patients is a 15-month-old female with a diagnosis of failure to thrive. The mother has stated that the child appears emotional, cries a lot, and does not like to be held. You have been taking care of the infants for 2 days since her admission, and she has smiled and laughed and held out her arms to everyone. She has eaten well.

There is something about the child's reaction to the mother's boyfriend that bothers you. The child appears to draw away from him when he visits. The mother is very young and seems to be rather immature but appears to care for the child.

This is the second hospital admission for this child. Although you were not on duty for the first admission 6 weeks ago, you check the records and see that the child was admitted with the same diagnosis. While you are on duty today, the child's father calls and inquires about her condition. He lives several hundred miles away and requests that the child be hospitalized until the weekend (it is Wednesday) "so that he can check things out." He tells you that he feels the child is mistreated. He says he also is concerned about his ex-wife's 4-year-old child from another marriage and is attempting to gain custody of that child in addition to his own child. From what little the father said, you are aware that the divorce was very bitter and that the mother has full custody.

You talk with the physician at length. He says that after the last hospitalization, he requested that the community health agency call on the family. Their subsequent report to him was that the 4-year-old appeared happy and well and that the 15-month-old appeared clean, although underweight. There was no evidence to suggest child abuse. However, the community health agency plans to continue following the children. He says the mother has been good about keeping doctor appointments and has kept the children's immunizations up to date.

The pediatrician proceeds to write an order for discharge. He says that although he also feels somewhat uneasy, continued hospitalization is not justified, and the state medical aid will not pay for additional days.

When the mother and her boyfriend come to pick her up, the baby clings to you and refuses to go to the boyfriend. She also is very reluctant to go to the mother. All during the discharge, you are extremely uneasy. When you see the car drive away, you feel very sad.

After returning to the unit, you talk with your supervisor who listens carefully and questions you at length. Finally she says, "It seems as if you have nothing concrete on which to act and are only experiencing feelings. I think you would be risking a lot of trouble for yourself and the hospital if you acted rashly at this time. Accusing people with no evidence and making them go through a traumatic experience is something I would hesitate to do."

You leave the supervisor's office still troubled. She did not tell you that you must do nothing, but you feel she would disapprove of further action on your part. The doctor also felt strongly that there was no reason to do more than was already being done. The child will be followed by community health nurses. Perhaps the disgruntled ex-husband was just trying to make trouble for his ex-wife and her new boyfriend. You would certainly not want anyone to have reported you or created problems regarding your own children. You remember how often your 5-year-old bruised himself when he was that age. He often looked like an abused child. You go about your duties and try to shake off your feeling. What should you do?

(continued)

LEARNING EXERCISE 22.1 (Continued)

Assignment:

1. Solve the case in small groups using the traditional problem-solving process. Identify the problem and several alternative solutions to solving this ethical dilemma. What should you do and why? What are the risks? How does your value system play a part in your decision? Justify your solution. After completing this assignment, solve part B.
2. Assume this was a real case. One week after the child's discharge, she is readmitted with critical head trauma. Police reports indicate that the child suffered multiple skull fractures after being thrown up against the wall by her mother's boyfriend. The child is not expected to live. Does knowing the outcome change how you would have solved the case? Does the outcome influence how you feel about the quality of your group problem solving?

The MORAL Decision-Making Model

Crisham (1985) has developed a model for ethical decision making, incorporating the nursing process and principles of biomedical ethics. This model is especially useful in clarifying ethical problems that result from conflicting obligations. This model is represented by the mnemonic MORAL, representing the following:

M—Massage the dilemma. Collect data about the ethical problem and who should be involved in the decision-making process.

O—Outline options. Identify alternatives, and analyze the causes and consequences of each.

R—Review criteria and resolve. Weigh the options against the values of those involved in the decision. This may be done through a weighting or grid.

A—Affirm position and act. Develop the implementation strategy.

L—Look back. Evaluate the decision making.

The Murphy and Murphy Approach to Ethical Decision Making

Murphy and Murphy (1976) have developed a systematic approach to ethical decision making.

1. Identify the problem.
2. Identify why the problem is an ethical problem.
3. Identify the people involved in the ultimate decision.
4. Identify the role of the decision maker.
5. Consider the short- and long-term consequences of each alternative.
6. Make the decision.
7. Compare the decision with the decision maker's philosophy of ethics.
8. Follow up on the results of the decision to establish a baseline for future decision making.

ONE APPLICANT TOO MANY

The reorganization of the public health agency has resulted in the creation of a new position of community health liaison. A job description has been written, and the job opening has been posted. As the chief nursing executive of this agency, it will be your responsibility to select the best person for the position. Because you are aware that all hiring decisions have some subjectivity, you want to eliminate as much personal bias as possible. Two people have applied for the position; one of them is a close personal friend.

Analysis

ASSESS

As the nursing executive, you have a responsibility to make personnel decisions as objectively as you can. This means that the hiring decision should be based solely on which employee is best qualified for the position. You do recognize, however, that there may be a personal cost in terms of the friendship.

PLAN

You must plan how you are going to collect these data. The tools you have selected are applications, résumés, references, and personal interviews.

IMPLEMENT

Both applicants are contacted and asked to submit résumés and three letters of reference from recent employers. In addition, both are scheduled for structured formal interviews with you and two of the board members of the agency. Although the board members will provide feedback, you have reserved the right to make the final hiring decision.

EVALUATE

As a result of your plan, you have discovered that both candidates meet the minimal job requirements. One candidate, however, clearly has higher level communication skills, and the other candidate (your friend) has more experience in public health and is more knowledgeable regarding the resources in your community. Both employees have complied with the request to submit résumés and letters of reference; they are of similar quality.

ASSESS

Your assessment of the situation is that you need more information to make the best possible decision. You must assess whether strong communication skills or public health experience and familiarity with the community would be more valuable in this position.

PLAN

You plan how you can gather more information about what the employee will be doing in this newly created position.

IMPLEMENT

If the job description is inadequate in providing this information, it may be necessary to gather information from other public health agencies with a similar job classification.

EVALUATE

You now feel that excellent communication skills are absolutely essential for the job. The candidate who had these skills has an acceptable level of public health experience

(continued)

and seems motivated to learn more about the community and its resources. This means that your friend will not receive the job.

ASSESS

Now you must assess whether a good decision has been made.

PLAN

You plan to evaluate your decision in 6 months, basing your criteria on the established job description.

IMPLEMENT

You are unable to implement your plan because this employee resigns unexpectedly 4 months after she takes the position. Your friend is now working in a similar capacity in another state. Although you correspond infrequently, the relationship has changed as a result of your decision.

EVALUATE

Did you made a good decision? This decision was based on a carefully thought-out process, which included adequate data gathering and a weighting of alternatives. Variables beyond your control resulted in the employee's resignation, and there was no apparent reason for you to suspect that this would happen. The decision to exclude or minimize personal bias was a conscious one, and you were aware of the possible ramifications of this choice. The decision making appears to have been appropriate.

This type of systematic decision making differs from problem-solving models already discussed because it does not attempt to solve the underlying problem. It does, however, require the person to make a decision. Specifically geared for ethical decision making, this approach helps clarify the basic beliefs and values of the individuals involved. Learning Exercise 22.3 should help you understand how the Murphy and Murphy approach could be used in making a human resource management decision with ethical ramifications.

ETHICAL FRAMEWORKS FOR DECISION MAKING

In addition to theoretical problem-solving and decision-making models, managers may use ethical frameworks to guide them in solving ethical dilemmas. These frameworks do not solve the ethical problem but assist the manager in clarifying personal values and beliefs. Four of the most commonly used ethical frameworks include utilitarianism, duty-based reasoning, rights-based reasoning, and intuitionism (Marquis & Huston, 1994).

Using an ethical framework of *utilitarianism* encourages the manager to make decisions based on what provides the greatest good for the greatest number of people. In doing so, the needs and wants of the individual are diminished (Deloughery, 1991). For example, a manager using a utilitarian approach might decide to use travel budget money to send many staff to local workshops rather than to fund one

Little White Lies

(From Huston & Marquis, 1989.)

Sam is the nurse recruiter for a metropolitan hospital that is experiencing an acute nursing shortage. He has been told to do whatever or to say whatever is necessary to recruit professional nurses so that the hospital will not have to close several units. He also has been told that his position will be eliminated if he does not produce a substantial number of applicants in the nursing career days to be held the following week. Sam loves his job and is the sole provider for his family. Because many organizations are experiencing severe personnel shortages, the competition for employees is keen. After his third career day without a single prospective applicant, he begins to feel desperate. On the fourth and final day, Sam begins making many promises to potential applicants regarding shift preference, unit preference, salary, and advancement that he is not sure he can keep. At the end of the day, Sam has a lengthy list of interested applicants but also feels a great deal of intrapersonal conflict.

Analysis

1. *Identify the problem.* In a desperate effort to save his job, Sam finds he has taken action that has resulted in high intrapersonal value conflict. Sam must choose between making promises he can't keep and losing his job.
2. *Identify why the problem is an ethical problem.* This is an ethical problem because it involves personal values and beliefs, has far-reaching implications for all involved, and presents several alternatives for decision making that are equally desirable or undesirable.
3. *Identify the people involved in the ultimate decision.* Sam has the ultimate responsibility for knowing his values and acting in a manner that is congruent with his value system. The organization is, however, involved in the value conflict in that its values and expectations conflict with Sam's. Sam and the organization have some type of responsibility to these applicants, although the exact nature of this responsibility is one of the values in conflict.
4. *Identify the role of the decision maker.* Because this is Sam's problem and an intrapersonal conflict, he must decide the appropriate course of action. His primary role is to examine his values and act in accordance with them.
5. *Consider the short-term and long-term consequences of each alternative.*
   Alternative 1—Quit his job immediately. This would prevent *future* intrapersonal conflict provided that Sam becomes aware of his value system and behaves in a manner consistent with that value system in the future. It does not, however, solve the immediate conflict about the action Sam has already taken. This action takes away Sam's livelihood.

   Alternative 2—Do nothing. Sam could choose not to be accountable for his own actions. This will require Sam to rationalize that the philosophy of the organization is in fact acceptable or that he has no choice regarding his actions. Thus, the responsibility for meeting the needs and wants of the new employees is shifted to the hospital. Although Sam will have no credibility with the new employees, there will be only a negligible impact on his ability to recruit at least on a short-term basis. Sam will continue to have a job and be able to support his family.

   Alternative 3—If after value clarification Sam has determined that his values

(continued)

LEARNING EXERCISE 22.3 (Continued)

confict with the hospital's directive to do whatever or say whatever is needed to recruit employees, he could approach his superior and share these concerns. Sam should be very clear about what his values are and to what extent he is willing to compromise them. He also should include in this meeting what, if any, action should be taken to meet the needs of the new applicant employees. Sam must be realistic about the time and effort usually required to change the values and beliefs of an organization. He also must be aware of his bottom line if the organization is not willing to provide a compromise resolution.

Alternative 4—Sam could contact each of the applicants and tell them that certain recruitment promises may not be possible. However, he will do what he can to see that the promises are fulfilled. This alternative is risky. The applicants will probably be justifiably suspicious of both the recruiter and the organization, and Sam has little formal power at this point to fulfill their requests. This alternative also requires a time and energy commitment by Sam and does not prevent the problem from recurring.

6. *Make the decision.* Sam chose alternative 3.

7. *Compare the decision with the decision maker's philosophy of ethics.* In value clarification, Sam discovered that he valued truth telling. Alternative 3 allows Sam to present a recruiting plan to his supervisor that includes a bottom line that this value will not be violated.

8. *Follow up on the results of the decision to establish a baseline for future decision making.* Sam approached his superior and was told that his beliefs were idealistic and inappropriate in an age of severe worker shortages. Sam was terminated. Sam did, however, feel that he made an appropriate decision. He did become self-aware regarding his values and attempted to communicate these values to the organization in an effort to work out a mutually agreeable plan. Although Sam was terminated, he knew that he could find some type of employment to meet immediate fiscal needs. Sam also used what he had learned in this decision-making process, in that he planned to evaluate more carefully the recruitment philosophy of the organization in relation to his own value system before accepting another job.

or two individuals to attend a national conference. Another example would be an insurance program that meets the needs of many but refuses coverage for expensive transplants. In Learning Exercise 22.3, the organization uses utilitarianism to justify lying to employee applicants because their hiring would result in good for many employees by keeping several units in the hospital open.

Duty-based reasoning is an ethical framework that says that some decisions must be made because there is a duty to do something or to refrain from doing something. In Learning Exercise 22.2, the supervisor feels a duty to hire the best qualified person for the job, even if the personal cost is high.

Rights-based reasoning is based on the belief that some things are a person's just due; that is, each individual has basic claims, or entitlements, with which there should be no interference. Rights are different from needs, wants, or desires. In

Learning Exercise 22.3, Sam felt that all individuals have the right to truth and, in fact, that he had the duty to be truthful. The supervisor in Learning Exercise 22.2 believes that both applicants have the right to fair and impartial consideration of their application.

The *intuitionist framework* allows the decision maker to review each ethical problem or issue on a case-by-case basis comparing the relative weights of goals, duties, and rights. This weighting is determined primarily by *intuition*—what the decision maker feels is right for that particular situation. Recently, some ethical theorists have begun questioning the appropriateness of intuitionism as an ethical decision-making framework because of the potential for subjectivity and bias. All of the cases solved in this chapter have involved some degree of decision making by intuition.

Another framework managers can use for guidance in ethical problem solving is a professional *code of ethics*. A code of ethics is a set of principles, established by a profession, to guide the individual practitioner. The first code of ethics for nurses was adopted by the American Nurses Association in 1950. Revisions in the Interpretive Statements since that time have reflected the change from physician-directed care to patient need-centered care. Professional codes of ethics do not have the power of law. They do, however, function as a guide to the highest standards of ethical practice for nurses. The International Code of Nursing Ethics is shown in Display 22.3 (Etziony, 1973).

PRINCIPLES OF ETHICAL REASONING

Deontological theories arise from the intent of the action that the decision maker takes. Duty-based, rights-based, and intuitionist ethical reasoning derive their framework from deontological theory. *Teleological* theories are used to support utilitarian ethical decision making. These are theories that support decisions that favor the common good. Both teleological and deontological theorists have developed a group of moral principles that is used for ethical reasoning. These *principles of ethical reasoning* further explore and define what beliefs or values form the basis for decision making. Six ethical principles have been identified.

Autonomy

A form of personal liberty, *autonomy* also is called freedom of choice or accepting the responsibility for one's choice. The legal right of self-determination supports this moral principle. The use of progressive discipline recognizes the autonomy of the employee. The employee, in essence, has the choice to meet organizational expectations or to be disciplined further. If the employee's continued behavior warrants termination, the principle of autonomy says that the employee has made the choice to be terminated by virtue of his or her actions, not the manager's.

Beneficence

This principle states that the actions one takes should be done in an effort to promote good. The concept of *nonmalificence*, which is associated with *beneficence*, says

---

Display 22.3 International Code of Nursing Ethics

---

1. The fundamental responsibility of the nurse is threefold: to conserve life, to alleviate suffering, and to promote health.
2. The nurse must maintain at all times the highest standards of nursing care and professional conduct.
3. The nurse must not only be well prepared to practice, but must maintain his or her knowledge and skill at a consistently high level.
4. The religious beliefs of a patient must be respected.
5. Nurses hold in confidence all personal information entrusted to them.
6. A nurse recognizes not only the responsibilities, but the limitations of her or his professional functions; recommends or gives medical treatment without medical orders only in emergencies; and reports such action to a physician at the earliest possible moment.
7. The nurse is under an obligation to carry out the physician's orders intelligently and loyally and to refuse to participate in unethical procedures.
8. The nurse sustains a confidence in the physician and other members of the health team; incompetence or unethical conduct of associates should be exposed but only to the proper authority.
9. A nurse is entitled to remuneration and accepts only such compensation as the contract, actual or implied, provides.
10. Nurses do not permit their names to be used in connection with the advertisement of products or with any other form of self-advertisement.
11. The nurse cooperates with and maintains harmonious relationships with members of other professions and with her or his nursing colleagues.
12. The nurse in private life adheres to standards of personal ethics, which reflect credit on his or her profession.
13. In personal conduct, nurses should not knowingly disregard the accepted patterns of behavior of the community in which they live and work.
14. A nurse should participate and share responsibility with other citizens and other health professions in promoting efforts to meet the health needs of the public—local, state, national, and international.

---

that if one cannot do good, then they should at least do no harm. For example, if a manager uses this ethical principle in planning performance appraisals, he or she is much more likely to view the performance appraisal as a means of promoting employee growth.

Paternalism

This principle is related to beneficence in that one individual assumes the authority to make a decision for another. Because *paternalism* limits freedom of choice, most ethical theorists feel paternalism is justified only to prevent a person from coming to harm. Unfortunately, some managers use the principle of paternalism in subordinate career planning. In doing so, managers assume they have greater knowledge of what an employee's short- and long-term goals should be than the employee does.

Utility

This principle reflects a belief in utilitarianism—what is best for the common good outweighs what is best for the individual. It justifies paternalism as a means of restricting individual freedom. Managers who use the principle of *utility* need to be careful not to become so focused on production that they become less humanistic.

Justice

This principle states that equals should be treated equally and unequals should be treated according to their differences. This principle is frequently applied when there are scarcities or competition for resources or benefits.

The manager who uses the principle of *justice* will work to see that pay raises reflect performance and not just time of service.

Truth Telling and Deception

These principles are used to explain how individuals feel about the need for *truth telling* or the acceptability of *deception*. A manager who feels that deception is morally acceptable if it is done with the objective of beneficence may tell all rejected job applicants that they were highly considered, whether they had been or not.

ETHICAL DIMENSIONS IN LEADERSHIP AND MANAGEMENT

Concerns about ethical conduct in American institutions abound in the media. Governmental agencies, both branches of congress, the stock exchange, and savings and loan institutions have all experienced problems with unethical conduct. Many members of society wonder what has gone wrong. Josephson (1989) suggests that although each new revelation of impropriety may be morally significant, the greatest danger is that American society has become less and less surprised. Americans are beginning to expect people to exploit opportunities for personal gain, act irresponsibly, and abuse their power.

Nursing managers, therefore, have a responsibility to create a climate in their organizations in which ethical behavior is the norm. Curtin (1993) believes that when managers develop an understanding of ethics and their own social responsibility, they will be able to risk doing the right thing and asking the right question. The need for ethical decisions occurs in every phase of the management process. Each chapter in this book could appropriately have included a section on ethical issues, such as the following.

Unit 2

- At what point do the needs of the organization become more important than those of the individual worker?
- Should employees ever be coerced into changing their stated values so that they more closely align with the organization's?
- How can managers fairly allocate resources when virtually all resources are limited?

LEARNING EXERCISE 22.4

(From Marquis & Huston, 1994).

You are the evening shift charge nurse of the recovery room. You have just admitted a 32-year-old woman who had been thrown from a jeep 2 hours ago. She had been a passenger in the vehicle. She had been rushed to the emergency room and subsequently to surgery where cranial burr holes were completed and an intracranial monitor was placed. No further cranial exploration had been attempted, because the patient had received extensive and massive neurological damage. She will probably not survive your shift. The plan is to hold her in recovery for 1 hour, and if she is still alive, transfer her to the intensive care unit.

Shortly after receiving the patient in the recovery room, you are approached by the evening house supervisor who says that the patient's sister is pleading to be allowed into the recovery room. Normally, visitors are never allowed in the recovery room, but occasionally exceptions have been made. Tonight the recovery room is empty except for this patient. You decide to bend the rules and allow the young woman's sister into the recovery room.

The visiting sister is near collapse; it is obvious that she had been the driver of the jeep. As the visitor continues to speak to the comatose patient, her behavior and words make you begin to wonder if she is indeed the sister.

Within 15 minutes, the house supervisor returns and states, "I have made a terrible mistake. The patient's family just arrived, and they say that the visitor we just allowed into the recovery room is not a member of the family but is the patient's lover. They are very angry and demand that this woman not be allowed to see the patient."

You approach the visitor and confront her in a kindly manner regarding the information you have just received. She looks at you with tears streaming down her face and says, "Yes, it is true. Mary and I have been together for 6 years. Her family disowned her because of it, but we were everything to each other. She has been my life, and I have been hers. Please, please let me stay. I will never see her again. I know the family will not allow me to attend the funeral. I need to say my goodbyes. Please let me stay. It is not fair that they have the legal right to be family when I have been the one to love and care for Mary."

Assignment: You must decide what to do. Recognize that your own value system will play a part in your decision. List several alternatives that are available to you. Identify which ethical frameworks or principles most greatly affected your decision making.

Unit 3
- Should quality or cost be the final determinant when selecting the most appropriate type of patient care delivery system?
- Should LVNs/LPNs be allowed to function in the primary nursing role?
- How should the manager protect clients from the inadequate primary nurse?
- When should the manager step outside the chain of command?
- Which should be more important to the organization—human relations or productivity?
- Does power or powerlessness corrupt?

Unit 4

- At what point does short staffing become unsafe?
- Should shift scheduling be used as a means of reward and punishment?
- Is seducing employees from other agencies ever ethical?
- How far can the truth be stretched in recruitment advertising before it becomes deceptive?
- Should pre-employment testing be required as a condition of employment?
- Is it ethical for employees to take a position in an organization if they know they are planning to leave in a short time?
- Is it ever justified for an employee to lie in an interview?
- Who has the responsibility for socializing the new graduate into the professional nursing role: the nursing school, the hospital, or is it a joint process?
- What commitment does the organization have to the nurse who is reentering the profession after not practicing for many years?
- Should an employee's orientation be continued indefinitely until they feel ready to function autonomously?

Unit 5

- To whom do managers owe their primary allegiance: the organization or their subordinates?
- When is it appropriate to use money as the primary motivator?
- Which is more important to the organization: good leaders or good managers?
- If employees are producing at acceptable or higher levels, what new rewards and incentives should be introduced?
- Is it ethical to promote union organizers to management to reduce the possibility of union formation?
- Is affirmative action hiring to compensate for past discrimination ethically justifiable, or does it promote reverse discrimination?
- Is it ethical for nurses to strike?
- Should the national nursing organization also be a collective bargaining agent?

Unit 6

- Is it necessary for each employee to be assisted to achieve at optimal levels? Can the manager be selective in determining which employees are assisted to reach optimal productivity?
- At what point does the power to evaluate the work of others become dangerous?
- Should the individual be allowed total self-determination in short- and long-term career planning?
- Is it ethical to promote or transfer a less qualified individual to keep a valuable employee on a unit?
- Does the organization have an obligation to reemploy the chemically impaired employee who seeks rehabilitation?
- When does the employee's right to privacy regarding their drug or alcohol use stop and the manager's right to that information begin?

- Is it ever ethical to file a grievance against another individual for the purpose of harassment?
- Can discipline administered in anger be fair?
- In pursuing beneficence, is it more appropriate to discipline marginal employees progressively or to terminate them?

ADVOCACY

Advocacy—helping others to grow and self-actualize—is a leadership role. Managers, by virtue of their many roles, must be advocates for patients, subordinates, and the profession. When advocating for clients, Curtin (1982) maintains that nursing is a moral art and that the purpose of nursing is the welfare of human beings. She stresses that disease results in decreased independence, loss of freedom of action, and interference with the ability to make choices. Thus, advocacy becomes the foundation and essence of nursing, and nursing has a responsibility to promote human advocacy.

Kohnke (1986) maintains that advocacy differs from ethics or good nursing practice, although advocacy is often defined as one or both. She states that the actions of an advocate are to inform clients of their rights and to ascertain that clients have sufficient information on which to base their decisions. Kohnke also states that organizations frequently view advocates as troublemakers.

Managers also must advocate for patients with regard to distribution of resources and the use of technology. The advances in science and limits of financial resources have created new problems and ethical dilemmas. For example, although diagnosis-related groupings may have eased the strain on government fiscal resources, they have created ethical problems, such as patient dumping, premature patient discharge, and inequality of care (Huston & Marquis, 1989). The first- and middle-level manager is in the best position to advocate for patients affected by such problems.

The manager also is an advocate for subordinates. Subordinate advocacy is a neglected concept in management theory but an essential part of the leadership role. In this area of advocacy, although the organization provides some direction in solving ethical issues, the manager must resolve ethical problems and live with the solutions at the unit level. Carpenter (1994) suggests that managers have an obligation to assist staff in dealing with ethical issues and encourages that appropriate support groups, ethics committees, and channels for dealing with ethical problems be established.

Managers must recognize what subordinates are striving for and the goals and values subordinates consider appropriate (Quinn & Smith, 1987). The leader/manager should be able to guide subordinates toward actualization while defending their right to autonomy.

Upper-level managers can advocate for subordinates in a different way. For example, when the healthcare industry has faced the crisis of inadequate human resources and nursing shortages, many organizations have made quick, poorly thought-out decisions to find short-term solutions to a long-term and severe problem. New workers have been recruited at a phenomenally high cost, yet the problems that caused high worker attrition have not been solved (Huston & Marquis, 1989). Upper-level managers must advocate for subordinates in solving problems and making decisions about how best to use limited resources. These decisions must be made carefully, following a thorough examination of the political, social, economic, and ethical costs.

Managers also must be an advocate for the nursing profession. This type of advocacy is described by Quinn and Smith (1987):

> Choosing to enter a profession amounts to voluntarily biting off a chunk of the human condition. The professional chooses to become involved (with expertise and commitment) in an area of human life in which important elements of human welfare are at stake and in which people must depend on experts. In making that choice, the professional becomes committed to living with and wrestling with the problem of professional issues and, sometimes unavoidable consequences (p. 55).

Joining a profession requires making a very personal decision to involve oneself in a system of roles that is socially defined. Thus, entry into a profession involves a personal and public promise to serve others with the special expertise that a profession can provide and that society legitimately expects it to provide.

Professional issues are ethical issues. When nurses find a discrepancy between their perceived role and society's expectations, they have a responsibility to advocate for the profession. At times, individual nurses feel that the problems of the profession are too big for them to make a difference.

A professional commitment means that people cannot shrink from their duty to question and contemplate problems that face the profession. They cannot afford to become powerless or helpless or claim that one person cannot make a difference. Often, one voice is all it takes to raise the consciousness of colleagues within a profession.

If nursing is to advance as a profession, practitioners and managers must broaden their sociopolitical knowledge base to understand better the bureaucracies in which they live. This includes speaking out on consumer issues, continuing and expanding attempts to influence legislation, and increasing membership on governmental health policy-making boards and councils (Nelson, 1988). Only then will nurses be able to influence the tremendous problems facing society today in terms of the homeless, teenage pregnancy, drug and alcohol abuse, and the lack of adequate healthcare for the poor. These are essential advocacy roles for the profession.

SEPARATING ETHICAL AND LEGAL DECISION MAKING

Although they are not the same, separating legal and ethical issues is sometimes difficult. Legal controls are generally clear and philosophically impartial; ethical controls are much more unclear and individualized. In many ethical issues, courts have made a decision that may guide managers in their decision making. Often, however, these

---

LEARNING EXERCISE 22.5

Do you belong to your statewide nursing organization or student nursing organization? Why or why not? Make a list of six things *you* could do to advocate for the profession. Be specific. Is your list realistic in terms of your energy and commitment to nursing?

guidelines are either not comprehensive or differ from the manager's own philosophy. Managers must be aware of established legal standards and cognizant of possible liabilities and consequences for actions that go against the legal precedent.

Legal precedents are frequently overturned later and often do not keep pace with the changing needs of society. Additionally, certain circumstances may favor an illegal course of action as the "right" thing to do. If a man were transporting his severely ill wife to the hospital, it might be morally correct for him to disobey traffic laws. Therefore, the manager should think of the law as a basic standard of conduct, while ethical behavior requires a greater examination of the issues involved.

The manager may confront several particularly sensitive legal/ethical issues, including termination or refusal of treatment, living wills, abortion, sterilization, child abuse, and human experimentation. Most healthcare organizations have legal counsel to assist managers in making decisions in such sensitive areas. Many hospitals also have ethics committees to assist with problem solving in ethical issues. The new manager must consult with others when solving sensitive legal/ethical questions because an individual's own value system may preclude examining all possible alternatives. Because legal aspects of management decision making are so important, Chapter 23 is devoted exclusively to this topic.

INTEGRATING LEADERSHIP ROLES AND MANAGEMENT FUNCTIONS IN ETHICS

Leadership roles in ethics focus on the human element involved in ethical decision making. Leaders are self-aware regarding their values and basic beliefs about the rights, duties, and goals of human beings. As self-aware and ethical individuals, they exude confidence in their decision making and are role models to subordinates. They also are realists and recognize that some ambiguity and uncertainty must be a part of all ethical decision making. Leaders are willing to take risks in their decision making despite the fact that negative outcomes can occur with quality decision making.

Perhaps, however, the most important leadership role in ethics is that of advocate. Advocacy is considered one of the most vital roles of the nursing profession. Many of the leadership skills described in previous chapters, such as risk taking, vision, self-confidence, ability to articulate needs, and assertiveness, are used in the advocacy role.

In ethical issues, the manager is often the decision maker. Because ethical decisions are so complex and the cost of a poor decision may be high, management functions focus on increasing the chances that the best possible decision will be made at the least possible cost in terms of fiscal and human resources. This usually requires that the manager become expert at using systematic approaches to problem solving or decision making, such as theoretical models, ethical frameworks, and ethical principles. By developing expertise, the manager can identify universal outcomes that should be sought or avoided.

The integrated leader/manager recognizes that ethical issues pervade every aspect of leadership and management. Rather than being paralyzed by the complexity and ambiguity of these issues, the leader/manager accepts his or her limitations and makes the best possible decision at that time with the information and resources available.

KEY CONCEPTS

▼ *Ethics* is the systematic study of what a person's conduct and actions ought to be with regard to himself or herself, other human beings, and the environment; it is the justification of what is right or good, and the study of what a person's life and relationships ought to be—not necessarily what they are (Aroskar, 1987).

▼ In an era of markedly limited physical, human, and fiscal resources, nearly all decision making by nurse-managers involves some ethical component. Multiple advocacy roles and accountability to the profession further increase the likelihood that managers will be faced with ethical dilemmas in their practice.

▼ Much of the difficulty individuals have in making ethical decisions can be attributed to a lack of formal education in problem solving and decision making.

▼ *Ethical dilemmas* can be defined as having to choose between two equally desirable or undesirable alternatives.

▼ Curtin (1982) maintains that for a problem to be an ethical dilemma, it must have three characteristics. First, the problem cannot be solved using only empirical data. Second, the problem must be so perplexing that it is difficult to decide what facts and data need to be used in making the decision. Third, the results of the problem must affect more than the immediate situation; there should be far-reaching effects.

▼ Many systematic approaches to ethical problem solving are appropriate for the manager. These approaches include the use of theoretical problem-solving and decision-making models, ethical frameworks, and ethical principles.

▼ *Outcomes* should never be used as the sole criteria for assessing the quality of the problem solving, because many variables affect outcome that have no reflection on whether the problem solving was appropriate. The quality of ethical problem solving should be evaluated in terms of the *process* used to make the decision. If a structured approach to problem solving is used, data gathering is adequate, and multiple alternatives are analyzed, then regardless of the outcome, the manager should feel comfortable that the best possible decision was made at that time with the information and resources available.

▼ Four of the most commonly used ethical frameworks for decision making include utilitarianism, duty-based reasoning, rights-based reasoning, and intuitionism. These frameworks do not solve the ethical problem but assist the individuals involved in the problem solving to clarify their values and beliefs.

▼ Using an ethical framework of *utilitarianism* encourages the manager to make decisions based on what provides the greatest good for the greatest number of individuals. In doing so, the needs and wants of the individual are diminished.

▼ *Duty-based reasoning* is an ethical framework that says some decisions must be made because there is a duty to do what is right. There is a duty to do something or to refrain from doing something.

▼ *Rights-based reasoning* is based on the belief that some things are a person's just due; that is, each individual has basic claims or entitlements with which there should be no interference. Rights are different from needs, wants, or desires.

▼ The *intuitionist framework* allows the decision maker to review each ethical problem or issue on a case-by-case basis, comparing the relative weights of goals, duties, and rights. This weighting is determined primarily by intuition—what the decision maker feels is right for that particular situation.

▼ Principles of ethical reasoning explore and define what beliefs or values form the basis for our decision making. These principles include *autonomy, beneficence, nonmalificence, paternalism, utility, justice, truth telling,* and *deception.*

▼ Ethical issues are inherent throughout all aspects of the management process.

▼ Professional codes of ethics are a guide to the highest standards of ethical practice for nurses.

▼ Managers, by virtue of their many roles, must be advocates for clients, subordinates, and the profession. *Advocacy* is helping others to grow and self-actualize and is a leadership role.

▼ Professional issues are ethical issues. When nurses find a discrepancy between their perceived role and society's expectations, they have a responsibility to advocate for the profession.

▼ If nursing is to advance as a profession, practitioners and managers must broaden their sociopolitical knowledge base to understand better the bureaucracies in which they live.

▼ Sometimes it is very difficult to separate legal and ethical issues, although they are not the same. Legal controls are generally clear and philosophically impartial. Ethical controls are much more unclear and individualized.

◣ ADDITIONAL LEARNING EXERCISES

Learning Exercise 22.6

The Impaired Employee

Beverly, a 35-year-old, full-time nurse on the day shift, has been with your facility for 10 years. There have been rumors that she has been coming to work under the influence of alcohol. Staff have reported the smell of alcohol on her breath, unexcused absences from the unit, and an increase in medication errors. Although the unit supervisor suspected Beverly was chemically impaired, she had been unable to observe directly any of these behaviors.

After arriving at work last week, the supervisor walked into the nurses' lounge and observed Beverly covertly drinking from a dark-colored flask in her locker. She immediately confronted Beverly and asked her if she was drinking alcohol while on duty. Beverly tearfully admitted that she was drinking alcohol but stated this was an isolated incident and begged her to forget it. She promised not to ever consume alcohol at work again.

In an effort to reduce the emotionalism of the event and to give herself time to think, the supervisor sent Beverly home and scheduled a conference with her for later in the day. At this conference, Beverly was defensive and stated, "I do not have a drinking problem, and you are overreacting." The supervisor shared data she had gathered, supporting her impression that Beverly was chemically impaired. Beverly offered no explanation for these behaviors. The plan for Beverly was a 2-week suspension without pay and the requirement that she attend three alcohol support group meetings before she returns to work. She also was informed that failure to do so and further evidence of intoxication while on duty would result in immediate termination. Beverly again became very tearful and begged the supervisor to reconsider. She stated that she was the sole provider for her four small children and that her frequent sick days had taken up all available vacation and sick pay. The supervisor stated that she felt her decision was appropriate and again encouraged Beverly to seek guidance for her drinking. Four days later the supervisor read in the newspaper that Beverly committed suicide the day after this meeting.

Assignment: Evaluate the problem solving of the supervisor. Would your actions have differed if you were the manager? Are there conflicting legal and ethical obligations? To whom does the manager have the greatest obligation: patients, subordinates, or the organization? Could the outcome have been prevented? Does this outcome reflect on the quality of the problem-solving?

Learning Exercise 22.7

You are the evening house supervisor of a small, private, rural hospital. In your role, you are responsible for staffing the upcoming shift and for troubleshooting problems that cannot be handled at the unit level.

Because of legislative changes and reductions in federal money in the last couple of years, the hospital has developed a policy that says that indigent admissions (admission of patients who cannot pay for services) shall not exceed 30% of the total patient census. Thus, the emergency room is expected to screen carefully all patients and refer noncritical indigent patients requiring hospitalization to county facilities, which are approximately 30 minutes away.

Tonight you are called to the emergency room to handle a patient complaint. When you arrive, you find a woman in her mid-20s arguing vehemently with the emergency room charge nurse and physician. When you intercede, the patient introduces herself as Teresa and states, "There is something wrong with my father, and they won't help him because we can't pay. If we had money, you would be willing to do something." The charge nurse intercedes by saying, "Teresa's father began vomiting about 2 hours ago and blacked out approximately 45 minutes ago, following a 14-hour drinking binge." The physician added, "The father's blood alcohol level is 0.25 (two and one-half times the level required to be declared legally intoxicated), and my physical examination would indicate nothing other than that he is drunk and needs to sleep it off. Besides, I have seen him in the emergency room before, and it's always for the same thing."

Teresa persists in her pleas to you that there is something different this time and that she feels the hospital should evaluate her father further. She intuitively feels that something terrible will happen to her father if he is does not receive care immediately. The physician becomes angrier after this comment and states to you, "I am not going to waste my time and energy on someone who is just drunk, and I refuse to order any more expensive laboratory work or x-rays on this patient. If you want something else done, you will have to find someone else to order it." With that, he walks off to another examination room. The emergency room nurse is waiting for further directions.

Assignment: How will you handle this situation? Would your decision be any easier if resource allocation was not an issue? Describe your decision in terms of the ethical principle of justice and the distribution of scarce resources.

Learning Exercise 22.8

You are a perinatal unit coordinator at a large teaching hospital. In addition to your management responsibilities, you have been asked to fill in as a member of the hospital promotion committee, which reviews petitions from clinicians for a step-level promotion on the clinical specialist ladder. You feel you could learn a great deal on this committee and could be an objective and contributing member.

The committee has been convened to select the annual winner of the Outstanding Clinical Specialist Award. In reviewing the applicant files, you find that one file from a perinatal clinical specialist contains many overstatements and several misrepresentations. You know for a fact that this clinician did not accomplish all that she has listed, because she is a friend and close colleague. She did not, however, know that you would be a member of this committee and thus would be aware of this deception.

When the entire committee met, several members commented on this clinician's impressive file. Although you were able to dissuade them covertly from further considering her nomination, you are left with many uneasy feelings and some anger and sadness.

You recognize that she did not receive the nomination and thus there is little real danger regarding the deceptions in the file being used inappropriately at this time. You do recognize, however, that you will not be on this committee next year and that if she were to submit an erroneous file again, she could in fact be highly considered for the award. You also recognize that even with the best of intentions and the most therapeutic of communication techniques, that confronting your friend with her deception will cause her to lose face and will probably result in an unsalvageable friendship. You also recognize that even if you did confront her, there is little that you could do to stop her from doing the same in future nomination processes, other than formally reporting her conduct.

Assignment: Determine what you will do. Do the potential costs outweigh the potential benefits? Be realistic about your actions.

Learning Exercise 22.9

The Valuable Employee
(From Huston & Marquis, 1989.)

Gina has been the supervisor of a 16-bed intensive care unit/critical care unit (ICU/CCU) in a 200-bed urban hospital for 8 years. She is respected and well liked by her staff. Her staff retention level and productivity are higher than any other unit in the hospital. For the last 6 years, Gina has relied heavily on Mark, her permanent charge nurse on the day shift. He is bright, motivated, and has excellent clinical and management skills. Mark seems satisfied and challenged in his current position, although Gina has not had any formal career planning meetings with him to discuss his long-term career goals. It would be fair to say that Mark's work has greatly increased Gina's scope of power and enhanced the reputation of the unit.

Recently, one of the physicians approached Gina about a plan to open an outpatient cardiac rehabilitation program. The program will require a strong leader and manager who is self-motivated. It will be a lot of work but also provides many opportunities for advancement. He suggests that Mark would be an excellent choice for the job, although he has given Gina full authority to make the final decision.

Gina is aware that Lynn, a bright and dynamic staff nurse from the open-heart surgery floor, also would be very interested in the job. Lynn has only been employed at the hospital for 1 year but has a proven track record and would probably be very successful in the job. In addition, there is a staffing surplus right now on the open-heart surgery floor because two of the surgeons have recently retired. It would be difficult and time consuming to replace Mark as charge nurse in the CCU/ICU.

Assignment: What process should this supervisor pursue to determine who should be hired for the position? Should the position be posted? When does the benefit of using transfers/promotions as a means of reward outweigh the cost of reduced productivity?

REFERENCES:

Aroskar, M. A. (1987). The interface of ethics and politics in nursing. *Nursing Outlook, 35*(6).

Carpenter, M. A. (1994). Tutor or tyrant. In J. McCloskey & H. K. Grace (Eds.), *Current issues in nursing* (4th ed.). St. Louis: C.V. Mosby.

Crisham, P. (1985). MORAL: How can I do what is right? *Nursing Management, 16*(3).

Curtin, L. (1982a). Ethics in nursing administration. In A. Marriner (Ed.), *Contemporary nursing management.* St. Louis: C.V. Mosby.

Curtin, L. (1993). Doing the right thing. *Nursing Management, 24*(12), 17–19.

Deloughery, G. L. (1991). *Issues and trends in nursing.* St. Louis: C.V. Mosby.

Etziony, M. B. (Ed.) (1973). *The physician's creed.* Springfield, IL: Charles C. Thomas.

Huston, C. J., & Marquis, B. L. (1989). *Retention and productivity strategies for nurse managers.* Philadelphia: J.B. Lippincott.

Josephson, J. (1989). "Ethical obligations and opportunities in business: Ethical decision making in the trenches." *The Joseph & Edna Josephson Institute for Advancement of Ethics.* Marina del Rey, CA.

Kohnke, M. (1986). The nurse as advocate. In E. Hein & M. J. Nicholson (Eds.), *Contemporary leadership behavior: Selected readings* (pp. 145–148). Boston: Little Brown and Company.

Marquis, B. L., & Huston, C. J. (1994). *Management decision making for nurses: 118 case studies.* (2nd ed.). Philadelphia: J.B. Lippincott.

Murphy, M., & Murphy, J. (1976). Making ethical decisions—Systematically. *Nursing 76, 6,* 13–14.

McCloskey, J., & Grace, H. K. (1994). Ethics of caring decisions. In J. McCloskey & H. K. Grace (Eds.), *Current issues in nursing* (4th ed.). St Louis: C.V. Mosby.

Nelson, M. L. (1988). Advocacy in nursing. *Nursing Outlook, 36*(3).

Powers, C. W., & Vogel, D. (1980). *Ethics in the education of business managers, the teaching of ethics V.* New York: The Hastings Center.

Quinn, C. A., & Smith, M. D. (1987). *The professional commitment: Issues and ethics in nursing* (p. 53). Philadelphia: W.B. Saunders.

Veatch, R. M., & Fry, S. T. (1987). *Case studies in nursing ethics.* Philadelphia: J.B. Lippincott.

BIBLIOGRAPHY

Cooper, C. C. (1988). Covenantal relationships: Grounding for the nursing ethic. *Advances in Nursing Science, 10*(4), 48–59.

Corey, G., Corey, M. S., & Callanan, P. (1988). *Issues and ethics in the helping professions* (3rd ed.). Pacific Grove, CA: Brooks/Cole Publishing Company.

Curtin, L. (1993) Informed consent: Cautious calculated candor. *Nursing Management, 24*(4), 18–20.

Curtin, L. (1993) Conscience and clinical care. *Nursing Management, 24*(8), 26–28.

Fenton, M. (1988). Moral distress in clinical practice: Implications for the nurse administrator. *Canadian Journal of Nursing Administration, 1*(3), 8–11.

Fry, S. T. (1989). Whistle blowing by nurses: A matter of ethics. *Nursing Outlook, 37*(1), 56.

Gaines, C., et. al. (1989). Overtime: A professional responsibility. *Focus on Critical Care, 16*(4), 270–273.

Haddad, A. M. (1989). The dilemma of keeping confidences. *American Operating Room Nurses Journal, 50*(1), 159, 162–164.

Huggins, E. A., & Sclazi, C. C. (1988). Limitations and alternatives: Ethical practice theory in nursing. *Advances in Nursing Sciences, 10*(4), 43–47.

Jones, H. (1988). Desperate measures . . . Case of a newly qualified nurse. *Nursing Times, 84*(47), 59–61.

Mappes, T. A., & Zembatty, J. S. (1986). *Biomedical ethics* (2nd ed.). New York: McGraw Hill.

Omery, A. (1989). Values, moral reasoning, and ethics. *Nursing Clinics of North America, 24*(2), 499–508.

Parker, R. S. (1990). Nurses stories: The search for a relational ethic of care. *Advances in Nursing Science, 13*(1), 31–40.

Pownall, M. (1989). When care has to be rationed . . . Ethical problems nurses face . . . Choices in care have to be balanced against cost. *Nursing Times, 85*(5), 16–17.

Proctor, D. A. (1995). Ethical issues. In K. W. Vestal (Ed.), *Nursing management* (2nd ed.). Philadelphia: J.B. Lippincott.

Raatikainen, R. (1989). Values and ethical principles in nursing. *Journal of Advanced Nursing, 14*(2), 92–96.

Sullivan, P. A., & Brown, T. (1989). Unlicensed persons in patient care settings: Administrative, policy, and ethical issues. *Nursing Clinics of North America, 24*(2), 557–569.

Tamborini-Martin, S., & Hanley, K. V. (1989). The importance of being ethical: Essential skills for effective leadership. *Health Progress, 70*(5), 24–27, 82.

Viens, D. C. (1989). A history of nursing's code of ethics. *Nursing Outlook, 37*(1), 45–49.

Yarling, R. R., & McElmurr, B. J. (1986). The moral foundation of nursing. *Advances in Nursing Science, 8*(2), 63–73.

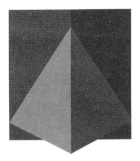

CHAPTER 23

Legal and Legislative Issues

Chapter 22 presents ethics as an internal control of human behavior and nursing practice. "Ethics has to do with actions we wish people would take, not actions they must take" (Hall, 1990). Once ethical behavior is written into law, it's no longer just desired; it's mandated. This chapter focuses on the external controls of legislation and law. Since the first mandatory Nurse Practice Act was passed in New York in 1938, nursing has been legislated, directed, and controlled to some extent.

The primary purpose of law and legislation is to protect the patient and the nurse. Laws and legislation define the scope of acceptable practice and protect individual rights. Nurses who are aware of their rights and duties in legal manners are better able to protect themselves against liability or loss of professional licensure.

This chapter is divided into four sections. The first section presents the four primary sources of law and how each affects nursing practice. The nurse's responsibility to be proactive in establishing and revising laws affecting nursing practice is emphasized. The next section presents specific doctrines used by the courts to define legal boundaries for nursing practice. The role of state boards in professional licensure and discipline is examined. The third section deals with the components of malpractice for the individual practitioner and the manager or supervisor. Legal terms are de-

Bessie L. Marquis and Carol J. Huston:
LEADERSHIP ROLES AND MANAGEMENT FUNCTIONS IN NURSING, 2nd ed.
Lippincott-Raven Publishers © 1996

fined. The last section in this chapter deals with issues such as informed consent, medical records, intentional torts, and patient rights.

This chapter is not meant to be a complete legal guide to nursing practice. There are many excellent legal textbooks and handbooks that accomplish that function. The primary function of this chapter is to emphasize the widely varying and rapidly changing nature of laws and the responsibility that each nurse-manager has to keep abreast of legislation and laws affecting nursing practice. Leadership roles and management functions inherent in legal and legislative issues are shown in Display 23.1.

Display 23.1 Leadership Roles and Management Functions in Legal and Legislative Issues

Leadership Roles

1. Serves as a role model by providing nursing care that meets or exceeds accepted standards of care.
2. Is current in the field and seeks professional certification to increase expertise in a specific field.
3. Reports substandard nursing care to appropriate authorities.
4. Fosters nurse/patient relationships that are respectful, caring, and honest, thus reducing the possibility of future lawsuits.
5. Joins and actively supports professional organizations to strengthen the lobbying efforts of nurses in healthcare legislation.
6. Practices nursing within the area of individual competence.
7. Prioritizes patient rights and patient welfare first in decision making.
8. Demonstrates vision, risk taking, and energy in determining appropriate legal boundaries for nursing practice, thus defining what nursing is and should be in the future.

Management Functions

1. Is knowledgeable regarding sources of law and legal doctrines that affect nursing practice.
2. Delegates to subordinates wisely, looking at the manager's scope of practice and that of those they supervise.
3. Understands and adheres to institutional policies and procedures.
4. Practices nursing within the scope of the state nurse practice act.
5. Monitors subordinates to ensure they have a valid, current, and appropriate license to practice nursing.
6. Uses foreseeability of harm in delegation and staffing decisions.
7. Increases staff awareness of intentional torts and assists them in developing strategies to reduce their liability in these areas.
8. Provides educational and training opportunities for staff on legal issues affecting nursing practice.

SOURCES OF LAW

The U.S. legal system can be somewhat confusing because not only are there four sources of the law, but also parallel systems at the state and federal levels. The sources of law include constitutions, statutes, administrative agencies, and court decisions. A comparison is shown in Table 23.1.

A *constitution* is a system of fundamental laws or principles that governs a nation, society, corporation, or another aggregate of individuals (Guido, 1988). The purpose of a constitution is to establish the basis of a governing system for the future and the present. The U.S. Constitution establishes the general organization of the federal government and grants and limits its specific powers. Each state also has a constitution that establishes the general organization of the state government and grants and limits its powers.

The second source of law is *statutes*—laws that govern and meet existing conditions (Guido, 1988). These laws are made by legislative bodies, such as the U.S. Congress, state legislature, and city councils. Statutes are officially enacted (voted on and passed) by the legislative body and compiled into codes, collections of statutes, and ordinances. The 51 nurse practice acts representing the 50 states and the District of Columbia are examples of statutes. These nurse practice acts define and limit the practice of nursing, thereby determining what constitutes unauthorized practice or practice that exceeds the scope of authority (Fiesta, 1990). Although nurse practice acts may vary between states, all must be consistent with provisions or statutes established at the federal level.

TABLE 23.1   Sources of Law

Origin	Use	Involvement With Nursing Practice
The Constitution	The highest law in the United States; interpreted by the United States Supreme Court; gives authority to other three sources of the law	Little direct involvement in the area of malpractice.
Statutes	Also called statutory law or legislative law; laws passed by the state or federal legislators and must be signed by the President or Governor	Prior to 1970s, very few state or federal laws dealt with malpractice. Since the malpractice crisis, many statutes affect malpractice.
Administrative agencies	The rules and regulations established by appointed agencies of the executive branch of the government (Governor or President)	Some of these agencies, such as the National Labor Relations Board or Health and Safety Boards can affect nursing practice.
Court decisions	Also called *tort law;* this is court mode law and the courts interpret the statutes and set precedents; in the United States, there are two levels of court: trial court and appellate court	Most malpractice law is addressed by the courts.

Administrative agencies, the third source of law, are given authority to act by the state legislative body and create rules and regulations that enforce statutory laws (Guido, 1988). For example, state boards of nursing are administrative agencies set up to implement and enforce the state nurse practice act by writing rules and regulations and by conducting investigations and hearings to ensure the law's enforcement. Administrative laws are valid only to the extent that they are within the scope of the authority granted to them by the legislative body.

The fourth source of law is *court decisions.* Judicial or decisional laws are made by the courts to interpret legal issues that are in dispute (Guido, 1988). Depending on the type of court involved, judicial or decisional law may be made by a single justice, with or without a jury, or by a panel of justices. Generally, initial trial courts have a single judge or magistrate, intermediary appeal courts have three justices, and the highest appeal courts have nine justices.

NURSING'S ROLE IN LEGISLATION AND LAWMAKING

A distinctive feature of American society is the manner in which citizens can participate in the political process (Quinn & Smith, 1987). Individuals have the right to express their opinions about issues and candidates by voting. Individuals also have relatively easy access to lawmakers and policy makers and can make their individual needs and wants known. Theoretically then, any one person can influence those in policy-making positions. In reality, this rarely happens; policy decisions are generally focused on group needs or wants.

Because they have been reluctant to become politically involved, nurses have failed to have a strong legislative voice in the past. Legislators and policy makers are more willing to deal with nurses as a group rather than as individuals, thus joining and supporting professional organizations allow nurses to become active in lobbying for a stronger nurse practice act or for the creation or expansion of advanced nursing roles. In this arena, professional organizations draft laws governing nursing practice, interpret their purpose to the community they will serve, and guide their passage through the legislature to subsequent approval by the governor (Betts, 1993; Guido, 1988).

In addition, professional organizations generally espouse standards of care that are higher than those required by law. Voluntary controls often are forerunners of legal controls (Mittelstadt & Hart, 1993). Nurses who participate in professional organizations are integral in determining whether voluntary or legal controls represent what nursing is and should be.

Nursing leaders are future oriented; they have vision. These leaders look not only at the needs of their patients and themselves at a particular time, but also are active in examining and setting policy for nurses in the future (Huston & Marquis, 1988). Not long ago, no one entered or left the healthcare system without the intervention of a physician. This closed system seriously limited rendering of complete healthcare services to patients. Through the work of future-oriented leaders, some nurses today are providing direct care to clients and families rather than just providing services for institutions.

The need for organized group efforts by nurses to influence legislative policy has long been recognized in this country. In fact, the first state associations were organized expressly for unifying nurses to influence the passage of state licensure laws (Quinn & Smith, 1987). Political Action Committees (PACs) of the Congress of Industrial Organizations attempt to persuade legislators to vote in a particular way. Lobbyists of the PAC may be a member of a group interested in a particular law or a paid agent of the group that wants a specific bill passed or defeated. Nursing must become more actively involved with PACs to influence healthcare legislation.

As a whole, the profession has not yet recognized the full potential of collective political activity. Nurses must exert their collective influence and make their concerns known to policy makers before they can have a major impact on political and legislative outcomes (Agnos, Snyder, & Evans, 1993).

LEARNING EXERCISE 23.1

List five things you would like to change about nursing or the healthcare system. Prioritize the changes you have identified. Write a one-page essay about the change you feel is most needed. Identify the strategies you could use individually and collectively as a profession to make the change happen. Be sure you are realistic about the time, energy, and fiscal resources you have to implement your plan.

LEGAL DOCTRINES AND THE PRACTICE OF NURSING

Two important legal doctrines guide courts in their decision making. The first of these, *stare decisis,* means to let the decision stand. *Stare decisis* uses precedents as a guide for decision making. This doctrine gives nurses insight into ways the court has previously fixed liability in given situations. However, the nurse must avoid two pitfalls in determining if *stare decisis* should apply to a given situation (Guido, 1988).

The first is that the previous case must be within the jurisdiction of the court hearing the current case. For example, a previous Florida case decided by a state court does not set precedent for a Texas appellate court. Although the Texas court may model its decision after the Florida case, it is not compelled to do so. The lower courts in Texas, however, would rely on Texas appellate decisions.

The other pitfall is that the court hearing the current case can depart from the precedent and set a *landmark* decision. Landmark decisions generally occur because societal needs have changed, technology has become more advanced, or following the precedent would further harm an already injured person (Guido, 1988). *Roe v. Wade,* the 1973 landmark decision to allow a woman to seek and receive a legal abortion during the first two trimesters of pregnancy is an example. Given changes in societal views about abortion in the 1990s, this precedent may change again in the near future. Indeed, Betts (1993) believes that the present Rehnquist court has already ignored the doctrine of *stare decisis* and has overturned many of the rights protected by the Warren and Burger courts.

The second doctrine that guides courts in their decision making is *res judicata*. *Res judicata* means a "thing or matter settled by judgment" and applies only when a legal dispute has been decided by a competent court and when no further appeals are possible (Guido, 1988). This doctrine keeps the same parties in the original lawsuit from retrying the same issues that were involved in the first lawsuit.

When using doctrines as a guide for nursing practice, the nurse must remember that all laws are fluid and subject to change. Laws cannot be static; they must change to reflect the growing autonomy and responsibility desired by nurses. It is critical that each nurse be aware of and sensitive to rapidly changing laws and legislation that affect their practice. The nurse also must recognize that state laws may differ from federal laws and that legal guidelines for nursing practice in the organization may differ from state or federal guidelines.

Boundaries for practice are defined in the nurse practice act of each state. These acts are general in most states to allow for some flexibility in the broad roles and varied situations in which nurses practice. Because this allows for some interpretation, many employers have established guidelines for nursing practice in their own organization. These guidelines regarding scope of practice cannot, however, exceed the requirements of the state nursing practice acts. Managers need to be aware of their organization's specific practice interpretations and ensure that subordinates are aware of the same and follow established practices. All nurses must understand the legal controls for nursing practice in their state.

PROFESSIONAL VERSUS INSTITUTIONAL LICENSURE

In general, a *license* is a legal document that permits a person to offer special skills and knowledge to the public in a particular jurisdiction, when such practice would otherwise be unlawful (Creighton, 1986). Licensure establishes standards for entry into practice, defines a scope of practice, and allows for disciplinary action (Northrup, 1987). Currently, licensing for nurses is a responsibility of state boards of nursing or state boards of nurse examiners, which also provide discipline as necessary. The manager, however, is responsible for monitoring that all licensed subordinates have a valid, appropriate, and current license to practice.

Licensure is a privilege and not a right. All nurses must safeguard this right by knowing the standards of care applicable to their work setting. Deviation from that standard should be undertaken only when nurses are prepared to accept the consequences of their actions, both in terms of liability and loss of licensure.

Nurses who violate specific norms of conduct, such as securing a license by fraud, performing specific actions prohibited by the nursing practice act, exhibiting unprofessional or illegal conduct, performing malpractice, and abusing alcohol or drugs, may have their licenses suspended or revoked by the licensing boards in all states (Creighton, 1986). Fiesta (1993a) states that drug and alcohol impairment and unprofessional conduct are the most common causes of license revocation for nurses, but there are many other causes, as shown in Display 23.2.

Typically, suspension and revocation proceedings are administrative. Following a complaint, the board of nursing completes an investigation, which generally takes 1

Display 23.2   Common Causes of Professional Nursing
License Suspension or Revocation.

- Being found guilty of professional negligence
- Practicing medicine or nursing without a license
- Obtaining a nursing license by fraud or allowing others to use your license
- Conviction of a felony for any offense substantially related to the function or duties of a registered nurse
- Participating professionally in criminal abortions
- Not reporting substandard medical or nursing care
- Providing patient care while under the influence of drugs or alcohol
- Giving narcotic drugs without an order
- Falsely holding oneself out to the public or to any healthcare practitioner as a "nurse practitioner"

---

to 4 months. Approximately 75% of these investigations reveal no grounds for discipline. If the investigation supports the need for discipline, nurses are notified of the charges and allowed to prepare a defense. At the hearing, which is very similar to a trial, the nurse is allowed to present evidence. Based on the evidence, an administrative law judge makes a recommendation to the state board of nursing, which makes the final decision. The entire process, from complaint to final decision, generally takes between 16 and 22 months (Anderson, 1982).

Some professionals have advocated shifting the burden of licensure, and thus accountability, from individual practitioners to an institution or agency. Proponents for this move feel that institutional licensure would provide more effective use of personnel and greater flexibility. Both the American Nurses Association (ANA) and the National League for Nursing (NLN) oppose this move strongly because they believe it has the potential for diluting the quality of nursing care (Creighton, 1986).

An alternative to institutional licensure has been the development of certification programs by the ANA. By passing specifically prepared written examinations, nurses are able to qualify for certification in at least 17 areas. This voluntary testing program represents professional organizational certification. Many nursing leaders today strongly advocate professional certification as a means of enhancing the profession.

PROFESSIONAL NEGLIGENCE

Historically, physicians were held liable for nursing care. As nurses have gained authority, autonomy, and accountability, they have assumed responsibility, accountability, and liability for their own practice. As roles have expanded, nurses have begun performing duties traditionally reserved for medical practice. As a result of an increased scope of practice, many nurses have begun to carry individual malpractice

> ## LEARNING EXERCISE 23.2
>
> *"Grandfathering"* is the term used to grant certain people working within the profession for a given period of time or prior to a deadline date the privilege of applying for a license without having to take the licensing examination (Guido, 1988). Grandfather clauses have been used to allow wartime nurses, those with on-the-job training and expertise, licensure, even though they did not graduate from an approved school of nursing or pass the licensure examination.
>
> With the American Nurses Association's (ANA's) proposal to make the BSN the entry level requirement for professional nursing, all nurses who have successfully passed the State Board of Registered Nursing licensure exam prior to the new legislation, regardless of educational preparation or experience, would retain the title of professional nurse. Nonbaccalaureate nurses after that time would be unable to use the title professional nurse.
>
> *Assignment:* If the purpose of the ANA's legislation is to improve the continuity and quality of nursing care, does grandfathering diminish its impact? Does grandfathering make professional nursing more a given than a privilege? Examine how your personal values have affected whether or not you support this principle.

insurance for the first time. Because of both the enhanced role of nurses and an increase in the number of insured nurses, the number of liability suits seeking damages from nurses as individuals has increased tremendously.

In all liability suits, there is a plaintiff and a defendant. In malpractice cases, the *plaintiff* is the injured party, and the *defendant* is the professional who is alleged to have caused the injury. *Negligence* has been defined as the omission to do something that a reasonable person, guided by the considerations that ordinarily regulate human affairs, would do or as doing something that a reasonable and prudent person would not do (Creighton, 1986). *Reasonable and prudent* generally mean the average judgment, foresight, intelligence, and skill that would be expected of a person with similar training and experience. *Malpractice*—the failure of a person with professional training to act in a reasonable and prudent manner—also is called *professional negligence*. Five elements must be present for a professional to be held liable for malpractice (Table 23.2).

First, a *standard of care* must have been established that outlines the level or degree of quality considered adequate by a given profession (Fiesta, 1993b). Standards of care outline the duties a defendant has to a plaintiff, or a nurse to a client. These standards represent the skills and learning commonly possessed by members of the profession and generally are the *minimal requirements* that define an acceptable level of care. Standards of care, which guarantee clients safe nursing care, include organizational policy and procedure statements, job descriptions, and student guidelines. (Guidelines for standards of care are shown in Display 23.3.)

Second, after the standard of care has been established, it must be shown that the standard was violated—there must have been a *breach of duty*. This breach is

TABLE 23.2 Components of Professional Negligence

Elements of Liability	Explanation	Example: Giving Medications
1. Duty to use due care (defined by the standard of care)	The care that should be given under the circumstances (what the reasonably prudent nurse would have done)	A nurse should give medications accurately completely, and on time.
2. Failure to meet standard of care (breach of duty)	Not giving the care that should be given under the circumstances	A nurse fails to give medications accurately, completely, or on time.
3. Forseeability of harm	The nurse must have reasonable access to information about whether the possibility of harm exists	The drug handbook specifies that the wrong dosage or route may cause injury.
4. A direct relationship between failure to meet the standard of care (breach) and injury can be proven	Patient is harmed because proper care is not given	Wrong dosage causes patient to have a convulsion.
5. Injury	Actual harm results to patient	Convulsion or other serious complication occurs.

shown by calling other nurses who practice in the same specialty or area as the defendant to testify as expert witnesses (Hogue, 1985).

Third, the nurse must have had the knowledge or availability of information that not meeting the standard of care could result in harm. This is called *foreseeability of harm*. If the average, reasonable person in the defendant's position could have anticipated the plaintiff's injury as a result of his or her actions, then the plaintiff's injury was foreseeable (Hogue, 1985). Being ignorant is not a justifiable excuse, but not having all the information in a situation may impede one's ability to foresee harm. An example might be a charge nurse who assigned another RN to care for a critically ill patient. The assigned RN makes a medication error that injures the patient in some way. If the charge nurse had reason to believe that the RN was incapable of adequately caring for the patient or failed to provide adequate supervision, foreseeability of harm is apparent, and the charge nurse also could be held liable. If the charge nurse was available as needed and had good reason to believe that the RN was fully capable, he or she could not be held liable.

The fourth element is that failure to meet the standard of care must have the *potential* to injure the patient. There must be a provable correlation between improper care and injury to the patient.

The final element is that actual *patient injury* must occur. This injury must be more than transitory. The plaintiff must show that the action of the defendant directly caused the injury and that the injury would not have occurred without the defendant's actions (Hogue, 1985).

Display 23.3 Guidelines for Standards of Care

1. Recognize that all professions have standards of care. Standards are the minimal level of expertise that may be delivered to the patient; they are a starting point for greater expectations.
2. Standards of care may be externally or internally set. The nurse is responsible for both categories of standards; those set by forces outside of nursing and those set by the role of nursing.
3. Standards of care can be found in the following:
   a. The state nurse practice act
   b. Published standards of professional organizations and specialty practice groups, such as the American Association of Critical Care Nurses or the Association of Operating Room Nurses
   c. Federal agency guidelines and regulations
   d. Hospital policy and procedure manuals
   e. The nurse's job descriptions
4. The nurse is accountable for all standards of care as they pertain to his or her profession. To remain competent and skillful, the nurse is encouraged to read professional journals and to attend pertinent continuing education and inservice programs.
5. Standards of care are determined for the judicial system by expert witnesses. Such people testify to the prevailing standards in the community—a standard that all nurses are accountable for matching and exceeding—thus ensuring that patients receive quality, competent nursing care.

(Reprinted with permission from Guido, G. W. [1988]. *Legal issues in nursing: A sourcebook for practice*. Norwalk, CT: Appleton and Lange, p. 93.)

EXTENDING THE LIABILITY

In recent years, the concept of *joint liability,* in which the nurse, physician, and employing organization are all held liable, has become the current position of the legal system. This probably more accurately reflects the higher level of accountability now present in the nursing profession. Before 1965, nurses were rarely held accountable for their own acts, and hospitals were usually exempt due to charitable immunity. However, following precedent-setting cases in the 1960s, employers are now held liable for the nurse's acts under a concept known as *vicarious liability*. One form of vicarious liability, called *respondeat superior*, is a Latin term that means "the master is responsible for the acts of his servants." *Respondeat superior* applies only when there is an employer-employee relationship and only with respect to negligent acts committed within the scope of employment (Goldstein, Perdew, & Pruitt, 1989). The theory behind the doctrine is that an employer should be held legally liable for the conduct of employees whose actions he or she has a right to direct or control.

The difficulty in interpreting *respondeat superior* is that many exceptions exist. The first and most important exception is related to the state in which the nurse practices. In some states, the doctrine of charitable immunity applies, which holds

LEARNING EXERCISE 23.3

You are a surgical nurse at Memorial Hospital. At 4 PM, you receive a patient from the recovery room who has had a total hip replacement. You note that the hip dressings are saturated with blood but are aware that total hip replacements frequently have some postoperative oozing from the wound. There is an order on the chart to reinforce the dressing as needed, and you do so. When you next check the dressing at 6 PM, you find the reinforcements saturated and drainage on the bed linen. You call the physician and tell her that you feel the patient is bleeding too heavily. The physician reassures you the amount of bleeding you have described is not excessive but encourages you to continue to monitor the patient closely. You recheck the patient's dressings at 7 PM and 8 PM. You again call the physician and tell her that the bleeding still looks too heavy. She again reassures you and tells you to continue to watch her closely. At 10 PM, the patient's blood pressure becomes nonpalpable and she goes into shock. You summon the doctor and she comes immediately.

Assignment: What are the legal ramifications of this case? Using the components of professional negligence outlined in Table 23.2, determine who in this case is guilty of malpractice. Justify your answer. At what point in the scenario should each character have altered his or her actions to reduce the probability of a negative outcome?

that a charitable (nonprofit) hospital cannot be sued by a person who has been injured as a result of a hospital employee's negligence (Goldstein, et al., 1989). Thus, liability is limited to the individual employee.

Another exception to *respondeat superior* occurs when the nurse is employed by the state or federal government. The common-law rule of governmental immunity provides that governments cannot be held liable for the negligent acts of their employees while carrying out government activities (Goldstein, et al., 1989). Some states have changed this rule by statute, however, and in these particular jurisdictions, *respondeat superior* continues to apply to the acts of nurses employed by the state government.

Nurses must remember that the purpose of *respondeat superior* is not to shift the burden of blame from the employee to the organization, but rather to share the blame, increasing the possibility of larger financial compensation to the injured party. Some nurses erroneously assume that they do not need to carry malpractice insurance because their employer will in all probability be sued as well and thus will be responsible for financial damages. Under the doctrine of *respondeat superior,* any employer required to pay damages to an injured person because of an employee's negligence has the legal right to recover or be reimbursed that amount from the negligent employee.

One rule that all nurses must know and understand is that of *personal liability,* which says that every person is liable for his or her own conduct (Goldstein, et al., 1989). The law does not permit a wrongdoer to avoid legal liability for his or her own wrongdoing, even though someone else also may be sued and held legally liable. For example, if a manager directs a subordinate to do something that both know to be improper, the injured party can recover damages against the subordinate, even if the supervisor agreed to accept full responsibility for the delegation at the time. In the end, each nurse is always held liable for his or her own negligent practice.

LEARNING EXERCISE 23.4

Have you ever been directed in your nursing practice to do something that you felt may have been unsafe or that you felt inadequately trained or prepared to do? What did you do? Would you act differently if the situation occurred now? What risks are inherent in refusing to follow the direct orders of a physician or superior?

Managers are not automatically held liable for all acts of negligence on the part of those they supervise but may be held liable if they were negligent in the supervision of those employees at the time they committed the negligent acts. Goldstein et al. (1989) state that the RN who is a manager or supervisor, unlike other categories of nurses, is legally and professionally responsible for directing and supervising the activities of LVNs, nurses' aides, and other nurses involved in direct patient care. Liability for negligence is generally based on the manager's failure to determine which of the patient needs can be assigned safely to a subordinate nurse or the failure to supervise a subordinate closely who requires such supervision.

Recently, however, hospitals have been found liable for assigning personnel who were unqualified to perform duties as shown by their evaluation reports (Fiesta, 1993c). Managers, therefore, need to be cognizant of their responsibilities in assigning and appointing personnel, because they could be found liable for ignoring organizational policies or for assigning employees duties that they are not capable of performing. However, the employee must provide the supervisor with the information that he or she is not qualified for the assignment. The manager does have the right to reassign employees as long as they are capable of discharging the anticipated duties of the assignment.

INCIDENT REPORTS

Incident reports are records of unusual or unexpected incidents that occur in the course of a client's treatment. Because attorneys use incident reports to defend the health agency against lawsuits brought by clients, the reports are considered confidential communications and cannot be subpoenaed by clients or used as evidence in their lawsuits (Anderson, 1982). However, incident reports that are inadvertently disclosed are no longer considered confidential and can be subpoenaed in court. Thus, a copy of an incident report should not be left in the chart. In addition, no entry should be made in the patient's record about the existence of an incident report. The chart should, however, provide enough information about the incident or occurrence that appropriate treatment can be given.

INTENTIONAL TORTS

Torts are legal wrongs committed against a person or property, independent of a contract, that render the person who commits them liable for damages in a civil action (Creighton, 1986). While professional negligence is considered to be an *unintentional tort,* assault, battery, false imprisonment, invasion of privacy, defamation, and slander are *intentional torts.* Intentional torts are a direct invasion of someone's legal rights. Managers are responsible for seeing that their staff are aware of and adhere to laws governing intentional torts. In addition, the manager must clearly delineate policies and procedures about these issues in the work environment.

Nurses can be sued for assault and battery. *Assault* is conduct that creates a reasonable apprehension of being touched in an injurious manner; *battery* is actual touching (Hogue, 1985). Unit managers must be alert to patient complaints of being handled in a rough manner or complaints of excessive force in restraining patients. Many battery suits have been won based on the use of restraints when dealing with confused patients.

The use of physical restraints also has led to claims of *false imprisonment.* Practitioners are liable for false imprisonment when they unlawfully restrain the movement of their patients. Physical restraints should be applied only with a physician's direct order. Likewise, the patient who wishes to sign out against medical advice should not be held against his or her will. This tort also is frequently applicable to involuntary commitments to mental health facilities (Hogue, 1985). Managers in mental health settings must be careful to institutionalize patients in accordance with all laws governing commitment.

Another area of the law that managers must understand is the right to *confidentiality.* Unauthorized release of information or photographs in medical records may make the person who discloses the information civilly liable for *invasion of privacy, defamation,* or *slander.* Written patient authorization to release information is needed to allow such disclosure. Many managers have been caught unaware by the telephone call requesting information about a patient's condition. It is extremely important that the manager not give out unauthorized information, regardless of the urgency of the person making the request. Likewise, managers must ensure that unauthorized individuals do not have access to patient charts or medical records and that unauthorized individuals are not allowed to observe procedures.

OTHER LEGAL RESPONSIBILITIES OF THE MANAGER

Managers also have some legal responsibility for *quality control* of nursing practice at the unit level, including such duties as reporting dangerous understaffing, checking staff credentials and qualifications, and carrying out appropriate discipline. Additionally, the manager, like all professional nurses, is responsible for reporting improper or substandard medical care, child and elder abuse, and communicable diseases specified by the Centers for Disease Control and Prevention.

Individual nurses also may be held liable for *product liability.* When a product is involved, negligence does not have to be proven (Fiesta, 1983). This *strict liability* is a somewhat gray area of nursing practice. Essentially, strict liability holds that a product may be held to a higher level of liability than a person. In other words, if it can be proven that the equipment or product had a defect that caused an injury, then it would be debated in court using all the elements essential for negligence, such as duty or breach. Therefore, equipment and other products fall within the scope of nursing responsibility. In general, if they are aware that equipment is faulty, nurses have a duty to refuse to use the equipment. If the fault in the equipment is not readily apparent, risks are low that the nurse will be found liable for the results of its use (Hogue, 1985).

Informed Consent

Informed consent (outlined in Display 23.4) is obtained by a physician from a person who is undergoing a procedure or surgery. The physician must describe the procedure to the patient in terms the patient can understand. The description must include potential benefits to the patient and possible risks, and it should not imply any guarantee of result. Only a competent adult can legally sign to show informed consent. Spouses or other family members cannot legally sign unless there is an approved guardianship or conservatorship.

In an emergency, the physician can invoke *implied consent,* in which the physician states in the progress notes of the medical record that the patient is unable to sign. Nurses frequently seek express consent from patients by witnessing patients sign a standard consent form. In *express consent,* the role of the nurse is to be sure that the patient has informed consent and to seek remedy if he or she does not.

Display 23.4 Guidelines for Informed Consent

Two Criteria Must Be Satisfied:
1. The person(s) giving consent must fully comprehend
   a. The procedure to be performed
   b. The risks involved
   c. Expected or desired outcomes
   d. Any complications of untoward side effects
   e. Alternative therapies, including no therapy at all
2. The consent is given by one who has the legal capacity for giving such consent
   a. Competent adult
   b. Legal guardian or representative for the incompetent adult
   c. Emancipated, married minor
   d. Mature minor
   e. Parent or legal guardian of a child
   f. Minor for the diagnosis and treatment of specific disease states or conditions
   g. Court order

(Reprinted with permission from Guido, G. W. [1988]. *Legal issues in nursing: A sourcebook for practice.* Norwalk, CT: Appleton and Lange, p. 86.)

Although they are obligated to provide teaching and to clarify information given to patients by their physicians, nurses must be careful not to give new information that contradicts information given by the physician, thus interfering in the physician-patient relationship. At times, this can be a cloudy issue both legally and ethically.

> ### LEARNING EXERCISE 23.5
>
> You are a staff nurse on a surgical unit. Shortly after reporting for duty, you make rounds on all your patients. Mrs. Jones is a 36-year-old woman scheduled for a bilateral salpingo-oophorectomy and hysterectomy. In the course of the conversation, Mrs. Jones comments that she is glad that she will not be undergoing menopause as a result of this surgery. She elaborates by stating that one of her friends had surgery that resulted in "surgical menopause" and that it was devastating to her. You return to the chart and check the surgical permit and doctor's progress notes. The operating room permit read "bilateral salpingo-oopherectomy and hysterectomy," and it is signed by Mrs. Jones. The physician has noted "discussed surgery with patient" in his progress notes.
>
> You return to Mrs. Jones' room and ask her what type of surgery she is having; she states, "I'm having my uterus removed." You phone the physician and relate your information to the surgeon. He says, "Mrs. Jones knows that I will take out her ovaries if necessary; I've discussed it with her. She signed the permit. Now, please get her ready for surgery—she is the next case."
>
> *Assignment:* Discuss what you should do at this point. Why did you select this course of action? What issues are involved here? Be able to discuss legal ramifications of this case.

Medical Records

One source of information people seek to help them make decisions about their healthcare is their medical record. Nurses have a legal responsibility for accurately recording appropriate information in the client's medical record. The alteration of medical records can result in license suspension or revocation.

Although the patient owns the information in that medical record, the actual record belongs to the facility that originally made the record and is storing it. Although patients must have "reasonable access" to their records, the method for retrieving the record varies greatly from one institution to another. Generally, a patient who wishes to inspect his or her records must make a written request and pay reasonable clerical costs to make such records available. The healthcare provider generally permits such inspection during business hours within 5 working days of the inspection request (Anderson, 1982). Nurses should be aware of the procedure for procuring medical records for patients at the facilities where they work. Often a patient's attempt to procure medical records results from a lack of trust or a need for additional teaching and education. Nurses can do a great deal to reduce this confusion and foster an open, trusting relationship between the patient and his or her healthcare providers.

(From Marquis & Huston, 1994.)

Mrs. Brown has been diagnosed as having invasive cancer. She has been having daily radiation treatments. Her husband is a frequent visitor and seems to be a devoted husband. They are both very interested in her progress and prognosis. Although they have asked many questions and you have given truthful answers, you know little because the physician has not shared much with the staff. Today, you walk into Mrs. Brown's room, and find Mr. Brown sitting at Mrs. Brown's bedside reading her chart. The radiation orderly had inadvertently left the chart in the room when Mrs. Brown returned from X-ray.

Assignment: Identify several alternatives that you have. Discuss what you would do and why. Is there a problem here? What follow-up is indicated? Attempt to solve this problem on your own before reading the sample analysis that follows.

Analysis

The nurse needs to determine the most important goal in this situation. Possible goals include 1) getting the chart away from Mr. Brown as soon as possible, 2) protecting the privacy of Mrs. Brown, 3) gathering more information, or 4) becoming a patient advocate for the Browns.

In solving the case, it is apparent that not enough information has been gathered. Mr. Brown now has the chart, and it seems pointless to take it away from him. Usually the danger in patients' families reading the chart lies in the direction of their not understanding the chart and thereby obtaining confusing information or the patient's privacy being invaded because the patient has not consented to family members' access to the chart.

Using this as the basis for rationale, the nurse should use the following approach.

1. Clarify that Mr. Brown has Mrs. Brown's permission to read the chart by asking her directly.
2. Ask Mr. Brown if there is anything in the chart that he did not understand or anything that he questioned. You may even ask him to summarize what he has read. Clarify the things that are appropriate for the nurse to address, such as terminology, procedures, or nursing care.
3. Refer questions that are inappropriate for the nurse to answer to the physician, and let Mr. Brown know that you will help him in talking with the physician regarding the medical plan and prognosis.
4. When done talking with Mr. Brown, the nurse should request the chart, and place it in the proper location. The incident should be reported to the immediate supervisor.
5. The nurse should follow through by talking with the physician about the incident and Mr. Brown's concerns and by assisting the Browns to obtain the information they have requested.

Conclusion

The nurse first gathered more information before becoming the adversary or advocate. It is possible that the Browns had only simple questions to ask and that the problem was a lack of communication between staff and their patients, rather than a physician-patient communication deficit. Legally, patients have a right to understand what is happening to them, and that should be the basis for the decisions in this case.

AVOIDING MALPRACTICE CLAIMS

Interactions between nurses and clients that are less businesslike and more personal are more satisfying to both. It has been proven that despite technical competence, nurses who have difficulty establishing positive interpersonal relationships with patients and their families are at greater risk of being sued. Communication done in a caring and professional manner has been shown repeatedly to be a major reason people do not sue, despite adequate grounds for a successful lawsuit. "It is *people* who sue, not the action or event that triggered a bad outcome" (Guido, 1988, p. 44). The importance of working to create respectful, honest, and positive nurse-patient relationships cannot be underestimated

Nurses can reduce their risk of being sued successfully for malpractice if they do the following (Goldstein, et al., 1989; Guido, 1988):

- Practice within the scope of the nurse practice act
- Observe agency policies and procedures
- Measure up to established practice standards
- Always put patient rights and welfare first
- Are aware of relevant law and legal doctrines and combine such with the biological, psychological, and social sciences that form the basis of all rational nursing decisions
- Stay within the area of their individual competence
- Upgrade technical skills consistently by attending continuing education programs and seeking specialty certification
- Purchase professional liability insurance and understand fully the limits of the individual policy

---

LEARNING EXERCISE 23.7

In small group, discuss the following questions.

1. Do you feel there are unnecessary lawsuits in the healthcare industry? What criteria can be used to distinguish between appropriate and unnecessary lawsuits?
2. Have you ever advised a friend or family member to sue to recover damages you felt they suffered as a result of poor quality healthcare? What motivated you to encourage them to do so?
3. Do you think you will make clinical errors in judgment as a nurse? If so, what type of errors should be considered acceptable (if any) and what types not acceptable?

PATIENT RIGHTS

The legislative controls of nursing practice primarily protect the rights of patients. Until the 1960s, patients had very few rights; in fact, patients often were denied basic human rights during a time when they were most vulnerable. Since that time, the NLN, the American Hospital Association, and many states have passed a bill of rights for patients (Display 23.5).

Display 23.5 List of Patient Rights in California

1. Exercise these rights without regard to sex or cultural; economic, education, or religious background; or the source of payment for care.
2. Considerate and respectful care.
3. Knowledge of the name of the physician who has primary responsibility for coordinating care and the names and professional relationships of other physicians who will see the patient.
4. Receive information from physician about illness, course of treatment, and prospects for recovery in terms the patient can understand.
5. Receive as much information about any proposed treatment or procedure as the patient may need to give informed consent or to refuse this course of treatment. Except in emergencies, this information shall include a description of the procedure or treatment, the medically significant risks involved in this treatment, alternate course of treatment or nontreatment and the risks involved in each, and the name of the person who will carry out the procedure or treatment.
6. Participate actively in decisions regarding medical care. To the extent permitted by law, this includes the right to refuse treatment.
7. Full consideration of privacy concerning medical care program. Case discussion, consultation, examination, and treatment are confidential and should be conducted discreetly. The patient has the right to be advised to the reason for the presence of any individual.
8. Confidential treatment of all communications and records pertaining to the patient's care and stay in the hospital. Written permission shall be obtained before medical records are made available to anyone not directly concerned with the patient's care.
9. Reasonable responses to any reasonable requests for service.
10. Ability to leave the hospital even against the advice of the physician.
11. Reasonable continuity of care and to know in advance the time and location of appointment and the physician providing care.
12. Be advised if hospital/personal physician proposes to engage in or perform human experimentation affecting care or treatment. The patient has the right to refuse to participate in such research projects.
13. Be informed by the physician or a delegate of the physician of continuing health-care requirements following discharge from the hospital.
14. Examine and receive an explanation of the bill regardless of source of payment.
15. Know which hospital rules and policies apply to the patient's conduct.
16. Have all patient's rights apply to the person who may have legal responsibility to make decisions regarding medical care on behalf of the patient.

(American Hospital Association)

A bill of rights that has become law or state regulation has the most legal authority because it provides the patient with legal recourse. A bill of rights issued by healthcare organizations and professional associations is not legally binding but may influence funding and certainly should be considered professionally binding.

Today, patients are more assertive and involved in their healthcare. They have more information to review when looking at treatment options and are demanding to be participants in decisions about their healthcare. The client's right to information and participation in medical care decisions has led to conflicts in the areas of informed consent and access to medical records. Although the manager has a responsibility to see that all patient rights are met in the unit, the areas that are particularly sensitive involve the right to privacy and personal liability, both guaranteed by the Constitution.

INTEGRATING LEADERSHIP ROLES AND MANAGEMENT FUNCTIONS IN LEGAL AND LEGISLATIVE ISSUES

Legislative and legal controls for nursing practice have been established to clarify the boundaries of nursing practice and to protect clients. The leader uses established legal guidelines to role model nursing practice that meets or exceeds accepted standards of care. Leaders also are role models in their efforts to expand expertise in their field and to achieve specialty certification. Perhaps the most important leadership roles in law and legislation are those of vision, risk taking, and energy. The leader is active in professional organizations and groups that define what nursing is and what it should be in the future. This is an internalized responsibility that must be adopted by many more nurses if the profession is to be a recognized and vital force in the political arena.

Management functions in legal and legislative issues are more directive. Managers are responsible for seeing that their practice *and* that of their subordinates is in accord with current legal guidelines. This requires that managers have a working knowledge of current laws and legal doctrines that affect nursing practice. Because laws are not static, this is an active and ongoing function. The manager has a legal obligation to uphold the laws, rules, and regulations affecting the organization, the patient, and nursing practice.

The integrated leader/manager reduces the personal risk of legal liability by creating an environment that prioritizes patient needs and welfare. In addition, caring, respect, and honesty as part of nurse-patient relationships are emphasized. If these functions and roles are truly integrated, the risk of patient harm and nursing liability are greatly reduced.

KEY CONCEPTS

▼ Sources of law include *constitutions, statutes, administrative agencies,* and *court decisions.*

▼ *Nurse practice acts* define and limit the practice of nursing, thereby determining what constitutes unauthorized practice or practice that exceeds the scope of authority.

▼ Because legislators and policy makers are more willing to deal with nurses as a group rather than as individuals, joining and actively supporting professional organizations allow nurses to lobby for a stronger nurse practice act or for the creation or expansion of advanced nursing roles.

▼ Professional organizations generally espouse standards of care that are higher than those required by law. These voluntary controls often are forerunners of legal controls.

▼ Nurses need to exert their collective influence and make their concerns known to policy makers before they can have a major impact on political and legislative outcomes.

▼ Two important legal doctrines guide courts in their decision making. The first of these is *stare decisis*, which means to "let the decision stand." The second is *res judicata*, which means a "thing or matter settled by judgment."

▼ Currently, licensing for nurses is a responsibility of state boards of nursing or state boards of nurse examiners. These state boards also provide discipline as necessary.

▼ Some professionals have advocated shifting the burden of licensure, and thus accountability, from individual practitioners to an institution or agency. Both the ANA and NLN oppose this move.

▼ In all malpractice suits, there is a plaintiff and a defendant. The *plaintiff* is the injured party. The *defendant* is the professional who is alleged to have caused the injury.

▼ *Negligence* has been defined as the omission to do something that a reasonable person, guided by the considerations that ordinarily regulate human affairs, would do or as doing something that a reasonable and prudent person would not do (Creighton, 1986).

▼ *Reasonable and prudent* generally mean the average judgment, foresight, intelligence, and skill that would be expected of a person with similar training and experience.

▼ *Malpractice* is the failure of a person with professional training to act in a reasonable and prudent manner. Malpractice also is called *professional negligence.*

▼ *Standards of care* represent the skills and learning commonly possessed by members of the profession and generally are the minimal requirements that define an acceptable level of care.

▼ Employers of nurses can now be held liable for an employee's acts under a concept known as *vicarious liability.* One form of vicarious liability is called *respondeat superior,* a Latin term meaning "the master is responsible for the acts of his servants."

▼ One rule that all nurses must know and understand is the rule of *personal liability,* which says that every person is liable for his or her own tortious conduct.

▼ Managers are not automatically held liable for all acts of negligence on the part of those they supervise, but they may be held liable if they were negligent in supervising those employees at the time they committed the negligent acts.

▼ *Incident reports* are records of unusual or unexpected incidents that occur in the course of a client's treatment. Because incident reports are prepared for attorneys defending healthcare agencies against lawsuits, they are considered confidential communications and cannot be subpoenaed by clients or used as evidence in their lawsuits.

▼ *Torts* are legal wrongs committed against a person or property, independent of a contract, that render the person who commits them liable for damages in a civil action. While professional negligence is considered to be an *unintentional tort,* assault, battery, false imprisonment, invasion of privacy, defamation, and slander are *intentional torts.*

▼ *Informed consent* is given by the person who is having a procedure or surgery done and is provided by the practitioner performing the procedure.

▼ Although the patient owns the information in a medical record, the actual record belongs to the facility that originally made it and is storing it.

▼ It has been proven that despite good technical competence, nurses who have difficulty establishing positive interpersonal relationships with clients and their families are at greater risk of being sued.

▼ Since the 1960s, the NLN, the American Hospital Association, and many states have passed bills of rights for patients.

 ## ADDITIONAL LEARNING EXERCISES

Learning Exercise 23.8

Mrs. Shin is a 68-year-old liver cancer patient who has been admitted to the oncology unit at Memorial Hospital. Her admitting physician has advised chemotherapy, even though he feels there is little chance of it working. The patient asks her doctor, in your presence, if there is an alternative treatment to chemotherapy. He replies, "Nothing else has been proven to be effective. Everything else is quackery, and you would be wasting your money." After he leaves, the patient and her family ask you if you know anything about alternative treatments. When you indicate that you do have some current literature available, they beg you to share your information with them.

Assignment: What do you do? What is your legal responsibility to your patient, the doctor, and the hospital? Using your knowledge of the legal process, the nurse practice act, patients' rights, and legal precedents (look for the case *Tuma v. Board of Nursing,* 1979), explain what you would do, and defend your decision.

Learning Exercise 23.9
(From Marquis and Huston, 1994)

You have been the evening charge nurse in the emergency room at Memorial Hospital for the last 2 years. Besides yourself, you have two LVNs and four RNs working in your department. Your normal staffing is to have two RNs and one LVN on duty Monday through Thursday and one LVN and three RNs on during the weekend.

It has become apparent that one of the LVNs, Maggie, resents the recently imposed limitations of LVN duties, because she has had 10 years of experience in nursing, including a long tour of duty as a medic in Vietnam. The emergency room physicians admire her and are always asking her to assist them with any major wound repair. Occasionally, she has exceeded her job description as an LVN in the hospital, although she has done nothing illegal of which you are aware. You have given her satisfactory performance evaluations in the past, even though everyone is aware that she sometimes pretends to be a "junior physician." You also suspect that the physicians sometimes allow her to suture wounds and perform duties outside her licensure, but you have not investigated this or actually seen it yourself.

Tonight you come back from supper and find Maggie suturing a deep laceration while the physician looks on. They both realize that you are upset, and the physician takes over the suturing. Later, the doctor comes to you and says, "Don't worry! She does a great job, and I'll take the responsibility for her actions." You are not sure what you should do. Maggie is a good employee, and taking any action will result in unit conflict.

Assignment: What are the legal ramifications of this case? Discuss what you should do, if anything. What responsibility and liability exist for the physician, Maggie, and yourself? Use appropriate rationale to support your decision.

Learning Exercise 23.10

You have been an obstetrical staff nurse at Memorial Hospital for 25 years. The obstetrical unit census has been abnormally low lately, although patient census in other areas of the hospital has been extremely high. When you arrive at work today, you are told to float to the thoracic surgery critical care unit. This is a highly specialized unit, and you feel ill-prepared to work with the equipment on the unit and the type of critically ill patients who are there. You call the staffing office and ask to be reassigned to a different area. You are told that the entire hospital is critically short staffed, that the thoracic surgery unit is four nurses short, and that you are at least as well-equipped to handle that unit as the other three staff who also are being floated. Now your anxiety level is even higher. You will be expected to handle a full RN patient load. You also are aware that more than half the staff on the unit today will have no experience in thoracic surgery. You consider whether or not to refuse to float. You do not want to place your nursing license in jeopardy, yet you feel conflicting obligations.

Assignment: To whom do you have conflicting obligations? You have little time to make this decision. Outline the steps you use to reach your final decision. Identify the legal and ethical ramifications that may result from your decision. Are they in conflict?

REFERENCES:

Agnos, I. C., Snyder, M. C., & Evans, N. (1993). Political appointments: Getting appointed. In D. J. Mason, S. W. Talbott, & J. K. Leavitt (Eds.), *Policy and politics for nurses* (2nd ed.). Philadelphia: W.B. Saunders.

Anderson, R. D. (1982). *Avoiding malpractice for the California nurse* (2nd ed.). Sacramento, CA: Robert D. Anderson Publishing.

Betts, V. T. (1993). Nursing and the courts: A strategy for shaping public policy. In D. J. Mason, S. W. Talbott, & J. K. Leavitt (Eds.), *Policy and politics for nurses* (2nd ed.). Philadelphia: W.B. Saunders.

Creighton, H. (1986). *Law every nurse should know* (5th ed.). Philadelphia: W.B. Saunders.

Fiesta, J. (1983). *The law and liability.* New York: John Wiley & Sons.

Fiesta, J. (1990). Safeguarding your nursing license. *Nursing Management, 21*(8), 20–21.

Fiesta, J. (1993a). Why nurses lose their licenses— Part III. *Nursing Management, 24*(12), 16.

Fiesta, J. (1993b). Legal aspects—Standards of care Part II. *Nursing Management, 24*(8), 16–17.

Fiesta, J. (1993c). Staffing implications: A legal update. *Nursing Management, 24*(6), 34–35.

Goldstein, A. S., Perdew, S., & Pruitt, S. (1989). *The nurse's legal advisor.* Philadelphia: J.B. Lippincott.

Guido, G. W. (1988). *Legal issues in nursing: A*

sourcebook for practice (p. 44). Norwalk, CT: Appleton and Lange.

Hall, J. K. (1990). Understanding the fine line between law and ethics. *Nursing 90, 20*(10), 37.

Hogue, E. (1985). *Nursing and legal liability: A case study approach.* Owing Mills, MD: National Health Publishing, Rynd Communications.

Huston, C. J., & Marquis, B. L. (1988). Attitudes and behaviors necessary for nurses to overcome powerlessness. *Nursing Connections, 1*(2), 39–47.

Mittelstadt, P. C., & Hart, M. A. (1993). Legislative and regulatory processes. In D. J. Mason, S. W. Talbott, & J. K. Leavitt (Eds.), *Policy and politics for nurses* (2nd ed.). Philadelphia: W.B. Saunders.

Northrup, C. E. (1987). *Legal issues in nursing.* New York: C.V. Mosby.

Quinn, C. A., & Smith, M. D. (1987). *The professional commitment: Issues and ethics in nursing.* Philadelphia: W.B. Saunders.

BIBLIOGRAPHY

Bellocq, J. A. (1989). Protecting your license. *Journal of Professional Nursing, 5*(1), 8.

Creighton, H. (1988). The nurse as an expert witness. *Nursing Management, 19*(8), 22–23.

Fiesta, J. (1992). Employers' liability for contagious disease. *Nursing Management, 23*(12), 18–22.

Greenslade, M. (1988). Informed consent: The nurse's responsibility. *Dimensions in Oncology Nursing, 2*(1), 5–8.

Kolpan, K. I. (1989). Disclosing medical records. *Journal of Head Trauma Rehabilitation, 4*(3), 95–96.

Mahrenholz, D. M. (1988). Nursing and the 100th Congress: Part 1. *Nursing Connections, 1*(4), 36–39.

Marquis, B. L., & Huston, C. J. (1994). *Management decision making for nurses: 118 Case studies* (2nd ed.). Philadelphia: J.B. Lippincott.

Miller, J. M. (1989). Medical malpractice and corporate responsibility. *Point of View, 26*(1), 21.

Murphy, E. K. (1989). Grounds for license revocation. *Association of Operating Room Nurses Journal, 49*(5), 1428, 1430, 1432.

Murphy, E. K. (1989). The definition and purpose of professional licensure. *Association of Operating Room Nurses Journal, 49*(4), 1106–1109.

Nichols, B. (1989). Regulatory initiatives: Instruments for leadership. *Nursing Outlook, 37*(2), 62–63.

Pohlman, K. J. (1988). Privacy, confidentiality, and privilege. *Focus on Critical Care, 15*(6), 60–61.

Rhodes, A. M. (1988). Emerging legal issues for the nurse executive. *Series on Nursing Administration, 1,* 138–153.

Rocereto L. R., & Maleski, C. (1984). All about rights to medical records. *Nursing Life, 4*(4), 50–51.

Sinback, M. F. (1988). Legislating solutions to the malpractice crisis. *Journal of the American Academy of Physician Assistants, 1*(2), 159–163.

Spohn, T. (1988). Liability insurance is essential to professional security. *Journal of Post Anesthesia Nursing, 3*(6), 423–424.

Stutheit, B. K. (1988). Patients access to medical records. *Colorado Medicine, 85*(4), 74.

Wong, D. L. (1989). Nursing practice acts and the scope of nursing practice. *School Nurse, 4*(3), 35–37, 39–42.

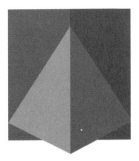

CHAPTER 24

Career Development Issues

Career development is the planning and implementation of career plans (Vogel, 1990). This can be accomplished through assessment, job analysis, education, training, job search and acquisition, and work experience. Before the 1970s, organizations did little to help employees plan and develop their careers. Since that time, however, the impact of career development programs has been documented as a positive force in successful businesses (Ouchi, 1981; Peters & Waterman, 1982; Kramer & Schmalenberg, 1988). This finding has led to an interest in career development by organizations and the recognition of a manager's responsibility for assisting subordinates with career development. Recently, organizational theorists have determined that to be competitive, organizations must develop a culture of learning—a philosophy in which everyone in the organization, executives and workers, is committed to the concept of continuous learning (Senge, 1990).

Unfortunately, most career planning efforts have centered around management development rather than activities that promote growth in nonmanagement employees. Generally, more than 80% of an organization's employees are nonmanagement, so it is imperative that attention also be paid to their career development.

This chapter examines appropriate management interventions for employee career management; responsibilities of the professional nurse for personal career planning; appropriate use of lateral, downward, and accommodating transfers; identify-

Bessie L. Marquis and Carol J. Huston:
LEADERSHIP ROLES AND MANAGEMENT FUNCTIONS IN NURSING, 2nd ed.
Lippincott-Raven Publishers © 1996

ing and selecting employees for promotion; and the components of management development. The leadership roles and management functions for career development are shown in Display 24.1.

JUSTIFICATIONS FOR CAREER DEVELOPMENT

The most obvious justification for an organization to include career development as part of its management functions is the impact it has on retention. White (1988) reports that 47% of employees would quit their jobs if no opportunity for advancement existed. Some authors, however, feel nurses traditionally have not had a career focus and in the past, generally viewed nursing as a job and not a career (Sharkley, 1988; Huston & Marquis, 1989). Therefore, White's findings might not hold true for nursing. The following list, however, includes retention and career advancement as justifications for a career development program.

1. *Reduces employee attrition.* Career development influences turnover of ambitious employees who would otherwise be frustrated and seek other jobs because of lack of job advancement.

Display 24.1 Leadership Roles and Management Functions in Career Development

Leadership Roles
1. Is self-aware of values influencing personal career development.
2. Encourages employees to take responsibility for their own career planning.
3. Identifies and develops future leaders.
4. Shows a genuine interest in the career planning and career development of all employees.
5. Encourages and supports the development of career paths within the organization.
6. Supports employees' personal career decisions based on each employee's needs and values.

Management Functions
1. Develops fair and well-communicated policies on promotions and transfers.
2. Uses organizational transfers appropriately.
3. Uses a planned system of long-term coaching for career development.
4. Disseminates career information.
5. Posts job openings.
6. Works cooperatively with other departments in arranging for release of employees to take other positions within the organization.

2. *Provides equal employment opportunity.* Minorities and women will have a better opportunity to move up in an organization if they are identified and developed early in their careers.
3. *Improves use of personnel.* When employees are kept in jobs they have outgrown, their productivity is often reduced. People perform better when they are placed in jobs that fit them and are provided with challenges.
4. *Improves quality of work life.* Nurses increasingly desire to control their own careers. They are less willing to settle for any role or position that comes their way and want greater job satisfaction and more career options.
5. *Improves competitiveness of the organization.* Highly educated professionals often prefer organizations that have a good record of career development. During nursing shortages, a recognized program of career development can be the deciding factor for professionals selecting a position.
6. *Avoids obsolescence and builds new skills.* Due to the rapid changes in the healthcare industry, especially in the areas of consumer demands and technology, employees may find their skills have become obsolete. A successful career development program begins to retrain employees proactively, providing them with the necessary skills to remain current in their field and therefore valuable to the organization.

A CAREER DEVELOPMENT PROGRAM

Before managers can plan a successful career development program, they need to understand the normal career stages of individuals, because people require different types of development in different stages of their career.

Van Maanen and Schein (1977) describe four successive career stages, including exploration, early establishment, career maintenance, and declining stage.

The Stage of Exploration

This occurs during early years as educational choices are made. With nurses, it is often during their senior year in nursing school that beginning career goals are formulated.

Early Establishment Stage

The first phase of this stage occurs when individuals seek their first job, are successfully hired, and begin working. Not only do individuals often experience reality shock at this time, but they also must often take positions with limited status and less desirable shift assignments.

Once the individual has been in the first job for several months, the second phase of the early establishment stage occurs. During this phase, the individual finds out if he or she is succeeding in the organization. If not succeeding, he or she may be terminated or may need remedial training. Most individuals will become competent during this stage, and they will begin to feel good about their chosen careers and often form a commitment to the organization and to their profession.

The final phase of the early establishment stage occurs as the individual internalizes his or her competence and worth in the chosen field. This is often referred to as the *granting of tenure* phase.

Career Maintenance

There are two phases to this stage. In the first phase, which occurs midcareer, individuals become proficient, and many become experts. They receive more important work assignments and are at their maximum productivity. It is often at this stage that nurses feel very good about their work. However, if continued stretching and challenges are not given, these individuals may become bored and look outside the organization for further advancement. This is frequently the time when nurses seek transfer to a new clinical area within the organization or when they may even leave nursing. People often move upward rapidly in an organization or in their career during this period.

During the second phase of career maintenance, which occurs in late career, job assignments usually reflect the judgment, wisdom, and broad perspective of a veteran. Many enjoy teaching at this stage. Problems often arise during this time for those who feel their past contributions were not appreciated. Many also feel threatened by younger, more recently trained professionals, especially if the younger person is assertive and better educated. At some point during this period, the individual must begin to adjust ambitions and dreams to what is realistic and possible to accomplish in the years remaining in the career.

Declining Stage of Career

This is the stage when retirement plans begin and individuals learn to accept a reduced role in their profession. It is often a time for a renewed interest in community, family, and friendships.

Although some correlation between age and career stage exists, there are many variances. Career stage and psychological development studies have received recent criticism because a majority of the population in many such studies have been white heterosexual males (Bailey, 1987; Schott, 1986), and therefore a predominantly female occupation may differ. Swanson (1994) believes that few studies of career development directly apply to women. Many women enter nursing in midlife, while other women interrupt their careers for childrearing, so there are obvious differences in male and female career patterns. However, as more women delay childbearing, the future might reveal greater similarities in male and female career stages.

In addition to a knowledge of career stages, the manager needs to be able to differentiate between the employee's personal responsibility for career development and the manger's responsibility. These areas of responsibility are shown in Display 24.2.

Career planning is the subset of career development that represents individual responsibility. It includes evaluating one's strengths and weaknesses, setting goals, examining career opportunities, preparing for potential opportunities, and using appropriate developmental activities (Rothrock, 1986). Sensitive managers and pro-

LEARNING EXERCISE 24.1

In a group, discuss the career stages listed in the chapter. What career stage most closely reflects your present situation? Do you believe that mature women are more apt to move more rapidly through these stages? How do the male and female nurses you know fit these patterns? What stages of their careers best represent your various nursing instructors?

Write a one-page essay describing whether you believe male and female nurses have similar or dissimilar career stages. Use examples of nurses you know to support your statements.

gressive organizations can assist employees in career planning through long-term coaching. Various career planning guides also can assist the individual in career planning. Managers should encourage the use of such tools and make them available to their staff.

Vestal (1987) maintains that career planning should be an ongoing process, conscious and deliberate; thus, it is much more difficult than it sounds. Vestal also suggests that career planning is easier when a career map is created to assist in developing a long-term master plan. Many novice professionals and most young people often neglect to make long-term career plans (Vestal, 1987; Marquis & Huston, 1988). Finn (1992) believes that taking a personal inventory and setting goals are the most important parts of career planning. Use the career guide shown in Figure 24.1 along with the steps in career planning outlined in Display 24.2, to assist with developing the personal plan described in Learning Exercise 24.2.

Display 24.2   The Components of Career Development

Career Planning
- Self-assess interests, skills, strengths, weaknesses, and values.
- Determine goals
- Assess the organization for opportunities.
- Assess opportunities outside the organization.
- Develop strategies.
- Implement plans.
- Evaluate plans.
- Reassess and make new plans as necessary, at least biannually.

Career Management
- Integrate individual employee needs with organizational needs.
- Establish, design, communicate, and implement career paths.
- Disseminate career information.
- Post and communicate all job openings.
- Assess employees.
- Provide work experience for development.
- Give support and encouragement.
- Develop new personnel policies as necessary.
- Provide training and education.

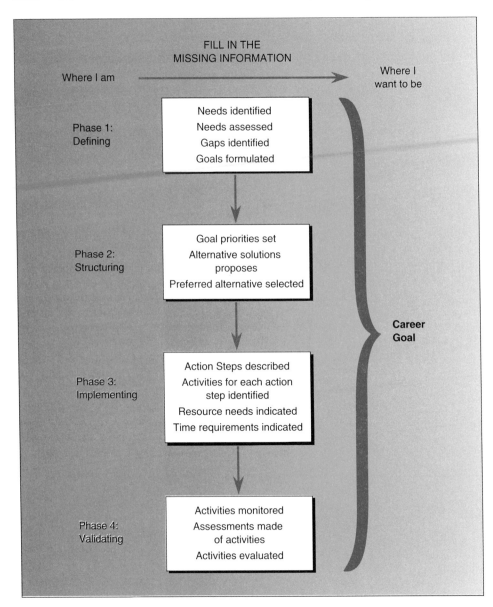

FIGURE 24.1 A career planning guide for a professional nurse.

Résumé Preparation

In addition to career mapping and self-assessment, the professional nurse is responsible for developing strategies that assist in realizing career goals. Such strategies include presenting a positive image by using good interviewing skills and a well-prepared résumé.

Résumés are discussed briefly in Unit 4. However, because of their importance

> ### ◢ LEARNING EXERCISE 24.2
>
> Develop a 20-year career plan taking into account the constraints of family responsibilities, such as marriage, children, and aging parents. Have your career plan critiqued to determine its feasibility and if the timelines and goals are realistic.

as a career planning tool, information on résumé preparation also is included in this unit. A survey of nurse recruiters has found that résumés are widely used as a screening mechanism for hiring (Graduating Nurse, 1993). They also are used for promotion decisions; therefore, maintaining an accurate and current résumé becomes a career planning necessity for the professional nurse.

Various acceptable styles and formats of résumés exist. However, because the résumé represents professionalism and is often used by recruiters as a summary of the applicant's qualifications, it must make an impression and quickly capture the reader's attention. The recruiters interviewed for *Graduating Nurse* (1993) stated that résumés should be of professional quality. The following are guidelines for résumé preparation:

1. The résumé should be typed in a format that is easy to read.
2. The résumé should maximize strong points and minimize weaknesses.
3. The style should reflect good grammar, correct punctuation, proper sentence structure, and simple direct language.
4. The content of the résumé should consist of educational history, work experience, personal characteristics, membership in professional organizations, community involvement, awards, honors and publications, professional objectives, health status, and license information. A sample résumé is shown in Display 24.3.

Career Management

Career management focuses on the responsibilities of the organization for career development. In career management, the organization creates career paths and advancement ladders. It also attempts to match position openings with appropriate individuals. This includes accurately assessing employee performance and potential to offer the most appropriate career guidance, education, and training.

Many of the organizational responsibilities outlined in Display 24.2 are discussed elsewhere in this book and therefore are only briefly mentioned here. These organizational responsibilities include the following:

- *Integration of needs.* The personnel department, nursing division, nursing units, and education department must work and plan together to match job openings with the skills and talents of present employees.
- *Establishment of career paths.* Not only must career paths be developed, but they must be communicated to the staff and implemented consistently. An often cited contributor to the nursing turnover is the lack of adequately com-

Display 24.3   Sample Résumé

SUSAN CARMEL GUEVARA

553-12-8456
628 Normal Street
Chico, CA 95928
(916) 555-3718

CAREER	To practice professional nursing within a progressive environment that will provide challenges and opportunities for personal and professional growth.
EDUCATION	Bachelor of Science in Nursing California State University, Chico December 1990 Public Health Certificate, January 1991
GPA	3.18—overall 3.34—within major
HONORS	Sigma Theta Tau International Society of Nursing, Kappa Omicron Chapter CSUS School of Nursing Scholarship Award Selection of one of my papers by the Writing Across the Discipline project for publication in *An Expression of Nursing, A Journal of Student Writing in The School of Nursing,* 1989, Vol. 1.
RELATED EXPERIENCE	June 1989—Present Nurse Attendant, Enloe Hospital, Chico, CA Perform nursing assignments and various aspects of nursing care under the supervision and guidance of a registered nurse. (Job description available on request.) July 1986—Present Home health aide/respite worker for various agencies and individuals throughout the academic school years and summers.
REFERENCES	Available on request.

---

pensated career paths in nursing (Schultz, 1993). Although various career ladders have been present for some time, they are still not widely used. This problem is not unique to nursing. Beach (1980) maintains that most organizations do not have in place systematically designed career paths.

Even when healthcare organizations design and use a career structure, the system often breaks down once the nurse leaves that organization. For example, nurses at the level of clinical nurse 3 in one hospital will usually lose that status when they leave the organization for another position.

When designing career paths, each successive job in each path should contain additional responsibilities and duties that are greater than the previous jobs in that path. Each successive job also must be related to and use previous skills. Once career paths are established, they must be communicated effectively to all concerned staff. What employees must do to advance in a particular path should be very clear.

- *Dissemination of career information.* The education department, personnel department, and unit manager are all responsible for sharing career information. Employees should not be encouraged to pursue unrealistic goals.
- *Posting of job openings.* Although this is usually the responsibility of the personnel department, the manager should communicate this information, even when it means that one of the unit staff may transfer to another area. Effective managers know who needs to be encouraged to apply for openings and who is ready for more responsibility and challenges.
- *Assessment of employees.* One of the benefits of a good appraisal system is the important information it gives the manager on the performance, potential, and abilities of all staff members. The use of long-term coaching will give managers insight into their employees' needs and wants so that appropriate career counseling will occur.
- *Provision of challenging assignments. Planned* work experience is one of the most powerful career development tools. This includes jobs that temporarily stretch the employee to their maximum skill, temporary projects, assignment to committees, shift rotation, assignment to different units, or shift charge duties.
- *Giving support and encouragement.* Because excellent subordinates make their job easier, managers are often reluctant to encourage these subordinates to move up the corporate ladder or to seek other more challenging experiences outside the manager's span of control. Thus, many managers hoard their talent. A leadership role requires that managers look beyond their immediate unit or department and consider the needs of the entire organization. Leaders recognize and share talent.
- *Development of personnel policies.* An active career development program often results in the recognition that certain personnel policies and procedures are impeding the success of the program. When this occurs, the organization should reexamine these policies and make necessary changes.
- *Provision of education and training.* The impact of education and training on career development and retention of subordinate staff is discussed previously. However, the need for organizations to provide for the development of leaders and managers is included later in this chapter.

LONG-TERM COACHING

Short-term coaching as a means to develop and motivate employees has previously been discussed. Short-term coaching should be a spontaneous part of the experienced manager's repertoire.

Long-term coaching, on the other hand, is a planned management action that occurs over the duration of employment. Because this form of coaching may cover a long period of time, it is frequently neglected unless the manager uses a systematic scheduling plan for coaching conferences and a form for documentation. Although long-term documentation has been used successfully to track an employee's deficiencies, documenting long-term coaching for career development has been less successful. Because employees and managers move frequently within an organization, the lack of record keeping regarding employees' career needs has deterred nursing career development.

Quick (1985) maintains that long-term coaching is a major step in building an effective team and an excellent strategy to increase productivity and retention. Long-term coaching has some of the same attributes of a mentoring relationship but is less intense and is not limited to one or a few subordinates.

The effective manager has at least one coaching session with each employee annually, in addition to any coaching that may occur during the appraisal interview. Although some coaching should occur during the performance appraisal interview, additional coaching should be planned at a less stressful time. Display 24.4 is an example of a long-term coaching progress form.

Quick (1985) states that effective coaching has several specific components. These components are discussed in the following three phases:

1. *Gathering data.* One of the best methods of gathering data about employees is to observe their behavior. When managers spend time observing employees, they are able to determine who has good communication skills, is well-organized, is able to use effective negotiating skills, and works collaboratively.

   Managers also should seek information about the employee's past work experience, performance appraisals, and educational experiences. Data also can include academic qualifications and credentials. Most of this information can be obtained by examining the personnel file. Finally, employees themselves are an excellent source of information that can assist the manager in the long-term coaching interview. All these sources of data should be reviewed prior to the coaching interview.

2. *What is possible.* As part of career planning, the manager should assess the department for possible changes in the future, openings or transfers, and potential challenges and opportunities. The manager should anticipate what type of needs lie ahead, what projects are planned, and what staffing and budget changes will occur.

   After carefully assessing the employee's profile and future opportunities, managers should consider each staff member and ask the following questions: How can each employee be helped so that he or she is better prepared to take advantage of the future? Who needs to be encouraged to return to school, to become credentialed, or to take a special course? Which employees need to be encouraged to transfer to a more challenging position, be given more responsibility on their present unit, or moved to another shift? Sossong et al. (1987) argue that managers are able to create a stimulating environment for career development by being aware of the uniqueness of their employees.

Display 24.4 Sample Long-Term Coaching Form

Name of employee _____

Name of supervisor _____

Date _____ Date of last coaching interview _____

1. What new challenges and responsibilities could be given to this employee that would utilize his or her special talents?

   _____

   _____

   _____

2. What events happening in the organization do you foresee affecting this employee? (Examples would be plans to go to an all-RN staff, changing the mode of patient care delivery, increasing emphasis on credentialing by the new CEO of the nursing division, changing the medication system, and changing the ratio of nonprofessionals to professionals for nursing staffing.)

   _____

   _____

   _____

3. How should the employee be preparing to meet new or changing expectations?

   _____

   _____

   _____

4. What specific suggestions and guidance for the future can you give this employee? (Examples would be taking specific courses to prepare for change, urging them to pursue an advanced degree, considering changing shifts, urging them to seek challenges outside of your unit, and suggesting that they apply for the next management opening.)

   _____

   _____

5. What specific organizational resources can you offer the employee?

   _____

   _____

6. What new information regarding this employee's long-term plans, aspirations, and potential have the perusal of the personnel record, your observations, and this interview given you?

   _____

   _____

   _____

7. Do the organizational and professional career plans held by the individual match your vision of his or her future? If not, how do they differ?

   _____

   _____

8. What developmental and professional growth has taken place since the last coaching session?

   _____

   _____

9. Date of next coaching interview _____

(From Huston & Marquis, 1994.)

3. *The coaching interview.* The goals of the career development coaching interview are to help employees increase their effectiveness, see where potential opportunities in the organization lie, and advance their knowledge, skills, and experience. Many of the techniques and guidelines listed in the postappraisal interview also are useful in the coaching interview. It is important not to intimidate employees as they are questioned about their future and their goals.

Although there is no standard procedure for conducting the interview, the main emphasis should be on employee growth and development. The manager can assist the employee in exploring future options. Coaching sessions give the manager a chance to discover potential future managers—employees who should then begin to be groomed for a future managerial role in subsequent coaching sessions.

Both the performance appraisal interview and the coaching session provide opportunities to assist employees in the growth and development necessary for expanded roles and responsibilities. A major leadership role is the development of subordinate staff. This interest in the future of individual employees plays a vital role in retention and productivity.

◢ LEARNING EXERCISE 24.3

You have been the evening charge nurse of a large surgical unit for the last 4 years. Each year you perform a career development conference with all your licensed staff.

These sessions are held separately from the performance appraisal interviews. You have been extremely pleased with the results of these conferences. Two of your practical nurses are now enrolled in an RN program. Several of your RNs from your unit have obtained advanced clinical positions, and many have returned to school. As a result of your encouragement and support, several of the nurses have taken charge positions on other units. You are quite proud of your ability to recognize talent and to perform successful career counseling.

This is the last time you will be performing career counseling, because you have resigned your position to return to graduate school. You have encouraged several of the staff to apply for your position but think one particular nurse, Beth, a 34-year-old, would be exceptional. She is extremely capable clinically, is very mature, is well respected by everyone, and has excellent interpersonal skills. Beth only works 4 days a week but has been invaluable to you in the 4 years since you have been charge nurse. However, Beth, is one of the few nurses who has never acted on any of your suggestions at previous career coaching interviews.

Last week you had another coaching interview with Beth and told her of your plans. You urged her to apply for your position and told her you would recommend her to your supervisor, although you would not be making the final selection. Beth told you she would think about it, and today she told you that she does not wish to apply for the position. You are very disappointed and feel that perhaps you have failed in some way.

Assignment: Examine this scenario carefully. Make a list of the possible reasons that Beth declined the promotion. Be creative. Why were the coaching conferences ineffective? Compare your findings with others in the group. After comparison, determine what influence, if any, values had on the development of the lists.

TRANSFERS

A *transfer* may be defined as a reassignment to another job within the organization. In a strict business sense, a transfer usually implies similar pay, status, and responsibility. Because of the variety of positions available for nurses in any healthcare organization, coupled with the lack of sufficient higher level positions available, two different terms have come into use. A *lateral transfer* is defined above and would describe one staff nurse moving to another unit within a hospital. A *downward transfer* occurs when someone takes a position within the organization that is below his or her previous level. This frequently happens in hospitals when a charge nurse decides to learn another nursing specialty. For example, the nurse may step down from a charge position on a medical-surgical unit to a staff position in labor and delivery.

Vestal (1987) suggests that it is in nurses' interest to consider a downward transfer because it often increases the chances of long-term career success. For example, a nurse's long-term career goal might be to hold a position in cardiac rehabilitation. The nurse determines that most of the cardiac rehabilitation staff are hired out of the hospital critical care unit (CCU). Although she has had previous experience in a cardiac care unit, she has not held that position in this organization. The nurse requests a downward transfer from an evening charge position on a surgical unit to day shift staff nurse in the CCU. This transfer will provide the nurse with current experience in CCU and more exposure to the manager of the cardiac rehabilitation unit. In this example, a downward transfer increases the likelihood that the nurse's long-term goal will be realized.

Downward transfers also should be considered when nurses are experiencing periods of stress, or role overload. Self-aware nurses often request such transfers by themselves. However, in some circumstances, the manager may need to intervene and use a downward transfer to alleviate temporarily a nurse's overwhelming stress.

Another type of transfer may accompany employees in the later stages of their career. Managers often assist valuable employees who desire a reduced role in their careers to locate a position that will use their talents and still allow them a degree of status. These *accommodating transfers* generally allow someone to receive a similar salary but with a reduction in energy expenditure. For example, a long-time employee might be given a position as ombudsman to use his or her expertise and knowledge of the organization and at the same time assume a status position that is less physically demanding.

Inappropriate Transfers

One deterrent to successful career development is the inappropriate transfer. One method managers use to solve unit personnel problems is to transfer problem employees to another unsuspecting department. Such transfers are harmful in many ways. They contribute to decreased productivity, are demotivating for all employees, and are especially destructive for the employee who is transferred.

This is not to say that employees who do not "fit" in one department won't do well in a different environment. It is not uncommon for an employee to start off poorly in one department but improve performance in a new department or unit.

Before such transfers, however, both managers and the employee must speak candidly with each other regarding the employee's capabilities and the manager's expectations. All types of transfers should be individually evaluated for appropriateness.

▶ LEARNING EXERCISE 24.4

You are the manager of a surgical unit. Many novice nurses apply to your unit for the purpose of perfecting their basic skills before transferring to a specialty unit. Although this is somewhat frustrating to you, you recognize that you can do little about it.

The hospital policy dictates that nurses requesting another position must fill out a "request for transfer" form when they apply for the new position. This form, which must be completed by their current manager, contains information regarding when they can be released from their present position for the new position and a current appraisal of their work performance.

Today you find another "request for transfer" form on your desk. However, when you read the name on the form, you feel a sense of relief rather than despair. The nurse requesting the transfer is one of your more difficult employees. Scott Powell is a very qualified nurse but is frequently absent from work, is very critical of the other nurses' work performance, and is generally unpleasant to be around.

During the 2 years he has worked on this unit, you have tried many different approaches in an effort to improve Scott's absenteeism and attitude. There would frequently be temporary improvement.

Scott has requested a transfer to the emergency room. His career goal is to be part of the flight rescue team. He certainly has the skills and intelligence to be part of this exciting and highly skilled group.

However, you feel that if you include all the negative aspects of Scott's performance, he may not be selected for the position. On one hand, you feel this job could be a turning point for Scott. It might be what he needs to overcome some of his work problems. On the other hand, the relief you feel at the possibility of transferring Scott off your unit indicates that there are some ethical issues present in this situation.

Assignment: Decide what you should do about Scott Powell's request to transfer to the emergency room. Outline your plan. Be specific about the alternatives open to you and what course of action you will take.

PROMOTIONS

Promotions are reassignments of individuals to a position of higher rank. It is normal for promotions to include a pay raise. Most promotions include increased status, title changes, more authority, and greater responsibility. Because of the importance American society places on promotions, certain guidelines must accompany promotion selection to ensure that the process is fair and equitable. Often organizations have poorly developed plans for handling promotions. When position openings occur, they are often posted and filled hastily with little thought of long-term organizational or employee goals. This frequently results in negative personnel outcomes. For this not to occur, the following elements should be determined in advance:

- *Recruitment from without or within.* There are obvious advantages and disadvantages to recruiting for promotions from within the organization. Johnson, Costa, Marshall, Moran, and Henderson (1994) put forth an excellent argument for recruiting from within, stating that it helps to develop individuals who are prepared to fill higher level positions as they become vacant. Developing and recruiting from within the organization are often termed succession management (Hansen & Wexier, 1988). Furthermore, promoting from within increases job satisfaction and retention (Swanson, 1994).

There are advantages to recruiting from outside the organization, however. When promotions are filled with individuals outside the organization, it allows the organization to seek people with new ideas. This prevents the stagnation that often occurs when all promotions are filled from within the organization.

Regardless of what the organization decides, the policy should be consistently followed and communicated to all employees. Some companies recruit from within first and only recruit from outside the organization if they are unable to find qualified individuals from among their own employees.

- *Establishment of promotion and selection criteria.* Employees should know in advance what the criteria for promotion are and what selection method is to be used. Some organizations use an interview panel as a selection method to promote all employees beyond the level of charge nurse. Decisions regarding selection method and promotion criteria should be justified with rationale. Additionally, employees need to know what place seniority will have in the selection criteria.

- *Identification of a pool of candidates.* When promotions are planned, as in succession management, there will always be an adequate pool of candidates identified and prepared to seek higher level positions. A word of caution must be given regarding the zeal with which managers urge subordinates to seek promotions. The leader's role is to identify and prepare such a pool. It is not the manager's role to urge the employee to seek a position in a manner that would lead the employee to think that he or she was guaranteed the job or to unduly influence him or her in the decision to seek such a job.

When employees actively seek promotions, they are making a commitment to do well in the new position. When they are pushed into such positions, the commitment to expend the energy to do the job well may be lacking. For many reasons, the employee may not feel ready, either due to personal commitments or because he or she feels inadequately educated or experienced.

- *Handling rejected candidates.* All promotion candidates that are rejected must be notified before the selected candidate. This is common courtesy. Candidates must be told of their nonselection in a manner that is not demotivating. They should be thanked for taking the effort to apply and when appropriate, be encouraged to apply for future position openings. Sometimes the employee should be told what deficiencies kept them from getting the position. For instance, employees should be told if they lack some educational component or work experience that would make them a stronger competitor for future promotions. This can be an effective way of encouraging career development.

• *How employee releases are to be handled.* Knowledge that the best candidate for the position is presently in a critical job or difficult position to fill should not influence decisions regarding promotions. Managers frequently find it difficult to release employees to another position within the organization. Policies regarding the length of time that a manager can delay releasing an employee should be written and communicated.

On the other hand, some managers are so good at developing their employees that they frequently become frustrated. Their success at career development results in constantly losing their staff to other departments. In such cases, higher level management should reward such leaders and set release policies that are workable and realistic.

MANAGEMENT DEVELOPMENT

Management development is a *planned* system of training and developing individuals so that they acquire the skills, insights, and attitudes to manage people and their work effectively within the organization. Marquis (1988) reports that the quality of supervision has a great impact on retention. Therefore, it is cost effective for organizations to have in place a planned program of management development.

Management development programs, as a part of career development, must be supported by top-level administration. The program also must be planned and systematically implemented. The program must include a means of developing appropriate attitudes through social learning theory and adequate management theoretical content.

Support for management development programs by the organization should occur in two ways. First, top-level management must do more than bear the cost of management development classes. Johnson et al. (1994) believe that streamlining the organizational structure is the first step in management development. Management training has little effect on improving the quality of supervision unless managers are allowed to apply their new knowledge. Therefore, for such programs to be effective, the organization must be willing to practice a management style that incorporates sound management principles.

Secondly, training outcomes will be improved if nursing executives are active in planning and developing the program. Whenever possible, nursing administrators should teach some of the classes and at the very least, make sure that the program supports top-management philosophy.

Just as nurses are required to be certified in critical care before they accept a position in a critical care unit, so too should nurses be required to take part in a management development program *prior* to their appointment to a management position. Potential managers should be identified and groomed early. The first step in this process would be an appraisal of the present management team and an analysis of possible future needs. The second step would be the establishment of a training and development program. This would require decisions, such as the following: How often should the formal management course be offered? Should outside educators be involved, or should it be taught by in-house staff? Who should be involved in teaching the didactic portion? Should there be two levels of classes, one for first-level and one for middle-level managers? Should the management development courses be open to all, or should individuals be recommended by someone from management? In addition to formal course content, what other methods should be used to develop managers? Should other methods, such as job rotation through an understudy system of pairing selected individuals with a manager and management coaching, be used?

The inclusion of social learning activities also is a valuable part of management development. Management development will not be successful unless learners have ample chance to try out new skills. Providing potential managers with didactic management theory alone inadequately prepares them for the attitudes, skills, and insights necessary for effective management. Case studies are an excellent technique for teaching management decision making and insight (Huston & Marquis, 1992). Management games, transactional analysis, and sensitivity training also are effective in changing attitudes and increasing self-awareness. All these techniques appropriately use social learning theory strategies.

INTEGRATING LEADERSHIP ROLES AND MANAGEMENT FUNCTIONS IN CAREER DEVELOPMENT

It is clear that appropriate career management should result in positive career development, alleviate burnout, reduce attrition, and promote productivity. Management functions in career development include disseminating career information and posting job openings. The manager should have a well-developed, planned system for career development for all employees; this system should include long-term coaching, the appropriate use of transfers, and how promotions are to be handled. These policies should be fair and communicated effectively to all employees.

With the integration of leadership, managers become more aware of how their own values shape personal career decisions. Additionally, the leader/manager shows genuine interest in career development of all employees. Career planning is encouraged, and potential leaders are identified and developed. Leaders develop and share talent.

Effective managers recognize that in all career decisions, the employee must decide when he or she is ready to pursue promotions, return to school, or take on greater responsibility. Leaders are aware that success is perceived by every individual in a different manner.

Although career development programs benefit all employees and the organization, there is an added bonus for the professional nurse. When professional nurses have the opportunity to experience a well-planned career development program, a greater viability for, and increased commitment to, the profession is often evident.

KEY CONCEPTS

▼ Many outcomes of a career development program justify its implementation, including the reduction of attrition, better use of personnel, increased recruitment, promotion of equal employment opportunity, and prevention of obsolescent skills.

▼ Career stage sequencing has been identified, which should assist the manager in career management.

▼ Career development programs consist of a set of personal responsibilities called *career planning* and a set of management responsibilities called *career management.*

▼ Employees often need to be encouraged to make more formalized long-term career plans.

▼ Designing *career paths* is an important part of organizational career management.

▼ Managers should plan specific interventions that promote growth and development in each of their subordinates.

▼ The transfer, when used appropriately, may be an effective way to provide career development.

▼ Policies regarding promotion should be in writing and communicated to all employees.

▼ Recruitment from within has been shown to have a positive effect on employee satisfaction.

▼ Recruitment from outside the organization allows for new ideas and prevents stagnation.

▼ To be successful, management development must be planned and supported by top-level management. This type of planned program is called *succession management.*

▼ If appropriate management attitudes and insight are goals of a management developmental program, social learning techniques need to be part of the teaching strategies used.

▼ *Long-term coaching* is a planned intervention on the part of the manager that results in the professional growth and development of subordinates.

▲ ADDITIONAL LEARNING EXERCISES

Learning Exercise 24.5

You have been appointed to a committee of staff nurses in your hospital to assist in developing a set of policies regarding how future promotions are to be handled. Lately, there has been some unhappiness about how employees have been selected for promotions. Your committee is to focus on how shift and day charge nurses are to be selected.

Assignment: Develop a list of five to seven policies regarding such promotions. Be able to justify your promotion criteria and policies.

Learning Exercise 24.6

The medical center where you have applied for a position has requested that you submit a résumé along with your application. Prepare a professional résumé using your actual experience and education. You may use any style and format you desire. The résumé will be critiqued on the basis of its professional appearance and appropriateness of included content.

Learning Exercise 24.7

You are serving on an ad hoc committee to construct a management development program. Your organization has requested that the charge nurses work with staff development and plan a 1-week training and education program that would be required of all new charge nurses prior to their appointment.

Because the organization will be bearing the cost of the program—that is, paying for the educators and employee time—you are required to select appropriate content and educational methods that will not exceed 40 hours, including actual orientation time, by a charge nurse.

Assignment: Develop such a plan, and share it with the class. Your plan should depict hours, content, and educational methods.

REFERENCES:

Bailey, M. T. (1987). Psychological development of adults: A comment. *Public administration Review, July/Aug,* 343–345.

Beach, D. S. (1980). *Personnel: The management of people out at work* (4th ed.). New York: Macmillan.

Finn, M. (1992) Discovering who you are and what you want from your career. *Healthcare Trends & Transition, 3*(4), 42–44.

Graduating Nurse (1993). Professional presentation. *Fall,* 51–53.

Hansen, R., & Wexier, M. (1988). Effective succession planning. *Employee Relations Today, 18*(1), 19–24.

Huston, C. J., & Marquis, B. L. (1989). *Retention and productivity strategies for nurse managers.* Philadelphia: J.B. Lippincott.

Huston, C. J., & Marquis, B. L. (1992). A collaborative teaching approach. *Literacy & Learning, 5*(3), 4.

Johnson, J. E., Costa, L. L., Marshall, S. B., Moran, M. J., & Henderson, C. S. (1994). Succession Management: A model for developing nursing leaders. *Nursing Management, 25*(6), 50–55.

Kramer, M., & Schmalenberg, C. (1988). Magnet hospitals: Institutions of excellence. Part II. *Journal of Nursing Administration, 18*(1), 11–19.

Marquis, B. L. (1988). Attrition: The effectiveness of retention activities. *Journal of Nursing Administration, 18*(3), 25–29.

Marquis, B. L., & Huston, C. J. (1988). Ten be-

haviors and attitudes necessary for nurses to overcome powerlessness. *Nursing Connections, 1*(2), 39–47.

Ouchi, W. C. (1981). *Theory Z: How American business can meet the Japanese challenge.* Reading, MA: Addison-Wesley.

Peters, T. J., & Waterman, R. H., Jr. (1982). *In search of excellence.* New York: Harper & Row.

Quick, T. L. (1985). *The manager's motivation deskbook.* New York: Ronald Press for John Wiley & Sons.

Rothrock, J. C. (1986). Career development: Steps to achieving your goals. *American Operating Room Nurses Journal, 43.*

Schott, R. L. (1986). The psychological development of adults: Implications for public administration. *Public Administration review, Nov/Dec,* 657–667.

Schultz, A. W. (1993). Evaluation of a clinical advancement system. *Journal of Nursing Administration, 23*(2), 13–19.

Senge, P. (1990). *The fifth discipline: The art and practice of the learning organization.* New York: Doubleday.

Sharkey, C. J. (1988). Decide to manage your career. *American Journal of Nursing, 88*(1), 105–106.

Sossong, A., Benson, M., Ballesteros, P., Dolley, P., Garrick, E., Gary, P., Couch, D., Miller, P., Pollard, A., & Smith, C. (1987). An expanding universe: Professional career opportunities. *Nursing Management, 18*(2), 46–48.

Sullivan, E. J., & Decker, P. J. (1990). *Effective management in nursing.* Menlo Park, CA: Addison-Wesley.

Swanson, E. A. (1994). Career development. In J. McCloskey & H. K. Grace (Eds.), *Current issues in nursing* (4th ed.). St. Louis: C.V. Mosby.

Van Maanen, J., & Schein, E. H. (1977). Career development. In J. R. Hackman & J. L. Suttle (Eds.), *Improving life at work.* Santa Monica, CA: Good Year Publishing.

Vestal, K. W. (1987). *Management concepts for the new nurse.* Philadelphia: J.B. Lippincott.

Vogel, G. (1990). Career development: An integrated process. *Holistic Nursing Practice, 4*(4), 46–53.

White, D. K. (1988). Few people quit jobs over money. *San Francisco Chronicle,* June 23.

BIBLIOGRAPHY

Alt, J. M., & Houston, G. R. (1986). *Nursing career ladders: A practical manual.* Rockville, MD: Aspen Systems Corp.

Billings, C. V. (1987). Employment setting barriers to professional actualization in nursing. *Nursing Management, 18*(11).

Chadwick, L. R. (1992). Professional nursing with a new focus: Staff nurse to research coordinator. *Journal of Neuroscience Nursing, 24*(3), 170–172.

Corley, M. C., Farley, B., Geddes, N., Goodloe, L., & Green, P. (1994). The clinical ladder. *Journal of Nursing Administration, 24*(2), 42–48.

(1990). From A to Z: Tips and time-savers for career development. *Nursing 90,* 139–149.

Gardner, D. (1992). Career commitment in nursing. *Journal of Professional Nursing, 8*(3), 155–160.

Hudek, K. (1990). Nursing: Making it a career. *Canadian Nurse, 86*(2), 18–19.

Huston, C. J. (1988). A guide to publication for nurses. *Nursing Connections, 1*(1), 85–91.

Jernigan, D. K. (1988). *Human resource management in nursing.* East Norwalk, CT: Appleton and Lange.

Johnston, M. (1988). Developing potential. *Nursing Times, 84*(48), 34–37.

Kirk, R. (1986). Professional development negotiations: Getting what you want. *Journal of Nursing Education, 28*(2), 79–81.

Murray, M. (1993). Where are career ladders going in the 90s? *Nursing Management, 24*(6), 46–48.

Ponte, P. R., Higgins, J. M., James, J. R., Fay, M., & Madden, M. J. (1993). Development needs of advance practice nurses in a managed care environment. *Journal of Nursing Administration, 23*(11), 13–19.

Rankin, E. A. D. (1991). Mentor, mentee, mentoring: Building career development relationships. *Nursing Connections, 4*(4), 49–57.

Peters, T., & Austin, N. (1985). *A passion for excellence.* New York: Random House.

Sanford, R. C. (1987). Clinical ladders: Do they serve their purpose? *Journal of Nursing Administration, 17*(5).

Vezina, M. L. (1986). A new approach to professional development nurse career counseling. *Journal of Nursing Staff Development, 2*(1), 38–39.

INDEX

INDEX

An italic *t* following a page number indicates a table; an italic *d* indicates a display; an italic *f* indicates a figure.

Solution to Learning Exercise 14.3 on page 299.
Crossword Puzzle: *A Review of Motivational Theory*

1 HIERARCHY
2 GELLERMAN
3 POWER
4 THEORY X
5 MCGREGOR
6 HAWTHORNE
7 HYGIENE
8 VROOM
9 SKINNER